Beginning J2EE 1.4:
From Novice to Professional

James L. Weaver, Kevin Mukhar, and Jim Crume

Apress™

Beginning J2EE 1.4: From Novice to Professional
Copyright © 2004 by James L. Weaver, Kevin Mukhar, and Jim Crume

ISBN (pbk): 1-59059-341-3

Printed and bound in the United States of America 12345678910

Additional Material: Rick Leander, Jim MacIntosh, Ron Phillips, Andrew Watt

Technical Reviewers: James L. Weaver, Kevin Mukhar, Jim Crume, Tom Marrs, Steve Anglin

Editorial Board: Dan Appleman, Craig Berry, Gary Cornell, Tony Davis, Steven Rycroft, Julian Skinner, Martin Streicher, Jim Sumser, Karen Watterson, Gavin Wray, John Zukowski

Assistant Publisher: Grace Wong

Project Manager: Kylie Johnston

Copy Editor: Ami Knox

Production Manager: Kari Brooks

Production Editor: Kelly Winquist

Proofreader: Katie M. Stence

Compositor: Katy Freer

Indexer: John Collin

Artist: April Milne

Cover Designer: Kurt Krames

Manufacturing Manager: Tom Debolski

Distributed to the book trade in the United States by Springer-Verlag New York, Inc., 175 Fifth Avenue, New York, NY 10010 and outside the United States by Springer-Verlag GmbH & Co. KG, Tiergartenstr. 17, 69112 Heidelberg, Germany.

In the United States: phone 1-800-SPRINGER, email orders@springer-ny.com, or visit http://www.springer-ny.com. Outside the United States: fax +49 6221 345229, email orders@springer.de, or visit http://www.springer.de.

For information on translations, please contact Apress directly at 2560 Ninth Street, Suite 219, Berkeley, CA 94710. Phone 510-549-5930, fax 510-549-5939, email info@apress.com, or visit http://www.apress.com.

The source code for this book is available to readers at http://www.apress.com in the Downloads section.

Contents at a Glance

Contents

Chapter 5: Servlets   151

Contents

Foreword

Once you have a good grasp of the Java language and feel comfortable with applying the class libraries using the Standard Edition of the Java System Development Kit, you'll almost certainly be looking at where to go next. Progression to the Enterprise Edition of the SDK is likely to be a natural choice for many, simply because so much professional Java programming effort is deployed in developing network-based applications. However, getting into developing Web Services and Enterprise Applications generally is more of a giant leap than a small step, simply because of the vast range of programming topics, technologies, and standards you have to master. This book is a very good starting point because it provides you with a structured introduction to most of what you need to know.

The previous edition of this book provided an excellent introduction to server-side programming using the Java 2 Platform, Enterprise Edition, J2EE, and this new edition is even better, having been fully updated to cover the latest version, J2EE 1.4. In a single book package, it covers all of the key capabilities provided by the J2EE 1.4 that you are most likely to need in a real-world Java development context. Because it starts by carefully explaining what J2EE is all about and how it relates to the Java 2 Platform, Standard Edition, you'll have an appreciation of the inter-relationships between the specific topics that you need for effective server-side programming in Java from the outset. This will enable you to better see how the various technologies involved can be combined when you get into the detail.

After guiding you through the process of setting up a development environment for web applications, it continues with introductory tutorials on the core topics in server-side programming, JSP and servlets. It doesn't end there. A whole range of supportive web programming technologies are discussed, each with working examples that show you how they can be applied. These include JDBC for database access, Enterprise JavaBeans, XML of course, SOAP, WDSL, and many others.

The book is the product of a cooperative effort by several authors who are each experts in their field. Each topic has the benefit of being explained by the author who is best equipped to provide an effective tutorial on that subject. As a professional Java programmer, you need to be conversant with the latest Java technologies for the development of Web applications. You also need a good overall perspective on the most up-to-date version of J2EE and what its capabilities are. This is precisely what you get in this book.

Ivor Horton, best-selling author of computer programming books on Java, C, and C++

About the Authors

James L. Weaver

Jim Weaver is chief scientist at Learning Assistant Technologies, a company that specializes in developing learner-centric tools. He is also the President of JMentor (http://www.jmentor.com), which is a Java mentoring, training, and consulting practice.

This book is dedicated to my wife, Julie, daughters, Lori and Kelli, and "son," Marty. Thanks for your constant love and support. Thanks to Merrill and Barbara Bishir, Ken and Marilyn Prater, and Walter Weaver for being such wonderful examples. Thanks also to Laura Lee and Steve Brown, Jill Weaver, Shari and Doug Beam, Wade and Dawn Weaver, Dan and David Wright, Jerry and Cheryl Bishir, and Pastor Steve Colter. I appreciate Gary Cornell, Steve Anglin, and Kylie Johnston for the great experience of writing for Apress. Psalm 37:4

Kevin Mukhar

Kevin Mukhar is a software developer from Colorado Springs, Colorado. On his most recent project, he was on a team where the ratio of men to women was almost one to one. (Hi to Karen, Judy, Sondra, Jennifer, Vui, and Elyssa!) In the world of software development, that's like the 500-year flood, or winning the Irish Sweepstakes. For the past 5 years, he has worked on various software systems using different J2EE technologies. He has coauthored several other books, including *Beginning Java Databases* (ISBN 1-86100-437-0), which is one of the more popular JDBC books available today. In addition to developing software during the day, he is working on a masters degree in computer science. He recently passed the certification exam for the Java Web Component Developer Certification, and his web page is at http://home.earthlink.net/~kmukhar/.

I get a kick out of writing a program that helps someone do their job better or easier; I get a thrill when tracking down and stamping out bugs; I think it's magic when programming turns ideas into software. And I want to share what I know with other programmers. That's why I'm grateful to the editors at Apress for letting me contribute to this book. I hope that what we've written in this book will help you do your job a little bit better or easier. Finally, I dedicate my chapters to my wife, Anne, and my daughter.

Jim Crume

Jim Crume (jcrume@fusionalliance.com) is a Java architect at Fusion Alliance, an Indianapolis-based consulting company that specializes in web application development. Jim has spent many years as a consultant, and specializes in architecting and developing web-based systems, but particularly enjoys Java.

This book is dedicated to my wife, Cindy, the light of my life, who has been more than patient with all of my projects; my son, Chris, and daughter, Liz, who gave up my time for this project; and my future daughter-in-law, Michelle, who helps me laugh when it gets stressful. Thanks can't even come close to expressing my appreciation. I love you all, and always will! Thanks to Steve Anglin and Kylie Johnston for the help and guidance, and to all the great people at Apress for taking a chance on me. And thanks to Jim Weaver for trusting me enough to ask me to help. Joshua 24:15

Introduction

First things first before we dive in. We, the authors, have read a lot of books on designing and developing software–some better than others–and spent a lot of time and money in the process. We had some very specific thoughts as we put this book together.

First and foremost, the focus of this book is on the *practical* aspects of getting started with developing distributed software for the J2EE platform. J2EE is a broad and deep subject, and getting started can be like getting a drink from a fire hose. We wanted to put together a practical approach to getting started, and spend most of our time talking about the topics that you'll use 90% (or more) of the time. We are serving up meat and potatoes here.

When we pick up a book on software development, we like to have the option of reading straight through, or to skip around and pick up the topics that we're interested in at a given time. As an introduction to J2EE, you'll learn the most if you first read through each chapter in order. Later, as you go back to particular sections, you'll find it easy to skip back to refresh your memory, so feel free to skip around in this book–we hope that we've done a good job of making each topic stand on its own, and provided examples that are straightforward and relevant.

The authors of this book are software engineers first. Like you, we have more projects than time to do them in, and we understand that you don't have extra time to waste when it comes to learning new technologies. We hope the result is a book that you will pick up frequently, highlight, bookmark, and consider a valued addition to your development resources.

Like J2SE, J2EE is comprised of several packages containing classes and interfaces that define the J2EE framework. You're already familiar with J2SE, and you got that expertise by taking the J2SE framework one topic at a time. We'll take J2EE the same way–one topic at a time.

Who Is This Book For?

This book is mainly aimed at people who already have knowledge of basic Java, and have been developing small, client-side applications for the desktop. If you have read and absorbed the information contained in an entry-level book such as *Beginning Java 2* written by Ivor Horton, then you will be well placed to begin your journey to developing server-side applications using J2EE.

If you are coming from another object-oriented language, such as C++ or C#, and you wish to begin developing enterprise-level applications with Java, then you will also benefit greatly from this book. The coding concepts, principles, and constructs are similar; you just need to watch out for the syntax differences and, obviously, the different code architecture for the different technology areas of J2EE.

What Does This Book Cover?

This book will take you from having a good grip of the basic Java language to being able to create reusable and scaleable components of J2EE, such as JavaServer Pages, Enterprise JavaBeans, and web services. At the end of the book, we will also point you in which direction to go to find out more information on your chosen areas of interest, and how you could land yourself the perfect job developing enterprise applications.

Here's a rundown of what you can expect to see as you work through the book.

❑ **Chapter 1: J2EE Essentials**–This chapter will lay out a roadmap of what J2EE is and how it is used as an application foundation. You'll get an introduction to the primary components of J2EE and how they fit together.

❑ **Chapter 2: Getting Set**–Having your machine configured correctly is essential if you want to be able to run the sample code presented in this book. This chapter walks through the installation, configuration, and testing of the core components of J2EE.

❑ **Chapter 3: JavaServer Pages**–An introduction to the world of server-side web programming using JSP pages. This chapter covers how to write simple JSP pages, covering the fundamentals of the technology and how they can be very useful in your web applications.

❑ **Chapter 4: Advanced JSP Topics**–In this chapter, we follow on from the basics of JSP, and look at some deeper features of the technology, such as the expression language, custom actions, and the JSP Standard Tag Library.

❑ **Chapter 5: Servlets**–Next, we cover another highly used component in J2EE web applications–servlets, which are designed to be extensions to servers and to extend the capabilities of servers and provide dynamic behavior.

❑ **Chapter 6: Working with Databases**–At some point in developing a J2EE application, you will very likely need to store and manipulate data stored in a data source. This is where JDBC comes in, and this chapter introduces this functionality where we access the Cloudscape database.

❑ **Chapter 7: Advanced Topics in JDBC**–After learning the basic data access functionality in the previous chapter, you will see deeper topics of JDBC in this chapter, covering prepared statements and stored procedures, transactions, and locking.

❑ **Chapter 8: EJB Fundamentals**–In this part of the book, we begin to look at a feature of J2EE dedicated to expressing the business logic of an application–Enterprise JavaBeans or EJBs. This chapter mainly focuses on an overview of EJB technology and looks at session beans in detail.

❑ **Chapter 9: EJB Entity Beans**–This second chapter on EJBs looks at another type of EJB, entity beans, and how they relate and fit in with other types of bean. We cover two different types of persistence and take a look at the EJB Query Language.

❑ **Chapter 10: More EJB Topics**–Creating container-managed relationships and combining the use of JDBC and EJBs are the two topics of this chapter. We also build on the EJB-QL knowledge gleaned from the previous chapter by looking at EJB-QL select methods.

❑ **Chapter 11: Design Patterns and Message-Driven Beans**–In the final EJB chapter of the book, we look at what design patterns are, and how they can be applied to your EJB applications and what benefits they bring. We also cover the final type of bean–message-driven beans.

❑ **Chapter 12: Web Services and JAX-RPC**–The next major topic in the book covers concepts of enabling distributed applications via the magic of web services. We will look at topics such as the fundamentals, guidelines and good practices, and other issues that you should be aware of when creating web services.

❑ **Chapter 13: More J2EE Web Services Topics**–In the second web services chapter of this book, we move on to combining different J2EE technologies. You will see how to implement a session bean as a web service, and also how to implement a stateful web service.

What You Need to Use This Book

The prerequisite system and software requirements for this are very small. Since you already have a background in Java, then you will no doubt have a version of the J2SE SDK installed on your machine already. In this book, we've used the latest version of the Standard Edition software development kit, which was J2SE 1.4.2. Throughout the book, we have used Microsoft Windows as our operating system but since Java has a "write once, run anywhere" motto, you can use another platform such as Solaris or Linux without any major changes to the code you see.

The only other piece of software you need to download and install to run the examples and follow the discussions in this book is the J2EE 1.4 SDK. We used the final version, released in November 2003, when writing this book.

Style Conventions

We have used certain layout and font styles in this book that are designed to help you to differentiate between the different kinds of information. Here are examples of the styles that are used, with an explanation of what they mean.

As you'd expect, we present code in two different ways: code used inline with text, and code that is displayed on its own. When we need to mention keywords and other coding specifics within the text (for example, in discussion relating to an `if...else` construct or the `beans` package) we use the single-width font as shown in this sentence. If we want to show a more substantial block of code, then we display it like this:

```
package beans;
import java.rmi.RemoteException;
import javax.ejb.EJBHome;
import javax.ejb.CreateException;

public interface SimpleSessionHome extends EJBHome {
   // The create() method for the SimpleSession bean
   public SimpleSession create()
      throws CreateException, RemoteException;
}
```

Sometimes, you will see code in a mixture of gray and white backgrounds, like this:

```
package beans;

import java.rmi.RemoteException;
import javax.ejb.EJBObject;

public interface SimpleSession extends EJBObject {
   // The public business method on the SimpleSession bean
   public String getEchoString(String clientString)
      throws RemoteException;
}

   private void Page_Load(object sender, System.EventArgs e)
   {
      HeaderIconImageUrl = Request.ApplicationPath + "/Images/winbook.gif";
      HeaderMessage = "Informative Page";
   }
```

In cases like this, we use the gray shading to draw attention to a particular section of the code—perhaps because it is new code, or it is particularly important to this part of the discussion.

Sometimes, you will need to type in commands on the command line. We will display situations like that using the following style:

```
> set classpath=.;%J2EE_HOME%\lib\j2ee.jar
> javac -d . client/*.java
```

We show the prompt using a > symbol and then highlight in the **bold** commands you need to type.

Advice, hints, and background information come in this type of font.

> **Important pieces of information come in boxes like this.**

Bullets appear indented, with each new bullet marked as follows:

❑ **Important Words** are in a bold type font.

❑ Words that appear on the screen, or in menus like File or Window, are in a similar font to the one you would see on a Windows desktop.

❑ Keys that you press on the keyboard like *Ctrl* and *Enter*, are in italics.

How to Download the Online Code for the Book

When you visit the Apress web site, http://www.apress.com/, simply locate the title through our search facility or by using the Online Catalog button on the left-hand side. Then you simply need to click on Download Code on the book's detail page to obtain all the code for the book.

1

J2EE Essentials

The word "enterprise" has magical powers in computer programming circles. It can increase the price of a product by an order of magnitude, and double the potential salary of an experienced consultant. Your application may be free of bugs, and cleanly coded using all the latest techniques and tools, but is it enterprise ready? What exactly is the magic ingredient that makes enterprise development qualitatively different from run-of-the-mill development?

Enterprise applications solve business problems. This usually involves the safe storage, retrieval, and manipulation of business data: customer invoices, mortgage applications, flight bookings, and so on. They might have multiple user interfaces: a web interface for consumers, and a GUI application running on computers in the branch offices, for example. They have to deal with communication between remote systems, co-ordination of data in multiple stores, and ensure the system always follows the rules laid down by the business. If any part of the system crashes, the business loses part of its ability to function, and starts to lose money. If the business grows, the application needs to grow with it. All this adds up to what characterizes enterprise applications: robustness in the face of complexity.

When we set out to build a GUI application, we don't start out by working out how to draw pixels on the screen, and build our own code to track the user's mouse around the screen; we rely on a GUI library, like Swing, to do that for us. Similarly, when we set out to create the components of a full-scale enterprise solution, we'd be crazy to start from scratch. Enterprise programmers build their applications on top of systems called **application servers**. Just as GUI toolkits provide services of use to GUI applications, application servers provide services of use to enterprise applications – things like communication facilities to talk to other computers, management of database connections, the ability to serve web pages, and management of transactions.

Just as Java provides a uniform way to program GUI applications on any underlying operating system, nowadays Java can provide a uniform way to program enterprise applications on any underlying application server. The set of libraries developed by Sun Microsystems and the Java Community Process that represent this uniform application server API is what we call the **Java 2 Platform, Enterprise Edition**, and is the subject of this book.

This chapter provides a high-level introduction to J2EE, and an introduction on how to get the most benefit from this book. After reading this chapter, you will:

❑ Have an understanding of the reasons why the concepts underlying J2EE are compelling and enabling technologies for large-scale applications

❑ Understand how J2EE relates to J2SE

❑ Be introduced to the cornerstone technologies of J2EE

❑ Be introduced to some of the essential architectural patterns that J2EE facilitates

So, without further ado, let's get started!

What Is J2EE?

Since you're reading this book you've got some interest in J2EE, and probably have some notion of what you're getting into. For many fledgling J2EE developers, J2EE equates to Enterprise JavaBeans. J2EE is a great deal more than just EJBs, though.

While perhaps an oversimplification, J2EE is a suite of specifications for application programming interfaces, a distributed computing architecture, and definitions for packaging of distributable components for deployment. It's a collection of standardized **components**, **containers**, and **services** for creating and deploying distributed applications within a well-defined distributed computing architecture.

As its name pretty much spells out, Java 2 Enterprise Edition is targeted at large-scale business systems. Software that functions at that level doesn't run on a single PC–it requires significantly more computing power and throughput than that. For that reason, the software needs to be partitioned into functional pieces and deployed on the appropriate hardware platforms to provide the necessary computing power. That is the essence of distributed computing. J2EE provides a collection of standardized components that facilitate software deployment, standard interfaces that define how the various software modules interconnect, and standard services that define how the different software modules communicate.

How J2EE Relates to J2SE

J2EE isn't a replacement for the Java 2 Standard Edition. The J2SE provides the essential language framework that the J2EE builds upon. It is the core upon which J2EE is based. As you'll see, J2EE consists of several layers, and J2SE is right at the base of that pyramid for each component of J2EE.

As a Java developer, you've probably already learned how to build user interfaces with the JFC/Swing and AWT components. You'll still be using those to build the user interfaces for your J2EE applications, as well as HTML-based user interfaces. Since J2SE is at the core of J2EE, everything that you've learned so far remains useful and relevant.

In fact, J2EE provides pretty much nothing in the way of user interfaces. You'll also see that the J2EE platform provides the most significant benefit in developing the "middle tier" portion of your application—that's the business logic and the connections to back-end data sources. You'll use familiar J2SE components and APIs in conjunction with the J2EE components and APIs to build that part of your applications.

Why J2EE?

J2EE defines a number of services that, to someone developing enterprise-class applications, are as essential as electricity and running water. Life is simple when you simply turn the faucet and water starts running, or flip the switch and lights come on. If you have ever been involved with building a house, you'll know that there is a great deal of effort, time, and expense in building in that infrastructure of plumbing and wiring that is then so nicely hidden behind freshly painted walls. At the points where that infrastructure is exposed, there are standard interfaces for controlling (water faucets and light switches, for example) and connecting (power sockets, lamp sockets, and hose bibs, for example).

In the same vein, there is a great deal of infrastructure required to write enterprise-class applications. There are a bunch of different system-level capabilities that you need in order to write distributed applications that are scaleable, robust, secure, and maintainable. Some vital pieces of that infrastructure include security, to ensure that a user is who they claim to be, and can only access the parts of the application that they're entitled to access. Database access is also a fundamental component so that your application can store and retrieve data. Transaction support is required to make sure that the right data is updated at the right time. If you're not familiar with some of these concepts, don't worry—you'll be introduced to them one at a time throughout this book.

Suppose, though, that the wiring and plumbing in your home wasn't there. You'd need to put in your own plumbing and electricity. Without standard components and interfaces, though, you'd have to fabricate your own pipes, wiring, and so on—it'd be terrifically expensive and an awful lot of work.

Putting in a distributed computing infrastructure—the plumbing and wiring of an architecture that supports enterprise applications—is no simple feat. That's why J2EE-based architectures are so compelling—the hard system-level infrastructure is already in place. But why not custom build (or pay someone to custom build) an infrastructure that is designed around your particular application? Well, for starters, it would take a fantastic amount of time, money, and effort. And even if you were to build up that infrastructure, it would be different from anyone else's infrastructure, so you'd not be able to share components or interoperate with anyone else's distributed computing model. That's a lot of work for something that sounds like a dead end. Even if you were lucky enough to find a vendor that could sell you a software infrastructure, you should be wary about any solution that would lock you into any single vendor's implementation that would preclude you from switching vendors at some point in the future.

The good news is, no surprise, that J2EE defines a set of containers, connectors, and components that fill that gap. J2EE not only fills the gap, but it's based on well-known, published specifications. That means that applications written for J2EE will run on any number of J2EE-compliant implementations. The reference implementation supplied with the J2EE Software Development Kit from Sun (J2SDKEE) provides a working model that we'll use throughout this book, since it's the implementation that Sun has built from the specification, and is freely available. In the next chapter you'll get an introduction to installing and testing the J2SDKEE.

It's important to note that the reference implementation is a working *model* but it's not designed to be used for enterprise-level deployment. It doesn't provide some of the enterprise-level features that are outside of the scope of the J2EE specification, such as clustering (the ability to have multiple servers handling requests at the same time) or failover (the ability to have a group of servers that can recover when one crashes). Working with the reference implementation, though, ensures that you'll get exposure to the core J2EE concepts that apply to ALL vendor implementations, and you won't get bogged down with vendor-specific details.

For production deployment, you'll want to select one of a number of J2EE solutions available from a number of different vendors, which have been optimized for high volume throughput and are designed for your particular application. Sun (http://www.sun.com/software), IBM (http://www.ibm.com/websphere), Borland (http://www.borland.com/besappserver) and BEA (http://www.bea.com/products/weblogic/server) are high-profile examples–but certainly not all–of the commercial implementations. JBoss (http://www.jboss.org) is an open source implementation that has a huge following. You get to choose which one works best for you–that's an exercise that's beyond the scope of this book.

> **Building a J2EE application for one J2EE implementation and deploying it on another is cheap, but it's not free, nor is each vendor's implementation of J2EE completely free of defects and operational quirks. Although Java and J2EE go a long way towards providing platform independence, that isn't a guarantee that you can develop on one platform and deploy on another without any hiccups or surprises. Bugs, differences in performance, and other little "gotchas" can seriously delay or derail your project. When you are developing systems that will be deployed in a production environment, it is always a good idea to do your development and staging using the same platforms and technologies that the production environment is based upon. This will help to avoid unnecessary surprises during and after the rollout.**

Multi-Tier Architecture

One of the recurring themes that you'll run into with J2EE is the notion of supporting applications that are partitioned into several levels, or **tiers**. That is an architectural cornerstone of J2EE and merits a little explanation. If you are already familiar with n-tier application architectures, feel free to skip ahead. Otherwise, the overview presented here will be a good introduction or review that will help lay the foundation for understanding the rationale behind much of J2EE's design and the services it provides.

If you think about what a software application is composed of, you can break it down into three fundamental concerns, or logical layers. The first area of concern is displaying stuff to the user and collecting data from the user. That user interface layer is often called the **presentation** layer, since its job is to present stuff to the user and provide a means for the user to present stuff to the software system. The presentation layer includes the part of the software that creates and controls the user interface and validates the user's actions.

Underlying the presentation layer is the logic that makes the application work, and handles the important processing. The logic in a payroll application that, for example, multiplies the hours worked by the salary to determine how much to pay someone, is one example of this kind of logic. This logical layer is called the **business rules** layer, or more informally the **middle tier**.

All non-trivial business applications need to read and store data, and the part of the software that is responsible for reading and writing data–from whatever source that might be–forms the **data access** layer.

Simple software applications are written to run on a single computer. All of the services provided by the application–the user interface, the persistent data access, and the logic that processes data that's input by the user and read from storage–all exist on the same physical machine and are often lumped together into the application. That monolithic architecture is called "single tier" because all of the logical application services–the presentation, the business rules, and the data access layers–exist in a single computing layer.

User interface logic, business rules, file/ database access

More significant applications may take advantage of a database server and access persistent data by sending SQL commands to a database server to save and retrieve data. In this case, the database runs as a separate process from the application, or even on a different machine than the machine that runs the rest of the program. The components for data access are segregated from the rest of the application logic. The rationale for this approach is to centralize data to allow multiple users to simultaneously work with a common database, and to provide the ability for a central database server to share some of the load associated with running the application. This architecture is usually referred to as "client-server."

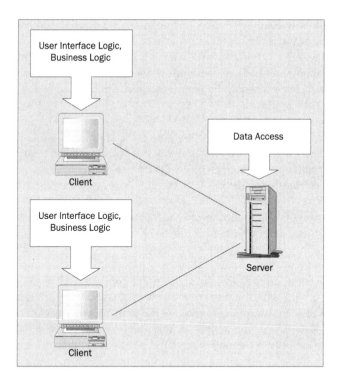

It's convenient and more meaningful to conceptualize the division of the responsibility into layers, or tiers. This software architecture can be shown in two tiers:

One of the disadvantages of two-tier architecture is the fact that the logic that manipulates the data and applies specific application rules concerning the data is lumped into the application itself. This poses a problem when multiple applications are needed to use a shared database. Consider, for example, a database that contains customer information that is used for order fulfillment, invoicing, promotions, and general customer resource management. Each one of those applications would have to be built with all of the logic and rules to manipulate and access customer data. For example, there might be a standard policy within a company that any customer whose account is more than 90 days overdue will be subject to a credit hold. It seems simple enough to build that rule into every application that's accessing customer data, but when the policy changes to reflect a credit hold at 60 days, updating each application becomes a real mess.

You might be tempted to try to solve this problem by building a reusable library that encapsulates the business rules, and when the rules change just replace that library, rebuild the application, and redistribute it to the computers running the application. There are some fundamental problems with that strategy though. First, that strategy assumes that all of the applications have been created using the same programming language, run on the same platform, or at least have some strategy for gluing the library to the application. Next, the applications may have to be recompiled or reassembled with the new library. Moreover, even if the library is a drop-in replacement without recompiling, it's still going to be a royal pain to make sure that each installation of the application has the right library installed simultaneously (it wouldn't do to have conflicting business rules being enforced by different applications at the same time).

In order to get out of that mess, the logical thing to do is to physically separate those business rules out from the computers running the applications onto a separate server so that the software that runs the business rules only needs to be updated once, not for each computer that runs the application. This adds a third tier to our two-tier client-server model:

In this model, all of the business logic is extracted out of the application running at the desktop. The application at the desktop is responsible for presenting the user interface to the end user, and for communicating to the business logic tier. It is no longer responsible for enforcing business rules or accessing databases–its job is solely as the presentation layer. Bear in mind that at this point we're talking somewhat abstractly and theoretically. In a perfect world without performance and other implications, the division of responsibility would be very clear-cut. You'll see throughout this book that you will make practical, balanced implementation decisions about how responsibilities are partitioned in order to create an application that is flexible and performs well.

Typically, in a deployed application, the business logic tier executes on a server apart from the workstation (you'll see shortly that this isn't absolutely required, though). The business logic tier provides the logical glue to bind the presentation to the database. Since it's running on a server, it's accessible to any number of users on the network running applications that take advantage of its business rules. As the number of users demanding those services increases, and the business logic becomes increasingly complex and processor-intensive, the server can be scaled up, or additional servers added. Scaling a single server is a lot easier–and cheaper–than upgrading everyone's workstations.

One of the really great things that this architecture makes possible is the ability to start to build application models where the classes defined in the business logic tier are taken directly from the application domain. The code in the business logic layer can work with classes that model things in the real world (like Customers) rather than working with complex SQL statements. By pushing implementation details into the appropriate layer, and designing applications that work with classes modeled from the real world, applications become much easier to understand and extend.

It's possible to continue the process of partitioning the application functionality into increasingly thin functional layers. You'd reach a point of diminishing returns fairly quickly, since the performance penalty for the network communication between the layers would start to chew up any gains in performance. There are some very effective application architectures based on "n-tier" architecture–the application architect is free to partition the application into as many layers as appropriate–based on the capabilities of the computing and network hardware that the system will be deployed on.

The J2EE architecture is based on the notion of n-tier applications. J2EE makes it very easy to build industrial-strength applications based on 2, 3, or n application layers, and provides all of the plumbing and wiring to make that possible.

I should mention that n-tier architecture does not demand that each of the application layers run on separate machines. It's certainly possible to write n-tier applications that execute on a stand-alone machine, as you'll see. The merit of the application design, however, is that the layers can be split apart and deployed on separate machines, as the application requires.

> **Labeling a particular architecture as "three-tier," "five-tier," etc. is almost guaranteed to spur some academic debate. Some insist that tiers are defined by the physical partitioning, so if the application components live on client workstations, an application server and a database server machine, it's definitely a three-tier application. Others will classify applications by the logical partitioning where the potential exists for physical partitioning. For the discussions in this chapter, I'll take the latter approach with apologies in advance for those who subscribe to the former.**

Vendor Independence

Sun Microsystems–the company that created the Java platform and plays a central role in Java technologies including the J2EE specification–has promoted the Java platform as a solid strategy for building applications that aren't locked into a single platform. In the same way, the architects of J2EE have created it as an open specification that can be implemented by anyone. To date, there are scores of J2EE-based "application servers" that provide a platform for building and deploying scaleable n-tier applications. Any application server that bills itself as J2EE compliant must provide the same suite of services using the interfaces and specifications that Sun has made part of J2EE.

This provides the application developer with a number of choices when implementing a project, and down the road as more applications are added to an organization's suite of solutions. Building an application atop the J2EE architecture provides substantial decoupling between the application logic that you write, and the "other stuff"–transaction support, security, database access–all the distributed computing infrastructure software of the J2EE server that supplies the plumbing and wiring that makes multi-tier applications tick. Remember that all J2EE servers have to support the same interfaces defined in the J2EE specification–that means you can design your application on one server implementation and deploy it on a different one. You can decide later that you want to change which J2EE server you use in your production environment. Moving your application over to the new production environment can be almost trivial.

The vendor and platform independence is something that you can take advantage of in your development. I find myself away from the office quite a bit, and will often use my notebook computer running Windows to do development. It's pretty easy to use that configuration to build, test, and debug (J2EE has great support for pool-side computing). When I am back in the office and happy with a particular component, I can deploy it to the Linux-based servers with little effort, despite the fact that those servers are running a different operating system and different J2EE implementation (after gratuitous testing, of course!).

Bear in mind that each J2EE vendor provides some added value to its particular J2EE implementation. After all, if there weren't market differentiators, there'd be no competition. The J2EE specification covers a lot, but there is also a lot that is not specified in J2EE. Performance, reliability, and scaleability are just a few of the areas that aren't part of the J2EE spec but are areas where vendors have focused a great deal of time and attention. That added value may be ease of use in its deployment tools, highly optimized performance, support for server clustering (which makes a group of servers able to serve application clients as if it were a single super-fast, super-big server), and so on. The key point here is to keep two issues in mind: first, your production applications can potentially benefit from capabilities not supported in the Sun J2EE reference implementation. Just because your application's performance stinks on the reference implementation running on your laptop doesn't mean that J2EE is inherently slow. The second issue is that any vendor-specific capabilities that you take advantage of in your production applications may impact the vendor-independence of your application.

Scaleability

Defining throughput and performance requirements is a vital step in requirements definition. Even the best of us get caught off-guard sometimes, though. Things can happen down the road—unanticipated numbers of users that will use a system at the same time, increased loading on hardware, unsatisfactory availability in the event of server failure, and so on—that can throw a monkey wrench into the works.

The J2EE architecture provides a lot of flexibility to accommodate changes as the requirements for throughput, performance, and capacity change. The n-tier application architecture allows software developers to apply additional computing power where it's needed. Partitioning applications into tiers also enables refactoring of specific pain points without impacting adjacent application components.

Clustering, connection pooling, and failover will become familiar terms to you as you build J2EE applications. Several providers of J2EE application servers have worked diligently to come up with innovative ways to improve application performance, throughput, and availability—each with its own special approach within the J2EE framework.

Features and Concepts in J2EE

Getting your arms around the whole of J2EE will take some time, study, and patience. There are a lot of concepts that you'll need to get started, and these concepts will be the foundation of more concepts to follow. The journey through J2EE will be a bit of an alphabet soup of acronyms, but hang tough—you'll catch on, and we'll do our best on our end to help you make sense of it.

Up to this point, I've been using terms like "client" and "server" fairly loosely and liberally. These terms represent fairly specific concepts in the world of distributed computing and J2EE.

A J2EE client can be a console (text) application written in Java, or a GUI application written using JFC/Swing or AWT. These types of clients are often called "fat" clients because they tend to have a fair amount of supporting code for the user interface.

J2EE clients may also be "web-based" clients. That is, they are clients that live inside a browser. Because these clients offload much of their processing to supporting servers, these clients have very little in the way of supporting code. This type of client is often called a "thin" client. A thin client may be a purely HTML-based interface, a JavaScript-enriched page, or may contain a fairly simple applet where a slightly richer user interface is needed.

It would be an oversimplification to describe the application logic called by the J2EE clients as the "server." While it is true that from the perspective of the developer of the client-side code, that illusion is in no small way the magic of what the J2EE platform provides. In fact, the J2EE application server is the actual "server" that connects the client application to the business logic.

The server-side components created by the application developer can be in the form of web components and business components. Web components come in the form of **JavaServer Pages** (**JSPs**) or **servlets**. Business components, in the world of J2EE, are **Enterprise JavaBeans** (**EJBs**).

These server-side components, of course, rely on the J2EE framework. J2EE provides support for the server-side components in the form of "containers."

Containers

Containers are a central theme in the J2EE architecture. Earlier in this chapter I talked about application infrastructure in terms of the plumbing and electricity that a house provides for its inhabitants. Containers are where those infrastructure services interface with, and provide a host for, application logic.

In the same way that application developers can partition application logic into tiers of specific functionality, the designers of J2EE have partitioned the infrastructure logic into logical tiers. They have done the work of writing the application support infrastructure–things that you'd otherwise have to build yourself. These include things like security, transaction handling, naming, and resource location, and of course the guts of network communications that connect the client to the server. J2EE provides a set of interfaces that allow you to plug your application logic into that infrastructure and access those services. Those interface layers are the J2EE containers.

Think of containers as playing a role much like a video gaming console that you plug game cartridges into. The gaming console provides a point of interface for the game, a suite of services that lets the game be accessed by the user and allows the game to interact with the user. The game cartridge itself needs only be concerned with itself–it doesn't need to concern itself with how the game is displayed to the user, nor what sort of controller is being used, or even if the household electricity is 120VAC or 220VAC–the console provides a container that abstracts all of that stuff out for the game, allowing the game programmer to focus solely on the game and not the infrastructure:

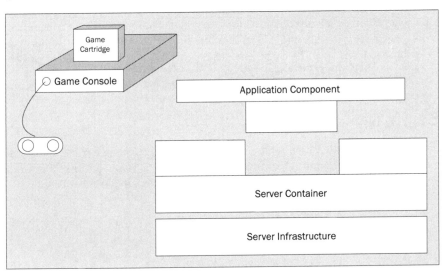

If you've ever created an applet, you're already familiar with the concept of containers. Most web browsers provide a container for applet components. The browser's container for applets provides a defined site for your application component in the form of the `java.applet.Applet` class interface. That site provides services through the `AppletContext` interface. When you develop applets, you are relieved of the burden of interfacing with a web browser and are free to spend your time and effort on the applet logic–not the issues associated with making your application appear to be an integral part of the web browsers.

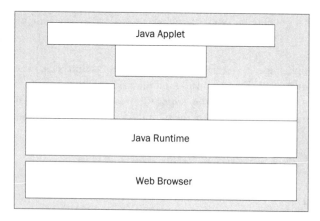

J2EE provides server-side containers in the same vein: they provide a well-defined interface, along with a host of services that allow application developers to focus on the business problems they're trying to solve, and alleviating the need to worry about the plumbing and electricity. Containers handle all of the monkey motion involved with starting up services on the server side, activating your application logic, and cleaning up after you.

J2EE and the Java platform provide containers for web components and business components. These containers–like the gaming console–provide an interface site for components that conform to the container's established interfaces. The containers defined in J2EE include a container for EJBs, JavaServer Pages, servlets, and J2EE clients.

Java Servlets

You are no doubt familiar with accessing simple, static HTML pages using a browser that sends a request to a web server, which in turn sends back a web page that's stored at the server. In that role, the web server is simply being used as a virtual librarian that returns a document based on a request.

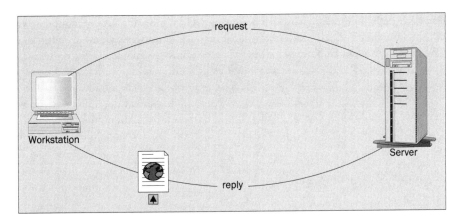

That model of serving up static web pages doesn't provide for dynamically generated content, though. For example, suppose that the web client wants the server to return a list of HTML documents based on some query criteria. In that case, some means of generating HTML on the fly and returning it to the client is needed.

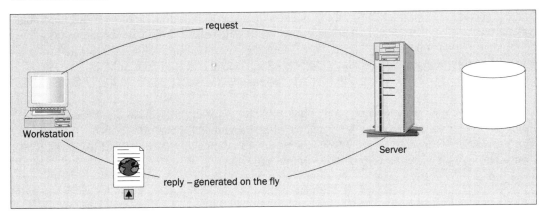

A servlet is a Java component implementing the `javax.servlet.Servlet` interface. It gets invoked as a result of a client request for that particular servlet. The servlet model is pretty generic and not necessarily bound to the Web and HTTP, but nearly all of the servlets that you'll encounter will fall into that category. The web server receives a request for a given servlet in the form of an HTTP query. The web server in turn invokes the servlet and passes back the results to the requesting client. The servlet can be passed parameters from the requesting web client. The servlet is free to perform whatever computations it cares to, and spits out results in the form of HTML back to the client.

The servlet itself is managed and invoked by the J2EE servlet container. When the web server receives the request for the servlet, it notifies the servlet container, which in turn will load the servlet as necessary, and invoke the appropriate `javax.servlet.Servlet` interface service method to satisfy the request.

If you've done any web application programming using CGI (common gateway interface), you'll be familiar with the limitations of that mechanism including lack of portability and no intrinsic support for session management (a much-overused example is the ability to maintain a list of items in a virtual shopping cart). If you've not done any development using CGI, consider yourself lucky and take my word for it–life with J2EE is a whole lot better! Java servlets are portable, and as you will see in later chapters, the servlet containers provide support for session management that allows you to write complex web-based applications. Servlets can also incorporate JavaBean components (which share little more than a name with Enterprise JavaBeans) that provide an additional degree of application compartmentalization.

Servlets are covered in detail in Chapter 5.

JavaServer Pages

JavaServer Pages, like servlets, are concerned with dynamically generated Web content. These two web components comprise a huge percentage of the content of real-world J2EE applications.

Building servlets involves building Java components that emit HTML. In a lot of cases that works out well, but isn't very accessible for people who spend their time on the visual side of building web applications but don't necessarily care to know much about software development. Enter the JavaServer Page. JavaServer Pages are HTML-based text documents with Java code with **scriptlets**–or chunks of Java code–embedded into the HTML document within XML tags.

When JSPs are deployed, something pretty remarkable happens–the contents of the JSP are rolled inside out like a sock, and a servlet is created based on the embedded tags and Java code scriptlets. This happens pretty much invisibly. If you care to, you can dig under the covers and see how it works (which makes learning about servlets all the more worthwhile):

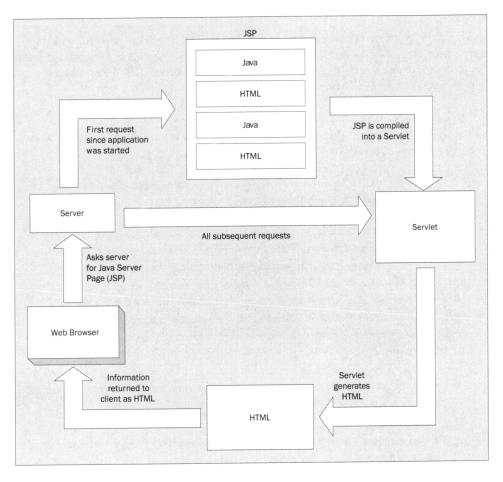

You may have had some exposure to JavaScript—that's a Java-like scripting language that can be included within a web page, and is executed by the web browser when a page containing JavaScript code is browsed to by the user. JSP is a little like that, but the code is compiled and executed at the *server*, and the resulting HTML is fed back to the requesting client. JavaServer Pages are lightweight and fast (after the initial compilation to the servlet), and provide a lot of scaleability for web-based applications.

The developer of a JavaServer Page can create both static and dynamic content in a JSP. Because content based on HTML, XML, etc. forms the basis of a JSP, a non-technical person can create and update that portion of a page. A more technical Java developer can create the snippets of Java code that will interface with data sources, perform calculations, and so on—the dynamic stuff.

Since an executing JSP is a servlet, JSP provides the same support for session management as servlets. JSPs can also load and call methods of JavaBean components, access server-based data sources, or perform complex calculations at the server.

JSPs are introduced in detail in Chapter 3. Chapter 4 continues with more advanced JSP concepts.

Enterprise JavaBeans

Enterprise JavaBeans are to J2EE what Mickey Mouse is to Disney—it's the flagship technology of the platform. When J2EE is mentioned, EJB is what immediately comes to mind. I mentioned earlier that J2EE is a whole lot more than EJB, but my intention isn't to trivialize EJBs—the attention that the technology gets is certainly merited.

In order to better understand what EJBs are and do, it helps to start out with Java's Remote Method Invocation (RMI). If you're not already familiar with RMI, or if you need a quick overview or a refresher, you may want to refer to http://java.sun.com/rmi.

RMI is Java's native means of allowing a Java object to run on one computer, and have its methods called by another object running on a separate computer across a network.

> In order to create a remote object with RMI, you'd first design an interface that extends the java.rmi.Remote interface. This interface defines the operations that you want to expose on your remote object. The next step is to design the remote object as a Java class that implements the interface you've defined. This class extends the java.rmi.server.UnicastRemoteObject class, which will provide the necessary network communications between this object and the objects that call it. Finally, you'd write an application that creates an instance of this class and registers that instance with the RMI registry. The registry is a simple lookup service that allows remote computers to find the remote object using a name-based lookup. The same service is used by the client application, which requests a named object from the registry and casts it into the remote interface designed in the first step.

What RMI provides is a bare-bones client-server implementation. It provides the basic stuff: a registry for lookup, the guts of network communication for invoking operations and passing parameters to and from remote objects, and a basic mechanism for managing access to system resources as a safeguard against malicious code running on a remote computer.

RMI is lightweight, though. It's not designed to satisfy the requirements of enterprise-class distributed applications. It lacks the essential infrastructure that enterprise-class applications rely on, such as security, transaction management, and scaleability. While it supplies base classes that provide networking, it doesn't provide a framework for an application server that hosts your server-side business components and scales along with your application—you have to write the client and the server applications.

Enter Enterprise JavaBeans. EJBs are Java components that implement business logic. This allows the business logic of an application (or suite of applications) to be compartmentalized into EJBs and kept separate from the front-end applications that use that business logic.

The J2EE architecture includes a server that is a container for EJBs. The EJB container loads the bean as needed, invokes the exposed operations, applies security rules, and provides the transaction support for the bean. If it sounds to you like the EJB container does a lot of work, you're right–the container provides all of the necessary plumbing and wiring needed for enterprise applications. As you'll see in Chapter 7, building Enterprise JavaBeans follows the same basic steps as creating an RMI object, but since the EJB container provides all of the enterprise plumbing, you get to spend more time building your application and less time messing around with trying to shoehorn in services like security and transaction support.

Enterprise JavaBeans come in a few different flavors: session beans, entity beans, and message beans. Session beans, like the name implies, live only as long as the conversation or "session" between the client application and the bean lasts. The session bean's primary reason for being is to provide application services, defined and designed by the application developer, to client applications. Depending on the design, a session bean may maintain state during the session (that is, it keeps its internal member variables' values so it can maintain sort of a conversation with the client), or it may be "stateless," meaning that it provides business rules through its exposed operations but doesn't provide any sense of "state"–that responsibility is delegated to the client.

Entity beans represent business objects–such as customers, invoices, and products– in the application domain. These business objects are persisted so they can be stored and retrieved at will. The J2EE architecture provides a lot of flexibility for the persistence model that allows you to defer all of the work of storing and retrieving the bean's state information to the container, or lets you control it all (very useful when you're dealing with interfacing your J2EE system to a legacy application!).

The third type of EJB, the message bean, provides a component model for services that listen to Message Service messages. The J2EE platform includes a messaging queue that allows applications to post messages to a queue, as well as to "subscribe" to queues that get messages. The advantage to this particular way of doing things is that the sender and the receiver of the message really need know nothing about each other–they only need to know about the message queue itself.

One example use of a message queue is an automated stock trading system. Stock prices are sent as messages to a message queue, and things that are interested in stock prices consume those messages.

With message-driven EJBs, it is possible to create an EJB that responds to messages concerning stock prices and makes automatic trading decisions based on those messages.

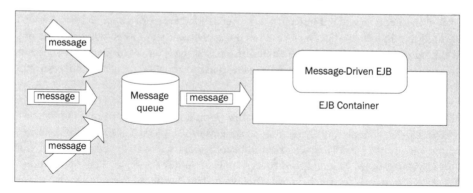

You will learn a lot about the ins and outs of using session and entity beans in Chapter 7. Your J2EE applications will typically be comprised of both session and entity beans. Message beans will come later in the book–they're not used as frequently as the other flavors in most applications, but they're still pretty darn cool!

XML Support

Extensible Markup Language (XML) is a significant cornerstone for building enterprise systems that provide interoperability and are resilient in the face of changes. There are several key technologies in J2EE that rely on XML for configuration and integration with other services.

J2EE provides a number of APIs for developers working with XML. Java API for XML Processing (JAXP) provides support for generating and parsing XML with both the Document Object Model (DOM), which is a tree-oriented model, and SAX (Simple API for XML), which is a stream-based event-driven processing model.

The Java API for XML Binding (JAXB) provides support for mapping XML to and from Java classes. It provides a compiler and a framework for performing the mapping so you don't have to write custom code to perform those transformations.

The Java API for XML Registries (JAXR), Java API for XML Messaging (JAXM), and Java API for XML-based Remote Procedure Calls (JAX-RPC) round out the XML API provisions. These sets of APIs provide support for SOAP and web services (discussed in the following section).

This book assumes that you've got a basic familiarity with XML. If you need a refresher on XML, you might want to review Chapters 21 and 22 of *Beginning Java 2* (*Apress, ISBN 1-86100-569-5*).

Web Services

The World Wide Web is becoming an increasingly prevalent backbone of business applications. The end points that provide web applications with server-side business rules are considered "web services." The W3C consortium, in an effort to unify how web services are published, discovered, and accessed, has sought to provide more concrete definitions for web services:

> *"A web service is a software system identified by a URI, whose public interfaces and bindings are defined and described using XML. Its definition can be discovered by other software systems. These systems may then interact with the web service in a manner prescribed by its definition, using XML-based messages conveyed by internet protocols."*
>
> *[Web Services Architecture, Working Draft 14:* http://www.w3.org/TR/ws-arch*]*

This specifies some specific requirements:

- ❑ XML is used to publish the description of the services.

- ❑ Those descriptions are discoverable through some form of registry.

- ❑ XML messages are used to invoke those services and to return the results to the requestor.

The W3C has established Web Service Description Language (WSDL) as the XML format that is used by web services to describe their services and how clients access those services. In order to call those services, clients need to be able to get their hands on those definitions. XML registries provide the ability to publish service descriptions, search for services, and obtain the WSDL information describing the specifics of a given service.

There are a number of overlapping XML registry service specifications, including ebXML and Universal Description, Discovery, and Integration (UDDI). The JAXR API provides an implementation-independent API for accessing those XML registries.

Simple Object Access Protocol (SOAP) is the lingua franca used by web services and their clients for invocation, parameter passing and obtaining results. SOAP defines the XML message standards and data mapping required for a client application to call a web service and pass it parameters. The JAX-RPC API provides an easy-to-use developer interface that masks the complex underlying plumbing.

Not surprisingly, the J2EE architecture provides a container that hosts web services, and a component model for easily deploying web services. Chapters 12 and 13 in the book cover SOAP and web services.

Transaction Support

One of the basic requirements of enterprise applications is the ability to allow multiple users of multiple applications to simultaneously access shared databases and to absolutely ensure the integrity of that data across those systems. Maintaining data consistency is no simple thing.

Suppose that your application was responsible for processing bank deposits, transfers, and withdrawals. Your application is processing a transfer request from one account to another. That process seems pretty straightforward: deduct the requested amount from one account and add that same amount to the other account. Suppose, however, that immediately after deducting the sum from the source account, something went horribly wrong–perhaps a server failed or a network link was severed–and it became impossible to add the transfer to the target account. At that point, the data's integrity has been compromised (and worse yet, someone's money is now missing).

Transactions can help to address this sort of problem. A transaction represents a set of activities that collectively will either succeed and be made permanent, or fail and be reverted. In the situation described above, we could define the transaction boundaries to start as the transfer amount is withdrawn from the source account, and end after the target account was updated successfully. When the transaction had been made successfully, the changes are committed. Any failure inside of the transaction boundary would result in the changes being rolled back and the account balances restored back to the original values that existed before the start of the transaction.

J2EE–and EJB in particular–provides substantial transaction support. The EJB container provides built-in support for managing transactions, and allows the developer to specify and modify transaction boundaries without changing code. Where more complex transaction control is required, the EJB can take over the transaction control from the container and perform fine-grained or highly customized transaction handling.

Security

Security is a vital component in enterprise applications, and J2EE provides built-in security mechanisms that are far more secure than home-grown security solutions that are typically added as an afterthought.

J2EE allows application resources to be configured for anonymous access where security isn't a concern. Where there are system resources that need to be secured, however, it provides authentication (making sure your users really are who they say they are) and authorization (matching up users with the privileges they are granted).

Authorization in J2EE is based on roles of users of applications. You can classify the roles of users who will be using your application, and authorize access to application components based on those roles. J2EE provides support for declarative security that is specified when the application is deployed, as well as programmatic security that allows you to build in fine-grained security into the Java code. These security mechanisms are discussed in the online chapter that comes as part of the download package for this book, available from the Apress web site at http://www.apress.com.

Sample J2EE Architectures

There is no such thing as a single software architecture that fits all applications, but there are some common architectural patterns that reappear frequently enough to take note of. The following architectures are ones that you're likely to run into as you examine and develop J2EE-based systems.

Each one of these has its own merits and strong points. I present them here to illustrate that there are a number of ways to put together applications and as a short "field guide" for identifying these architectures as you spot them in the wild.

n-Tier Architecture

n-Tier application architecture is intended to address a number of problems, including:

❑ High cost of maintenance when business rules change

❑ Inconsistent business rule implementation between applications

❑ Inability to share data or business rules between applications

❑ Inability to provide web-based front ends to line-of-business applications

❑ Poor performance and inability to scale applications to meet increased user load

❑ Inadequate or inconsistent security across applications

Two tier applications address sharing of data between applications and, to a lesser degree, touch on performance scalability, but do not address any of the other concerns. The business rules still must be coded into the client applications, leaving the problems of high maintenance costs and inconsistency in business rules and security.

J2EE provides a platform that enables developers to easily create n-tier applications in a number of different configurations. The following examples illustrate some typical J2EE application configurations.

Application Client with EJB

The client application is built as a stand-alone (JFC/Swing or console) application. The application relies on business rules implemented as EJBs running on a separate machine.

JSP Client with EJB

The client in this architecture is a web browser. JavaServer Pages access business rules and generate content for the browser.

Applet Client with JSP and Database

Again, the client application is a web browser, but in this case a Java applet is used within a web page to provide a more interactive, dynamic user interface for the user. That applet accesses additional content from JSPs. Data is accessed from the JSP via the JDBC API.

Using Web Services for Application Integration

In this final example, a client application implemented in C# accesses data from a web service implemented in Java.

Summary

In this opening chapter to the book, we have covered an overview of the J2EE and how all the various bits fit together to enable you to create powerful business components. We first looked at what *exactly* J2EE is and tackled the obvious issue of moving from creating desktop applications with Java 2 Platform, Standard Edition (J2SE) to building enterprise-level applications and dynamic, data-driven web sites using the Enterprise Edition of the Java 2 Platform, J2EE. We covered how the two relate to each other and how they differ from each other, as well as looking at how applications are built using J2EE.

Next we looked at what makes up a J2EE application. J2EE architecture is based on the idea of building applications around multiple tiers of responsibility. The application developer creates components, which are hosted by the J2EE containers. Containers play a central theme in the J2EE architecture.

Servlets are one type of J2EE web component. They are Java classes that are hosted within, and invoked by the J2EE server by requests made to, a web server. These servlets respond to those requests by dynamically generating HTML, which is then returned to the requesting client.

JavaServer Pages (JSPs) are very similar in concept to servlets, but differ in that the Java code is embedded within an HTML document. The J2EE server then compiles that HTML document into a servlet, and that servlet generates HTML in response to client requests.

Enterprise JavaBeans are the centerpiece of J2EE and are the component model for building the business rules logic in a J2EE application. EJBs can be designed to maintain state during a conversation with a client, or can be stateless. They can also be designed to be short-lived and ephemeral, or can be persisted for later recall. EJBs can also be designed to listen to message queues and respond to specific messages.

The J2EE platform provides a number of services beyond the component hosting of servlets, JSPs, and EJBs. Fundamental services include support for XML, web services, transactions, and security.

Extensive support for XML is a core component of J2EE. Support for both document-based and stream-based parsing of XML documents forms the foundation of XML support. Additional APIs provide XML registry service, remote procedure call invocation via XML, and XML-based messaging support.

Web services, which rely heavily on XML, provide support for describing, registering, finding, and invoking object services over the Web. J2EE provides support for publishing and accessing J2EE components as web services.

Transaction support is required in order to ensure data integrity for distributed database systems. This allows complex, multi-step updates to databases to be treated as a single step with provisions to make the entire process committed upon success, or completely undone by rolling back on a failure. J2EE provides intrinsic support for distributed database transactions.

J2EE provides configurable security to ensure that sensitive systems are afforded appropriate protection. Security is provided in the form of authentication and authorization.

After reading through the chapter, you might think that J2EE is *just* about EJBs. The truth is that it is about a lot more than EJBs, although EJBs do play a prominent role within J2EE. J2EE provides a platform for developing and deploying multi-tiered, distributed applications that are designed to be maintainable, scaleable, and portable.

Just as an office building requires a lot of hidden infrastructure of plumbing, electricity, and telecommunications, large-scale applications require a great deal of support infrastructure. This infrastructure includes database access, transaction support, and security. J2EE provides that infrastructure and allows you to focus on application.

Building distributed applications (software with components that run as separate processes, or on separate computers) allows you to partition the software into layers of responsibility, or tiers. Distributed applications are commonly partitioned into three primary tiers: presentation, business rules, and data access. Partitioning applications into distinct tiers makes the software more maintainable and provides opportunities for scaling applications up as the demand on those applications increases.

That's it for your first taster of how J2EE works and why it is so popular. In the next chapter, you'll see the extra steps required to set up your environment, ready for developing powerful J2EE applications.

2

Getting Set

Since this is a book for developers by developers, you'll get the most from this book by running the examples and experimenting. This chapter will help you to make sure that you've properly installed the J2EE 1.4 SDK and will walk you through the steps of setting up the environment and writing a simple application. This is vital to ensuring that you don't encounter needless frustration as you work through the examples. You'll also get a taste of the essential steps of creating a J2EE application, what those steps do, and why they're needed.

In this chapter, you will learn:

❑   What the exact prerequisites for installing the J2EE 1.4 SDK are, and how to configure your system to run enterprise Java applications

❑   How to construct a simple JSP application, and how to deploy and run this application

Even if you already have your environment set up, it's probably a good idea to read through the development steps in this chapter not only to ensure that your environment is set up correctly, but also to give you some essential insight into the fundamentals of building a J2EE application.

All of the installation files are available from the Sun web site. Both the J2EE SDK and the J2SE SDK (required to run the J2EE SDK) are freely available at http://java.sun.com. The URL for the J2EE SDK 1.4 is http://java.sun.com/j2ee/1.4/, and the URL for the J2SE SDK 1.4 is http://java.sun.com/j2se/1.4/

Installing the J2EE 1.4 SDK

> This chapter assumes that you're running Windows 2000 Professional or XP
> Professional. The J2EE 1.4 SDK does not support earlier versions of Windows.
> The Sun web site (http://java.sun.com/j2ee) has installation details of other
> supported operating systems (Solaris SPARC 8 & 9, and RedHat Linux 7.2).

Installing the J2EE 1.4 SDK couldn't be much easier. As we saw in Chapter 1, the J2EE environment
is based on the Java 2 Standard Edition platform, so you need to have that installed before following
the steps described in this chapter. You'll need to ensure that you've got the Java Development Kit for
J2SE (Java Standard Edition) 1.4 (or later) installed. If you've got an earlier JDK, you need to update
it. If you're not certain which version of Standard Edition you have, you can try running the J2EE
SDK 1.4 installation anyway. If you don't have the correct version of J2SE installed, you'll see a
warning message, and have to abort the installation. You should then install the correct version of the
J2SE SDK and run the J2EE SDK installation again.

Alternatively, you can simply go to a command line prompt and type java —version at the command
prompt. The Java interpreter should print out the version information:

```
> java —version
java version "1.4.0"
Java(TM) 2 Runtime Environment, Standard Edition (build 1.4.0-b92)
Java HotSpot(TM) Client VM (build 1.4.0-b92, mixed mode)
```

The version listed in the first line should be at least "1.4.0".

Problems and Solutions

Problem	Solution
Java version is lower than 1.4.0	Obtain and install the latest version of the J2SE SDK. You may want to uninstall the older version before installing the newer version. (You don't have to, but unless you have some compelling reason to keep it around, it's just dead weight).
java —version returns the message: 'java' is not recognized as an internal or external command, operable program or batch file.	The J2SE SDK is not installed, or the PATH environment variable does not include the path to the java executables. Check the PATH, and correct the problem, or reinstall the J2SE SDK.

Once you've done that, installing J2EE is a breeze—just run the installation program. The installation program will firstly check to make sure you've got the right version of the J2SE SDK. Then, make a note of where you're installing the J2EE SDK on your system—you'll need to know that path after the installation is complete in order to update and add some environment variables.

Environment variables are used by the Windows operating system as a shortcut to selected directories on your system. You can set either user-specific environment variables, or (provided you're logged in as a user with administrative rights) system-wide environment variables. Once you set an environment variable for your Java installation, you will find it much quicker and easier to compile and run your Java applications from the command line, as you'll see shortly.

Once the installation is complete, it's time to set up the environment variables you'll need to run the examples in this book. You can check and set these from the System properties. From the Control Panel, choose the System applet. Select the Advanced tab and click on Environment Variables:

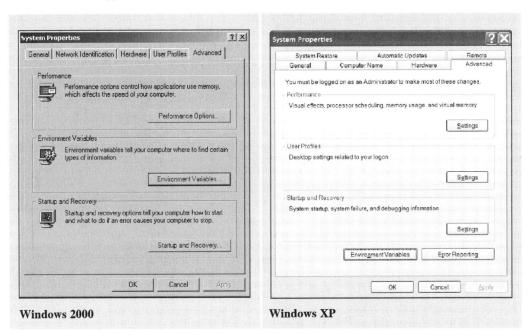

Windows 2000   Windows XP

When you click the Environment Variables button, a dialog will allow you to check and set the values for environment variables:

Make sure that the following environment variables are set either in your local user variables, or in the system variables. If they don't already appear in the list, you can add them by clicking the New button. If they need to be modified, edit them by clicking the Edit button. Click OK when you've finished.

Variable Name	Settings
JAVA_HOME	Contains the path to the directory where J2SE is installed, for example: `c:\j2sdk1.4`
J2EE_HOME	Contains the path to the directory where J2EE SDK is installed, for example: `c:\Sun\AppServer`

PATH	This should include the path to the bin directories of the J2SE SDK and the J2SDKEE. For example:
	`c:\j2sdk1.4\bin;c:\Sun\AppServer\bin;...`
	You can alternatively use the JAVA_HOME and J2EE_HOME environment variables in your path to make things a little simpler, for example:
	`%JAVA_HOME%\bin;%J2EE_HOME%\bin;...`
	Note that the system will search through for executable files using the PATH variable, starting with the directories that appear first in the path. In order to ensure that there aren't other versions of the J2SE or J2EE interfering on this machine, make sure that these new entries go at the front of the PATH variable.

You'll also want to download the free J2EE SDK 1.4 documentation at http://java.sun.com/j2ee/1.4/docs/.

Testing the J2EE 1.4 SDK Installation

If everything went according to plan, your system should be set up and ready to use, so we're now going to walk through some quick tests to ensure that you're ready to run the code in this book.

Starting the Database Server

When you install the J2EE 1.4 SDK, a sample database called PointBase is also installed. We'll be using this database later on in the book, so we need to ensure that the database is ready for use by starting it and testing it out.

From the Windows Start menu, choose the following option:

Start | All Programs | Sun Microsystems | J2EE 1.4 SDK | Start PointBase

After a second or two you should see a command window with the message:

```
Server started, listening on port 9092, display level: 0 ...
>
```

This indicates that the database server has started. The next step is for you to work with the database server from the console of the interactive SQL tool for the PointBase database. To do this, open a new command window and start the PointBase Console by invoking the following command at the command line:

```
> %J2EE_HOME%\pointbase\tools\serveroption\startconsole.bat
```

The dialog shown below should appear, in which you should select the Open specified Database radio button, and enter the following into the labeled text boxes:

❏ Driver: com.pointbase.jdbc.jdbcUniversalDriver

❏ URL: jdbc:pointbase:server://localhost:9092/sun-appserv-samples

❏ User: PBPUBLIC

❏ Password: PBPUBLIC

After a second or two you will see the PointBase Console, shown below:

We'll create a database table and test it. Enter the SQL commands shown below into the **Enter SQL Commands** panel, and click the **Execute All** icon. Make sure that each line ends with a semicolon, which tells the interactive that the command is complete. These commands create the zootable and insert three rows into it. The results should be similar to what you see in the **ExecuteAll** tab of the screenshot above.

```
create table zootable (animal varchar(12) primary key, legcount int);
insert into zootable values ('duck',2);
insert into zootable values ('horse',4);
insert into zootable values ('aardvark',4);
```

Now you can run a SQL query to see the data that you've added. Type the following SQL query into the **Enter SQL Commands** panel, and click the **Execute All** icon to execute the query:

```
select * from zootable;
```

The interactive tool will query the database and print the results of the query:

```
SQL> select * from zootable;

ANIMAL          LEGCOUNT
------------    ------------
duck            2
horse           4
aardvark        4

3 Rows Selected. select * from zoot..., Total 0.391 secs, Compile 0.13 secs
```

One last step—we want to delete the table before we exit. Type the SQL command, followed by a semicolon, and click the Execute All icon:

```
drop table zootable;
```

Exit the PointBase Console by choosing Exit from the File menu.

When you are finished with PointBase, you can stop it by choosing the following option from the Start menu:

Start | All Programs | Sun Microsystems | J2EE 1.4 SDK | Stop PointBase

Starting the J2EE Server

The next step to verifying that your installation is working correctly is to start the J2EE server. The server is launched from menus that are automatically created during installation, so choose the following option from the Start menu:

Start | All Programs | Sun Microsystems | J2EE 1.4 SDK | Start Default Domain

A command window should open with messages similar to the following, the last one prompting you to Press any key to continue as shown below:

```
Starting Domain domain1, please wait.
Log redirected to C:\Sun\AppServer\domains\domain1\logs\server.log.
Domain domain1 started.
Press any key to continue . . .
```

At this point the J2EE server is started. Go ahead and press any key as requested, open a browser, and go to the following URL:

http://localhost:8080

The web browser should display the default J2EE web page:

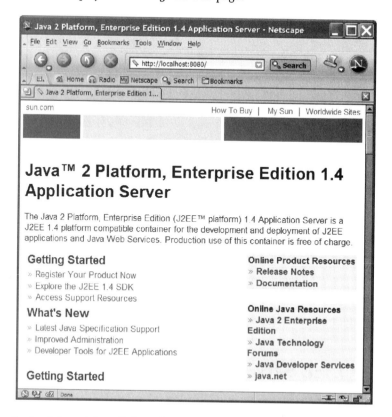

Pat yourself on the back for a job well done. Let's go shred a little code for a final test.

Problems and Solutions

Here is a possible problem you might come up against when running through the previous steps to test your J2EE 1.4 SDK installation:

Problem	Solution
The web browser reports "Page cannot be displayed" when trying to open the URL http://localhost:8080	Make certain that there weren't any errors reported when starting the J2EE server. If you see messages indicating that the server couldn't start because TCP ports were in use by other processes, you may either have another web server using port 8080, or have another instance of the J2EE server running.
	Also, make certain that you've specified the port "8080" in the URL (this is the default port used by the J2EE server).

Compiling and Deploying "Hello J2EE World"

As a final test, we're going to walk through the process of creating and deploying a JavaServer page. This is going to make certain that the J2EE server is working properly first, and give you your first taste of building, deploying, and testing a J2EE application.

This will consist of the following steps:

❑ Create a working directory. This will give us a sandbox for creating the application files and editing them.

❑ Create a text file for the JavaServer Page. This will be a text file of HTML with snippets of Java code, which will be compiled by the J2EE server into a servlet.

❑ Using the Deployment Tool utility, select the components for the application and package them up into a Web Archive. The Web Archive is a jar file that bundles all of the application components into a single file for easy deployment.

❑ Verify the contents of the Web Archive. The Deployment Tool has a utility that will test the contents of the Web Archive before it's distributed to catch problems beforehand.

❑ Distribute the Web Archive to the J2EE server. Once this is done, the application is available and ready to be run.

❑ Test the application.

So, let's get started!

Try It Out Hello J2EE World

1. Create a directory on your machine that will be your sandbox for this exercise. I'll use `C:\3413\Ch02` for mine.

2. Create a new file in that directory called `index.jsp` using your favorite text editor. Here's the code for that file:

```
<%--
    file: index.jsp
    desc: Test installation of J2EE SDK 1.4
--%>
<html>
<head>
  <title>Hello World - test the J2EE SDK installation
  </title>
</head>
<body>
<%
  for (int i = 1; i < 5; i++)
  {
%>
```

```
    <h<%=i%>>Hello World</h<%=i%>>
 <%
    }
 %>
 </body>
 </html>
```

3. Start up the J2EE server if it's not already running, by following the instructions given above.

4. Start the J2EE Deployment Tool application that comes with the J2EE SDK. This tool is a utility that is used to assemble application components into distributable archives, and also to distribute the application to the J2EE server. You can invoke this tool by choosing the following option from the Start menu:

Start | All Programs | Sun Microsystems | J2EE 1.4 SDK | Deploytool

When the Deployment Tool has finished initializing, you'll see its main window:

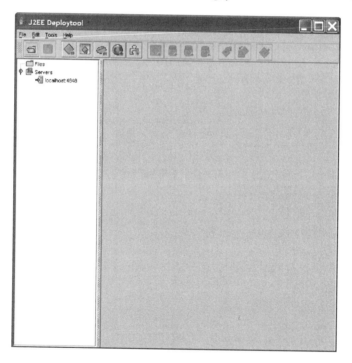

5. We need to create a new **Web Archive** (WAR). A WAR file is an archive file that will contain the web components of a J2EE application, along with a descriptor or "table of contents" that describes what is in the archive. Web applications frequently consist of many more files than our simple application, and the WAR is a very convenient means of bundling up all of those files into a single file for deployment. Select File | New | Web Component from the menu. This will start the New Web Application Wizard:

6. On the War File page of this wizard, shown above:

❑ Make certain that the radio button labeled **Create New Stand-Alone WAR Module** is checked.

❑ In the **WAR Location** text field, enter (or browse to) the path to your working directory, followed by `hello.war` (in my case, `C:\3413\ch02\hello.war`). This tells the Deployment Tool what to name the WAR file.

❑ Enter Hello in the **WAR Name** field, which is the name that will be displayed in the Deployment Tool for this WAR file.

❑ Enter hello into the **Context Root** field. This sets what's called the "context root" (kind of a "home base") for your WAR file when it gets deployed to the server.

You can think of the context root as sort of like a logical directory that's part of the URL. For example, a hypothetical web application located at www.apress.com/codesamples/index.jsp *has a root context of "codesamples". Note that this doesn't necessarily correspond to a directory on the server called "codesamples"—it's a name that the server recognizes and maps to a specific application.*

Next, click the "Edit" button on the right hand side of the dialog. This will open a dialog to select files to add to the Web Archive:

7. In the dialog shown above, set the starting directory (using the top textbox) to your working directory. This simply points the dialog to where your application files are. You should see a folder tree with index.jsp appearing below your working directory folder. Select index.jsp and click the Add button. You should now see index.jsp in the Contents tree at the bottom of the dialog. Click the OK button to close this dialog. Click the Next button to go to the next page of the wizard:

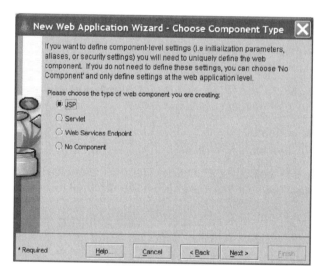

8. You learned in Chapter 1 that there are several different kinds of components in J2EE. This particular application includes a JavaServer Page component, and this is where we tell the Deployment Tool what kind of component we're building. Select the radio button labeled JSP to indicate that you are creating a JavaServer Page component. Click on the Next button to go to the next page of the wizard:

The Deployment Tool's tree navigator now displays the Web Archive you've just created, and its contents.

Save your work now. With the Hello WAR highlighted in the tree on the left, select File | Save All.

9. The next step is to verify the WAR. This step will catch problems with bad code in the JSP, and make sure that the WAR doesn't have obvious problems before it's deployed to the server. Make sure the Hello WAR is still highlighted, and select Tools | Verify J2EE Compliance from the menu. This will bring up a window that will help you verify that your WAR complies with the J2EE specification.

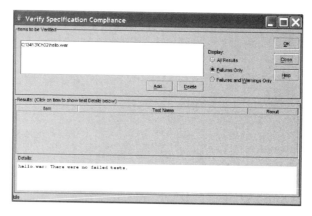

The Display group of radio buttons, shown above, lets you select how much detail you care to see about the tests that are run. If you want to only see messages about failures, select the radio button labeled Failures Only (try not to take it personally–it's not the best phrasing in the world). Click the OK button.

If all went well, you should see a message at the bottom indicating that no tests failed. If your JSP had problems with its code, you will get compilation error messages. If you see compilation errors, go back to your JSP file and check it carefully to make sure it matches the code in the book.

10. We're almost done. Next, we need to deploy the WAR to the J2EE server. With the hello WAR selected in the tree navigator, select Tools | Deploy from the menu. This will bring up the Deploy Module dialog:

11. You'll supply the user name and password that you specified when installing the J2EE SDK 1.4. Click **OK**, and when the dialog closes a window will appear and will show the status of the deployment process. You should see something like:

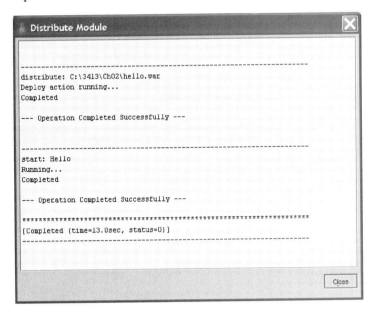

Wait until you see the **Completed** message, and click **Close**.

12. It's time to test your first JSP. Start a web browser and open the following URL:

   http://localhost:8080/hello

After a couple of seconds, you should see the web page:

Congratulations! Your first JSP is a success!

Before we look at what we've done in this example, you should stop the J2EE server by selecting the following option from the Windows Start menu:

Start | All Programs | Sun Microsystems | J2EE 1.4 SDK | Stop Default Domain

How It Works

The JSP file that you created is a text file that consists of HTML and embedded snippets of code. Notice in this file that there are tags with enclosed Java code, as we discussed in Chapter 1:

```
<%--
    file: index.jsp
    desc: Test installation of J2EE SDK 1.4
--%>
<html>
<head>
  <title>Hello World - test the J2EE SDK installation
  </title>
</head>
<body>
<%
  for (int i = 1; i < 5; i++)
  {
%>
  <h<%=i%>>Hello World</h<%=i%>>
<%
  }
%>
</body>
</html>
```

When the JSP is compiled into a servlet, that servlet code expands the JSP's code snippets and HTML into code that writes HTML to an output stream:

```
out.write("\n\n");
out.write("<html>\n");
out.write("<head>\n");
out.write("  <title>Hello World - test the J2EE SDK installation");
out.write("  </title>\n");
out.write("</head>\n");
out.write("<body>\n");
for (int i = 1; i < 5; i++)
{
  out.write("\n    ");
  out.write("<h");
  out.write(String.valueOf(i));
  out.write(">Hello World");
  out.write("</h");
  out.write(String.valueOf(i));
```

```
   out.write(">\n");
   }
out.write("</body>\n");
out.write("</html>\n");
```

That code, when executed, will write the following HTML code to the stream that is sent back to the requesting browser:

```
<html>
<head>
   <title>Hello Hello World - test the J2EE SDK installation
   </title>
</head>
<body>

   <h1>Hello World</h1>

   <h2>Hello World</h2>

   <h3>Hello World</h3>

   <h4>Hello World</h4>

</body>
</html>
```

That's how the JSP code works. The process of packaging and deployment has a few more steps. Let's dig in a bit and see what's happening:

In order to deploy a J2EE application to a server, it has to be bundled up into an archive–that's a single file that packages up all the requisite files. The Web Archive (WAR) has to contain the components that we've created for the application (the JSP file), as well other support files. Those support files include a deployment descriptor that tells the server what's contained in the WAR and how to run it, a manifest for the archive, which is an application table of contents, and a file containing deployment information specific to the J2EE reference implementation server:

Once those contents have been assembled into a WAR file, that WAR can then be deployed to the J2EE server. That process sends the archive to the server, which then reads the deployment descriptor to determine how to unbundle the contents. In the case of this application, it sees that the WAR contains a JSP, and so it compiles that JSP into a servlet.

In order to run the application once it is deployed, you have to request the JSP by requesting an URL with your web browser. Notice that the URL consists of the protocol (http), the server name (localhost), the root context of the application (hello) and the requested resource (index.jsp):

The server receives the incoming HTTP request, and uses the deployment information to invoke the appropriate servlet in a servlet container. The servlet writes HTML to an output stream, which is returned to the web browser by the server.

Problems and Solutions

If you run into any difficulties, the following table lists some common problems and how to fix them:

Problem	Solution
Verifier reports errors.	Carefully retrace your steps and ensure that the steps are followed correctly as described.
When testing the JSP, the web browser reports "Page cannot be displayed" when trying to open the URL http://localhost:8080.	Make certain that there weren't any errors reported when starting the J2EE server. Make certain that you've specified the port "8080" in the URL (this is the default port used by the J2EE server).
When testing the JSP, it reports a compilation error in the web browser.	Double-check the code in index.jsp. If you've mistyped something, the server won't be able to compile the JSP. The message in the web browser should give you a hint where to look.

Summary

This chapter described how to get the J2EE SDK installed, and to verify that the installation was successful. You also got your first taste of creating and running a J2EE application, as well as looking at some of the core concepts involved in building J2EE applications:

❑ JavaServer Pages (JSPs) consist of HTML, with embedded snippets of Java code. The JSP is compiled into a servlet by the J2EE server which, when executed, emits HTML back to the requesting client.

❑ WARs (Web Archives) are deployment components that contain the Web components of a J2EE application. The WAR contains the components themselves (such as JSPs), and the deployment descriptor that defines the contents of the WAR. The WAR can also contain server-specific deployment information.

At this point in the book, you should now be familiar with the following procedures:

❑ How to install and configure the J2EE environment

❑ How to start and stop the PointBase database server

❑ How to start the PointBase Console

❑ How to start and stop the J2EE server

❑ How to start the Deployment Tool

❑ The essential steps of building a J2EE application:

    ❑ Create the application components

    ❑ Bundle the components into an archive

    ❑ Verify the contents of the archive to catch problems before deploying

    ❑ Distribute the archive to the J2EE server

    ❑ Test the application

If you've been able to get through this exercise, you're more than ready to dive into more detail. The next chapter will take you deeper into the details of JavaServer Pages—you'll learn the essential structure of JSPs, and how to enable users to interact with your JSPs.

JavaServer Pages

In the previous chapters, we briefly introduced the J2EE and JavaServer Pages (JSP) technologies; in this chapter, we'll start to take a much more detailed look at JSP.

JSP pages are components in a web, or J2EE, application that consist of HTML with Java code added to the HTML. You might ask, "What's so different about that? I've been putting JavaScript into my HTML for years." The difference is that JavaScript runs on the client, whereas the code in a JSP runs on the server. JavaScript can only affect the particular page in which it is embedded; code in a JSP can access data across the entire web application.

In this chapter we will begin to look at how to create JSP pages for your web application. We will look at:

❑ The basic structure of JSP pages, and how to write a JSP page

❑ How to use directive, scripting, and action elements

❑ How to access the implicit objects of the page

❑ How servers translate and compile JSP pages

❑ How to handle errors and exceptions

❑ How to forward and include pages from a JSP page

Introduction to JSP

As components in a J2EE application, JSP pages run on a server and respond to requests from clients. These clients are usually users accessing the web application through a web browser. The protocol used by clients to call the HTML and JSP pages in our J2EE application is HTTP, the same protocol used by browsers to get HTML pages from a web server.

For the moment we'll concentrate on the basics of creating JSP pages, but we'll look at the underlying HTTP protocol in Chapter 5.

Developing JSP Pages

In order to create a JSP page that can respond to client requests, there are a number of things we need to do. Firstly, of course, we need to write the JSP page. At some point, this page is translated and compiled into a Java class. This can happen before the page is loaded to a server, or it can happen at the time the client makes a request. The page executes inside a JSP container. A container is a piece of software that loads and manages J2EE components, in this case JSP pages. This container can be part of the web server, or it can run separately from the web server.

We can divide this process into three steps:

❑ Creation–The developer creates a JSP source file that contains HTML and embedded Java code.

❑ Deployment–The JSP is installed into a server. This can be a full J2EE server or a stand-alone JSP server.

❑ Translation and compilation–The JSP container translates the HTML and Java code into a Java code source file. This file is then compiled into a Java class that is executed by the server. The class file created from the JSP is known as the JSP page implementation class.

Note that this last step can actually occur at various times. Even though it is listed last here, you can translate and compile the JSP prior to deployment, and deploy the class file directly. Compiling first allows us to catch and fix syntax errors in our code prior to deployment. Alternatively, the JSP container can compile the JSP when it is deployed to the server. Finally, the usual process is that when the first request is made for the JSP, the server translates and compiles the JSP. This is known as translation at request time.

Basic JSP Lifecycle

Once compilation is complete, the JSP lifecycle has these phases:

❑ Loading and instantiation–The server finds the Java class for the JSP page and loads it into the Virtual Machine. After the class is loaded, the JVM creates one or more instances of the page. This can occur right after loading, or it can occur when the first request is made.

❑ Initialization–The JSP page is initialized. If you need to execute code during initialization, you can add a method to the page that will be called during initialization.

❑ Request processing–The page responds to a request. After performing its processing, a response is returned to the client. The response consists solely of HTML tags or other data; none of the Java code is sent to the client.

❑ End of life–The server stops sending requests to the JSP. After all current requests are finished processing, any instances of the class are released. If you need code to execute and perform any cleanup actions, you can implement a method that will be called before the class instance is released.

When a client sends a request for a JSP, the web server gives the request to the JSP container, and the JSP container determines which JSP page implementation class should handle the request. The JSP container then calls a method of the JSP page implementation class that processes the request and returns a response through the container and web server to the client:

Although we've seen how JSP works, we haven't yet addressed the question of *why* we need JSP. The JSP home page (http://java.sun.com/products/jsp/) says, "Web developers and designers use JavaServer Pages technology to rapidly develop and easily maintain information-rich, dynamic web pages that leverage existing business systems." JSP pages can be rapidly developed and easily maintained because they are based on HTML and XML. Documents with markup such as HTML are easy to understand and there are many automated tools for dealing with HTML and XML documents. JSP pages are dynamic because they can contain Java code, which can process the request and tailor the response based on the request. All the power of Java sits behind every JSP page.

Writing JSP Pages

So, now that we've seen how JSP pages work, let's look at what they contain, and how we go about writing them. Take a look at the following line of code:

```
<html><body><p>Hello, World!</p></body></html>
```

Admittedly, this example is not a very good JSP example. However, these HTML tags do form a correct and valid JSP file. You could save the above file as `HelloWorld.jsp`, install it into a web application, and the server would access it as a JSP resource. The point I want to make is that JSP pages tend to look a lot like HTML pages. To make these pages dynamic, you can embed special tags and Java code in them. You can think of JSP pages as web pages with little bits of Java embedded in them.

The reason the example above is not very good is that it isn't dynamic in any way. If your JSP pages don't contain Java code, you might as well just make them static HTML pages. JSP pages are intended to have dynamic behavior; they are supposed to change in response to specific client requests. You give the page dynamic behavior by embedding Java code into the page.

JSP Elements

You can't just write Java code wherever you want in the page, though. You need some way to tell the server which bits are code, and which bits are regular HTML. To do this, the JSP specification defines HTML-like or XML tags that enclose the code in the JSP. Those tags come in three categories:

❑ Directive elements

❑ Scripting elements

❑ Action elements

The original JSP specification used tag formats for these elements that were not compatible with XML; that is, they were not well-formed according to the XML specification. With the JSP 1.2 specification, alternative XML-compliant versions of all the above tags were introduced. You will see both formats in this book, with the original style referred to as JSP style, and the newer as XML style.

Directive Elements

Directive elements provide information to the JSP container about the page. There are three directives available: page, include, and taglib. We will look at page and include here, deferring discussion of taglib to the next chapter. The page and include directives have these forms:

JSP Style	XML
`<%@ page` `attributes %>`	`<jsp:directive.page` `attributes />`
`<%@ include` `attributes %>`	`<jsp:directive.include` `attributes />`

You can find the complete list of attributes and their meanings in the JSP specification, which you can download at http://java.sun.com/products/jsp. Shown below are the attributes you are most likely to be using as you start developing JSP pages:

Directive	Attribute	Description
Page	import	Lists the Java packages to be imported into the page. Just as with a Java source file, the Java code embedded in a JSP page must import the packages of the classes used with the code. Multiple package statements are delimited by commas, for example import="java.io.*,java.util.*".
	session	The valid values are "true" or "false". The default value is "true". If "true", the page participates in a session; if "false", then it does not, and cannot access any session information. Sessions are covered later in the chapter.
	isThreadSafe	Whether the page is thread-safe or not. If "true", the container can use the JSP for multiple concurrent request threads. The default is "true".
	info	An arbitrary string. This can have any value. It is provided so that the JSP can provide information to a management tool about its contents, purpose, name, etc.
	errorPage	The URL of the web page that should be sent to the client if an error occurs in a page.
	isErrorPage	Whether the current page is an error page. The default is false.
	contentType	Defines the content type of the page. The content type can appear as a simple type specification, or as a type specification and a charset. The default value is "text/html" for JSP-style JSP tags and "text/xml" for XML-style JSP tags. When including the charset, the syntax for the attribute is contentType="text/html;charset= char_set_identifier". Whitespace can follow the semicolon in the attribute value. Charsets indicate how written characters are encoded, so that pages can support languages that use different scripts. Information about charsets can be found at http://www.w3.org/TR/REC-html40/charset.html.
	pageEncoding	The charset of the current page. The default is ISO-8859-1 (Latin script) for JSP-style and UTF-8 (an 8-bit Unicode encoding) for XML-style tags.
include	file	The file to be included at the current position in the file. The included file can be any HTML or JSP page or fragment of a page. The file is specified using a URI to a file within the web application.

A single JSP page can have multiple instances of the page directive.

The include directive is used, as stated in the table, to include another page within the current page. This might typically be a standard header or footer, but it can include any content. You would use this when you have standard data that you want to include in multiple JSP pages. The file is included when the page is translated into its Java form. Later we will see a function that allows you to include content at request time.

Scripting Elements

The scripting elements are the elements in the page that include the Java code. There are three subforms of this element: declarations, scriptlets, and expressions. Their forms are:

JSP Style	XML
<%! declaration %>	<jsp:declaration>declaration</jsp:declaration>
<% scriptlet code %>	<jsp:scriptlet>code fragment</jsp:scriptlet>
<%= expression %>	<jsp:expression>expression</jsp:expression>

Declarations

A declaration is used to declare, and optionally define, a Java variable or a method. It works just like any declaration within a Java source code file. The declaration only appears within the translated JSP page, but not in the output to the client. For example, to declare a Vector in your JSP, you would use one of these forms:

```
<%! Vector v = new Vector(); %>
<jsp:declaration>Vector v = new Vector();</jsp:declaration>
```

This JSP fragment declares a variable v of type Vector and initializes it by calling the Vector constructor. Any variable you declare within a declaration element becomes an instance variable of the JSP page implementation class, and thus is global to the entire page. Thus, you must take care when initializing variables with a declaration, because instance variables are not thread-safe. By default, the server can send multiple requests to the same page simultaneously. You don't want one thread to change the variable while another thread is using the variable.

You can also declare and define methods within a declaration element:

```
<%!
public int void countTokens(String s) {
   StringTokenizer st = new StringTokenizer(s);
   return st.countTokens();
}
%>
<jsp:declaration>
public int countTokens(String s) {
```

```
    StringTokenizer st = new StringTokenizer(s);
    return st.countTokens();
}
</jsp:declaration>
```

Variables or methods in a declaration element can be called by any other code in the page.

Scriptlets

Scriptlets contain Java code statements. The code in the scriptlet appears in the translated JSP, but not in the output to the client. Any legal Java code statements can appear within a scriptlet. For example, to repeat the phrase "Hello, World!" ten times in the output page, you could use this scriptlet:

```
<%
   for (int i = 0; i < 10; i++) {
%>
Hello, World!
<%
   }
%>
```

As in this code snippet, we can freely interleave Java code and HTML and/or text data. Everything between the scriptlet markers (<% and %>) is script code; everything outside the markers is template data, which is sent to the client as written. Notice that in the above example the Java code block does not need to begin and end within the same scriptlet element. This allows you complete freedom to mix Java code and HTML elements as needed within the page.

The above example is relatively simple. However, as your application gets more complicated and involved, you'll get more and more code mixed in with the HTML and the page will tend to get complicated. In the next chapter, we will see how tag libraries can give the same rich behavior as above, but using only XML tags.

Since scriptlets can contain Java statements, the following is a legal scriptlet:

```
<%
Vector v = new Vector();
// more code...
%>
```

This looks very similar to the code snippet in the declaration section that preceded this section. This might lead you to wonder what the difference between scriptlets and declarations is, since they appear to be the same. Despite that seeming similarity, they are different in the following ways:

❏ Scriptlets cannot be used to define a method; only declarations can be used for that.

❏ Variables declared in a declaration are instance variables of the JSP page implementation class. These variables are visible to all other code statements or methods in the page.

❏ Variables declared in a scriptlet are local to a method in the JSP page implementation class. They are visible only within their defining code block.

Expressions

Expressions are used to output the value of a Java expression to the client. For example, this code fragment in a JSP:

```
The number of tokens in this statement is <%= countTokens("The number of
tokens in this statement is n") %>.
```

would result in the text "The number of tokens in this statement is 9." being displayed in the browser. The code snippet above calls the hypothetical countTokens(String) method that was shown in the declaration section previously. To count the number of tokens in the statement, a literal copy of the statement is passed to the method. In the code snippet above, the method call returned an int value, which was printed to the client's browser. Here is the same expression using XML style:

```
The number of tokens in this statement is
<jsp:expression>
    countTokens("The number of tokens in this statement is n")
</jsp:expression>.
```

Any legal Java expression can be used with an expression element. An expression could contain a method call, as shown above, or a literal expression such as '2 + 2', or an expression using Java variables or keywords such as 'v instanceof Vector', or any combination of these. Notice also that because declarations and scriptlets contain Java code, the lines of Java code must be terminated with a semicolon. Expressions, however, will not necessarily be legal code statements (but they will be valid expressions), so they do not need a terminating semicolon.

Comments

You can use standard HTML comments within the JSP and those comments will appear in the page received by the client browser. Standard HTML comments have this form:

```
<!-- This comment will appear in the client's browser -->
```

You can also include JSP-specific comments that use this syntax:

```
<%-- This comment will NOT appear in the client's browser --%>
```

JSP comments will not appear in the page output to the client.

Template Data

Everything that is not a directive, declaration, scriptlet, expression, or JSP comment (usually all the HTML and text in the page) is termed **template data**. This data is output to the client as if it had appeared within a static web page.

Try It Out Creating a JSP Web Application

OK, now we really will develop an example JSP page using the information seen so far. This page will provide a welcome page to an application that manages a Frequently Asked Questions (FAQ) forum. Once we've written the code, we will use this example to show how to deploy a JSP application to the J2EE reference implementation server and to a stand-alone Tomcat server.

1. Start by creating a directory structure to match the web application. If you are planning to deploy this application to Tomcat stand-alone, you can create this directory directly in the Tomcat /webapps directory. Here is the directory structure, with the files that will be created:

    ```
    Ch03/
      welcome.jsp
      WEB-INF/
        web.xml
        footer.jspf
        errorPage.jsp
        classes/
          Ch03/
            FaqCategories.java
            FaqCategories.class
    ```

    As you go through the following steps and create each file, refer to the directory structure above to determine where to save each file.

2. Let's start with the page that welcomes users to the web application. This is the welcome.jsp file:

    ```jsp
    <%@ page errorPage="/WEB-INF/errorPage.jsp"
             import="java.util.Iterator,Ch03.FaqCategories" %>

    <!DOCTYPE HTML PUBLIC "-//W3C//DTD HTML 4.01 Transitional//EN">
    <html>
      <head>
        <title>Java FAQ Welcome Page</title>
      </head>

      <body>
        <h1>Java FAQ Welcome Page</h1>
        Welcome to the Java FAQ

    <%! FaqCategories faqs = new FaqCategories(); %>
    Click a link below for answers to the given topic.
    <%
      Iterator categories = faqs.getAllCategories();
      while (categories.hasNext()) {
        String category = (String) categories.next();
    %>
        <p><a href="<%= replaceUnderscore(category) %>.jsp"><%= category
    %></a></p>
    <%
      }
    %>
    ```

```
<%@ include file="/WEB-INF/footer.jspf" %>
   </body>
</html>

<%!
public String replaceUnderscore(String s) {
   return s.replace(' ','_');
}
%>
```

3. The welcome.jsp page above has a JSP include directive to add a standard footer. Because the include file is just a fragment and not a complete JSP file, we use the convention of naming the file with a .jspf extension as recommended by the JSP specification. Here is the footer.jspf file:

```
<hr>
Page generated on <%= (new java.util.Date()).toString() %>
```

4. Now create errorPage.jsp:

```
<%@ page isErrorPage="true" import="java.io.PrintWriter" %>

<!DOCTYPE HTML PUBLIC "-//W3C//DTD HTML 4.01 Transitional//EN">
<html>
   <head>
     <title>Error</title>
   </head>
   <body>
     <h1>Error</h1>
     There was an error somewhere.
     <%@ include file="/WEB-INF/footer.jspf" %>
   </body>
</html>
```

5. And finally, we have a helper file that will be used by welcome.jsp. This file is FaqCategories.java. After entering the source, compile the file into a class file.

```
package Ch03;

import java.util.Iterator;
import java.util.Vector;

public class FaqCategories {
   private Vector categories = new Vector();

   public FaqCategories() {
     categories.add("Dates and Times");
     categories.add("Strings and StringBuffers");
     categories.add("Threading");
   }
   public Iterator getAllCategories() {
     return categories.iterator();
   }
}
```

How It Works

The `welcome.jsp` file demonstrates many of the features that have been introduced in this chapter so far. It begins with the `page` directive. This directive has two attributes, as shown below. First, an `errorPage` is defined, to which the browser will be redirected if an error occurs on the page. The other attribute used with the page directive is the `import`. The page imports two Java classes: the `Iterator` class from the Java API and the `FaqCategories` class that is part of this application:

```
<%@ page errorPage="/WEB-INF/errorPage.jsp"
         import="java.util.Iterator,Ch03.FaqCategories" %>
```

Note that the page can also use this syntax for the `import`:

```
<%@ page errorPage="/WEB-INF/errorPage.jsp"
         import="java.util.*,Ch03.*" %>
```

This is followed by some straight HTML. Further down in the page is a declaration scripting element. This element declares a variable called `faqs` and initializes it by calling the constructor of the `FaqCategories` helper class. You can see that declaration elements must follow Java coding rules, including the use of a semicolon to terminate the statement:

```
<%! FaqCategories faqs = new FaqCategories(); %>
```

The next JSP element in the page is a scriptlet. This scriptlet gets an `Iterator` from the `FaqCategories` instance. We use this `Iterator` to loop through each of the categories defined in the `FaqCategories` class. Each category is loaded into a `String` variable called `category`, and this is used to create an HTML link. Each category is printed out twice using expression elements—first within the `href` attribute of the `<a>` tag to set the page that the link refers to, and then within the body of the link. The first expression element calls the `replaceUnderscore()` method (defined later in the page) and prints the result; the other expression element simply prints the category value:

```
<%
   Iterator categories = faqs.getAllCategories();
   while (categories.hasNext()) {
   String category = (String)categories.next();
%>
      <p><a href="/<%= replaceUnderscore(category) %>"><%= category %></a></p>
<%
     }
%>
```

Notice that with the scriptlet, Java syntax must be used. However, within an expression element, you only need to use the expression itself, without a semicolon to end the statement.

At the bottom of the page, an include directive includes a standard footer:

```
<%@ include file="/WEB-INF/footer.jspf" %>
```

The last thing in the file is another declaration element. This element, shown below, declares the `replaceUnderscore()` method, which replaces the spaces in a string with underscores. It was called by the scriptlet earlier in the file:

```
<%!
public String replaceUnderscore(String s) {
  return s.replace(' ','_');
}
%>
```

The next file is `footer.jspf`:

```
<hr>
Page generated on <%= (new java.util.Date()).toString() %>
```

You will see that this is not a complete JSP file. This file uses an expression element to print out the current date and time at the server when the page is served to the user. I used the extension `.jspf` as recommended by the specification to indicate that this file is a fragment. Also, because it is a fragment and is not meant to be publicly available, the file was put into the **WEB-INF** directory. Files in this directory are not publicly available. This means that you cannot enter an address into a browser to access this file. Only code within the application can access files within the **WEB-INF** directory.

The `errorPage.jsp` is meant to be used when an uncaught exception occurs in the `welcome.jsp` page. It includes the standard footer. However, assuming everything in the page is correct, it will not be called in this application. This page is not meant to be publicly available, so it too resides in the **WEB-INF** directory:

```
<%@ page isErrorPage="true" import="java.io.PrintWriter" %>

<!DOCTYPE HTML PUBLIC "-//W3C//DTD HTML 4.01 Transitional//EN">
<html>
  <head>
    <title>Error</title>
  </head>
  <body>
    <h1>Error</h1>
    There was an error somewhere.
    <%@ include file="/WEB-INF/footer.jspf" %>
  </body>
</html>
```

Since this is an error page, notice that we set the `isErrorPage` attribute of the `page` directive to `true`. Apart from that directive, this page contains just straight HTML and an `include` directive to include our `footer.jspf` file.

The final source file is `FaqCategories.java`. This is a helper class that supplies three categories to the `welcome.jsp` page. In a real-world application, the categories would come from some persistent store such as a database or a directory. For this example, we use the helper class to "hard-code" the categories for `welcome.jsp`:

```
package Ch03;

import java.util.Iterator;
import java.util.Vector;

public class FaqCategories {
  private Vector categories = new Vector();

  public FaqCategories() {
    categories.add("Dates and Times");
    categories.add("Strings and StringBuffers");
    categories.add("Threading");
  }
  public Iterator getAllCategories() {
    return categories.iterator();
  }
}
```

The categories are stored in a `Vector` object, which is an instance member of the class. In the class constructor, we just add our hard-coded categories to this `Vector`. Finally, we define a `getAllCategories()` method, which simply returns the `Iterator` for our `Vector`. Our JSP page uses this `Iterator` to loop through each of the categories in turn.

Try It Out Deploying the Web Application in J2EE

That finishes the code for our application, but before it can actually be accessed by clients, we need to deploy our application to an application server. We'll look at two application servers in this book–the reference implementation server that comes with the J2EE SDK, and the Tomcat stand-alone server. First, let's see how we do it with the J2EE server.

1. Ensure the J2EE server is running, and start up the J2EE Deployment Tool that we looked at in the previous chapter.

2. Select File | New | Application EAR from the menu to create a new Application EAR file. EAR stands for Enterprise Archive.

3. In the dialog that results, enter a filename for the application. I used JavaFAQ.ear for this example:

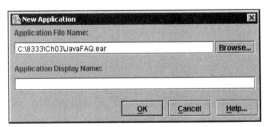

4. Select File | New | Web Application WAR from the menu to create a new web application. This will start the Web Application Wizard:

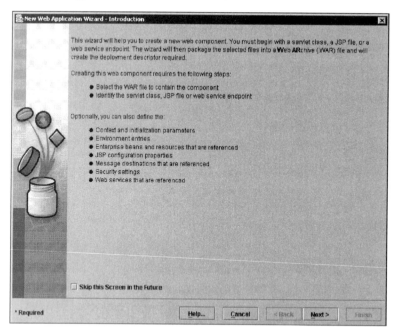

5. At the first screen of the wizard, shown below, ensure the correct application is selected in the Create New WAR Module in Application drop-down box. Click the Edit button in the Contents panel and add these files to the WAR:

- ❑ FaqCategories.class

- ❑ errorPage.jsp

- ❑ footer.jspf

- ❑ welcome.jsp

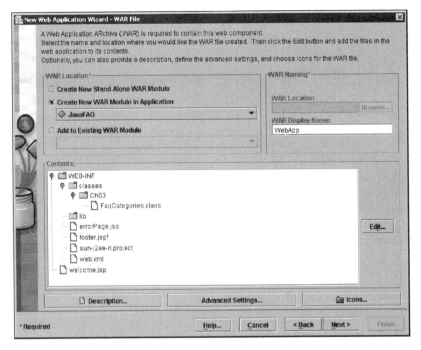

Make sure that the `errorPage.jsp` and `footer.jspf` files appear in the correct location underneath the WEB-INF directory. If they do not, you can drag and drop them into the correct location. Note that the wizard will create the deployment descriptor, `web.xml`, for you. You do not need to add `web.xml` to the application.

6. At the next dialog, select the JSP radio button and click the Next button:

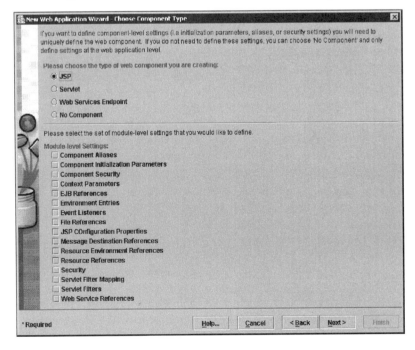

7. In the JSP Filename drop-down box, select /welcome.jsp as the JSP to define. The Web Component Name and Web Component Display Name fields will be automatically filled. Click the Finish button:

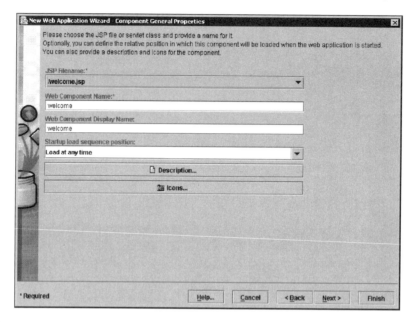

8. In the navigation pane on the left, ensure the application is selected. In the screenshot below, the web application has been named JavaFAQ, and you can see it is selected. In the right pane, select the Web Context tab, and double-click in the Context Root field. Enter Ch03 as the context root and press *Enter*:

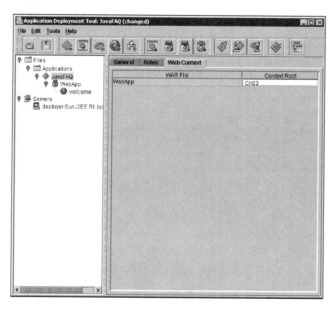

9. Now select the WebApp label in the left pane. Select the File Refs tab in the right pane. Add an entry for a Welcome File. Enter the `welcome.jsp` page.

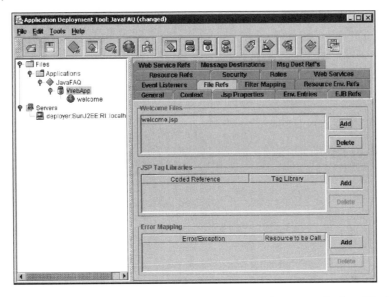

10. Ensure the JavaFAQ application is selected in the left-hand pane, and select File | Save As to save the Application EAR. The location doesn't matter, as long as you remember where you save it.

11. Select Tools | Deploy from the menu. The Deployment Tool allows you to select the server to which the web application is deployed. Most likely you are deploying to the localhost and will not have any other servers. You can add servers from the File | Add Server selection on the menu. You may also need to enter the admin username and password for the server (hopefully you wrote those down when you installed the J2EE server). When you are ready, click the OK button; the Deployment Tool will deploy your web application.

12. A window will open in which the results of the deployment are listed.

13. When the tool is finished, open a browser window. Enter the address http://localhost:1024/Ch03. The `welcome.jsp` page will automatically load:

The address and port you use in the web browser depend on where the server is located and which port it uses to listen for HTTP requests. If you installed the J2EE server to the same machine as the web browser, then you can access it using localhost, or you can use the localhost IP address 127.0.0.1 or the actual IP address of the machine. The default HTTP port for the J2EE reference implementation is 1024, so if you did not keep the default port during installation, you will access the web application using the URL listed previously.

If, however, you installed the J2EE server to a different machine, or selected a different port for the server to listen for HTTP requests, you will need to change the URL to use the name or IP address of that machine, and the correct port for the server.

Try It Out Deploying the Web Application in Tomcat

Deploying applications to a Tomcat stand-alone server is simpler, but it does require us to write a special XML file, known as a **deployment descriptor**. This file is also required by the J2EE server, but the Deployment Tool creates it for us, so we don't need to write it by hand.

1. Firstly, then, if you are deploying to a Tomcat stand-alone, you need to write a deployment descriptor for the web application. Development descriptors are XML files that contain configuration information about the entire web application. We will look at development descriptors in more detail in Chapter 5. Here is the deployment descriptor for our JavaFAQ application. This file is called web.xml and is placed in the application's WEB-INF directory:

```
<?xml version="1.0" encoding="ISO-8859-1"?>

<!DOCTYPE web-app
    PUBLIC "-//Sun Microsystems, Inc.//DTD Web Application 2.3//EN"
    "http://java.sun.com/dtd/web-app_2_3.dtd">

<web-app>
    <!-- this is the deployment descriptor for Chapter 3
         Try It Out example 1                                      -->

    <welcome-file-list>
      <welcome-file>welcome.jsp</welcome-file>
    </welcome-file-list>
</web-app>
```

2. If the J2EE server is running, shut it down.

3. If you created the directory structure we described earlier in the chapter (when we looked at the source code for the application) within the Tomcat /webapps directory, then you are finished. Go to step 5.

4. If the application directory is not under the Tomcat /webapps directory, you can do one of two things:

    Either copy the directory structure to Tomcat /webapps.

Or navigate to the top-level directory of the web application. For example, if the highest directory of the application is /Ch03, you would navigate into that directory.

Now create the Web Archive manually:

```
> jar cf Ch03.war *
```

Copy the .war file to the Tomcat /webapps directory.

5. Start the Tomcat server. When it is started, open a browser window and enter the address http://localhost:8080/Ch03. The welcome.jsp file will load as shown in the J2EE example.

How It Works

Since you'll need to write a deployment descriptor for any web applications you want to deploy to a Tomcat stand-alone, let's take a moment to look at the web.xml file in this example. First come the standard XML declaration and document type declaration, which you can use for any JSP deployment descriptors:

```
<?xml version="1.0" encoding="ISO-8859-1"?>
<!DOCTYPE web-app
    PUBLIC "-//Sun Microsystems, Inc.//DTD Web Application 2.3//EN"
    "http://java.sun.com/dtd/web-app_2_3.dtd">
```

Next, comes the XML content of the file. The root XML element is called <web-app>, and in this case contains only a single child element, <welcome-file-list>:

```
<web-app>
  <welcome-file-list>
    <welcome-file>welcome.jsp</welcome-file>
  </welcome-file-list>
</web-app>
```

This element lists the files that will be served to any client that simply enters the application context from a browser. These files are referred to as welcome files. For example, an address like http://localhost:8080/Ch03 does not reference any resource within the web application root context, /Ch03. Anyone who enters a URL like this will be served a welcome file from the list. If multiple files are listed in the welcome file list, the server will respond with the first file in the welcome file list that it finds.

I will cover specific elements of the deployment descriptor as they apply, but we will look at deployment descriptors in more detail in Chapter 5. You can also find more information about the deployment descriptor in the documentation for Tomcat, and the JSP and Servlet specifications.

When you load the welcome page, you probably saw that the links in that page do not reference actual resources within the application. If you clicked on one of the links, you probably received an HTTP 404 error in the browser. You did not see the error page, because the problem was a Resource Not Found in the server, not an uncaught exception in the page.

> **The elements in the deployment descriptor must follow a particular order specified by a Document Type Definition (DTD) (JSP 1.2 and earlier), or an XML Schema (JSP 2.0). If the elements are not in the correct order, the server will not start the application. In Chapter 5 in this book, we'll look at the correct order as defined by the DTD in the Servlet 2.3 specification.**

To actually deploy the application to Tomcat, we need to copy the files to Tomcat's /webapps directory. If you don't want to store the application's files directly in this directory, you can deploy the application by packaging all the files into a web archive, or WAR, file. The WAR is a convenient way to package all the files and components that make up a web application into one archive. All JSP containers know how to read and deploy web applications from the WAR. Thus, deploying a web application is as simple as creating the archive with the correct application directory structure and putting it into the correct directory location for the container. The directory structure of the web application, and thus the WAR, is defined in the servlet specification. Likewise, the deployment descriptor is defined by the specification. When you use a tool like the J2EE Deployment Tool, it takes care of creating the correct directory structure and deployment descriptor for you, but you need to create it manually if you're deploying to a Tomcat stand-alone.

In general, the structure of your application will look like this:

```
app_context/
  public web resources
  WEB-INF/
    web.xml
    tlds/
      tld files
    lib/
      archives used by application
    classes/
      class files used in application
```

The directory at the top of the structure defines the web application context. The application context provides a separation between different web applications. Under the application context directory are the public files of the application. This will generally include the HTML and JSP pages of the application. Under the application context is the WEB-INF directory. This directory contains the deployment descriptor web.xml and other files that are not publicly accessible by clients of the application. There can be any number of directories under WEB-INF, but three common ones are shown above. The tlds directory is not required, but is a commonly used directory for keeping tag library descriptor files (see Chapter 4). The lib directory is used for Java archives (.jar files) that are used by the web application. Finally, the classes directory is used for class files in the web application.

Action Elements

The last set of JSP elements we will look at are the action elements. These elements are also known as **Standard Actions**. Standard actions are defined by the JSP specification (which is one reason why they are called standard).

> *As we will see in the next chapter, we can define our own actions that can be used in a JSP page.*

The JSP 2.0 specification defines these standard actions:

- ❑ `<jsp:useBean>`
- ❑ `<jsp:setProperty>`
- ❑ `<jsp:getProperty>`
- ❑ `<jsp:param>`
- ❑ `<jsp:include>`
- ❑ `<jsp:forward>`
- ❑ `<jsp:plugin>`, `<jsp:params>`, `<jsp:fallback>`
- ❑ `<jsp:attribute>`
- ❑ `<jsp:body>`
- ❑ `<jsp:invoke>`
- ❑ `<jsp:doBody>`

We will look at `<jsp:include>`, `<jsp:forward>`, and `<jsp:param>` later in the chapter.

The `<jsp:plugin>`, `<jsp:params>`, and `<jsp:fallback>` elements are used to include applets or JavaBeans in the HTML page generated by a JSP page. Using these over hand-coding the HTML allows the server to create browser-specific HTML from the JSP tags. These tags are not discussed further in this book.

The elements `<jsp:attribute>` and `<jsp:body>` are used with standard and custom actions. The elements `<jsp:invoke>` and `<jsp:doBody>` are only valid in tag libraries, which we will cover in the next chapter.

The <Jsp:useBean> Action

This element makes a JavaBean available to the page. A JavaBean (which is not the same as an Enterprise JavaBean, or EJB) is simply a Java class that follows certain requirements. The two requirements that are important for our purposes are:

❑   The JavaBean class has a no-argument constructor.

❑   Every property of the bean that is provided for client use has a method to set the value of the parameter, and a method to get the value of the parameter. The methods have this form:

```
public type getSomeParameter() { return someParameter; }
public boolean isSomeParameter() { return someBooleanParameter; }
public void setSomeParameter(type someParameter) {
  // Set the parameter
}
```

The name of every setter and getter uses the name of the parameter, with the first letter capitalized, appended to the token set, get, or is. The getter method has the form isXXX() for boolean properties, and getXXX() otherwise.

The <jsp:useBean> element has these attributes:

Attribute	Description
id	The name used to access the bean in the rest of the page. It must be unique. It is essentially the variable name that references the bean instance.
scope	The scope of the bean. Valid values are page, request, session, or application. The default is page. See the *Scope* section below for more information.
class	The fully qualified class name of the bean class.
beanName	The name of a bean, as expected by the instantiate() method of the java.beans.Beans class. Most often you will use the class attribute, rather than beanName. Refer to the JavaBeans specification at http://java.sun.com/products/javabeans for more information on how to supply a name to the instantiate() method.
type	The type to be used for the variable that references the bean. This follows Java rules, so it can be the class of the bean, any parent class of the bean, or any interface implemented by the bean or by a parent class.

The <jsp:useBean> element causes the container to try to find an existing instance of the object in the specified scope and with the specified id. If no object with the specified id is found in that scope, and a class or bean name is specified, the container will try to create a new instance of the object. You can use the class, beanName, and type attributes in these combinations:

❑   class–Creates an instance of the class that can be referred to by the given id.

❑   class, type–Creates an instance of the given class; the variable that refers to the bean will have the given type.

❑   beanName, type–Creates an instance of the given bean; the variable that refers to the bean will have the given type.

❑   type–If an object of the given type exists in the session, the id will refer to that object.

You must create a reference to a JavaBean using the `<jsp:useBean>` element before you can use `<jsp:setProperty>` or `<jsp:getProperty>`.

The <jsp:setProperty> Action

Sets the property for a JavaBean. The `<jsp:setProperty>` element has these attributes:

Attribute	Description
name	The id of the bean.
property	The name of the property to set. The value can explicitly name a property of the bean, in which case the setXXX() method for the property will be called. The value can also be "*", in which case, the JSP will read all the parameters that were sent by the browser with the client's request, and set the properties in the bean that have the same names as the parameters in the request. We will see an example of this in the next *Try It Out* section.
param	The parameter name in the browser request whose value will be used to set the property. Allows the JSP to match properties and parameters with different names.
value	The value to assign to the property.

The name and property attributes are always required. The param and value elements are mutually exclusive. If neither param nor value are used, the jsp:setProperty element attempts to use the request parameter with the same name as the property attribute. I will show examples of request parameters in the next section.

Suppose we have a JavaBean that holds information about a user of the system. This bean might look like this:

```
public class User {
   private String id;
   private String surname;
   public void setId(String id) { this.id = id; }
   public String getId() { return id; }
   public void setSurname(String surname) { this.surname = surname; }
   public String getSurname() { return surname; }
}
```

Here is one simple example of using the `<jsp:setProperty>` element with a literal value, and an expression:

```
<jsp:useBean id="userA" class="User" />
<jsp:setProperty id="userA" property="surname" value="Smith" />
<jsp:setProperty id="userA" property="id"
                 value="<%= validateId("86753") %>" />
```

After this code in the compiled JSP executes, the surname property of the instance of `User` has a value of `"Smith"` and the id property has whatever value is returned by the hypothetical `validateId()` expression. What occurs is that the JSP translator takes the elements above and translates them into code that creates an instance of the `User` class, and then calls the `setSurname()` and `setId()` methods of the object.

The <jsp:getProperty> Action

This element retrieves the value of a property from a JavaBean. The `<jsp:getProperty>` element has these attributes:

Attribute	Description
name	The id of the bean.
property	The name of the property to get.

The `name` and `property` attributes are always required. When used within a JSP, the value of the property will be output as part of the response. Given the example in the previous section, you could write template data that used `<jsp:getProperty>` like this:

```
The user with id <jsp:getProperty id="userA" property="id" />
has a surname of <jsp:getProperty id="userA" property="surname" />
```

When the JSP page is translated into Java code, this will result in calls to the `getSurname()` and `getId()` methods of the object. The return values are then output with the template data to the response, so that the client sees this in his browser:

The user with id 86753 has a surname of Smith

JSP Initialization and End-of-Life

In the JSP lifecycle section above, I mentioned that you can add methods to your JSP that will be called when the JSP is initialized and when the JSP is destroyed. These methods are declared using the declaration scripting element.

When you need to perform one-time initialization of the JSP, you would add this method to the JSP:

```
<%!
public void jspInit() {
    // ...perform one time initialization.
    // ...this method is called only once per JSP, not per request
}
%>
```

If you need to clean up any resources used by the JSP, you would add this method to the JSP:

```
<%!
public void jspDestroy() {
  // ...perform one time cleanup of resources
}
%>
```

If you don't need to perform initialization or cleanup, you do not need to add these methods to the JSP.

Implicit Objects

The previous section stated that the properties of a JavaBean can be set from the parameters in the request sent by the client browser. Your JSP can also access the client's request directly. You access the client's request through an object named `request`. In addition to the `request` object, the JSP model provides you with a number of other implicit objects. These objects are implicit because a JSP has access to and can use them without needing to explicitly declare and initialize the objects. Implicit objects are used within scriptlet and expression elements. In this section, we will look at these implicit objects:

- ❏ request

- ❏ response

- ❏ out

- ❏ session

- ❏ config

- ❏ exception

- ❏ application

In this section, I will show the methods of these objects that you will be using the most. You should consult the Javadoc for the complete list and explanation of all the available methods.

The request Object

JSP pages are web components that respond to and process HTTP requests. The `request` implicit object represents this HTTP request. Through the `request` object, you can access the HTTP headers, the request parameters, and other information about the request. You will most often use this object to read the request parameters.

When a browser submits a request to a server, it can send information along with the request in the form of request parameters. These take two forms:

❏ URL-encoded parameters–These are parameters appended to the requested URL as a query string. The parameters begin with a question mark, followed by the name-value pairs of all the parameters, with each pair delimited by an ampersand (&):

```
http://www.myserver.com/path/to/resource?name1=value1&name2=value2
```

❏ Form-encoded parameters –These parameters are submitted as a result of a form submission. They have the same format as URL-encoded parameters, but are included with the body of the request and not appended to the requested URL.

These parameters can be read through various methods of the request object:

```
String request.getParameter(String name);
String[] request.getParameterValues(String name);
Enumeration request.getParameterNames();
Map getParameterMap();
```

The getParameter(String) method returns the value of the parameter with the given name. If the named parameter has multiple values (for example, when a form submits the value of checkboxes), this method returns the first value. For multi-valued parameters, getParameterValues(String) returns all the values for the given name. The getParameterNames() method returns all the parameter names used in the request, while getParameterMap() returns all the parameters as name-value pairs.

Information can also be passed to the server using extra path information. This data is appended to the requested URL. For example, suppose /Ch03/MyComponent was the context and name of a web application component; additional information could be appended to the path like this: Ch03/MyComponent/extraPathInfo. With the correct configuration, the server would send the request to MyComponent, and MyComponent would get the extra path information using this method:

```
String request.getPathInfo();
```

The request object has request scope. That means that the implicit request object is in scope until the response to the client is complete. It is an instance of javax.servlet.HttpServletRequest. For further information about the methods of request, see Chapter 5.

The response Object

The response object encapsulates the response to the web application client. Some of the things you can do using the response are set headers, set cookies for the client, and send a redirect response to the client. You can perform those functions with these methods:

```
public void addHeader(String name, String value)
public void addCookie(Cookie cookie)
public void sendRedirect(String location)
```

It is an instance of javax.servlet.HttpServletResponse and it has page scope.

The out Object

The out implicit object is a reference to an output stream that you can use within scriptlets. Using the out object, the scriptlet can write data to the response that is sent to the client. For example, we could rewrite the earlier welcome.jsp to use the out object like this:

```
<%
    Iterator categories = faqs.getAllCategories();
    while (categories.hasNext()) {
      String category = (String)categories.next();
      out.println("<p><a href=\"" + replaceUnderscore(category) + "\">" +
                  category + "</a></p>");
    }
%>
```

The scriptlet above would cause the same HTML to be sent to the client as was sent in the original version of welcome.jsp. Note that one of the purposes of JSP is to separate the HTML from the Java code, so the above example is not the best use of the out object.

The out object is an instance of javax.jsp.JspWriter. It has page scope.

The session Object

HTTP is a stateless protocol. As far as a web server is concerned, each client request is a new request, with nothing to connect it to previous requests. However, in web applications, a client's interaction with the application will often span many requests and responses. To join all these separate interactions into one coherent conversation between client and application, web applications use the concept of a session. A session refers to the entire conversation between a client and a server.

The JSP components in a web application automatically participate in a given client's session, without needing to do anything special. Any JSP page that uses the page directive to set the session attribute to false does not have access to the session object, and thus cannot participate in the session.

Using the session object, the page can store information about the client or the client's interaction. Information is stored in the session, just as you would store information in a Hashtable or a Hashmap. This means that a JSP page can only store objects in the session, and not Java primitives. To store Java primitives, you need to use one of the wrapper classes such as Integer, or Boolean. The methods for storing and retrieving session data are:

```
Object setAttribute(String name, Object value);
Object getAttribute(String name);
Enumeration getAttributeNames();
void removeAttribute(String name);
```

When other components in the web application receive a request, they can access the session data that was stored by other components. They can change information in the session or add new information to it. Also, be aware that sessions are not inherently thread-safe. You should consider the possibility that two or more web components could access the same objects from the same session simultaneously. If this could be a problem for your application, you must synchronize access to the objects stored in the session.

Normally, you don't need to write code in your page to manage the session. The server creates the `session` object, and associates client requests with a particular session. However, this association normally happens through the use of a cookie that is sent to the client. The cookie holds a session ID; when the browser sends the cookie back to the server, the server uses the session ID to associate the request to a session. When the browser does not accept cookies, the server falls back to a scheme called **URL rewriting** to maintain the session. If there is the possibility that the server will be using URL rewriting, your page needs to rewrite any embedded URLs. This is actually done with a method of the `response` object:

```
response.encodeURL(String);
response.encodeRedirectURL(String);
```

The second method is used when the URL will be sent as a redirect to the browser using the `response.sendRedirect()` method. The first method is used for all other URLs.

The `session` object has session scope, and all the objects stored in the `session` object also have session scope. The session object is an instance of `javax.servlet.http.HttpSession`.

The config Object

This object is used to obtain JSP-specific `init` parameters. These initialization parameters are set in the deployment descriptor, but are specific to a single page. JSP `init` parameters are set in the `<servlet>` element of the deployment descriptor. This is because the page implementation class of the JSP (the Java class which is compiled from the JSP page) is a servlet class. The `<servlet>` element with the `<init-param>` element will look like this:

```
<servlet>
  <servlet-name>StockList</servlet-name>
  <servlet-class>web.StockListServlet</servlet-class>
  <init-param>
    <param-name>name</param-name>
    <param-value>value</param-value>
  </init-param>
</servlet>
```

See Chapter 5 for more information on how to use the `<servlet>` element.

If JSP initialization parameters are defined in the deployment descriptor, you can access them using:

```
config.getInitParameter(String name);
```

The exception Object

This implicit object is only available within error pages. It is a reference to the `java.lang.Throwable` object that caused the server to call the error page.

The application Object

This object represents the web application environment. You will use this object to get application-level configuration parameters. Within the deployment descriptor, you can set application parameters using this element:

```
<webapp>
  <context-param>
    <param-name>name</param-name>
    <param-value>value</param-value>
  </context-param>
</webapp>
```

The value of the parameter can be accessed using:

```
application.getInitParameter(String name);
```

Scope

Objects that are created as part of a JSP have a certain scope, or lifetime. That scope varies with the object. In some cases, such as the implicit objects, the scope is set and cannot be changed. With other objects (JavaBeans for example), you can set the scope of the object. Valid scopes are page, request, session, and application.

❑ **page**–Page scope is the most restrictive. With page scope, the object is only accessible within the page in which it is defined. JavaBeans created with page scope and objects created by scriptlets are thread-safe. (Recall, though, that Java objects created by declaration elements are not thread-safe.)

❑ **request**–With request scope, objects are available for the life of the specific request. This means that the object is available within the page in which it is created, and within pages to which the request is forwarded or included. Objects with request scope are thread-safe. Only the execution thread for a particular request can access these objects.

❑ **session**–Objects with session scope are available to all application components that participate in the client's session. These objects are not thread-safe. If multiple requests could use the same session object at the same time, you must synchronize access to that object.

❑ **application**–This is the least restrictive scope. Objects that are created with application scope are available to the entire application for the life of the application. These objects are not thread-safe and access to them must be synchronized if there is a chance that multiple requests will attempt to change the object at the same time.

Try It Out   Using JavaBeans in JSP Pages

In this example, we will expand the earlier example. This example will add a registration page to the application. Using the registration page, we will see some examples of using a JavaBean in the page. This example will also use the implicit request object to read request parameters.

1. Here is the application structure for this example:

```
Ch03/
    registration.jsp
    registrationform.html
    welcome.jsp
    WEB-INF/
        errorPage.jsp
        footer.jspf
        web.xml
        classes/
            Ch03/
                FaqCategories.java
                User.java
                FaqCategories.class
                User.class
```

2. Start by creating the JavaBean. This bean consists of a class called User, and represents a user of our application. After entering the source, compile it into a class file:

```java
package Ch03;

public class User {
    private String firstName;
    private String surname;
    private String loginName;
    private int age;

    public String getFirstName() { return firstName; }
    public void setFirstName(String newFirstName) {
        this.firstName = newFirstName;
    }

    public String getSurname() { return surname; }
    public void setSurname(String newSurname) {
        this.surname = newSurname;
    }

    public String getLoginName() { return loginName; }
    public void setLoginName(String newLoginName) {
        this.loginName = newLoginName;
    }
    public int getAge() { return age; }
    public void setAge(int newAge) {
        this.age = newAge;
    }
}
```

3. Next, we'll modify `welcome.jsp` from the earlier example. This page will ask users to register, if they haven't already done so:

```jsp
<%@ page errorPage="/WEB-INF/errorPage.jsp"
    import="java.util.Iterator,Ch03.*" %>

<!DOCTYPE HTML PUBLIC "-//W3C//DTD HTML 4.01 Transitional//EN">
<html>
  <head>
    <title>Java FAQ Welcome Page</title>
  </head>

  <body>
    <h1>Java FAQ Welcome Page</h1>

<%
  User user = (User) session.getAttribute("user");
  if (user == null) {
%>
    You are not yet registered, please
    <a href="registrationform.html">register</a>.
<%
  } else {
%>
    Welcome to the Java FAQ

<%! FaqCategories faqs = new FaqCategories(); %>
Click a link below for answers to the given topic.
<%
    Iterator categories = faqs.getAllCategories();
    while (categories.hasNext()) {
      String category = (String) categories.next();
%>
      <p><a href="<%= replaceUnderscore(category) %>.jsp"><%= category
%></a></p>
<%
    }
%>

<%@ include file="/WEB-INF/footer.jspf" %>
<%
  }
%>
  </body>
</html>

<%!
public String replaceUnderscore(String s) {
  return s.replace(' ','_');
}
%>
```

4. Next, create the `registrationform.html` page that collects the user information:

```html
<!DOCTYPE HTML PUBLIC "-//W3C//DTD HTML 4.01 Transitional//EN">
<html>
  <head>
    <title>Registration Page</title>
  </head>
  <body>
    <h1>Registration Page</h1>

    <form action="registration.jsp" method="POST">
      <table>
        <tr>
          <td align="right">First name:</td>
          <td align="left"><input type="text"
              name="firstName" length="30"/></td>
        </tr>
        <tr>
          <td align="right">Surname:</td>
          <td align="left"><input type="text"
              name="surname" length="30"/></td>
        </tr>
        <tr>
          <td align="right">Login Name:</td>
          <td align="left"><input type="text"
              name="loginName" length="30"/></td>
        </tr>
        <tr>
          <td align="right">Age:</td>
          <td align="left"><input type="text"
              name="age" length="5"/></td>
        </tr>
      </table>

      Which topics are you interested in?
      <br><input type="checkbox" name="topics"
                 value="Dates and Times">
        Dates and Times</input>
      <br><input type="checkbox" name="topics"
                 value="Strings and StringBuffers">
        Strings and StringBuffers</input>
      <br><input type="checkbox" name="topics"
                 value="Threading">
        Threading</input>
      <p><input type="submit" value="Submit"/></p>
    </form>
  </body>
</html>
```

5. This form submits to a JSP page that gathers the form data and populates the User bean. This page is registration.jsp:

```
<!DOCTYPE HTML PUBLIC "-//W3C//DTD HTML 4.01 Transitional//EN">
<html>
   <head>
      <title>Register User</title>
   </head>
   <body>
      <h1>Register User</h1>

      <jsp:useBean id="user" scope="session" class="Ch03.User">
        <jsp:setProperty name="user" property="*" />
      </jsp:useBean>

      Welcome new user, these are the values you submitted:
      <p>Your first name is <%= user.getFirstName() %>.</p>
      <p>Your last name is
         <jsp:getProperty name="user" property="surname" />.</p>
      <p>Your user id is
         <jsp:getProperty name="user" property="loginName" />.</p>
      <p>Your age is
         <jsp:getProperty name="user" property="age" />.</p>
      You selected these topics:

<%
   String[] topics = request.getParameterValues("topics");
   if (topics == null) { topics = new String[] {"No topics"}; }
   for (int i = 0; i < topics.length; i++) {
%>
      <br><%= topics[i] %>
<%
   }
%>
      <p>Go to <a href="welcome.jsp">Topic List Page</a></p>
      <%@ include file="/WEB-INF/footer.jspf" %>
   </body>
</html>
```

6. The other files for this application remain the same as before.

7. Deploy this application to the server of your choice, using the same steps as in the first example in this chapter. If you want to update an existing EAR using the Deployment Tool, there are a couple of things you can do. Update the existing files by selecting the specific application in the left pane, and then selecting Tools | Update Files from the menu. If you also need to add new files, select the web application entry in the left pane, then click the Edit button on the General tab in the right pane, and add the new files (registration.jsp, registrationform.html, and User.class). Finally, redeploy the application by selecting Tools | Deploy.

8. If you're using a Tomcat stand-alone and the application files are stored in the Tomcat /webapps directory, you just need to update the files and add the extra ones in this directory structure. If they're stored outside this directory, delete the existing .war file and the /Ch03 directory in /webapps, recreate the .war file by calling jar cf Ch03.war * from the application's root directory as before, and copying this file to /webapps. Tomcat does not automatically deploy a .war file that has been replaced, so you will need to restart Tomcat.

9. Enter the URL for the welcome.jsp. You should see this page in your browser:

10. Click on the register link to load the registration page.

11. Fill out the fields and check one or more of the boxes. Click the Submit button.

12. Clicking the Submit button will cause the registration information to be passed to registration.jsp. That JSP will display this page:

13. Finally, clicking the link in this page will send you to welcome.jsp again. This time, welcome.jsp will display the topic list:

How It Works

As in the first example, the entry into the application is the `welcome.jsp` page. However, this time, the page checks for the existence of a `User` object in the session using this code:

```
User user = (User)session.getAttribute("user");
```

Recall that all JSP pages have access to the implicit `session` object, unless specified otherwise with the `page` directive. Using the `getAttribute()` method, the page attempts to get the named object from the session. Notice that `getAttribute()` returns a reference of type `Object`, which must be cast to the proper type to assign it to the `user` variable.

If there is no `user` object in the session (that is, if `user` is `null`), `welcome.jsp` outputs the HTML with a link for the `registrationform.html` page. Later, when returning to this page, the `user` object will exist, and the welcome page displays the topic list. The remainder of this page is unchanged.

The `registrationform.html` page is a standard web page with a form that submits form data to the server. The resource that it submits to is given in the `<form>` tag:

```
<form action="registration.jsp" method="POST">
```

The `action` attribute contains the URI for the server resource that should receive the data. This URI can be relative as shown, or absolute. The `method` attribute indicates which HTTP method should be used for the submission. The form includes some text fields and some checkboxes. The form submits all its data to `registration.jsp`.

The first interesting thing about `registration.jsp` is the `<jsp:useBean>` tag shown here:

```
<jsp:useBean id="user" class="Ch03.User">
  <jsp:setProperty name="user" property="*" />
</jsp:useBean>
```

This tag creates an instance of the class given by the `class` attribute. Throughout the rest of the page, the object can be referred to using the variable `user`. Enclosed within the `<jsp:useBean>` element is a `<jsp:setProperty>` element. This element uses the `property="*"` attribute, which causes the page to find each `setXXX` method of the given bean, and call each method with the same named parameter in the request. If you look at the `User` class, you will see it has four public `setXXX` methods: `setFirstName(String)`, `setSurname(String)`, `setLoginName(String)`, and `setAge(int)`. These methods must be matched by four request parameters. If you examine `registrationform.html`, you will see that it does have four form fields with the correct names: `firstName`, `surname`, `loginName`, and `age`. The value from each of these request parameters is used to set the properties of the `User` bean.

You may recall that the <jsp:setProperty> tag also has an attribute named param. This attribute is used when the names in the request do not match the names in the bean. For example, suppose that the web page form had a field lastName instead of surname and that you were not allowed to change the web form or the bean. The JSP could not use the property="*" syntax, because the JSP is not able to match request parameters to bean properties in this case. The way to set the properties would be to use this syntax:

```
<jsp:useBean id="user" class="Ch03.User">
   <jsp:setProperty name="user" property="surname" param="lastName"/>
</jsp:useBean>
```

Using this syntax, the page knows that it can set the bean's surname property using the value of the request parameter called lastName.

Although it is shown enclosed within the <jsp:useBean> element, you can use <jsp:setProperty> any time after the bean is created.

Next, registration.jsp stores the newly created bean in the implicit session object. This makes it available to every component in the application. Thus, when the welcome.jsp is called again, it will find the bean object.

Then the page prints out the values of the User bean's properties. For the first property, a JSP expression is used to print the property. For the remainder of the properties, the <jsp:getProperty> element is used:

```
<p>Your first name is <%= user.getFirstName() %></p>
<p>Your last name is
    <jsp:getProperty name="user" property="surname" />.</p>
```

The page then prints out the remainder of the request parameters. These are the values of the checkboxes that were checked in the form. The page calls the request.getParameterValues() method and then prints every element in the String array returned by the method. Notice that the web browser only submits values for the boxes that were checked. Finally, the JSP prints a link to the welcome.jsp page.

When welcome.jsp is called this time, the User object exists in the session, so the JSP outputs the topic list.

Translation and Compilation

As you develop and test JSP pages, you may have noticed that the first time you access a new page, there is some delay before the page is sent to the browser. This is a result of the server translating and compiling the page at request time. After the page has been translated and compiled, subsequent requests to the page are processed more quickly.

The Servlet API

When a page is translated, whether at request time, or earlier, it is translated into a Java source file. This Java class is known as a **servlet**. You may have noticed the term "servlet" earlier in the chapter. Much of what a JSP does is based on the Servlet API, another API within J2EE. In fact, the Servlet API predates the JSP API.

Servlets were developed to allow a server's capabilities to be extended by Java code that ran inside the server. `HttpServlets` are servlets that run inside an HTTP server. A servlet accepts HTTP requests from clients, and creates dynamic responses to those requests. It sends response data to the client through an `OutputStream`. The servlet uses a `session` object to store data about a client and the client's interactions with the server. The servlet has access to the application through a `ServletContext` object, and it can access servlet parameters through a `ServletConfig` object. In fact, all the features of JSP pages that we will see in this chapter are based on the servlet model.

The JSP API

So, if servlets can do everything JSP pages can do, why do we need JSP?

If a JSP page is an HTML page with bits of embedded code, a servlet is Java code with bits of HTML. However, the larger the web application, the more HTML tends to be in the Java code. This becomes very hard to maintain, especially if your team has web experts who are not programmers.

Servlets tend to be good at computations and processing, while JSP pages tend to be good at data presentation. If only there were a way to get all the HTML out of servlets, and all the Java code out of JSP pages. That way, programmers could work on the servlets, and web designers could develop the JSP pages. In the next chapter, we will see one way to move the code out of JSP pages.

So, although you don't need to be a servlet expert to work with JSP, if you know how servlets work it can help to understand what is happening with the page. We'll look at servlets in detail in Chapter 5.

A Translated JSP

Let's take a quick look at a translated JSP to see how the JSP page is translated into code that implements a Java servlet. Most servers will keep the translated `.java` source file in the file system, so you can examine it if you need to. For J2EE 1.4, that location is *J2EE_HOME*\domains*{domain}*\server\generated\jsp\j2ee-apps*{app name}*\war-ic_war\ where *J2EE_HOME* is the appropriate location of the J2EE installation on your system, *{domain}* is the domain name used when you start your server (domain1 is the default), and *{app name}* is the name of the application. For the Tomcat stand-alone, that location is *TOMCAT_HOME*\work\Standalone\localhost*application_context*, where *TOMCAT_HOME* is the appropriate location of the Tomcat installation on your system. If you have deployed the examples in this chapter, navigate to the appropriate directory and open the source file for the `welcome.jsp` page. The J2EE reference implementation and Tomcat both name the source file as `welcome_jsp.java`. If you are using a different server, the name may be different. We will not look at every line in the file, but only some of the lines that show the relation between the JSP source and the Java source. For this section, I looked at the welcome_jsp.java source file created by Tomcat 5.0 for the last *Try It Out* example. Your Java source file may differ, depending on which server you have and which source file you are looking at.

One of the first things you will notice is that the import attribute of the page directive has been turned into import statements:

```
import java.util.Iterator;
import ch3.*;
```

This is followed by the class statement:

```
public final class welcome_jsp
    extends org.apache.jasper.runtime.HttpJspBase
    implements javax.servlet.jsp.el.FunctionMapper,
               org.apache.jasper.runtime.JspSourceDependent {
```

Notice that the class extends HttpJspBase. In the servlet chapter, we will see that servlets in a web application extend HttpServlet.

Next, you will see that the two declarations in the JSP page have been turned into a variable declaration and a public method declaration in the Java source. Note that the variable is declared as a member variable of the class, and so is accessible from all the methods in the class:

```
FaqCategories faqs = new FaqCategories();

public String replaceUnderscore(String s) {
  return s.replace(' ','_');
}
```

The main body of the JSP is contained in the _jspService() method as shown here. In the Servlet API, the analogous method is service(). This method starts by declaring the implicit objects that are used when servicing a request. Of course, they are not so implicit now that the translator has added the code to declare and initialize them:

```
public void _jspService(HttpServletRequest request,
                        HttpServletResponse response)
             throws java.io.IOException, ServletException {

  JspFactory _jspxFactory = null;
  javax.servlet.jsp.PageContext pageContext = null;
  HttpSession session = null;
  ServletContext application = null;
  ServletConfig config = null;
  JspWriter out = null;
  Object page = this;
  JspWriter _jspx_out = null;
```

Following the previous code is code that initializes all the implicit objects. Although we will not explicitly look at all the code in this chapter, I do want to show one last snippet from the `_jspService()` method:

```
out.write("<body>\n    ");
out.write("<h1>Java FAQ Welcome Page");
out.write("</h1>\n\n");

User user = (User) session.getAttribute("user");
if (user == null) {
   out.write("\n    You are not yet registered, please \n    ");
   out.write("<a href=\"registrationform.html\">register");
   out.write("</a>.\n");
```

This is part of the code that outputs the template data to the client. Notice that the translated code uses the same implicit out object that the JSP can use. Also, notice that the whitespace from the JSP source file is preserved in the Java source file. A servlet implementing the same page would similarly output the HTML template data using print statements. However, with a servlet, you would need to code those statements manually. With a JSP page, it is much easier to write the template data as HTML, and let the container perform the translation to Java code.

Earlier in the chapter, I stated that you could declare and define a `jspInit()` method and a `jspDestroy()` method. If you define those methods in the JSP, they will appear as additional methods in the Java source file.

Errors and Exceptions

If you've typed in any of the examples in this chapter, or if you have created any JSP pages of your own, you have probably run into the situation where you've had bugs in your page. Whether these bugs occur at translation time or at request time affects the response that you see in the browser when you attempt to test your page. Sometimes you see a very ugly stack trace. Well, maybe not ugly to you, as the developer, but you don't want any of the users of your application to see anything so unfriendly.

Java web applications can deal with exceptions in a number of ways. Obviously, some exceptions can be handled as you develop the web application by adding data validation and try-catch blocks into the code. This technique avoids the exceptions. However, you need a way to deal with unexpected exceptions. Two ways to deal with unexpected exceptions are through:

❑   The page directive

❑   The deployment descriptor

The page Directive

We have already seen how to include a page directive in your JSP page. The page directive can have an attribute named errorPage. Whenever an uncaught exception occurs in that particular page, the server sends the specified error page to the client. This allows you to use different error pages for different components in the application. The errorPage attribute looks like this:

```
<%@ page errorPage="/WEB-INF/errorPage.jsp" %>
```

where the value of the errorPage attribute is the path to the error page file. The drawback is, of course, that you can only specify a single error page for all exceptions in the JSP page.

The Deployment Descriptor

The deployment descriptor allows you to specify application-wide error handlers for errors in the application. This provides a way to specify different error pages for exceptions that might occur within a single page. If a given exception or HTML error occurs anywhere in the application, the deployment descriptor identifies an error page that can be served to the client. Of course, a specific error page identified in a JSP page takes precedence over the error page identified in the deployment descriptor.

You can specify error pages for Java exceptions, and error pages for HTML errors. Error page elements come immediately after the <welcome-file-list> element in the deployment descriptor.

To specify an error page for a Java exception, use this element in the deployment descriptor:

```
<error-page>
  <exception-type>java.lang.NumberFormatException</exception-type>
  <location>/WEB-INF/BadNumber.html</location>
</error-page>
```

To specify an error page for an HTML error, use this element:

```
<error-page>
  <error-code>404</error-code>
  <location>/WEB-INF/NoSuchPage.html</location>
</error-page>
```

A complete list of the HTML error codes can be found in the HTTP specification at http://www.w3.org/Protocols/rfc2616/rfc2616-sec10.html.

Try It Out Exception Handling in JSP Pages

In this example, we will add error handling to the Java FAQ application.

1. The structure of the web application looks like this:

```
Ch03/
  welcome.jsp
  Dates_and_Times.jsp
  registration.jsp
  registrationform.html
  Threading.jsp
  WEB-INF/
    footer.jspf
    errorPage.jsp
    web.xml
    BadNumber.html
    NoSuchPage.html
    classes/
      Ch03/
        FaqCategories.java
        FaqCategories.class
        User.java
        User.class
```

2. Add this page to the `JavaFAQ` application. This page is `Threading.jsp`, and it is located in the root directory of the application (the same directory in which `welcome.jsp` is located):

```
<%@ page errorPage="/WEB-INF/errorPage.jsp" %>

<!DOCTYPE HTML PUBLIC "-//W3C//DTD HTML 4.01 Transitional//EN">
<html>
  <head><title>Threading FAQs</title></head>
  <body>
<% Integer i = new Integer("string"); %>
  </body>
</html>
```

3. Modify `errorPage.jsp` as shown here:

```
<%@ page isErrorPage="true" import="java.io.PrintWriter" %>

<!DOCTYPE HTML PUBLIC "-//W3C//DTD HTML 4.01 Transitional//EN">
<html>
  <head>
    <title>Error</title>
  </head>
  <body>
    <h1>Error</h1>
    There was an error somewhere.
    <p>Here is the stack trace
    <p><% exception.printStackTrace(new PrintWriter(out)); %>
<%@ include file="/WEB-INF/footer.jspf" %>
  </body>
</html>
```

4.   Create the JSP `Dates_and_Times.jsp` in the root directory:

```
<!DOCTYPE HTML PUBLIC "-//W3C//DTD HTML 4.01 Transitional//EN">
<html>
  <head>
    <title>Dates and Times FAQ</title>
  </head>

  <body>
    <h1>Dates and Times FAQ</h1>
<% Integer i = new Integer("string"); %>
<%@ include file="/WEB-INF/footer.jspf"%>
  </body>
</html>
```

5.   Create two HTML pages that will be used as error pages. The first is `NoSuchPage.html`, and it is located in the **WEB-INF** directory:

```
<!DOCTYPE HTML PUBLIC "-//W3C//DTD HTML 4.01 Transitional//EN">
<html>
  <head>
    <title>Resource Not Found</title>
  </head>

  <body>
    <h1>Resource Not Found</h1>
    You are attempting to go to a page that does not exist
    or is not available. If you entered the address by hand,
    please go to the <a href="welcome.jsp">Welcome Page</a>.

    <p>If you clicked on a link on this site, the page is
       temporarily unavailable. Try again later.
<%@ include file="/WEB-INF/footer.jspf"%>
  </body>
</html>
```

6.   The second error page is `BadNumber.html`. It too is located in the **WEB-INF** directory:

```
<!DOCTYPE HTML PUBLIC "-//W3C//DTD HTML 4.01 Transitional//EN">
<html>
  <head>
    <title>Invalid Number</title>
  </head>

  <body>
    <h1>Invalid Number</h1>
    You entered a number that is incorrect.
    Only digits are allowed. Please press the
    back button and try again.
<%@ include file="/WEB-INF/footer.jspf"%>
  </body>
</html>
```

7. Modify the deployment descriptor. If you are using J2EE, go to step 8. If you are using Tomcat, edit the `web.xml` file as shown here:

```xml
<?xml version="1.0" encoding="ISO-8859-1"?>

<!DOCTYPE web-app
    PUBLIC "-//Sun Microsystems, Inc.//DTD Web Application 2.3//EN"
    "http://java.sun.com/dtd/web-app_2_3.dtd">

<web-app>

  <!-- this is the deployment descriptor for Chapter 3
       Try It Out example 3                               -->

  <welcome-file-list>
    <welcome-file>welcome.jsp</welcome-file>
  </welcome-file-list>
  <error-page>
    <exception-type>java.lang.NumberFormatException</exception-type>
    <location>/WEB-INF/BadNumber.html</location>
  </error-page>

  <error-page>
    <error-code>404</error-code>
    <location>/WEB-INF/NoSuchPage.html</location>
  </error-page>

</web-app>
```

8. If you are using the J2EE Deployment Tool, modify the File Refs tab for the WebApp as shown below. You need to add two entries to the Error Mapping list. Add the same mappings that are shown in the `web.xml` file in step 4:

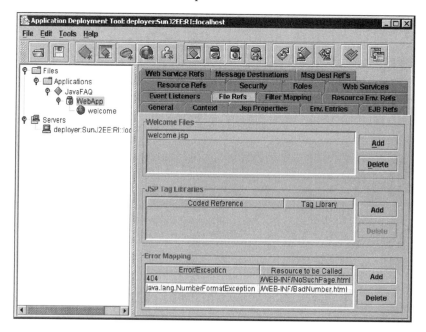

9. Deploy the application.

10. Open a browser and navigate through the screens until you reach the topic list page as shown below:

11. Click the link for Threading. The browser should look something like this:

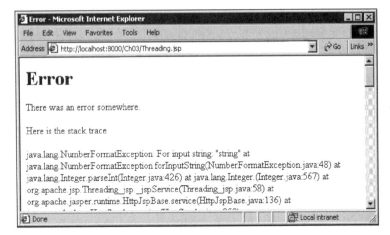

12. Click the link for Dates and Times. You will see this:

13. Click the link for Strings and StringBuffers. You will see this:

How It Works

We've added three pages to the application, each of which causes a different error-handling mechanism to control the page flow.

The Threading.jsp page included a page directive that specified the error page. Since Threading.jsp attempts to create an Integer object with an invalid argument to the constructor, an exception is thrown, and the page does not have an error handler to catch the exception. This causes the server to call the error page specified by the page directive, and that page is sent to the client.

The error page, errorPage.jsp, has access to the implicit exception object. This is because the page includes the page directive with the isErrorPage attribute set to true. Pages that don't have this attribute do not have access to the exception object. We can use this object together with the implicit out object to print out the stack trace to the response like this:

```
<p><% exception.printStackTrace(new PrintWriter(out)); %>
```

This works because the java.lang.Throwable interface defines a printStackTrace(PrintWriter) method. The PrintWriter constructor can take an OutputStream instance, which is exactly the type of the implicit out object. The method prints the stack trace to the given PrintWriter. (Keep in mind that you wouldn't print a stack trace in a live page meant for a user of the application. It provides no useful information for users, and just gives them a bad feeling about your application. The example above is used to show that you can access the implicit exception object in an error page.)

The Date_and_Times.jsp also uses an Integer object to cause an exception to be thrown from the page. However, this page does not specify an error handler in the page directive. In this case, the server matches the exception thrown to an exception specified in an <error-page> element in the deployment descriptor. The server sends the BadNumber.html page to the client. If the exception did not match a specification in the deployment descriptor, the server would probably have sent an HTTP 500 error to the client.

Finally, the `Strings_and_StringBuffer.jsp` page does not exist. This creates an HTTP 404 error in the server. Since this error code matches an error code specified in an `<error-page>` element in the deployment descriptor, the server sends the specified page to the client. If the error code had not matched a specification in the deployment descriptor, the server would have taken some server-specific action. Some servers, such as Tomcat, may send a server-specific page back to the client with the error; other servers might simply send the error code to the browser and let the browser decide how to display the error to the user.

Including and Forwarding from JSP Pages

JSP pages have the ability to include other JSP pages or servlets in the output that is sent to a client, or to forward the request to another page or servlet for servicing. This is accomplished through the standard actions `<jsp:include>` and `<jsp:forward>`.

include Action

Including a JSP page or servlet through a standard action differs from the `include` directive in the time at which the other resource is included, and how the other resource is included. Recall that an `include` directive can be used in either of the two formats below, anywhere within the JSP:

```
<%@ include file="/WEB-INF/footer.jspf">
<jsp:directive.include file="/WEB-INF/footer.jspf"/>
```

When the JSP container translates the page, this directive causes the indicated page to be included in that place in the page, and become part of the Java source file that is compiled into the JSP page implementation class. That is, it is included at translation time. Using the `include` directive, the included file does not need to be a complete and valid JSP.

With the `include` standard action, the JSP file stops processing the current request and passes the request to the included file. The included file passes its output to the response. Then control of the response returns to the calling JSP, which finishes processing the response. The output of the included page or servlet is included at request time. Components that are included via the `include` action must be valid JSP pages or servlets.

The included file is not allowed to modify the headers of the response, nor to set cookies in the response.

forward Action

With the `forward` action, the current page stops processing the request and forwards the request to another web component. This other component completes the response. Execution never returns to the calling page. Unlike the `include` action, which can occur at any time during a response, the `forward` action must occur prior to writing any output to the `OutputStream`. In other words, the `forward` action must occur prior to any HTML template data in the JSP, and prior to any scriptlets or expressions that write data to the `OutputStream`. If any output has occurred in the calling JSP, an exception will be thrown when the `forward` action is encountered.

Using include and forward

The format of the `include` action is:

```
<jsp:include page="URL" flush="true|false">
  <jsp:param name="paramName" value="paramValue"/>
</jsp:include>
```

For the `include` element, the `page` attribute is required, and its value is the URL of the page whose output is included in the response. The `flush` attribute is optional, and indicates whether the output buffer should be flushed before the included file is called. The default value is `false`.

If the JSP needs to pass parameters to the included file, it does so with the `<jsp:param>` element. One element is used for each parameter. This element is optional. If it is included, both the `name` and `value` attributes are required. The included JSP can access the parameters using the `getParameter()` and `getParameterValues()` methods of the `request` object.

The format of the `forward` element is similar:

```
<jsp:forward page="URL">
  <jsp:param name="paramName" value="paramValue"/>
</jsp:forward>
```

The meaning and use of the attributes and of the `<jsp:param>` element are the same as for the `include` action.

Try It Out Including and Forwarding to JSP Pages

In this last example of the chapter, we will modify the `JavaFAQ` application to use `forward` actions to control the application flow. Here is the application structure:

```
Ch03/
    welcome.jsp
    Dates_and_Times.jsp
    registration.jsp
    registrationform.html
    Threading.jsp
    WEB-INF/
        footer.jspf
        errorPage.jsp
        web.xml
        BadNumber.html
        NoSuchPage.html
        formatStackTrace.jsp
        classes/
            Ch03/
                FaqCategories.java
                FaqCategories.class
                User.java
                User.class
```

1. Start by modifying `welcome.jsp` as shown here:

```jsp
<%@ page errorPage="/WEB-INF/errorPage.jsp"
   import="java.util.Iterator,Ch03.*" %>

<%
   User user = (User)session.getAttribute("user");
   String reqType = request.getParameter("reqType");
   if (user == null && reqType == null) {
%>
   <jsp:forward page="registrationform.html"/>
<%
   } else if (user == null && reqType != null) {
%>
   <jsp:forward page="registration.jsp">
       <jsp:param name="submitTime"
                      value="<%=(new java.util.Date()).toString()%>" />
   </jsp:forward>
<%
   }
%>

<!DOCTYPE HTML PUBLIC "-//W3C//DTD HTML 4.01 Transitional//EN">
<html>
  <head>
    <meta name="Cache-control" content="no-cache">
    <title>Java FAQ Welcome Page</title>
  </head>

  <body>
    <h1>Java FAQ Welcome Page</h1>
    Welcome to the Java FAQ

<%! FaqCategories faqs = new FaqCategories(); %>
Click a link below for answers to the given topic.
<%
     Iterator categories = faqs.getAllCategories();
     while (categories.hasNext()) {
       String category = (String) categories.next();
%>
       <p><a href="<%= replaceUnderscore(category) %>.jsp">
          <%= category %></a></p>
<%
     }
%>

<%@ include file="/WEB-INF/footer.jspf" %>
    </body>
</html>

<%!
public String replaceUnderscore(String s) {
  return s.replace(' ','_');
}
%>
```

2. The next modified file is registrationform.html. Only the single line that contains the form tag needs to be modified as shown here:

```
<!DOCTYPE HTML PUBLIC "-//W3C//DTD HTML 4.01 Transitional//EN">
<html>
  <head>
    <title>Registration Page</title>
  </head>
  <body>
    <h1>Registration Page</h1>

    <form action="welcome.jsp?reqType=register" method="POST">
      <table>

<!-- The remainder of registrationform.html is the same as before,
     so it is not shown here -->
```

3. A single new line of code has been added to the registration.jsp file; only the applicable snippet is shown here:

```
<%    String[] topics = request.getParameterValues("topics");
      if (topics == null) { topics = new String[] {"No topics"}; }
      for (int i = 0; i < topics.length; i++) {
%>
        <br><%= topics[i] %>
<%
      }
%>
      <p>This request was submitted at
        <%= request.getParameter("submitTime") %>
      <p>Go to <a href="welcome.jsp">Topic List Page</a></p>
    <%@ include file="/WEB-INF/footer.jspf" %>
  </body>
</html>
```

4. This next file is errorPage.jsp. This file now has an include action in addition to the include directive for the standard footer:

```
<%@ page isErrorPage="true" import="java.io.PrintWriter" %>

<!DOCTYPE HTML PUBLIC "-//W3C//DTD HTML 4.01 Transitional//EN">
<html>
  <head>
    <title>Error</title>
  </head>
  <body>
    <h1>Error</h1>
    There was an error somewhere.
    <p>Here is the stack trace
    <p>
      <% request.setAttribute("ex", exception); %>
      <jsp:include page="formatStackTrace.jsp" />
  <%@ include file="/WEB-INF/footer.jspf" %>
  </body>
</html>
```

5. The JSP page included by the `include` action in `errorPage.jsp` is shown here. It is named `formatStackTrace.jsp`:

```jsp
<%@ page import="java.io.PrintWriter" %>
<%
   out.println("<pre>");
   Throwable t = (Throwable) request.getAttribute("ex");
   if (t != null) {
      t.printStackTrace(new PrintWriter(out));
   }
   out.println("</pre>");
%>
```

6. Create the web application with these new files, and the files developed in previous examples. Deploy the application to the J2EE server or the Tomcat stand-alone server. For the J2EE server, use the same web application settings as in the previous *Try It Out* example. For Tomcat, you can use the same deployment descriptor as in the previous *Try It Out* example.

7. Open a browser and enter the appropriate address for the `welcome.jsp` page. The browser will display the registration form page.

8. Enter the appropriate parameters, and click the Submit button. The browser will display the registration page.

9. Click the link in the registration page, and the browser will display the welcome page with the topic list. If the topic list is not displayed, your browser has probably cached the welcome page. Click the refresh button to get the correct page.

10. Click the Threading topic link. The browser will display the errorPage.jsp with a nicely formatted stack trace:

How It Works

The first thing the welcome.jsp does now is to check for the existence of the user object, as previously, and for a request parameter with the name reqType. As before, the user object is put into the session by the registration.jsp; the reqType parameter will be added to the request by the registrationform.html page. If both of these are null, neither the registrationform.html nor registration.jsp pages has been called, so the welcome.jsp forwards the request to the registrationform.html page:

```
<%
   User user = (User)session.getAttribute("user");
   String reqType = request.getParameter("reqType");
   if (user == null && reqType == null) {
%>
      <jsp:forward page="registrationform.html"/>
```

If you look at the registrationform.html, you will see that the action attribute of the <form> tag has been modified to add a request parameter to the URL. When the Submit button is clicked, the form submits to welcome.jsp. This method of submitting request parameters in the URL is known as URL encoding. This time, welcome.jsp finds that the user object is still null, but that the reqType has a value. Since this indicates that the registrationform.html page has been visited, but the registration has not been submitted, welcome.jsp forwards the request to registration.jsp; it includes another request parameter with the request using the <jsp:param> element:

```
<%
   } else if (user == null && reqType != null) {
%>
      <jsp:forward page="registration.jsp">
         <jsp:param name="submitTime"
                     value="<%=(new java.util.Date()).toString()%>" />
      </jsp:forward>
<%
   }
%>
```

This flow is artificially complicated, because it probably makes more sense to have registrationform.html submit directly to registration.jsp. The main reason for submitting to welcome.jsp is to provide several different examples of the use of the <jsp:forward> action. However, there is a little justification for having all requests go through the welcome.jsp page: this is a very simple example of something known as a Model 2, or Model View Controller, architecture. With a Model 2 architecture, one component acts as a controller, directing the requests to the component that is set up to handle a particular request. We will look at the Model 2 architecture in more detail in Chapter 5.

The `registration.jsp` page performs the same actions as in previous examples, with the addition of reading the new request parameter added by `welcome.jsp`, and displaying the value of that parameter. When the user clicks the link, the request is again sent to `welcome.jsp`. This final time, both `user` and `reqType` are not null, so `welcome.jsp` does not forward the request, but completes the response itself.

Clicking the Threading topic link again calls `Threading.jsp`, which still causes a `NumberFormatException`. This time, however, `errorPage.jsp` includes `formatStackTrace.jsp`. The `formatStackTrace.jsp` outputs the stack trace as older versions of `errorPage.jsp` did, but it wraps it in a `<pre>` tag, so that the stack trace is nicely formatted.

Summary

In this chapter, we've taken a tour of many of the basic features of JSP pages. With the information in this chapter, you should be able to easily begin creating JSP web applications of your own. After completing this chapter you should have learned:

❑ JSP pages consist of HTML data, also known as template data, and Java code.

❑ You can specify an error page for a JSP using `<%@page errorPage=""%>`. Error pages are used to provide a meaningful error page to a user when something bad happens to the web application.

❑ You can import Java packages for the page using `<% page import="" %>`.

❑ Java code is included in the page using a declaration `<%! declaration %>`, a scriptlet `<% scriptlet %>`, or an expression `<%= expression %>`. These elements allow you to mix Java code with the template data in the page.

❑ JavaBean instances can be created using the `<jsp:useBean>` standard action; properties of the bean can be set using `<jsp:setProperty>`; and the value of a bean's properties can be obtained using `<jsp:getProperty>`. JavaBeans are one way to encapsulate business or domain logic so that JSP pages can be used primarily for presentation.

❑ Various implicit objects such as `request`, `response`, `out`, `session`, and so on, are always available to the JSP to help process a request. The `session` object is particularly useful because it enables the web application to keep track of user information. One example of the usefulness of this is an e-commerce application that needs to keep track of a user's shopping cart.

❑ Servers translate and compile JSPs into Java classes that behave like servlets.

❑ You can specify error handlers for the entire application using the `<error-page>` element in the deployment descriptor.

❑ A JSP can include the output of other JSPs or servlets in the response to clients. This is done through the `<jsp:include>` standard action.

❑ A JSP can forward a request to another JSP or servlet for processing. This is done through the `<jsp:forward>` standard action.

That's quite a lot. All these features put together allow application developers to create dynamic and powerful web applications that can be used for many purposes from chat rooms to e-commerce, from virtual communities to business applications. However, you may have noticed that as the examples in this chapter became more dynamic, more featured, they also tended to have more and more Java code interspersed in the JSP pages. This tends to be a problem because web page developers are often not Java developers.

What would be ideal is a way to create JSP pages that hide the Java code from the page developers. This would allow the page developer to concentrate on the format and structure of the markup, and leave Java developers free to work on only the Java code. There are several ways to do this, and we will see some of them in the next chapter, where we explore some of the new JSP features introduced in the latest version of the JSP specification.

Exercises

1. Declare an init and a destroy method in a JSP. Include some debug output so that you can see when these methods are called. Deploy the JSP and determine when these methods are called. (You may not see the output from the destroy method.)

2. Write additional JSP pages for the `JavaFAQ` application that allow a user to submit a question, and answer a question.

3. Create a JSP web application that presents a quiz to the user. Use a JSP page to present each question one at a time to the user. Use the same page to accept the answer submitted by the user. (That is, the HTML created by the page should submit the answer to the same `.jsp` page.) The page should determine whether the answer is correct or not, compute the current score of the user, and select a graphic that illustrates the current status, and select the next question; this is all put into the response back to the client.

Advanced JSP Topics

The previous chapter introduced you to JSPs and provided enough information to enable you to begin writing and using those web components. However, the previous chapter only scratched the surface of what can be done with JSP.

In this chapter, we'll stretch our JSP wings a little further and explore some more advanced topics. Some of the material in this chapter has been in use for a while as part of earlier JSP specifications. Other material, though, comes from the JSP 2.0 specification, and so is quite new. For the examples in this chapter that rely on new JSP 2.0 features, you will need to use a server that supports JSP 2.0, such as J2EE 1.4 or Tomcat 5.0.

We won't cover every aspect of JSP, because that would take up a whole book in itself, and would mean going into details that you'll probably never need to know. Instead, we'll focus on learning some of the new or advanced features that will help you the most when writing real-world JSP pages.

The topics we'll look at in this chapter are:

❑ **Expression language**–Expression language was developed as a way to simplify expressions in a JSP. It provides a way to use run-time expressions outside JSP scripting elements. Expression language is a new feature of JSP 2.0.

❑ **Custom actions**–Standard actions were introduced in the previous chapter. Standard actions provide a way to encapsulate Java code so that the page designer only has to know the syntax of the tag. JSP provides a way for Java developers to create their own actions, known as **custom actions** or **tag extensions**. We'll look at both **classic** and **simple** custom actions and how to use them in JSPs. Classic tag extensions are from JSP 1.2 and prior; Simple tag extensions are a part of JSP 2.0.

❑ **JSTL**–To avoid multiple developers creating conflicting tag libraries for basic actions, the **JSP Standard Tag Library** specification was developed. It doesn't stop multiple developers creating the same tag extensions, but if they follow the specification, at least the libraries will work the same. The JSTL is compatible with JSP 1.2. We'll look at what it is and how to use it in your JSPs.

Expression Language

In the previous chapter, we saw how we can create scripting elements that can be used to embed Java code in the JSP file. Scripting elements included JSP tags for declarations, scriptlets, and expressions:

```
<%! int a = 5; %> <%-- declaration --%>
<% while (x < 10) { out.write("x=" + x); } %> <%-- scriptlet --%>
<%= user.getFirstName() %> <%-- expression --%>
```

JSP 2.0 adds **Expression Language** (EL) statements to the JSP toolkit. Expression language statements provide a somewhat simpler syntax for performing some of the same actions as the JSP elements above. Further, you can use EL expressions in scriptless JSP pages. Scriptless JSP pages are those pages that, for whatever reason, are not allowed to use JSP declarations, scriptlets, or scripting expressions.

You can, of course, write any JSP page without using any declarations, scriptlets, or expressions. We saw an example of one such page at the beginning of the previous chapter: HelloWorld.jsp. That page was scriptless by choice. You can also force a page to be scriptless. One reason for doing this is to enforce a separation between display elements and business logic. By enforcing scriptless pages, the dynamic behavior of JSP pages must be provided through other elements such as JavaBeans (see the previous chapter), EL expressions, custom actions, and standard tag libraries (we will see custom actions and standard tag libraries later in this chapter). By encapsulating business logic in JavaBeans and custom actions, the page designers do not need to learn any Java code. Whether or not your application should have scriptless JSP pages is a decision you must make based on the requirements and needs of your application.

There are two ways to ensure a page doesn't contain any scripting elements: through a page directive, or through an element of the deployment descriptor. You can also specify whether EL expressions are allowed or not through the same two mechanisms. The page directive looks like this:

```
<%@ page isScriptingEnabled="true|false" isELEnabled="true|false" %>
```

The default for isScriptingEnabled is true. The container sets the default isELEnabled value to true for JSP 2.0; false for JSP 1.2 or earlier. The container determines the JSP version based on the deployment descriptor. Descriptors that have a DOCTYPE declaration that includes "web-app_2_3.dtd" imply JSP 1.2. Descriptors with a web-app attribute of version="2.4" are JSP 2.0.

Under JSP 2.0 you can also specify JSP configuration information in the deployment descriptor. Where the page directive applies to a single page, the deployment descriptor can apply to whole sets of pages. For example:

```
<web-app xmlns="http://java.sun.com/xml/ns/j2ee"
    xmlns:xsi="http://www.w3.org/2001/XMLSchema-instance"
    xsi:schemaLocation="http://java.sun.com/xml/ns/j2ee/web-app_2_4.xsd"
    version="2.4">

  <welcome-file-list>
    <welcome-file>TopicList.jsp</welcome-file>
  </welcome-file-list>
```

```
<jsp-config>
  <jsp-property-group>
    <url-pattern>*.jsp</url-pattern>
    <el-enabled>true</el-enabled>
    <scripting-enabled>true</scripting-enabled>
  </jsp-property-group>
</jsp-config>
</web-app>
```

Within the <web-app> element of the deployment descriptor, the <jsp-config> element supplies configuration information for the JSP pages in a web application. This element only applies in a deployment descriptor where the web-app version is 2.4.

The version number is based on the Servlet specification version.

Within the <jsp-property-group> element of <jsp-config>, the <url-pattern> identifies which JSP pages the configuration applies to. The <el-enabled> element defines whether EL expressions are enabled or not. The <scripting-enabled> element defines whether scripting is enabled or not. The default for both elements is true.

> **The elements in the deployment descriptor must follow a specific order. When using the elements shown above, they must be used in the order shown.**

You can have multiple <jsp-property-group> elements within the <jsp-config> element. If a resource matches more than one group, the pattern that is most specific applies.

Syntax of EL

The basic syntax for an EL expression is:

```
${expr}
```

where *expr* is a valid expression. Valid expressions can include literals, operators, object references (variables), and function calls.

Literals

The EL syntax provides for a number of literal values that can be used in expressions. These literal values are:

❑ Boolean literals—`true`, `false`.

❑ String literals—Any string delimited by single or double quotes. The backslash is used as an escape character for quotes and backslashes. For, example, `'This string\'s value has an escaped single quote'` or `"the directory is c:\\My Documents\\apress"`. You need to escape quotes only when they are enclosed by a quote of the same kind (in other words `'\''` or `"\""`). If double quotes had been used around the string example earlier in this paragraph, the single quote would not need to be escaped: `"This string's value has a single quote"`.

❑ Integer literals—Any positive or negative integer number (−13, 45, 2374, and so on).

❑ Floating-point literals—Any positive or negative floating-point number (`-1.3E-30`, `3.14159`, `2.00000000000001`, `.45`, `.56e2`, etc.).

❑ Null literal—`null`.

Here are some examples:

```
${true} <%-- evaluates to true --%>
${"Single quotes inside 'double quotes' do not need to be escaped"}
   <%-- evaluates to Single quotes inside 'double quotes'
        do not need to be escaped --%>
${2*4} <%-- evaluates to 8 --%>
```

Operators

Most of the usual operators available in Java are available in Expression Language:

Type	Operator
Arithmetic	+, −, *, /, div, %, mod
Relational	== and eq
	!= and ne
	< and lt
	> and gt
	<= and le
	>= and ge

Type	Operator
Logical	&& and and
	|| and or
	! and not
Other	(), empty, [], .

You should be familiar with most of the operators in the table above. In the next few paragraphs, we will look at the last four "other" operators in the list. However, note that many of the operators have both symbolic and word variants (such as / and div, or < and lt). These equivalents are provided so that if your JSP page needs to be XML-compliant, you can avoid using entity references (such as < for <). Within an XML document, an EL expression for "less than" could be coded ${2 lt 3} rather than ${2 < 3}.

As with most expressions, the parentheses can be used to change the precedence of the expression:

```
${ (2 * 4) + 3 } <%-- evaluates to 11 --%>
${ 2 * (4 + 3) } <%-- evaluates to 14 --%>
```

The empty operator can be used to test for various conditions. An expression such as:

```
${empty name}
```

will return true if name references a null object or if name references an empty String, List, Map, or array. Otherwise empty returns false. The object referenced by name is an object stored in the page, request, session, or application implicit objects. For example:

```
<% Vector vec = new Vector();                  // Create empty vector
pageContext.setAttribute("someName", vec); %> // Store vector in pageContext
${empty someName}   // Evaluates to true; notice the operator acts on the
                    // attribute name someName, not the variable name vec
```

Keep in mind that this works for any object in one of the contexts, not just objects you explicitly add using setAttribute() or some other method. For example, as we will see later, custom actions can create variables that are accessible through EL expressions. The empty operator can be applied to these variables. Another way to add objects to a context is by creating a JavaBean; JavaBeans are stored in a context based on the scope attribute of the <jsp:useBean> action. The point is that the empty operator can be applied to any object that can be referenced by name in one of the contexts.

The final two operators are the dot operator (.) and the operator []. These are used to access the attributes of an object in the page. The left-value (lvalue) of the operator is interpreted to be an object in the page; the right-value (rvalue) is a property, key, or index. For example, if you have defined a bean in the page using the <jsp:useBean> standard action, you can access the properties of the bean using either notation. Given a bean with the properties firstName and surname, you could access its properties using either notation like this:

```
${user.firstName}
${user[surname]}
```

The two notations are equivalent when accessing the properties of an object in the page. Either expression above results in the page attempting to find the given object in the page and call the getXXX() method for the given property.

The two operators can also be used for Maps, Lists, or arrays. When either operator is applied to a Map (such as Hashtable or HashMap) the page class attempts to access the Map attribute with the key given by the rvalue. That is, given:

```
${myObject[name]} <%-- myObject is a Hashtable or HashMap --%>
```

the equivalent code statement is:

```
myObject.get("name");
```

If the operator is applied to a List or array, the page attempts to convert the rvalue into an index and access the value using:

```
myObject.get(name);         // myObject is a List
Array.get(myObject, name);  // myObject is an array
```

When myObject is an object that implements List, the page class uses the get(int) method of List to get the value of the expression. When myObject references an array, the get(Object, int) method of Array is used.

Implicit Objects

EL expressions also have implicit objects available to them. Many of these implicit objects are the same implicit objects that are available in JSP scriptlets and expressions. Through the implicit objects, the EL expression can perform many of the actions that can be performed through scriptlets and JSP expressions. In the *Try It Out* section, we will see examples of how to use some of these objects. The implicit objects are:

❑   pageContext–The javax.servlet.jsp.PageContext object for the page. Can be used to access the JSP implicit objects such as request, response, session, out, etc. For example, ${pageContext.request} evaluates to the request object for the page.

❑   pageScope–A Map that maps page-scoped attribute names to their values. In other words, given an object, such as a bean, that has page scope in the JSP, an EL expression can access the object with ${pageScope.objectName} and an attribute of the object can be accessed using ${pageScope.objectName.attributeName}. In this code snippet, the bean has been given page scope, and it has a property named topic:

```
<jsp:useBean id="questions" scope="page" class="Ch04.Questions">
  <jsp:setProperty name="questions" property="topic"/>
</jsp:useBean>
${pageScope.questions.topic} <%-- Evaluates to the topic property of the
                               bean referenced by the id 'questions' --%>
```

❏ requestScope—A Map that maps request-scoped attribute names to their values. This object allows you to access the attributes of the request object.

❏ sessionScope—A Map that maps session-scoped attribute names to their values. This object is used to access the session objects for the client. For example, if you've added an object to the session, you can access it as shown here:

```
<% session.put("address", "123 Maple St."); %>
${sessionScope.address}          <%-- evaluates to 123 maple St. --%>
<%= session.get("address"); %>   <%-- equivalent scripting expression --%>
```

❏ applicationScope—A Map that maps application-scoped attribute names to their values. Use this object to access objects with application scope.

❏ param—A Map that maps parameter names to a single String parameter value (obtained by calling ServletRequest.getParameter(String name)). Recall that a request object contains data sent by the client. The getParameter(String) method returns the parameter with the given name. The expression ${param.name} is equivalent to request.getParameter(name). (Note that name is not the literal string 'name', but the name of the parameter.)

❏ paramValues—A Map that maps parameter names to a String[] of all values for that parameter (obtained by calling ServletRequest.getParameterValues(String name)). Similar to the previous implicit object, but it retrieves a String array rather than a single value. For example, the expression ${paramValues.name} is equivalent to request.getParameterValues(name).

❏ header—A Map that maps header names to a single String header value (obtained by calling ServletRequest.getHeader(String name)). Requests always contain header information such as the content type and length, cookies, the referring URL, and so on. The expression ${header.name} is equivalent to request.getHeader(name).

❏ headerValues—A Map that maps header names to a String[] of all values for that header (obtained by calling ServletRequest.getHeaders(String)). Similar to the header implicit object. The expression ${headerValues.name} is equivalent to request.getHeaderValues(name).

❏ cookie—A Map that maps cookie names to a single Cookie object. A client can send one or more cookies to the server with a request. The expression ${cookie.name.value} returns the value of the first cookie with the given name. If the request contains multiple cookies with the same name, you should use ${headerValues.name}.

❏ initParam—A Map that maps context initialization parameter names to their String parameter value (obtained by calling ServletContext.getInitParameter(String name)). To access an initialization parameter, use ${initParam.name}.

Using EL Expressions

EL expressions can be used as attribute values in standard and custom actions. They can also be used anywhere there is template text (such as HTML or non-JSP elements) in the JSP file.

This next code snippet shows the use of an EL expression in the attribute value of the `<jsp:forward>` standard action:

```
<jsp:forward page="${param.nextPage}" />
```

In this example, the `<jsp:forward>` action will forward the request to the URL specified by the request parameter named `nextPage`. If the request parameter does not exist, or if its value is not a valid URL, an error will occur in the page.

Errors and Default Values

Because of their use in display-oriented JSP pages, EL expressions do not throw the same exceptions that you might expect from the equivalent Java expression. For example, given this expression:

```
${user.surname}
```

The analogous Java expression is:

```
user.getSurname();
```

Now, if you were writing this Java code manually, and you had not defined the `user` variable, or did not provide a `getSurname()` method, the compiler would warn you of this situation. Before the code was ever executed, you would be able to correct the problem. If you did not initialize the variable `user` at run-time, the code would throw a `NullPointerException`.

However, in a JSP page, many of these requirements cannot be checked until run-time. Since the JSP page is usually used for presentation, many EL expressions result in **default values** rather than thrown exceptions. For example, in the expression above, if `user` is `null`, the value of the EL expression is `null`. With many of the operators, if either the `lvalue` or the `rvalue` is `null`, the default value of the expression is `null` (rather than a thrown exception). You should consult the JSP specification for the full list of default values. When an EL expression does result in an exception, the exception is handled via the normal JSP exception-handling mechanisms.

Try It Out   Using EL Expressions

In this example, we'll create a few JSPs that use EL expressions. Note that you must deploy this example to a server that supports JSP 2.0. If you are trying this example with J2EE or Tomcat, you will need to use J2EE 1.4 or Tomcat 5.0. Here is the directory structure of the application:

```
Ch04/
   TopicList.jsp
   Questions.jsp
   WEB-INF/
      web.xml
      EL_1.jsp
        classes/
           Ch04/
              Questions.java
```

We will be creating the files `TopicList.jsp`, `Questions.jsp`, `EL_1.jsp`, and `Questions.java`. If you are deploying to Tomcat, you will also need to create a `web.xml` deployment descriptor. The basic flow of the application is shown below. In fact, we will use this same flow for several examples in this chapter:

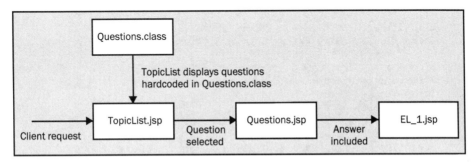

1. Although this example builds on the Java FAQ example application from the previous chapter, you will not need to use any of the files from previous examples. Since we're not using the `welcome.jsp` from the previous chapter, we need another entry point into this part of the Java FAQ application. That entry point is this file, `TopicList.jsp`:

```
<!DOCTYPE HTML PUBLIC "-//W3C//DTD HTML 4.01 Transitional//EN">
<html>
   <head><title>Topic Questions</title></head>
   <body>
      <h1>Topic Questions</h1>

      <jsp:useBean id="questions" class="Ch04.Questions">
         <jsp:setProperty name="questions" property="topic" />
      </jsp:useBean>

The number of questions in topic ${questions.topic} is ${questions.numTopics}
<%
   for (int i = 1; i <= questions.getNumTopics(); i++) {
      pageContext.setAttribute("count", ""+i);
%>
<p>Question <a href="Questions.jsp?qid=${questions.topic}_${count}">
      ${questions.topic}_${count}</a>:
      ${questions.questions[count]}
<%
   }
%>
   </body>
</html>
```

2. The `TopicList.jsp` above displays a list of questions for a given topic. These questions are hard-coded into the `Questions.java` class:

```java
package Ch04;

import java.util.Map;
import java.util.HashMap;

public class Questions {
    private String topic;
    private int numTopics;
    private Map questions = new HashMap();

    public String getTopic() { return topic; }
    public void setTopic(String t) { topic = t; }

    public int getNumTopics() { return numTopics; }
    public void setNumTopics(int n) { numTopics = n; }

    public Map getQuestions() { return questions; }
    public void setQuestions(Map m) { questions = m; }

    public Questions() {
        questions.put("1", "How do I use implicit objects?");
        questions.put("2", "How do I use the JSTL?");
        questions.put("3", "How do I use the 'empty' operator?");
        setNumTopics(questions.size());
    }
}
```

3. Compile this file into `Questions.class`.

4. After displaying the list of questions, the user can click a link for a particular question. The request is posted to the `Questions.jsp` file, shown here (yes, this really is the whole file!):

```jsp
<jsp:include page="/WEB-INF/${param.qid}.jsp" />
```

5. As you can see, `Questions.jsp` simply includes the appropriate question file based on the user's selection. For this example, we will only create the JSP page for the first question. In a later example, we will see `EL_2.jsp`; `EL_3.jsp` will not be presented here, but it is included with the code download for this book at http://www.apress.com. Here is `EL_1.jsp`:

```jsp
<!DOCTYPE HTML PUBLIC "-//W3C//DTD HTML 4.01 Transitional//EN">
<html>
  <head>
    <title>Expression Language Q1</title>
  </head>

  <body>
    <h1>Expression Language Question 1</h1>
    <h2>How do I use implicit objects?</h2>
```

```
<p>The explicit objects are</p>
<ul>
  <li>pageContext</li>
  <li>pageScope</li>
  <li>requestScope</li>
  <li>sessionScope</li>
  <li>applicationScope</li>
  <li>param</li>
  <li>paramValues</li>
  <li>header</li>
  <li>headerValues</li>
  <li>cookie</li>
  <li>initParam</li>
</ul>

<p>Implicit objects form the lvalue of an EL expression, and their
properties are accessed using the . or [] operator. Here are some exam-
ples:</p>
<%-- The four lines after this comment contain special expression syntax
     needed to display a literal ${} in the output of a JSP. This is done
     by using an expression to evaluate the literal '${'. That is, the
     expression ${ '${' } evaluates to ${, and whatever follows the
     expression is treated as normal template text.                    --%>
<p>${'${'}pageContext.request.requestURI} evaluates to
   "${pageContext.request.requestURI}"</p>
<p>${'${'}param.qid} evaluates to "${param.qid}"</p>
<p>${'${'}header.referer} evaluates to "${header.referer}"</p>
<p>${'${'}cookie.JSESSIONID.value} evaluates to
   ${cookie.JSESSIONID.value}</p>
</body>
</html>
```

6. Finally, if you are deploying to Tomcat, or some other stand-alone JSP container, you will need a deployment descriptor. Here is a very simple web.xml file that will do the job:

```
<?xml version="1.0" encoding="ISO-8859-1"?>

<web-app xmlns="http://java.sun.com/xml/ns/j2ee"
    xmlns:xsi="http://www.w3.org/2001/XMLSchema-instance"
    xsi:schemaLocation="http://java.sun.com/xml/ns/j2ee/web-app_2_4.xsd"
    version="2.4">

  <!-- This is the deployment descriptor for Chapter 4 -->

  <!-- Expression Language example, welcome file list  -->

  <welcome-file-list>
    <welcome-file>TopicList.jsp</welcome-file>
  </welcome-file-list>
</web-app>
```

7. If you are deploying to Tomcat 5.0, you can copy the entire directory structure into the Tomcat /webapps directory. Alternately, you can create a .war file and place that into /webapps. You create the .war file by navigating to the top-level directory of the application (/Ch04 in this example) and executing this command:

```
> jar cvf Ch04.war *
```

After deploying, go to step 15.

8. If you are deploying to J2EE, start the J2EE server. After the server has started, run the Deploytool.

9. Create a new Application EAR by selecting File | New | Application EAR from the menu. Enter a name for the EAR and click OK.

10. Create a new Web Application Archive in the EAR by selecting File | New | Web Application WAR from the menu.

11. Add the files TopicList.jsp, Questions.jsp, EL_1.jsp, and Questions.class to the WAR. Ensure you place the EL_1.jsp file into the /WEB-INF directory. Click Next. Select the JSP radio button, and click Next. At the screen that follows, select TopicList.jsp as the component to create. Click Finish.

12. In the main Deployment Tool window, select the application in the left pane, and select the Web Context tab in the right pane. Set the context root for the EAR to be Ch04.

13. Save the EAR file. Then select File | Deployment Settings | Create New File to create a new deployment settings file. Select File | Deployment Settings | Close File to close and save the settings file.

14. Deploy the application using Tools | Deploy from the menu.

15. After the application is deployed, open a web browser and enter the address http://localhost:1024/Ch04/TopicList.jsp?topic=EL (or, if you are using Tomcat stand-alone as the server, use port 8080).

16. Note that because this is an example, not all the links will work correctly. Additionally, you must enter the correct value for the topic (EL) for it to work correctly. When you enter the correct URL, you will see this display:

17. Click on the EL_1 link, and you will see this display:

How It Works

Let's take a quick look at the deployment descriptor first. One big change between JSP 2.0 and previous JSP versions is that you no longer need the DOCTYPE declaration. If you use a DOCTYPE declaration that specifies version 2.2 or 2.3 of the DTD, as we did in the previous chapter, the container will not allow EL expressions or other JSP 2.0 features to be used. To activate JSP 2.0 support, you need to include the web-app attributes shown in the example here:

```
<web-app xmlns="http://java.sun.com/xml/ns/j2ee"
    xmlns:xsi="http://www.w3.org/2001/XMLSchema-instance"
    xsi:schemaLocation="http://java.sun.com/xml/ns/j2ee/web-app_2_4.xsd"
    version="2.4">
```

The questions that are displayed on the page for each topic are hard-coded into the Questions JavaBean. This class has a member called questions, of type Map, which is used to store the individual questions together with a name that holds the number for each question.

```
public class Questions {
  private String topic;
  private int numTopics;
  private Map questions = new HashMap();
```

This property has standard JavaBean setter and getter methods. This means that in an EL expression, we can access the property using the dot notation:

```
${questions.questions}
```

When the bean is instantiated, we add our questions to this Map, together with its name—a String literal that has an integer value:

```
questions.put("1", "How do I use implicit objects?");
questions.put("2", "How do I use the JSTL?");
questions.put("3", "How do I use the 'empty' operator?");
```

Since the property is actually a data structure that stores name-value pairs, we can access any particular value if we know the name.

TopicList.jsp is similar to the welcome.jsp page we used in the previous chapter. It begins by using the <jsp:useBean> standard action to create an object in the page:

```
<jsp:useBean id="questions" class="Ch04.Questions">
  <jsp:setProperty name="questions" property="topic" />
</jsp:useBean>
```

Because this object automatically has page context, we can reference it in an EL expression. That is the next thing the file does, accessing the topic and numTopics properties using this template data with EL expressions:

```
The number of questions in topic ${questions.topic} is ${questions.numTopics}
```

The EL expression references the bean using its id from the <jsp:useBean> action. It accesses the properties using the dot notation. The expression ${questions.topic} evaluates to the value of the topic property of the bean, which happens to be "EL". The expression ${questions.numTopics} evaluates to the value of the numTopics property, which is "3". Next, the page uses a scriptlet to perform a loop. Notice that each time through the loop, it stores the current index as a pageContext attribute using the name count. This allows another EL expression to access the current index using ${count}.

```
    for (int i = 1; i <= questions.getNumTopics(); i++) {
      pageContext.setAttribute("count", ""+i);
%>
<p>Question <a href="Questions.jsp?qid=${questions.topic}_${count}">
  ${questions.topic}_${count}</a>:
```

Not only does the page access the value of count to create a link in the page, it uses count to access the value of the question stored by the Questions object:

```
${questions.questions[count]}
```

Since we can access any particular value if we know the name, we can retrieve a particular question held by the questions object like this:

```
<p>Question <a href="Questions.jsp?qid=${questions.topic}_${count}">
    ${questions.topic}_${count}</a>:
    ${questions.questions[count]}
```

Because the value of count is a String that has an integer value, the code ${questions.questions[count]} is equivalent to:

```
Map m = questions.getQuestions();
String q = (String)questions.get(count);
```

The value of the expression after evaluation is simply the question string stored by the class. This is output to the response.

When you click one of the links in the page created by TopicList.jsp, the request is sent to the Questions.jsp page. This is a very simple page consisting of a single standard action, the <jsp:include> action:

```
<jsp:include page="/WEB-INF/${param.qid}.jsp" />
```

Notice that this file has no template text in it. JSP files can consist solely of JSP elements and still be valid JSP pages. The include action uses an EL expression in the page attribute to determine which JSP page to include. It does this using the implicit param object and the name of the parameter that is being accessed. The TopicList.jsp page outputs a link that looks like this:

```
<a href="Questions.jsp?qid=EL_1">EL_1</a>
```

This link sends the request to the Questions.jsp file with a request parameter of qid=EL_1. The Questions.jsp page can access the value of that parameter with the EL expression:

```
${param.qid}
```

What we want to do is to use this value to include the answer to the selected question in the response to the user. In this case, the answer is found in a page called EL_1.jsp in the WEB-INF directory, so the page directive for our <jsp:include> action is set to "/WEB-INF/${param.qid}.jsp".

This answer page also uses EL expressions. One interesting thing to note is that the specification provides a way to have a literal ${expr} in the output of a page. This is done by placing the quoted expression '${' in an EL expression. The EL expression ${'${'} evaluates to ${ in the page, and the rest of the string is output without evaluation. For example, the line:

```
<p>${'${'}param.qid} evaluates to "${param.qid}"</p>
```

will generate the HTML:

```
<p>${param.qid} evaluates to "EL_1"</p>
```

The remainder of the page uses various EL expressions to show how to use some of the implicit objects available in an EL expression.

Custom Actions and Tag Libraries

Several times in the previous chapter, we talked about removing Java code from the JSP to further separate the display elements from the business logic. In reality, the Java code is not removed from the page, but it is hidden from the page developer. For example, in the previous chapter, we saw some standard actions defined by the JSP specification. Standard actions are actions that must be implemented by every JSP container. A standard action appears in a JSP page as an XML-style tag. Here is the tag for a useBean standard action with an enclosed setProperty action:

```
<jsp:useBean id="questions" class="Ch04.Questions">
  <jsp:setProperty name="questions" property="topic"/>
</jsp:useBean>
```

At the start of the tag is the namespace prefix, jsp (a namespace is analogous to a Java package). This is followed by the action name. The standard action can have attributes, and some actions have bodies between the start and end tag. Tag bodies can include other tags (as shown above) and/or template data. To anyone familiar with XML, this looks like a standard XML tag (but even though the tag looks like an XML tag, it is used in a JSP file, which does not have to be an XML document).

However, the JSP translator "sees" the tag a little differently. The translator sees the tag as a token that is to be replaced by Java code. This Java code implements the functionality specified by the tag. Thus, the Java code is not removed from the page, but it is "encapsulated" within the tag. For example, when the JSP translator for Tomcat 5.0 sees the tag above, it generates the code below:

```
questions = (Ch04.Questions)java.beans.Beans.instantiate(
                this.getClass().getClassLoader(), "ch04.Questions");
```

Now, if the only actions you had available were the standard actions, you would still need to use Java code embedded in your JSP. Fortunately, the JSP specification provides a way for developers to create their own actions. These actions are known as **custom actions**. Custom actions are deployed to the web application using a **tag library**. The mechanism for defining, implementing, deploying, and executing custom actions is known as **tag extension**. Using standard and custom actions, a web designer can build a dynamic web page without needing to know how to program in Java.

Custom Actions

When we use the term **custom action** (or standard action), we are generally referring to the tag in the JSP file. Custom actions, like standard actions, can be used just like any other tag in a JSP file. Custom actions are identified by a prefix and a name:

```
<prefix:name />
```

The prefix is used to avoid name collisions between tags with the same name. The *prefix* is selected and used by the page developer, although the tag developer can suggest a prefix, as we will see later. The *name* is the name of the action. This is specified by the tag developer.

Custom actions can be empty (they have no body):

```
<x:MyCustomAction />  <%-- Start and end tags combined into single tag --%>
<x:MyCustomAction></x:MyCustomAction>   <%-- Separate tags --%>
```

Or they can have bodies:

```
<x:MyCustomAction>
   Body content
</x:MyCustomAction>
```

The Java code that implements the tag can direct the page to evaluate the body or skip the body. Actions can be nested. Here is an example using the `<jsp:useBean>` and `<jsp:setProperty>` standard actions:

```
<jsp:useBean id="user" class="Ch03.User">
   <jsp:setProperty name="user" property="*"/>
</jsp:useBean>
```

Also, as shown with the `<jsp:useBean>` and `<jsp:setProperty>` actions, an action can have attributes that customize the action. Actions can access the implicit objects of JSPs (request, response, and so on), and use these objects to modify the response to the client. Objects can be created by a custom action, and these objects can be accessed by other actions or scriptlets in the JSP.

The actual behavior of a custom action is provided at run-time by an instance of a Java class. This Java class is also known as a **tag handler**.

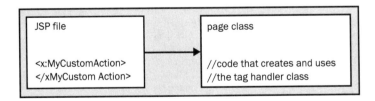

Tag Handlers

The tag handler is the Java class that implements the behavior of a custom action. The tag handler class follows the requirements of a JavaBean, and it will implement one of the tag extension interfaces. There are several tag handler interfaces available.

JSP 1.1 had two interfaces, `Tag` and `BodyTag`, for tag handlers. `Tag` handles a simple action with no iteration and no need to process the body of the tag; `BodyTag` is used when the body of the tag is processed (rather than simply output) as part of the action. JSP 1.2 introduced the `IterationTag` to deal with iteration (JSP 1.1 used `BodyTag` to handle iteration). These three interfaces—`Tag`, `IterationTag`, and `BodyTag`—are known as **classic tag handlers**. JSP 2.0 adds the `SimpleTag` interface to make tag handling easier, and the `JspFragment` interface to encapsulate the body content of a tag in an object. `SimpleTag` and `JspFragment` are known as **simple tag handlers**.

JSP Specification	Reference Implementation	JSP Interfaces
JSP 1.1	Tomcat 3, J2SDKEE 1.2	`Tag`, `BodyTag`
JSP 1.2	Tomcat 4, J2SDKEE 1.3	`IterationTag`
JSP 2.0	Tomcat 5, J2SDKEE 1.4	`SimpleTag`, `JspFragment`

Simple tag handlers are called simple, because they simplify the process of developing a tag handler. They are no less capable than classic tag handlers in dealing with iteration and processing of body content. You are more likely to be using simple tag handlers than the more complicated classic tag handlers in your development, so we will look at those first.

Simple Tag Handlers

The tag extension mechanism of JSP 1.2 was powerful, but it was also relatively complicated to use, as we will see later. JSP 2.0 introduces the `SimpleTag` interface and a base class, `SimpleTagSupport` that implements this interface:

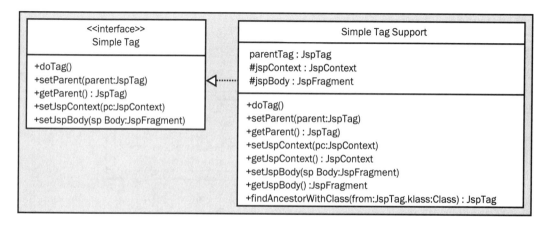

We can use this interface and base class to implement any tag handlers in JSP 2.0, regardless of whether the tag needs to be processed multiple times, or whether it has a body that needs to be processed. To create a custom action, you would create a tag handler class that extends the `SimpleTagSupport` base class, overriding the methods as necessary to provide the behavior for a custom action. Usually, all you will need to do is override the `doTag()` method. This method provides all the behavior of the custom action, including tag logic, iterations, and body evaluation. As we will see later, classic tag handlers used three methods to do everything that is done within the single `doTag()` method of `SimpleTag`.

When the tag appears in a JSP file, the translator creates code that:

❑   Creates an instance of the tag handler

❑   Calls `setJspContext()` and `setParent()`

❑   Initializes the tag handler attributes

❑   Creates a `JspFragment` object and calls `setJspBody()`

For the page implementation code to be able to create the tag handler instance and initialize its properties, all tag handlers follow the JavaBean conventions. You may recall that for our purposes, this means two things:

❑   The tag handler class must have a no-argument constructor.

❑   Properties of the class that can be used by clients must be exposed through public `setXXX` methods to set the value; and must have `getXXX` or `isXXX` methods to retrieve the value.

This provides a standard way for JSP containers to create instances of tag handlers and set the properties of tag handlers from attributes of the custom action element in the JSP. Each attribute in the custom action tag must correspond to a property of the tag handler that can be set using some `setXXX()` method.

After the tag handler class is created and initialized, the page class calls `doTag()`. This method is called only once for the tag; if the body content needs to be evaluated, it does that through the `JspFragment` object that was passed to the class through `setJspBody()`.

JspFragment

Like `SimpleTag`, `JspFragment` is also an interface, but the implementation of the interface is left entirely to the JSP container to implement. As a developer, you only need to know how to call a fragment to evaluate its contents. If your `SimpleTag` tag handler needs to evaluate the body of the tag, it calls the `invoke()` method of `JspFragment`:

```
public void invoke(java.io.Writer out)
```

As you can see, invoke() takes a single argument. If the Writer argument is null, the fragment will write its output to the current output stream of the client response; otherwise, the fragment will write its output to the given Writer. JspFragments can contain template text, JSP action elements, and EL expressions, but they cannot contain JSP scriptlets or scriptlet expressions. Variables used in EL expressions are set through context attributes, which you will see in the next example.

Tag Library Descriptor

After creating one or more classes that implement a tag, you need to inform the container which tag handlers are available to the JSP pages in an application. This is done through a descriptor file called a **Tag Library Descriptor** (TLD). The TLD is an XML-compliant document that contains information about the tag handler classes in a tag library.

A TLD for JSP 2.0 will provide information about the tag library using a <taglib> element as shown here:

```
<?xml version="1.0" encoding="UTF-8" ?>

<taglib xmlns="http://java.sun.com/xml/ns/j2ee"
        xmlns:xsi="http://www.w3.org/2001/XMLSchema-instance"
        xsi:schemaLocation="http://java.sun.com/xml/ns/j2ee/web-

jsptaglibrary_2_0.xsd"
        version="2.0">

  <tlib-version>1.0</tlib-version>
  <short-name>simplefaq</short-name>

  <tag>
    <name>simplelist</name>
    <tag-class>Ch04.SimpleList</tag-class>
    <body-content>scriptless</body-content>
    <attribute>
      <name>topic</name>
      <required>yes</required>
      <rtexprvalue>true</rtexprvalue>
    </attribute>
  </tag>
</taglib>
```

The <taglib> element can have a number of sub-elements. The mandatory elements are:

Element	Meaning
tlib-version	The version number of the library.
short-name	A simple default name. It may be used as the preferred prefix value in taglib directives.
tag	Information about a tag handler.

The <tag> element has several sub-elements. The mandatory sub-elements are:

Element	Meaning
name	The name of the tag handler.
tag-class	The fully qualified class name of the tag handler class.

In addition, you will often need to use these optional sub-elements of the <tag> element:

Element	Meaning
body-content	Whether the body of the tag can have content. Valid values are tagdependent, scriptless, or empty. The default is scriptless. If the value is empty, the tag is not allowed to have a body.
variable	Defines the scripting variables created by this tag handler and made available to the rest of the page. This element must contain one of two sub-elements: name-given or name-from-attribute. If name-given is used, the value of this element defines the name that other JSP elements can use to access the created scripting variable. If name-from-attribute is used, the value of the attribute with the name given by this element defines the name of the scripting variable.
attribute	Defines attributes for the tag. This element has three sub-elements: name, required, and rtexprvalue.

The value of the name element will be the name of the attribute.

The element named required is optional, and must be one of true, false, yes, or no. The default value is false.

The rtexprvalue element is optional, and must be one of true, false, yes, or no. The default value is false, which means that the attribute can only be set using a static value known at compile time. If the element contains true or yes, the attribute can be set using a runtime expression. |

This may be a bit daunting, especially near the end of that last table, so let's look at an example.

```xml
<?xml version="1.0" encoding="UTF-8" ?>

<taglib xmlns="http://java.sun.com/xml/ns/j2ee"
        xmlns:xsi="http://www.w3.org/2001/XMLSchema-instance"
        xsi:schemaLocation="http://java.sun.com/xml/ns/j2ee/web-

jsptaglibrary_2_0.xsd"
        version="2.0">
  <tlib-version>1.0</tlib-version>
  <short-name>apress</short-name>

  <tag>
    <name>example</name>
    <tag-class>Ch04.Example</tag-class>
    <body-content>empty</body-content>
    <variable>
       <name-given>script1</name-given>
    </variable>
    <variable>
       <name-from-attribute>attr1</name-from-attribute>
    </variable>
    <attribute>
       <name>attr1</name>
       <required>yes</required>
       <rtexprvalue>true</rtexprvalue>
    </attribute>
    <attribute>
       <name>attr2</name>
       <required>no</required>
       <rtexprvalue>false</rtexprevalue>
    </attribute>
  </tag>
</taglib>
```

The TLD above is for a tag library that the developer has identified as version 1.0. It relies on JSP 2.0. The suggested prefix for tags from the library is apress. However, note that page developers can use whatever prefix they desire. This is so that name conflicts between libraries with the same suggested prefix can be avoided.

The TLD defines one tag with the name "example". The tag handler class for the tag is Ch04.Example. The tag must have an empty body, because the value of the <body-content> element is empty.

The tag creates two objects that are made available to the rest of the page as scripting variables. The JSP accesses the first object using the name script1 (from the <name-given> element). The second object is accessed by the name given in the attr1 attribute of the tag.

The tag takes two attributes. The attribute attr1 is required, and can be set by a run-time expression. The attribute attr2 is optional, and cannot be set at run-time from an expression.

Packaging Tag Libraries

After creating the tag handler classes and the TLD, there are a few final steps that need to be accomplished to use the tags in a JSP.

Application Structure

Although some parts of the structure of a web application are not specified, locations for tag libraries and TLDs are specified.

```
context-root
  META-INF/
    jar_that_contains_TLD.jar
  WEB-INF/
    lib/
      taglib.jar
    tlds/
      descriptor.tld
    classes/
      path/to/tag/handler.class
```

Tag handler classes must be placed in the /classes subdirectory of WEB-INF or in a .jar file in the /lib subdirectory of WEB-INF. TLD files must be placed under WEB-INF, although the actual location under WEB-INF is unspecified. In the example above, a TLD is located in the /tlds directory of WEB-INF. If a TLD is in a .jar file, it must be in the META-INF directory of the application.

Deployment Descriptor

Within the web.xml deployment descriptor, you can create a mapping from a URI to a TLD location. This is done through the <taglib> element. For example, this element:

```
<taglib>
  <taglib-uri>/examples</taglib-uri>
  <taglib-location>/WEB-INF/tlds/descriptor.tld</taglib-location>
</taglib>
```

maps the URI /examples to the TLD descriptor.tld. This mapping can then be used in the JSP files, as we will see next.

> **The order of elements in the deployment descriptor must follow the order specified by the DTD. See Chapter 5 for the correct order.**

Importing a Taglib into a Page

To use a custom action, you need to "import" the tag library into the JSP. This is done with the `taglib` directive. The `taglib` directive has this form:

```
<%@ taglib uri="URI_of_library" prefix="tag_prefix"%>
```

This element must appear in the JSP file prior to any custom action that uses a tag from the tag library.

The `uri` attribute is either an absolute or relative path to the TLD file. Alternately, if the `web.xml` deployment descriptor has a `<taglib>` element, you can refer to the TLD using the value of the `<taglib-uri>` element from like this:

```
<%@ taglib uri="/examples" prefix="ex"%>
```

Combined with the `<taglib>` element of the previous section, this directive would "import" the tag library defined by `descriptor.tld`. Within the particular JSP file that used this `taglib` directive, the custom actions would be referenced using the prefix given. For example, the TLD above defined a tag handler named `example`. With the taglib directive above, the action would be referenced in a JSP as:

```
<ex:example />
<%-- or as --%>
<ex:example></ex:example>
```

Try It Out   Defining a Simple Tag Handler

In this example, we'll develop a tag handler using the simple tag handler interfaces of JSP 2.0. This tag handler will perform iteration and process the body content of the tag. When this example is complete, you will see that custom actions and simple tag handlers can make your JSP files extremely easy to develop. This example has the following structure:

```
Ch04/
  TopicList2.jsp
  Questions.jsp
  WEB-INF/
    web.xml
    EL_1.jsp
    tlds/
      simplefaq.tld
    classes/
      Ch04/
        SimpleList.java
        Questions.java
```

1. Start with a new tag handler class that extends `SimpleTagSupport`. This file is called `SimpleList.java`, and is located in the /WEB-INF/classes/Ch04 directory. Since this class uses the JSP API, when you compile the class, your `classpath` will need to include the correct libraries. If you are using J2EE, your `classpath` must include `J2EE.jar`. If you are using Tomcat 5.0, your `classpath` must include `jsp-api.jar`. If you are using some other JSP container, check your documentation for the correct `.jar` file to include on the `classpath`.

```java
package Ch04;

import java.util.*;
import javax.servlet.jsp.tagext.*;
import javax.servlet.jsp.*;
import java.io.*;

public class SimpleList extends SimpleTagSupport {
   private String topic;
   public void setTopic(String s) { topic = s; }
   public String getTopic() { return topic; }

   public void doTag() throws JspException {
      Questions questions = new Questions();
      questions.setTopic(getTopic());

      // Get list of questions, TreeMap will sort them by key
      Map qmap = new TreeMap(questions.getQuestions());
      Iterator faqs = qmap.values().iterator();
      int count = 1;

      while (faqs.hasNext()) {
        try {
          // Store the parameters for invoke()
          getJspContext().setAttribute("qid", topic + "_" + count);
          getJspContext().setAttribute("question", faqs.next());
          count++;
          // Process the body
          getJspBody().invoke(null);
        } catch (IOException e) {
          throw new JspException("Exception processing body");
        }
      }
   }
}
```

2. Now we need to create a TLD for this tag handler. This is `simplefaq.tld`, and in this example, it will be saved to the /WEB-INF/tlds directory.

```xml
<?xml version="1.0" encoding="UTF-8" ?>

<taglib xmlns="http://java.sun.com/xml/ns/j2ee"
        xmlns:xsi="http://www.w3.org/2001/XMLSchema-instance"
        xsi:schemaLocation="http://java.sun.com/xml/ns/j2ee/web-

jsptaglibrary_2_0.xsd"
        version="2.0">
```

```
      <tlib-version>1.0</tlib-version>
      <short-name>simplefaq</short-name>

      <tag>
        <name>simplelist</name>
        <tag-class>Ch04.SimpleList</tag-class>
        <body-content>scriptless</body-content>
        <attribute>
          <name>topic</name>
          <required>yes</required>
          <rtexprvalue>true</rtexprvalue>
        </attribute>
      </tag>
  </taglib>
```

3. If you are using Tomcat, you'll need to edit web.xml as shown here:

```
<?xml version="1.0" encoding="ISO-8859-1"?>

<web-app xmlns="http://java.sun.com/xml/ns/j2ee"
    xmlns:xsi="http://www.w3.org/2001/XMLSchema-instance"
    xsi:schemaLocation="http://java.sun.com/xml/ns/j2ee/web-app_2_4.xsd"
    version="2.4">

  <!-- this is the deployment descriptor for Chapter 4 -->

  <welcome-file-list>
    <welcome-file>TopicList2.jsp</welcome-file>
  </welcome-file-list>
  <jsp-config>
    <!-- This element is for the simple tag handler example -->
    <taglib>
      <taglib-uri>/simplequestions</taglib-uri>
      <taglib-location>/WEB-INF/tlds/simplefaq.tld</taglib-location>
    </taglib>

    <jsp-property-group>
      <url-pattern>*.jsp</url-pattern>
      <el-enabled>true</el-enabled>
      <scripting-enabled>false</scripting-enabled>
    </jsp-property-group>
  </jsp-config>

</web-app>
```

If you are using the J2EE Deployment Tool, the mapping shown above between the URI /simplequestions and the TLD simplefaq.tld is set in the JSP Tag Libraries section of the File Refs tab for the Web Application.

4. Finally, we'll create a new version of `TopicList.jsp` that uses this new tag. This is `TopicList2.jsp`:

```
<!DOCTYPE HTML PUBLIC "-//W3C//DTD HTML 4.01 Transitional//EN">
<%@ taglib uri="/simplequestions" prefix="faq"%>
<html>
  <head><title>Topic Questions 2</title></head>
  <body>
    <h1>Topic Questions 2</h1>

    <faq:simplelist topic="${param.topic}">
      <p>Question <a href="Questions.jsp?qid=${qid}">${qid}</a>
         ${question}</p>
    </faq:simplelist>
    <p>Click a link to get the answer.</p>
  </body>
</html>
```

5. Deploy these new files and access `TopicList2.jsp` from a browser. Don't be shocked when you see that it looks the same as the first example of this chapter. (Or it should, assuming everything is correct.)

> If you encounter problems running this example after updating the previous example using the Deployment Tool, try creating a new application from scratch.

How It Works

As stated earlier, all the processing for a SimpleTag happens in the doTag() method. The doTag() method starts by instantiating our Questions bean, and setting its topic property to the value of the topic property of our tag handler:

```
Questions questions = new Questions();
questions.setTopic(getTopic());
```

As we'll see shortly, this value is set through an attribute in our <jsp:simplelist> tag.

Next, we set up the Iterator that will be used to step through the questions. We do this by calling the getQuestions() method and passing the returned set of questions to a TreeMap constructor. A TreeMap sorts a collection based on the name in the name-value pairs stored in the map. If you look at the Questions class, you will see that the names are the strings "1", "2", and "3". After the TreeMap is constructed, the iterator() method is called to get an Iterator:

```
Map qmap = new TreeMap(questions.getQuestions());
faqs = qmap.values().iterator();
```

The class then iterates over each question in the collection. For each question, two pieces of data used by the body of the tag are saved as attributes in the JspContext. First, the question itself is saved as an attribute value using the name "question" as the attribute name. The ID value is then stored with the name "qid", and is constructed by appending the topic "EL", an underscore, and a digit based on a counter:

```
getJspContext().setAttribute("question", faqs.next());
getJspContext().setAttribute("qid", topic + "_" + count);
```

After the parameters for a single question are saved in the JspContext, the doTag() method gets a reference to the JspFragment for the tag and calls its invoke() method:

```
getJspBody().invoke(null);
```

Since null is passed as the argument, the body content is passed to the client's output response stream. That is, it is sent directly to the client.

Now let's look at the tag as it is used in TopicList2.jsp. This page uses the taglib directive to specify the TLD. The URI /simplequestions is mapped by the deployment descriptor to simplefaq.tld. The prefix used for the tag is faq. Notice that this is not the short-name used in the TLD. As has been mentioned several times, the page developer chooses the prefix. The name of the tag is the name given in the TLD, and the tag has a single attribute, called topic. This attribute was specified in the TLD as a required attribute that could be set using an expression. In our TopicList2.jsp page, the value of the attribute is indeed set with an expression, ${param.topic}. This is the attribute that is used to set the topic property of our tag handler:

```
<faq:simplelist topic="${param.topic}">
  <p>Question <a href="Questions.jsp?qid=${qid}">${qid}</a>
      ${question}</p>
</faq:simplelist>
```

The tag has a body, which is allowed by the TLD. The body content is represented by the JspFragment instance in the doTag() method. When the invoke() method is called, the body is evaluated and sent as part of the response to the client. You can see that the body of the tag includes two EL expressions. The value of these expressions comes directly from the parameters that the doTag() method added to the JspContext. The doTag() method placed data into the JspContext using the names question and qid; when the EL expressions are evaluated, their value is obtained by getting the value of the attribute with the same name as the expression body.

Classic Tag Handler Design

Prior to JSP 2.0, three interfaces and two implementing classes provided the basic design for tag handlers. As you will see here, using classic tag handlers is somewhat more involved than using simple tag handlers. For that reason, you will probably always use simple tag handlers. However, you may be working a project that still uses a server that only supports JSP 1.2, or you may need to work with tag handlers that were written under JSP 1.2 or the greater flexibility provided by classic tag handlers. For that reason, we will look at how to use classic tag handlers.

The javax.servlet.jsp.tagext.Tag interface is the primary interface for classic tag handlers. It provides an interface for simple tag handler classes that do not need to manipulate their body content. IterationTag extends Tag to provide an interface for tag handlers that need to perform some iteration or looping. Finally, BodyTag extends IterationTag for tag handlers that manipulate their body content. These interfaces are shown in the class diagram below:

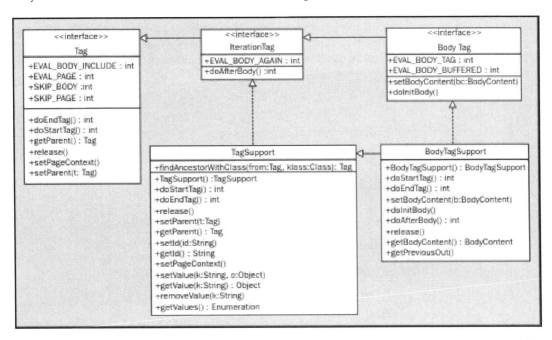

The tag extension API includes two classes that implement the interfaces above. **TagSupport** implements **IterationTag**; BodyTagSupport implements BodyTag.

Tag

Tag is the interface to implement when the tag handler does not need to process multiple times and does not need to manipulate its body. As an alternative to implementing the **Tag** interface, your tag handler can extend TagSupport (since TagSupport implements IterationTag, which extends Tag). In fact, this is the usual way you will implement a tag handler for a simple tag. When you extend TagSupport, you will only need to override doStartTag() or doEndTag(). So a simple tag handler class that has no properties will look like this:

```
public class MySimpleTag extends TagSupport {
   public int doStartTag() { // method body }
   public int doEndTag() { // method body }
}
```

The doStartTag() method is called by the page class at the point where the start tag appears in the JSP file. When you implement a tag handler, you implement the doStartTag() method with code that you want to have executed before the body of the tag is processed. When your code is finished, it returns one of two values defined by the Tag interface. If it returns Tag.SKIP_BODY, the body of the tag, which can include template (HTML) data, JSP elements, or other tag extensions, is not evaluated. Earlier, we saw that a descriptor file contains information about the tag extensions. If the <body-content> element of the descriptor has the value empty, this indicates that a tag *must* be empty, and SKIP_BODY is the only allowed return value. If your doStartTag() method returns Tag.EVAL_BODY_INCLUDE, the body of the tag is evaluated.

The doEndTag() method is called by the page class at the point where the end tag appears in the JSP file. When you implement a tag handler, you implement the doEndTag() method with code that you want to have executed after the body of the tag is processed. After your doEndTag() completes, it returns Tag.SKIP_PAGE or Tag.EVAL_PAGE. The value SKIP_PAGE indicates that the remainder of the JSP should not be evaluated; EVAL_PAGE indicates the opposite.

This execution flow is illustrated below:

Note that when extending TagSupport, you can, but do not need to, implement both doStartTag() and doEndTag(). If the tag handler does not need to perform any action prior to the body, and the tag must have an empty body, you do not need to implement doStartTag(). However, because the TagSupport implementation of doStartTag() returns SKIP_BODY, if the tag can have a body you should implement a minimal doStartTag() that returns EVAL_BODY_INCLUDE. If the tag handler does not need to perform any action after the body, you do not need to implement doEndTag(). The TagSupport implementation of doEndTag() returns EVAL_PAGE.

IterationTag

When you need a tag handler class to iterate or loop its actions, your tag class will implement IterationTag. Of course, as with Tag, you will usually just extend TagSupport. IterationTag adds one method and one property, which are used to provide the looping behavior. Here is a simple tag handler class without any properties:

```
public class ListQuestions extends TagSupport {
    public int doStartTag() throws JspTagException { // method body }
    public int doAfterBody() throws JspTagException { // method body }
    public int doEndTag() throws JspTagException { // method body }
}
```

This time, the example includes the new method: doAfterBody().

After calling doStartTag() and after evaluating the body of the tag, the page class calls the doAfterBody() method. The doAfterBody() method allows the tag handler class to determine whether the page class should evaluate the body another time. If so, doAfterBody() should return a value of IterationTag.EVAL_BODY_AGAIN, which indicates that the page class should evaluate the body of the tag again; if not, it returns Tag.SKIP_BODY. The page class then calls doEndTag() and proceeds as with a Tag.

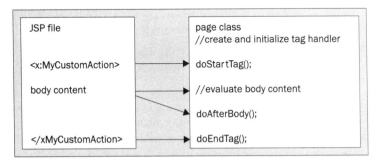

BodyTag

With `Tag` and `IterationTag`, the implementing class can indicate whether the body of the tag should be evaluated by the page class. However, the tag handler classes that implement `Tag` or `IterationTag` have no way of actually manipulating the contents of the tag body. This is possible through the `BodyTag` interface and its implementing class, `BodyTagSupport`:

```
public class ListQuestionsInBody extends BodyTagSupport {
    public int doStartTag() throws JspTagException { // method body }
    public void setBodyContent(BodyContent bc) { // method body }
    public void doInitBody() { // method body }
    public int doAfterBody() throws JspTagException { // method body }
    public int doEndTag() throws JspTagException { // method body }
}
```

For the most part, the `doStartTag()` method is the same as for `Tag` or `IterationTag`. The difference is that the `BodyTag` interface defines an additional return value for the method. That return value is `BodyTag.EVAL_BODY_BUFFERED`. When your code returns `EVAL_BODY_BUFFERED`, the page class calls the `setBodyContent()` and `doInitBody()` methods. This makes the body content available to your code in the `doAfterBody()` and `doEndTag()` methods. When the return value of `doStartTag()` is `EVAL_BODY_BUFFERED`, the page class evaluates the tag body and stores the result in an instance of `BodyContent`. (Thus, an instance of `BodyContent` will not contain actions, scriptlets, and so on—only the results of those elements.) The page class then needs to pass the `BodyContent` instance to the tag handler so that it can manipulate the body content. It does this by calling `setBodyContent()`; the page class then calls `doInitBody()`. Inside the `doInitBody()` method, the tag handler class can perform any initialization that depends on the body of the tag:

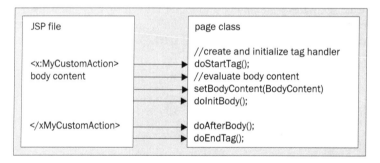

Normally, you will manipulate the body content in the `doAfterBody()` method. However, the `BodyContent` object is also available to the `doEndTag()` method, so you can use the `BodyContent` object there. The `BodyContent` class defines various methods for getting the body content, and writing the body content to an output stream. For example, this code snippet shows how to write the body content to the response:

```
public void doAfterBody() {
    // bodyContent is an instance variable of BodyTagSupport
    // Call the getEncloseingWriter() method to get the enclosing JspWriter
    Writer writer = bodyContent.getEnclosingWriter();
    // Call the writeOut(Writer) method to send the body content
    // to the writer
    bodyContent.writeOut(writer);

    if (need_to_eval_body_again) {
        return EVAL_BODY_AGAIN;
    } else {
        return SKIP_BODY;
    }
}
```

The page class will evaluate the body again if the doAfterBody() method returns EVAL_BODY_AGAIN; otherwise, if doAfterBody() returns SKIP_BODY, then the page class calls doEndTag().

Try It Out Defining a Classic Tag Handler

In this example, we'll create a custom action using classic tag handlers to list the FAQ questions in the TopicList.jsp page. As with the simple tag handler example previously, by putting the iteration into the custom action, all the Java code will be eliminated from the JSP page and encapsulated in the tag handler. This will make the page simpler than the version introduced in the first example of the chapter. Encapsulating the Java code in beans and tag handlers also makes the page easier for page developers to develop and maintain. Here's the application structure:

```
Ch04/
    Questions.jsp
    TopicList3.jsp
    WEB-INF/
        EL_1.jsp
        web.xml
        tlds/
            faq.tld
        classes/
            Ch04/
                Questions.java
                Questions.class
                ListQuestions.java
                ListQuestions.class
```

Most of the files above are the same as in the previous example. The new files are TopicList3.jsp, faq.tld, and ListQuestions.java.

1. Here's the tag handler, ListQuestions.java. The tag handler will need to iterate over a collection of questions, so it extends TagSupport. Since this class uses the JSP API, when you compile the class, your classpath will need to include the correct libraries. If you are using J2EE, your classpath must include J2EE.jar. If you are using Tomcat 5.0, your classpath must include jsp-api.jar. If you are using some other JSP container, check your documentation for the correct .jar file to include on the classpath.

131

Also, you will need to ensure that Questions.class either exists or is compiled at the same time. You can do that by using javac *.java (assuming the classpath is set):

```java
package Ch04;

import java.util.*;
import javax.servlet.jsp.tagext.*;
import javax.servlet.jsp.*;
import java.io.*;

public class ListQuestions extends TagSupport {
   private String topic;
   private Iterator faqs;
   private int count;
   public void setTopic(String s) { topic = s; }
   public String getTopic() { return topic; }

   public int doStartTag() throws JspTagException {
      Questions questions = new Questions();
      questions.setTopic(getTopic());
      Map qmap = new TreeMap(questions.getQuestions());

      // Get an Iterator for the questions
      // The Iterator is an instance variable because we will access
      // it in the doAfterBody()method
      faqs = qmap.values().iterator();
      count = 0;
      try {
         // Write some preliminary data to the response
         pageContext.getOut().write("<h2>Questions for Topic</h2>");
         pageContext.getOut().write("\nThe number of questions in topic " +
                              getTopic() + " is " + qmap.size());

      } catch (IOException e) {
         throw new JspTagException("Error writing to out");
      }
      return EVAL_BODY_INCLUDE;
   }

   public int doAfterBody() throws JspTagException {
      // Create the link for a single question
      // Each time this method is called by the page class,
      // the Iterator advances to the next question
      if (faqs.hasNext()) {
         String question = (String) faqs.next();
         String s = "<p>Question <a href=\"Questions.jsp?qid=" + getTopic() +
            "_" + ++count + "\">" + getTopic() + "_" + count + "</a>: " +
            question + "</p>";
         try {
            pageContext.getOut().write(s);
         } catch (IOException e) {
            throw new JspTagException("Error writing to out");
         }
         // Tell the page class to evaluate the body again
         return EVAL_BODY_AGAIN;
      } else {
```

```
            // faqs.next() was false, so no more questions
            return SKIP_BODY;
    }
}

    public int doEndTag() throws JspTagException {
        try {
            pageContext.getOut().write("<p>Click a link to see the answer</p>");
        } catch (IOException e) {
            throw new JspTagException("Error writing to out");
        }
        return EVAL_PAGE;
    }
}
```

2. The tag library descriptor (`faq.tld`) for this tag is next:

```
<?xml version="1.0" encoding="UTF-8" ?>

<taglib xmlns="http://java.sun.com/xml/ns/j2ee"
        xmlns:xsi="http://www.w3.org/2001/XMLSchema-instance"
        xsi:schemaLocation="http://java.sun.com/xml/ns/j2ee/web-

jsptaglibrary_2_0.xsd"
        version="2.0">

    <tlib-version>1.0</tlib-version>
    <tag>
      <name>listFaqs</name>
      <tag-class>Ch04.ListQuestions</tag-class>
      <body-content>scriptless</body-content>
      <attribute>
         <name>topic</name>
         <required>yes</required>
         <rtexprvalue>true</rtexprvalue>
      </attribute>
    </tag>
</taglib>
```

3. If you are deploying to Tomcat, you will need to add a `<taglib>` element to the deployment descriptor. Here is the modification to `web.xml`:

```
<?xml version="1.0" encoding="ISO-8859-1"?>

<web-app xmlns="http://java.sun.com/xml/ns/j2ee"
    xmlns:xsi="http://www.w3.org/2001/XMLSchema-instance"
    xsi:schemaLocation="http://java.sun.com/xml/ns/j2ee/web-app_2_4.xsd"
    version="2.4">

    <!-- this is the deployment descriptor for Chapter 4 -->

    <welcome-file-list>
      <welcome-file>TopicList3.jsp</welcome-file>
    </welcome-file-list>
```

```
<!-- this element is for the custom action example -->
<taglib>
    <taglib-uri>/questions</taglib-uri>
    <taglib-location>/WEB-INF/tlds/faq.tld</taglib-location>
</taglib>
</web-app>
```

4. If you are deploying to J2EE using the Deployment Tool, you will need to set the `<taglib>` element of the deployment descriptor through the J2EE Deployment Tool. This is done in the File Refs tab of the right pane when the web application is selected in the left pane:

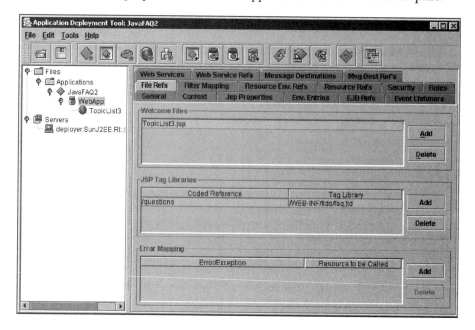

The section where you need to add the taglib mapping is in the JSP Tag Libraries section as seen above. Enter /questions for the Coded Reference and /WEB-INF/tlds/faq.tld for the Tag Library.

5. Finally, here is the JSP page. Save this as `TopicList3.jsp`:

```
<!DOCTYPE HTML PUBLIC "-//W3C//DTD HTML 4.01 Transitional//EN">
<%@ taglib uri="/questions" prefix="faq"%>
<html>
    <head><title>Topic Questions</title></head>
    <body>
        <h1>Topic Questions</h1>

        <faq:listFaqs topic="${param.topic}">
        </faq:listFaqs>


    </body>
</html>
```

6. Deploy the application to your server. Open a browser window and enter the address http://localhost:1024/Ch04/TopicList3.jsp?topic=EL (use port 8080 for Tomcat). If everything is correct, you will see the same display as in the previous two examples of this chapter.

How It Works

The tag handler class, `ListQuestions`, extends the `TagSupport` class. Since that class implements `IterationTag`, the tag handler can perform iterations, but it can't manipulate the body of the tag. Thus, the tag handler class needs to perform all the output to the response itself. `ListQuestions` provides implementations for the `doStartTag()`, `doAfterBody()`, and `doEndTag()` methods.

The `doStartTag()` creates an instance of the `Questions` class, and gets the `Map` consisting of the list of questions. This `Map` is used to create a `TreeMap` instance. We use `TreeMap` because that provides a sorted collection. Since the keys used in `Questions` are strings representing numbers, this means the `TreeMap` will sort the data with "1" first, followed by "2", and so on. Finally, it sets up an iterator for the values (the questions), and prints out some preliminary text. Notice that to do this, it gets an output stream from the `pageContext` object:

```
Map qmap = new TreeMap(questions.getQuestions());
faqs = qmap.values().iterator();
count = 0;
try {
    // Write some preliminary data to the response
    pageContext.getOut().write("<h2>Questions for Topic</h2>");
    pageContext.getOut().write("\nThe number of questions in topic " +
                                getTopic() + " is " + qmap.size());
```

The `doAfterBody()` method actually uses the `Iterator` to create the links and text of each question. As it iterates through each question, it returns a value of `EVAL_BODY_AGAIN`. This signals that the page class should call `doAfterBody()` again. When it has iterated through all the values, `doAfterBody()` returns `SKIP_BODY`:

```
if (faqs.hasNext()) {
    String question = (String) faqs.next();
    String s = "<p>Question <a href=\"Questions.jsp?qid=" + getTopic() +
        "_" + ++count + "\">" + getTopic() + "_" + count + "</a>: " +
        question + "</p>";
    try {
        pageContext.getOut().write(s);
    } catch (IOException e) {
        throw new JspTagException("Error writing to out");
    }
    // Tell the page class to evaluate the body again
    return EVAL_BODY_AGAIN;
} else {
    // faqs.next() was false, so no more questions
    return SKIP_BODY;
}
```

The TLD tells the application about the tag handler class. This TLD only has one <tag> element in it. This <tag> element provides the name of the custom action, listFaq, and the name of the class that implements the action. As in the previous example, the action has one attribute named topic, which is required and which can be set through an expression:

```
<tag>
  <name>listFaqs</name>
  <tag-class>Ch04.ListQuestions</tag-class>
  <body-content>scriptless</body-content>
  <attribute>
    <name>topic</name>
    <required>yes</required>
    <rtexprvalue>true</rtexprvalue>
  </attribute>
</tag>
```

We.also added a <taglib> element to the deployment descriptor. This <taglib> element specified that a URI of /questions referred to the TLD at /WEB-INF/tlds/faq.tld.

And now we get to the JSP page. Because all of the work is now done by the tag handler, the JSP has become incredibly simple. Notice that there is no Java scriptlet in the page at all. At the top of the page, the tag library is "imported" using the taglib directive. The taglib directive specifies that the TLD is at the URI /questions. Because of the mapping in the web.xml file, this resolves to the file faq.tld.

```
<%@ taglib uri="/questions" prefix="faq" %>
```

The taglib directive specifies that the prefix for custom actions from that library would be faq. In this case, the prefix is the same as the short name, but remember that the page developer can set the prefix to any value regardless of the short name of the library. The single custom action that causes the tag handler to be called is:

```
<faq:listFaqs topic="${param.topic}">
</faq:listFaqs>
```

We have the prefix, faq, followed by the tag name, and the topic attribute. Notice that we set this attribute using an EL expression. This is allowed because the TLD specified that the attribute could be set by a run-time expression.

So, the JSP has become much simpler, and that's good, but at what cost? The ListQuestions class now has HTML tags and data in it. This could become a maintenance problem. Recall that one of the reasons for JSP pages was to remove template data from code. Although it's nice that TopicList3.jsp is so simple, it would be better to put presentation data back into the JSP, and leave the tag handler to do non-presentation tasks. One way to do that is through the BodyTag interface.

Try It Out Classic Tag Handler with Body Tag Support

1. Here's a revised version of the tag handler; this time it's called `ListQuestionsInBody`. Add
    this class to the /WEB-INF/classes/Ch04 directory.

```java
package Ch04;

import java.util.*;
import javax.servlet.jsp.tagext.*;
import javax.servlet.jsp.*;
import java.io.*;

public class ListQuestionsInBody extends BodyTagSupport {
  private String topic;
  private Iterator faqs;
  private int count;
  public void setTopic(String s) { topic = s; }
  public String getTopic() { return topic; }

  public int doStartTag() throws JspTagException {
    Questions questions = new Questions();
    questions.setTopic(getTopic());
    Map qmap = new TreeMap(questions.getQuestions());
    faqs = qmap.values().iterator();
    count = 1;

    if (faqs.hasNext()) {
      setVariables();
      return EVAL_BODY_INCLUDE;
    } else {
      return SKIP_BODY;
    }
  }

  public int doAfterBody() throws JspTagException {
    if (faqs.hasNext()) {
      setVariables();
      return EVAL_BODY_BUFFERED;
    } else {
      return SKIP_BODY;
    }
  }

  public int doEndTag() throws JspTagException {
    return EVAL_PAGE;
  }

  void setVariables() {
    pageContext.setAttribute("question", faqs.next());
    pageContext.setAttribute("qid", topic + "_" + count);
    count++;
  }
}
```

2. We need to add another entry to the TLD for this new tag handler. Modify the `faq.tld` file as shown here:

```xml
<?xml version="1.0" encoding="UTF-8" ?>

<taglib xmlns="http://java.sun.com/xml/ns/j2ee"
        xmlns:xsi="http://www.w3.org/2001/XMLSchema-instance"
        xsi:schemaLocation="http://java.sun.com/xml/ns/j2ee/web-
                                         jsptaglibrary_2_0.xsd"
        version="2.0">

   <tag>
     <name>listFaqs</name>
     <tag-class>ch04.ListQuestions</tag-class>
     <body-content>scriptless</body-content>
     <attribute>
       <name>topic</name>
       <required>yes</required>
       <rtexprvalue>true</rtexprvalue>
     </attribute>
   </tag>

   <tag>
     <name>faqData</name>
     <tag-class>Ch04.ListQuestionsInBody</tag-class>
     <body-content>scriptless</body-content>
     <variable>
       <name-given>qid</name-given>
     </variable>
     <variable>
       <name-given>question</name-given>
     </variable>
     <attribute>
       <name>topic</name>
       <required>yes</required>
       <rtexprvalue>true</rtexprvalue>
     </attribute>
   </tag>
</taglib>
```

3. And we need a new version of the topic list page. This is `TopicList4.jsp`:

```jsp
<!DOCTYPE HTML PUBLIC "-//W3C//DTD HTML 4.01 Transitional//EN">
<%@ taglib uri="/questions" prefix="faq"%>
<html>
   <head><title>Topic Questions 4</title></head>
   <body>
     <h1>Topic Questions 4</h1>

     <faq:faqData topic="${param.topic}">
       <p>Question <a href="Questions.jsp?qid=${qid}">${qid}</a>
         ${question}</p>
     </faq:faqData>
     <p>Click a link to get the answer.</p>
   </body>
</html>
```

4. Modify `web.xml` so that the value for `<Welcome-File>` is now `TopicList4.jsp`. No other additions or modifications are needed to the existing files in the application. After deploying the new files, enter the URL http://localhost:1024/Ch04/TopicList4.jsp?topic=EL (again, use port 8080 for Tomcat).

5. You should see the same behavior as occurred with the previous examples.

How It Works

The `ListQuestionsInBody` class does not have any more template data in it, and does not need to output anything to the response. All it does is process the collection of questions, exposing each one to the rest of the page through the `setVariables()` method. This method adds two attributes to the page context. This makes the variables accessible to the rest of the page. Within the page, these variables are accessed using the EL expressions `${question}` and `${qid}`. To cause the body of the tag to be evaluated, `doStartTag()` returns `EVAL_BODY_INCLUDE` and `doAfterBody()` returns `EVAL_BODY_BUFFERED`. These return values cause the page class to call the `setBodyContent()` and `doInitBody()` methods of the class. Since our tag handler didn't need to do anything special with the body content, the default implementations of these methods in the parent class were sufficient.

To make the variables created by the tag handler accessible to the page, the TLD specifies that the tag handler should create two scripting variables that are then available to the rest of the page (although they are only used within the body of the tag). It did this through the `<variable>` element:

```
<variable>
  <name-given>qid</name-given>
</variable>
<variable>
  <name-given>question</name-given>
</variable>
```

Each of these elements used the `<name-given>` element to specify the name by which the scripting variables could be accessed. These are the same names that the tag handler class must use when adding the attributes to the page context.

Finally, there is the topic page. Our new tag is called in the same way as the simple tag example, so `TopicList4.jsp` is simpler than the original `TopicList.jsp`, but not quite as simple as `TopicList3.jsp`. The body of the tag consists of template data and EL expressions:

```
<faq:faqData topic="${param.topic}">
  <p>Question <a href="Questions.jsp?qid=${qid}">${qid}</a>
    ${question}</p>
</faq:faqData>
```

The EL expressions access the scripting variables created by the custom action. Each time the page class evaluates the body, it gets the current values of these variables from the page context and inserts them into the response.

This allows page designers to easily change the presentation of the data without needing to edit and recompile the tag handler.

JavaServer Pages Standard Tag Library (JSTL)

Much of this chapter has been devoted to information about creating your own custom actions and tag libraries. However, you are not limited to using just the tags you create. You can use any tag library that is available. While there are many such libraries distributed, in this section we will look at the JavaServer Pages Standard Tag Library, or JSTL.

The JSTL grew out of the realization that with many developers creating tag libraries, many actions would be duplicated among the various libraries. Because these libraries were developed separately, the duplicated actions would probably have different names, syntaxes, or behaviors. The JSTL standardizes a number of common actions. In theory, then, if you use one implementation of a standard tag library, switching to another standard tag library should be as easy as adding the `.jar` files to your application and changing the `web.xml` file to map the `taglib-uri` to the new different TLD. In this section, we will look at some of the actions in the JSTL.

Getting an Implementation

If you want to experiment with the JSTL, one place where you can get an implementation of the library is the Jakarta project. You can get a copy of the latest version at http://jakarta.apache.org/taglibs/index.html.

Using the JSTL is as simple as:

1. Unpacking the distribution into your application. The `.jar` files containing the tag handlers should go into /WEB-INF/lib, and the TLDs into a directory under /WEB-INF/.

2. Changing the `web.xml` file to map `taglib-uris` to the location of the TLDs.

3. Adding the `taglib` directive to the pages that will use the JSTL tags.

What's in the JSTL?

The JSTL tags have been divided into four categories. These categories with their associated TLDs are:

❑ Core actions (`c.tld` and `c-rt.tld`)

❑ XML processing (`x.tld` and `x-rt.tld`)

❑ Internationalization-capable formatting (`fmt.tld` and `fmt-rt.tld`)

❑ Relational database access (`sql.tld` and `sql-rt.tld`)

To simplify the support for both EL expressions and JSP scripting expressions, there are two TLDs for each of the categories above. If your page uses JSP scripting expressions (<%! %>, <%= %>, or <% %>), then you will use the rt version of each TLD (rt is short for rtexprvalues, which is short for "runtime expression values"). If your page uses EL expressions, then you will use the other version. If your page uses both, then you will need both TLDs. You can freely mix actions from either library in the same JSP.

Core Actions

The core actions provide tag handlers for manipulating variables and dealing with errors, performing tests and conditional behavior, and executing loops and iterations.

General-Purpose Actions

The general-purpose actions provide support for dealing with variables and errors.

Tag	Meaning
`<c:out value="" default="">`	Sends the value to the response stream. We can specify an optional default value so that if the value attribute is set with an EL expression, and the expression is null, the default value will be output.
`<c:set var="" value="">`	Sets the JSP-scoped variable identified by var to the given value.
`<c:set target="" property="" value="">`	Sets the property of the given JavaBean or Map object to the given value.
`<c:remove var="" scope="">`	Removes the object identified by var from the given scope. The scope attribute is optional. If the scope is not given, each scope will be searched in the order page, request, session, application, until the object is found or all scopes are searched. If scope is given, the object is removed only if it is in the given scope. If the object is not found, an exception will be thrown.
`<c:catch var="">`	Encloses a block of code that might throw an exception. If the exception occurs, the block terminates but the exception is not propagated. The thrown exception can be referenced by the variable named by var.

Conditional Actions

Conditional actions allow you to test expressions and evaluate tags based on the result of the test.

Tag	Meaning
`<c:if test=""` `var="">`	Used like a standard Java if block. The `var` attribute is optional; if present, the result of the test is assigned to the variable identified by var. If the test expression evaluates to true, the tag is evaluated; if false, it is not.
`<c:choose>`, `<c:when test="">`, `<c:otherwise>`	The analog to a Java if...elseif...else block. The `<c:choose>` action starts and ends the block. The test in each `<c:when test="">` tag is evaluated; the first test that evaluates to `true` causes that tag to be evaluated. If no `<c:when>` action evaluates to `true`, the `<c:otherwise>` tag is evaluated.

Iterator Actions

Iterator actions allow you to loop over a set of values:

Tag	Meaning
`<c:forEach var=""` `items="">`	Iterates over each item in the collection identified by `items`. Each item can be referenced by var. When `items` is a Map, the value of the item is referenced by `var.value`.
`<c:forEach var=""` `begin=""` `end=""` `step="">`	The tag for a for loop. The `step` attribute is optional.
`<c:forTokens items=""` `delims="">`	Iterates over the tokens in the `items` string.

Formatting Actions

Formatting actions are part of the I18N library. As you might guess, they provide support for formatting output. Among the actions for setting locales and time zones, are actions for formatting numbers. Here are two of them:

Tag	Meaning
```<fmt:formatDate value="date" [type="{time｜date｜both}"] [dateStyle="{default｜short｜medium｜long｜full}"] [timeStyle="{default｜short｜medium｜long｜full}"] [pattern="customPattern"] [timeZone="timeZone"] [var="varName"] [scope="{page｜request｜session｜application}"]/>```	Only the value attribute is required. The other attributes define how to format the data. The pattern attribute can contain a custom pattern for formatting the date string.
```<fmt:formatNumber value="numericValue" [type="{number｜currency｜percent}"] [pattern="customPattern"] [currencyCode="currencyCode"] [currencySymbol="currencySymbol"] [groupingUsed="{true｜false}"] [maxIntegerDigits="maxIntegerDigits"] [minIntegerDigits="minIntegerDigits"] [maxFractionDigits="maxFractionDigits"] [minFractionDigits="minFractionDigits"] [var="varName"] [scope="{page｜request｜session｜application}"]/>```	Formats the number given by value. Various styles are possible, including currency formats and custom formatting styles. You can also use this tag without the value attribute, in which case the number to be formatted is passed in the body of the tag.

SQL Actions

The JSTL SQL actions allow page authors to perform database queries, access query results, and perform inserts, updates, and deletes. We will look at just one of the actions `<sql:query>`.

Tag	Meaning
```<sql:query var="" dataSource=""> SQL Command </sql:query>```	Queries the database given by the dataSource attribute. The query that is performed is given in the body of the tag. The results of the query can be accessed by var.rows. You can use the `<c:forEach>` tag to iterator over the collection of rows. The dataSource attribute can identify the database in two ways. It can use the JDBC URL to access the database, or it can use the JNDI Data Source Name to look up the database. See Chapters 6 and 7 for more information on these techniques.

Try It Out   Using the JSP Standard Tag Library

In this example, we will finally add another FAQ answer to the FAQ application we have been
developing in this chapter. This JSP will show various uses of the JSTL. Here is the structure of the
web application:

```
Ch04/
    Questions.jsp
    TopicList.jsp
    WEB-INF/
        EL_1.jsp
        EL_2.jsp
        web.xml
        lib/
            jstl.jar
            standard.jar
        tlds/
            simplefaq.tld
            c-rt.tld
            fmt.tld
        classes/
            SimpleList.class
            Questions.class
```

For the most part, this example will reuse the files created for the example used earlier to demonstrate
simple tag handlers. Start by finding the files for the simple tag handler example and putting them into
the directory structure shown above. The new files that need to be added are EL_2.jsp and the .jar
and .tld files from the JSTL.

1. Download the JSTL from the Jakarta web site http://jakarta.apache.org/taglibs/doc/standard-
   doc/intro.html. Extract all the TLDs into the /tlds directory you've been using for the examples
   in this chapter. Extract the following .jar files into the lib directory: standard.jar and
   jstl.jar. You can add the others if you like, but they are not needed for this example.

2. Create the following EL_2.jsp file. Save this file in the same place as EL_1.jsp:

```
<!DOCTYPE HTML PUBLIC "-//W3C//DTD HTML 4.01 Transitional//EN">
<%@ taglib uri="http://java.sun.com/jstl/core_rt" prefix="c_rt" %>
<%@ taglib uri="http://java.sun.com/jstl/format" prefix="fmt" %>

<html>
  <head>
    <title>JSTL Q2</title>
  </head>

  <body>
    <h1>JSTL Question 2</h1>
    <h2>How do I use the JSTL?</h2>

    <jsp:useBean id="questions" class="Ch04.Questions">
      <jsp:setProperty name="questions" property="topic" value="EL"/>
    </jsp:useBean>

    <table border="1">
      <!-- the literal JSTL tag will be in left column of table -->
      <!-- the evaluated JSTL tag will be in right column of table -->
```

```
<tr><th>tag</th><th>result</th></tr>

<!-- This tag uses c_rt:out to send the value of an EL
     to the response -->
<tr>
  <td>&lt;c_rt:out value="${'${'}questions.topic}"/&gt;</td>
  <td><c_rt:out value="questions.topic=${questions.topic}"/></td>
</tr>

<!-- this tag uses c_rt:set to set the property of a JavaBean -->
<tr>
  <td>
    &lt;c_rt:set target="${'${'}questions}" property="topic"
                 value="JSTL" /&gt;
    <c_rt:set target="${questions}" property="topic" value="JSTL" />
  </td>
  <td><c_rt:out value="questions.topic=${questions.topic}"/></td>
</tr>

<!-- This tag uses c_rt:if to determine whether to create
     another row -->
<c_rt:if test="${questions.topic} == 'EL'">
  <tr><td>This row will not be created</td><td></td></tr>
</c_rt:if>

<c_rt:if test="${questions.topic == 'JSTL'}">
  <tr>
    <td>This row was created because the c_rt:if tag result was
true</td>
    <td></td>
  </tr>
</c_rt:if>
</table>

<p>Multiplication table, 1 - 5</p>

<!-- Use the forEach tag to create a table -->
<table border="1">
  <tr>
    <td></td><td>1</td><td>2</td><td>3</td><td>4</td><td>5</td>
  </tr>
  <c_rt:forEach var="i" begin="1" end="5">
    <tr>
      <td><c_rt:out value="${i}"/></td>
      <c_rt:forEach var="j" begin="1" end="5">
        <td><c_rt:out value="${i*j}"/></td>
      </c_rt:forEach>
    </tr>
  </c_rt:forEach>
</table>

<h2>Formatting numbers</h2><br>
&lt;fmt:formatNumber value="23.456" type="number" /&gt;
results in <fmt:formatNumber value="23.456" type="number" /><br>
&lt;fmt:formatNumber type="currency"&gt;23.456&lt;/fmt:formatNumber&gt;
results in <fmt:formatNumber type="currency">23.456</fmt:formatNumber>
```

145

```
<br>&lt;fmt:formatNumber value=".23456" type="percent"/&gt;
results in <fmt:formatNumber value=".23456" type="percent"/><br>

&lt;fmt:formatNumber value=".23456" type="percent"
                    minFractionDigits="2" /&gt;
results in <fmt:formatNumber value=".23456" type="percent"
                             minFractionDigits="2" />

    </body>
</html>
```

3. If you are using Tomcat, modify the `web.xml` file as shown below. If you are using the J2EE Deployment Tool, set the `taglib` mapping through the Deployment Tool.

```xml
<?xml version="1.0" encoding="ISO-8859-1"?>

<web-app xmlns="http://java.sun.com/xml/ns/j2ee"
    xmlns:xsi="http://www.w3.org/2001/XMLSchema-instance"
    xsi:schemaLocation="http://java.sun.com/xml/ns/j2ee/web-app_2_4.xsd"
    version="2.4">

  <!-- this is the deployment descriptor for Chapter 4
       Expression Language example                      -->

  <welcome-file-list>
    <welcome-file>TopicList.jsp</welcome-file>
  </welcome-file-list>

  <!-- this element is for the custom action example -->
  <taglib>
    <taglib-uri>/questions</taglib-uri>
    <taglib-location>/WEB-INF/tlds/faq.tld</taglib-location>
  </taglib>

  <!-- this element is for the simple tag handler example -->
  <taglib>
    <taglib-uri>/simplequestions</taglib-uri>
    <taglib-location>/WEB-INF/tlds/simplefaq.tld</taglib-location>
  </taglib>

  <!-- these elements are for the JSTL example -->
  <taglib>
    <taglib-uri>http://java.sun.com/jstl/core_rt</taglib-uri>
    <taglib-location>/WEB-INF/tlds/c-rt.tld</taglib-location>
  </taglib>
  <taglib>
    <taglib-uri>http://java.sun.com/jstl/format</taglib-uri>
    <taglib-location>/WEB-INF/tlds/fmt.tld</taglib-location>
  </taglib>

</web-app>
```

4. That should be all that's required to make the tags available. Deploy the new files and enter the URL http://localhost:1024/Ch04/TopicList.jsp?topic=EL in a browser. Click the link for EL_2 and you should see this:

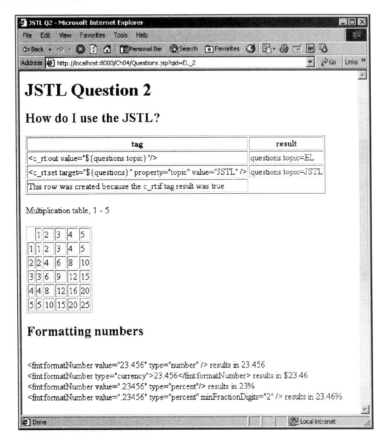

How It Works

This page demonstrates a few of the JSTL tags available to you. We've seen the TLD and the web.xml entries several times now, so I won't cover those at all. The EL_2.jsp file begins by "importing" the tag library:

```
<%@ taglib uri="http://java.sun.com/jstl/core_rt" prefix="c_rt" %>
<%@ taglib uri="http://java.sun.com/jstl/format" prefix="fmt" %>
```

I am using the rt version of the core library and the EL version of the format library. The prefix follows the JSTL suggestion; however, recall that I can make the prefix any value I want. The prefix is set by the page designer.

The page then creates a JavaBean from the Questions class and prints out the value of its topic property. It then sets the topic property to a different value and prints that out. Next it uses two <c:if> tags to control the creation of another row in the table.

The next part of the page uses nested <c:forEach> tags to create a two-dimensional table and to fill the table with the result of multiplying the numbers one through five against themselves.

This example should give you a fair idea of how to start using some of the other tags in the JSTL. There is, of course, much more information in the JSTL specification, available at the Jakarta web site and at http://java.sun.com.

Other Tag Libraries

The JSTL is certainly not the only tag library available to you. There are many more commercial and free tag libraries available. Here is a short listing of a few:

❏ Struts–This is another tag library from the Jakarta web site. The struts taglib provides tags that are useful in building Model View Controller (MVC) applications. (We saw a simplistic MVC at the end of the last chapter, and we'll see MVC again in the next chapter.)

❏ JNDI–This library is also available from Jakarta. It provides tags for using the Java Naming and Directory Interface API. As we will see throughout this book, you will often use JNDI to look up resources in your web applications.

❏ BEA WebLogic Portal JSP Tag Libraries–This tag library from BEA provides standard tags for working with BEA's web portal.

❏ Coldjava Bar Charts–This is one of many tag libraries available from http://www.servletsuite.com/jsp.htm. This library provides tags for creating horizontal and vertical bar charts.

❏ Orion EJB–Available at http://www.orionserver.com/tags/ejbtags/, this library provides tags for using Enterprise JavaBeans.

❏ jsptags.com–Not a taglib, but a whole collection of taglibs, can be found at http://jsptags.com/tags/index.jsp. If you can't find what you need here, you will probably need to develop it yourself.

We could spend an entire book just looking at the different tag libraries out there. We obviously don't have room for that here. However, with the information in this chapter on deploying custom actions and using the JSTL, you should have enough information to be able to tackle any taglibs you find.

Summary

So that's the nickel tour of advanced topics in JSPs. We spent some time getting to know Expression Language in some detail, and we spent a lot of time with custom actions and seeing how to implement tag extensions. After that, we took a quick look at the JSP Standard Tag Library.

By no means, though, did we cover everything on those topics. There are many other features of Expression Language, Tag Extensions, and the JSTL that we just didn't have time to cover. What we did look at, though, was the fundamental information, the information that will allow you to sit down and start using these technologies. After you have spent a little time writing tag extensions or EL expressions, you can start delving into the really advanced material.

So, what should you know after having read this chapter?

❑ EL expressions provide a simple syntax for using expressions with attributes and template text.

❑ EL expressions are very Java-like in their syntax.

❑ Custom actions provide a way to hide the Java code from the page designer.

❑ Tag handlers are the Java classes that implement a custom action. You will usually extend `SimpleTagSupport`, `TagSupport`, or `BodyTagSupport` when creating a tag handler.

❑ Deploying a tag library is as easy as 1, 2, 3 (copy `jars` and `tlds`, add mapping to `web.xml`, add a `taglib` directive to the JSP page).

❑ JSTL provides a library of standard tags that can be used for many basic functions.

Exercises

1. When using a classic tag handler, investigate if there is any difference in how the tag handler methods are called for the two different forms of the empty tag: `<empty/>` and `<empty></empty>`.

2. Develop a JSP that uses the `sql` taglib of JSTL to talk to a database.

5

Servlets

Along with JSPs, servlets are the other highly used component in J2EE web applications. Servlets are server-side applications in much the same way that way applets are client-side applications. Like JSP pages, servlets are Java classes that are loaded and executed by a servlet container that can run stand-alone or as a component of a web server or a J2EE server. In fact, as we saw in Chapter 3, JSP pages are actually compiled by the container into a servlet class that is then executed by the container. However, while JSP pages are usually HTML pages with bits of embedded Java code, servlets are Java classes with bits of embedded HTML.

Servlets are designed to be extensions to servers, and to extend the capabilities of servers. Notice that I say "servers" rather than "web servers." Servlets were originally intended to be able to extend any server such as an FTP server, or an SMTP (e-mail) server. However, in practice, only servlets that respond to HTTP requests have been widely implemented. Servlets extend the capabilities of a web server and provide dynamic behavior for web applications. Servlets are designed to accept a response from a client (usually a web browser), process that request, and return a response to the client. Although all the processing can occur within the servlet, usually helper classes or other web components such as Enterprise JavaBeans (EJBs) will perform the business logic processing, leaving the servlet free to perform the request and response processing.

After JDBC, servlets were the second J2EE technology invented. Since they were also developed before JSP, early servlets had to handle display processing. This mixture of page design mixed into code was one of the reasons JSP was introduced. When servlets were first introduced, if you were developing a web application in Java, you were using just servlets in the middle tier, and JDBC if you had a database. Now, of course, servlets are just one aspect of the whole J2EE architecture.

In this chapter, we'll introduce you to servlets and show you how to use them correctly in your web application. Specifically, we will look at:

❏   How HTTP requests are made to servers

❏   How servlets are designed to respond to HTTP requests

❏   The phases in the servlet lifecycle

❏   Ways to make your servlet thread-safe

❏   Handling exceptions in your servlet

❏   How to create and use sessions

❏   How to use filters in your web application

❏   What the Model View Controller (MVC) architecture is, and how it makes better applications

HTTP and Server Programs

Although servlets were originally intended to work with any server, in practice servlets are only used with web servers, so in a J2EE application, you will only be developing servlets that respond to HTTP requests. As we will see later, the Servlet API provides a class named `HttpServlet` specifically for dealing with these requests. The `HttpServlet` class is designed to work closely with the HTTP protocol. This protocol was developed years before servlets were designed, and the basic HTTP protocol has been very stable. The HTTP protocol defines the structure of the requests that a client sends to a web server, the format for the client to submit request parameters, and the way the server responds. `HttpServlets` use the same protocol to handle the service requests they receive and to return responses to clients. So understanding the basics of HTTP is important to understanding how to use servlets.

Request Methods

The HTTP specification defines a number of requests that a web client, typically a browser, can make upon a web server. These are called methods, and there are seven methods defined. They are:

❏   GET—Retrieves information identified by a request Uniform Resource Identifier (URI).

❏   POST—Requests that the server pass the body of the request to the resource identified by the request URI for processing.

❏   HEAD—Returns only the header of the response that would be returned by a GET request.

❏   PUT—Uploads data to the server to be stored at the given request URI. The main difference between this and POST is that the server should not further process a PUT request, but simply store it at the request URI.

❑ DELETE–Deletes the resource identified by the request URI.

❑ TRACE–Causes the server to return the request message.

❑ OPTIONS–Asks the server for information about a specific resource, or about the server's capabilities in general.

These methods are defined in the HTTP specification at http://www.ietf.org/rfc/rfc2068.txt?number=2068. When developing web applications, we are concerned primarily with GET and POST requests.

GET

Simply stated, the GET method means that the browser sends a formatted string to the server, and the server returns the content identified by that string. This string is known as a Uniform Resource Identifier (URI). One specific type of URI is a string that specifies the location of a resource in relation to the server. This is a Uniform Resource Locator (URL). The resource can be a static web page, or the result of a web application. A GET request usually results when a user clicks a link in a web page, or enters a URL in the address bar of the browser. However, there are other ways this can occur. For example, you can send a GET request through a telnet session or programmatically send a GET request to a server; you can even create a web page form that uses GET for its requests.

When sending a GET request, additional information can be passed to the web server. For GET requests, this usually takes the form of request parameters that are appended to the URL. For example, when you perform a web search using the web site http://www.google.com, the search parameters are passed to the search engine using request parameters as shown here:

http://www.google.com/search?hl=en&q=Beginning+Java+Server

The request parameters are prefixed by a question mark (?), the parameters are passed as name-value pairs (hl=en, for example), and each pair is delimited by an ampersand (&). This format is also known as **URL encoding**.

Another way to pass parameters to a server is by appending the data as additional path information to the URL. The additional information looks like a continuation of the URL, but the web application interprets the path information as parameters that it can act upon. For example, suppose we had a stock brokerage application identified by the URL /stock/StockList. We could append additional information to the URL, which the StockList application would interpret as a parameter. It might look like this:

http://localhost:1024/stock/StockList/AddRating

The /AddRating part of the URL appears to be part of the URL for the web application; however, it does not identify any resource installed on the server. The resource is StockList, and the StockList application knows how to interpret the additional path information.

153

Try It Out   Sending an HTTP Request via Telnet

1. You can create a GET request from the command line to see the basic structure of such a request. Start by ensuring that the J2EE server or Tomcat is running. If you need to start the server, use the appropriate script file in the J2EE bin or Tomcat bin directories, or select the Start J2EE shortcut from the Start menu if you are using Windows.

2. Start a telnet client. On Windows, open a command window. For Unix, open a terminal or console window. Then enter the following command to connect to the J2EE server on the default port:

    ```
    > telnet localhost 1024
    ```

    or this command to connect to Tomcat on its default port:

    ```
    > telnet localhost 8080
    ```

    You can replace localhost with an IP address or a hostname, and the port number should be replaced with the correct port for your system, as necessary.

3. For J2EE, enter the following command followed by two *Return* characters:

    ```
    > GET /index.html HTTP/1.0
    >
    ```

    If you are attempting to connect to Tomcat, use:

    ```
    > GET /index.jsp HTTP/1.0
    >
    ```

    If you wait too long before entering the request, the connection will be automatically closed. Try again, but type more quickly.

4. Don't forget to press the *Return* key twice. The second *Return* creates a blank line; this tells the server that the request is complete. The server should respond with the appropriate information. Here is what was returned when I connected to the J2EE server:

    ```
    HTTP/1.1 200 OK
    ETag: W/"1406-1035567554000"
    Last-Modified: Fri, 25 Oct 2002 17:39:14 GMT
    Content-Type: text/html
    Content-Length: 1406
    Date: Sun, 05 Jan 2003 19:14:53 GMT
    Server: Apache Coyote/1.0
    Connection: close

    ...remainder of response not shown...
    ```

How It Works

The telnet command line includes the name of the telnet program (which just happens to be `telnet`), followed by the hostname for the connection, and the port.

The actual request consists of the method (`GET`) followed by the relative URI of the desired resource, followed by the HTTP identifier for the HTTP version that the telnet program supports. The URI is just /index.html (or /index.jsp), which is the URI for the root resource of the server. Press *Enter* to complete the request line, and then press *Enter* again. The blank line tells the server that the header is complete. Since a `GET` request has no body, the request is sent to the server.

A general HTTP message has this format:

```
Request-Line
Headers
<Carriage Return/Line Feed>
[ message-body ]
```

Each request begins with the request line. In our example, that was `GET /index.html HTTP/1.0`. This is followed by header data. In our example, we did not use any header data. A blank line created by entering just a carriage return/line feed sequence signals the end of the headers. This is followed by an optional message body. Since our example was a `GET` request, there was no message body. `POST` requests will have message bodies.

You can see this entire structure in the response from the server, which has the same message format as a request. The first line of the response is the status line, which consists of the HTTP version, a response code (200), and a response message (OK). This is followed by the response headers: the date, content length, and other information added by the server. The headers, whether part of the request or response, are in the format *name* : *value*. This is followed by the actual body of the resource. In the example above, the server returns the J2EE home page.

So, whether you are clicking a link, entering an address in a browser address bar, using telnet, or connecting to a server programmatically (using code), the request that is sent to the server must ultimately follow the format prescribed by the HTTP specification. Most of the time, however, formatting the request is handled for you.

POST

If the request is sent using the `POST` method, the request can include a message body, and the server should pass this message body to the resource in the URI for processing. `POST` requests are typically generated by users submitting a form through their web browser. Forms can be used with either `GET` or `POST` requests, although they tend to be used with `POST`s. Additionally, like `GET` requests, `POST` requests can be generated manually using a program such as telnet, or programmatically using classes in the `java.net` package.

Also, while data can be passed to the server using the same techniques as with GET requests (appending parameters or adding additional path information), a POST request usually submits data to the server in the body of a request. For example, using the hypothetical StockList application, the POST request to submit stock ratings might look like this:

```
POST /stock/servlet/StockList/AddRating HTTP/1.0
Content-type: application/x-www-form-urlencoding
Content-length: 39

analysts=3&stocks=DDC&ratings=Smashing!
```

Now, if a browser had submitted the above POST request, it would pass more information than I have shown above. However, the commands shown above are sufficient for sending data to a web application. The request starts with the method and URL, and the head of the request includes Content-type and Content-length parameters. This is followed by two pairs of <CRLF> characters, followed by the request data in the message-body. In this example, the POST data consists of 39 characters, formatted using URL-encoding. The data does not need to be URL-encoded, however. POST data can be in any format that the web application understands. The point is that request data for a POST request is usually included in the body of the request, rather than appended to the URL.

How a Server Responds to Requests

We already know how a server responds when the GET request is for a static HTML web page. When you enter an address or click a link, the server locates the resource identified by the URI and returns that resource as part of an HTTP message to the web browser. In the case of a web page, the browser displays the web page for you.

What happens, however, when the resource is a server-side program? In this case, the server needs to interpret the URI as a request for a server-side program, format the request parameters in a form the program recognizes, and pass the request to that program. In the early days of the web, a standardized format for doing this was developed called Common Gateway Interface, or CGI; whenever you see a URL that has /cgi/ as part of the address, you are creating a request to a server-side program of that type. The program must interpret the request parameters, execute the appropriate processing, and return a response to the server, which returns it to the client.

In the early days of the Web, the server program was usually a program written in a language such as C or Perl, which executed in a separate process from the server. Every request caused a new process to be spawned; when the program completed processing the request, it was terminated. This was usually resource intensive.

A process is a running program and all the data associated with it.

Java servlets, and specifically `HttpServlets`, provide several advantages over CGI programs for server-side applications:

❏ They can run in the same process as the server, so new processes don't need to be spawned for every request.

❏ They are portable between servers (as long as they don't use any platform-specific code). CGI programs written and compiled in C, for example, would need to be recompiled for a different operating system.

The Servlet Model and HttpServlets

The following diagram presents a slightly simplified view of what happens when a client makes a request that is processed by a servlet:

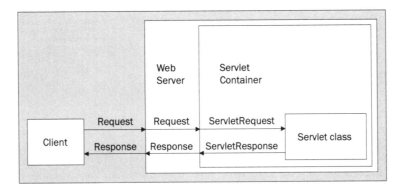

When a client (usually, but not necessarily, a web browser) makes a request to the server, and the server determines the request is for a servlet resource, it passes the request to the servlet container. The container is the program responsible for loading, initiating, calling, and releasing servlet instances. The servlet container takes the HTTP request, parses its request URI, the headers, and the body, and stores all of that data inside an object that implements the `javax.servlet.ServletRequest` interface. It also creates an instance of an object the implements `javax.servlet.ServletResponse`. The response object encapsulates the response back to the client. The container then calls a method of the servlet class, passing the request and response objects. The servlet processes the request, and sends a response back to the client.

If you read the JSP chapters of this book, you will realize that this request-response flow is very similar to the request-response flow for JSP pages. In fact, since JSP pages are translated into servlets, it is almost identical. Is there any difference between the two? Or put another way, when should we use servlets, and when JSP pages? In general, JSP pages are better suited for web components that contain a large amount of presentation logic. Servlets are better suited for web components that perform processing or business logic. Servlets can send display data directly through the response as shown above, but in many web applications the servlet will accept and process the request, using some other component to generate the response back to the client. In the next few sections, we'll look at how a servlet receives the request and returns a response.

Basic Servlet Design

Like CGI programs, HTTP servlets are designed to respond to GET and POST requests, along with all the other requests defined for HTTP, although you will probably never need to respond to anything other than GET or POST. When writing servlets, you will usually extend a class named `javax.servlet.http.HttpServlet`. This is a base class provided by the Servlet API that provides support for HTTP requests. The `HttpServlet` class, in turn, extends `javax.servlet.GenericServlet`, which provides some basic servlet functionality. Finally, `GenericServlet` implements the primary Servlet API interface, `javax.servlet.Servlet`. It also implements an interface called `ServletConfig`, which allows it to provide easy access to servlet configuration information. This is shown in the class diagram below:

The service() Method

Notice that `Servlet` only defines a small number of methods. You can probably guess that `init()` and `destroy()` don't handle any requests. We'll look at these methods later when we discuss the servlet lifecycle in more detail. Likewise, `getServletConfig()` and `getServletInfo()` don't handle requests either. That leaves only `service()` to handle requests. When a servlet container receives a request for a servlet, it calls the `service()` method of the servlet. So a servlet that implements the `Servlet` interface must implement the `service()` method to handle requests.

The doPost() and doGet() Methods

`HttpServlet` is intended to respond to HTTP requests, and it has to handle requests for GET, POST, HEAD, etc. Thus `HttpServlet` defines additional methods. It defines a `doGet()` to handle GET requests; `doPost()` to handle POST requests, and so on: there is a `doXXX()` method for every HTTP method. What these methods really do, rather than processing the request, is to return an error message to the client saying the method is not supported. You, as the developer, are expected to write your servlet to extend `HttpServlet` and override the methods you want to support. Usually this will be `doPost()` and/or `doGet()`.

You will often see servlet examples in books or tutorials that show a servlet class that extends `HttpServlet` and overrides the `service()` method to process an HTTP request. This is acceptable for simple example servlets, and you really won't cause any problems if you do this in a real J2EE application. However, `HttpServlet` already implements a `service()` method and it determines the correct `doXXX()` method to call for the HTTP request. In a real-world application, you should avoid overriding `service()` in your servlet, and instead override `doPost()` and/or `doGet()`.

When the servlet container receives the HTTP request, it maps the URI to a servlet. It then calls the `service()` method of the servlet. Assuming the servlet extends `HttpServlet`, and only overrides `doPost()` or `doGet()`, the call to `service()` will go to the `HttpServlet` class. The `service()` method determines which HTTP method the request used, and calls the correct `doXXX()` method. If your servlet has that method, it will be called because it overrides the same method in `HttpServlet`. Your `doXXX()` method processes the request, generates an HTTP response, and returns it to the client. Here is an illustration of that process, with an HTTP GET request:

In this illustration, note that even though `HttpServlet` and `MyServlet` are shown in separate boxes, together they constitute a single object in the system, an instance of `MyServlet`.

Request and Response Objects

The actual signature of all of the `doXXX()` methods is:

```
public void doXXX(HttpServletRequest req, HttpServletResponse res)
```

Each method—`doPost()`, `doGet()`, etc.—accepts two parameters. The `HttpServletRequest` object encapsulates the request to the server. It contains the data for the request, as well as some header information about the request. Using methods defined by the `request` object, the servlet can access the data submitted as part of the request. The `HttpServletResponse` object encapsulates the response to the client. Using the response object and its methods, you can return a response to the client.

Since we know the basic objects at this point, let's look at a simple example servlet. We'll use some of the methods of `HttpServletRequest` and `HttpServletResponse`, even though they have not been introduced yet. We'll look at those methods in more detail after the example.

Try It Out Creating a Servlet

1. In this example, we'll create a servlet that can respond to HTTP POST requests. Start by creating the simple servlet shown here:

```
package web;

import javax.servlet.http.*;
import java.io.*;

public class Login extends HttpServlet {
  public void doPost(HttpServletRequest request,
                     HttpServletResponse response)
  {
    String username = request.getParameter("username");
    try {
      response.setContentType("text/html");
      PrintWriter writer = response.getWriter();
      writer.println("<html><body>");
      writer.println("Thank you, " + username +
                     ". You are now logged into the system.");
      writer.println("</body></html>");
      writer.close();
    } catch (Exception e) {
      e.printStackTrace();
    }
  }
}
```

2. Compile the servlet. You will need to include the correct library for the compilation. There are two possible libraries to choose from, depending on whether you are using the J2EE reference implementation or the Tomcat server. It doesn't matter which one you use. If you have the J2EE SDK, you can use the j2ee.jar library; if you have Tomcat you can use servlet.jar. Assuming J2EE_HOME is the environment variable for the location of the J2EE SDK, then compile the servlet with the appropriate command line below:

```
> javac —classpath %J2EE_HOME%\lib\j2ee.jar Login.java    # For Windows
> javac —classpath $J2EE_HOME/lib/j2ee.jar Login.java      # For Linux/UNIX
```

If you're using Tomcat 4, then assuming CATALINA_HOME is the location of the Tomcat installation, compile the servlet with the appropriate command below:

```
> javac —classpath %CATALINA_HOME%\common\lib\servlet.jar Login.java # Windows
> javac —classpath $CATALINA_HOME/common/lib/servlet.jar Login.java  # Linux
```

If you're using Tomcat 5, then assuming CATALINA_HOME is the location of the Tomcat installation, compile the servlet with the appropriate command below:

```
> javac —classpath %CATALINA_HOME%\common\lib\servlet-api.jar Login.java
> javac —classpath $CATALINA_HOME/common/lib/servlet-api.jar Login.java
```

3. The root of this application will be named Ch05. So, to call the servlet above, the path will be Ch05/Login. Create the HTML page below (login.html), which has a form that posts to the servlet:

```
<!DOCTYPE HTML PUBLIC "-//W3C//DTD HTML 4.01 Transitional//EN">
<html>
  <head>
    <title>Login</title>
  </head>

  <body>
    <h1>Login</h1>

    Please enter your username and password
    <form action="/Ch05/Login" method="POST">
      <p><input type="text" name="username" length="40">
      <p><input type="password" name="password" length="40">
      <p><input type="submit" value="Submit">
    </form>
  </body>
</html>
```

How It Works

The Login servlet illustrates some of the main points developed in this chapter so far. The class itself is just like any other Java class. In this case, it is a subclass of HttpServlet. As a subclass of HttpServlet, the Login class only needs to override the methods of HttpServlet that it needs to implement its behavior, or alternately, add new methods for new behavior. In this example, Login only needs to override the doPost() method of HttpServlet.

When you click the Submit button of the login.html static page, the web browser submits a POST request to the Tomcat server. Web forms can be used to submit either GET or POST requests. The <form> tag in the web page has a method attribute that has the value POST. This tells the browser to submit a POST request to the resource indicated by the action attribute of the <form> tag. If no method attribute is used, the form defaults to the GET method.

When the Tomcat server receives the POST request, it parses the URL to determine which resource to send the request to. The /Ch05 portion tells Tomcat that this is a resource in the Ch05 application; the /Login portion maps to the web.Login class. Tomcat constructs instances of HttpServletRequest and HttpServletResponse, and calls the service() method of Login. Since Login does not implement service(), the parent class method is called; the service() method of HttpServlet determines that the request is a POST request and calls the doPost() method. Since Login does define doPost(), it is that method which is used to process the request.

Within the doPost() method, the Login servlet reads a request parameter from the HttpServletRequest object. The method that it uses to do this is getParameter(String), which returns a String that has the value of the request parameter with the given name. If no such parameter exists, then null is returned. The name used by the servlet:

```
String username = request.getParameter("username");
```

is the same as the name used in the web form:

```
<p><input type="text" name="username" length="40">
```

There are several other methods used to retrieve the request parameters from the request object. I will cover these methods later in the chapter.

The Login servlet then uses the response object to return a response to the client. It starts by setting the Content-type of the response to "text/html":

```
response.setContentType("text/html");
```

> The content type must be set before getting an OutputStream or Writer object
> from the response object, since the content type is used to create the
> OutputStream or Writer.

After setting the content type, the servlet gets a Writer object from the response object. This Writer is used to send the strings that constitute the response to the client:

```
try {
  response.setContentType("text/html");
  PrintWriter writer = response.getWriter();
  writer.println("<html><body>");
  writer.println("Thank you, " + username +
                 ". You are now logged into the system");
  writer.println("</body></html>");
  writer.close();
} catch (Exception e) {
  e.printStackTrace();
}
```

Because writing to a stream can throw an IOException, the whole block is wrapped in a try...catch block. However, this try...catch block just prints out the stack trace for any exception thrown. While this is OK for this example, it is generally a bad practice to ignore exceptions in the servlet. I will show why this is so in the *Handling Exceptions* section later in the chapter. Also, as with the request object, I will show the other methods of the response object later in the chapter.

Try It Out Deploying a Servlet to the J2EE Server

At this point, we are ready to deploy the servlet. The next set of steps will show how to deploy the servlet with the J2EE SDK. These steps are virtually identical to the steps used in the previous JSP chapters. If you want to deploy to Tomcat, go to the next *Try It Out* section. Make sure the J2EE server is running, and open the Deployment Tool from the Start menu (for Windows) or by typing deploytool at a command prompt.

1. Create a new Application EAR. Select File | New | Application EAR as shown below. Alternatively, you can click the toolbar button for creating a new EAR.

2. In the dialog that results, enter a filename for the EAR. I used `StockBrokerage.ear`. The Deployment Tool will set the display name automatically:

3. Next select File | New | Web Application WAR (alternatively, you can click the toolbar button for creating a new Web Application WAR).

4. The New Web Application Wizard will now run. Click Next on the opening splash screen. In the Contents pane of the next screen, click the Edit button and add the `login.html` and `Login.class` files to the application. Click the Next button:

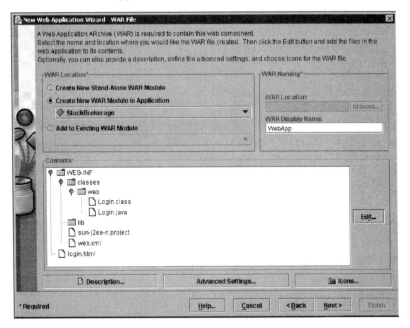

5. The following dialog selects the component to create. Servlet should already be selected, so click Next.

6. The dialog that follows allows you to select the Servlet Class and the Web Component Name. There should only be one selection in the class drop-down box, web.Login, so select this. The wizard will automatically fill in the component name to be Login. Click Finish (or, if you want to see the generated deployment descriptor, select Next, then Finish).

163

7. With the Login WebApp selected, click on the Aliases tab. Click on Add to add a new alias, and enter the alias /Login for the servlet:

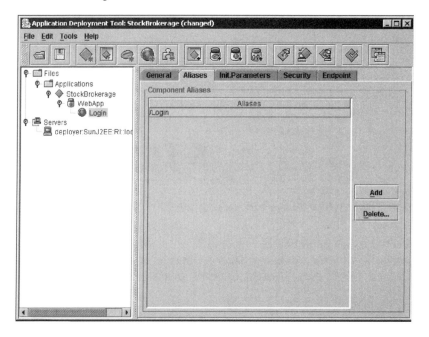

8. You will now see the main Deployment Tool window. Ensure the StockBrokerage EAR entry is selected in the left navigation pane, and select the tab named Web Context in the right pane. Enter Ch05 for the Context Root as shown below:

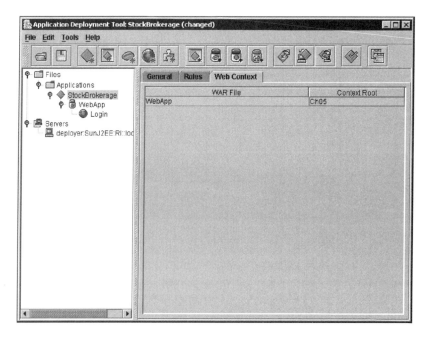

9. Save the application using File | Save As. Put the EAR into a location you can remember, such as the directory where you have the Login.java or Login.class file.

10. You are now ready to deploy the servlet. Select Tools | Deploy. Enter the admin username and password in the deploy dialog and click OK. As the deployment process proceeds, the progress is reported in a new dialog box. After the deployment is complete, close the progress dialog.

11. Open a browser and enter the URL http://localhost:1024/Ch05/login.html into the address bar. (If you selected a different context root, then use that context root in place of "Ch05".) The browser will load the login page:

12. Enter a username and password into the dialog and click the Submit button. The servlet will process the request and return this to the browser:

Try It Out Deploying a Servlet to a Tomcat Stand-Alone

1. In the next few steps, I will show how to manually deploy the Login servlet to a Tomcat stand-alone. To deploy to Tomcat, the application needs an appropriate directory structure. Start by creating this directory structure:

```
Ch05/
   login.html
   WEB-INF/
     web.xml
     classes/
       web/
         Login.class
```

This is the same directory structure created automatically by the Deployment Tool in the previous step 4. You can create this directory structure anywhere in your file system, but if you create it in the /webapps directory of your Tomcat installation, you'll be one step ahead of the game.

2. The web.xml file shown in the previous directory structure is also known as the deployment descriptor. For this example, it will look like this:

```
<?xml version="1.0" encoding="ISO-8859-1"?>

<!DOCTYPE web-app
    PUBLIC "-//Sun Microsystems, Inc.//DTD Web Application 2.3//EN"
    "http://java.sun.com/dtd/web-app_2_3.dtd">

<web-app>
  <display-name>Beginning J2EE Ch 5</display-name>
  <servlet>
    <servlet-name>Login</servlet-name>
    <servlet-class>web.Login</servlet-class>
  </servlet>
  <servlet-mapping>
    <servlet-name>Login</servlet-name>
    <url-pattern>/Login</url-pattern>
  </servlet-mapping>
</web-app>
```

3. If you created the directory structure above in the /webapps directory of Tomcat, you can go to the next step. Otherwise, you need to install the application in one of two ways:

Copy the entire directory structure to the /webapps folder of the Tomcat installation.

Create a Web Application Archive (WAR) file and copy the WAR file to Tomcat. If you created the directory structure in step 1, navigate into the /Ch05 directory and create the WAR file using the jar tool:

```
C:\8333\Ch05\>jar cf stock.war *
```

Copy the WAR file to the Tomcat /webapps directory. If you used a different directory for your application, navigate into the root directory for your application, create the WAR file, and copy it to the /webapps directory.

4. Start the Tomcat server. If it is already running, you will need to stop and restart it.

5. Open a browser and enter the URL http://localhost:8080/Ch05/login.html into the address bar. The browser will load the login page as shown in the previous step 12. Enter a username and password and click the Submit button. The web browser will display a welcome message returned by the servlet as shown in the previous step 13.

How It Works

The deployment descriptor for this application has two important elements under the `<web-app>` element:

```
<servlet>
  <servlet-name>Login</servlet-name>
  <servlet-class>web.Login</servlet-class>
</servlet>
<servlet-mapping>
  <servlet-name>Login</servlet-name>
  <url-pattern>/Login</url-pattern>
</servlet-mapping>
```

The `<servlet>` element tells the container the class that is used for a given servlet name, and the `<servlet-mapping>` element maps a URL to a servlet name. Thus, when the servlet container receives a URL that matches the given pattern, it will know which class to send the request to.

Using the request Object

In the example above, the servlet got information from the `request` object by calling the `getParameter()` method:

```
String username = request.getParameter("username");
```

The `getParameter()` method is unique in that it is the only method ever undeprecated by Sun. In the second version of the specification, `getParameter()` was deprecated and replaced by `getParameterValues()`. Enough developers expressed the opinion that the method was in fact still useful, and Sun undeprecated the method.

The `ServletRequest` interface defines a few other methods for getting and using request data from the client's request. Those methods are:

```
public Enumeration getParameterNames()
public String[] getParameterValues(String name)
public Map getParameterMap()
```

The `getParameterValues()` method returns the request parameters with the given name. The `getParameterValues()` method is used when the named parameter may have multiple values. For instance, if an HTML form contains a `<select>` list that allows multiple selections, the request will contain all the selected values keyed by a single name, the name of the `<select>` list. If you call `getParameter()` on a parameter with multiple values, the value returned is the same as the first element returned by `getParameterValues()`. If you call either `getParameter()` or `getParameterValues()` and the name does not exist in the request, `null` is returned. Also, keep in mind that web browsers only send non-null values. In other words, if an HTML form has a checkbox, and the user does not select the checkbox, the checkbox name is not sent in the request.

The getParameterNames() returns an enumeration of all the names in the request.

The getParameterMap() method returns all the parameters stored in a Map object. Each parameter name is a key in the Map; the value can be either a String or a String[] array, depending on whether the parameter has multiple values.

You can also get information about the request using ServletRequest methods. Here is a listing of a few of the more useful methods:

❑ public String getProtocol()–The protocol used by the request; this will usually be "HTTP".

❑ public String getServerName()–The host name of the server that received the request. This is useful if the server uses virtual servers.

❑ public String getRemoteAddr()–The IP address of the client that made the request.

❑ public String getRemoteHost()–The host name of the client that made the request.

You can also get access to the request stream containing the unparsed request parameters. There are two methods available for accessing the request stream:

```
public BufferedReader getReader()
public ServletInputStream getInputStream()
```

You can only use one of the methods with a single request. Once you access the request input stream using one of these methods, the stream cannot be accessed again. Attempting to call either of them for the same request will result in an exception being thrown. Also, note that if you use one of these methods, and the request has a message body, the getParameter() and getParameterValues() methods may not work.

Earlier, we looked at the format of an HTTP message. Recall that it looked like this:

```
Request-Line
Headers
<Carriage Return/Line Feed>
[ message body ]
```

The HttpServletRequest object provides a number of methods for reading the header data from the HTTP message:

```
long getDateHeader(String name)
String getHeader(String name)
Enumeration getHeaders(String name)
Enumeration getHeaderNames()
int getIntHeader(String name)
```

Two special methods are provided for getting a header value as a date or an `int`. Headers that are not dates or `int`s can be accessed using the general `getHeader(String)` method. The name argument passed to any of these methods should be the name of the header. Here again is part of the header portion of the response we got from the J2EE server in the first example of the chapter:

```
Last-Modified: Fri, 25 Oct 2002 17:39:14 GMT
Content-Length: 1406
Server: Apache Coyote/1.0
```

A servlet could get the value of the `Last-Modified` header by calling `getDateHeader("Last-Modified")`. It could get the `Content-Length` by calling `getIntHeader("Content-Length")`. A header like `Server`, neither date nor `int`, would be obtained by calling `getHeader("Server")`.

Earlier in the chapter, I mentioned that browsers can append request parameters to the URL. The servlet can obtain those parameters by calling `getQueryString()`.

```
public String getQueryString()
```

Thus, suppose you have a request URL that looks like this:

```
http://localhost/ch05/Login?name=Kevin
```

In this case, calling `getQueryString()` will return `"name=Kevin"`.

I also mentioned that information could be added to the URL that looks like a continuation of the path. This extra path information can be obtained by calling `getPathInfo()`:

```
public String getPathInfo()
```

For example, suppose you have a request URL like this:

```
http://localhost/ch05/Login/extra/path/info
```

In this case, `getPathInfo()` will return `"/extra/path/info"`.

Using the response Object

In the previous example, we used two methods of the `response` object:

```
response.setContentType("text/html");
PrintWriter writer = response.getWriter();
```

Using the `Writer` obtained from the `response`, the servlet sent HTML data to the client browser for it to display. There is another object that can be used to send response data. You will normally use the `Writer` to send character data, but you can also send data to the client using an output stream obtained through this method:

```
public ServletOutputStream getOutputStream()
```

While the `OutputStream` can be used for text data, its primary purpose is to send binary data to the response. However, that topic is beyond the scope of this chapter. Briefly, the servlet would get binary data (an image, for example) and store it in a byte array, then set the content type (`"image/jpeg"`, perhaps), set the content length, and then write the binary data to the output stream.

The three methods above are defined by the `ServletResponse` interface. The `HttpServletResponse` interface adds methods that are useful for responding to HTTP requests. These methods allow the servlet to add or set header data in the response:

```
void addDateHeader(String name, long date)
void addHeader(String name, String value)
void addIntHeader(String name, int value)
void setDateHeader(String name, long date)
void setHeader(String name, String value)
void setIntHeader(String name, int value)
```

Deployment Descriptors

Throughout the last couple of chapters, we've seen several examples of deployment descriptors for our web applications contained in a file called `web.xml`. However, we've postponed a full coverage of deployment descriptors until now, because many of the elements involved relate to servlets rather than JSP pages. So, now you know what a servlet is, we can take a deeper look at the deployment descriptor.

As well as the application-specific deployment descriptors that we've been using so far, Tomcat also has a default `web.xml` file used for applications that do not provide their own deployment descriptor. This file is located in the Tomcat /conf directory. Note that the servlet specification only requires an application `web.xml`. Servlet containers other than Tomcat may or may not support a global `web.xml` file; you should consult the documentation for your servlet container or server to see if it has such a feature.

Your servlet container probably has a tool that automates the process of creating the deployment descriptor. For example, the Deployment Tool that comes with J2EE can automatically create the deployment descriptor for a web application. In this section we will look at some of the more important elements of the deployment descriptor. This will be useful if you need to understand a deployment descriptor, or if you need to manually create one.

Because the deployment descriptor is contained in an XML file, it must conform to the XML standard. This means it should start with the XML declaration (`<?xml version="1.0"?>`) and a DOCTYPE declaration, as shown here:

```
<?xml version="1.0" encoding="ISO-8859-1"?>

<!DOCTYPE web-app
    PUBLIC "-//Sun Microsystems, Inc.//DTD Web Application 2.3//EN"
    "http://java.sun.com/dtd/web-app_2_3.dtd">

<web-app>
</web-app>
```

The root element of the deployment descriptor is the `<web-app>` element. The Servlet 2.3 specification defines these sub-elements that can be used within the `<web-app>` element:

Element	Description
icon	Contains a path to icons that can be used by a graphical tool to represent the web application
display-name	A name that can be used by an application management tool to represent the web application
description	A description of the web application
distributable	Describes whether the web application can be distributed across servers; the default value is `false`
context-param	Contains parameter values that are used across the application
filter	Defines filter classes that are called prior to the servlet
filter-mapping	Defines aliases for filters
listener	Defines listener classes that are called by the container when certain events occur
servlet	Defines a servlet by name and class file
servlet-mapping	Defines aliases for servlets
session-config	Defines a timeout value for sessions
mime-mapping	Defines a mapping for the public files of the web application to mime types
welcome-file-list	Defines the file to return to the client when no resource is specified in the URL
error-page	Defines the error page returned to the client when a particular error occurs
taglib	Defines the location of tag libraries
resource-env-ref	Configures an external resource that can be used by the servlet
resource-ref	Configures an external resource that can be used by the servlet
security-constraint	Describes the roles or users that can access the web application
login-config	Configures the authentication method
security-role	Defines a security role for the application
env-entry	Defines the name of a resource that be accessed through the JNDI interface
ejb-ref	Defines a remote reference to an Enterprise JavaBean (EJB)
ejb-local-ref	Defines a local reference to an EJB

Note that the servlet container will expect the elements above to be given in the same order as defined in the DTD (for version 2.3 or earlier of the Servlet specification) or the XML Schema (Servlet 2.4). That order is the same as shown in the table above. Let's take a brief look at some of those elements. I will not cover all the elements, or all the options for each element, but rather enough to get you going. We'll look at a couple of these later on in the chapter: in the *Filters* section we will look at `<filter>` and `<filter-mapping>`, and in the *Handling Exceptions* section, we will look at `<error-page>`.

The `<context-param>` Element

The `<context-param>` element allows you to define context parameters. These parameters specify values that are available to the entire web application context. The element is used like this:

```
<web-app>
  <context-param>
    <param-name>debug</param-name>
    <param-value>true</param-value>
  </context-param>
</web-app>
```

The deployment descriptor can contain zero or more of these elements. Each web component that has access to the servlet context can access these parameters by name. I will show how this is done later in the chapter. Notice that because the `web.xml` file is in text format, you can only pass parameters to the application as strings.

The `<servlet>` Element

The `<servlet>` element is the primary element for describing the servlets in your web application. The `<servlet>` element can have the following sub-elements:

❑   `<icon>`

❑   `<servlet-name>`

❑   `<display-name>`

❑   `<description>`

❑   `<servlet-class>`

❑   `<jsp-file>`

❑   `<init-param>`

❑   `<load-on-startup>`

❑   `<run-as>`

❑   `<security-role-ref>`

The only required sub-elements are `<servlet-name>` and one of the sub-elements `<servlet-class>` or `<jsp-file>`. The `<servlet-name>` sub-element defines a user-friendly name that can be used for the resource. The `<servlet-class>` or `<jsp-file>` sub-elements define the fully qualified name of the servlet class or JSP file. In the previous example, we used this for the `<servlet>` element:

```
<servlet>
  <servlet-name>Login</servlet-name>
  <servlet-class>web.Login</servlet-class>
</servlet>
```

By defining the servlet name as Login, and using the `<servlet-mapping>` element to map URLs such as /Login to the name Login, we were able to access the servlet using the simple URL /stock/Login. Okay, that's not such a big deal when the servlet-name and class name are both Login; but suppose your class name were com.mycompany.subdivision.MyServletWithAReally ReallyLongName. Then it makes much more sense to be able to access the servlet using SimpleName.

The `<servlet-class>` sub-element told the servlet container that all requests for Login should be handled by the web.Login class.

The other elements of servlet that you will often use are `<load-on-startup>` and `<init-param>`.

```
<load-on-startup>5</load-on-startup>
```

The `<load-on-startup>` element, if used, contains a positive integer value that specifies that the servlet should be loaded when the server is started. The relative order of servlet loading is determined by the value; servlets with lower values are loaded before servlets with higher values; servlets with the same value are loaded in an arbitrary order. If the element is not present, the servlet is loaded when the first request for the servlet is made.

The `<init-param>` element is similar to the `<context-param>` element. The difference is that `<init-param>` defines parameters that are only accessible to the given servlet.

```
<init-param>
  <param-name>jdbc.name</param-name>
  <param-value>jdbc/CloudscapeDB</param-value>
</init-param>
```

The `<servlet-mapping>` Element

This element is used to define mappings from a particular request URI to a given servlet name. For example, in the Login servlet, I defined this mapping:

```
<servlet-mapping>
  <servlet-name>Login</servlet-name>
  <url-pattern>/Login</url-pattern>
</servlet-mapping>
```

This told Tomcat that if it received any URI that matched the pattern /Login, it should pass the request to the servlet with the name Login.

> *There is a standard mapper that you can use in Tomcat for all servlets. This mapping sends all requests that match /servlet/* to a Tomcat-specific servlet named* invoker. *The* invoker *servlet reads the URL and sends the request to the correct application servlet. The mapping is defined in the default* web.xml *file, but is commented out. This means that individual web applications must explicitly decide how to map servlet requests. You can easily make the* invoker *servlet the default for all Tomcat web applications by uncommenting the servlet mapping for* invoker *in the* web.xml *file in the Tomcat* /conf *directory.*

Servlet Lifecycle

In the previous example, we looked at a simple servlet that processed a POST request. This processing encompassed just a small portion of a servlet's lifecycle (although that's the most important portion from the client's point of view). Now, let's look at the complete lifecycle of a servlet.

The servlet specification defines the following four stages of a servlet's lifecycle:

- ❑ Loading and instantiation
- ❑ Initialization
- ❑ Request handling
- ❑ End of life

These four stages are illustrated below, along with the methods that correspond to the change between each stage. It is through these methods that the servlet lifecycle is realized:

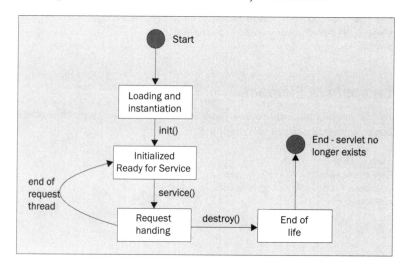

Loading and Instantiation

In this stage of the life cycle, the servlet class is loaded from the classpath and instantiated. The method that realizes this stage is the servlet constructor. However, unlike the other stages, you do not need to explicitly provide the method for this stage. I will show why in a moment.

How does the servlet container know which servlets to load? It knows by reading the deployment descriptors from a well-known location. For example, for Tomcat, that location is the webapps directory. Each subdirectory under webapps is a web application. Within each subdirectory that uses servlets will be a WEB-INF directory that contains a web.xml file. The servlet container reads each web.xml file, and loads the servlet classes identified in the deployment descriptor. Then it instantiates each servlet by calling its no-argument constructor.

Since the servlet container dynamically loads and instantiates servlets, it does not know about any constructors you create that might take parameters. Thus, it can only call the no-argument constructor and it is useless for you to specify any constructor other than one that takes no arguments. Since the Java compiler provides this constructor automatically when you do not supply a constructor, there is no need for you to write any constructor at all in your servlet. This is why your servlet class does not need to define an explicit constructor.

If you do not provide a constructor, how does your servlet initialize itself? This is handled in the next phase of the lifecycle, servlet initialization.

Initialization

After the servlet is loaded and instantiated, the servlet must be initialized. This occurs when the container calls the init(ServletConfig) method. If your servlet does not need to perform any initialization, the servlet does not need to implement this method. The method is provided for you by the GenericServlet class. That is why the Login servlet class earlier in the chapter did not have an init() method. The init() method allows the servlet to read initialization parameters or configuration data, initialize external resources such as database connections, and perform other one-time activities. GenericServlet provides two overloaded forms of the method:

```
public void init() throws ServletException
public void init(ServletConfig) throws ServletException
```

As I mentioned above, the deployment descriptor can define parameters that apply to the servlet through the <init-param> element. The servlet container reads these parameters from the web.xml file and stores them as name-value pairs in a ServletConfig object. Because the Servlet interface only defines init(ServletConfig), this is the method the container must call. GenericServlet implements this method to store the ServletConfig reference, and then call the parameterless init() method that it defines. Therefore, to perform initialization, your servlet only needs to implement the parameterless init() method. If you implement init(), your init() will be called by GenericServlet; and because the ServletConfig reference is already stored, your init() method will have access to all the initialization parameters stored in it.

If you do decide to implement init(ServletConfig) in your servlet, the method in your servlet must call the superclass init(ServletConfig) method:

```
public class LoginTUS extends HttpServlet {

    public void init(ServletConfig config) throws ServletException {
        super.init(config);

      // ...Remainder of init() method
    }

    //...Rest of servlet
}
```

> If you implement init(ServletConfig) without calling
> super.init(ServletConfig), the ServletConfig object won't be saved, and
> neither your servlet nor its parent classes will be able to access the
> ServletConfig object during the remainder of the servlet lifecycle.

The servlet specification requires that init(ServletConfig) successfully complete before any requests can be serviced by the servlet. If your code encounters a problem during init(), you should throw a ServletException, or its subclass UnavailableException. This tells the container that there was a problem with initialization and that it should not use the servlet for any requests. Using UnavailableException allows you to specify an amount of time that the servlet is unavailable. After this time, the container could retry the call to init(). You can specify the unavailable time for the UnavailableException using this constructor:

```
public UnavailableException(String msg, int seconds)
```

The int parameter can be any integer: negative, zero, or positive. A non-positive value indicates that the servlet cannot determine when it will be available again. For example, this could occur if the servlet determines that an outside resource is not available; obviously, the servlet cannot estimate when the outside resource will be available. A positive value indicates that the server should try to initialize the servlet again after that number of seconds.

How the container handles the ServletException is container-dependent. Tomcat, for example, will return an HTTP 500 error to the client if init() throws a ServletException when it is called as a result of a client request. Subsequent client requests will receive an HTTP 404 (resource unavailable) error.

After the servlet successfully initializes, the container is allowed to use the servlet to handles requests.

Request Handling

As we saw in the chapter, the primary method defined for servicing requests during this phase of the servlet lifecycle is the `service()` method. As each request comes to the servlet container, the container calls the `service()` method to handle the request. Since you will almost always be subclassing `HttpServlet`, however, your servlet only needs to override `doPost()` and/or `doGet()` to handle requests. Here are the signatures of those two methods:

```
protected void doGet(HttpServletRequest req, HttpServletResponse res)
    throws ServletException, IOException
protected void doPost(HttpServletRequest req, HttpServletResponse res)
    throws ServletException, IOException
```

As with `init()`, the servlet can throw a `ServletException` or `UnavailableException` during the processing of a request. If your servlet throws either exception, then the servlet container is required to stop sending requests to the servlet. For a `ServletException` or for an `UnavailableException` that indicates a permanent unavailability (it was created with no value for seconds unavailable), the servlet container must end the servlet's lifecycle. If the servlet throws an `UnavailableException` with some value for seconds unavailable (see the *Initialization* section above), the servlet specification permits the container to keep or destroy the servlet at its choosing. If it keeps the servlet, it must not route any requests to the servlet until it is again available; if it destroys the servlet, it will presumably create a new servlet instance when the servlet is estimated to be available again.

End of Service

When the servlet container needs to unload the servlet, either because it is being shut down, or for some other reason such as a `ServletException`, the servlet container will call the `destroy()` method. However, prior to calling `destroy()`, the container must allow time for any request threads that are still processing to complete their processing. After they are complete, or after a server-defined timeout period, the container is allowed to call `destroy()`. Note that `destroy()` does not actually destroy the servlet or cause it to be garbage collected. It is simply an opportunity for the servlet to clean up any resources it used or opened. Obviously, after this method is called, the container will not send any more requests to the servlet. The signature of the `destroy()` method is:

```
public void destroy()
```

The `destroy()` method allows the servlet to release or clean up any resources that it uses. For example, it can close database connections or files, flush any streams, or close any sockets. If there is no cleanup that your servlet needs to perform, your servlet does not need to implement this method. After the `destroy()` method completes, the container will release its references to the servlet instance, and the servlet instance will be eligible for garbage collection.

Although this method is public, it is meant only to be called by the servlet container. You should never call the `destroy()` method from within your servlet, and you should not allow other code to call this method.

The Login Servlet

Even though we did not explicitly see it, the Login servlet in the last example followed all the steps of the servlet lifecycle. Since the deployment descriptor did not have a <load-on-startup> element, the servlet was loaded when the first request for the Login servlet was made. After the class was loaded, the init() method was called. Since the Login.class did not have an init() method, this call was handled by the GenericServlet class, the parent class of HttpServlet. After initialization completed successfully, the request was sent to the service() method of HttpServlet, which called the doPost() method of Login. When and if you stop the server, the destroy() method is called, again to be handled by GenericServlet.

Event Logging in Servlets

In addition to the methods of GenericServlet that were presented earlier, you will find two other methods useful:

```
public void log(String)
public void log(String, Throwable)
```

Although you can use the poor man's debug tool (System.out.println()) with servlets, GenericServlet provides two log() methods. Rather than sending their output to System.out, these methods write the log information to the servlet's log. This provides a more convenient and permanent logging mechanism than System.out.println(). We will use these methods in the next example, and the remainder of the examples in this chapter.

Servlets Are Multi-Threaded

This statement may seem obvious—or maybe it doesn't. It's obvious because all Java classes are inherently multi-threaded. That is, whether you use them as such or not, they have the potential to have multiple threads executing their methods. (Unless, of course, a method is marked as synchronized.) On the other hand, it's not obvious because most of the time, you don't think about multi-threading when you are writing your Java classes. Think about your first "Hello, World!" class (or whatever you wrote as your first Java class). You probably wrote it with a single static main() method, in which all the processing occurred. When you ran the class, the JVM created a single thread of execution, and this thread executed the main() method. Even today, unless you are writing GUI applications with Swing or AWT or web applications, most of the classes you write are usually executed by only a single thread.

With servlets, you need to change that mindset. Since servlets are firmly in the web world of HTTP protocol, where concurrent requests are the norm and not the exception, you need to plan for multiple concurrent requests being sent to your servlet.

Try It Out A Thread-Unsafe Servlet

In this example, we will see how a servlet that is not thread-safe can cause problems for a web application. This application will be very similar to the previous example; the difference between the two is that we will use a different servlet class for this example.

1. With some simple changes to the Login servlet, we can easily demonstrate the danger of not making your servlet thread-safe. Create this new class, LoginTUS (for Thread-UnSafe), based on the previous Login class:

```java
package web;

import javax.servlet.*;
import javax.servlet.http.*;
import java.io.*;

public class LoginTUS extends HttpServlet {
  private String username;
  private String password;

  public void init(ServletConfig config) throws ServletException {
    super.init(config);
  }

  public void doPost(HttpServletRequest request,
                     HttpServletResponse response)
  {
    String username = request.getParameter("username");
    String password = request.getParameter("password");

    this.username = username;
    this.password = password;

    try {
      String sleeptime = getInitParameter("sleep.time");
      int sleep = Integer.parseInt(sleeptime);
      Thread.sleep(sleep);
    }catch(Exception e){
      log("", e);
    }

    try {
      response.setContentType("text/html");
      PrintWriter writer = response.getWriter();
      writer.println("<html><body>");
      writer.println("<p>METHOD LOCAL");
      writer.println("<br>username=" + username);
      writer.println("<br>password=" + password);
      writer.println("<p>SERVLET MEMBER VARIABLES");
      writer.println("<br>username=" + this.username);
      writer.println("<br>password=" + this.password);
      writer.println("</body></html>");
      writer.close();
    } catch (Exception e) {
      e.printStackTrace();
    }
  }
}
```

2. Compile this class.

3. If you used the J2EE Deployment Tool and the J2EE server, use the same steps as in the original Login example to create and deploy the stock web application. Create this new web application by removing the Login.class from the web application created in the previous example and replacing it with LoginTUS.class; alternately, you can create an entirely new web application using LoginTUS.class and login.html. Use the same alias (/Login) for the servlet, and don't forget to set the context root. Add an initialization parameter to the servlet through the Init.Parameters tab of the servlet window. The parameter's name is sleep.time and the value is 10000:

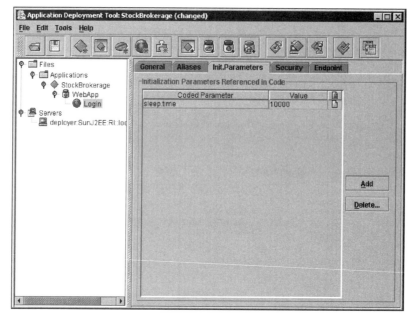

4. If you used a Tomcat stand-alone, you need to add the class file to the web application that was created in the earlier example. If you created the /Ch05 context directly in webapps, simply copy the new servlet class to that directory. If you created a WAR package and copied it to webapps, you will need to delete the /Ch05 context in /webapps and add the new class file to the WAR.

5. For Tomcat, edit the web.xml deployment descriptor as shown here:

```
<?xml version="1.0" encoding="ISO-8859-1"?>

<!DOCTYPE web-app
    PUBLIC "-//Sun Microsystems, Inc.//DTD Web Application 2.3//EN"
    "http://java.sun.com/dtd/web-app_2_3.dtd">

<web-app>
  <display-name>Beginning J2EE Ch 5 Thread-UnSafe Login</display-name>
  <servlet>
    <servlet-name>Login</servlet-name>
```

```
      <servlet-class>web.LoginTUS</servlet-class>
      <init-param>
         <param-name>sleep.time</param-name>
         <param-value>10000</param-value>
      </init-param>
   </servlet>
   <servlet-mapping>
      <servlet-name>Login</servlet-name>
      <url-pattern>/Login</url-pattern>
   </servlet-mapping>
</web-app>
```

6. Add this deployment descriptor to the /Ch05 context or to the WAR.

7. If you are using Tomcat, stop the server if it is running, and then restart it. If you are using J2EE, that server should already be running.

8. Open two browser windows. Load the login.html page into each browser. Enter usernames and passwords into both windows, but do not click Submit.

9. After entering data into both web pages, click the Submit button in one browser; wait approximately four to five seconds and then click the Submit button in the other browser. This screenshot shows the two browser windows on my system prior to clicking the Submit button:

10. Here is my output. Looks like there's a problem: some data from Anne's request is mixed up with the response to Kevin's request:

How It Works

In this servlet, I've created a situation that allows multiple concurrent request threads to interfere with each other. This was done by using member variables in the servlet class. Member variables, also known as instance variables, are inherently not thread safe. Each thread that enters a Java class has access to the same instance variables. Our servlet has two instance variables, `username` and `password`:

```
public class LoginTUS extends HttpServlet {
    private String username;
    private String password;
```

The `LoginTUS` class defines two instance variables, `username` and `password`. The `doPost()` method also defines two local variables with the same names. When a thread is inside `doPost()`, the local variables hide the instance variables of the same name if you use the simple names `username` and `password`. You can access the member variables by using the `this` keyword: `this.username` or `this.password`.

```
public void doPost(HttpServletRequest request,
                 .          HttpServletResponse response)
{
    // These variables are local to the method. Because they have the same
    // name as the instance variables, they hide the instance variables
    // inside the method
    String username = request.getParameter("username");
    String password = request.getParameter("password");

    // Here we use the keyword this. By using this we can access the instance
    // variable of the class. These lines assign the value of the local
    // variables to the instance variables.
    this.username = username;
    this.password = password;
```

Inside doPost(), the code reads the username and password parameters from the request and assigns the strings to both the member variables and the local variables. It then sleeps by calling the Thread.sleep() method.

To determine how long to sleep for, the servlet reads an init parameter by calling the getInitParameter(String) method. The init parameter is set through the deployment descriptor:

```
<servlet>
  <servlet-name>Login</servlet-name>
  <servlet-class>web.LoginTUS</servlet-class>
  <init-param>
     <param-name>sleep.time</param-name>
     <param-value>10000</param-value>
  </init-param>
</servlet>
```

You can define any number of init parameters for a servlet using one or more <init-param> elements. The <param-name> is the name that the servlet will use in the getInitParameter(String) method. The <param-value> element is the value for the init parameter. Each init parameter is servlet-specific; this means that no servlet can access the init parameters defined for anther servlet. Notice that parameter values can only be passed as Strings to the servlet. So, if you need to pass a number to the servlet, the servlet will have to convert the string to a numeric type:

```
String sleeptime = getInitParameter("sleep.time");
int sleep = Integer.parseInt(sleeptime);
```

By sleeping, the two requests that you generate, one from each browser window, have a chance to interact with each other. The first request sets the instance variables to a certain value. The second request then changes the same instance variables. The first request sees those changes because it shares the instance variables with every other request thread.

Now this example was pretty simple. We simply read some strings from the request and changed some String variables. Imagine what would happen, however, if you used member variables for a more important resource. One problem I've seen is servlet developers who use a member variable to hold a database connection. Concurrent requests end up writing data with the same connection and the database gets corrupted with bad data. That is why it is so important not to use instance variables for request-specific data.

How to Make Your Servlets Thread-Safe

In the example above, I showed one way to make servlets thread-unsafe: I used a member variable for data that was specific to a request. What you need to know, however, is how to make your servlet thread-safe. Here is the list of techniques that I use:

❑ Use method variables for request-specific data. Whenever you need to access data from a request, that data should be stored in method variables, also known as local variables. These are variables defined within the scope of a method. Each thread that enters a method gets its own copy of the method variables. Thus, no thread can change the member variables of any other thread.

❑ As far as possible, use the member variables of the servlet only for data that does not change. (However, there are exceptions: see the next two bullets.) Usually you would use member variables for data that is initialized at startup, and does not change for the life of the servlet. This might be data such as lookup names for resources such as database connections (see the *Data Source* section of the JDBC chapter), paths to other resources, or paths to other web components, etc. In the example, I could have made the sleep time a member variable, because this value will not change during the lifetime of the servlet.

❑ Protect access to member variables that may be changed by a request. Occasionally, you may need to use a member variable for data that could be changed by a request. Or, you may have a context attribute that can be changed by a request. For example, I once worked on a web application that allowed an administrator to pause the application via a servlet request. Information about how the application was paused needed to persist across requests. So I saved the data in objects that were instance variable of the servlet. Since I didn't want two administrators trying to pause or unpause the application at the same time, I synchronized access to the objects; thus, while one administrator was pausing or unpausing the application, no other request could use those objects, and therefore could not pause or unpause the application at the same time. When you are using member variables or context attributes that can be changed by a request, you need to synchronize access to that data so that different threads aren't changing the data simultaneously.

❑ If your servlet accesses outside resources, consider protecting access to that resource. For example, suppose you decide to have your servlet read and write data to a file in the file system. One request thread could be reading or writing to that file while some other request thread is writing or reading the file. File access is not inherently thread-safe, so you must include code that manages synchronized access to this resource.

How Not to Make Your Servlets Thread-Safe

In addition to the above list, you may see two other suggestions for making your servlet thread-safe, which we'll look at next. However, do *not* follow them. They will either not solve your problem, or will be too unpractical for a real-world application.

1. Use `SingleThreadModel`

This is a common, but incorrect, solution attempted by servlet developers. `SingleThreadModel` is a marker interface. You use it like this:

```
public class MyServlet implements SingleThreadModel
```

Marker interfaces, such as `Serializable`, have no methods to implement. What `SingleThreadModel` does is signal to the servlet container that only a single thread should be allowed in the class at a time. There are various ways for the servlet container to do this. The usual way to do this is to create a pool of servlet instances. The servlet specification allows the servlet container to create multiple instances of any servlet that implements `SingleThreadModel`.

As each request comes to the container, an instance of the servlet from the pool is used to satisfy the request. While any request thread is executing in a servlet instance, no other thread is allowed to execute in the same instance.

However, this does not guarantee that your servlet is thread-safe. Remember that static member variables are shared by all instances of a servlet; moreover, external resources, such as files, may be accessed concurrently by request threads. If your servlet uses static member variables, uses outside resources, or uses context attributes, using `SingleThreadModel` does not make your servlet thread-safe. You would still need to synchronize access to these resources.

An even more important reason not to use `SingleThreadModel` is because it is not scaleable. There is a limit to the number of servlet instances that can be created. All those instances need to be managed. The larger the number of concurrent requests, the more unusable this solution becomes. It is always easier to create new threads rather than to create new objects. Again, I don't recommend it, but if you must use `SingleThreadModel`, you should only use it where the number of concurrent requests is relatively small (but remember, you still need to make the servlet thread-safe).

2. Synchronize `service()`, `doPost()`, or `doGet()`

This attempt at making the servlet thread-safe is even worse than attempting to use `SingleThreadModel`. If you override `service()` and make it synchronized at the same time, you have limited your servlet to handling only a single request at a time (remember that the specification allows only a single instance of servlet per JVM for non-`SingleThreadModel` servlets). That may be fine while you are reading this book, and you are the only client of the servlets you write, but as soon as you move to any real-world application this will become totally unworkable. As the number of requests increases, your clients are more and more likely to spend their time watching the little progress icon go around and around. As you probably know, it won't take much of that for users to abandon your web site.

Synchronizing `doPost()` and `doGet()` is just as bad. Since the `service()` method of `HttpServlet` almost always calls `doPost()` or `doGet()`, synchronizing `doPost()` and `doGet()` has the same effect as if you had synchronized `service()`.

Of course, as I mentioned in the previous section, you must sometimes synchronize access to resources used by your servlet. If you must synchronize code within your servlet, you should attempt to synchronize the smallest block of code possible. The less code that is synchronized, the better your servlet will execute.

Handling Exceptions

This chapter has tried to concentrate on how to use the various features of the Servlet API, so exception handling has consisted simply of logging the exception stack trace. In a real-world application, though, you will need to be more vigilant in the way you handle exceptions.

Poor Exception Handling

Look at this code for a very simple servlet:

```java
package web;

import java.io.*;
import javax.servlet.http.*;

public class BadServlet extends HttpServlet {
  public void doPost(HttpServletRequest req, HttpServletResponse res)
    throws IOException
  {
    res.setContentType("text/html");
    PrintWriter writer = res.getWriter();

    writer.println("<html><body>");
    String num = req.getParameter("number");
    Integer i = new Integer(num);
    writer.println("You entered the number " + i.intValue());
    writer.println("</body></html>");
    writer.close();
  }
}
```

Can you see the problem in the code above? Try creating an HTML form that includes a field named number, and which calls the servlet. Deploy the application and test various values.

What happened when you entered anything other than a non-numeric value? If a non-numeric value is entered, the Integer constructor throws an exception. What happens on the client side depends on the exception and the server. Sometimes the user might get an ugly (from the user's point of view) stack trace; other times the user might get no response from the server. To the client, it appears as though your application is broken (which it is). You probably should have checked the request parameters to ensure they were valid.

This brings up the question: where should data validation be done, the client side or the server side? The answer to this question depends in part on the requirements of your application. However, you will probably need to do data validation on both sides. You need to validate some data on the client side so that errors can be corrected prior to making the HTTP request. You need to validate data on the server side in case the user bypasses client-side validation.

Your servlet also needs to attempt to provide error handling for every error that could occur. Let's look at a common attempt at error handling and why it is not the best solution. Suppose we take the example above and add a `try...catch` block:

```
try {
    res.setContentType("text/html");
    PrintWriter writer = res.getWriter();

    writer.println("<html><body>");
    String num = req.getParameter("number");
    Integer i = new Integer(num);
    writer.println("You entered the number " + i.intValue());
    writer.println("</body></html>");
    writer.close();
} catch (Exception e) {
    log("", e);
}
```

Looks OK, right? No, there is still a problem. What happens when the `Integer` constructor throws an exception? No output is sent back to the client, because the exception causes the thread of execution to immediately jump to the `catch` block. The client gets to stare at a blank screen.

Unless the exception is an `IOException` thrown while writing the response, you should always attempt to return some kind of response to the client. That could mean putting `try...catch` blocks around the code that you anticipate could throw exceptions, or adding output statements that would be called from the `catch` block to send a response back to the client.

Error Pages

One other way to make your application more robust is to define error pages for your application. For example, given the `BadServlet` above, we might create a web page or JSP that tells the user that they must enter digits only. Then we can specify that the application serve this page whenever a `NumberFormatException` occurs. This is done with the `<error-page>` element of the deployment descriptor:

```
<web-app>
    <!- This is the deployment descriptor for the BadServlet example ->

    <servlet>
        <servlet-name>BadServlet</servlet-name>
        <servlet-class>web.BadServlet</servlet-class>
    </servlet>
    <servlet-mapping>
        <servlet-name>BadServlet</servlet-name>
        <url-pattern>/BadServlet</url-pattern>
    </servlet-mapping>

    <error-page>
        <exception-type>java.lang.NumberFormatException</exception-type>
        <location>/BadNumber.html</location>
    </error-page>
</web-app>
```

Using this deployment descriptor, the BadNumber.html page will be sent to the client whenever the servlet container catches a NumberFormatException. You can also specify error pages for HTTP error codes. The <error-page> element in the deployment descriptor looks like this:

```
<error-page>
    <error-code>404</error-code>
    <location>/NoSuchPage.html</location>
</error-page>
```

When a user attempts to access a page or resource that does not exist, the server generates a 404 error. Because the deployment descriptor says to send the NoSuchPage.html page whenever a 404 error occurs, this is what will be sent to the client. You can find the complete list of error codes at http://www.w3c.org/Protocols/HTTP/HTTPRESP.html.

The one error page you should specify for every application is for error code 500. An error code of 500 indicates an error in the server that the server was unable to deal with. This could be anything from a JSP page that can't be compiled to an uncaught exception in a servlet. By specifying a page to be sent to the client for a 500 error, you can be sure that if an error of this type occurs, the client will get a nicely formatted error page, rather than an ugly stack trace.

Session Management

There's one big challenge with relying on HTTP for web applications. HTTP is a stateless protocol. Each request and response stand alone. Without session management, each time a client makes a request to a server, it's a brand new user with a brand new request from the server's point of view.

To deal with that issue, web applications use the concept of a session. A session refers to the entire interaction between a client and a server from the time of the client's first request, which generally begins the session, to the time the session is terminated. The session could be terminated by the client's request, or the server could automatically close it after a certain period of time. A session can last for just a few minutes, or it could last days or weeks or months (if the application were willing to let a session last that long).

The Servlet API provides classes and methods for creating and managing session. In this section, we'll look in detail at session creation and management.

Creating and Using Sessions

Two methods of the HttpServletRequest object are used to create a session. They are:

```
HttpSession getSession();
HttpSession getSession(boolean);
```

If a session already exists, then getSession(), getSession(true), and getSession(false) will all return the existing session. If a session does not exist, then getSession() and getSession(true) will cause one to be created; getSession(false) will return null. Note that you must call one of these methods before writing any data to the response. This is because the default technique for session tracking is to use cookies. Cookies are sent in the header part of an HTTP message, so they must be set in the response prior to writing any data to the response.

In addition, HttpServletRequest provides a few other methods for dealing with sessions:

Method	Description
String getRequestedSessionId()	Gets the ID assigned by the server to the session
Boolean isRequestedSessionIdValid()	Returns true if the request contains a valid session ID
Boolean isRequestedSessionIdFromCookie()	Returns true if the session ID was sent as part of a cookie
Boolean isRequestedSessionIdFromURL()	Returns true if the session ID was sent through URL rewriting (we'll look at URL rewriting very shortly)

Session Tracking with Cookies

All the data for the session, and all the data stored with the session, is maintained on the server. The server therefore needs some way to associate a client's request with a session on the server. The primary technique for doing this is to use cookies. When the server creates a session, it sends a session ID to the client in the form of a cookie. When the client makes another request and sends the cookie with the session ID, the server can select the correct session for the client based on the session ID.

When the client is accepting cookies, there is nothing your servlet needs to do as far as session tracking is concerned. The servlet container and the server handle all the session tracking for you.

Session Tracking with URL Rewriting

Some users don't like cookies. If you are working with a public web application, you can accept as fact that some users of your application will not accept the cookies sent to them by the server. When that occurs, the server resorts to another technique to track a user's session: URL rewriting. With this technique, the server appends the session ID to the URLs of the pages it serves.

When that occurs, the servlet does need to do something. In this case, the URLs embedded within the HTML pages of the application need to be modified for each client by rewriting the URL. This can be done with these methods of the HttpServletResponse:

```
encodeURL(String)
encodeRedirectURL(String)
```

These methods will rewrite the URL given by the `String` argument when the client is not accepting cookies. If the client does accept cookies, then the URLs are returned unchanged. You use `encodeRedirectURL()` for URLs that will be used with the `sendRedirect()` method of `HttpServletResponse`. Use `encodeURL()` for all other URLs.

What Can You Do with a Session?

All kinds of stuff, it turns out. Primarily, though, sessions are useful for persisting information about a client and a client's interactions with an application. To do that, the `HttpSession` interface defines a number of methods.

The methods you will probably use most often are methods for setting and getting attributes from the session. You would store information in the session using the `setAttribute(String, Object)` method. Since the session is common to the entire application, this data then becomes available to every component in the application (and you therefore need to consider synchronizing access to the session and session data). The stored data is retrieved with the `getAttribute(String)` method.

```
public Object getAttribute(String name)
public Enumeration getAttributeNames()
public void setAttribute(String name, Object value)
public void removeAttribute(String name)
```

You can store anything at all in the session. You could store text information about the user or the user's preferences. If you were working on an e-commerce application, you could store the user's shopping cart in the session.

The next set of methods deal with session creation and lifecycle:

```
public long getCreationTime()
public String getId()
public long getLastAccessedTime()
public boolean isNew()
public void setMaxInactiveInterval(int interval)
public int getMaxInactiveInterval()
public void invalidate()
```

The `isNew()` method returns `true` when the client has refused the session (usually by rejecting the cookie with the session ID), or when the session ID has not been sent to the client yet. The `setMaxInactiveInterval(int)` method is used to tell the servlet container how long a session can be inactive before it is invalidated. When that time limit is reached without activity, the session is invalidated. Using a negative value for the argument tells the container never to expire a session. A session is considered active when a client makes a request and sends the session ID with the request. Finally, the servlet can actively expire the session by calling the `invalidate()` method.

Lastly, there is a method that returns the `ServletContext` for the session:

```
public ServletContext getServletContext()
```

Session Management with Cookies

Using the `session` object provided through the Servlet API is the preferred method for using and managing sessions. However, there is another method for session management that can be used in conjunction with, or in place of, `session` objects. That method is to use cookies for session management.

Cookies are strings of text that a server can send to a client. The client can either accept and store the cookie, or reject the cookie. Cookies should contain information relevant to the client. When the client makes a request to a given server, it sends the cookies it has from the server back with the request.

The `session` object has two advantages over cookies. First, as I mentioned earlier, clients can reject cookies sent by a server; `session` objects live on the server, and can always be created, either by setting the session ID in a cookie, or through URL rewriting. Second, cookies can only store text data, so you are limited to storing text information, or information that can be represented by text. Using a `session` object, you can store any Java object in a session. For these reasons, you should always use the Session API for session management.

However, there is one place where cookies make sense. Have you ever registered at a web site, and then the next time you went back to the site, the site logged you in automatically? This was probably accomplished by sending a cookie to your browser. The cookie contained an ID that the server could use to identify you. When your browser sends the request, it sends the cookie, and the server is able to identify you, retrieve your personalization information from some persistent store, and preload a `session` object with your data before your browser has actually joined the session.

Let's look briefly at how a cookie might be used to do this. Using the `Cookie` object in the Servlet API is straightforward. Cookie data comes in name-value pairs, so the `Cookie` constructor takes a name and a value:

```
Cookie(String name, String value)
```

You could then set a number of properties of the cookie. The two that you are most likely to use are:

```
public void setMaxAge(int expiry)
public void setValue(String newValue)
```

The `setMaxAge(int)` method specifies how long, in seconds, the cookie should be kept by the client. If you do not set a maximum age, the cookie is discarded when the client exits the browser. The `setValue(String)` method allows you to change the value held by the cookie.

After creating a cookie, you can add it to the response using the `addCookie()` method of the `HttpServletResponse` class:

```
void addCookie(Cookie cookie)
```

Cookies are added to the header of the response message, so the servlet must call the `addCookie()` method before any message body data is written to the response.

When a client sends a request to the servlet, the servlet can access the cookies using the HttpServletRequest's getCookies() method:

```
Cookie[] getCookies()
```

This returns an array containing Cookie objects for all the cookies sent by the client. Note that the client only sends the name-value pairs of the cookies, and not any other information such as maximum age. The servlet can access the names and values of each Cookie using the Cookie methods getName() and getValue(String name).

Finally, even though we have discussed the Cookie object and its methods in terms of session management, cookies can be used to send any text data to the client browser, regardless of whether it is used for session management or not.

Try It Out Maintaining State with the session Object

In the first servlet example in this chapter, we created a simple Login servlet. That Login servlet did not really validate the user credentials, did not use a secure connection for receiving the username and password, and did not store the Login information. In a real application, all those things would probably be done. We still won't perform a real validation, but we can show how to store login credentials in a session.

1. Modify the Login servlet from the beginning of the chapter:

```
package web;

import javax.servlet.http.*;
import java.io.*;

public class LoginSES extends HttpServlet {
  public void doPost(HttpServletRequest request,
                     HttpServletResponse response)
  {
    String username = request.getParameter("username");
    String password = request.getParameter("password");

    HttpSession session = request.getSession(true);
    session.setAttribute("username", username);
    session.setAttribute("password", password);

    try {
      response.setContentType("text/html");
      PrintWriter writer = response.getWriter();
      writer.println("<html><body>");
      writer.println("Thank you, " + username +
                     ". You are now logged into the system");
      String newURL = response.encodeURL("/Ch05/GetSession");
      writer.println("Click <a href=\"" + newURL +
                     "\">here</a> for another servlet");
      writer.println("</body></html>");
```

```
            writer.close();
        } catch (Exception e) {
            e.printStackTrace();
        }
    }
}
```

2. Create a new servlet that will check for the session:

```
package web;

import javax.servlet.http.*;
import java.io.*;
import java.util.*;
public class GetSession extends HttpServlet {
    public void doGet(HttpServletRequest request,
                        HttpServletResponse response)
    {
        HttpSession session = request.getSession(false);
        try {
            response.setContentType("text/html");
            PrintWriter writer = response.getWriter();
            writer.println("<html><body>");

            if (session == null) {
                writer.println("You are not logged in");
            } else {
                writer.println("Thank you, you are already logged in");
                writer.println("Here is the data in your session");
                Enumeration names = session.getAttributeNames();
                while (names.hasMoreElements()) {
                    String name = (String) names.nextElement();
                    Object value = session.getAttribute(name);
                    writer.println("<p>name=" + name + " value=" + value);
                }
            }
            writer.println("<a href=\"/Ch05/login.html\">Return" +
                            "</a> to login page");
            writer.println("</body></html>");
            writer.close();
        } catch (Exception e) {
            e.printStackTrace();
        }
    }
}
```

3. Compile these servlets.

4. Here is the deployment descriptor for Tomcat:

```
<?xml version="1.0" encoding="ISO-8859-1"?>

<!DOCTYPE web-app
    PUBLIC "-//Sun Microsystems, Inc.//DTD Web Application 2.3//EN"
    "http://java.sun.com/dtd/web-app_2_3.dtd">

<web-app>
  <display-name>Beginning J2EE Ch 5</display-name>
  <servlet>
    <servlet-name>Login</servlet-name>
    <servlet-class>web.LoginSES</servlet-class>
  </servlet>
  <servlet>
    <servlet-name>GetSession</servlet-name>
    <servlet-class>web.GetSession</servlet-class>
  </servlet>
  <servlet-mapping>
    <servlet-name>Login</servlet-name>
    <url-pattern>/Login</url-pattern>
  </servlet-mapping>
  <servlet-mapping>
    <servlet-name>GetSession</servlet-name>
    <url-pattern>/GetSession</url-pattern>
  </servlet-mapping>
</web-app>
```

5. If you are using Deployment Tool and J2EE, ensure that both the servlets have aliases as shown in the deployment descriptor above. Through the New Web Application WAR wizard (File | New | WebApplication WAR) create components for both servlets. Make sure that you add both servlet .class files to the first WAR module, and for the second component, select Add to Existing WAR Module on the second screen, instead of creating a new WAR module. Select each component in the left pane, and select the Aliases tab in the right pane to set the alias.

6. Create and deploy the application using the two servlets and the login.html page that was created earlier in the chapter. You can either create a new EAR with a new application context, or modify the earlier application. You may need to edit both servlets and the HTML page so that they use the correct application context.

7. Open a browser and ensure that it is accepting cookies. Enter the URL http://localhost:port/Ch05/GetSession (assuming that you set the context root to Ch05). Use the correct value (1024 or 8080) for port. Because you do not have a session yet, this servlet should respond with a page that tells you to go to the login.html page.

8. On the login page, enter a username and password and click Submit. The next page prints a short message that includes a link to the GetSession servlet. If you examine the link, you will see that it has the session ID embedded in it. Click the link.

9. On the next page, the `GetSession` servlet printed out the value of the attributes in your session. If you look at the address bar, you will see a URL with the session ID. Click the link to return to the login page:

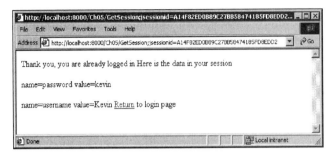

10. Enter a username and password and click Submit again. This time, the link on the welcome page does not include the session ID. If you click the link, the URL for the page generated by `GetSession` does not have the session ID either:

How It Works

Our new version of the login servlet starts by trying to access any existing session by calling the `request.getSession()` method. Since we pass in `true` as the parameter, a new session will be created if one doesn't already exist. Once we've got the session, we store the username and password in it that the user entered in `login.html`:

```
HttpSession session = request.getSession(true);
session.setAttribute("username", username);
session.setAttribute("password", password);
```

A client does not have a session until the server creates a session for the client, the server has sent the session ID to the client, *and* the client has returned the session ID in a cookie or URL. Because the `LoginSES` servlet is the first web component to create the session, the session has not been joined when `LoginSES` generates the page that has the link for the `GetSession` servlet. The `LoginSES` servlet calls `encodeURL()` for the link, and since the client has not joined the session, the URL is rewritten to append the session ID:

```
String newURL = response.encodeURL("/Ch05/GetSession");
writer.println("Click <a href=\"" + newURL +
                "\">here</a> for another servlet");
```

This is the session ID that appears in the browser address window for the page generated by GetSession servlet. When you click the link that sends the request to GetSession, you have finally joined the session.

When you link back to the login.html page again, you have joined the session, and the server knows that the browser accepts cookies. That is why the second time you log in, the server does not rewrite the URL.

Filters

So, you've finished writing the Login servlet for your application, and it's working great. When users submit their credentials, your code checks them against the user information stored by the application. The servlet creates a session for the user, so that other components in the application know that the user has logged in properly. Everything's great.

Until the customer comes to you and asks you to log each login attempt to the file system. So you edit the servlet code and redeploy it. Then the customer asks you to log the attempt to a database table. Edit the code and redeploy. Then the customer...

Pretty soon your servlet is filled with lots of code that's useful but is outside the scope of the core job of a servlet: receiving and responding to requests. There's got to be an easier way.

Why You Need Filters

Filters are a way to provide a plug-in capability to your web application. Using filters you can encapsulate different behaviors needed to help process a request. Filters also make it easy to change the functionality of a web application with just a change to the deployment descriptor.

The Javadoc for Filter suggests a number of situations in which you might use filters. Some of these include:

❑ Authentication filters

❑ Logging and auditing filters

❑ Data compression filters

❑ Encryption filters

The primary job of a servlet is to accept requests and provide responses to clients. Anything outside that scope is the candidate for other classes. So, whether you need the functionality suggested by the list in the Javadoc, or you have some other functionality your application needs to provide, filters provide an excellent way to encapsulate functionality. Further, by encapsulating that functionality in a filter, the same filter can easily be used with several servlets.

Implementing a Filter

To implement a filter for your web application, you need to do two things. The first is to write a class that implements the `Filter` interface; the second is to modify the deployment descriptor to tell the container when to call the filter.

The Filter API

The Filter API consists of three interfaces: `Filter`, `FilterChain`, and `FilterConfig`. `javax.servlet.Filter` is the interface you will use to implement a filter. It has three methods:

Method	Description
`void init(` `    FilterConfig filterConfig)`	Called by the web container to indicate to a filter that it is being placed into service.

`void doFilter(`
`    ServletRequest request,`
`    ServletResponse response,`
`    FilterChain chain)`
	The `doFilter()` method is called by the container each time a request/response pair is passed through the chain due to a client request for a resource at the end of the chain.

`void destroy()`	Called by the web container to indicate to a filter that it is being taken out of service.

You can see that this interface is very similar to the `Servlet` interface. Based on this interface, you won't be surprised to learn that a filter lifecycle is very similar to a servlet lifecycle. When the filter is created, the container will call the `init()` method. Inside the `init()` method, you can access init parameters through the `FilterConfig` interface. However, unlike a servlet, if you need to access the `FilterConfig` in the `doFilter()` method, you will need to save the reference yourself. To service requests, the container calls the `doFilter()` method. When the container needs to end the filter lifecycle, it will call the `destroy()` method.

`javax.servlet.FilterConfig` is fairly straightforward and almost identical to `ServletConfig`. If you need to use init parameters or other features of the `FilterConfig`, you can get more details from the Javadoc.

The `javax.servlet.FilterChain` interface represents a chain of filters. It defines a method that each filter can use to call the next filter in the chain:

Method	Description

void doFilter(
    ServletRequest request,
    ServletResponse response)
	Causes the next filter in the chain to be invoked, or if the calling filter is the last filter in the chain, causes the resource at the end of the chain to be invoked.

If you look above at the `Filter` interface, you can see that when a filter's `doFilter()` method is called, one of the arguments passed is a reference to a `FilterChain`. When the filter calls `chain.doFilter()`, the next filter in the chain is called. Filter code before the `chain.doFilter()` method call is executed prior to the servlet processing. Thus, any processing that the filter needs to do to the request should occur prior to the call to `chain.doFilter()`. Code that occurs after the `chain.doFilter()` method returns executes after the servlet, so that code performs processing on the response. If you need to do processing both before and after the servlet, then you put code both before and after the `chain.doFilter()` call. On the other hand, if any of the filters needs to abort processing (think of a filter that provides user authentication), it can easily abort the processing by not calling `doFilter()`. If all this sounds a little confusing, the illustration below should make it clearer:

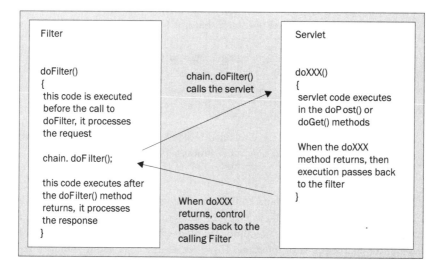

The Deployment Descriptor

The deployment descriptor is used to tell the container which, if any, filters to call for each servlet in the application. Two tags within the deployment descriptor describe the filters and indicate to which servlet requests the filters should be applied.

The first element is `<filter>`. A `<filter>` element including all sub-elements looks like this:

```
<filter>
  <icon>path to an icon file</icon>
  <filter-name>the name of the filter for the application</filter-name>
  <display-name>named for use by management tool</display-name>
  <description>a description</description>
  <filter-class>fully qualified class name</filter-class>
  <init-param>
     <param-name>some_name</param-name>
     <param-value>a_value</param-value>
  </init-param>
</filter>
```

Only two of these sub-elements are required: the `<filter-name>` and the `<filter-class>`. If you use an `<init-param>`, then `<param-name>` and `<param-value>` are required. These init values can be accessed through the `FilterConfig` object.

The second element is the `<filter-mapping>` element. It looks like this:

```
<filter-mapping>
    <filter-name>same name as filter element</filter-name>
    <url-pattern>URL pattern that the filter applies to</url-pattern>
</filter-mapping>
```

or like this:

```
<filter-mapping>
    <filter-name>Same name as filter element</filter-name>
    <servlet-name>Name of servlet from servlet element</servlet-name>
</filter-mapping>
```

Recall that the order of tags in the deployment descriptor must follow the DTD. All the `<filter>` tags must occur prior to any `<filter-mapping>` tags. The `<filter-mapping>` tags must occur prior to the `<servlet>` tags.

If multiple filters are needed for a request, then each filter is listed in separate `<filter-mapping>` elements. The filters are applied in the same order that the `<filter-mapping>` elements appear in the deployment descriptor. For example, if you had this deployment descriptor:

```
<filter-mapping>
    <filter-name>FilterD</filter-name>
    <servlet-name>Login</servlet-name>
</filter-mapping>

<filter-mapping>
    <filter-name>FilterA</filter-name>
    <servlet-name>Login</servlet-name>
</filter-mapping>

<filter-mapping>
    <filter-name>FilterW</filter-name>
    <servlet-name>Login</servlet-name>
</filter-mapping>
```

Then any request for the `Login` servlet would first be sent to `FilterD`, since the filter-mapping element for that filter appears first in the deployment descriptor. When `FilterD` calls `chain.doFilter()`, `FilterA` would be called. After that, `FilterW` is called. Finally, when `FilterW` calls `doFilter()`, the `Login` servlet would be invoked.

Try It Out Using Filters

1. Create the following filter. This filter will perform request logging for the `Login` servlet:

```
package web;

import javax.servlet.*;

public class LogB implements Filter {
   public void init(FilterConfig filterConfig) {}

   public void doFilter(ServletRequest request,
                        ServletResponse response,
                        FilterChain chain)
   {
      System.out.println("Entered LogB doFilter()");
      System.out.println("protocol is " + request.getProtocol());
      System.out.println("remote host is " + request.getRemoteHost());
      System.out.println("content type is " + request.getContentType());
      System.out.println("content length is " + request.getContentLength());
      System.out.println("username is " + request.getParameter("username"));

      try {
         chain.doFilter(request, response);
      } catch (Exception e) {
         e.printStackTrace();
      }
   }

   public void destroy() {}
}
```

2. Create this second filter. This filter will do its processing after the servlet has responded to the request (we've deliberately called the `LogB` filter before `LogA`, just to prove that the filters are called in the order in which they appear in the deployment descriptor, not in alphabetical or some other order):

```
package web;

import javax.servlet.*;

public class LogA implements Filter {
   public void init(FilterConfig filterConfig) {}

   public void doFilter(ServletRequest request,
                        ServletResponse response,
                        FilterChain chain)
   {
```

```
      System.out.println("LogA passing request to next filter");

      try {
        chain.doFilter(request,response);
      } catch (Exception e) {
        e.printStackTrace();
      }

      System.out.println("The servlet has processed the request");
      System.out.println("LogA filter is now working to process");
      System.out.println("the response");
    }

    public void destroy() {}
}
```

3. If you are using Tomcat, you will need to modify the web.xml file as shown here. You need to
    add the <filter> and <filter-mapping> elements. If you are using J2EE, skip to step 4:

```xml
<?xml version="1.0" encoding="ISO-8859-1"?>

<!DOCTYPE web-app
    PUBLIC "-//Sun Microsystems, Inc.//DTD Web Application 2.3//EN"
    "http://java.sun.com/dtd/web-app_2_3.dtd">

<web-app>

<!- this is the deployment descriptor for the Filter example ->

    <display-name>Beginning J2EE Ch 5</display-name>
    <filter>
      <filter-name>LogA</filter-name>
      <filter-class>web.LogA</filter-class>
    </filter>

    <filter>
      <filter-name>LogB</filter-name>
      <filter-class>web.LogB</filter-class>
    </filter>

    <filter-mapping>
      <filter-name>LogA</filter-name>
      <url-pattern>/Login</url-pattern>
    </filter-mapping>

    <filter-mapping>
      <filter-name>LogB</filter-name>
      <url-pattern>/Login</url-pattern>
    </filter-mapping>

    <servlet>
      <servlet-name>Login</servlet-name>
      <servlet-class>web.Login</servlet-class>
    </servlet>

    <servlet-mapping>
      <servlet-name>Login</servlet-name>
      <url-pattern>/Login</url-pattern>
    </servlet-mapping>

</web-app>
```

4. If you are using Tomcat, package the web application into a WAR file and drop it into the Tomcat /webapps directory. Proceed to step 11. If you are using J2EE, proceed to step 5.

5. Start by opening the StockBrokerage application that was created earlier in the first example of this chapter. If you did not create that application earlier, use the Deployment Tool to create it now, adding Login.class, LogA.class, LogB.class, and login.html to the EAR. Refer to the earlier Login example for further instructions on how to create the application. Don't forget to alias the Login servlet as /Login.

6. When creating the application with the Deployment Tool, you need to specify the filter mappings through the Filter Mapping tab of the WebApp window. Start by clicking the Edit Filter List button:

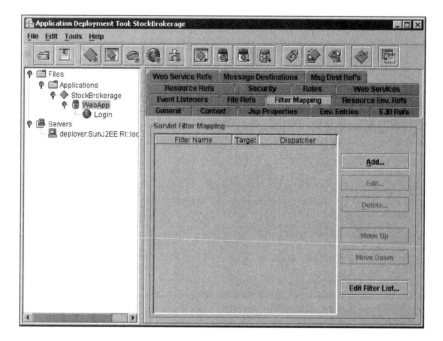

7. Clicking the Edit Filter List button will bring up a dialog through which you specify the available filter classes. Click the Add button and add each of the filter classes, LogA and LogB, to the list:

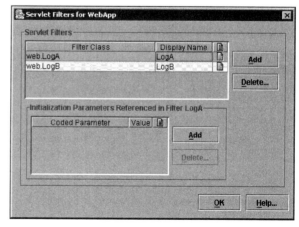

8. When both the classes have been added, click the OK button. When you are back in the main window, you can add filter mappings by clicking the Add button in the Filter Mapping tab. In the Add Servlet Filter Mapping dialog, you specify the filter name, and the target using either a URL pattern or a servlet name. In the Dispatcher Options section, choose Request:

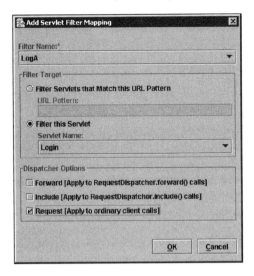

9. When complete, the list of filter mappings should look like this:

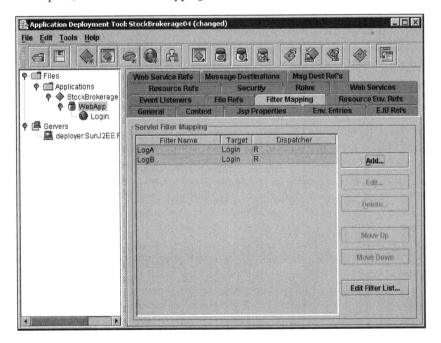

10. Now deploy the application.

11. To see the output in J2EE, you need to have the server in verbose mode. If it is not, rerun the J2EE server in verbose mode by running the **j2ee** script file from the command line and passing the command line parameter **–verbose**. If you start Tomcat from the command line with the script file, you should be able to see the output in the Tomcat console window. Open a browser window. For J2EE, use the address http://localhost:1024/Ch05/login.html. For Tomcat, use http://localhost:8080/Ch05/login.html. Enter a username and password, and click the Submit button. You will see the output from the filters. Here is what I saw on my system:

```
LogA passing request to next filter
Entered LogB doFilter()
protocol is HTTP/1.1
remote host is 127.0.0.1
content type is application/x-www-form-urlencoded
content length is 21
username is k
The servlet has processed the request
LogA filter is now working to process the response
```

How It Works

The `LogA` filter calls the `chain.doFilter()` method almost immediately. This calls the next filter in the chain, `LogB`. The `LogB` filter reads some of the request headers and request parameter from the request and prints them to the console. Then `LogB` calls `chain.doFilter()`. Since it is the last chain in the filter, this calls the servlet, which performs its processing of the request. The code in `LogB` executes before the `doFilter()` method is called, so it executes before the servlet is called:

```
System.out.println("Entered LogB doFilter()");
System.out.println("protocol is" + request.getProtocol());
System.out.println("remote host is " + request.getRemoteHost());
System.out.println("content type is " + request.getContentType());
System.out.println("content length is " + request.getContentLength());
System.out.println("username is " + request.getParameter("username"));

try {
  chain.doFilter(request, response);
} catch (Exception e) {
  e.printStackTrace();
}
```

When the `doPost()` method of the servlet completes, the thread of execution returns to the caller, which in this case is the `LogB` filter. The thread of execution returns to the `doFilter()` method of `LogB`; however, `LogB` performs no other processing. Its `doFilter()` method completes, and execution returns to `LogB`'s caller, `LogA`. When the thread of execution returns to `LogA`, execution continues from the method call `chain.doFilter()`. Since there is code following that method call, it now executes. In a real filter, the code would perform some processing on the response. In the example, all that the filter does is write some strings to `System.out`:

```
System.out.println("The servlet has processed the request");
System.out.println("LogA filter is now working to process");
System.out.println("the response");
```

The MVC Architecture

In the previous JSP chapters, and previously in this chapter, we used an architectural model known as Model 1. In a Model 1 architecture, HTTP requests are handled primarily by web components, which process the request and then return a response to a client. That is, a single web component (or small number of components) handles both the business logic and display logic. There is a second model used for J2EE applications. Unsurprisingly, this model is known as Model 2; it is also known as **Model-View-Controller**, or MVC. In a Model 2 architecture there is a division of functionality: the business data is separated from the display logic, and components that process the data do not manage the display of the data, and vice versa.

Model 1 vs. Model 2

A Model 1 system mixes both application and business logic with display logic. While this is probably OK for small applications, this becomes more and more of a problem as your application grows. This model leads to JSP pages interspersed with a lot of Java code, or servlets that have a lot of print statements that output HTML text to the client. While the examples we've used previously aren't too bad (the first Login servlet example in this chapter only had three println statements), imagine an HTML-heavy application written entirely with servlets, or a code-intensive application written with JSP pages. Your application will become less maintainable as changes to display logic affect business logic and vice versa.

There are various solutions to this problem. On one of the systems I worked on, before the days of JSPs, we solved this problem by creating template files for all the web pages in the application. The template files contained HTML with special place markers for request-specific data. When a servlet needed to send a response to a client, it used a utility class that had methods for reading a template, and replacing the markers with strings. The toString() method of the utility class returned a String that contained the entire HTML web page. Then it was just a simple matter of one println statement to send the response to the client. While this solution was workable, it starts to break down when you have lists, tables, or combo boxes in the web page. You don't know ahead of time how many list items or table rows you might have. Thus, HTML strings start appearing in your servlet code again.

Model 2, or MVC, separates the display from the business logic in another way. In an MVC application, separate components handle the business logic and the display logic. As long as the interface between the two is stable and well defined, the business logic can be changed without affecting the view components, and vice versa.

MVC

In an MVC application, the components of the application are divided into three categories: the model, the view, and the controller.

❏ **Model**–The model includes both the data and the business logic components that operate on that data. Again, any class can act as a model component, and many web applications use only JSPs or servlets with regular (not J2EE API) classes providing business logic. As we will see from Chapter 8 onwards, EJBs make excellent components for the model category.

❏ **View**–After the request is processed, the controller determines which view component should be used to display the data to the user. In simpler applications, the controller component may also act as the view component. In more complex systems, view and controller objects are separate. JSP pages tend to make good view components.

❏ **Controller**–Components in this category receive the client requests, process the request, or forward the request to other components that process the data, and then direct the request to a view component. Any web application component, such as a JSP, a servlet, or an EJB, could be a controller component. However, servlets tend to make good controllers due to their basic structure. A servlet is intended to receive requests from clients and return responses to clients, and that matches the purpose of the controller.

Let's take a quick look at an example design that uses MVC. Imagine that you are working on an application that displays stock market analysts and the ratings they have made on certain stocks.

In this example, we would probably want to have a web page that shows the names of the stock market analysts, with actions to add or delete an analyst. We also would want to have a page that showed the different stocks and the ratings given to them by an analyst, with an action to add a new rating. That's the view side of our simple application.

What about the controller side? For this application, we'll use a servlet to be the controller. The primary job of the controller servlet is to route requests to the appropriate JSP page or to another servlet. The other servlet in this application will be a servlet that responds to the "add rating" request from a JSP page.

Finally, for the model side, in a real application, we would probably use a robust data persistence tier. This might include both a database and objects such as EJBs to access the data. Here's a simple diagram illustrating what this application might look like:

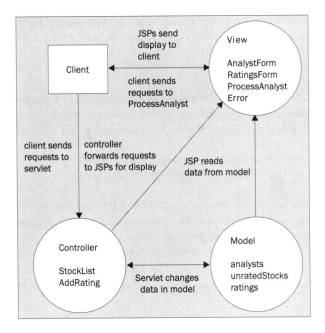

Forwarding and Including Requests

If a servlet is going to be a controller in an MVC application, it needs some way to forward requests to the display components of the application, since the display components create the response back to the client. This is accomplished by getting an object called a RequestDispatcher. Through a request dispatcher, a servlet can forward the request to another web component or include the response of another web component in the current response. This is the same as the JSP standard actions <jsp:forward> and <jsp:include>, which we looked at in Chapter 4.

Getting a RequestDispatcher

You can get a RequestDispatcher from the ServletRequest object or from the ServletContext object. The method signature for the ServletRequest method is:

```
RequestDispatcher getRequestDispatcher(String path)
```

This method returns a RequestDispatcher for the web component at the given location. The path argument is the path to the web application resource. This path can be a relative path or an absolute path. For example, the path to the Login servlet earlier in the chapter was /Login. This path starts with a forward slash (/), so it is interpreted as an absolute path that is relative to the application context. For example, if the application context is /Ch05, then /Login would be the resource at /Ch05/Login. If the path does not start with a slash, it is a relative path that is interpreted relative to the current web component location. For example, if the web component were /Ch05/reports/DisplayReport, then the path PrintReport would be the resource /Ch05/reports/PrintReport. If the resource does not exist, the method returns null.

You can also get a `RequestDispatcher` using a `ServletContext` object. The `GenericServlet` class defines a method to get a reference to the `ServletContext` object for your servlet:

```
ServletContext getServletContext()
```

Since your servlet is a subclass of `GenericServlet`, you can just call this method directly from your servlet. The `ServletContext` represents the application context in which the servlet executes. Next, your servlet can call one of two methods of the `ServletContext` to get a `RequestDispatcher`:

```
RequestDispatcher getNamedDispatcher(String name)
RequestDispatcher getRequestDispatcher(String path)
```

Either method can be used to return a `RequestDispatcher` for the resource at the given path or name. If the resource does not exist, the methods return `null`. The `path` argument for `getRequestDispatcher(String)` must begin with a slash (`"/"`), and is interpreted relative to the application context. The name argument for `getNamedDispatcher(String)` must be the same name used in the `<servlet-name>` sub-element of `<servlet-mapping>` in the deployment descriptor. So, using the `Login` servlet example again, the deployment descriptor for this servlet had this entry:

```
<servlet-mapping>
  <servlet-name>Login</servlet-name>
  <url-pattern>/Login</url-pattern>
</servlet-mapping>
```

The call to `getNamedDispatcher("Login")` would return a `RequestDispatcher` for the web resource /Ch05/Login (remember /Login is interpreted relative to the application context).

Using a Request Dispatcher

Request dispatchers can be used either to forward a request to another resource, or to include another resources' response in the current response. To forward a request, use this method:

```
void forward(ServletRequest request, ServletResponse response)
        throws ServletException, java.io.IOException
```

Since this method relies on another resource to generate the response output, the calling servlet should not write any data to the response stream before calling this method. If response data is sent to the client before this method is called, this method will throw an exception. Also, since the response stream will be complete when the other resource is finished, the calling servlet should not attempt to use the response object after the `forward()` method returns.

Alternatively, you can call another resource and include its response data in the current response. This is done with the method:

```
void include(ServletRequest request, ServletResponse response)
        throws ServletException, java.io.IOException
```

Since this method includes another response in the current response, you can safely write response data to the client both before and after calling this method.

Adding Parameters to the Request

At times, you may need to add additional information to the request object that you use in a `forward()` or `include()` method call. The `ServletRequest` interface defines a number of methods for adding, getting, and removing data from the request object:

```
Object getAttribute(String name)
Enumeration getAttributeNames()
void setAttribute(String name, Object o)
void removeAttribute(String name)
```

The calling servlet can add attributes to the request using `setAttribute(String name, Object o)`. Take care not to duplicate names already used for attributes; if you use a duplicate name, the new attribute will replace the previous attribute. The receiving servlet will use the `getAttribute(String name)` method to get the attribute, using the same name that the calling servlet used to set the attribute.

Try It Out   Using the MVC Architecture

Let's take the simple design above and turn it into a working web application. We will develop view and controller segments as described above. For the model layer, we will simply use some `ArrayList` and `Vector` objects to store the data.

1. Start by creating a directory structure for the web application:

    ```
    stock/
       WEB-INF/
          classes/
             web
    ```

2. We'll start with one view component not shown above–a static HTML page that will be the entry point into the application. Save this file into the /stock directory with the name `index.html`. This web page provides two links into the application:

    ```html
    <!DOCTYPE HTML PUBLIC "-//W3C//DTD HTML 4.01 Transitional//EN">
    <html>
      <head>
        <title>Stocks and Analysts</title>
      </head>
      <body>
        <h1>Stocks and Analysts</h1>
        <p>
          <a href="StockList/AnalystForm">See all Analysts</a>
        <p>
          <a href="StockList/RatingsForm">See all Ratings</a>
        <hr>
      </body>
    </html>
    ```

3. Now we'll create the controller for this application. Name this code `StockListServlet.java`. Notice that it is in a package named web. Save it into the /classes/web directory:

```java
package web;

import javax.servlet.*;
import javax.servlet.http.*;
import java.util.*;

public class StockListServlet extends HttpServlet {
  static ArrayList analysts = new ArrayList();
  static ArrayList unratedStocks = new ArrayList();
  static ArrayList ratings = new ArrayList();

  public void init() {
    analysts.add("Fred");
    analysts.add("Leonard");
    analysts.add("Sarah");
    analysts.add("Nancy");
    unratedStocks.add("ABC");
    unratedStocks.add("DDBC");
    unratedStocks.add("DDC");
    unratedStocks.add("FBC");
    unratedStocks.add("INT");
    unratedStocks.add("JIM");
    unratedStocks.add("SRI");
    unratedStocks.add("SRU");
    unratedStocks.add("UDE");
    unratedStocks.add("ZAP");
    Vector v = new Vector();
    v.add("Fred");
    v.add("ZZZ");
    v.add("Smashing!");
    ratings.add(v);
  }

  public void doPost(HttpServletRequest request,
                     HttpServletResponse response)
  {
    doGet(request, response);
  }

  public void doGet(HttpServletRequest request,
                    HttpServletResponse response)
  {
    try {
      ArrayList data = null;
      RequestDispatcher dispatcher;
      ServletContext context = getServletContext();
      String name = request.getPathInfo();
      name = name.substring(1);

      if ("AnalystForm".equals(name)) {
        data = analysts;
        request.setAttribute("data", data);
      } else if ("RatingsForm".equals(name)) {
```

```
              request.setAttribute("data", ratings);
              request.setAttribute("analysts", analysts);
              request.setAttribute("unrated", unratedStocks);
          } else if ("AddRating".equals(name)) {
              request.setAttribute("data", ratings);
              request.setAttribute("analysts", analysts);
              request.setAttribute("unrated", unratedStocks);
          } else if ("ProcessAnalyst".equals(name)) {
              //no need to set any attributes for this resource
          } else {
              name = "Error";
          }

          dispatcher = context.getNamedDispatcher(name);
          if (dispatcher == null) {
              dispatcher = context.getNamedDispatcher("Error");
          }
          dispatcher.forward(request, response);
      } catch (Exception e) {
          log("Exception in StockListServlet.doGet()");
      }
  }
}
```

4. We're now ready for the first JSP view component. This is a page that will show all the analysts in the application. Name this file `AnalystForm.jsp`, and save it into the /stock directory:

```
<!DOCTYPE HTML PUBLIC "-//W3C//DTD HTML 4.01 Transitional//EN">
<html>
  <head>
    <title>Analyst Management</title>
  </head>
  <body>
    <%@ page import="java.util.*" %>
    <h1>Analyst Management Form</h1>
    <form action="ProcessAnalyst" method="POST">
      <table>
      <%
      ArrayList analysts = (ArrayList)request.getAttribute("data");
      if (analysts == null) {
      %>
        <h2> Attribute is null </h2>
      <%
      } else {
        for (int i = 0; i < analysts.size(); i++) {
          String analyst = (String)analysts.get(i);
      %>
        <tr>
          <td>
            <input type="checkbox" name="checkbox" value="<%= analyst %>"
          </td>
          <td>
            <%= analyst %>
          </td>
        </tr>
      <%
```

211

```
          }
        }
      %>
      </table>
      <input type="submit" value="Delete Selected" name="delete"><p>
      <input type="text" size="40" name="addname">
      <input type="submit" value="Add New Analyst" name="add">
    </form>
  </body>
</html>
```

5. When the user attempts to add or delete an analyst from `AnalystForm.jsp`, the request is sent directly to another JSP. That JSP is `ProcessAnalyst.jsp`, although you will see it does not really add or delete an analyst. Save this file into the /stock directory too:

```
<!DOCTYPE HTML PUBLIC "-//W3C//DTD HTML 4.01 Transitional//EN">
<html>
  <head>
    <title>Process Analyst Request</title>
  </head>

  <body>
    <h1>Process Analyst Request</h1>
    Adding or deleting an analyst from the database is not currently
    implemented. Implementation of this feature is left as an exercise
    for the reader.
  </body>
</html>
```

6. The other functionality provided by this application is to show the ratings the analysts have given to certain stocks. This view of the data is handled by the `RatingsForm.jsp`. Again, since this is a JSP, save it to the /stocks directory:

```
<!DOCTYPE HTML PUBLIC "-//W3C//DTD HTML 4.01 Transitional//EN">
<html>
  <head>
    <title>Stock Ratings</title>
  </head>

  <body>
    <h1>Stock Ratings</h1>

    <%@ page import="java.util.*" %>
    <%
    ArrayList stocks = (ArrayList) request.getAttribute("data");
    if (stocks != null && stocks.size() > 0) {
    %>
    <form action="AddRating" method="post">
      <table border="1">
          <tr>
            <th>Ticker</th>
            <th>Analyst</th>
            <th>Rating</th>
          </tr>
        <%
```

```
        for (int i = 0; i < stocks.size(); i++) {
          Vector v = (Vector) stocks.get(i);
          String ticker = (String)v.elementAt(0);
          String analyst = (String)v.elementAt(1);
          String rating = (String)v.elementAt(2);
        %>
        <tr>
          <td><%= ticker %></td>
          <td><%= analyst %></td>
          <td><%= rating %></td>
        </tr>
        <%
        }
        %>
  </table>
  <table>
      <tr>
        <td>
          <select name="analysts">
            <%
            ArrayList analysts =
              (ArrayList) request.getAttribute("analysts");
            for (int i = 0; i < analysts.size(); i++) {
              String analyst = (String)analysts.get(i);
            %>
            <option value="<%= analyst %>">
              <%= analyst %>
              <%
              }
              %>
          </select>
        </td>
        <td>
          <select name="stocks">
            <%
            ArrayList unratedStocks =
              (ArrayList) request.getAttribute("unrated");
            for (int i = 0; i < unratedStocks.size(); i++) {
              String ticker = (String)unratedStocks.get(i);
            %>
            <option value="<%= ticker %>">
              <%= ticker %>
              <%
              }
              %>
          </select>
        </td>
        <td>
          <select name="ratings">
            <option value="Run away! Run away!">Run away! Run away!
            <option value="Could be worse!">Could be worse!
            <option value="A bit of OK!">A bit of OK!
            <option value="Take a chance!">Take a chance!
            <option value="Smashing!">Smashing!
          </select>
        </td>
```

```
                </tr>
                <tr>
                  <td>
                     <input type="submit" value="Submit Rating">
                  </td>
                </tr>
          </table>
        </form>
        <%
        } else {
        %>
        No stock information found
        <%
        }
        %>
     </body>
  </html>
```

7. Now, we need a servlet to process the request to add a stock rating from an analyst. After adding the rating, the servlet will send the request back to the RatingsForm.jsp to display the new model of the data. This servlet needs to be saved to the /web directory:

```
package web;

import javax.servlet.*;
import javax.servlet.http.*;
import java.util.*;

public class AddRating extends HttpServlet {
   public void doPost(HttpServletRequest request,
                        HttpServletResponse response)
   {
      try {
         String analyst = request.getParameter("analysts");
         String ticker = request.getParameter("stocks");
         String rating = request.getParameter("ratings");

         Vector v = new Vector();
         v.add(analyst);
         v.add(ticker);
         v.add(rating);

         ArrayList ratings = (ArrayList)request.getAttribute("data");
         ratings.add(v);

         ArrayList unratedStocks =
           (ArrayList)request.getAttribute("unrated");
         unratedStocks.remove(unratedStocks.indexOf(ticker));

         ServletContext context = getServletContext();
         RequestDispatcher dispatcher =
           context.getNamedDispatcher("RatingsForm");
         dispatcher.forward(request, response);
      } catch (Exception e) {
         log("Exception in AddRating.doPost()", e);
      }
   }
}
```

8. Create a simple `Error.jsp` page to handle bad request URLs. If you are using Tomcat stand alone, you need to change the port number shown below from 1024 to 8080. Save this page in the root directory of the web application:

```
<!DOCTYPE HTML PUBLIC "-//W3C//DTD HTML 4.01 Transitional//EN">
<html>
  <head>
    <title>Error!</title>
  </head>

  <body>
    <h1>Error!</h1>
    The URL you submitted was not recognized. Please go to the
    <a href="../index.html">start page</a>
    and try again.
  </body>
</html>
```

9. Lastly, if you plan to deploy this application to Tomcat stand-alone, you need to create the deployment descriptor. The `web.xml` file I used is shown below. Save this file into the /WEB-INF directory. If you are deploying this application to the J2EE server, you can skip this step because the J2EE Deployment Tool will create an appropriate deployment descriptor for you:

```
<?xml version="1.0" encoding="ISO-8859-1"?>

<!DOCTYPE web-app
      PUBLIC "-//Sun Microsystems, Inc.//DTD Web Application 2.3//EN"
      "http://java.sun.com/dtd/web-app_2_3.dtd">

<web-app>
  <display-name>Beginning J2EE Ch 5</display-name>
  <servlet>
   <servlet-name>StockList</servlet-name>
   <servlet-class>web.StockListServlet</servlet-class>
  </servlet>

  <servlet>
    <servlet-name>AddRating</servlet-name>
    <servlet-class>web.AddRating</servlet-class>
  </servlet>

  <servlet>
    <servlet-name>ProcessAnalyst</servlet-name>
    <jsp-file>/ProcessAnalyst.jsp</jsp-file>
  </servlet>

  <servlet>
    <servlet-name>Error</servlet-name>
    <jsp-file>/Error.jsp</jsp-file>
  </servlet>

  <servlet>
    <servlet-name>AnalystForm</servlet-name>
    <jsp-file>/AnalystForm.jsp</jsp-file>
  </servlet>
```

```
    <servlet>
      <servlet-name>RatingsForm</servlet-name>
      <jsp-file>/RatingsForm.jsp</jsp-file>
    </servlet>

    <servlet-mapping>
      <servlet-name>StockList</servlet-name>
      <url-pattern>/StockList/*</url-pattern>
    </servlet-mapping>

    <servlet-mapping>
      <servlet-name>ProcessAnalyst</servlet-name>
      <url-pattern>/ProcessAnalyst</url-pattern>
    </servlet-mapping>

  </web-app>
```

10. Compile the servlet classes.

11. The directory structure of your application should now look like this:

```
stock/
    AnalystForm.jsp
    Error.jsp
    index.html
    ProcessAnalyst.jsp
    RatingsForm.jsp
    WEB-INF/
      web.xml
      classes/
        web/
          AddRating.java
          AddRating.class
          StockListServlet.java
          StockListServlet.class
```

12. Deploy the application.

Tomcat–Copy the entire directory structure into the /webapps directory of the Tomcat installation; or create the WAR file, and copy the WAR file into the /webapps directory.

J2EE–Use the J2EE Deployment Tool as shown earlier in this chapter and in the JSP chapter. Create a web component for each of the JSP pages and servlet classes by selecting File | New | Web Application War from the menu and adding components to an existing WAR module rather than creating a new WAR module. Alias the StockListServlet to /StockList/*, and set the context root for the EAR to stock.

13. If you are using Tomcat, start, or restart, the server.

14. Fire up the browser and start playing with your new little MVC application.

Use this URL for J2EE:

http://localhost:1024/stock/index.html

Or this URL for Tomcat:

http://localhost:8080/stock/index.html

Use the links or buttons to navigate around and try different requests. Here's a screenshot of the RatingsForm.jsp web page after adding a rating:

How It Works

Although a simple example, there is a lot of code here. Rather than go over each servlet and JSP line by line, I'll cover some of the more interesting points of each.

The index.html static HTML page contains links that create two slightly different requests. Each link goes to the same servlet, StockListServlet, but each link uses the additional path technique to pass information to the controller servlet. In the first link, /AnalystForm is the additional path information; in the other link it is /RatingsForm:

```
<a href="StockList/AnalystForm">See all Analysts</a>
<a href="StockList/RatingsForm">See all Ratings</a>
```

When StockListServlet is initialized, it populates the various ArrayLists and Vectors that are being used as the model in this MVC application. When it gets a request, it parses the extra path information using the request.getPathInfo() method. It uses this information to determine what model data to add to the request using the setAttribute() method. Then it uses the extra path information to forward the request to the appropriate view or other controller servlet:

```
String name = request.getPathInfo();
//.....some code not shown
dispatcher = context.getNamedDispatcher(name);
//.....some code not shown
dispatcher.forward(request, response);
```

The dispatcher is obtained with a `getNamedDispatcher()` call; the name used to obtain the dispatcher is the same name assigned to the component in the deployment descriptor. Notice also that the `doPost()` method in this servlet simply calls `doGet()`. This is a common technique when you want to support both GET and POST with the same processing. You could also have `doGet()` call `doPost()`.

The `AnalystForm.jsp` view component reads the data from the model and displays it to the user. The controller servlet (`StockListServlet`) added the model data to the request with `setAttribute()`. The data is obtained in the JSP page by calling the `getAttribute()` method. The JSP page creates a form, and when the user clicks one of the buttons on the page, the controller servlet sends the request to `ProcessAnalyst.jsp` (which does nothing in this example):

```
<%
ArrayList analysts = (ArrayList)request.getAttribute("data");
if (analysts == null) {
%>
   <h2> Attribute is null </h2>
<%
} else {
   for (int i = 0; i < analysts.size(); i++) {
      String analyst = (String) analysts.get(i);
%>
   <tr>
     <td>
        <input type="checkbox" name="checkbox" value="<%= analyst %>"
     </td>
     <td>
        <%= analyst %>
     </td>
   </tr>
<%
   }
}
%>
```

The `RatingsForm.jsp` view component displays the analyst, stock ticker, and rating for all stocks that currently have ratings. It gets the model data from the request by calling the `getAttribute()` method of the `request` object. Then it lists all the analysts, all unrated stocks, and the valid ratings. This allows the user to select a stock and assign it a rating. Clicking the Submit button sends the request to `StockListServlet`, which forwards the request to the `AddRating` servlet.

`AddRating` is the controller servlet that adds a rating to the model. The servlet gets the model components from the request, and calls a method to change their data. Notice that it does not need to add the model components back to the request. The request already holds a reference to the model; calling the `add()` or `remove()` methods of `ArrayList` does not change the reference held by the request—it only changes the state of the object. After changing the model, this servlet forwards the request back to `RatingsForm.jsp`, so that it can display the new model:

```
String analyst = request.getParameter("analysts");
String ticker = request.getParameter("stocks");
String rating = request.getParameter("ratings");

Vector v = new Vector();
v.add(analyst);
v.add(ticker);
v.add(rating);

ArrayList ratings = (ArrayList) request.getAttribute("data");
ratings.add(v);

ArrayList unratedStocks =
   (ArrayList) request.getAttribute("unrated");
unratedStocks.remove(unratedStocks.indexOf(ticker));

ServletContext context = getServletContext();
RequestDispatcher dispatcher =
   context.getNamedDispatcher("RatingsForm");
dispatcher.forward(request, response);
```

Finally, the Error.jsp page handles the case of a user typing an incorrect address into the browser.

You should see now the basics of a simple MVC application. You would not want to use this example directly, though. For one thing, because the data is held in member variables in the servlet–there is no persistence. As soon as the servlet is destroyed, any changes to the model are lost. In later chapters, we will extend the example here with a more robust model.

Summary

We've covered quite a lot of information in this chapter. After reading this chapter, you should have learned:

❏ Servers respond to requests and specifically that web servers respond to HTTP requests such as GET and POST.

❏ Servlets extend a server's functionality by providing a server-side program that can respond to HTTP requests. HttpServlets live inside servlet containers.

❏ A servlet lifecycle consists of four phases: loading and creating, initialization, request handling, and end of service. For each of those phases, specific servlet methods realize those phases. The servlet will spend most of its lifecycle in the request-handling phase.

❏ You can make your servlet thread-safe: use local variables for request data, and use instance variables for constant data. If you need to change instance variables or outside resources, synchronize access to them. Making your servlet implement SingleThreadModel does not guarantee that your server is thread-safe. Synchronizing service(), doGet(), or doPost() will make your servlet thread-safe, but doing this is very, very impractical.

❑ You should always handle exceptions and never allow an exception to bypass the servlet's response (unless it is an IOException that occurs during the response).

❑ The Servlet API facilitates session tracking, which allows you to create a web application that can keep track of a client's interactions with the application.

❑ Filters provide a pluggable architecture for processing requests and responses. They encapsulate processing that is outside the scope of the servlet.

❑ The Model-View-Control architecture can help create more easily maintainable applications. Code is kept away from JSPs; HTML is kept away from servlets.

With the information above, you should be able to tackle most of the servlet challenges that you will face as you begin to develop web applications. As usual, though, there is so much more that just could not be covered within the chapter. If you will be doing extensive work with servlets, you may want to obtain a copy of *Professional Java Servlets 2.3* (ISBN 1-86100-561-X) from Apress. In addition, there are several online forums that cover servlet technology. Sun's developer forum hosts a servlet forum at http://forum.java.sun.com/.

Exercises

1. Using one of the servlet examples in this chapter that accepts a POST request, experiment with sending a POST request using a telnet client. Hint: you need to set the content-length header.

2. In the section on *Using the response Object*, we very briefly outline the basic steps for using a servlet to send binary data to a client. Create a servlet that accepts a request from a client for an image file. The name of the image file can be passed as a form parameter, part of the URL, or as extra path information. Write the servlet to load the named image into a byte array, set the content type for an image, set the content length (the number of bytes in the array), and write the image to the response.

3. In the session tracking example, remove the code that performs the URL rewriting, set your browser to reject cookies, and experiment with the example to see how it behaves in this situation.

4. Expand the session tracking example to write a cookie with the user ID to the client browser. Use this cookie to "recognize" the user and initialize some session data.

5. If you have read the JSP chapters, rewrite the final example to use custom actions in the JSP pages.

Working with Databases

Many J2EE applications that you work on will be dependent on a **database**. Search engines use databases to store information about web resources, e-commerce sites use databases to store information about customers and orders, geo-imaging sites that provide photographic images of the world from space use databases to store images and information about those images...the list goes on and on.

In this chapter, we will be using the PointBase database that comes with the J2EE SDK as our example database. PointBase is an example of a **relational database**. Data in a relational database is stored in a series of **tables**. Each table consists of **rows** and **columns**. For example, you can use a table to store information about customers of an e-commerce web application. Each row in the table represents a user; each column in the row represents a particular piece of data about that user. You might also have a separate table that records data about customer orders. Rather than repeating the information about a customer in the orders table, the orders table will have a column that identifies the customer from the customer table. This creates a relationship between the two tables, and thus is why the database is called a relational database.

Java has an API for working with databases, and this technology is known as **JDBC**. JDBC provides the developer with tools that allow clients to connect to databases, and send commands to the database. These commands are written in the **Structured Query Language**, or **SQL**. (For more on SQL, see Appendix B.) Relational databases are not the only kind of database, but they are the most common. However, JDBC can be used with any kind of database. That is because JDBC abstracts common database functions into a set of common classes and methods. Database-specific code is contained in a code library, commonly called a driver library. If there is a driver library for a database, you can use the JDBC API to send commands to the database and extract data from the database.

There is a lot of information about JDBC that can be covered. Clearly, we can't cover everything in this single chapter, but what we will attempt to cover is enough topics to get you started. In the next chapter, we will look at some advanced topics that you need to be aware of as you begin to develop J2EE applications.

Here are the topics we'll cover in this chapter:

❑   How to specify which **driver** your code will use so that you can communicate with the correct database

❑   How your Java code can get a **connection** to a database server

❑   How to use a `Statement` object to insert, update, and delete data from a database

❑   How to read the results of a query from a **resultset**

❑   How to use `PreparedStatements` and `CallableStatements`

If you want to take your understanding of databases beyond that which is presented in these two chapters, you should consider, as your next step, reading Beginning Java Database, by Apress, 1-86100-437-0.

Connecting to Databases

The first step in being able to work with a database is to connect to that database. It's a process that's analogous to a web browser making a connection to a web server. The browser makes a connection to a server, sends a specially formatted message to the server, and receives a response back from the server. When working with a database, your code will use the JDBC API to get a connection to a database server, send a specially formatted message to the server, and receive a response back from the server. As mentioned in the introduction, the JDBC API is an abstraction, and it uses a database-specific code library to communicate with a particular database. A high-level diagram of that process is shown here:

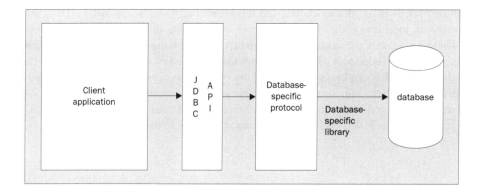

When making a database connection, your code does not need to open any sockets, or use any classes of the `java.net` package to make a connection to the database. All the connection details are handled primarily by a class in the database-specific library. This class is known as a driver. Your code simply tells a class known as the DriverManager that it needs a connection, and the DriverManager works with the driver to create a connection to the database that your code can use.

Drivers

JDBC provides a database-neutral set of classes and interfaces that can be used by your Java class. The database-specific code is included in a driver library that is developed by the database vendor or third parties. The primary advantage of using a driver library is that your code can use the same JDBC API to talk to many different databases simply by changing the library used by your code. Also, by using a driver library, your code is simpler to develop, debug, and maintain, since the lower-level networking details are handled by the driver.

Driver Types

The JDBC specification identifies **four** types of drivers that can be used to communicate with databases. We will briefly look at each of the four types in this section:

Type 1 Driver

This driver provides a mapping between JDBC and some other data access API. The other data access API then calls a native API library to complete the communication to the database. Since native APIs are platform specific, this type of driver is generally less portable. One of the most common Type 1 drivers you will see is the JDBC-ODBC bridge because this driver comes as a standard part of the Java SDK. Like JDBC, ODBC is an API for talking to databases. The JDBC-ODBC Type 1 driver provides a translation layer between your application and the ODBC driver. Thus, if an ODBC driver exists for a database, you can use the JDBC-ODBC bridge driver to communicate with that database. Here is what the communication between client and database looks like using the JDBC-ODBC bridge driver.

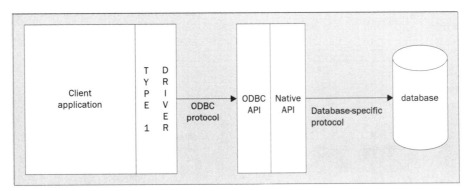

Note that Sun's web site says that the JDBC-ODBC driver should not be used for production applications. Specifically, they say:

> *"The JDBC-ODBC Bridge driver is recommended for use in prototyping efforts and for cases where no other JDBC technology-based driver exists. If a commercial, all-Java JDBC driver is available, we recommend that it be used instead of the Bridge."*

This is taken from http://java.sun.com/j2se/1.3/docs/guide/jdbc/getstart/bridge.doc.html.

Type 2 Driver

This type of driver is similar to the Type 1 driver because it communicates to the database through a native API. However, because it makes calls directly to the native API and bypasses the additional data access layer, this type of driver tends to be more efficient than Type 1. Like a Type 1 driver, it is dependent upon the existence of the native API library. The communication between client and database looks like this:

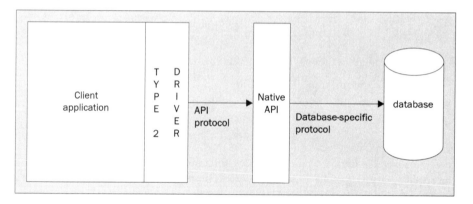

Type 3 Driver

This type of driver sends database calls to a **middleware component** running on another server. This communication uses a database-independent net protocol. The middleware server then communicates with the database using a database-specific protocol. The communication between client and database looks like this:

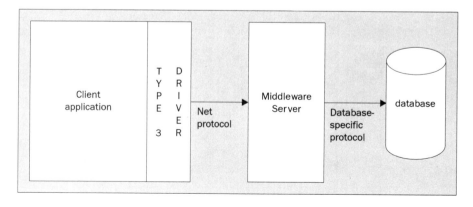

Note that for this driver, the middleware server usually resides on a different computer from the client application, but it may or may not be on a different computer from the database. Also, this driver does not imply that the middleware server uses a native library. The middleware server could be an all-Java piece of code. All that is required is that it translates the JDBC call received from the client into a database call.

Type 4 Driver

The type 4 driver, also commonly known as a **thin driver**, is *completely* written in Java. It communicates directly with a database using the database's native protocol. Since it is written completely in Java without any platform-specific code, it can be directly used on any platform with a Java virtual machine. The driver translates JDBC directly into the database's native protocol without the use of ODBC or native C APIs. The communication between client and database looks like this:

Thus, the thin driver makes an excellent choice for distributed database applications. If you are developing a client application that must communicate with a database, and the client could be installed on various platforms (Windows, Unix, Mac), then you would almost certainly use a Type 4 driver. Using a Type 4 driver, you could deploy the same client code (including the driver) to each platform and the client would work without any other modifications. If, however, you were using the Type 2 driver with this client, you would need to ensure that the native library used by the driver was installed to each client platform. You can see that deploying an application with a Type 4 driver is easier than deploying an application that uses one of the other drivers.

Choosing a Driver

In general you will want to choose either a Type 2 or a Type 4 driver for your web application. Type 1 and Type 3 drivers add a communication layer between the JDBC driver and the database, so they tend to be less efficient. The difference between a Type 2 and a Type 4 driver depends on whether you need to support a single platform or multiple platforms. If you must support multiple platforms, and native libraries do not exist for all platforms, then you will have to use a Type 4 driver. If a native library exists for all platforms, then there is no great difference between a Type 2 and a Type 4 driver. I have seen tests for Oracle's drivers that show the Type 2 performs better in some situations, and the Type 4 performs better in other situations. If performance is an important requirement for your system, you should conduct tests using all the drivers available to you, and then choose the driver that performs best.

225

The DriverManager Class

The DriverManager class is responsible for managing the JDBC drivers available to an application. The other important job of the driver manager is to hand out connections to client code. When you need a connection to a database, you hand the driver Manager a URL, and the driver manager returns a connection to you. To do this, the driver manager maintains a reference to an instance of each driver class that is available. When you ask for a connection, it polls each driver to determine if the driver can handle the URL. As soon as it finds a driver that can handle the URL, it asks the driver for a connection, and returns that connection to you.

For all this to work, two things need to happen:

❏ The driver manager needs to know which drivers are available.

❏ You need to provide a valid URL to the DriverManager class.

We'll look at loading driver classes in the next section, and how to provide a URL in the *Connections* section of the chapter.

Loading a Driver

Before the driver manager can provide connections, a driver class must be loaded by your application and registered with the driver manager. There are various ways to accomplish this:

❏ You can load and register the class dynamically using Class.forName().

❏ You can let the system load and register the class automatically using a system property.

The first technique is the one you will see most often. The second technique is the one I recommend. Interestingly, even though the driver manager needs to know about the driver class, you do not need to interact directly with it when loading the driver class. Regardless of which technique you use, when the driver class is loaded, the driver class will register itself with the driver manager.

Using Class.forName()

This technique uses the method forName(String) from java.lang.Class. Calling forName(String) instructs the JVM to find, load, and link the class file identified by the String parameter. As part of initialization, the driver class will register itself with the driver manager. Thus, your code does not need to create an instance of the class, nor does it need to call the registerDriver(Driver) method. The JVM creates the instance for you, and the driver itself does the registration. The code to do this will look like this:

```
try {
  Class.forName("com.pointbase.jdbc.jdbcUniversalDriver");
} catch (Exception e) {
  e.printStackTrace();
}
```

Note that with the code above, you do not need to import any driver-specific packages at the top of your class. The name of the class is given as a literal String, so the driver class does not need to be present as compile time. The other step you could take to make your class more database-independent would be to replace the literal String with a String variable. Then, you just need to pass the string to the application. For example, you could pass it on the command line:

```
> java JDBCClient com.pointbase.jdbc.jdbcUniversalDriver
```

In the command line above, the jdbcUniversalDriver class is passed as a command line parameter to the JDBCClient class. To change the driver, and thus the database, used by your application, you simply change the string that is passed to the application. When you hard-code the driver name into the class, you must edit and recompile the class to change the driver. By specifying the driver from *outside* the class, there is no need to edit and recompile the class to change the driver.

However, using Class.forName() is a technique that I do not recommend. If there are many developers working on a major J2EE application, they each tend to put the Class.forName() method call into their code to ensure the driver is loaded. This leads to code duplication, which reduces the maintainability of your application.

Using a System Property

The other way to load the driver is to put the driver name into the jdbc.drivers system property. When any code calls one of the methods of the driver manager, the driver manager looks for the jdbc.drivers property. If it finds this property, it attempts to load each driver listed in the property. You can specify multiple drivers in the jdbc.drivers property. Each driver is listed by full package specification and class name. A colon is used as the delimiter between each driver.

> *Properties, as you may recall, are name-value pairs that allow you to associate a value with a given name. They are usually stored in an instance of* java.util.Properties. *System properties can be set and read through the* java.lang.System *class.*

So, for example, you can specify system properties on the command line of a Java application. You do this with the –D command line option. You probably already know this, but to use it, you put –D on the command line, followed immediately by the name of the property to be set, then the assignment operator =, and finally the value of the property. It might look something like this:

```
> java –Djdbc.drivers=com.pointbase.jdbc.jdbcUniversalDriver MyApplication
```

In the line above, jdbc.drivers is the name of the property, and com.pointbase.jdbc.jdbcUniversalDriver is the value of the property. The first time any code calls a driver manager method, such as getConnection(), the DriverManager class will load and link the drivers specified by the jdbc.drivers property and then execute the method. Note that there are other ways of setting a system property, such as reading a property file or resource bundle, but the DriverManager only loads driver classes once, so the system property must be set before any DriverManager method is called. Setting the system property from the command line guarantees the property is set before any code is executed.

Of the two techniques for loading a driver, this is the best for any non-trivial application. Using this technique, the driver classes are automatically loaded. No code needs to create an instance of the driver or call `Class.forName()`. If the driver needs to be changed, it's a simple change in only one place in the application, on the command line, with no need to edit or recompile code. In the next section, we will use this technique to load the driver and get a connection to a database.

Connections

Once we have loaded our driver, the next step is to create a connection to the database. In this section we look at the methods for getting a connection.

Getting a Connection

You get connections from the driver manager, as we mentioned earlier. One of the few times you need to interact with the driver manager is when you need a connection to a database. The driver manager acts as a **factory** for `Connection` objects. The method used to get a `Connection` object is `getConnection()` and there are three overloaded forms of this method:

❑   getConnection(String url)

❑   getConnection(String url, String username, String password)

❑   getConnection(String url, Properties properties)

Common to each of the methods is the url parameter. Just as with an HTTP URL, the JDBC URL provides a means to identify a resource (the database) that the client wishes to connect to.

The URL for each database will vary depending on the database and the driver. However, all URLs will have the general form `jdbc:<subprotocol>:<subname>`, with the `<subprotocol>` usually identifying the vendor and `<subname>` identifying the database and providing additional information needed to make the connection.

Here is one example of a PointBase URL:

```
jdbc:pointbase:embedded:sample
```

The subprotocol is `pointbase` and the subname consists of PointBase-specific information. The keyword `embedded` indicates the connection is to the embedded database (the other valid database is `server`), and `sample` is the name of the database. Notice that PointBase uses a semicolon as the delimiter between the parts of the subname.

Be aware that the driver for a database might be able to accept different URLs. PointBase, for example, recognizes other URLs in addition to the one shown above. You can consult the documentation that comes with your driver to find the various forms of the URL to use with that driver.

Some databases allow you to pass a username and password to the data as part of the URL. If the username and password are part of the URL, you would use the getConnection(String) method to get a connection to the database.

PointBase, however, does not let you include a username and password in the URL. If you use the getConnection(String) method, PointBase uses the default username and password to create the connection. If you need to pass a different username or password, then you will need a different getConnection() method. The other two forms of getConnection() allow you to pass parameters without including them in the URL. Those two forms are:

```
DriverManager.getConnection(sourceURL, myUserName, myPassword);
DriverManager.getConnection(sourceURL, myProperties);
```

You would use the first of those methods with the example PointBase URL shown above. Both methods have a parameter for the URL. The method that takes a username and password as method arguments is pretty straightforward, you just pass the username and password as arguments to the method, so we will not look at it in detail. Rather, let's examine the last form of the getConnection() method:

```
getConnection(String url, Properties properties)
```

This method is used when you want to pass additional information to the driver (which can also include username and password).

The additional information is passed as a property in a java.util.Properties object. To supply the properties required by your JDBC driver, you can create a Properties object, and then set the properties that you need by calling its setProperty() method.

The properties that can be set are dependent on the database. For example, another database, the Cloudscape database, lists the following attributes that can be set with a Properties object:

❑ autocommit

❑ bootPassword

❑ create

❑ current

❑ databaseName

❑ dataEncryption

❑ encryptionProvider

❑ encryptionAlgorithm

❑ locale

❑ logDevice

❑ Password

❑ Shutdown

❑ Unicode

❑ Upgrade

❑ user

The documentation for your particular driver will list the properties it accepts. In general, you need to set the user name and password at a minimum. The code fragment below illustrates using a `Property` object to create a connection to a Cloudscape database named `CloudscapeDB`:

```
String sourceURL = "jdbc:cloudscape:CloudscapeDB";
Properties prop = new Properties();
prop.setProperty("user", "cloudscape");
prop.setProperty("password", "cloudscape");
Connection conn = DriverManager.getConnection(sourceURL, prop);
```

Now in real code, you wouldn't hard-code the username and password as shown above. The point is to show how to use a properties file to pass parameters to the driver.

Releasing Connections

I was working on a web application recently where the application locked up every time we stress tested it with thousands of database transactions. We were getting very frustrated because we couldn't release the application to production until it could reliably handle thousands of transactions per hour.

The database vendor included a management utility for their system that showed how many database connections had been opened, and how many had been released. Whenever we tested our application, the utility would show that the number of opened connections slowly but steadily diverged from the number of released connections. It turned out that the developer who had written the JDBC code hadn't understood how to release connections properly. Sometimes the connections were not released; sometimes the same connection was released more than once. Whenever we tested the code, it didn't take long for the defects in the code to cause the system to be starved for connections. After enough time, the application just locked up, waiting for connections that were no longer available.

By now you should see the importance of releasing connections. The `Connection` class has a method for releasing the connection:

```
public void close() throws SQLException
```

Many beginners will try to use it like this:

```
Connection conn = DriverManager.getConnection(url);
// Then some JDBC code that works with the database
conn.close();
```

This is a mistake! Almost all JDBC methods throw SQLExceptions (which are discussed in the next section). If the JDBC code between the getConnection() method call and the close() method call throws a SQLException, the call to close() is completely skipped.

The correct way to use close() , when the close() method is in the same method as the connection code, is to put it inside the finally block of a try...catch...finally exception handler. Thus, you are ensured that close() will be called no matter what happens with the JDBC code. And since close() also throws an SQLException, it needs to be inside a try...catch block as well. So, JDBC code begins to look something like this:

```
try {
    conn = DriverManager.getConnection(url);
    // Then some JDBC code that works with the database
} catch (SQLEXception e) {
    // Handle the exception
} finally {
    try {
        conn.close();
    } catch (SQLException e2) {
        // Usually this is ignored
    }
}
```

And of course, this needs to be in every class that uses a connection. Pretty soon, you have finally blocks with enclosed try...catch blocks all over the place, and things are starting to look pretty cluttered!

That's the situation I faced with that web application I just spoke of; the developer had written many long methods inside a gigantic class, and all of these methods were opening connections at the top of a try block, and many hundreds of lines later closing them inside their own try...catch blocks (if they were getting closed at all).

To fix this code, I wrote one *single* method inside the class that was responsible for closing a connection. Whenever there was a try...catch block with conn.close(), I replaced it with a call to the new method. This eliminated all the duplicate code that closed connections. Then I went through the class line-by-line and ensured that every time a connection was opened inside a try block, there was a corresponding finally block that called the new method to close the connection.

When we tested the new code, I paid a lot more attention to that system diagnostic that compared open and released connections. When the code was finally correct, the two numbers were always equal when all the transactions were completed. Next time we sent the code to test, the system did not lock up. Mission successful!

Setting the Login Timeout

One other way we might have narrowed down the problem above is by setting a **login timeout**. Our application appeared to lock up because the code was waiting for a connection that never became available. It waited and it waited...and it would have waited forever if we let it.

There is a way to tell the driver manager to wait only a certain amount of time for a connection. To do this, the DriverManager class provides the following method:

```
public static void setLoginTimeout(int)
```

The int parameter indicates the number of seconds that the driver manager should wait for a connection. If the driver does not return a connection in that amount of time, then the manager throws a SQLException.

SQLException

Earlier I mentioned that almost all JDBC methods declare that they throw SQLExceptions. In most respects, SQLExceptions are the same as the other exception objects that you encounter in your Java code. Your methods that use JDBC code will either need to handle these exceptions in try...catch...finally blocks, or declare that they throw SQLExceptions.

However, SQLExceptions are different from other exceptions in that they can be **chained**. What this means is that the SQLException you catch in your code, may contain a reference to another SQLException, which in turn may contain a reference to another SQLException, and so on, and so on. It's a linked list of exceptions. The SQLException class adds a method for dealing with chained exceptions:

```
public SQLException getNextException()
```

Another difference is that the SQLException can contain additional information about the error that occurred *inside* the database. Databases have their own error codes that identify the problem that occurred. These error codes are returned inside the SQLException object, and you can get the error code with a call to this method:

```
public int getErrorCode()
```

Here is a small snippet of code showing these two methods:

```
try {
  // Some JDBC code
} catch (SQLException e) {
  while (e != null) {
    System.out.println("The error code is " + e.getErrorCode();
    e = e.getNextException();
  }
}
```

Inside the while loop, the error code from the database is printed, then getNextException() is called. The reference returned by getNextException() is assigned back to the variable e. When the last exception is reached, getNextException() returns null and the while loop will terminate.

Try It Out   Talking to a Database

At this point, we have enough information to start building some classes that communicate with database. We'll create two classes here. The first class will be a utility class that manages JDBC resources for clients. We will use the system property technique for loading the driver, and we will use the PointBase demonstration database that comes with the J2EE SDK. We will run PointBase as a server that executes separately from your application. The second class is simply the client class that uses the first to get a connection to the database.

1. The first class is the utility class that manages our JDBC resources, which is called
    `DriverLoader.java`:

```java
package Ch06;

import java.sql.*;
import java.util.*;

public class DriverLoader {
  private DriverLoader() {}

  public static Connection getConnection(String url)
    throws SQLException
  {
    DriverManager.setLoginTimeout(10);
    return DriverManager.getConnection(url);
  }

  public static Connection getConnection(
    String url, String user, String password) throws SQLException
  {
    return DriverManager.getConnection(url, user, password);
  }

  public static Connection getConnection(String url, Properties props)
    throws SQLException
  {
    return DriverManager.getConnection(url, props);
  }

  public static void close(Connection conn) {
    if (conn != null) {
      try {
        conn.close();
      } catch (Exception e) {
        e.printStackTrace();
      }
    }
  }
}
```

You might notice something unusual about the class above: its one and only constructor is `private`. I'll explain why this is so in the *How It Works* section later.

2. Now we need a client that will use the `DriverLoader` class to get a connection to a database. Here's our client code, in a file called `JDBCClient.java`:

```java
package Ch06;

import java.sql.*;

public class JDBCClient {
  public static void main(String[] args) {
    Connection conn = null;
    try {
      String url =
        "jdbc:pointbase:server://localhost/pointbaseDB,new";
      String username = "PBPUBLIC";
      String password = "PBPUBLIC";
      conn = DriverLoader.getConnection(url, username, password);
      DatabaseMetaData dbmd = conn.getMetaData();

      System.out.println("db name is " + dbmd.getDatabaseProductName());
      System.out.println(
        "db version is " + dbmd.getDatabaseProductVersion());
      System.out.println("db driver name is " + dbmd.getDriverName());
      System.out.println("db driver version is " + dbmd.getDriverVersion());
    } catch (SQLException e) {
      e.printStackTrace();
    } finally {
      DriverLoader.close(conn);
    }
  }
}
```

3. Compile both the `DriverLoader` and `JDBCClient` classes using this simple line at the command prompt located in the directory you are currently working in:

```
> javac *.java
```

4. Before you can test out the client, you need to start the database server. In server mode, the database runs separately from the client application. In this mode, the database is started before your program runs, and continues to run after your program ends. You can find scripts for running the PointBase server in the `/pointbase/tools/serveroption` directory of your J2EE installation, or on the Start menu, if you are running Windows. Select Start | Sun Microsystems| J2EE 1.4 SDK | Start PointBase to start the server. To run the server in Windows using the script directly, you would use the following command line in that directory:

```
> startserver
```

5. For Unix/Linux, use:

```
> startserver.ksh
```

If this works correctly, you should see a simple one-line response from the server like this:

```
> startserver.bat
Server started, listening on port 9092, display level: 0 ...
```

6. Now that the server is running, you can run the client. First, you need to ensure your classpath is set correctly. The classpath must be set to include the directory structure up to the start of the package for the `JDBCClient` class. It also needs to include the `pbclient.jar` library. On my system, I've put the class files into `C:\3413\Ch06` and PointBase is installed in `C:\sun\j2sdkee1.4_final2\pointbase`. So, assuming that we're working in the directory `C:\3413`, my classpath statement looks like this:

```
> set classpath=C:\sun\j2sdkee1.4_final2\pointbase\lib\pbclient.jar
> set classpath=%classpath%;C:\3413
```

7. If you are trying this code with a different database, you will need to change the lines above so that they are correct for your setup. In general, your classpath needs to include the `.jar` file that contains the JDBC driver for your database, and the path to the top of the package structure for your class files.

8. Now you are ready to run the client. Remember that we will pass the driver class name as a system property on the command line for the application. The command you need to type looks like this:

```
> java —Djdbc.drivers=com.pointbase.jdbc.jdbcUniversalDriver Ch06.JDBCClient
```

Again, if you are using a different database, you would pass a different driver name on the command line.

9. Here is an example of the output you should see:

```
C:\8333> java -Djdbc.drivers=com.pointbase.jdbc.jdbcUniversalDriver
Ch06.JDBCClient
db name is PointBase
db version is 4.5 RE build 219
db driver name is PointBase JDBC Driver
db driver version is 4.5 RE build 219
```

How It Works

Let's start by looking at the `DriverLoader` class. This is a class that manages JDBC resources for us. We'll actually modify it several times in the course of this chapter. In developing the `DriverLoader`, I've started to apply some of the practices I recommended earlier. The class uses the system property technique for loading the driver. It also provides a central location for handing out and releasing resources.

Now, like the driver class, you really only need one instance of `DriverLoader` in the entire application. You don't need other developers creating instances of `DriverLoader` in their code; they just need to call the static methods we've provided. So, how do you prevent just anyone from creating instances of `DriverLoader`? The way to do that is to create one *private* constructor. Recall that if you don't provide any constructor, the compiler provides a public no-argument constructor for you.

So, you have to provide at least one constructor to stop the compiler from adding a constructor, and make it private so that no other code can call the constructor. Now, anyone who wants a JDBC resource can get it from your class, and they cannot create an instance of this class, but can only call the static methods.

The class then has three methods that return connection objects to the caller. At the moment, these three methods are simply a pass-through to the similar methods of java.sql.DriverManager. Although they have no behavior of their own at this time, we will modify these methods later in the chapter to give them a little behavior.

Finally, the class includes the close() method for the connection. As I mentioned above, it is important to release database resources as soon as you no longer need them. Usually, what you will see in an application is that there are try...catch blocks surrounding method calls to the close() method of the connection in every class that does some JDBC work. Again, we want to avoid code duplication, so we put a close(Connection) method inside the DriverLoader class. This way, there is one central class that can close connections, it tests for null before attempting to close the connection, and when used properly, the application code does not need to be littered with duplicate try...catch blocks.

The DriverLoader class is simple to use. Assuming the system property jdbc.drivers is set, you call one of the getConnection() methods to get a connection, and call close(Connection) when you are finished with the connection. getConnection() calls the same named method in driver manager, and driver manager automatically loads the driver before it returns the first Connection object.

The JDBCClient class shows how to use the DriverLoader class. It consists of a single static main() method in which all the code executes. We start by assigning the URL string to a variable. Note that for a real application, you should not hard-code the URL into the class, but rather pass it in as a String using the command line, or prompt the user for it, or some other technique. Here is the URL:

```
String url =
    "jdbc:pointbase:server://localhost/pointbaseDB,new";
```

If your PointBase server is running on some other machine, you will need to replace localhost with the correct name or IP address for the server.

❑   jdbc:pointbase is the JDBC protocol and subprotocol.

❑   server://localhost/pointbaseDB,new is a URL that specifies the host machine of the server. Since the URL does not include a port, the driver uses the default PointBase port of 9092. If the server is running on a different port, you would append it to the host name like this: hostname:port.

❑   pointbaseDB is the name of the database.

❑   new is a property that tells the server to create the database if it doesn't exist yet.

Next, we use getConnection(String) to get a connection. We used the form getConnection( ), which takes url, username, and password as arguments.

```
conn = DriverLoader.getConnection(url, username, password);
```

Next, we wanted to show that we actually had connected to the database, so we made a call to a method of conn that returns an object that contains data about the database. This object is an instance of DatabaseMetaData. From the DatabaseMetaData object, we were able to get the name and version of both the database and the driver:

```
DatabaseMetaData dbmd = conn.getMetaData();

System.out.println("db name is " + dbmd.getDatabaseProductName());
System.out.println(
    "db version is " + dbmd.getDatabaseProductVersion());
System.out.println("db driver name is " + dbmd.getDriverName());
System.out.println("db driver version is " + dbmd.getDriverVersion());
```

The DatabaseMetaData object contains many other methods that return information about the database. However, since it's not often that you'll be in a situation where you need to use this class, we'll not look at it in detail in this book. If you are interested in the other methods available, you can check the Javadoc for DatabaseMetaData.

The last part of the client class is the finally block. Remember that you want to ensure that you always release JDBC resources when you are finished with them. Since several of the methods that we called in the client class could have thrown a SQLException, if we had put the call to close( ) at the end of the try block, it would have been skipped over when an exception is thrown. Putting the close( ) call into the finally block ensures that it will always be called before the method terminates. Generally, you will always want to close the JDBC resources in a finally block.

Notice also, that we closed the connection in the same method in which we obtained the connection. In general, you should attempt to have the object that gets the connection be responsible for releasing the connection, preferably within the same method. When you obtain the connection and close the connection in the same method, it is much easier to verify you are releasing all your resources, than if you obtain the connection in one method, and release it in some other method.

Logging with the DriverManager

In the code example above, we used a System.out.println( ) to display the database information. This prints directly to the console. If you've done much development with Java, you probably know the problem that can happen with this. You'll have so many System.out.println( ) commands, that what is printed scrolls right off the screen, or is lost among the hundreds of lines of debug.

The DriverManager class provides a method that can be used to redirect debug output, and a method to send strings to the output through the driver manager. These methods are:

```
public static void setLogWriter(PrintWriter)
public static void println(String)
```

Using setLogWriter(), you can direct the DriverManager object's debug statements to an instance of PrintWriter. The PrintWriter can be a wrapper for any Writer or OutputStream, such as a file, a stream, or a PipedWriter. You can also send your own debug statements to the log by calling the println() method. Here is a snippet of code showing how we could have used this feature in the example above:

```
// At the top of the try block
FileWriter fw = new FileWriter("mydebug.log");
PrintWriter pw = new PrintWriter(fw);
DriverManager.setLogWriter(pw);

// After getting the Connection and the DatabaseMetaData objects
DriverManager.println("db name is " + dbmd.getDatabaseProductName());
```

Statements

In the previous section, you saw how to get a connection to a database. However, the connection does *not* provide any methods that allow us to do anything to the database. To actually create, retrieve, update, or delete data from the database, we need the Statement class.

Statement objects are your primary interface to the tables in a database. We will look at using statements to insert new rows into a table, update a row in a table, and delete a row from a table. In the next section on resultsets, we will see how to use a statement to query tables in a database.

Creating and Using Statement Objects

Statement objects are creating from methods of the Connection class:

Connection Method	Description
public Statement createStatement()	Creates a Statement object. If the statement is used for a query, the resultset returned by the executeQuery() method is a non-updateable, non-scrollable resultset.
public Statement createStatement(int, int)	Creates a Statement object. If the statement is used for a query, the two parameters determine whether the resultset returned by the executeQuery() method is updateable or scrollable.
public Statement createStatement(int, int, int)	JDBC 3.0–creates a Statement object. If the statement is used for a query, the two parameters determine whether the resultset returned by the executeQuery() method is updateable or scrollable and the third parameter determines holdability.

For now, don't worry what **updateable**, **scrollable**, and **holdable** mean. These apply to statements used to execute an SQL SELECT command. We will cover those topics in the *Resultsets* section. When executing any other SQL command, we only need a statement created with the createStatement() method that takes no parameters.

Once you have a Statement object, you use it to send SQL to the database with one of ~~three~~ four methods:

Statement Method	Description
public int executeUpdate(String)	Used to any execute SQL that is not a query. Those will primarily be create, insert, update, and delete SQL operations.
public ResultSet executeQuery(String)	Used for querying database tables.
public int[] executeBatch()	Used for sending multiple SQL commands in a single operation.
public boolean execute(String)	Used for executing unknown SQL or SQL that could return either ints or resultsets.

We will look at executeQuery(String) in the section on resultsets. The execute(String) method is rarely used—when the SQL could return either a resultset (as from a query) or an int (as from some kind of update) or both, and you don't know which it will return. Since you are not as likely to encounter this situation day-to-day, we'll not be covering this in detail in this book. If you're interested in learning more, you may consider reading *Professional Java Data*, by Apress, ISBN 1-86100-410-9.

Single Statement Execute

The executeUpdate(String) method is fairly straightforward. It is used to execute a *single* SQL command. The String parameter is the SQL that you want to execute in the database. It can be any SQL *except* for a query. The return value of the method is the number of rows affected by the SQL. This value can range from 0 to the number of rows in the database table. The number of rows returned by various types of SQL commands is shown below:

SQL Type	Number of Rows Affected
Statements such as CREATE, ALTER, and DROP that affect tables, indexes, and so on.	0
INSERT statements	1...n where n is any number
DELETE statements	0...n where n is the number of rows in the table
UPDATE statements	0...n where n is the number of rows in the table

If you attempt to execute a SQL query through the `executeUpdate(String)` method, an `SQLException` will be thrown.

Batch Updates

One way that you can improve the performance of your JDBC application is to execute a number of SQL commands in a **batch**. With batch execution, you add any number of SQL commands to the statement. The statement holds these SQL commands in memory until you tell it that you are ready for the database to execute the SQL. When you call `executeBatch()`, the statement sends the entire batch of SQL in one network communication. In addition to the `executeBatch()` method listed above, two other methods are needed for batch execution:

Statement Method	Description
`public void addBatch(String)`	Adds a SQL command to the current batch of commands for the `Statement` object
`public void clearBatch()`	Makes the set of commands in the current batch empty

The use of batch updating is straightforward. You add SQL commands to the statement with the `addBatch(String)` command. When you are ready for the commands to be executed, you call the `executeBatch()` method. This causes the statement to send all the SQL commands to the database for execution. In code, it would look like this:

```
// Each variable in the method call is an SQL command
stmt.addBatch(sqlCreateTable);
stmt.addBatch(sqlInsert);
stmt.addBatch(sqlUpdate);
stmt.addBatch(sqlDelete);
int[] results = stmt.executeBatch();
```

As you can see in the snippet above, the `executeBatch()` method returns an `int` array which contains the number of rows affected by each of the commands. The result of the first SQL command that was added to the statement is returned in the first element of the array, the result of the second SQL command is in the second element, and so on. Since the `executeBatch()` methods returns an `int` array, the one type of SQL command that cannot be executed by batching is a SQL SELECT command, which returns a `ResultSet` object, not an `int`.

Releasing Statements

Just as with `Connection` objects, it is equally important to release `Statement` objects when you are finished with them. This does not mean that you must immediately release the statement after executing an SQL command–you can use the same `Statement` object to execute multiple SQL commands. However, when you no longer need the statement to execute SQL, you should release it. The `Statement` class has its own `close()` method.

If you're near a computer, take a moment to read the JavaDoc for the Statement class (http://java.sun.com/j2se/1.4.2/docs/api/). You'll see that for the close() method, the JavaDoc states:

> *Releases this Statement object's database and JDBC resources immediately instead of waiting for this to happen when it is automatically closed.*

This means that when the Statement object goes out of scope or is otherwise no longer reachable, it is eligible for garbage collection; when the object is garbage collected, its resources will be released. However, there's always the potential that objects that you think are out of scope are still reachable. In addition, even if an object is eligible for garbage collection, it may not be collected immediately.

> *Garbage collection of objects relies on the* **reachability** *of objects. An object is* **reachable** *if there is a chain of references that reach the object from some root reference. More information can be found at*
> http://java.sun.com/docs/books/performance/1st_edition/html/JPAppGC.fm.html.

Even different databases may handle closing resources differently. For example, with the Cloudscape database, the garbage collector does not close resources. Finally, since database resources are limited, it's never a good idea to hold onto them longer than you need. That is why the Javadoc for close() also states:

> *It is generally good practice to release resources as soon as you are finished with them to avoid tying up database resources.*

Just as with the Connection objects, the close() method call for Statement objects should be in a finally block, and since it too throws a SQLException, it needs to be wrapped inside its own try...catch block. And since developers usually close the connection right after the statement, this usually leads to code that looks something like this:

```
    ...
} finally {
    try {
        stmt.close();
        conn.close();
    } catch (Exception e) {}
}
```

Can you see the potential problem here? There is the possibility that the stmt.close() method call will throw an exception. When that occurs, the call to conn.close() will be skipped, and now your application has unclosed connections lying around.

The solution is to create a method similar to the close(Connection) method in the DriverLoader class. This method will have its own try...catch block, but any exception thrown in the new method will not prevent the close(Connection) method from being called. We'll look at the code for doing that in the next example.

Try It Out Using Statements

1. In this example, we will modify the DriverLoader class from the previous example. Make a copy of the DriverLoader.java source code, which we created in the previous example, and make the following modifications to it:

```
package Ch06;

import java.sql.*;
import java.util.*;

public class JDBCManagerV1 {
  private JDBCManagerV1() {}

  // Several methods are not shown in this listing (they are
  // the same as the ones used in the DriverLoader class):
  // getConnection(String url)
  // getConnection(String url, String user, String password)
  // getConnection(String url, Properties props)
  // close(Connection conn)

    public static void close(Statement stmt) {
      if (stmt != null) {
        try {
          stmt.close();
        } catch (Exception e) {
          e.printStackTrace();
        }
      }
    }
  }
}
```

Notice that I have changed the name of the class—since it is providing some significant methods to manage our database resources, I have decided to call this class JDBCManagerV1. The V1 is because this version will be modified later in the chapter to produce our final JDBCManager class. Don't forget to save your new code in a file named JDBCManagerV1.java.

2. Now enter the client class below that will use the JDBC manager class to get a connection to a database, use the connection to create a Statement object, and finally use the statement to insert, update, and delete data in a database. The code should be placed in a file called JDBCClient2.java:

```
package Ch06;

import java.sql.*;

public class JDBCClient2 {
  static Connection conn = null;
  static Statement stmt = null;

  static String sqlCreateTable = "create table COUNTRIES " +
    "(COUNTRY VARCHAR(26), COUNTRY_ISO_CODE VARCHAR(2) NOT NULL, " +
    "REGION VARCHAR(26))";
  static String sqlInsert = "insert into COUNTRIES " +
```

```
      "(COUNTRY, COUNTRY_ISO_CODE, REGION) " +
      "values ('Kyrgyzstan', 'KZ', 'Asia')";
  static String sqlUpdate = "update COUNTRIES set COUNTRY_ISO_CODE='KG'" +
      " where COUNTRY='Kyrgyzstan'";
  static String sqlDelete = "delete from COUNTRIES " +
      "where COUNTRY='Kyrgyzstan'";
  static String sqlDropTable = "drop table COUNTRIES";

  public static void main(String[] args) {
    try {
      String url =
        "jdbc:cloudscape:rmi://localhost:1099/CloudscapeDB;create=true";
      String username = "PBPUBLIC";
      String password = "PBPUBLIC";
      conn = JDBCManagerV1.getConnection(url, username, password);
      stmt = conn.createStatement();

      createTable();
      doInsert();
      doUpdate();
      doDelete();
      dropTable();
      doBatch();
    } catch (SQLException e) {
      e.printStackTrace();
    } finally {
      JDBCManagerV1.close(stmt);
      JDBCManagerV1.close(conn);
    }
  }

  public static void createTable() throws SQLException {
    int result = stmt.executeUpdate(sqlCreateTable);
    System.out.println("Create affected " + result + " rows (expected 0)");
  }

  public static void doInsert() throws SQLException {
    int result = stmt.executeUpdate(sqlInsert);
    System.out.println("Inserted " + result + " rows (expected 1)");
  }

  public static void doUpdate() throws SQLException {
    int result = stmt.executeUpdate(sqlUpdate);
    System.out.println("Updated " + result + " rows (expected 1)");
  }

  public static void doDelete() throws SQLException {
    int result = stmt.executeUpdate(sqlDelete);
    System.out.println("Deleted " + result + " rows (expected 1)");
  }

  public static void dropTable() throws SQLException {
    int result = stmt.executeUpdate(sqlDropTable);
    System.out.println("Drop affected " + result + " rows (expected 0)");
  }
```

```
public static void doBatch() throws SQLException {
   stmt.addBatch(sqlCreateTable);
   stmt.addBatch(sqlInsert);
   stmt.addBatch(sqlUpdate);
   stmt.addBatch(sqlDelete);

   int[] results = stmt.executeBatch();
   for (int i = 0; i < results.length; i++) {
     System.out.println("result[" + i + "]=" + results[i]);
   }
 }
}
```

3. Compile the two classes. This shouldn't require any special classpath and a simple command in execute in the directory in which the two `.java` files live should suffice:

```
> javac *.java
```

4. If it is not already running, run the PointBase server as shown in the previous example. To do this, pick the Start PointBase option on the Start menu, or open a command line window and run the `startserver` script located in the `PointBase/tools` directory of your J2EE installation:

```
> startserver.bat
```

5. Set the classpath to include the `pbclient.jar` library. This library is contained in the `PointBase/lib` directory of the J2EE installation.

```
> set classpath=c:\Sun\j2sdkee1.4_final2\pointbase\lib\pbclient.jar
> set classpath=%classpath%;C:\3413
```

6. After setting the classpath, run the `JDBCClient2` class using the following command line:

```
> java -Djdbc.drivers=com.pointbase.jdbc.jdbcUniversalDriver Ch06.JDBCClient2
```

This is the output you should see when you run the code:

```
> java -Djdbc.drivers=com.pointbase.jdbc.jdbcUniversalDriver Ch06.JDBCClient2
Create affected 0 rows (expected 0)
Inserted 1 rows (expected 1)
Updated 1 rows (expected 1)
Deleted 1 rows (expected 1)
Drop affected 0 rows (expected 0)
result[0]=0
result[1]=1
result[2]=1
result[3]=1
```

```
C:\8333>java -Djdbc.drivers=COM.cloudscape.core.RmiJdbcDriver Ch06.JDBCClient2
Create affected 0 rows (expected 0)
Inserted 1 rows (expected 1)
Updated 1 rows (expected 1)
Deleted 1 rows (expected 1)
Drop affected 0 rows (expected 0)
result[0]=0
result[1]=1
result[2]=1
result[3]=1

C:\8333>_
```

How It Works

The JDBCManagerV1 class (previously known as the DriverLoader class) has only one new method, the close(Statement) method. Putting this method here provides a central location for closing statements, and provides a way to avoid putting try...catch blocks in every bit of code that needs to close a statement.

The JDBCClient2 class demonstrates many of the features of statements that were presented in this section. It starts by defining variables for the connection and statement, and then defines a number of strings that contain SQL commands. The main() method gets the connection, and creates a statement, as shown below. You will notice that even though we don't use the connection after the statement is created, we cannot close the connection yet. The connection must remain open as long as you are working with the Statement object:

```
String url =
  "jdbc:pointbase:server://localhost/pointbaseDB,new";
String username = "PBPUBLIC";
String password = "PBPUBLIC";
conn = JDBCManagerV1.getConnection(url, username, password);
stmt = conn.createStatement();
```

You can also see that we're using the same URL as we used with JDBCClient, with the new parameter. Recall that this instructs the PointBase server to create the given database if it does not exist. If you created the database with JDBCClient, you do not need to include this parameter with the URL.

Next, the main() method calls various other methods. These other methods create the table, insert a row, update the row, and then delete the row. Notice that the CREATE TABLE command and the DROP TABLE command do not directly affect any rows, so the executeUpdate() returns a 0 as the result. The other commands affect a single row, so the return value from executing the INSERT, UPDATE, and DELETE commands is 1. Each of these methods execute the SQL command as *single* statements (that is, *without* batch update). Then, the code calls a method that drops the table, so that it can do the same actions, this time with batching.

Here's the method that performs the batch update:

```
public static void doBatch() throws SQLException {
  stmt.addBatch(sqlCreateTable);
  stmt.addBatch(sqlInsert);
  stmt.addBatch(sqlUpdate);
  stmt.addBatch(sqlDelete);

  int[] results = stmt.executeBatch();
  for (int i = 0; i < results.length; i++) {
    System.out.println("result[" + i + "]=" + results[i]);
  }
}
```

Each SQL command is added to the Statement object with the addBatch() method. When all the commands have been added, the code calls the executeBatch() command. The results are returned in an int array. Each element in the array contains the number of rows affected by the corresponding SQL command (first command added is the first element, and so on). The first command was again the CREATE TABLE–this returns a 0, as expected. The other commands each return 1, which you can see in the screen output above.

Lastly, in a finally block, we release the Statement and Connection objects:

```
  } finally {
    JDBCManagerV1.close(stmt);
    JDBCManagerV1.close(conn);
  }
}
```

Notice that we close the objects in the opposite order from which they were created. The object created first is closed last, and vice versa. Notice how clean this looks–you don't have to put a try...catch block inside the finally block and you don't have to worry about the close(Statement) method throwing an exception that prevents close(Connection) from executing.

The last method of Statement object that we're going to look at is the executeQuery() method. Unlike the executeUpate() or executeBatch() methods, executeQuery() does not return a simple int value. The method is used to execute a SQL SELECT command, and the SELECT command returns zero or more rows of data from one or more tables. These rows are returned in an object known as ResultSet, which is the subject of the next section.

Resultsets

When you perform a query of a table in a database, the results of the query are returned in a ResultSet object. The ResultSet object allows you to scroll through each row of the results, and read the data from each column in the row.

Moving Through the Results

The `ResultSet` interface defines a number of methods that can be used for moving through the results returned. However, not all methods are available for every resultset. Here again are the three methods that create `Statement` objects:

❑   public Statement createStatement()

❑   public Statement createStatement(int, int)

❑   public Statement createStatement(int, int, int)

When you use the first method to create a `Statement` object, the `ResultSet` object that is returned by `executeQuery()` is a nonscrollable `ResultSet`, or one that is of type forward-only. This means that you can only move from the first row to the last row, and cannot scroll backwards through the results. The only method for moving through the `ResultSet` object that can be used is:

```
public boolean next()
```

Assuming no problems with the SQL command, the `executeQuery()` method will always return a non-null `ResultSet`. When the `executeQuery()` method returns the `ResultSet`, the **cursor** is positioned *prior* to the first row of data.

> **Cursor** *is a database term. It generally refers to the set of rows returned by a query. When a cursor is positioned at a row, we mean that we are accessing a particular row in the set.*

To get to the first row of data, you must call the `next()` method. Each time you need to get the following row of data, you call `next()` again. The `next()` method returns a `boolean` value. If there is another row of data, the cursor is positioned at that row and the method returns `true`; if there are no more rows of data, the cursor is positioned after the last row and the `next()` method returns `false`. If there are no results at all in the resultset, then `next()` will return `false` the first time it is called. If you use any of the other movement methods (which we will see shortly) with a nonscrollable resultset, the resultset will throw a `SQLException`.

Now, let's take a look at the other two forms of `createStatement()`. These two forms have method parameters, and the first parameter sets the type. The type refers to whether you can move backwards through the resultset. The second parameter defines whether you can update the table through the resultset. We'll talk about **updateable** resultsets later in the chapter. For the first parameter, you can pass one of these three arguments:

❑   ResultSet.TYPE_SCROLL_SENSITIVE

❑   ResultSet.TYPE_SCROLL_INSENSITIVE

❑   ResultSet.TYPE_FORWARD_ONLY

The first two values create a **scrollable resultset**, a resultset through which you can move forward or backward. If changes occur to the database while you are going through a `ResultSet`, `TYPE_SCROLL_SENSITIVE` means you will see those changes; `TYPE_SCROLL_INSENSITIVE` means you will not see the changes. The third value creates a non-scrollable resultset. With a scrollable resultset, you can use these methods for moving the cursor:

boolean next()	boolean previous()	boolean first()
boolean last()	void afterLast()	void beforeFirst()
boolean absolute(int)	boolean relative(int)	
boolean isFirst()	boolean isBeforeFirst()	boolean isLast()
boolean isAfterLast()	int getRow()	
void moveToInsertRow()	void moveToCurrentRow()	

Because these methods are fairly self-explanatory, and since the use of these methods is documented in the JavaDoc (http://java.sun.com/j2se/1.4.1/docs/api/), we will not cover them here, but we'll use them in the next example.

Reading Data from the Resultset

The resultset also contains a number of methods for reading the data in a query result. These methods allow you to reference the column by number or by name, and to retrieve just about any data type. Here are two of the methods:

```
double getDouble(int)
double getDouble(String)
```

These methods allow you to read a double from the resultset. The first method gets a double from the column with the index given by the int parameter. The second method gets the double from the column with the name given by the String parameter. There are getXXX() methods for every Java primitive, and for several objects. Here is a short list of some of the methods:

Array getArray(int i)	float getFloat(int columnIndex)
BigDecimal getBigDecimal (int columnIndex)	int getInt(int columnIndex)
boolean getBoolean (int columnIndex)	long getLong(int columnIndex)
byte getByte(int columnIndex)	short getShort(int columnIndex)
Date getDate(int columnIndex)	String getString(int columnIndex)
double getDouble (int columnIndex)	Time getTime(int columnIndex)

You should consult the JavaDoc for the complete list of available methods.

Like the getDouble() methods above, each getXXX() method comes in two overloaded forms. One form takes an int argument. The parameter you pass to the method is the column number of the column you wish to retrieve. One important point to know here is that columns returned from a table are numbered starting from one, *not* zero. If you call one of these methods, and pass a zero as the argument, or pass a column number that is too great, a SQLException is thrown.

> Note that the first column is index 1. With SQL, all column numbering begins at 1 and not 0. Likewise, row numbering starts with 1. So, the first column is 1 and the first row is 1.

The second form takes a String parameter. The argument you pass is the name of the column you wish to retrieve. If you pass an invalid name, a SQLException will be thrown.

Whether you use the int parameter or the String parameter depends on your application. Using the int parameter is more efficient. However, the String parameter is more flexible. This is because column indexes sometimes change but column names rarely do. If you hard-code the column number into your code, you'll have problems as soon as the database analysts change the schema of the database tables so that the column numbers change.

Working with Null Values

NULL is a special value in the world of SQL. NULL is not the same thing as an empty string for text columns, nor is it the same thing as zero for a numeric field. NULL means that no data is defined for a column value within a relation. However, for primitive types and for Booleans, the JDBC driver cannot return a null. When the column data for a row is a SQL NULL, the getXXX() method returns a value that is appropriate for the return type. For all the methods that return an object, getDate() for example, the methods return a Java null for SQL NULL. All of the getXXX() numeric methods, getFloat() for example, return the value 0 for SQL NULL. The getBoolean() method returns false for SQL NULL.

This creates a potential problem. If you call getFloat(), and the return value is 0, how do you know if the column value is really 0 or NULL? The ResultSet instance provides a method that can give you this information. Here is its signature:

```
public Boolean wasNull()
```

It does not take a column number or a column name. It provides its answer based on the most recently read column.

Try It Out   Using ResultSet Objects

1. The `ResultSet` object is yet another JDBC resource that we need to manage. Here is version 2 of the JDBCManager. This one contains the method for releasing `ResultSet` objects. Note that to conserve space the methods that have not changed are not shown:

```
package Ch06;

import java.sql.*;
import java.util.*;

public class JDBCManagerV2 {
  private JDBCManagerV2() {}

// The following methods are not shown in this listing:
// getConnection(String url)
// getConnection(String url, String user, String password)
// getConnection(String url, Properties props)
// close(Connection conn)
// close(Statement stmt)

  public static void close(ResultSet rset) {
    if (rset != null) {
      try {
        rset.close();
      } catch (Exception e) {
        e.printStackTrace();
      }
    }
  }
}
```

2. The client will create a scrollable resultset and move through the `ResultSet` object, reading the data from it. Enter and save the `JDBCClient3.java` source for the class:

```
package Ch06;

import java.sql.*;

public class JDBCClient3 {
  static Connection conn = null;
  static Statement stmt = null;
  static ResultSet rset = null;

  static String sqlInsert00 = "insert into COUNTRIES " +
    "(COUNTRY, COUNTRY_ISO_CODE, REGION) " +
    "values ('Kyrgyzstan', 'KG', 'Asia')";
  static String sqlInsert01 = "insert into COUNTRIES " +
    "(COUNTRY, COUNTRY_ISO_CODE, REGION) " +
    "values ('Great Britain', 'GB', 'Europe')";
  static String sqlInsert02 = "insert into COUNTRIES " +
    "(COUNTRY, COUNTRY_ISO_CODE, REGION) " +
    "values ('United States', 'US', 'North America')";
  static String sqlInsert03 = "insert into COUNTRIES " +
```

```
       "(COUNTRY, COUNTRY_ISO_CODE, REGION) " +
       "values ('Canada', 'CA', 'North America')";
    static String sqlInsert04 = "insert into COUNTRIES " +
       "(COUNTRY, COUNTRY_ISO_CODE, REGION) " +
       "values ('France', 'FR', 'Europe')";
    static String sqlQuery = "select * from COUNTRIES";

    public static void main(String[] args) {
       try {
          String url = "jdbc:pointbase:server://localhost/pointbaseDB";
          String username = "PBPUBLIC";
          String password = "PBPUBLIC";
          conn = JDBCManagerV2.getConnection(url, username, password);
          stmt = conn.createStatement(
             ResultSet.TYPE_SCROLL_INSENSITIVE, ResultSet.CONCUR_READ_ONLY);

          doBatch();
          doQuery();
       } catch (SQLException e) {
          e.printStackTrace();
       } finally {
          JDBCManagerV2.close(rset);
          JDBCManagerV2.close(stmt);
          JDBCManagerV2.close(conn);
       }
    }
    public static void doBatch() throws SQLException {
       stmt.addBatch(sqlInsert00);
       stmt.addBatch(sqlInsert01);
       stmt.addBatch(sqlInsert02);
       stmt.addBatch(sqlInsert03);
       stmt.addBatch(sqlInsert04);
       int[] results = stmt.executeBatch();
    }

    public static void doQuery() throws SQLException {
       rset = stmt.executeQuery(sqlQuery);
       System.out.println("rset.next()=" + rset.next());
       System.out.println(
          "Should be on first row: isFirst()=" + rset.isFirst());
       // Now move forward two rows
       rset.next();   // Row 2
       rset.next();   // Row 3
       System.out.println("row num should be 3, getRow()=" + rset.getRow());
       rset.next();   // Row 4
       System.out.print("Row 4 - ");
       System.out.print(rset.getString(1) + " - ");
       System.out.print(rset.getString(2) + " - ");
       System.out.println(rset.getString(3));
       rset.next(); //row 5
       System.out.println("Should be on last row: isLast()=" + rset.isLast());
       rset.previous();
       System.out.println(
          "Should not be on last row: isLast()=" + rset.isLast());
       rset.beforeFirst();
       System.out.println(
          "Should be before first row: isBeforeFirst()=" + rset.isBeforeFirst());
    }
}
```

3. If it is not running, run the PointBase server as shown in the previous example. As a reminder, to do this, select Start PointBase from the Start menu, or open a command line window and run the pointbase script located in the PointBase/tools directory of your J2EE installation:

```
> startserver.bat
```

4. This class relies on the table created by the JDBCClient2 class. If you did not run that class, you will need to do so before running this class.

5. After compiling the class files, make sure that the classpath contains pbclient.jar, and the current working directory up to the directory that contains the two class files. Now we can run the class and see the results:

```
> java -Djdbc.drivers=Com.pointbase.jdbc.jdbcUniversalDriver Ch06.JDBCClient3
rset.next()=true
Should be on first row: isFirst()=true
row num should be 3, getRow()=3
Row 4 - Canada - CA - North America
Should be on last row: isLast()=true
Should not be on last row: isLast()=false
Should be before first row: isBeforeFirst()=true
```

How It Works

Most of the client class is the same as that we have used in the previous two examples. The client gets a connection from the JDBC manager, and creates a Statement object from the connection. The Statement object is created so that it is scrollable. We used the createStatement(int,int) method as shown here:

```
stmt = conn.createStatement(ResultSet.TYPE_SCROLL_INSENSITIVE,
                            ResultSet.CONCUR_READ_ONLY);
```

To ensure we used the correct arguments, we used the static variables defined in the ResultSet class to define the scroll type and updateability of the resultset.

You will need to consult your database and driver documentation to see if the driver supports scrollable resultsets. In our case, PointBase does support scrollable and updateable resultsets. However, we didn't need to update the table in this example, which is why the second argument to the createStatement() method above is ResultSet.CONCUR_READ_ONLY. We will see how to use updateable resultsets in the next section.

Then the main() method calls a doBatch() method to insert five rows of data into the table that was created by the JDBCClient2 class. If you did not run the JDBCClient2 class, this table will not be available to you and the code will not work. You can either enter and run JDBCClient2, or modify JDBCClient3 to create the table itself.

The interesting part of the JDBCClient3 class is in the doQuery() method. Here, I used various movement methods to jump around in the resultset. I also printed the column values for the fourth row of data. Here is a table showing what was printed out by the various lines of code:

Code	Output
`System.out.println("rset.next()=" + rset.next());`	`rset.next()=true`
`System.out.println("Should be on first row: isFirst()=" + rset.isFirst());`	`Should be on first row: isFirst()=true`
`// Now move forward two rows`	
`rset.next();  // Row 2`	
`rset.next();  // Row 3`	
`System.out.println("row num should be 3, getRow()=" + rset.getRow());`	`row num should be 3, getRow()=3`
`rset.next();  // Row 4`	

`System.out.print("Row 4 - ");`
`System.out.print(rset.getString(1) + " - ");`
`System.out.print(rset.getString(2) + " - ");`
`System.out.println(rset.getString(3));`
	`Row 4 - Canada - CA - North America`

`rset.next(); //row 5`	
`System.out.println("Should be on last row: isLast()=" + rset.isLast());`	`Should be on last row: isLast()=true`
`rset.previous();   S`	
`ystem.out.println("Should not be on last row: isLast()=" + rset.isLast());`	`Should not be on last row: isLast()=false`
`rset.beforeFirst();`	
`System.out.println("Should be before first row: isBeforeFirst()=" + rset.isBeforeFirst());`	`Should be before first row: isBeforeFirst()=true`

In the `finally` block, we called the new method of `JDBCManagerV2` to release the `ResultSet` object. We then released the `Statement` and `Connection` objects. They are closed in reverse order of their creation. As with the `Statement` objects, you should close the `ResultSet` as soon as your code is finished with it. One important point to remember is that you must not close the `Statement` or `Connection` objects until after you are finished with the `ResultSet` object, since closing the `Statement` or `Connection` objects will automatically close the `ResultSet` object. Just as with `Statements`, though, you shouldn't rely on closing the `Connection` to close the `ResultSet`. You should close resources as soon as you are finished with them.

> **Always close the resultset before you close its corresponding Statement or Connection. Likewise, close the Statement before closing the Connection that created it.**

Updateable Resultsets

The second parameter in the `createStatement(int, int)` and `createStatement(int, int, int)` methods determines whether you can update the database through the resultset. Prior to JDBC 2.0, resultsets could only be used to select data, move forward through the data, and read the data in each column. To update the data, you needed to execute another SQL command through a statement object.

JDBC 2.0 introduced the ability to update the data in the table directly through the resultset, so as you move through the data, you can call methods that insert, update, or delete the data. Here are some of the methods you would use:

Methods for Inserting, Updating, or Deleting Data	
void updateRow()	void cancelRowUpdates()
void moveToInsertRow()	void moveToCurrentRow()
void insertRow()	void deleteRow()
void updateBoolean(int, boolean)	void updateBoolean(String, boolean)
void updateByte(int, byte)	void updateByte(String, byte)
void updateDate(int, Date)	void updateDate(String, Date)
void updateDouble(int, double)	void updateDouble(String, double)
void updateFloat(int, float)	void updateFloat(String, float)
void updateInt(int, int)	void updateInt(String, int)
void updateLong(int, long)	void updateLong(String, long)
void updateNull(int)	void updateNull(String)
void updateString(int, String)	void updateString(String, String)

The table does not list all the updateXXX() methods available, but only the ones you are most likely to use. You should consult the JavaDoc for the other update methods.

When you move through a resultset using the methods presented previously, you can update whichever row you are currently positioned at. You update the data in the current row with the updateXXX() methods. There is an updateXXX() method for every data type supported by JDBC. Each method comes in two overloaded versions. The first parameter of one version takes a String argument that gives the name of the column to be updated; the other version uses the column number of the column to be updated. The column number refers to the index of the column in the resultset, *not* the table. The column that is named first in the SELECT command is column 1, and so on.

> **Check your driver documentation for the requirements for updating a resultset.**
> **Some databases do not allow you to use SELECT * FROM for an updateable**
> **resultset. You may need to explicitly name each column in the SELECT command.**

The second parameter in each method is the new value for the column. After you have updated all the columns that you want to update, you call the updateRow() method to write the updated row to the table. The code snippet below shows how this could be accomplished:

```
// Assume the COUNTRIES table has bad data in it for Canada
// Assume COUNTRY is Canada and COUNTRY_ISO_CODE is CS
// Update row with good data
static String sqlQuery = "select COUNTRY, COUNTRY_ISO_CODE, REGION " +
                         "from COUNTRIES where " + "COUNTRY_ISO_CODE='CS'";
rset = stmt.executeQuery(sqlQuery);
rset.next();

rset.updateString(1, 'Canada');
rset.updateString(2, 'CA');
rset.updateRow();
```

If, before you call updateRow(), you may decide that you don't want to update the row, you can call cancelRowUpdates().

You can also insert a new row of data through the resultset. This is accomplished by moving to a special row in the resultset; this row is known as the **insert row**. You move to the insert row by calling the following method:

```
rset.moveToInsertRow();
```

When you move to the insert row, the resultset remembers the position you were at; this remembered position is know as the **current row**. Then, you update each column with the appropriate value using the updateXXX() methods. When you are finished entering data for the new row, you call this method:

```
rset.insertRow();
```

After you have called insertRow( ), the resultset is still positioned at the insert row. You can insert another row of data, or move back to the remembered position (the current row) in the resultset. You move back to the current row by calling moveToCurrentRow( ). You also cancel an insert by calling moveToCurrentRow( ) before you call insertRow( ).

Finally, you can delete a row from the table and the resultset by calling:

```
rset.deleteRow();
```

Holdable Resultsets

When you execute another SQL command with a statement, any open resultsets are closed. Also, when commit( ) is called with a JDBC 2.0 or 1.0 driver, the resultset is closed. JDBC 3.0 adds a new ResultSet object feature called **holdability**, which refers to whether or not a resultset is closed when a new SQL command is executed by a statement or when commit( ) is called. JDBC 3.0 gives you the capability to keep the resultset open.

Two class constants were added to the ResultSet interface to provide parameters for the createStatement( ) method:

❏ ResultSet.HOLD_CURSORS_OVER_COMMIT–This specifies that the ResultSet object should *not* be closed when changes are committed.

❏ ResultSet.CLOSE_CURSORS_AT_COMMIT–The driver can close ResultSet object when changes are committed.

A new createStatement( ) method was added to the Connection class to support this feature:

```
createStatement(int resultSetType, int resultSetConcurrency, int
resultSetHoldability)
```

As of the time this chapter was written, Sun listed about a dozen drivers that support JDBC 3.0 Check your database documentation to see if it supports holdability functionality. PointBase does support holdability, if you are using a JVM of version 1.4 or above.

Summary

In this chapter we've looked at some of the ways you can communicate with databases. After finishing this chapter you should know:

❑   How to load a driver and how to get connections from the DriverManager. Loading driver classes can be done by calling `Class.forName(String)` with the fully qualified class name of the driver, or by setting the `jdbc.drivers` System property.

❑   `Statement` objects are used to send SQL commands to the database. `Statement` objects are created by `Connection` objects. SQL commands are sent using either `executeUpdate(String)` or `executeQuery(String)`.

❑   Resultsets are used to read the data returned by an SQL query. Resultsets can be scrollable or updateable. You move through a resultset using methods such as `next()`, `previous()`, `first()`, or `last()`. You read results using methods such as `getString(int)` or `getDouble(String)`.

This chapter has been mainly an introduction to the basics of JDBC. If you are brand new to JDBC programming, this chapter provided you enough information to start doing some JDBC programming. However, this book is about J2EE applications. As a J2EE developer, you are going to quickly encounter some more advanced situations. In the next chapter, we will look at some of the more advanced topics that you will need to know as a J2EE developer.

Exercises

1.   In the beginning of the chapter, the driver manager's `setLogWriter()` method was presented. Modify one of the examples from this chapter to use a log writer that writes to a file, and then run the class. After the class finishes executing, examine the log to see what was logged.

2.   In the *Statements* section, the example inserted, updated, and deleted a row in the CloudscapeDB COUNTRIES table. Modify the code so that you can verify that each operation actually did occur.

3.   If your driver supports updateable resultsets, write a class that uses a resultset to update a table.

7

Advanced Topics in JDBC

In the previous chapter, we looked at some basic features of JDBC: how to get a connection, how to query and update a database using `Statement` objects, and how to read the results of a query using a `ResultSet` object. Once you've gained an understanding of these fundamentals, you'll be able to write simple JDBC programs with no problem.

However, in the fast-paced world of web applications, you will soon find that you need more skills than those presented in the previous chapter. In this chapter, we will cover some advanced JDBC topics that you will find invaluable as a J2EE developer, and we will see how to use JDBC in a J2EE environment. As in the previous chapter, we will look at some problems you might encounter in a J2EE application and how to avoid them with well-designed JDBC code.

In this chapter you will learn:

- ❑ How to use `PreparedStatement` objects to make your JDBC more efficient and to insert non-primitive data types into a database.

- ❑ What sprocs are, why they are useful, and how you can call them with JDBC code.

- ❑ How to get a database connection in a J2EE environment; as this implies, it doesn't involve loading a driver or using a `DriverManager` to get a connection.

- ❑ How to ensure that your JDBC code takes the database from one valid and consistent state to another so that the database does not contain corrupted code.

- ❑ How to deal with the problem of multiple users trying to change data in the database at the same time.

Prepared Statements

One of the projects I recently worked on involved three different teams scattered across the country. Each team was responsible for a system, and the three systems were supposed to work together to solve the user's problem. In addition to developing one of the systems, the team I was on was responsible for integrating the whole mess together. As you'll see, the project provides an excellent example of the platform independence notion of Java and JDBC, but it also points out that there are differences between databases.

One of the teams was using MySql as its database for development, but the final system was using Sybase as the production database. As soon as I tried integrating their code, the method call I made threw an exception. It indicated that the problem was in one of the SQL commands in the JDBC code. What made it even more frustrating is that the error message did not seem to have any relation to what the problem was. PointBase reacts similarly to the problem I encountered. Let's run PointBase's console **tool** and look at it. Navigate to the PointBase/`tools/serveroption` directory of your J2EE installation and run the startconsole script:

```
> startconsole.bat
```

After the tool starts up, connect to the pointbaseDB database created in the last chapter by selecting DBA→Connect to Database from the menu, and entering the appropriate connection parameters. Find the schema that contains the COUNTRIES table. You can enter and execute SQL commands in the window with the title Enter SQL Commands. Enter the following SQL command, replacing "*SCHEMA*" with the correct schema on your system, in the window:

```
ij> update "SCHEMA"."COUNTRIES" set COUNTRY="Canada";
```

Now click the Execute button. On my system, a dialog box with this message was displayed:

Column "Canada" not found in table at position 41.

Okay, the error message is telling me that Canada is not a column in the table. I know that already, I created the table so I know what the column names are. The SQL appears to be correct. It certainly follows the syntax for an UPDATE command. It has:

❑ update–The command itself

❑ COUNTRIES–The table name

❑ set–Part of the syntax for an update command

❑ COUNTRY–Correct column name

❑ "Canada"–The new String value for the column

Even though the SQL looks correct, the problem is in that last quoted word. Look back at the JDBCClient3 class and see how we inserted the string data into the table. The SQL command used single quotes, ', to delimit string data. Most databases, PointBase included, only accept single quotes to delimit strings–MySql accepts double quotes.

> **The problem is that JDBC is platform-independent, but the SQL you use *may not* be platform-independent.**

Another place this occurs is when dealing with data that includes single quotes as part of the data. This question gets asked a lot on JDBC discussion forums. Every once in a while, someone new to SQL and databases asks, "How do I insert a name such as 'O'Grady' into my database, since the apostrophe in the name acts as a delimiter?" The common answer to that question is change the single quote in the name to two single quotes. Thus O'Grady becomes O''Grady (notice that it's not a double quote, it's two single quotes in a row). With MySql, you can escape the single quotes so O'Grady becomes O\'Grady. (Unfortunately, escaping the apostrophe does not work with Sybase or PointBase, so this was another problem we dealt with on my project.) The other part of the common answer is to write a little method that searches for single quotes in the strings and changes them to whatever works for the database in question.

There is a better answer though. Rather than worrying about how to delimit strings, or how to change single quotes into double quotes, JDBC provides a class that can do all this work for you. That class is the PreparedStatement class.

There is one other often-mentioned reason for using a PreparedStatement object. Most databases keep previously executed SQL in a cache. If you send a SQL command that matches one in the cache, the database reuses the SQL from the cache because it has already been compiled and optimized. This improves performance. To reuse a command, the SQL command you send must match one in the cache exactly. Suppose you send these two commands to a database:

```
insert into COUNTRIES values ('Kyrgyzstan', 'KG', 'Europe')
insert into COUNTRIES values ('Great Britain', 'GB', 'Europe')
```

You can easily see that these two SQL commands are essentially the same except for the literal values. For the database, however, these two SQL commands are entirely different. It cannot reuse the first SQL command when you send the second SQL command.

Suppose, however, you could pass the database an SQL command that had variables in it. Then the database could reuse the same SQL command any time you passed it new values for the variables. This is what the prepared statement does.

Creating a Prepared Statement

Creating a `PreparedStatement` object is similar to creating a `Statement` object. One difference is that with a prepared statement, you need to tell the database what SQL you intend to execute. You pass the SQL in the creation method, rather than in the execute method. The methods to create a `PreparedStatement` object are as follows:

Method	Description
`prepareStatement(String sql)`	Creates a prepared statement for the given SQL. If the prepared statement returns a resultset, the resultset has a type forward-only, is not updateable, and is not holdable.

`prepareStatement(`
`    String sql, int resultSetType,`
`    int resultSetConcurrency)`
	Create a prepared statement for the given SQL. If the prepared statement returns a resultset, the resultset has the given resultset type and concurrency, and is not holdable.

`prepareStatement(`
`    String sql, int resultSetType,`
`    int resultSetConcurrency,`
`    int resultSetHoldability)`
	JDBC 3.0: Create a prepared statement for the given SQL. If the prepared statement returns a resultset, the resultset has the given resultset type, concurrency, and holdability.

In the table above, `resultSetType` *refers to whether a resultset is scrollable.* `resultSetConcurrency` *is the ability to update a resultset.* `resultSetHoldability` *refers to whether a resultset is closed when changes are committed. Refer to the Statement and ResultSet sections in the previous chapter for more information on these concepts.*

The first argument in each method is a SQL string. The SQL string can have **placeholders** (variables) that represent data that will be set at a later time. The placeholder is represented by the question mark symbol (?). Let's take the SQL command presented above and change it so that it could be used as part of a prepared statement:

```
insert into COUNTRIES values (?, ?, ?)
```

Placeholders are referred to by their index in the SQL command. Placeholders are consecutively indexed starting with index 1 at the beginning of the SQL string. When the SQL in the prepared statement is sent to the database, the database compiles the SQL. Before you execute a prepared statement, you must set the placeholders with data. The driver sends the data to the database when the prepared statement is executed. Then, the database sets the variables with the data, and executes the SQL.

Using a Prepared Statement

After creating the PreparedStatement object, but before the SQL command can be executed, the placeholders in the command must be set. The PreparedStatement interface defines various methods for doing this. You can also use the PreparedStatement object for setting null values in a table. The other advantage of using a prepared statement is that the values you set do not need to be reset every time you want to execute the SQL command; that is, the values you set are persistent. Finally, you can perform batch updating with a prepared statement.

Setting Placeholders

The methods for setting placeholders take the form of setXXX() where XXX is a Java type name. Here is the method for setting a String:

```
void setString(int parameterIndex, String x)
```

There are other setXXX() methods available, one for each Java primitive, and methods for many object types such as Date, or BigDecimal. You should consult the JavaDoc for information on all the available methods.

The first argument in the setXXX() method will be the index of the placeholder in the SQL command. Each placeholder is referenced by its position in the SQL string. Starting from the beginning of the string, the first placeholder is at index 1, the second at 2, and so on.

The second argument is the data value that replaces the placeholder. So, using the same SQL INSERT from above, here's how the data values would be set:

```
String sdl = "insert into COUNTRIES values (?, ?, ?)"
// Placeholder index:                        1   2   3
PreparedStatement ps = conn.prepareStatement(sql);
ps.setString(1, "Canada");
ps.setString(2, "CA");
ps.setString(3, "North America");
ps.executeUpdate();
```

> If you do not set all the parameters before executing the SQL, the driver will throw a SQLException.

When the values have all been set, you execute the SQL command by calling the executeUpdate() method as shown above.

> If you call any of the executeQuery(String), executeUpdate(String), or execute(String) methods, the driver will throw a SQLException. You must call the "no parameter" versions of those methods with a prepared statement.

Setting Null Values

You might think that you can insert a NULL into a database table by not setting the placeholder that corresponds to the column that will have the null value. As the note above states, however, this will cause the driver to throw a SQLException. Null values are inserted into the database by using one of two methods named setNull():

```
void setNull(int parameterIndex, int sqlType)
void setNull(int parameterIndex, int sqlType, String typeName)
```

As with the other setXXX() methods, the first parameter is the index of the placeholder. The second parameter is defined in the Java class java.sql.Types. The java.sql.Types class contains int constants that correspond to every JDBC type. Thus if you want to set a String column to null, you would pass java.sql.Types.STRING; using java.sql.Types.DATE would set a Date to null. You would pass the appropriate constant for the column you are setting to null.

The typeName parameter in the second method above must be the *fully qualified* type name of the type being set to null. This method can be used for any type, but is provided primarily for user-named types and REF type parameters. When a database supports user-defined types, you can create your own type, like creating a class, and create a column of that type. In your Java code, you create a class that corresponds to that type. In the method, you would pass java.sql.Types.OBJECT as the sqlType parameter, and the fully qualified class name of the class as the typeName parameter.

Showing how to create and map Java classes to database types is beyond the scope of this chapter. You can find more information on mapping in section 3.6 of the advanced JDBC Tutorial at http://developer.java.sun.com/developer/Books/JDBCTutorial/index.html.

Reusing a Prepared Statement

Once a placeholder has been set with data, that data remains set for that placeholder until the code explicitly changes the value for the placeholder. In other words, you are not required to set every placeholder every time you want to execute some SQL using the same prepared statement. If you set the placeholder at some point in the code, and that value is reused in multiple rows, you only need to set the placeholder the first time. All the placeholders can be cleared by calling the PreparedStatement class' clearParameters() method. The value of a placeholder is changed by calling one of the setXXX() methods again with the appropriate index like this:

```
ps.setString(1, "United States");
ps.setString(2, "US");
ps.executeUpdate();
```

The third placeholder was previously set with the value North America, and since it was not changed, that value is reused when the command is executed.

Batch Updates

Just as with a statement, you can use a prepared statement to perform batch updating. The difference is that with the prepared statement, you set each placeholder with the setXXX() methods as shown above. After you have set the placeholders, you call addBatch(). This adds the data values to the batch. After you have added all the rows you want, you call executeBatch(). This sends all the data values to the database for execution with the already stored SQL command.

Try It Out Using Prepared Statements

In this example, we will modify the JDBCClient3 class that we used in the previous chapter to use a PreparedStatement object instead of a Statement object.

> *In order to compile this class, you need to have the JDBCManagerV2 class from the previous chapter. Simply copy and paste this class into the Ch07 folder, then make sure you change the package to Ch07 before you attempt to recompile.*

1. The JDBCClient3 class was presented in the previous chapter. Make the modifications to the code as shown below:

```java
package Ch07;

import java.sql.*;

public class JDBCClient4 {
    static Connection conn = null;
    static Statement stmt = null;
    static PreparedStatement pstmt = null;
    static ResultSet rset = null;

    static String sqlInsert = "insert into COUNTRIES " +
        "(COUNTRY, COUNTRY_ISO_CODE, REGION) " +
        "values (?, ?, ?)";

    static String sqlQuery = "select * from COUNTRIES";

    public static void main(String[] args) {
        try {
            String url = "jdbc:pointbase:server://localhost/pointbaseDB";
            String username = "PBPUBLIC";
            String password = "PBPUBLIC";
            conn = JDBCManagerV2.getConnection(url, username, password);
            doBatch();
            doQuery();
        } catch (SQLException e) {
            e.printStackTrace();
        } finally {
            JDBCManagerV2.close(rset);
            JDBCManagerV2.close(stmt);
            JDBCManagerV2.close(pstmt);
            JDBCManagerV2.close(conn);
```

```
        }
    }

    public static void doBatch() throws SQLException {
        pstmt = conn.prepareStatement(sqlInsert);

        pstmt.setString(1, "Kyrgyzstan");
        pstmt.setString(2, "KG");
        pstmt.setString(3, "Asia");
        pstmt.addBatch();

        pstmt.setString(1,"Great Britain");
        pstmt.setString(2,"GB");
        pstmt.setString(3,"Europe");
        pstmt.addBatch();

        pstmt.setString(1,"France");
        pstmt.setString(2,"FR");
        pstmt.addBatch();

        pstmt.setString(1,"United States");
        pstmt.setString(2,"US");
        pstmt.setString(3, "North America");
        pstmt.addBatch();

        pstmt.setString(1,"Canada");
        pstmt.setString(2,"CA");
        pstmt.addBatch();

        int[] results = pstmt.executeBatch();
        System.out.println("Results of inserts (value should be 1 for each):");
        for (int i = 0; i < results.length; i++) {
            System.out.println("results[" + i + "]=" + results[i]);
        }
    }

    public static void doQuery() throws SQLException {
        stmt = conn.createStatement();
        rset = stmt.executeQuery(sqlQuery);
        rset = stmt.executeQuery(sqlQuery);
        System.out.println("Checking the table:");
        int rownum = 1;
        while (rset.next()) {
            System.out.print("row " + rownum++ + " is ");
            System.out.print(rset.getString(1) + ", ");
            System.out.print(rset.getString(2) + ", ");
            System.out.println(rset.getString(3));
        }
    }
}
```

2. Compile the class using the usual command:

```
> javac *.java
```

and if the PointBase server is not running, start it from the Start menu or the PointBase/tools/serveroption directory of your J2EE installation:

```
> startserver.bat
```

3. If the COUNTRIES table has data in it from JDBCClient2, delete those rows through the PointBase console tool. If the table does not exist at all, you will need to create it. Check the JDBCClient2 class for the SQL to create the table.

4. As usual, make sure that the right classpath has been set. You need to include pbclient.jar, and the current working directory. Then, you can run the program and you should see something like the following:

```
> java -Djdbc.drivers=com.pointbase.jdbc.jdbcUniversalDriver Ch07.JDBCClient4
Results of inserts (value should be 1 for each):
results[0]=1
results[1]=1
results[2]=1
results[3]=1
results[4]=1
Checking the table:
row 1 is Kyrgyzstan, KG, Asia
row 2 is Great Britain, GB, Europe
row 3 is France, FR, Europe
row 4 is United States, US, North America
row 5 is Canada, CA, North America
```

How It Works

Instead of five separate SQL commands to insert the rows of the COUNTRIES table, this class uses a single SQL INSERT command with placeholders for data. In the doBatch() method, five rows of data are inserted by using the PreparedStatement and batch updating. Each placeholder in the SQL command is set with the value for the row. After each value has been set, the addBatch() method is called. After all five rows of data have been added to the batch, the SQL is executed with a call to executeBatch(). Notice that we only needed to set the value for the region column three times.

Callable Statements

In many enterprise applications, the business logic for the application will be encapsulated in **sprocs** (which is short for stored **proc**edures) inside the database. Stored procedures are just like methods in your Java code. They have names, they can have parameter lists, they have a body (containing SQL and procedural commands) that performs some work, and they can return values.

In this section, the term *stored procedure* is used generically to refer to both procedures and functions. The main difference between the two is that a function returns a value and a procedure does not return a value. If your database supports storing procedural and SQL statements in the database for execution, but uses a different term, you should consider "stored procedure" to be a synonym for the term used by your database.

There are many reasons why we would use stored procedures. Some of the services provided by stored procedures are encapsulation and reuse of functionality, control of transactions, and standardization of business rules:

❑ A sproc can encapsulate a common set of SQL commands. A client can access this functionality without needing to make many different JDBC calls.

❑ You can reuse sprocs that are already developed, rather than recreating their functionality from scratch in JDBC.

❑ The sproc makes transaction control easier. We look at transactions and transaction control in greater detail later in this chapter.

❑ Providing a given functionality in a sproc ensures that every part of the application that uses the functionality does so in the same way. If requirements change, only the procedure may need to be changed, and everyone who uses the procedure automatically gets the change.

❑ By having a procedure in a database, the code exists in one place only, yet is accessible to any client, Java or not, that can connect to the database.

Even though they provide useful features, not all databases implement stored procedures–MySQL does not have stored procedures (as of the time this chapter was written). Other databases may provide similar functionality in a different manner. Cloudscape, for example, doesn't support storing SQL statements, but does support storing and executing Java classes. PointBase and other enterprise database systems such as Oracle, SQL Server, and Sybase do have stored procedures.

JDBC code can call stored procedures using a `CallableStatement` object. A `CallableStatement` object is created in much the same way as the `PreparedStatement` object, by calling a method of the `Connection` object. The table below lists all the `Connection` interface methods for creating a `CallableStatement` object:

Method	Description
`prepareCall(String sql)`	Creates a `CallableStatement` object for the given SQL. If the `CallableStatement` returns a `ResultSet` object, the `ResultSet` has a **type** of forward-only, is not **updateable**, and is not **holdable**.

`prepareCall(`
    `String sql,`
    `int resultSetType,`
    `int resultSetConcurrency)`
	Create a `CallableStatement` object for the given SQL. If the `CallableStatement` returns a `ResultSet`, the `ResultSet` has the given `ResultSet` type and concurrency, and is not holdable.

`prepareCall(`
    `String sql, int resultSetType,`
        `int resultSetConcurrency,`
    `int resultSetHoldability)`
	JDBC 3.0: Create a `CallableStatement` object for the given SQL. If the `CallableStatement` returns a `ResultSet`, the `ResultSet` has the given `ResultSet` type, concurrency, and holdability.

See the "Statement" section in the previous chapter for information on scrolling, updating, and holding resultsets.

The first argument in each `prepareCall()` method is a SQL string. The SQL string for calling a stored procedure can take one of several forms. Common between all the forms is the SQL keyword `call` that appears before the procedure name, and the curly braces that surround the SQL. This signals the driver that the SQL is not an ordinary SQL statement and that the SQL must be converted into the correct form for calling a procedure in the target database. The most basic form is the SQL for calling a stored procedure that takes no parameters. The SQL string looks like this:

```
{ call procedure_name }
```

For example, suppose the database had a stored procedure named `adjust_prices`, which took no parameters and returned no value. The code to create a `CallableStatement` object for this stored procedure would look like:

```
String sql = "{ call adjust_prices }";
CallableStatement cs = connection.prepareCall(sql);
```

When a procedure or function takes parameters, the SQL will look something like this:

```
String sql = "{ call set_price(?, ?) }";
CallableStatement cs = connection.prepareCall(sql);
```

The `set_price` procedure takes two parameters and returns no value. Placeholders mark each parameter in the procedure call. We have already looked at placeholders in detail in the *Prepared Statements* section of this chapter.

Finally, the SQL for calling a stored function would look like this:

```
String sql = "{ ? = call get_price(?) }";
CallableStatement cs = connection.prepareCall(sql);
```

The return value of the function is marked by a placeholder, as is the parameter sent to the function.

Using Placeholders

Like the `PreparedStatement` object, the placeholders are numbered consecutively, starting with number 1 for the placeholder that appears in the left-most position in the string. Moving from left to right, each placeholder is given the next number in sequence.

If a placeholder is used to pass an argument to a stored procedure, this parameter is known as an `IN` parameter. Its value must be set before the statement can be executed. If you fail to set one of the placeholders, the driver will throw a `SQLException` when you attempt to execute the SQL. The `CallableStatement` interface inherits the `setXXX()` methods of the `PreparedStatement` interface for doing this.

A stored procedure can also set an input parameter to a new value, and that value is passed back to the caller through the parameter list. For example, this SQL command:

```
call set_price(?, ?)
```

has two parameters in the parameter list. If this were a Java method call, the method could set the value of either parameter inside the method, and that value is not visible to the caller. With a SQL stored procedure, the parameters can be set, and the new values can be visible to the caller. If the placeholder is used to pass data to the sproc, and the sproc passes data back through the parameter, this is an INOUT parameter. A placeholder that is only used to pass data back, or that is a return value, is an OUT parameter.

If any of the parameters in the SQL command are INOUT or OUT parameters, the JDBC type of the placeholder must be registered before the call can be executed. If you do not register a placeholder that returns a value, you will get a SQLException. This is done with the following methods:

```
void registerOutParameter(int parameterIndex, int jdbcType)

void registerOutParameter(int parameterIndex, int jdbcType, int scale)
```

Unlike the setXXX() methods, the registerOutParameter() method only has two forms. The first parameter in the method is the position of the placeholder in the SQL string. The second parameter is one of the constants defined in the java.sql.Types class. The Types class defines a constant for each generic JDBC type.

So, for example, if you were calling a stored procedure that passed a value through the second parameter in a parameter list, and the SQL type returned was a varchar (essentially a string), you would register the parameter like this:

```
cs.registerOutParameter(2, java.sql.Types.STRING);
```

If the return value of a function was a double, you could use this:

```
cs.registerOutParameter(1, java.sql.Types.DOUBLE);
```

For the complete list of the available java.sql.Types constants, consult the API Java documentation.

When registering a parameter that is one of the numeric types such as float, double, numeric, or decimal, you could also use the second form of the registerOutParameter() method. This method takes a third parameter that defines the scale of the returned value. For example, to register a return type that returned a number with two digits to the right of the decimal point, you could use:

```
cs.registerOutParameter(1, java.sql.Types.DOUBLE, 2);
```

Note that if any of the placeholders is an INOUT parameter, the JDBC code must call both a setXXX() method and a registerOutParameter() method prior to executing the callable statement. If you fail to set the value or register the parameter, the driver will throw a SQLException.

As with the PreparedStatement object, once a placeholder has been set with data, that placeholder remains set until the code explicitly changes the placeholder. All the placeholders can be cleared by calling the method clearParameters(). The value of a placeholder is changed by calling one of the setXXX() or registerOutParameter() methods, again with the appropriate index.

After the data values are set, the code calls one of the execute methods, executeUpdate(), executeQuery(), or execute(), to tell the database to execute the stored procedure.

> If you call any of the executeQuery(String), executeUpdate(String), or execute(String) methods, the driver will throw a SQLException. You must call the no parameter versions of those methods with a CallableStatement.

After executing the sproc, the return values of any placeholders are retrieved with getXXX() methods, similar to those used to retrieve the column values from a row in a resultset. The getXXX() methods only have one form, one that takes an int parameter. The parameter int is the index of the placeholder in the callable statement.

Data Sources and Connection Pools

Data sources were introduced as part of JDBC 2.0 and are currently the preferred method for obtaining database connections. The DataSource interface provides a more flexible architecture than using DriverManager for creating and using database connections. As you will see, by using a DataSource object to obtain a connection, you can access different databases without a single change in your client code. The data source hides the connection details so that you, as the client programmer, never need to worry about the connection URL, host, port, and so on.

Connection pools provide a *pool* of precreated database connections. This avoids the time-consuming activity of creating a new connection to a database. On the client side, there is little to no difference in how the connection is used. The difference lies in how connections are created, handed out, and returned to the pool.

Data Source Overview

A data source is usually obtained by performing a lookup in a **context**. A very simple definition of a context is that it is just a means to associate a *name* with a *resource*. One implementation of a context is a **directory**. There are numerous implementations of directory services and protocols. There is Active Directory, X.500, Lightweight Directory Access Protocol (LDAP), and your computer's directory (which associates a name with a file resource).

On the server side of the connection, some code will create a DataSource instance, and then **bind** that instance in the directory. Binding is the action that tells a directory that a particular name is associated with a particular resource. For example, when you created one of the examples in this chapter you caused a collection of bytes to be written to some media such as the hard drive; at the same time, you told the operating system to associate (or bind) that collection of bytes with some name. Thus, anyone that has access to the hard drive can get the collection of bytes by giving the correct name to the operating system. Likewise, a client can get a reference to a data source by giving the correct name to the directory server.

Just as JDBC provides a vendor-neutral interface to numerous databases, Java has provided a vendor-neutral interface to directory services: the **Java Naming and Directory Interface** (**JNDI**). This API provides a common set of functions for accessing directories. Your code uses the JNDI API to communicate with a directory; the details of talking to a particular directory are provided by directory specific libraries, in a similar fashion to JDBC drivers.

Using a DataSource Object

A DataSource object is similar to the DriverManager interface in that it provides methods for obtaining a connection to a database. In fact, the basic method for obtaining a connection has the same name: getConnection(). Before any client code can get a connection from a data source, however, a server must create a DataSource object and bind it to a directory. The exact steps will be different for every directory and database. In general, the data source will be created with parameters (the server, port, database name, and so on) for connecting to the database, and then the data source will be bound to a directory. In the next *Try It Out* section, we will see one way to create and bind a data source resource.

Using a data source to get a connection, the JDBC client code doesn't need to know anything about the database. The client does not need to know the server, the port, the database name, or any other connection parameters. It simply performs a directory lookup and obtains a connection from the data source it gets from the directory. Getting a DataSource object involves two steps. Within a J2EE server, you create an InitialContext object, and then call its lookup() method. This is shown in the code snippet below:

```
InitialContext context = new InitialContext();
DataSource dataSource =
    (DataSource) context.lookup("java:comp/env/jdbc/pointbaseDB");
```

The string passed to the lookup() method is the name which maps to a particular DataSource. Using a data source, a database administrator could change anything about the database such as the connection URL, username, password, and so on. By simply changing and rebinding the data source, the change would be completely transparent to the JDBC client code. As soon as the client code performs a lookup, it will automatically get the connection. The client will not know that anything about the connection has changed, because it only knows the lookup name, which does not change.

Once the client has the connection object, it is used in the same manner as connections that are obtained directly through a driver manager. The data source can even return a connection from a connection pool, and from the client's perspective, the code does not need to change at all.

Connection Pool Overview

In a distributed J2EE application, where different servers run on different machines, creating a network connection to a database is potentially a time-consuming operation. To alleviate this, many J2EE applications use **connection pools**. A connection pool is a collection of already-created connections to a database. When a client needs a connection, it gets one from the pool, performs the work it needs to do, then returns the connection to the pool.

In a J2EE environment, pooled connections are usually obtained using a data source, and the data source is provided through an application server. For example, both the J2EE server and Tomcat provide connection pooling for JSPs and servlets. Every pool implementation will be different in how the pool is created and how you get access to the pool. What is important for you, as a developer, is not how to set up the pool, but how to use the connection you get.

Interestingly, the way you use a pooled connection is exactly the same way you would use a normal connection. After obtaining a pooled connection, you can set its autocommit mode the same as with a normal connection. You can call `getStatement()`, `prepareStatement()`, and `prepareCall()`. You can even call its `close()` method. The difference is that when you call `close()` on a connection from a connection pool, the connection is returned to the pool without being closed.

There are several connection pool libraries that you can use with your JDBC code (for example, http://www.bitmechanic.com/projects/jdbcpool/). However, in a J2EE environment, you will use a `DataSource` to get a connection from a connection pool. Both the J2EE server and Tomcat server have `DataSources` through which you can get a pooled connection object. In this next example, we will use a `DataSource` to get a connection from a connection pool. As you will see, on the client side, this connection is used just as if it were a connection obtained from a `DriverManager`.

Try It Out   Using Data Sources with J2EE

1. First, a data source needs to be configured in the server. This procedure will be different for every J2EE server. So, if you are running a different server, you will need to consult your server documentation to find the correct procedure for your server. For J2EE final 2, ensure the J2EE server is running. Then, in a console window, run the asadmin tool located in the J2EE /bin directory. For Windows, run this script:

```
> asadmin.bat
```

For Solaris, run this script:

```
> asadmin.sh
```

You will see the asadmin prompt in the window. Enter the following series of commands at the asadmin prompt, replacing password with the correct admin password for your server. The commands you type are shown in bold, the asadmin response is shown unbolded.

```
asadmin> create-jdbc-connection-pool --user admin --password password
datasourceclassname com.pointbase.xa.xaDataSource --restype
javax.sql.XADataSource countrypool
Created the JDBC connection pool resource with id = countrypool
asadmin> set --user admin --password password server.jdbc-connection-
pool.countrypool.property.DatabaseName=jdbc:pointbase:server://localhost/point
baseDB
Attribute property.DatabaseName set to
jdbc:pointbase:server://localhost/pointbaseDB
asadmin> set --user admin --password password server.jdbc-connection-
pool.countrypool.property.User=PBPUBLIC
Attribute property.User set to PBPUBLIC
asadmin> set --user admin --password password server.jdbc-connection-
pool.countrypool.property.Password=PBPUBLIC
Attribute property.Password set to PBPUBLIC
asadmin> create-jdbc-resource --user admin --password password
--connectionpoolid countrypool --enabled=true jdbc/countries
Created the external JDBC resource with jndiname = jdbc/countries
asadmin> reconfig --user admin --password password server
Instance restart is required
Successfully reconfigured
asadmin> stop-domain --user admin --password password server --domain domain1
DomainStoppedRemotely
asadmin> start-domain
Starting Domain domain1, please wait.
Domain domain1 started.
```

All the commands above assume you have used the default values at the J2EE installation. If any of those values were changed during installation (e.g., the admin username or password, or the server instance), you will need to substitute the correct values into the commands above. Also, the commands above assume the asadmin tool is running on the same machine as the server. If you need to connect to a server on a different machine, add the following parameters to the commands:

```
--host server_hostname --port server_admin_port
```

I used countrypool for the pool name and jdbc/countries for the JNDI name to the connection pool. You can used a different pool name and different JNDI name. Ensure you use the same pool name and JNDI name in the commands above, and in the JSP and Deployment Tool.

2. Since this example will run inside the J2EE server, the client will be a JSP. Here's the JSP that will query the COUNTRIES table that we created in previous examples. The JSP will perform a lookup of a resource using a resource name. The name that the JSP uses is jdbc/countries (the same name used when creating the resource above). Save this file as PoolExample.jsp. Since we will use the J2EE Deployment Tool, you can save it anywhere in the file system (we've included it in the Ch07 folder in the code download):

```html
<html>
  <head>
    <title>Chapter 7 JSP Pool Example</title>
    <%@ page import="java.sql.*, javax.sql.*, java.io.*, javax.naming.*" %>
  </head>

  <body>
    <h1>Chapter 7 JSP Pool Example</h1>

    <%
      InitialContext context = new InitialContext();
      DataSource dataSource =
        (DataSource) context.lookup("java:comp/env/jdbc/countries");
      Connection conn = null;
      Statement stmt = null;
      ResultSet rset = null;
      try {
        Connection conn = dataSource.getConnection();
        Statement stmt = conn.createStatement();
        ResultSet rset = stmt.executeQuery("select * from COUNTRIES");
        if (rset.next()) {
    %>
      <table width="100%" border="1">
      <tr align="left">
        <th>Country</th><th>iso code</th><th>region</th>
      </tr>
    <%
        do {
    %>
      <tr><td><%= rset.getString(1) %></td>
      <td><%= rset.getString(2) %></td>
      <td><%= rset.getString(3) %></td></tr>
    <%
        } while (rset.next());
    %>
      </table>
    <%
        } else {
    %>
    No results from query
    <%
        }
      } catch (SQLException e) {
    %>
      <%= e.getMessage(); %>
    <%
        e.printStackTrace();
      } finally {
        if (rset != null) { rset.close(); }
        if (stmt != null) { stmt.close(); }
        if (conn != null) { conn.close(); }
        if (context != null) { context.close(); }
      }
    %>

  </body>
</html>
```

275

3. Since numerous JSPs have been deployed in previous chapters, detailed steps for using the Deployment Tool are not shown here. However, there are two specific steps you need to take to ensure the `DataSource` is available to the JSP. These will be shown in the following steps. Refer back to Chapter 2 if you need to learn how to deploy a JSP. Start by creating the Application EAR (which we called `PoolExample`), and use the New Web Application WAR wizard to add `PoolExample.jsp` to it.

4. You must set up a Resource Reference for the web component. This is done in the **Resource Refs** tab of the web application. After selecting the tab as shown below, click the **Add** button to add a Resource Reference. The name of the resource must match the name used in the JSP, and that is "`jdbc/countries`." Make sure that the case of the entered text is as shown here. Click in the type field and select **javax.sql.DataSource**. You can use the default entries for Authentication and Sharable. At the bottom of the panel, enter `jdbc/countries` as the JNDI name.

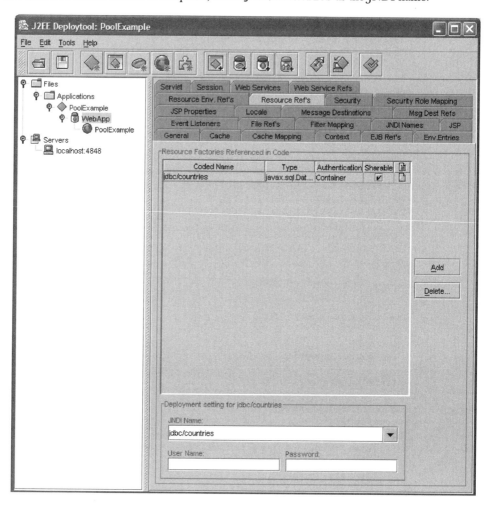

5. Set the Web Context for the application to have a context root of pe, as shown below:

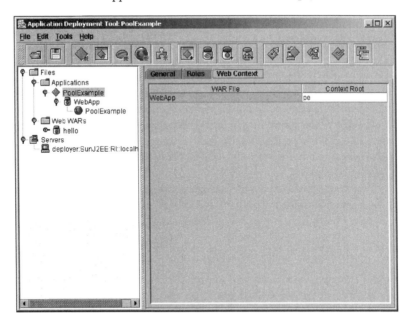

6. Save and deploy the application to the J2EE server. Access the application by using the correct URL for your deployment. Since we set the application context to be pe, the URL you should use is http://localhost:1024/pe/PoolExample.jsp. You should see the following output in your browser:

How It Works

In the JSP, we wanted to access the PointBase database. The reason we've been using this database throughout this chapter and the previous chapter is that it is the default example database for the J2EE server. To use the database through the J2EE server, I needed to set up a data source. The `asadmin` tool provides a number of commands for creating resources in the server. I used the `create-jdbc-pool` command to create a connection pool. Then I used the `set` command to set the url, username, and password for the connection pool. Finally, I used the `create-jdbc-resource` command to associate a JNDI name to the connection pool. While not required, a common practice is to prefix the resource name with a short word that describes the resource: for database resources we use "jdbc". In the EJB chapters later in the book, we will use "ejb" for EJB resources.

In the JSP code, we created an instance of `InitialContext`, and then used this context to perform a lookup using the name `jdbc/countries`:

```
DataSource dataSource =
    (DataSource) context.lookup("java:comp/env/jdbc/countries");
```

Notice that in this example, we actually had to prepend some additional information to the lookup name. The prefix `java:comp/env` is used when you are performing a lookup of resources provided by the server that your component is running in.

Then, to get this example to work, we had to ensure the deployment descriptors for the web component and the application were configured to map the lookup name to the JNDI name. First, in the deployment descriptor for the web application, we identified that the resource for the name `jdbc/countries` would be an instance of `javax.sql.DataSource`. Then we mapped the name `jdbc/countries` to the JNDI name `jdbc/countries`. This ensured that when the code performed the lookup, the server would locate the correct `DataSource` object and return it to the JSP.

After that, the JSP was able to use the connection object, just like any other client in the JDBC examples used a connection obtained from a Driver Manager. Looking at the code, you can see that even though there is no change in how the connection object is used, the code that obtains the connection is much simpler. You no longer need to know the JDBC connection URL, or the username or password for the database. All you need is a lookup name.

Now let's look at this same JSP running in a Tomcat stand-alone.

Try It Out   Using Data Sources with Tomcat

1.   We can use the same JSP from above with the Tomcat stand-alone server, but it takes a little more work. First, copy the PointBase `pbclient.jar` from the `%J2EE_HOME%\pointbase\lib` directory to `%CATALINA_HOME%/common/lib`.

2. Next, we need to configure Tomcat to talk to the PointBase database. Edit the `%CATALINA_HOME%/conf/server.xml` file. You are looking for the end of the `</Host>` tag. Insert the `<DefaultContext>` element shown below; it should be inserted immediately before the `</Host>` tag:

```
<!-- Example Server Configuration File -->
<!-- Note that component elements are nested corresponding to their
     parent-child relationships with each other -->

   ...lots of lines from the server.xml file not shown...

       <!-- Define the default virtual host -->
       <Host name="localhost" debug="0" appBase="webapps"
        unpackWARs="true" autoDeploy="true">

   ...more lines from the server.xml file not shown...

           <DefaultContext>
             <Resource name="jdbc/countries" auth="Container"
                       type="javax.sql.DataSource" />
             <ResourceParams name="jdbc/countries">
               <parameter>
                 <name>driverClassName</name>
                 <value>com.pointbase.jdbc.jdbcUniversalDriver</value>
               </parameter>
               <parameter>
                 <name>url</name>
               <value>jdbc:pointbase:server://localhost/pointbaseDB</value>
               </parameter>
               <parameter>
                 <name>username</name>
                 <value>PBPUBLIC</value>
               </parameter>
               <parameter>
                 <name>password</name>
                 <value>PBPUBLIC</value>
               </parameter>
             </ResourceParams>
           </DefaultContext>

       </Host>

     </Engine>

   </Service>

   ...more lines from the server.xml file not shown...

 </Server>
```

The `<DefaultContext>` section shown above configures Tomcat to create a `javax.sql.DataSource` object and bind it to the name `jdbc/countries`. Notice that both the `Resource` and `ResourceParams` elements use the same value for the name attribute. This is how Tomcat connects the resource parameters to the resource. The `DataSource` is created to talk to the database at the URL given by the `url` parameter, using the driver given by the `driverClassName` parameter.

3. Next create a web application directory in the Tomcat `/webapps` directory. Name this directory `/pe`, and copy the `PoolExample.jsp` file into this directory. Create this `web.xml` file and place it into the `webapps/pe/WEB-INF` directory:

    ```
    <?xml version="1.0"?>
    <web-app>
       <display-name>WebApp</display-name>
       <servlet>
          <servlet-name>PoolExample</servlet-name>
          <jsp-file>/PoolExample.jsp</jsp-file>
       </servlet>
       <resource-ref>
          <res-ref-name>jdbc/countries</res-ref-name>
          <res-type>javax.sql.DataSource</res-type>
       </resource-ref>
    </web-app>
    ```

4. Start Tomcat, open a browser, and navigate to this URL http://localhost:8080/pe/PoolExample.jsp. If everything is correct and running OK, you should see the same display as in step 5 of the previous *Try It Out* example.

How It Works

The `server.xml` and `web.xml` files identify the database and connection parameters to Tomcat. In the `server.xml`, we told Tomcat what name (`jdbc/countries`) to use for the resource and which parameters to use to create the `DataSource`. The `<Resource>` element has a name attribute that links it to the `<ResourceParams>` element with the same name, and that contains parameters for the data source. The following parameters are recognized:

Parameter	Description
driverClassName	The full name of the driver class
maxActive	The maximum number of active connections in pool
maxIdle	The maximum number of idle connections in pool
maxWait	The maximum wait for a connection in milliseconds, throws an exception if exceeded
user	The database username
password	The database password
url	The URL for the database
validationQuery	A query that can be sent to the database to ensure a valid active connection

When Tomcat starts up, it reads the `server.xml` file, and creates a data source based on the parameters in the `ResourceParams` list. It then makes it available to clients using a JNDI interface.

Note that Tomcat does not really use a directory to store the resource. It just uses JNDI semantics to make the resource available to clients. As clients, though, we really don't care how Tomcat stores the resource, as long as it fulfills the contract of the JNDI interface.

In `web.xml`, we told the web application the name and the type of the resource we would be using. The JSP then obtained the data source reference and used it to talk to the database. This code was the same code as used in the previous example. Here is the relevant part of the code:

```
InitialContext context = new InitialContext();
DataSource dataSource =
    (DataSource) context.lookup("java:comp/env/jdbc/countries");
Connection conn = dataSource.getConnection();
Statement stmt = conn.createStatement();
ResultSet rset = stmt.executeQuery("select * from COUNTRIES");
```

As shown previously in this section, the code creates an instance of `InitialContext`. This context object represents the directory of names and resources. Using the context, we then look up a resource that we want to use. To get the correct resource, we create a URL by appending the name of the resource, `jdbc/countries`, to the string `jdbc:/comp/env`. This string is used within the application server to identify resource names.

Then, just as we have done so many times previously, we call the `getConnection()` method. Unlike with the `DriverManager` class, we do not need to pass the URL to the `getConnection()` method of the data source. The URL and other parameters have already been set in the data source. If we wanted to change the database for the J2EE application, there would not need to be any code changes involved in the client code. We just change the `server.xml` and `web.xml` files, restart Tomcat, and every client gets the new connection the next time they use the data source. The rest of the JDBC is just like we have seen in the other examples in this chapter.

Notice also, that the client has no idea that they are dealing with a pooled connection. The client continues to access the database using the same `Connection` interface that we used when we created the connection directly. This means that even the `close()` method is the same from the client's point of view. However, when you close a pooled connection, rather than closing the physical connection to the database, the connection is returned to the pool.

Earlier, I stated that what's important about pooled connections is not how they are *created* (because that will differ between implementations) but how they are *used*. Now, you should see that from the client's point of view, there is no difference between how you use pooled connections and non-pooled connections. In fact, you could take the `JDBCManager` class developed in this chapter, and modify it to use `Context` and `DataSource` for getting connections. This new `JDBCManager` class could then be used from inside JSPs and servlets, and the JSP or servlet would then never need to know whether the connection came from a driver manager or a data source.

281

Transactions

So far in this chapter, every SQL command that we sent to the database was immediately executed and the change was made permanent in the database. In database terms, when the change is made permanent, we say that we **commit** the change, or that the change was **committed**. In an earlier example, we inserted a row into a table named COUNTRIES in the pointbaseDB database, and as soon as the SQL was sent to the database, the change was committed. If we had done a query on the table, the new data would be returned by the query. Suppose we were inserting 50 rows into that table, and halfway through the 50 inserts, our workstation suffered a power failure. Rather than having a total failure, with no changes made to the database, the half of the rows that had been sent to the table before the power failure would be in the table. Only half of the work would have been incomplete. In this case, that's probably okay; the fact that we're able to insert Kyrgyzstan, but not Zambia does not make the table invalid.

However, sometimes, a partial success would be bad and would make the table invalid. If you were working on an Internet stock trading application, and the "sell stock" process failed halfway through, the software may have deposited the funds, but not moved the stock, or vice versa. In either case, the database is in an invalid state: the client's account has both the proceeds and the stock, or neither the proceeds nor the stock. In this case, we want all the changes to be made to a database, or none of the changes to be made.

This is the main purpose of **transactions** in the database—they take the database from one consistent state to the next. That is their job. When you commit work in the database, you are assured that all of your changes have been saved; if you rollback the work, none of the changes are saved.

In some SQL dialects, the code must explicitly tell the database that a transaction is beginning before it executes SQL commands. In SQL Server, for example, the BEGIN TRAN command starts a transaction. JDBC does not require you to explicitly begin a transaction (and thus, does not provide any class or methods for you, the application programmer, to perform this action). The JDBC driver you are using will start a transaction for you automatically. The transaction can be ended automatically, or manually.

Whether the transaction is committed automatically or manually is determined by the **autocommit** status of the connection. For JDBC, the default autocommit status is true. That is, transactions are automatically committed by the connection. The point at which the transaction ends depends on what type of statement is being executed, as shown in the table below:

Statement Type	Transaction Committed When...
SQL INSERT, UPDATE, or DELETE	The statement has finished executing, from the client's view, as soon as executeUpdate(), or execute() returns
SQL SELECT	All the rows in the ResultSet object have been retrieved, or a Statement object is used to execute a new SQL command on the same connection

With autocommit enabled, the driver ends the transaction by automatically calling the commit method. Even with a SQL query, which has no changes to be saved, there is still a transaction. The driver still has to signal the database that the transaction has ended.

When the autocommit status is false, then it is the responsibility of the client to explicitly end transactions. The `Connection` class provides several methods to handle transactions:

Method	Description
`void setAutoCommit(boolean)`	Sets the autocommit mode to `true` (commit transaction automatically, the default setting) or `false` (require explicit transaction commit)
`void commit()`	Commits the current transaction. All changes made since the last commit or rollback are made permanent. Any database locks are released.
`void close()`	Not explicitly part of transaction management. However, closing the `Connection` may cause a transaction to be committed. The exact behavior is database dependent; the JDBC specification does not require a particular behavior.
`void rollback()`	Returns the database to the state that existed at the start of the current transaction.
`Savepoint setSavepoint()`	JDBC 3.0: Creates an unnamed `Savepoint` in the current transaction and returns that `Savepoint` object.
`Savepoint setSavepoint(String)`	JDBC 3.0: Creates a named `Savepoint` in the current transaction and returns that `Savepoint` object.
`void releaseSavepoint(Savepoint)`	JDBC 3.0: Removes the given `Savepoint` from the current transaction.
`void rollback(Savepoint)`	JDBC 3.0: Undoes all the changes that were performed after the given `Savepoint` was created.

We'll look at some of these methods in more detail in the next section and in the *Try It Out* that follows.

Connection Methods for Transaction Control

When your code gets a connection from the driver manager, a data source, or a connection pool, JDBC requires that the connection be in autocommit mode (autocommit enabled). When autocommit is enabled, each SQL command is treated as a transaction and the transaction is committed when the statement is complete as shown in the table above.

Having the driver in autocommit mode may be acceptable when you are learning JDBC or when you are using a single-user database. However, the fact that the JDBC (and ODBC) API defaults to autocommit enabled is problematic for any type of real-world application. Real-world database applications are almost always multi-user applications or applications that touch more than a single table to complete a given task. Thus, for almost any type of real-world application, the next method call after obtaining a connection should be a call to setAutoCommit(boolean) as shown here:

```
Connection conn = DriverManager.getConnection(strUrl);
conn.setAutoCommit (false);    // Autocommit disabled
```

Now, all the control of the transaction resides with the client, which is where it belongs. The developer can code the transaction so that it includes all the queries, inserts, updates, and deletes to take the database from one consistent state to another, and commit only after all the statements have succeeded (or rollback if there are problems).

When the autocommit mode is set to false, transaction management must now be performed explicitly by the code. SQL commands sent to the database will still be executed, but the transaction is not committed when the statement is complete. The transaction will be committed when the code calls the commit() method of the Connection object. Alternatively, the transaction could be rolled back if the code calls the rollback() method. Here is an example of code that shows how we might do this:

```
try {
   stmt = conn.createStatement();
   stmt.executeUpdate("delete from COUNTRIES");
   conn.commit();
} catch (Exception e) {
   JDBCManager.rollback(conn);
} finally {
   JDBCManager.close(stmt);
}
```

In addition to commit() or rollback(), you might be able to control transactions with a feature known as a **savepoint**. Savepoints have been available in databases for some time, but they are a new feature for JDBC. They are part of the JDBC 3.0 specification, so are not widely supported by drivers yet. Check your driver documentation to see if savepoints are supported.

Let's look at an example that shows how savepoints might be used. Suppose we have a transaction that manipulates data in two tables, A and B. If the changes to table A succeed, the database will be left in a consistent state and the transaction could be committed at that point; however, for business reasons, the changes to table B are required to be part of the transaction. However, if the SQL for table A succeeds but some or all of the SQL for table B fails, the database will be in an inconsistent state; if the transaction were committed, the database would contain bad data.

Here is what this scenario might look like:

Time	Transaction Without Savepoint
T0	Transaction begins
T1	SQL insert, update, or delete data into table A, SQL succeeds
T2	SQL insert, update, or delete data into table B, some SQL succeeds and some fails
T3	Client must ROLLBACK, all changes are lost

Without savepoints, all the changes in the transaction must be rolled back because there is no way to perform a partial rollback. Also, there is no easy way to know which parts of table B need to be fixed, so there is no way to recover from the failure and commit the changes to table A.

Now, let's try the same example, but with savepoints:

Time	Transaction with Savepoint
T0	Transaction begins
T1	SQL insert, update, or delete data into table A, SQL succeeds
T2	Savepoint s1 created
T3	SQL insert, update, or delete data into table B, SQL fails
T4	Client calls rollback to savepoint s1
T5	Client performs additional SQL
T6	Client commits transaction

With save points, the client is able to perform a partial rollback of data, perform some additional work, if needed, to put the database into a consistent state, and then commit the transaction. Thus, some of the work performed in a transaction is not lost. Below is an example of what this might look like in code. In the snippet below, insertIntoTable1() and insertIntoTable2() are methods that perform some database actions. If there is a problem, the methods will throw a SQLException. Based on whether or not an exception is thrown, and whether or not the savepoint is set, the code commits all the data, performs a partial rollback and commit, or does a complete rollback:

```
Savepoint sp1 = null;
try {
  insertIntoTable1();
  sp1 = conn.setSavepoint();

  insertIntoTable2();

  // No exceptions, so commit the changes
  conn.commit();
} catch (SQLException e) {
  // This exception means either insertIntoTable1()
  // or insertIntoTable2() failed
  try {
    // If Savepoint is NOT null, then insertIntoTable1() was good
    // but insertIntoTable2() failed, do partial rollback, then commit
    if (sp1 != null) {
      conn.rollback(recordSavepoint);
      conn.commit();
    } else {
      // insertIntoTable1() failed, do complete rollback
      connection.rollback();
    }
  } catch (SQLException e2) {
    e2.printStackTrace();
  }
}
```

Here are some additional points that you need to be aware of when using savepoints:

❑   Calling commit() or rollback() invalidates all savepoints created since the transaction started

❑   Calling releaseSavepoint(Savepoint) invalidates the given savepoint

❑   Calling rollback(Savepoint) invalidates any savepoints that had been created after the given savepoint

Transactions and Stored Procedures

I mentioned previously that transaction control belongs in the hands of the developer. The system requirements should provide information on the business rules for the application and the developer can use those requirements to make the best decision on what sequence of SQL constitutes the transactions for the system, and when those transactions should be committed. Another way to provide this control is to put all the statements that constitute a transaction into a stored procedure.

Stored procedures are perhaps the easiest and most accessible method to ensure correct transactions. If you follow a programming paradigm that says "a stored procedure call is a transaction," you'll have an easier time controlling your transactions and building new ones. You would code stored procedures that received all of the necessary inputs to perform its work. It would take the database from one consistent state to the next. When you invoke this procedure, you would wrap the procedure call in transaction control statements:

```
// Disable autocommit
connection.setAutoCommit(false);

String sql = "{ call MyProcedure }";
CallableStatement cs = connection.prepareCall(sql);

// Call procedure
cs.executeUpdate();
connection.commit();
```

Now, if `MyProcedure` completes successfully, we will commit all of the work it did. If it fails we'll roll back the work (although that is not shown in the snippet above). The reason we would not put the commit directly into `MyProcedure` itself is because at some later date we might need to combine two or three procedures into one transaction. By leaving transaction control to the client (which is where the choice belongs) we can assemble larger transactions as a collection of stored procedures.

Try It Out Using Transaction Control

Let's modify the `JDBCManager` class one final time in this chapter. This will be the last version of `JDBCManager`. With this change, we'll give the class the ability to give the client a connection that is configured to return a connection with autocommit already enabled or disabled, depending upon the user's preference.

1. First, make the following changes to the code:

```
package Ch07;

import java.sql.*;
import java.util.*;

public class JDBCManager {
  private JDBCManager() {}

    //Returns a connection with autocommit true
  public static Connection getConnection(String url)
    throws SQLException
  {
    return getConnection(url, true);
  }

    //Returns a connection with autocommit set by the autocommit parameter
  public static Connection getConnection(String url, boolean autocommit)
    throws SQLException
  {
    Connection connection = DriverManager.getConnection(url);
    connection.setAutoCommit(autocommit);
    return connection;
  }

    //Returns a connection with autocommit true
  public static Connection getConnection(
    String url, String user, String password)
```

```
          throws SQLException
       {
         return getConnection(url, user, password, true);
       }


        //Returns a connection with autocommit set by the autocommit parameter
       public static Connection getConnection(
         String url, String user, String password, boolean autocommit)
           throws SQLException
       {
         Connection connection =
           DriverManager.getConnection(url, user, password);
         connection.setAutoCommit(autocommit);
         return connection;
       }


        //Returns a connection with autocommit true
       public static Connection getConnection(String url, Properties props)
           throws SQLException
       {
         return getConnection(url, props, true);
       }


        //Returns a connection with autocommit set by the autocommit parameter
       public static Connection getConnection(
         String url, Properties props, boolean autocommit)
           throws SQLException
       {
         Connection connection = DriverManager.getConnection(url, props);
         connection.setAutoCommit(autocommit);
         return connection;
       }


       public static void rollback(Connection conn) {
         try {
           conn.rollback();
         } catch (Exception e) {
           e.printStackTrace();
         }
       }

     // close(Connection conn) not shown
     // close(Statement stmt) not shown
     // close(ResultSet rset) not shown


     }
```

2.   Now create the following client class:

```
     package Ch07;

     import java.sql.*;

     public class JDBCClient5 {
       static Connection conn = null;
       static PreparedStatement pstmt = null;
```

```java
static ResultSet rset = null;

static String sqlInsert =
  "insert into COUNTRIES "
    + "(COUNTRY, COUNTRY_ISO_CODE, REGION) "
    + "values (?, ?, ?)";

static String sqlQuery = "select * from COUNTRIES";

public static void main(String[] args) {
  try {
    String url = "jdbc:pointbase:server://192.168.1.103/pointbaseDB";
    String username = "PBPUBLIC";
    String password = "PBPUBLIC";
    conn = JDBCManager.getConnection(url, username, password, false);
    pstmt = conn.prepareStatement(sqlInsert);

    // Transaction begins here
    cleanupTable();
    doEUBatch();
    doNABatch();
    System.out.println(
      "\nChecking the table before " + "commit or rollback:");
    doQuery();

    // Pretend we need to roll back
    JDBCManager.rollback(conn);
    System.out.println("\nChecking the table after rollback:");
    doQuery();
    JDBCManager.close(pstmt);

    pstmt = conn.prepareStatement(sqlInsert);
    doEUBatch();
    doNABatch();
    conn.commit();
    System.out.println("\nChecking the table after commit:");
    doQuery();
  } catch (SQLException e) {

    // An exception means something failed, so do rollback
    JDBCManager.rollback(conn);
    e.printStackTrace();
  } finally {
    JDBCManager.close(rset);
    JDBCManager.close(pstmt);
    JDBCManager.close(conn);
  }
}

public static void cleanupTable() {
  // If there is data in the COUNTRIES table from previous examples
  // then delete this old data
  Statement stmt = null;

  try {
    stmt = conn.createStatement();
```

```
      stmt.executeUpdate("delete from COUNTRIES");
      conn.commit();
      System.out.println("Database has been cleaned");
    } catch (Exception e) {
      JDBCManager.rollback(conn);
    } finally {
      JDBCManager.close(stmt);
    }
  }

  public static void doEUBatch() throws SQLException {
    pstmt.setString(1, "Kyrgyzstan");
    pstmt.setString(2, "KG");
    pstmt.setString(3, "Asia");
    pstmt.addBatch();

    pstmt.setString(1, "Great Britain");
    pstmt.setString(2, "GB");
    pstmt.setString(3, "Europe");
    pstmt.addBatch();

    pstmt.setString(1, "France");
    pstmt.setString(2, "FR");
    pstmt.addBatch();

    pstmt.executeBatch();
  }

  public static void doNABatch() throws SQLException {
    pstmt.setString(1, "United States");
    pstmt.setString(2, "US");
    pstmt.setString(3, "North America");
    pstmt.addBatch();

    pstmt.setString(1, "Canada");
    pstmt.setString(2, "CA");
    pstmt.addBatch();

    pstmt.executeBatch();
  }

  public static void doQuery() throws SQLException {
    Statement stmt = null;
    try {
      stmt = conn.createStatement();
      rset = stmt.executeQuery(sqlQuery);
      int rownum = 1;
      if (rset.next()) {
        do {
          System.out.print("row " + rownum++ +" is ");
          System.out.print(rset.getString(1) + ", ");
          System.out.print(rset.getString(2) + ", ");
          System.out.println(rset.getString(3));

        } while (rset.next());
      } else {
```

```
            System.out.println("No results in table");
        }
    } catch (SQLException e) {
        e.printStackTrace();
    } finally {
        JDBCManager.close(rset);
        JDBCManager.close(stmt);
    }
  }
}
```

3.   Compile the classes and run the PointBase server.

4.   As usual, check that the classpath includes the pbclient.jar file as well as the directory above the working directory. Then, you can run the program:

```
> set classpath=c:\Sun\j2sdkee1.4_beta2\pointbase\lib\pbclient.jar

> java -Djdbc.drivers=com.pointbase.jdbc.jdbcUniversalDriver Ch07.JDBCClient5
Database has been cleaned

Checking the table before commit or rollback:
row 1 is Kyrgyzstan, KG, Asia
row 2 is Great Britain, GB, Europe
row 3 is France, FR, Europe
row 4 is United States, US, North America
row 5 is Canada, CA, North America

Checking the table after rollback:
No results in table

Checking the table after commit:
row 1 is Kyrgyzstan, KG, Asia
row 2 is Great Britain, GB, Europe
row 3 is France, FR, Europe
row 4 is United States, US, North America
row 5 is Canada, CA, North America
```

How It Works

This class uses the COUNTRIES table that was created in earlier examples. If you did not run those earlier examples, you should refer back to the JDBCClient3 example for the SQL to create the table. This code also assumes there is data in the table, so it uses the cleanupTable() method to delete any existing rows in the table.

Then, the class calls two methods that insert data into the table. This shows that transactions within a single connection can span multiple methods; you don't need to confine a transaction to a single method in a class.

After both methods complete, the code queries the table. Since this occurs within the same transaction, the changes the code made are visible in a query. (Other transactions may or may not be able to see these changes before the commit. See the *Locking and Isolation* section later for more information.) Now, the code pretends there was some problem and calls rollback(). This ends the transaction, and since a rollback discards the changes, a subsequent query finds no rows in the table.

The code then inserts the data again, this time calling commit when all inserts are complete. Calling commit() ends the transaction, but since it saves all the changes, a subsequent query finds all five rows in the table.

Introduction to Distributed Transactions

Previously in this section, we've been looking at transactions involving a single connection to a single database. In your work with J2EE applications, you may be faced with a situation where you need to use **distributed transactions**.

Distributed transactions can include two or more databases:

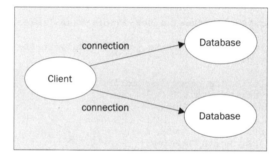

or transactions can span multiple connections to the same data source:

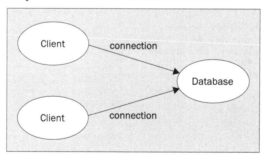

Just as for single connection transactions, all the changes made by each connection in the distributed transaction must be successful for the transaction to be committed.

From the client's point of view, coding a distributed transaction is almost the same as coding for a single connection transaction, so we will be able to look at distributed transactions from that perspective.

While you can use multiple data sources or connections within your JDBC application, the term "distributed transactions" usually applies to applications or classes that have distributed components. One place where you are likely to run into distributed applications is, of course, a J2EE application, where various components may execute on different servers. We've seen some of these components already–JSPs, servlets, and databases. In the following chapters, we'll look at other J2EE components such as Enterprise JavaBeans (EJBs). These components will most likely be running inside a container called an **application server**. You'll learn more about application servers in the EJB chapters. For now, we'll define an application server as an application that acts as a container for J2EE components and provides the infrastructure support to business logic components.

When separate components provide part of a transaction, no single component can determine when or how to commit or roll back changes. This then becomes the responsibility of the transaction manager. Since we're working in the Java world, that manager will be an implementation of the **Java Transaction API (JTA)**.

> *You can learn more about the JTA at* http://java.sun.com/products/jta.

The application server will use a transaction manager to provide distributed transaction support to the components in a J2EE application. As part of providing transaction support, the application server will use special JDBC classes. Those classes will implement the XADataSource, XAConnection, and XAResource interfaces. The application server vendor or the database vendor will provide these classes. At least one of these classes might look vaguely familiar: the XAConnection. Its name is similar to Connection, but it's got that XA bit on the front. As its name suggests, the XAConnection interface represents connections. However, in this case, it represents a connection that can be used in a distributed transaction. Likewise, XADataSource and XAResource represent data sources and resources used in distributed transactions.

However, the client does not need to use or be aware of these classes. At the client level, the code will use the same interfaces that we have seen throughout this chapter: Connection, Statement, and ResultSet. Just like when the JDBCClient1 or JDBCClient2 classes got a Connection object, the reference was of type java.sql.Connection. Even though the underlying object may have been a com.pointbase.jdbc.jdbcUniversalDriver, the client simply used a Connection object. Likewise, even though the underlying object may be an XAConnection, the client will still use a reference of type Connection. The client code used to talk to the database will not look very different from code we have seen previously in this chapter. For example, the code to get a connection might look like this:

```
Context context = new InitialContext();
DataSource dataSource = context.lookup("jdbc/oracle");
Connection connection = dataSource.getConnection();
```

If you look at the *Data Source and Connection Pools* section earlier in this chapter, you will see that the code used to get a "normal" data source is essentially the same that an application involved in a distributed transaction will use. Under the covers, the application server will likely use an XAConnection implementation to get the connection that is passed to the client, but in the client, the object will be referenced as a Connection. After getting the connection, the code would use one of the statement objects to send SQL to the data source. The difference between a nondistributed and a distributed transaction is in how the transaction is committed or rolled back.

Since the transaction is being controlled by a transaction manager outside the client, any class involved in a distributed transaction is prohibited from calling any of these methods:

- ❑ commit()

- ❑ rollback()

- ❑ setSavepoint()

- ❑ setAutoCommit(true)

Committing or rolling back a transaction is entirely under the control of the transaction manager. The client does not need to do anything special other than call the close() method of the Connection interface when it has completed its work. After all the components involved in the transaction have completed, the transaction manager will commit or roll back the transaction.

This commit (or rollback) is called a **two-phase commit**. It has two phases because the transaction manager must poll all the data sources before deciding to commit or roll back. As each data source is polled, it throws an exception if it cannot commit its changes. If no data source throws an exception in the polling phase, the transaction manager instructs the data sources to commit their changes. Suppose we have two clients involved in a distributed transaction. Here's an illustration of how the two-phase commit would proceed:

Time	
T0	Both clients have called close() to signal that they have completed their work.
T1	Transaction manager calls the prepare() method of XAResource. There is an XAResource for each data source.
T2	If neither XAResource throws an exception, then each is ready to commit.
T3	Transaction manager calls the commit() method of each XAResource. This message is passed to each data source, which then commits.

Note that the above would all occur outside the client code. It is entirely handled by the transaction manager. If no data sources throw an exception in the polling phase, the transaction manager tells all the data sources to commit their changes. If any data source throws an exception, all the data sources are notified to roll back the changes.

We've seen in this section how to deal with situations where you are updating more than a single table. These are situations where you might be making numerous changes to a database, and all the changes must succeed for the database to be in a consistent state at the end of the transaction.

Often, though, in a web application, your client application will only be one of many that are trying to perform a transaction simultaneously. In the few minutes it took me to write this paragraph, during the busy shopping season of December, Amazon.com just processed 1,324 transactions. That's 1,324 transactions potentially touching the same rows in the database. (Well, let's caveat that; more likely for the top ranked sellers, almost nil for the bottom ranked sellers.) Using transaction control will ensure that all of the changes in a transaction are committed or rolled back, but it says nothing about what happens when two or more transactions are dealing with the same data. To deal with that situation, we need to look at the topic of locking.

Locking and Isolation

In any application where you must be concerned with two or more clients interacting with the database (and that includes almost every J2EE application with a database) you need to be concerned with the problem of **concurrency**. That is, how do allow multiple users to interact with the database, and yet prevent their actions from interfering with each other.

Databases handle this problem through **isolation** and some type of concurrency control that usually involves **locking** the data in the database. However, different databases handle isolation and locking differently. You can tell the database what level of isolation to use, and thus have some control over isolation. Locking, however, is totally under the control of the database. There is no way for you, as a JDBC developer, to tell the database how to lock the data. The database chooses to lock or not, based on the SQL commands you are executing. For this reason, we will not discuss the locking behavior of any particular database.

> **Locking is highly database-dependent. You *must* check the database documentation to determine how your database handles concurrency control and locking.**

Isolation

Isolation refers to the degree to which actions taken in one transaction can be seen by other transactions. At the highest level of isolation, any actions taken in a transaction cannot be seen by any other transaction. This applies to both reads and writes. That is, if one transaction reads a row or rows of data, no other transaction is impacted by the first transaction. At the lowest level of isolation (as defined by the SQL specification) everything done in any transaction, whether committed or not, can be seen by any other transaction.

The ANSI/ISO SQL92 standard identifies three different types of interactions between transactions. From the lowest to the highest levels of isolation, these types are dirty reads, non-repeatable reads, and phantom reads:

❏ **Dirty reads**–Changes made in one transaction can be seen in other transactions, whether committed or not.

❏ **Non-repeatable reads**–Updates to existing rows made in one transaction are seen by other transactions as soon as they are committed. Thus, multiple queries that are the same may retrieve different data within a single transaction.

❏ **Phantom reads**–Inserts to tables made in one transaction are seen by other transactions as soon as they are committed.

The transaction level you select will depend on the business requirements of your application. The SQL specification identifies four isolation levels that indicate which interactions above are allowed or prevented. Those levels are read uncommitted, read committed, repeatable read, and serializable:

❏ **Read uncommitted**–Lowest level, allows all interactions

❏ **Read committed**–Prevents dirty reads

❏ **Repeatable read**–Prevents nonrepeatable reads

❏ **Serializable**–Highest level, prevents all interactions

Most databases have a default level of read committed, and this will be sufficient for most applications. You can select a higher level with the method from the `Connection` interface:

```
void setTransactionIsolation(int level)
```

This method is called before a transaction begins. You pass one of four arguments to the method. The arguments are defined as constants in the `Connection` interface. They are:

❏ `TRANSACTION_READ_UNCOMMITTED`

❏ `TRANSACTION_READ_COMMITTED`

❏ `TRANSACTION_REPEATABLE_READ`

❏ `TRANSACTION_SERIALIZABLE`

A database may not support all levels of isolation. For example, the PointBase server that comes with J2EE final 2 does not support the read uncommitted level. Check your database documentation to see which levels are supported.

Locking

Even though you can't control how the database locks data, the SQL commands you execute and how you execute them can have a big impact on how separate concurrent transactions in a database interfere, or don't interfere, with each other.

Let's look at what might happen if two transactions attempt to modify the same data when the application is not properly designed for concurrency and isolation. Let's assume that we are working on an online reservation system for a small bed & breakfast style hotel. A guest can log on to the site, see which rooms are available, and make reservations for an available room:

Time	Transaction A	Transaction B
T0	Beth logs onto the web site and queries the application for available rooms. The system reads from the database and shows that the Pikes Peak Room is available.	Jennifer logs onto the web site and performs the same query. Again, the Pikes Peak room is shown as available.
T1		Jennifer makes a reservation for the Pikes Peak room. The application updates the database to show that the Pikes Peak room is reserved for Jennifer.
T2	Beth makes a reservation for the Pikes Peak room. The application updates the database, this time setting the data to show that the room is reserved for Beth.	

You can see that at T1, the database has been placed into a particular state. In this state, a table has been updated to show certain information. However, because transaction A was operating on the database based on its original view of the data, when it updates the same table, the updates from transaction B are overwritten or lost. This is known as a lost update.

Either transaction could have prevented this problem by the proper use of locking. If **pessimistic locking** had been used, then the first transaction to perform the original query would have locked that data, preventing the other transaction from modifying the data. If **optimistic locking** had been used, then the second transaction to attempt to update the table would have been prevented from doing so because it would have found that the table had changed since the original query. In the next two sections, we'll look at each type of locking in more detail.

Pessimistic Locking

Pessimistic locking is usually used when there is a high likelihood that other transactions might want to change the table between a query and an update. For example, in an online concert ticketing system, if the user selects a particular seat, there is an implicit promise that the user can buy that seat before any other user. The application should give that user the option of completing the purchase; only if the user declines to purchase the ticket should it be re-offered to anyone else. Thus, the application should somehow lock that data at the time the seat is selected. We call it pessimistic locking because we are pessimistic about the chances of no one wanting to buy the same tickets (or access the same data) between the times the user checks the availability of seats and purchases the tickets.

In SQL, you indicate that you intend to update some data using the FOR UPDATE clause of your SELECT statement. When you use FOR UPDATE with SELECT, it signals to the database that it should lock the data against other updates until your transaction is complete. Remember, however, that every database will do this differently.

In the next example, we'll see how PointBase performs this pessimistic locking.

Try It Out   Using Pessimistic Locking

We need two client classes for this example, one for each simulated transaction.

1. Create the PessimisticLockerA.java class using the code shown below. Notice that it uses the final version of the JDBCManager class from earlier in this chapter. You will need to create that class also, if you have not already done so. This class creates the table for this example, in addition to querying and updating the table:

```java
package Ch07;

import java.sql.*;
import java.io.*;

public class PessimisticLockerA {
    static Connection conn;
    static Statement stmt;
    static Statement stmtA;
    static PreparedStatement pstmt;
    static ResultSet rsetA;

    static String sqlCreate = "create table RESERVE " +
        "(ROOMID varchar(5), RES_DATE date, RES_FLAG boolean, " +
        "RES_NAME varchar(30))";
    static String sqlInsert = "insert into RESERVE values " +
        "(?, ?, ?, ?)";
    static String sqlUpdate = "update RESERVE set RES_FLAG=?, " +
        "RES_NAME=? WHERE ROOMID=? AND RES_DATE=?";
    static String sqlSelect = "select ROOMID, RES_DATE, " +
        "RES_FLAG, RES_NAME from RESERVE WHERE RES_FLAG=false FOR UPDATE";

    static String roomName;
    static java.sql.Date roomDate;

    public static void main(String[] args) {
        try {
            String url = "jdbc:pointbase:server://localhost/pointbaseDB";
            String username = "PBPUBLIC";
            String password = "PBPUBLIC";
            conn = JDBCManager.getConnection(url, username, password, false);
            System.out.println("conn autocommit is " + conn.getAutoCommit());
            setup();
            userAQuery();
            System.out.println("Sleeping for 15 seconds, " +
                        "run PessimisticLockerB");
```

```
      try {Thread.sleep(15000);} catch (Exception e) {}
        System.out.println("PessimisticLockerA is awake");
        userAUpdate();
      } catch (Exception e) {
        e.printStackTrace();
      } finally {
        JDBCManager.close(conn);
    }
}

static void setup() throws SQLException {
  System.out.println("Creating RESERVE table");
  try {
    stmt = conn.createStatement();
    stmt.addBatch(sqlCreate);
    stmt.executeBatch();
    System.out.println("Inserting row of data");
    pstmt = conn.prepareStatement(sqlInsert);
    pstmt.setString(1, "PIKE");
    pstmt.setDate(2, new java.sql.Date(System.currentTimeMillis()));
    pstmt.setBoolean(3,false);
    pstmt.setNull(4, java.sql.Types.VARCHAR);
    pstmt.executeUpdate();
    conn.commit();
  } finally {
    JDBCManager.close(pstmt);
    JDBCManager.close(stmt);
  }
}

static void userAQuery() throws SQLException {
  System.out.println("User A is querying for rooms");
  stmtA = conn.createStatement();
  rsetA = stmtA.executeQuery(sqlSelect);
  if (rsetA.next()) {
    System.out.println("Query returned one row");
    roomName = rsetA.getString(1);
    roomDate = rsetA.getDate(2);
  }
  // Neither the statement nor resultset are closed here
  // We need them open for the userAUpdate() method
}

static void userAUpdate() throws SQLException {
  try {
    if (roomName != null && roomDate != null) {
      System.out.println("User A is attempting to reserve room");
      pstmt = conn.prepareStatement(sqlUpdate);
      pstmt.setBoolean(1, true);
      pstmt.setString(2, "User A");
      pstmt.setString(3,roomName);
      pstmt.setDate(4, roomDate);
      int result = pstmt.executeUpdate();
      if (result == 0) {
        System.out.println("Reservation did NOT succeed!");
        System.out.println("The user will have to try " +
```

```
                                        "another room, or another date");
             } else {
                System.out.println("Calling commit for user A");
                conn.commit();
             }
          }
       } catch (SQLException e) {
          e.printStackTrace(DriverManager.getLogWriter());
          System.out.println(e.getErrorCode());
          System.out.println(e.getMessage());
       } finally {
          JDBCManager.close(pstmt);
          JDBCManager.close(rsetA);
          JDBCManager.close(stmtA);
       }
    }
 }
```

2.   Now we create the PessimisticLockerB class. This class simply queries the table and
     attempts to update it:

```
package Ch07;

import java.sql.*;
import java.io.*;

public class PessimisticLockerB {
   static Connection conn;
   static Statement stmt;
   static Statement stmtB;
   static PreparedStatement pstmt;
   static ResultSet rsetB;

   static String sqlUpdate = "update RESERVE set RES_FLAG=?, " +
      "RES_NAME=? WHERE ROOMID=? AND RES_DATE=?";
   static String sqlSelect = "select ROOMID, RES_DATE, " +
      "RES_FLAG, RES_NAME from RESERVE WHERE RES_FLAG=false FOR UPDATE";

   static String roomName;
   static java.sql.Date roomDate;

   public static void main(String[] args) {
      try {
         String url = "jdbc:pointbase:server://localhost/pointbaseDB";
         String username = "PBPUBLIC";
         String password = "PBPUBLIC";
         conn = JDBCManager.getConnection(url, username, password, false);
         System.out.println("conn autocommit is " + conn.getAutoCommit());
         userBQueryAndUpdate();
      } catch (Exception e) {
         e.printStackTrace();
      } finally {
         JDBCManager.close(conn);
      }
   }
```

```
static void userBQueryAndUpdate() throws SQLException {
  System.out.println("User B is querying for rooms");
  try {
    stmtB = conn.createStatement();
    rsetB = stmtB.executeQuery(sqlSelect);
    if (rsetB.next()) {
      System.out.println("User B is reserving room");
      pstmt = conn.prepareStatement(sqlUpdate);
      pstmt.setBoolean(1, true);
      pstmt.setString(2, "User B");
      pstmt.setString(3,rsetB.getString(1));
      pstmt.setDate(4, rsetB.getDate(2));
      pstmt.executeUpdate();
      System.out.println("Calling commit for user B");
      conn.commit();
    } else {
      System.out.println("User B found no available rooms");
    }
  } catch (SQLException e) {
    e.printStackTrace();
    System.out.println(e.getErrorCode());
    System.out.println(e.getMessage());
  } finally {
    JDBCManager.close(pstmt);
    JDBCManager.close(rsetB);
    JDBCManager.close(stmtB);
  }
}
}
```

3. Compile the classes and start the PointBase server if it isn't already running, using the usual commands at the prompt.

4. These two classes need to be run at the same time, so you will need to open two windows, one for each class. Open the windows and prepare the usual classpath for each class:

```
> set classpath=C:\Sun\j2sdkee1.4_beta2\pointbase\lib\pbclient.jar
> set classpath=%classpath%;C:\3413
```

5. PessimisticLockerA needs to be run first, and then after it performs the query, PessimisticLockerB is run. I've inserted a sleep into the code for PessimisticLockerA so that you have time to run PessimisticLockerB. In each window, prepare the command line for running the class. In the first window enter the following:

```
> java -Djdbc.drivers=com.pointbase.jdbc.jdbcUniversalDriver
Ch07.PessimisticLockerA
```

And in the second window, enter this command:

```
> java -Djdbc.drivers=com.pointbase.jdbc.jdbcUniversalDriver
Ch07.PessimisticLockerB
```

Now execute the command for `PessimisticLockerA`. You will see this output:

```
conn autocommit is false
Creating RESERVE table
Inserting row of data
User A is querying for rooms
Query returned one row
Sleeping for 15 seconds, run PessimisticLockerB
```

When you see the message that `PessimisticLockerA` is sleeping, run `PessimisticLockerB`, and you will see this output:

```
conn autocommit is false
User B is querying for rooms
```

Then, `PessimisticLockerB` will appear to freeze while it waits for the query to return. Its query is blocked because the database has locked the table row as a result of user A's query. After 15 seconds have passed, the code for `PessimisticLockerA` wakes up and continues to execute. This is what you see:

```
PessimisticLockerA is awake
User A is attempting to reserve room
Calling commit for user A
```

After the code calls commit, PointBase releases the lock on the row, and `PessimisticLockerB`'s query returns. Unfortunately for B, user A got the last room:

```
User B found no available rooms
```

How It Works

This is probably the most complicated of the examples in this chapter, since it relies on the timing between the two client classes and the locking behavior of the database.

> **Locking is very dependent on the database. This example may or may not work with other databases. Even if it does work with different databases, the behavior you see may be different. Consult the database documentation to understand how locking works so that you understand how the database deals with multiple users in the database and how to control their interactions.**

First, the code in `PessimisticLockerA` creates the `RESERVE` table that represents a room reservation system. The table has four columns, a room ID, a reservation date, a flag for whether the room is reserved, and the name of the person reserving the room. The code also inserts a single row of data into the table. Notice that because the table includes a date and a boolean column, and a null value is inserted, it uses a prepared statement to insert the row. As we saw in the *Prepared Statement* section of this chapter, with some data types, such as date, it's easier to use a prepared statement; with other data values such as boolean or null, using a prepared statement may be the only way to insert those values into the table with JDBC.

Each of the classes shown above queries the database to find a row of data. This query is performed with this SQL SELECT command:

```
SELECT ROOMID, RES_DATE, RES_FLAG, RES_NAME
   from RESERVE
WHERE RES_FLAG=false FOR UPDATE
```

The FOR UPDATE clause tells the database that the transaction intends to update the table, and that the database should perform locking to ensure that no other transaction can modify the data until the first transaction is complete. However, notice that there is no way to tell the database how to lock the data. This is one of the features of a declarative language like SQL. You instruct the database to execute a command, such as select, insert, or update, and the database determines how to execute the command. PointBase, for example, has row locks and table locks, but which lock it decides to use depends on several factors, and there is no way to tell which lock will be used.

After user A queries the table, the code saves the value of the ROOMID and RES_DATE columns. Also, it does not close the statement or resultset; this is because the code is simulating a real-world situation in which a client may keep those objects open while updating the data. The code then executes a Java sleep() method. This simulates the real-world behavior of some lag in time between when a user queries some data and submits new data for updating the database. It also provides a time gap in which the PessimisticLockerB class can be run.

Like user A, user B executes a query that looks for rooms in the database that have not yet been reserved. If user B finds such a row, user B attempts to reserve the room. However, user B's query is blocked, apparently because the database has locked the RESERVE table for update by user A.

After 15 seconds, the code for PessimisticLockerA wakes, and continues executing. The code performs an SQL UPDATE to reserve the room for user A, and then commits the transaction. At this point, user B's query unblocks. Unfortunately, because no rows now match the query, rset.next() returns false. User B finds no rooms available.

In this example, we allowed one transaction to get access to and update data from the database. With the proper use of pessimistic locking, the first user to access the data was the user that got to update the data. However, that came at a cost. With the particular way this example was structured, any other user was completely prevented from accessing the table at all. Suppose user A had walked away from their computer for 15 minutes, or even 15 hours. User B's application may have been frozen for that entire length of time. That's a heavy price to pay to ensure a good user experience (for user A, not B). It's very important to stress, though, that other situations or other databases may not have prevented B from querying the table. That's why it's so important for you to understand how your database handles this situation.

Optimistic Locking

Optimistic locking is usually used when there is a low likelihood that other transactions might want to change the table between a query and an update. In fact, unlike pessimistic locking, it really does not involve locking at all, but it still prevents the problem of lost updates. We call it optimistic because we are optimistic about the chances of no one wanting to access the same data (or reserve the same room) between the time the user queries the data and attempts to update the data.

To implement optimistic locking in your code, when your code performs a query, it keeps a local copy of all the data it retrieved. It then presents this data to the user for him to modify. Then when your code issues the update statement, it includes a WHERE clause in the SQL command which checks that the data in the table still matches the data originally retrieved. If it does not, that means some other user has modified the data between your query and your update. Your update command fails, but the other user's update is not lost. We can see how this works with the following example.

Try It Out   Using Optimistic Locking

1. Here is a client class that demonstrates how optimistic locking might be used. Enter and save this file as OptimisticLocker.java:

```java
package Ch07;

import java.sql.*;
import java.io.*;

public class OptimisticLocker {
   static Connection conn;
   static Statement stmt;
   static PreparedStatement pstmt;
   static ResultSet rset;

   static String sqlCreate = "create table RESERVE " +
      "(ROOMID varchar(5), RES_DATE date, RES_FLAG boolean, " +
      "RES_NAME varchar(30))";
   static String sqlInsert = "insert into RESERVE values " +
      "(?, ?, ?, ?)";
   static String sqlUpdate = "update RESERVE set RES_FLAG=?, " +
      "RES_NAME=? WHERE ROOMID=? AND RES_DATE=? AND RES_FLAG=?";
   static String sqlSelect = "select ROOMID, RES_DATE, " +
      "RES_FLAG, RES_NAME from RESERVE WHERE RES_FLAG=0";

   static String roomName;
   static java.sql.Date roomDate;
   static boolean reserveStatus;

   public static void main(String[] args) {
      try {
         String url = "jdbc:pointbase:server://localhost/pointbaseDB";
         String username = "PBPUBLIC";
         String password = "PBPUBLIC";
         conn = JDBCManager.getConnection(url, username, password);        stmt =
```

```
conn.createStatement();
        setup();
        userAQuery();
        userBQueryAndUpdate();
        userAUpdate();
      } catch (Exception e) {
      e.printStackTrace();
      } finally {
        JDBCManager.close(rset);
        JDBCManager.close(pstmt);
        JDBCManager.close(stmt);
        JDBCManager.close(conn);
      }
    }

    static void setup() throws SQLException {
      System.out.println("Creating RESERVE table");
      stmt.addBatch(sqlCreate);
      stmt.executeBatch();
      System.out.println("Inserting row of data");
      pstmt = conn.prepareStatement(sqlInsert);
      pstmt.setString(1, "PIKE");
      pstmt.setDate(2, new java.sql.Date(System.currentTimeMillis()));
      pstmt.setBoolean(3,false);
      pstmt.setNull(4, java.sql.Types.VARCHAR);
      pstmt.executeUpdate();
      JDBCManager.close(pstmt);
    }

    static void userAQuery() throws SQLException {
      System.out.println("User A is querying for rooms");
      rset = stmt.executeQuery(sqlSelect);
      rset.next();
      roomName = rset.getString(1);
      roomDate = rset.getDate(2);
      reserveStatus = rset.getBoolean(3);
      JDBCManager.close(rset);
    }

    static void userBQueryAndUpdate() throws SQLException {
      System.out.println("User B is querying for rooms");
      rset = stmt.executeQuery(sqlSelect);
      rset.next();
      System.out.println("User B is reserving room");
      pstmt = conn.prepareStatement(sqlUpdate);
      pstmt.setBoolean(1, true);
      pstmt.setString(2, "Jennifer");
      pstmt.setString(3,rset.getString(1));
      pstmt.setDate(4, rset.getDate(2));
      pstmt.setBoolean(5, rset.getBoolean(3));
      pstmt.executeUpdate();
      JDBCManager.close(rset);
      JDBCManager.close(pstmt);
    }

    static void userAUpdate() throws SQLException {
```

```
        System.out.println("User A is attempting to reserve room");
        pstmt = conn.prepareStatement(sqlUpdate);
        pstmt.setBoolean(1, true);
        pstmt.setString(2, "Beth");
        pstmt.setString(3,roomName);
        pstmt.setDate(4, roomDate);
        pstmt.setBoolean(5, reserveStatus);
        int result = pstmt.executeUpdate();
        if (result == 0) {
           System.out.println("Reservation for User A did NOT succeed!");
           System.out.println("User A will have to try " +
                              "another room, or another date");
        }
        JDBCManager.close(pstmt);
     }
  }
```

2. Note that before this code can be run, you need to delete the reservations table we created in the previous example. Using either the PointBase commander or console (in the PointBase\tools directory), enter the following command:

```
> startcommander.bat
...startup information is entered...
SQL> drop table RESERVE
```

3. Compile the class using the usual compile command, make sure the PointBase server is running, set the relevant classpath and then run the program using:

```
> java -Djdbc.drivers=com.pointbase.jdbc.jdbcUniversalDriver
Ch07.OptimisticLocker
```

4. Here is the output from running the program on my system:

```
Creating RESERVE table
Inserting row of data
User A is querying for roooms
User B is querying for rooms
User B is reserving room
User A is attempting to reserve room
Reservation did NOT succeed!
The user will have to try another room, or another date
```

5. You can also verify that one reservation occurred and the other did not by running the PointBase commander or console tool. Scripts to run either of these tools are in the PointBase \tools\serveroption directory. Here's the output from my system:

```
> startcommander.bat
...startup information is entered...
SQL> SELECT * from RESERVE;
SQL>

ROOMID          RES_DATE        RES_FLAG        RES_NAME
----------      ----------      ----------      -----------------------------------
PIKE            2003-11-11      TRUE            Jennifer

1 row selected
```

You can see from the output of the SELECT command, that the table was updated with the reservation for user B, but not for user A.

How It Works

The four methods called by main(), demonstrate how optimistic locking works. The first method is the setup() method. This method creates the table and inserts a row of data into the table. The table simulates a room reservation system and it has four columns, one for a room ID, one for reservation date, one for a flag that indicates whether the room is reserved, and one for the name of the person who has the room reserved. The reservation name column is expected to be null when the room is not reserved. If you created the RESERVE table previously in the pessimistic locking example, you should drop that table using the PointBase console or commander tool:

```
> startcommander.bat
...startup information is entered...
SQL> drop table RESERVE;
```

The setup() method has to use a prepared statement to insert the row of data because of the special values used by the table. For instance, to set the reservation name column to null, the code has this line:

```
pstmt.setNull(4, java.sql.Types.VARCHAR);
```

As we saw in the *Prepared Statement* section of this chapter, with some data types, such as Date, it's easier to use a prepared statement; with other data values such as boolean or null, using a prepared statement is the only way to insert those values into the table with JDBC.

Next, the userAQuery() method is called. This simulates a user querying for data from the table. To do the optimistic locking, this method also saves the values of the row it retrieved from the query. This can be done in this simple manner because I only inserted a single row into the table, and I knew that the query would return only a single row. In a real world application, the original query might return many rows, so you would want to wait until the user had selected a particular row before your code saves the data. At the completion of this method, the resultset is no longer needed, so the code closes it.

The userBQueryAndUpdate() method simulates a second user querying and retrieving the same row as user A, and then updating that row. Since there is no lock on the data queried by user A, user B is not restricted from querying or updating the same data that user A is working with. This method also uses the prepared statement to update the data in the table. This time, however, the SQL command is an UPDATE command that uses optimistic locking. When the placeholders in the prepared statement are set with values, the SQL looks like this:

```
UPDATE RESERVE
    set RES_FLAG=true, RES_NAME='Jennifer'
    WHERE ROOMID='Pike' AND RES_DATE='2002-12-20' AND RES_FLAG=false
```

The SQL command that updates the two fields RES_FLAG and RES_NAME has a WHERE clause that checks that no one else has changed the row since user B queried the table. Since no one has, the WHERE clause matches the row, and the update proceeds.

Finally, user A attempts to reserve the room. The code in userAUpdate() uses the same UPDATE command with optimistic locking. When this SQL command is executed, the WHERE condition does not match any data in the table, because RES_FLAG is now true whereas it was false when user A first queried the table. Thus, there are no rows that can be updated and the update fails. The code checks for the return value, and when it sees that zero rows were updated, it logs the failure. If the SQL UPDATE command had only included the ROOM_ID and RES_DATE fields, the update would have proceeded and user B's update would have been lost.

Note that even though the example code executed step by step with no pauses, this does not need to be the case for lost updates to occur. All that need happen is for two or more users to query and attempt to change the same data in the same relative order as shown above: one user reads the data, a second user updates the data, the first user then attempts to update his view of the data which no longer matches what is in the database.

Notice also the differences between pessimistic locking and optimistic locking. With pessimistic locking, the first user to query the data gets to commit his changes. With optimistic locking, the first user to update the table gets to commit his changes. Pessimistic locking works better from the user's point of view; with optimistic locking, the user may expend significant effort to input all the changes he wants only to be told that the update failed when he tries to submit the data. On the other hand, pessimistic locking ties up a database resource, and depending on the database, can prevent other users from working with the database. Which method you choose will depend on the business rules of your application, and the type of locking supported by your database.

Summary

In this chapter we've looked at some advanced topics in JDBC, and how to use JDBC in a J2EE environment. If you are working in a real-world J2EE application, you will almost certainly find that you will be using at least some of the concepts in this chapter. Still, as mentioned in the overview of the first JDBC chapter of this book, there's so much more that wasn't covered. If you find yourself deeply into database programming, you should definitely explore some of the more advanced books that focus on the subject of databases and JDBC programming. If you're not heavily into JDBC, then hopefully this chapter has given you enough to keep you from becoming overwhelmed.

After finishing this chapter you should have learned:

❑ That connections in a J2EE environment are obtained from a DataSource. Data sources hide the connection details away from the client, making it easier to change databases. From the client's point of view, it doesn't matter where the connection comes from.

❑ PreparedStatement objects are used to send SQL commands to the database. PreparedStatement objects are useful when you are sending many SQL commands to the database, and only the data values are changing. Because the database caches the SQL, PreparedStatements can be more efficient that Statement objects. PreparedStatements are also useful when you need to insert non-primitive data into a table. PreparedStatements make it easy to insert Dates, Nulls, Strings, and so on, because the driver formats the data for you.

❑ CallableStatement objects are used to call stored procedures, aka sprocs, in a database. Stored procedures have many advantages, so if your system contains sprocs, you should consider using them rather than recreating their behavior in JDBC.

❑ Connection pools provide a way to avoid the time-consuming creation of new connections. Although you can use connection pools with or without data sources, in a J2EE environment, you will get pooled connections from a DataSource. Pooled connections are used just like non-pooled connections.

❑ Transactions are used to ensure that databases move from one consistent state to another. Properly using transactions can ensure that all the changes your code makes all succeed, or are all rolled back.

❑ A J2EE application needs to deal with problems of isolation and locking. Setting the proper isolation level can prevent one transaction from seeing changes made to the database by other transactions. Preventing two users from changing the same data such that one update is lost is usually done through pessimistic or optimistic locking.

Exercises

1. If your database does support stored procedures, find an existing stored procedure, or create one of your own, and write JDBC code that calls the stored procedures.

2. Write a stored procedure for the PointBase database and call it from JDBC code. One possible stored procedure is one that would add a row to the COUNTRIES table.

3. Rewrite the JDBCManager class to use the Tomcat data source for getting connections. Rewrite the JSP presented in this chapter to use this new JDBCManager class.

8

EJB Fundamentals

So far we've discussed the user interface, business logic, and database connection aspects of developing J2EE applications. The primary mechanism discussed to this point for expressing business logic has been JavaBeans accessed from JSP and servlet code. J2EE has a powerful facility dedicated to expressing the business logic of an application, and for accessing a database using a JavaBeans-like concept. That facility is **Enterprise JavaBeans**, also know as **EJBs** for short.

In this chapter, we'll begin exploring the world of EJBs, which is a very important capability of the J2EE platform. EJBs provide infrastructure for developing and deploying mission-critical, enterprise applications.

Throughout the chapter, you will learn:

- ❏ The benefits of using EJBs
- ❏ The three kinds of EJBs: session, entity, and message-driven beans
- ❏ What an EJB container is
- ❏ How to develop session beans
- ❏ How to use **Java Naming and Directory Interface** (**JNDI**) to locate EJBs
- ❏ Differences between stateful and stateless session beans

Understanding EJBs

Application architectures often consist of several **tiers** that each have their own responsibilities. One such architecture that consists of three tiers is illustrated in the Unified Modeling Language (UML) diagram below:

The two elements on the left-hand side of the diagram are called **components** *in the Unified Modeling Language (UML) notation. Components represent software modules. An overview of the UML is given as part of the download bundle with this book, available on the Apress web site.*

Multi-tiered, or **layered**, architectures have many advantages, not the least of which is the ability to change any one of the layers *without* affecting all of them. In the illustration above, if the *Database* layer is changed, only the *Application Logic* layer is affected. The *Application Logic* layer shields the *User Interface* layer from changes to the *Database* layer. This facilitates ongoing maintenance of the application, and increases its ability to incorporate new technologies in its layers. EJBs provide an application logic layer and a JavaBeans-like abstraction of the database layer. The application logic layer is also known as the middle tier.

> JavaBeans and *Enterprise* JavaBeans are two different things, but because of their similarities (and for marketing reasons) they share a common name. JavaBeans are components built in Java that can be used on any tier in an application. They are often thought of in relationship to servlets, and as GUI components. Enterprise JavaBeans are special, server-based components used for building the business logic and data access functionality of an application.

Why Use EJBs?

Not too long ago, when system developers wanted to create an enterprise application, they would often start by "rolling their own" (or purchasing a proprietary) application server to support the functionality of the application logic layer. Some of the features of an application server include:

❑ **Client communication**—The client, which is often a user interface, must be able to call the methods of objects on the application server via agreed-upon protocols.

❑ **Session state management**—You'll recall our discussions on this topic in the context of JSP and servlet development back in Chapter 5.

❑ **Transaction management**–Some operations, for example when updating data, must occur as a unit of work. If one update fails, they all should fail. Recall that transactions were discussed in Chapter 7.

❑ **Database connection management**–An application server must connect to a database, often using **pools** of database connections for optimizing resources.

❑ **User authentication and role-based authorization**–Users of an application must often log in for security purposes. The functionality of an application to which a user is allowed access is often based upon the role associated with their user ID.

❑ **Asynchronous messaging**–Applications often need to communicate with other systems in an **asynchronous manner**, that is, without waiting on the other system to respond. This requires an underlying messaging system that provides guaranteed delivery of these asynchronous messages.

❑ **Application server administration**–Application servers must be **administered**. For example, they need to be monitored and tuned.

The Enterprise JavaBeans specification defines a common architecture, which has prompted several vendors to build application servers that comply with this specification. Now we can get off-the-shelf application servers that comply with a common standard, benefiting from the competition (in areas such as price, features, and performance) among those vendors. Some of the more common commercial Enterprise JavaBeans application servers are: WebLogic (BEA), Sun ONE (Sun), and WebSphere (IBM).

There are also some very good open-source entries in this market such as JBoss and JOnAS. As you know, Sun provides a freeware Reference Implementation (J2EE SDK) of the J2EE 1.4 and EJB 2.1 specifications that may be used to develop as well as to test an application for compliance with those specifications. The Reference Implementation may not, however, be used to deploy production systems.

> *The Sun Reference Implementation was used to develop all of the examples and exercises contained in this book.*

These application servers, in conjunction with the capabilities defined in the EJB specification, support all of the features listed above and many more. Since they all support the EJB specification, we can develop full-featured enterprise applications and still avoid application server, operating system, and hardware platform vendor lock-in.

Yes, things sure have improved! We now have a standard, specifications-based way to develop and deploy enterprise-class systems. We are approaching the Java dream of developing an application that can run on any vendor platform as-is. This is in contrast to the vendor-specific way we used to develop where each server had its own way of doing things, and where the developer was locked into the chosen platform once the first line of code was written!

For more information on the EJB specification, see the http://java.sun.com/products/ejb/docs.html web site.

313

The Three Kinds of EJBs

As we mentioned briefly at the start of this chapter, there are actually three kinds of EJBs:

- ❑ Session beans
- ❑ Entity beans
- ❑ Message-driven beans

When referring to them in the general sense in this book, we'll use the term **EJBs**, **enterprise beans**, or simply **beans**. Here is a brief introduction to each type of bean. The balance of this chapter will then focus on **session beans**.

Session Beans

One way to think about the application logic layer (middle tier) in the example architecture described above is as a set of objects that, together, implement the business logic of an application. Session beans are the construct in EJBs designed for this purpose. In the diagram below, we see that that there may be multiple session beans in an application and each handles a subset of the application's business logic. A session bean tends to be responsible for a group of related functionality. For example, an application for an educational institution might have a session bean whose methods contain logic for handling student records. Another session bean might contain logic that maintains the lists of courses and programs available at that institution.

There are two types of session bean, which are defined by their use in a client interaction:

- ❑ **Stateless**–These beans do not declare any instance (class-level) variables so that the methods contained within can only act upon any local parameters. There is no way to maintain state across method calls.

- ❑ **Stateful**–These beans can hold client state across method invocations. This is possible with the use of instance variables declared in the class definition. The client will then set the values for these variables and then use these values in other method calls.

Stateless session beans provide excellent scaleability because the EJB container does not have to keep track of their state across method calls. However, storing the state of an EJB is a very resource-intensive process. There may be more work involved for the server to share stateful session beans than stateless beans. So the use of stateful beans in your application may not make it as easily scaleable as using stateless beans.

All EJBs, session beans included, operate within the context of an **EJB server**, shown in the diagram below. An **EJB server** contains constructs known as **EJB containers** that are responsible for providing an operating environment for managing and providing services to the EJBs that are running within it.

In a typical scenario, the user interface (UI) of an application calls the methods of the session beans as it requires the functionality that they provide. Session beans can call other session beans and entity beans. The diagram below illustrates typical interactions between the user interface, session beans, entity beans, and the database:

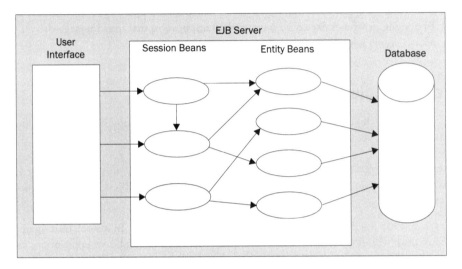

Entity Beans

Before object orientation became popular, programs were usually written in procedural languages and often employed relational databases to hold the data. Because of the strengths and maturity of relational database technology, it is now often advantageous to develop object-oriented applications that use relational databases. The problem with this approach is that there is an inherent difference between object-oriented and relational database technologies, making it less than natural for them to coexist in one application. The use of entity beans is one way to get the best of both of these worlds, because:

❑ Entity beans are objects, and they can be designed using object-oriented principles and utilized in applications as objects.

❑ The data in these entity bean objects are usually persisted in relational databases. All of the benefits of relational technologies, including maturity of products, speed, reliability, ability to recover, and ease of querying, can be leveraged.

In a typical EJB scenario, when a session bean needs to access data it calls the methods of an entity bean. Entity beans represent the persistent data in an EJB application. For example, an application for an educational institution might have an entity bean named Student that has one instance for every student that is enrolled in an institution. Entity beans, often "backed" by a relational database, read and write to tables in the database. Because of this, they provide an object-oriented abstraction to a relational database. Entity beans will be covered in detail in the next chapter.

Message-Driven Beans

When an EJB-based application needs to receive asynchronous messages from other systems, it can leverage the power and convenience of **message-driven beans**. Asynchronous messages between systems can be analogous to the events that are fired from a UI component to an event handler in the same JVM. One example application that could use message-driven beans is in the business to business (B2B) domain: a wholesaler could have an EJB application that uses message-driven beans to listen for purchase orders issued electronically from retailers.

Decisions, Decisions

So, how do you decide whether a given enterprise bean should be a session bean, entity bean, or a message-driven-bean? A set of rules to remember here:

❑   Session beans are great at implementing business logic, processes, and workflow. For example, a StockTrader bean with buy() and sell() methods, among others, would be a good fit for a session bean.

❑   Entity beans are the persistent data objects in an EJB application. In a stock trading application, a Stock bean with setPrice() and getPrice() methods would be an appropriate use of an entity bean. The buy() method of the previously mentioned StockTrader session bean would interact with instances of the Stock entity bean by calling their getPrice() methods for example.

❑   Message-driven beans are used for the special purpose of receiving asynchronous messages from other systems, like the fictitious wholesaler application mentioned above that listens for purchase orders.

By the way, as seen in the diagram above, it is a good practice to call only session beans directly from the client, and to let the session beans call the entity beans. Here are some reasons for this:

❑   This practice doesn't circumvent the business logic contained in the session beans. Calling entity beans directly tends to push the business logic into the UI logic, which is usually a bad thing.

❑   The UI doesn't have to be as dependent upon changes to the entity beans. The UI is shielded from these changes by the session beans.

❑   In order for a client to interact with a bean on the EJB server, there must be a remote reference to the bean, which takes resources. There tends to be far more (orders of magnitude) entity bean instances in an application than session bean instances. Restricting client access to session beans conserves server and network resources considerably.

A Closer Look at Session Beans

Now that we've covered some basics concerning the three types of EJBs, we'll use the rest of this chapter to take a closer look at the first type mentioned–session beans.

The Anatomy of a Session Bean

To develop a session bean, you actually need to create two Java interfaces and a Java class. These interfaces and the class are called the **home interface**, **bean interface**, and **bean class**, respectively. These are illustrated in the following diagram:

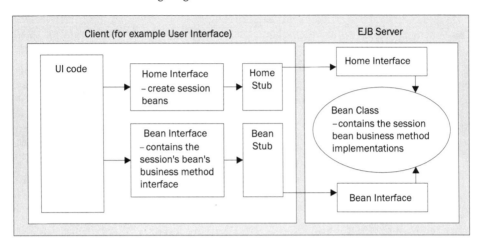

It is worth noting that developing entity beans also requires that you create a home interface, a bean interface, and a bean class. We'll make some entity beans in the next chapter.

The Home Interface

In order for the client of a session bean to get a reference to that bean's interface, it must use the bean's home interface. Incidentally, the home interface for an EJB extends the EJBHome interface of the javax.ejb package; the package that EJB-related classes reside in.

As a naming convention for this book, we'll append the word Home to the name of a bean to indicate that it is a home interface. For example, a session bean with the name StockTrader would have a home interface named StockTraderHome.

The Bean Interface

Session beans have an interface that exposes their business methods to clients. This bean interface extends the EJBObject interface of the javax.ejb package.

As a naming convention for this book, we'll use the name of a bean as the name of its bean interface. For example, a session bean with the name StockTrader would have a bean interface named StockTrader.

The Bean Class

The implementation of the business logic of a session bean is located in its bean class. The bean class of a session bean extends the SessionBean interface of the javax.ejb package.

As a naming convention for this book, we'll append the word Bean to the name of a bean to indicate that it is a bean class. For example, a session bean with the name StockTrader would have a bean class named StockTraderBean.

The Home and Bean Stubs

Also in the previous diagram are the **home stub** and the **bean stub** classes. These stubs are the mechanism by which the UI code on the client can invoke methods of the EJBs that are located on the server. The stubs invoke their respective interfaces on the server side via Java Remote Method Invocation (RMI). RMI is a protocol, included in J2SE 1.4, for invoking the Java methods of a class that exists on another JVM, perhaps on a different machine.

These stubs are created for you by the Deployment Tool that has been used in this book to build and deploy JSPs and servlets. We will use it to build and deploy EJBs as well.

Here is a UML class diagram that depicts the classes, interfaces, and relationships described above:

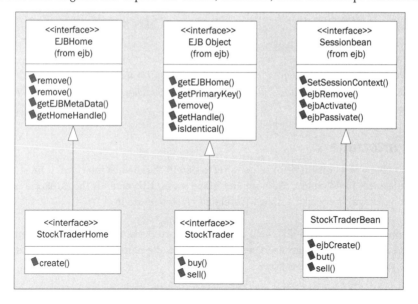

Developing Session Beans

Well, it is now time to put all this theory into practice. In this section, we're going to develop our first session bean in an example that's on par with the traditional "Hello World!" example program.

First, we'll walk through the bean creation code in a good bit of detail, reinforcing concepts we just learned, and covering new ones. Then, we'll explain how to compile the example. For this, we'll use the Java compiler that comes with the Java 2 SDK Standard Edition 1.4 (J2SE SDK 1.4). Then, we'll show you how deploy the example. For this we'll use the Deployment Tool. Finally, we'll run the application.

Try It Out Creating a Session Bean

Since this is the first EJB example, and we haven't learned to build and deploy EJBs yet, we're going to walk through the code now and then run it later. There are four Java source files for this example:

❑   `SimpleSessionHome.java`

❑   `SimpleSession.java`

❑   `SimpleSessionBean.java`

❑   `SimpleSessionClient.java`

1. The first source file contains the code for the home interface, and should be named `SimpleSessionHome.java`. The code that this file contains should be as follows:

```
package beans;
import java.rmi.RemoteException;
import javax.ejb.EJBHome;
import javax.ejb.CreateException;

public interface SimpleSessionHome extends EJBHome {
    // The create() method for the SimpleSession bean
    public SimpleSession create()
        throws CreateException, RemoteException;
}
```

2. This is the code for the bean interface, `SimpleSession.java`:

```
package beans;

import java.rmi.RemoteException;
import javax.ejb.EJBObject;

public interface SimpleSession extends EJBObject {
    // The public business method on the SimpleSession bean
    public String getEchoString(String clientString)
        throws RemoteException;
}
```

3. Next is the code for the bean class, `SimpleSessionBean.java`:

```
package beans;

import javax.ejb.SessionBean;
import javax.ejb.SessionContext;
public class SimpleSessionBean implements SessionBean {
    // The public business method. This must be coded in the
    // remote interface also.
    public String getEchoString(String clientString) {
        return clientString + " - from session bean";
    }

    // Standard ejb methods
```

```
    public void ejbActivate() {}
    public void ejbPassivate() {}
    public void ejbRemove() {}
    public void ejbCreate() {}
    public void setSessionContext(SessionContext context) { }
}
```

4. And this is the client code to test our session bean, `SimpleSessionClient.java`:

```
package client;

import beans.SimpleSession;
import beans.SimpleSessionHome;
import javax.naming.InitialContext;
import javax.rmi.PortableRemoteObject;

public class SimpleSessionClient {
    public static void main(String[] args) {
        try {
            // Get a naming context
            InitialContext jndiContext = new InitialContext();

            // Get a reference to the SimpleSession JNDI entry
            Object ref = jndiContext.lookup("ejb/beans.SimpleSession");

            // Get a reference from this to the Bean's Home interface
            SimpleSessionHome home = (SimpleSessionHome)
            PortableRemoteObject.narrow(ref, SimpleSessionHome.class);

            // Create a SimpleSession object from the Home interface
            SimpleSession simpleSession = home.create();

            // Loop through the words
            for (int i = 0; i < args.length; i++) {
                String returnedString = simpleSession.getEchoString(args[i]);
                System.out.println("sent string: " + args[i] +
                                ", received string: " + returnedString);
            }
        } catch(Exception e) {
            e.printStackTrace();
        }
    }
}
```

These files should be organized in the following subdirectory structure:

he SimpleSessionApp directory.

ing that the classpath is set to contain the j2ee.jar library. At

IOME%\lib\j2ee.jar

directory that the client and beans directories are located, ds from the command prompt:

va

mpiler to place the class files in subdirectories matching their to the given directory. In this case, the given directory is the he period. As a result, the Java class files should end up in the iles.

Server (Start Default Domain) using the instructions in Chapter 2.

l running we need to start the Deployment Tool using the

looks something like this:

The first thing that we need the Deployment Tool to do is create the J2EE application, which will be bundled together in an **enterprise application resource** (**EAR**) file. EAR files are JAR files that contain all of the components of a J2EE application, including other JAR files and application deployment information. These other JAR files could contain:

❑   Enterprise beans and their deployment information

❑   Web application components and deployment information (recall our earlier discussion about WAR files in Chapter 7)

❑   Application client components and deployment information.

10.   To create the application EAR file, from the File menu choose New | Application.

11.   A dialog box will be displayed, prompting you to enter the name of the EAR file, and the application name that you want displayed. Let's name the EAR file SimpleSessionApp.ear, and the application display name SimpleSessionApp:

Click OK to accept the changes to this dialog.

12.   Now we'll create the JAR file in which the session bean classes and resources will be packaged. To do this, choose File | New | Enterprise Bean menu item.

13.   This will start the Enterprise Bean Wizard. On the page shown below you will be asked to choose where you want the bean jar to be placed. We're going to put it in our newly created SimpleSessionApp EAR file. Also on this page is a place to enter the name for the bean jar, we will call it SimpleSessionJar. Finally, click the Edit button on the page to pick the bean class files that you want to put in the bean jar.

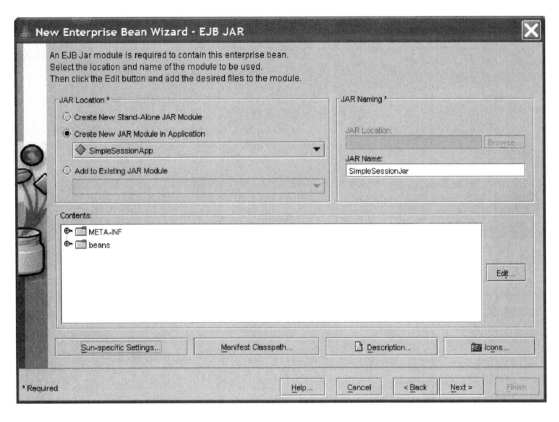

14. In the Available Files panel of the dialog box shown below, navigate to the beans directory of this SimpleSessionApp example. Choose the bean interface, the bean class, and the home interface, and click the Add button. Those bean classes will appear in the Contents of <EJB Bundle> panel as seen below:

15. Click OK in the dialog box and then click the **Next** button to see the page shown below. You will then have four drop-down lists in which to make choices:

❑ From the Enterprise Bean Class drop-down list, choose beans.SimpleSessionBean.

❑ The bean in the `SimpleSessionApp` example is a stateless session bean. To remind you, stateless means it is not capable of storing any information within itself. We'll go into more detail about stateless session beans soon. From the Enterprise Bean Type drop-down list, go ahead and choose Stateless Session.

❑ From the Remote Home Interface drop-down list, choose beans.SimpleSessionHome.

❑ From the Remote Interface drop-down list, choose beans.SimpleSession.

The Enterprise Bean Name is the name for the bean that you'd like to appear in EJB tools. The convention that we'll use is the name of the bean interface concatenated with Ejb, so enter SimpleSessionEjb into this field. When you're done with all this, your window should look like the one shown here:

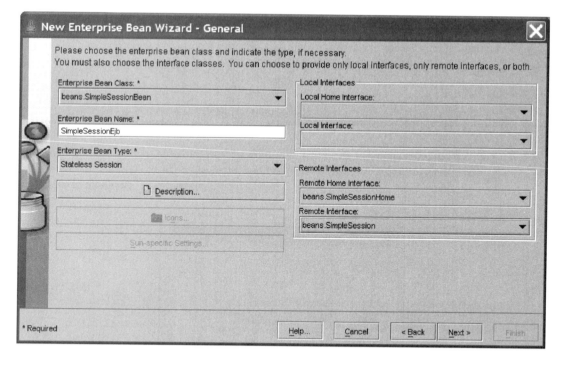

16. Click Next and the resulting dialog asks if you want the bean to be exposed as a **web service**; a concept that we'll cover in detail in Chapter 12 and Chapter 13. For this example, we don't, so just click Next.

17. The last page of the Enterprise Bean Wizard suggests some steps to do next. Click the Finish button to leave the wizard:

Remember the discussion we had about JNDI and how it helped the client get a reference to the home interface of the session bean? The next step deals with this JNDI name.

18. Make sure that SimpleSessionApp is selected in the left-hand panel, as shown below. In the JNDI Name tab, type the same JNDI name that the client application uses in the lookup() method to obtain the bean's home reference. In this case, it is ejb/beans.SimpleSession.

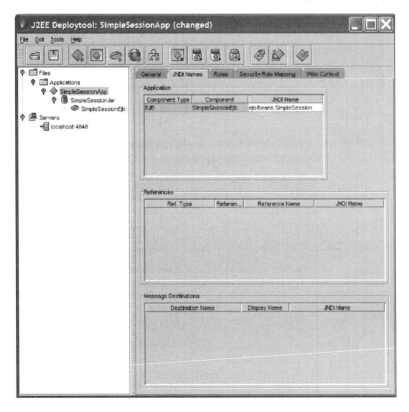

There is one more thing to do before deploying the application: run the Verifier Tool to check whether we've configured the beans according to the EJB specifications.

19. Select the SimpleSessionApp node from the tree on the left panel and choose Verify J2EE Compliance from the Tools menu. You may be prompted to save the application.

20. To run the verification tests against the application, choose one of the Display options and click the OK button. We usually choose Failures Only option as shown below so that only the failed tests show up. The Results and the Details panels show the results of the tests and details of any problems encountered, respectively. If there are any problems encountered, then read the Details and go to the Deployment Tool page in which that detail is configured.

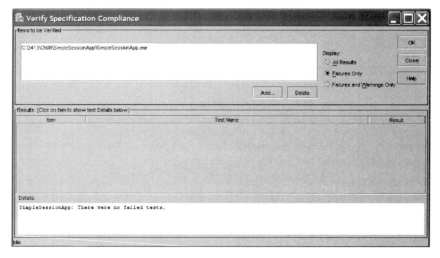

21. If there were no failed tests, close the Verifier Tool. Then go ahead and deploy the application by selecting the SimpleSessionApp node in the tree in the left panel and selecting the Tools | Deploy menu item.

22. As a result, you should see the Deploy Module dialog, shown below. In this dialog, you are prompted for your User Name and Password:

The Deploy Module dialog also asks if you want to create a client JAR file. We need to create a client JAR file that contains the stubs that we discussed earlier. Recall that these stubs live on the client and implement the home interface and bean interface. The client can call the methods defined by those interfaces, and the stubs propagate the method invocations to the home interface and bean interface on the server.

23. To create the client JAR file, check the **Return Client Jar** checkbox in the dialog shown above. Enter the directory in which you want the client JAR file to be located. Choose the same directory that the client directory is rooted in. For this example, specify the name of the directory as `C:\3413\Ch08\SimpleSessionApp`. The tool will name the client JAR file `SimpleSessionAppClient.jar`, which is the name of the application's display name with "`Client.jar`" appended.

24. Click OK, and the following dialog will appear. With any luck, your bean should successfully deploy and start up, ready for clients to invoke its methods. Click the Close button when it becomes enabled:

If there were any error messages when trying to deploy, please read the section called *Troubleshooting the Deploy.*

25. To see a list of the modules that are deployed in the server, select the localhost:4848 node in the Servers tree in the left panel. The right panel will display all of the deployed objects, including the SimpleSessionApp that you just deployed.

Note: As a good housekeeping measure, when you no longer need an application deployed, you should visit this page, select the deployed object, and click Undeploy.

Running the Application

The directory structure should now have the following files:

To run the example client, set the CLASSPATH to:

❑ The current directory (this example has used SimpleSessionApp)

❑ The j2ee.jar file that is in the lib directory of the Java 2 SDK, Enterprise Edition 1.4 (J2EE SDK 1.4) installation

❑ The appserv-rt.jar file that is in the lib directory of the Java 2 SDK, Enterprise Edition 1.4 (J2EE SDK 1.4) installation

❑ The SimpleSessionAppClient.jar file of the current directory

Note that it is important to use the same filename for the client JAR in the CLASSPATH as the Deployment Tool named it when creating it. In future examples, if you ever get a ClassCastException when first running the client, check to make sure that you used the same name.

1. On a default J2EE SDK 1.4 Windows installation, ensure the CLASSPATH is set correctly by using the following command:

```
> set CLASSPATH=.;%J2EE_HOME%\lib\j2ee.jar;%J2EE_HOME%\lib\appserv-
rt.jar;SimpleSessionAppClient.jar
```

2. With SimpleSessionApp as the current directory, execute the following command from the command prompt:

```
> java -Dorg.omg.CORBA.ORBInitialHost=localhost -
Dorg.omg.CORBA.ORBInitialPort=3700 client.SimpleSessionClient now is the time
```

3. When you run the `SimpleSessionClient` client program, it will produce the following output:

```
sent string: now, received string: now - from session bean
sent string: is, received string: is - from session bean
sent string: the, received string: the - from session bean
sent string: time, received string: time - from session bean
```

Not much output for all that work!

How It Works

We have four Java source files to walk through here. We'll start with the client and work our way back up to the session bean interfaces and class.

Using JNDI to Phone Home

The `main()` method of the `SimpleSessionClient` class kicks things off by using the Java Naming and Directory Interface (JNDI) to help us get a reference to the home interface of the session bean. JNDI provides a common interface to directories. The directory that we're dealing with here is internal to the EJB server and holds the reference to the home interface of our session bean. That reference is accessed using the JNDI name `ejb/beans.SimpleSession` which is the name we'll give it when we configure it using the Deployment Tool. The "/" and "." characters are used here as separators in the JNDI name.

```
InitialContext jndiContext = new InitialContext();

Object ref    = jndiContext.lookup("ejb/beans.SimpleSession");
```

After we get the reference, the following statement casts the reference to type `SimpleSessionHome`:

```
SimpleSessionHome home = (SimpleSessionHome)
PortableRemoteObject.narrow(ref, SimpleSessionHome.class);
```

Creating and Using the Session Bean Instance

A reference to the home interface of the session bean now exists on the *client*. We use that client-held home interface to create an instance of that bean on the *server* so that its methods may be invoked. The `create()` method creates an object that implements the bean interface on the client and returns it. In this example, that reference is stored in the variable named `simpleSession`:

```
SimpleSession simpleSession = home.create();
```

The client code for this example, which is shown below, demonstrates that we can pass an argument to a method of a session bean that exists on the server, operate on the argument in the method, and return a different value to the client. More specifically, the code loops through the arguments that were passed to the client's `main()` method via the command line, and passes them one at a time to the `getEchoString()` method of the session bean class. This is accomplished by calling the `getEchoString()` method of the bean interface that exists on the client:

```
for (int i = 0; i < args.length; i++) {
  String returnedString = simpleSession.getEchoString(args[i]);
  System.out.println("sent string: " + args[i] +
                           ", received string: " + returnedString);
}
```

Note that invoking the getEchoString() method of the bean interface on the client invokes the getEchoString() method of the session bean class on the server. This is possible due to the **stub classes** described above. These stub classes are also the reason that invoking the create() method of the bean's home interface on the client was able to cause the session bean to be created on the server. When the create() method of the home interface was called using the following line of code:

```
SimpleSession simpleSession = home.create();
```

it called the home stub class that was generated by the Deployment Tool. This home stub class implements the home interface that is defined in the SimpleSessionHome.java code listing, which we'll turn our attention to now. This interface extends the EJBHome interface located in the javax.ejb package:

```
public interface SimpleSessionHome extends EJBHome {
```

The EJBHome interface defines three methods:

❑ getEJBMetaData()

❑ getHomeHandle()

❑ remove()

SimpleSessionHome defines an additional method:

```
public SimpleSession create()
    throws CreateException, RemoteException;
```

The create() method is analogous to a constructor in a normal Java class. This particular create() method takes no arguments, but it is valid to define this method with parameters when it is desirable to pass in values at bean creation time. Like constructors, the create() method may be overloaded. When the bean is created in the EJB server, the ejbCreate() method of the bean class (SimpleSessionBean.java) will be called by the EJB container:

```
public void ejbCreate() {}
```

In this example, the ejbCreate() method is empty, so no additional initialization will take place apart from what the EJB container will perform. Note that if we had defined a create() method with parameters in the home interface, an ejbCreate() with matching parameters would be required in the bean class.

Since `SimpleSessionBean` implements the `SessionBean` interface of the `javax.ejb` package, it is necessary to implement the other session bean lifecycle methods defined by that interface as well. The EJB container is responsible for calling these methods at various points in the session bean's life cycle. In this case, they are implemented with empty methods:

```
public void ejbActivate() {}
public void ejbPassivate() {}
public void ejbRemove() {}
public void setSessionContext(SessionContext context) { }
```

The one and only business method in this particular session bean takes the argument passed in, appends a string of characters to it, and returns the result:

```
public String getEchoString(String clientString) {
   return clientString + " - from session bean";
}
```

This method is also defined in the bean interface specified in the `SimpleSession.java` code listing:

```
public String getEchoString(String clientString)
   throws RemoteException;
}
```

Note that the `getEchoString()` method defined in the bean interface declares that it throws a `RemoteException`, but the same method in the `SimpleSessionBean` class does need to declare that it throws that exception. This is because the business methods of the bean class are called by the EJB container, and not via RMI.

It may be helpful to refer again to the UML class diagram that depicts these classes, interfaces, and relationships. Now that we've looked at the session bean's Java source code, let's look at another source file that is necessary for session beans, the **deployment descriptor**.

About Bean Jars and Deployment Descriptors

A **bean jar** is a JAR file that is used by an EJB server, and which contains the class files for the EJBs and other resources. A **deployment descriptor** is an XML file that tells the EJB server how to deploy the beans that are in the **bean jar** file by defining their characteristics. Example characteristics include bean names, home interface names, transaction types, and bean method security access. Characteristics can be changed by editing the deployment descriptor without having to recompile the beans, which makes EJBs very flexible and maintainable. The deployment descriptor for this example was generated by the J2EE SDK 1.4 Deployment Tool, but it is possible to create and maintain it manually via a text or XML editor, and with other EJB server vendors' tools. The filename of the deployment descriptor is `ejb-jar.xml`, which is the EJB deployment descriptor that is portable across EJB server implementations. This XML file gets packaged and placed into the bean jar file by the Deployment Tool. The deployment descriptor for the `SimpleSession` example is shown below:

There are platform-specific deployment descriptors as well, which you could see by cracking open jar files that are created by various EJB tools.

331

```xml
<?xml version='1.0' encoding='UTF-8'?>
<ejb-jar
    version="2.1"
    xmlns="http://java.sun.com/xml/ns/j2ee"
    xmlns:xsi="http://www.w3.org/2001/XMLSchema-instance"
    xsi:schemaLocation="http://java.sun.com/xml/ns/j2ee
                        http://java.sun.com/xml/ns/j2ee/ejb-jar_2_1.xsd"
    >
    <display-name>SimpleSessionJar</display-name>
    <enterprise-beans>
        <session>
            <ejb-name>SimpleSessionEjb</ejb-name>
            <home>beans.SimpleSessionHome</home>
            <remote>beans.SimpleSession</remote>
            <ejb-class>beans.SimpleSessionBean</ejb-class>
            <session-type>Stateless</session-type>
            <transaction-type>Bean</transaction-type>
            <security-identity>
                <use-caller-identity>
                </use-caller-identity>
            </security-identity>
        </session>
    </enterprise-beans>
</ejb-jar>
```

Since the ejb-jar.xml file is portable across EJB server implementations, we will examine it in conjunction with the EJB code examples to learn about configuring enterprise bean characteristics. Let's look at a few characteristics in this example.

A bean jar's display-name is the name that would appear in a given vendor's EJB tools, for example an EJB server administration tool:

```xml
<display-name>SimpleSessionJar</display-name>
```

A bean's ejb-name is a unique name for that bean within the ejb-jar.xml file:

```xml
<ejb-name>SimpleSessionEjb</ejb-name>
```

The class names of the home interface, bean interface, and bean class are specified as well:

```xml
<home>beans.SimpleSessionHome</home>
<remote>beans.SimpleSession</remote>
<ejb-class>beans.SimpleSessionBean</ejb-class>
```

We mentioned briefly that a bean interface can be a *remote* interface or a *local* interface. This will be covered in detail in the next chapter, but for now, note that the <remote> element indicates that the bean interface is a remote interface. This indicates that the bean's methods can be called from outside the JVM that it resides in.

Another bean characteristic in the `ejb-jar.xml` file is the `session-type`. In this example, the `SimpleSessionBean` is `Stateless`, which means that it can't be relied upon to remember anything after each method invocation. Anyway, we'll have more to say about **stateless** (and **stateful**) session beans later in this chapter.

Troubleshooting the Deployment

We know that it's hard to believe, but occasionally your application may not deploy successfully on the first try. This is exacerbated by the fact that we're using a reference implementation deployment tool. So if you get an exception in the Distribute Module dialog after attempting deployment, there are a few things you can do to rectify the situation:

❑ Obviously, go back and verify that all the instructions were followed, and run the Verifier Tool.

❑ If you are still getting exceptions when deploying, then try the following steps until you get a successful deploy.

1. Select the applications in the tree on the left, and select Close from the File menu. Exit the Deployment tool. Stop the J2EE application (closing the J2EE window will usually accomplish this). Start the J2EE application again. Start the Deployment Tool. Open your application again by selecting the Open from the File menu and finding your application EAR file. Try to deploy again.

2. If it still doesn't deploy, then repeat the above step, rebooting your machine after stopping the J2EE application.

3. If it still doesn't deploy, then uninstall the J2EE SDK (backing up anything that you care about in the J2EE SDK directory structure) and reinstall. This may seem like a drastic measure, but we've had to take this step on rare occasions.

4. If the application still won't deploy, then it seems reasonable that a bean configuration detail has been missed or incorrectly performed.

When the bean is successfully deployed, we'll get the client ready to access it.

What Did We Learn from This?

In this `SimpleSessionApp` example, we learned how to develop a session bean, including how to deploy and start it in a J2EE application server. We also learned how to develop a client application that uses session beans. As we briefly mentioned in the deployment descriptor discussion, the `SimpleSessionBean` was deployed as a stateless session bean, which means that it can't be counted on to retain data between method invocations. The next section will introduce the idea of a **stateful** session bean, and compare these two types.

Stateful vs. Stateless Session Beans

As mentioned previously, session beans are great choice for implementing business logic, processes, and workflow. When you choose to use a session bean to implement that logic, you have yet another choice to make: whether to make that session bean **stateful** or **stateless**.

Choosing Between Stateful and Stateless Beans

Consider a fictitious stock trading application where the client uses the `buy()` and `getTotalPrice()` methods of a `StockTrader` session bean. If the user has several different stocks to buy and wants to see the running total price on the tentative purchases, then that state needs to be stored somewhere. One place to store that kind of transient information is in the instance variables of the session bean itself. This requires that the session bean be defined as stateful, as we learned previously, in the `ejb-jar.xml` (EJB deployment descriptor) file.

There are advantages for choosing that a session bean be stateful, and some for it being stateless. Some advantages of being stateful are:

❑ Transient information, such as that described in the stock trading scenario, can be stored easily in the instance variables of the session bean, as opposed to defining and using entity beans (or JDBC) to store it in a database.

❑ Since this transient information is stored in the session bean, the client doesn't have to store it and potentially waste bandwidth by sending the session bean the same information repeatedly with each call to a session bean method. This bandwidth issue is a big deal when the client is installed on a user's machine that invokes the session bean methods over a phone modem, for example. Bandwidth is also an issue when the data is very large or needs to be sent many times repeatedly.

The main disadvantage of being stateful is:

❑ Stateful session beans don't scale up as well on an EJB server, because they require more system resources than stateless session beans do. A couple of reasons for this are that:

❑ Stateful session beans require memory to store the state.

❑ Stateful session beans can be swapped in and out of memory (activated and passivated) as the EJB container deems necessary to manage server resources. The state gets stored in a more permanent form whenever a session bean is passivated, and that state is loaded back in when the bean is activated.

By the way, you may recall that the `SessionBean` interface defines several session bean lifecycle methods, including `ejbActivate()` and `ejbPassivate()`. A stateful session bean class can implement these methods to cause special processing to occur when it is activated or passivated.

Let's look at an example of using stateful session beans in the context of a device that stores state—a calculator.

Try It Out   Creating a Stateful Session Bean

This example mimics some very simple operations on a calculator: adding, subtracting, and keeping a running total. Not very impressive by today's standards, but you would have paid good money for a calculator with those functions in the early 1970s! That "keeping a running total" part is what we'll be demonstrating with the help of a stateful session bean. A screenshot of the GUI client follows the instructions to build and run the example.

There are four Java source files in this example:

❑   Calculator.java (in the beans package)

❑   CalculatorBean.java (in the beans package)

❑   CalculatorHome.java (in the beans package)

❑   CalculatorClient.java (in the client package)

Listed below are the bean-related classes only. The source code for CalculatorClient.java, as well as the source code for all the examples in this book, may be downloaded from the Apress web site.

1.   Add the following code files to a new application directory called SimpleCalculatorApp. Within the directory add beans and client subdirectories. Copy the code for CalculatorClient.java into the client directory.

Here is the code for the home interface, CalculatorHome.java:

```
package beans;

import java.rmi.RemoteException;
import javax.ejb.EJBHome;
import javax.ejb.CreateException;
public interface CalculatorHome extends EJBHome {
  // The create method for the Calculator bean.
  public Calculator create()
    throws CreateException, RemoteException;
}
```

As in the previous example, we supply a no-argument create() method.

This is the code for the bean interface, `Calculator.java`:

```java
package beans;

import java.rmi.RemoteException;
import javax.ejb.EJBObject;

public interface Calculator extends EJBObject {
   // The public business methods on the Calculator bean
   public void clearIt() throws RemoteException;
   public void calculate(String operation, int value)
      throws RemoteException;
   public int getValue() throws RemoteException;
}
```

It defines the three business methods of the calculator.

The code for the bean class, `CalculatorBean.java`:

```java
package beans;

import java.rmi.RemoteException;
import javax.ejb.SessionBean;
import javax.ejb.SessionContext;

public class CalculatorBean implements SessionBean {
   // Holds the calculator value
   private int _value = 0;

   // The public business methods. These must be coded in the
   // remote interface also.

   // Clear the calculator
   public void clearIt() {
      _value = 0;
   }

   // Add or subtract
   public void calculate(String operation, int value)
      throws RemoteException {
      // If "+", add it
      if (operation.equals("+")) {
        _value = _value + value;
        return;
      }

      // If "-", subtract it
      if (operation.equals("-")) {
        _value = _value - value;
        return;
      }

      // If not "+" or "-", it is not a valid operation
      throw new RemoteException("Invalid Operation");
   }
```

```
    // Return the value
    public int getValue() throws RemoteException {
      return _value;
    }

    // Standard ejb methods
    public void ejbActivate() {}
    public void ejbPassivate() {}
    public void ejbRemove() {}
    public void ejbCreate() {}
    public void setSessionContext(SessionContext context) { }
}
```

2. Now compile the java files following the same instructions as in the previous example. At the command line type:

```
> set classpath=.;%J2EE_HOME%\lib\j2ee.jar
```

3. Within the `SimpleCalculatorApp` directory that the `client` and `beans` directories are located, execute the following commands from the command prompt:

```
> javac -d . client/*.java
> javac -d . beans/*.java
```

4. Now start the J2EE Server and then the Deployment Tool.

5. Create a new EAR file for the application, from the File menu choose New | Application.

6. In the New Application dialog box, name the Application File Name `SimpleCalculatorApp.ear`. As before, this file should be located in the base directory of the example. In the same New Application dialog box, make the Application Display Name SimpleCalculatorApp.

7. Now create the JAR file for the session bean classes and resources. Choose the File | New | Enterprise Bean menu item.

8. In the EJB JAR page of the Edit Enterprise Bean Wizard, make the JAR Display Name SimpleCalculatorJar. We will create the JAR in the SimpleCalculatorApp EAR file.

9. Press the Edit button in the Contents section of the page. In the Available Files dialog that appears, navigate to the `beans` directory and add the three Calculator bean-related classes.

10. Once these have been added, click Next.

11. You will then have four drop-down lists in which to make choices:

❑ From the Enterprise Bean Class drop-down list, choose beans.CalculatorBean.

❑ From the Enterprise Bean Type drop-down list, choose Stateless Session.

❑ From the Remote Home Interface drop-down list, choose beans.CalculatorHome.

❑ From the Remote Interface drop-down list, choose beans.Calculator.

Enter SimpleCalculatorEjb as the Enterprise Bean Display Name, and then click Next.

12. Again leave the Configuration Options page at its default setting and click Next.

13. Click Finish on the Next Steps page.

14. Select the SimpleCalculatorApp node of the tree in the left-hand panel. Enter `ejb/beans.SimpleCalculator` in the JNDI Name column of the table that is in the JNDI Names tab.

15. Again run the Verifier Tool to check your application.

16. We can now deploy the application by selecting the SimpleCalculatorApp node in the tree in the left panel and selecting the Tools | Deploy menu item. Be sure to select the Return Client Jar checkbox and type the `C:\3413\Ch08\SimpleCalculatorApp` directory path into the text box.

After doing all of the above steps, we can now get on with running the application.

Running the Application

1. On a default J2EE SDK 1.4 Windows installation, the CLASSPATH would be set correctly by using the following command:

```
> set CLASSPATH=.;%J2EE_HOME%\lib\j2ee.jar;%J2EE_HOME%\lib\appserv-
rt.jar;SimpleCalculatorAppClient.jar
```

2. With `SimpleCalculatorApp` as the current directory, execute the following command from the operating system prompt:

```
> java -Dorg.omg.CORBA.ORBInitialHost=localhost -
Dorg.omg.CORBA.ORBInitialPort=3700 client.CalculatorClient
```

The graphical user interface (GUI) of the client should appear like this when run:

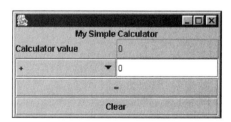

To operate the calculator, type a number into the text box, select an operation (+ or −) from the drop-down, and click the = button. The running total will be displayed beside the Calculator value label.

How It Works

To understand how this example works, we'll walk through some of the GUI client code contained in the `CalculatorClient.java` source file, and then we'll take a closer look at some of the EJB code shown above. By the way, in the code examples you'll notice that some of the import statements are wildcards and some explicitly name the class or interface.

For instructional purposes, we've chosen to be explicit on the imports that are relevant to J2EE, the subject of this book. We've chosen to be more frugal with lines of code by using wildcards, the more familiar ones that are relevant to J2SE.

The client is a standard Java Swing application, complete with GUI components and event handler methods. The client needs to call methods of the stateful session bean, so as in the previous example it gets a reference to the bean's home interface and creates the session bean on the server. The code that performs this is in the getCalculator() method of the CalculatorClient class, which is called from the constructor:

```
private Calculator getCalculator() {
  Calculator calculator = null;
  try {
    // Get a naming context
    InitialContext jndiContext = new InitialContext();

    // Get a reference to the Calculator JNDI entry
    Object ref  = jndiContext.lookup("ejb/beans.SimpleCalculator");

    // Get a reference from this to the Bean's Home interface
    CalculatorHome home = (CalculatorHome)
      PortableRemoteObject.narrow(ref, CalculatorHome.class);

    // Create a Calculator object from the Home interface
    calculator = home.create();
  } catch(Exception e) {
    e.printStackTrace();
  }
  return calculator;
}
```

When the = button is clicked, two things are passed to the calculate() method of the calculator session bean: the operator (either + or –), and the value to be added or subtracted from the running total:

```
_calculator.calculate(oper, operVal);
```

Since it is a stateful session bean, it is able to store the running total in an instance variable. The client then calls the getValue() method of the calculator session bean to retrieve the running total and subsequently display it:

```
_topNumber.setText("" + _calculator.getValue());
```

When the user presses the Clear button, the clearIt() method of the calculator session bean is called, which sets the running total to 0.

And Now the Bean Code

The implementations of the three calculator business methods of the CalculatorBean class are shown below. They manipulate the instance variable named _value, which holds the running total between invocations of any of these calculator session bean methods.

```
// Clear the calculator
public void clearIt() {
  _value = 0;
}

// Add or subtract
public void calculate(String operation, int value)
  throws RemoteException {
  // If "+", add it
  if (operation.equals("+")) {
    _value = _value + value;
    return;
  }

  // If "-", subtract it
  if (operation.equals("-")) {
    _value = _value - value;
    return;
  }

  // If not "+" or "-", it is not a valid operation
  throw new RemoteException("Invalid Operation");
}

// Return the value
public int getValue() throws RemoteException {
  return _value;
}
```

There are a couple of more points to take away from this example:

❏ There is no indication in any of the session bean code that it is stateful–that is controlled by the ejb-jar.xml file (deployment descriptor). An excerpt of the ejb-jar.xml file for the calculator stateful session bean appears below.

❏ A session bean that holds values in instance variables should never be configured as stateless, because the values of the instance variables are not predictable. This is because the EJB container has complete control over managing stateless (and stateful) session beans, including initializing the values of instance variables as the bean is shared among various clients. This is a common trap because sometimes the values are retained, giving a false indication that everything is OK, and then one day you can't figure out why the program isn't working correctly. From personal experience, that's a fun one to diagnose!

Indicating Stateful In the Deployment Descriptor

Here is an excerpt of the `ejb-jar.xml` file for the calculator example. Note that the `session-type` is `Stateful`:

```
    ...
<display-name>SimpleCalculatorJar</display-name>
<enterprise-beans>
  <session>
    <ejb-name>SimpleCalculatorEjb</ejb-name>
    <home>beans.CalculatorHome</home>
    <remote>beans.Calculator</remote>
    <ejb-class>beans.CalculatorBean</ejb-class>
    <session-type>Stateful</session-type>
    <transaction-type>Bean</transaction-type>
    <security-identity>
      <use-caller-identity>
      </use-caller-identity>
    </security-identity>
  </session>
</enterprise-beans>
</ejb-jar>
```

Summary

In this chapter, we learned what Enterprise JavaBeans are, and built a case for using them. We touched on the three types of EJBs: session beans, entity beans, and message-driven beans. Then we covered when to use each type.

The balance of this chapter was then devoted to session beans, and we started that discussion by explaining that session beans are made up of three parts; the home interface, the bean interface, and the bean class. During the session bean discussions we experienced the following concepts in the context of code examples:

- ❑ Java Naming and Directory Interface (JNDI)

- ❑ Creating session beans

- ❑ Application EAR, bean jar, and client JAR files

- ❑ Deployment descriptors

- ❑ Compiling, configuring, and deploying session beans

- ❑ Using the J2EE SDK Deployment Tool to configure EJBs

- ❑ Stateless and stateful session beans

Now that we've explored session beans, in the next chapter we'll turn our attention to another type of enterprise bean–the entity bean.

Exercises

1. Write a stateless session bean that takes a word and returns it spelled backwards.

2. Write a stateful session bean that takes one word at a time and appends it to the previous words received to make a sentence. Return the entire sentence each time a word is added.

3. Modify the previous exercise, adding a stateless session bean with a method that counts the number of letters in a word. Call this method from the builder bean to count the number of letters in each word. Show this number in the returned string.

EJB Entity Beans

The previous chapter gave us an introduction to enterprise beans, including an overview of the different types of enterprise beans. These types are session beans, entity beans, and message-driven beans. We previously looked at session bean development in a good level of detail.

In this chapter and the following one, we'll focus on developing the second type of enterprise beans, **entity beans**, which are the persistent data objects in an EJB application.

In this chapter you will learn:

❏ More about what an entity bean is

❏ Similarities and differences between entity bean and session beans

❏ How to develop entity beans

❏ Finding an entity bean via its primary key

❏ Local vs. remote interfaces

❏ Container-managed persistence

❏ Finding entity beans with the EJB Query Language

A Closer Look at Entity Beans

As mentioned in the previous chapter, entity beans can provide an object-oriented abstraction of a relational database. They are essentially JavaBeans that are backed by a persistent data store. Entity beans work well with session beans in providing the server-side functionality of the application. The following diagram from Chapter 8 depicts how session and entity beans work together for this purpose:

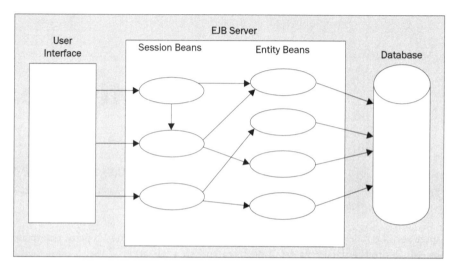

Session beans generally implement the business logic, processes, and workflow of an application, and entity beans are the persistent data objects. For example, the first example in this chapter is an application that manipulates stocks. We will create a session bean named `StockList` that implements the processes that a stockbroker might use for manipulating stocks. We will also create an entity bean named `Stock` whose instances represent individual stocks.

For the reasons discussed in the previous chapter, it is a good practice for the client to call session beans methods, and for session beans to manipulate the entity beans. These reasons are:

❑   Calling entity bean methods directly circumvents the business logic contained in session beans, and tends to push the business logic into the UI code.

❑   Session beans can protect the UI from changes to the entity beans.

❑   Restricting client access to session beans conserves server and network resources.

The Anatomy of an Entity Bean

Since entity beans are *enterprise* beans, they have some anatomy in common with their session bean siblings. Some of these commonalities are the entity bean's home interface, bean interface, and bean class. The following diagram illustrates these:

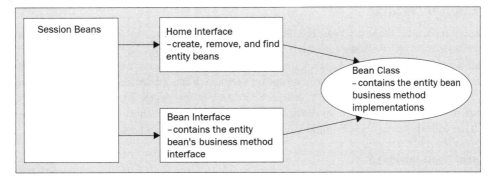

Session beans use an entity bean's home and bean interfaces to create, find, remove, and use entity beans. Strictly speaking, other clients such as user interfaces and external systems could use these interfaces as well, although as we stated previously, this is not usually the best practice.

The Home Interface

The home interface of an entity bean is used to create a new entity bean, remove one, or find an existing one. Because entity beans are backed by an underlying database, these methods cause the database to be queried and/or updated. This will be covered in the upcoming *Container-Managed Persistence* section.

❑   Calling a `create()` method creates a new entity bean instance. As with session beans, `create()` methods in EJBs are analogous to constructors in regular classes, and can be overloaded.

❑   Calling a `remove()` method of the home interface deletes the specified entity bean.

Calling a **find** method of the home interface finds the appropriate entity bean instances and returns them. Entity beans have at least one such find method, named `findByPrimaryKey()`, and more find methods can be defined by the developer.

As with session beans, the home interface for an entity bean extends the `EJBHome` interface of the `javax.ejb` package. As a naming convention, we'll append the word `Home` to the name of an entity bean to indicate its home interface. For example, an entity bean with the name `Stock` would have a home interface named `StockHome`.

The Local Home Interface

When two beans are in the same EJB container, a leaner variation of the home interface theme may be used, called the **local home interface**. Local home interfaces have less overhead because they don't require the use of Java RMI and stubs to communicate, since the beans exist within the same JVM. By the way, when a home interface isn't a local one, it is sometimes referred to as a **remote home interface**. The home interfaces that we developed in the previous chapter were remote home interfaces, characterized by the fact that they utilize Java RMI and stubs.

The Bean Interface

The bean interface for an entity bean is analogous to the bean interface for a session bean. They both are interfaces that expose a bean's methods. In the case of entity beans, however, the exposed methods are primarily setters and getters for the fields of the entity bean, but they often contain business logic as well. In this way, entity beans are very much like traditional JavaBeans. Like session beans, the **bean interface** extends the EJBObject interface of the javax.ejb package. As a naming convention, we'll use the name of an entity bean as the name of its bean interface. For example, an entity bean with the name Stock would have a bean interface named Stock.

The Local Bean Interface

Similar to the local home interface introduced earlier, there is a variation of the bean interface called the **local bean interface**, or more commonly, the **local interface**. By the way, when a bean interface isn't a local one, it is sometimes referred to as a **remote bean interface**, or more commonly, a **remote interface**. The interfaces that we developed in the previous chapter were remote interfaces, characterized by the fact that they utilize Java RMI and stubs. Local interfaces and local home interfaces can be used with both session and entity beans. We'll discuss local interfaces and local home interfaces in more detail a little later in the chapter.

The Bean Class

The bean class of an entity bean contains:

❑ The getter and setter methods specified in the bean interface. For example, a StockBean class might have a field named tickerSymbol, with a getter method named getTickerSymbol() and a setter method named setTickerSymbol(). We sometimes call entity bean fields **virtual fields** because it is not required that there is actually a field in the entity bean named tickerSymbol. The getter and setter method names just imply the name of a field, similar to JavaBean properties.

❑ Methods specified in the bean interface that contain business logic. These methods typically access and manipulate the fields of the entity bean. For example, if we had an entity bean named StockTransactionBean with a price field and a quantity field, a method named getTransactionAmount() could be created to multiply the two fields and return the amount of the transaction.

❑ Lifecycle methods that are called by the EJB container. For example, as with session beans, the ejbCreate() method is called by the container when the create() method of the home interface is called. These are analogous to constructors in normal Java classes, and can be overridden to pass in initialization values.

The bean class of an entity bean extends the EntityBean interface of the javax.ejb package. As with session beans, we'll append the word Bean to the name of a bean to indicate that it is a bean class. For example, an entity bean with the name Stock would have a bean class named StockBean.

Here is a UML class diagram that depicts some of the classes, interfaces, and relationships described above. It will also serve as the class diagram of the first *Try It Out* example a little later in this chapter:

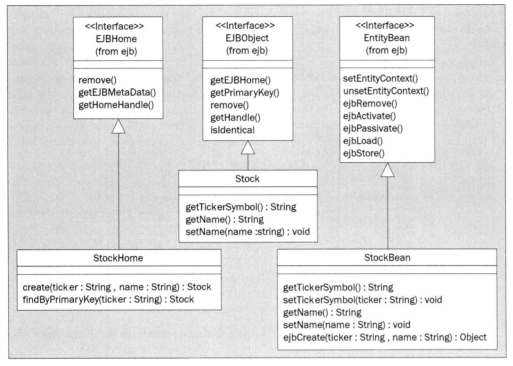

Other Features of Entity Beans

We've been discussing the features of entity beans that have some commonality with session bean features. Now let's turn our attention to some features that are *unique* to entity beans.

Container-Managed Persistence

Entity beans are backed by some type of persistent data store, often a relational database. There is a feature of entity beans that makes this persistence automatic, which is called **container-managed persistence** (**CMP**). Recall from the previous chapter that an EJB **container** is a facility within an EJB server that manages, and provides services to, the EJBs running within it. With CMP, an entity bean is mapped to a database table that is dedicated to the purpose of storing instances of that entity bean. For example, an entity bean named `Stock` might have a table named `stock`, `stock_table`, or perhaps `StockBeanTable` dedicated to it. Each record in the table would represent an instance of the entity bean. So, using a table named `StockBeanTable` and looking back at the home interface methods:

❑ Calling a `create()` method of the home interface of the `Stock` bean not only creates the entity bean–it also creates a row in the `StockBeanTable` table to persist it. Note that the EJB container manages this process for you, including choosing at what point in time to create the new row.

❑ Calling a `find()` method of the home interface finds the appropriate row(s) in the `StockBeanTable` table and returns an entity bean from each of those rows. The fields of the entity beans are loaded from the columns in the corresponding row of the `StockBeanTable` table.

Calling a `remove()` method of the home interface deletes the entity bean, and deletes the associated row from the `StockBeanTable` table. Again, it is up to the EJB container to choose when the row gets deleted.

Also, calling the getter and setter methods corresponding to the fields of the entity bean causes the fields of the database table to be read from, and written to, respectively. These fields are often called **CMP fields**, as they are managed by the container. In the class diagram above, the `Stock` entity bean has two CMP fields: `tickerSymbol` and `name` as indicated by its getters and setters. When using CMP, the schema of the database directly reflects the design of the entity beans, as shown below:

The alternative to container-managed persistence is **bean-managed persistence** (**BMP**), in which you get to write all that persistence logic yourself. This should be considered in situations where:

❑ A database already exists in a legacy system, and you are building an EJB-based application on top of that database. If the design of the entity beans do not match the existing database schema, then a BMP would be required.

❑ There is no database, but rather, the entity beans are "wrapper" for an external system.

❑ The EJB server doesn't support CMP with the database that you are using.

Because of their simplicity, we prefer to use CMP whenever possible. Note that most of the entity bean discussions and examples in this book are of the CMP variety, and are in accordance with the EJB 2.1 specification. There is one BMP example coming up, however, to give you an idea of how to develop this type of entity bean. Now let's look at another enterprise bean feature that is unique to entity beans; **primary keys**.

Primary Keys

A requirement of an entity bean is that one or more of its CMP fields must make it unique. This field (or combination of fields) is known as the **primary key**, which is useful in finding a particular entity bean. A primary key may be any serializable object, such as a `String` or an `Integer`. Primary keys also enable another nice feature of entity beans: the ability of the EJB container to manage the relationships between entity beans. This feature is called **container-managed relationships**, or **CMR**.

Container-Managed Relationships

Like a relational database, entity beans have an **abstract schema** that defines the CMP fields of each entity bean and the container-managed relationships between entity beans. For each relationship, there are corresponding methods in the related entity beans that refer to each other. Container-managed relationships will be covered in more detail in the next chapter.

EJB Query Language

There is a feature of entity beans called the EJB Query Language (EJB-QL) that enables SQL-like queries to be run against entity beans. These queries are encapsulated in entity bean methods so that developers that use an entity bean can call methods instead of constructing SQL queries.

We'll work through code that demonstrates the entity bean features described above in the *Try It Out* examples, so let's get busy!

Developing CMP Entity Beans

As mentioned above, entity beans can have their data persistence managed by the EJB container through the use of a database. Consequently, designing the entity beans in an application can be very much like designing the tables in a relational database, keeping in mind that entity beans are objects and therefore can have business methods as well as data.

During analysis, the entities, which are often "nouns", in a problem domain are analyzed as candidates for being represented as entity beans. For example, an application that helps students manage their education might have entity beans such as Student, Institution, Counselor, Course, and Program.

Another logical step is to discover what persistent fields each entity bean should have. For example, the Course entity bean could have CMP fields such as name of the course, and the course abstract.

Let's now work through an example to get some experience with entity beans that have container-managed persistent fields.

Try It Out Creating an Entity Bean That Uses CMP

This example application demonstrates the container-managed persistence feature of entity beans. It is a very simple application in which the user can create, find, update, and delete stocks. This application uses two enterprise beans:

❑   An entity bean named Stock that holds information about stocks. There is one instance of this entity bean per stock.

❑   A session bean named StockList that uses the Stock beans and provides business methods to the UI that enables it to maintain the Stock beans.

A screenshot of the GUI client, and a description of its behavior, follows the instructions to build and run the example. Let's go ahead and build the application so that you can use it yourself.

The source files involved in this example used to define the Stock entity bean are contained in the beans subfolder:

- ❑ Stock.java
- ❑ StockBean.java
- ❑ StockHome.java

The source files that define the StockList session bean are also contained in the beans subfolder:

- ❑ StockList.java
- ❑ StockListBean.java
- ❑ StockListHome.java

The source file that defines the user interface client lives in the client subfolder:

- ❑ StockClient.java

1. Add the following code files to their respective subfolders in the StockListApp application directory.

    First is Stock.java:

    ```
    package beans;

    import java.rmi.RemoteException;
    import javax.ejb.EJBObject;

    public interface Stock extends EJBObject {
        // The public business methods on the Stock bean
        // These include the accessor methods from the bean
        // Get the ticker. Do not allow ticker to be set through the
        // interface because it is the primary key.
        public String getTickerSymbol() throws RemoteException;

        // Get and set the name
        public String getName() throws RemoteException;
        public void setName(String name) throws RemoteException;
    }
    ```

Next is StockBean.java:

```java
package beans;

import javax.ejb.CreateException;
import javax.ejb.EntityBean;
import javax.ejb.EntityContext;

public abstract class StockBean implements EntityBean {

  // Keeps the reference to the context
  private EntityContext _context;

  // The abstract access methods for persistent fields
  public abstract String getTickerSymbol();
  public abstract void setTickerSymbol(String ticker);

  public abstract String getName();
  public abstract void setName(String name);

  // Standard entity bean methods

  public String ejbCreate(String ticker, String name)
    throws CreateException {

    setTickerSymbol(ticker);
    setName(name);
    return null;
  }

  public void ejbPostCreate(String ticker, String name)
    throws CreateException { }

  public void setEntityContext(EntityContext ctx) {
    _context = ctx;
  }

  public void unsetEntityContext() {
    _context = null;
  }

  public void ejbRemove() { }
  public void ejbLoad() { }
  public void ejbStore() { }
  public void ejbPassivate() { }
  public void ejbActivate() { }
}
```

Then StockHome.java:

```
package beans;

import java.rmi.RemoteException;
import javax.ejb.CreateException;
import javax.ejb.EJBHome;
import javax.ejb.FinderException;

public interface StockHome extends EJBHome {
   // The create method for the Stock bean
   public Stock create(String ticker, String name)
      throws CreateException, RemoteException;

   // The find by primary key method for the Stock bean
   public Stock findByPrimaryKey(String ticker)
      throws FinderException, RemoteException;
}
```

Then StockList.java:

```
package beans;

import java.rmi.RemoteException;
import javax.ejb.CreateException;
import javax.ejb.EJBObject;
import javax.ejb.FinderException;

public interface StockList extends EJBObject {
   // The public business methods on the StockList bean
   public String getStock(String ticker)
      throws FinderException, RemoteException;
   public void addStock(String ticker, String name)
      throws CreateException, RemoteException;
   public void updateStock(String ticker, String name)
      throws FinderException, RemoteException;
   public void deleteStock(String ticker)
      throws FinderException, RemoteException;
}
```

Next is StockListBean.java:

```
package beans;

import javax.ejb.CreateException;
import javax.ejb.FinderException;
import javax.ejb.SessionBean;
import javax.ejb.SessionContext;
import javax.naming.InitialContext;
import javax.naming.NamingException;
import javax.rmi.PortableRemoteObject;

public class StockListBean implements SessionBean {

   // The public business methods. These must be coded in the
   // remote interface also.
```

```
public String getStock(String ticker) throws FinderException {
  try {
    StockHome stockHome = getStockHome();
    Stock stock = stockHome.findByPrimaryKey(ticker);
    return stock.getName();
  } catch (FinderException fe) {
    throw fe;
  } catch (Exception ex) {
    throw new RuntimeException(ex.getMessage());
  }
}

public void addStock(String ticker, String name) throws CreateException {
  try {
    StockHome stockHome = getStockHome();
    stockHome.create(ticker, name);
  } catch (CreateException ce) {
    throw ce;
  } catch (Exception ex) {
    throw new RuntimeException(ex.getMessage());
  }
}

public void updateStock(String ticker, String name)
 throws FinderException {
  try {
    StockHome stockHome = getStockHome();
    Stock stock = stockHome.findByPrimaryKey(ticker);
    stock.setName(name);
  } catch (FinderException fe) {
    throw fe;
  } catch (Exception ex) {
    throw new RuntimeException(ex.getMessage());
  }
}

public void deleteStock(String ticker) throws FinderException {
  try {
    StockHome stockHome = getStockHome();
    Stock stock = stockHome.findByPrimaryKey(ticker);
    stock.remove();
  } catch (FinderException fe) {
    throw fe;
  } catch (Exception ex) {
    throw new RuntimeException(ex.getMessage());
  }
}

private StockHome getStockHome() throws NamingException {
  // Get the initial context
  InitialContext initial = new InitialContext();

  // Get the object reference
  Object objref = initial.lookup("ejb/beans.Stock");
  StockHome home = (StockHome)
```

```
          PortableRemoteObject.narrow(objref, StockHome.class);
        return home;
    }

    // Standard ejb methods
    public void ejbActivate() {}
    public void ejbPassivate() {}
    public void ejbRemove() {}
    public void ejbCreate() {}
    public void setSessionContext(SessionContext context) {}
}
```

And finally `StockListHome.java`:

```
package beans;

import java.rmi.RemoteException;
import javax.ejb.CreateException;
import javax.ejb.EJBHome;

public interface StockListHome extends EJBHome {
    // The create method for the Stock List bean.
    public StockList create() throws CreateException, RemoteException;
}
```

We're not going to show the complete client code here due to its size since it is available in the code download from the Apress web site. However, the code contained in the file will be discussed later.

2. Now compile the source code for the application:

    ❑   As pointed out in the previous example, on a default J2EE SDK 1.4 Windows installation the classpath would be set correctly by using the following command:

    ```
    > set classpath=.;%J2EE_HOME%\lib\j2ee.jar
    ```

    ❑   Within the directory that the client and beans directories are located, execute the following commands from the command prompt:

    ```
    > javac -d . client/*.java
    > javac -d . beans/*.java
    ```

3. We now need to start the J2EE Server and the Deployment Tool as before. In addition, we need to start up the PointBase database server. PointBase is a lightweight database server that comes with the J2EE SDK 1.4, and will serve as the database in which our entity beans will be persisted. Go ahead and start PointBase using the instructions in Chapter 2.

4. Once these are all running we can then create the application EAR file by choosing New | Application from the File menu. Set the Application File Name to StockListApp.ear in the application directory, and the Application Display Name to StockListApp.

5. We can now create the bean JAR. Start the Edit Enterprise Bean Wizard by choosing the File | New | Enterprise Bean menu item.

Set the JAR Display Name to StockListJar. You will see the class files for the Stock entity bean, but you only need to choose the three EJB class files for the StockList session bean. For your convenience you can use the drop-down list in the dialog shown below to show only the files with the .class extension:

6. After clicking Next, in the General dialog choose the bean class in the Enterprise Bean Class drop-down, make the session bean Stateless, choose the Remote Interfaces for the session bean, and set the Enterprise Bean Display Name to StockListEjb. Click Next.

7. Don't change the default on the Configuration Options page, and finish the wizard.

8. Now we're going to create another bean JAR, this time for the Stock entity bean. You'll start this process the same way that you created the bean JAR for the session bean: by choosing the New menu item from the File menu, and then choosing Enterprise Bean. When the following page appears:

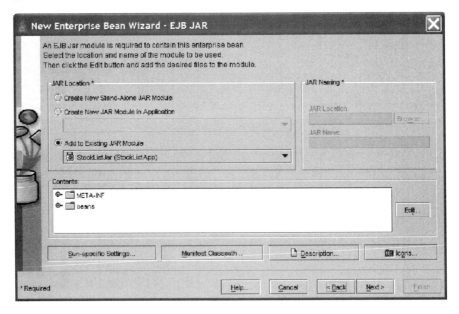

We will need to do the following:

❑ Choose the Add to Existing JAR Module option if it isn't already selected. This is because we're going to put our entity bean in the same bean JAR file as the session bean.

❑ Verify that the application shown in the drop-down is StockListApp.

❑ Then click the Edit button to select only the three Stock entity bean .class files (`Stock.class`, `StockBean.class`, and `StockHome.class`) to be put into this JAR. In the dialog box (not shown), don't forget to click the Add button before clicking OK.

9. When you click the Next button, select the Enterprise Bean Class, Enterprise Bean Type, and Remote Interfaces from the drop-downs as shown below. Also, set the Enterprise Bean Display Name to StockEjb. Note: If the Enterprise Bean Name drop-down is disabled when you get to this page, then deselect and reselect the beans.StockBean option in the Enterprise Bean Class drop-down.

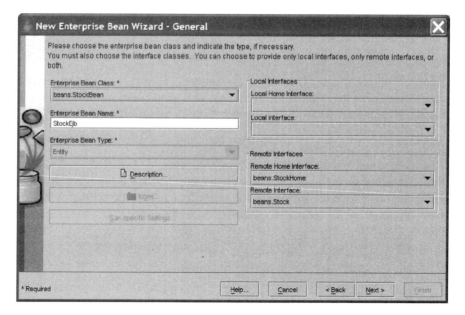

10. Click Next on the Configuration Options page.

11. The next page in this wizard is the Entity Settings page:

❑ Our entity bean is going to use Container-Managed Persistence 2.0, so select that option from the Persistence Management drop-down. Version 1.1 of the EJB specification, by the way, didn't support **container-managed relationships**, a feature that we'll be discussing a little later.

❑ The Deployment Tool used reflection to discover the getter/setter methods so that it could offer the Fields To Be Persisted choices shown. We'll choose both fields to be CMP fields because we want both of them to be persisted.

❑ We're going to use the tickerSymbol field as the primary key for the Stock bean since ticker symbols are unique, so select it in the Primary Key Field Name drop-down. The setter and getter methods for this field accept and return a String, so select java.lang.String in the Primary Key Class drop-down.

❑ You'll recall from our earlier discussion that the CMP fields of entity beans define an **abstract schema**, which is sometimes referred to as an **abstract persistence schema**. The Deployment Tool creates tables in a database, for persistence purposes, that matches the schema defined by our entity beans and fields. Let's make Stock the Abstract Schema Name for this entity bean. We'll be able to use that name in EJB-QL queries later in the chapter.

The page should now look like below:

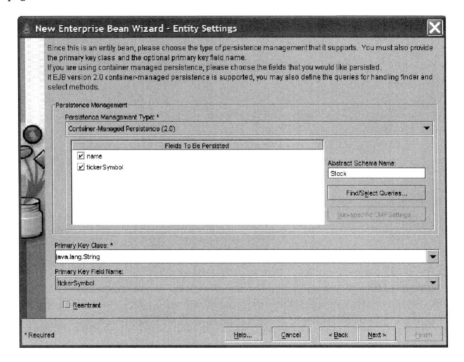

12. It is recommended for many of the methods of container-managed entity beans to run in the auspices of a transaction. So, after finishing the wizard, select StockEjb in the left-hand panel, and the Transactions tab on the right. The Transaction Management page should appear:

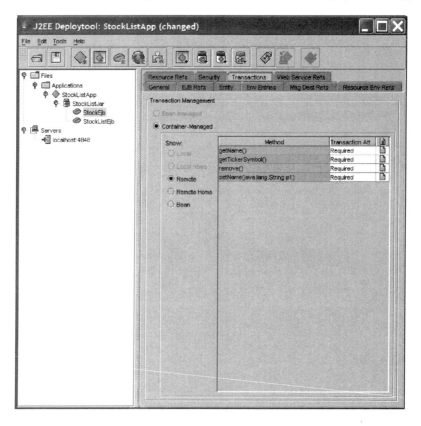

Container-Managed should be selected, and we'll specify that transactions are required for all of this entity bean's methods. To do this, select Remote, and then Remote Home, verifying that the Transaction Attribute of each method is set to Required.

13. Now select StockListApp in the left-hand panel, as shown on the following page.

In the JNDI Name tab:

❑ Give the Stock entity bean the JNDI Name ejb/beans.Stock.

❑ Give the StockList session bean the JNDI Name ejb/beans.StockList.

14. Select the File | Save All menu option. It is important in this reference implementation to save your work often in order for the settings that you've entered to be stored, which leads to a successful deployment.

15. Select StockListJar in the left-hand panel, and click the Sun-specific Settings button at the bottom of the page. The Sun-specific Settings page shown on the next page will appear, and in it we'll take care of some database-related issues:

❑ We'll be using the PointBase database, so enter jdbc/PointBase as the Database JNDI Name in the CMP Resource panel.

❑ Click the Create Field Mappings button.

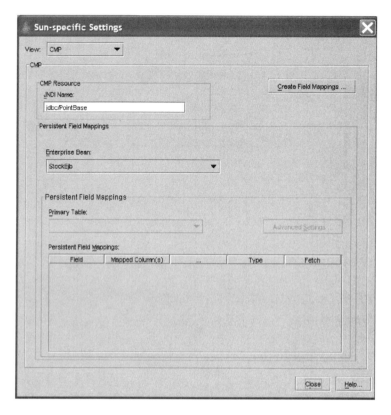

16. In the Create Field Mappings dialog shown below, make sure that:

❏ The Automatically Generate Necessary Tables option is selected.

❏ PointBase is selected in the Datasource Vendor drop-down list.

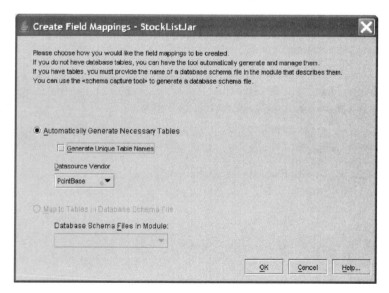

17. The Sun-specfic Settings dialog (not shown) will reappear with the database table and field names that will be used to persist the data in the Stock entity bean. Click the Close button.

18. Before deploying the application, let's get in the habit of making sure that no other applications are deployed. The main reason for doing this is that some of these examples use the same JNDI name for a session bean, and we want the correct session bean reference to be found. Also, we want this reference implementation of the J2EE server to be stable as long as possible. To verify that no other applications are deployed, select localhost:4848 in the tree in the left panel, and click the Undeploy button for any applications that you deployed that are listed in the table. Leave any applications that you didn't deploy alone.

19. Save the application by choosing the File | Save All menu item. Select the StockListApp node from the tree on the left panel and choose Verify J2EE Compliance from the Tools menu. Choose the Failures Only option and click OK. Note: There were two failed tests for this example when we ran the Verifier, and the application deployed successfully. One was EJB-QL–related, which we haven't covered yet, and one was a CMP mapping test.

20. Now we can deploy the application. With the StockListApp node selected in the left panel, choose the Tools | Deploy menu item. In the Deploy Module dialog, check the Return Client Jar checkbox and enter the directory path in which the bean and client directories are rooted.

21. To run the client, first set the classpath to use the client JAR. To do this, enter the following from the command prompt:

```
> set CLASSPATH=.;%J2EE_HOME%\lib\j2ee.jar;%J2EE_HOME%\lib\
→ appserv-rt.jar;StockListAppClient.jar
```

You can enter the following command to run the client that uses the beans we've built:

```
> java -Dorg.omg.CORBA.ORBInitialHost=localhost -
→ Dorg.omg.CORBA.ORBInitialPort=3700 client.StockClient
```

Here is a screenshot of the Stock List application user interface that was taken while the user was adding an entry for Sun Microsystems stock:

After at least one stock name has been added, the user can enter a symbol and click the Get button, which causes the desired entity bean to be found and its name displayed. Changing the Name text field and clicking the Update button causes the CMP name field of the entity bean to be updated. Clicking the Delete button results in the entity bean being deleted.

Now that we've built, deployed, and run the application, let's see how it works.

How It Works

We're going to examine the code for this example from the inside out, beginning with the entity bean. A diagram of these entity bean classes is contained in the section titled *The Bean Class*, which we passed through earlier in the chapter. Let's first look at the entity bean home interface, `StockHome.java`:

```
...
public interface StockHome extends EJBHome {
  // The create method for the Stock bean
  public Stock create(String ticker, String name)
    throws CreateException, RemoteException;

  // The find by primary key method for the Stock bean
  public Stock findByPrimaryKey(String ticker)
    throws FinderException, RemoteException;
}
```

There are two methods defined in the `Stock` entity bean's home interface.

❏ The `create()` method acts like a constructor in that it creates a new instance of the `Stock` entity bean, allowing initialization arguments to be passed in. As we'll see in the bean class code, these arguments will be tucked away into CMP fields of the new entity bean instance. Note that if the entity bean couldn't be created, a `CreateException` will be thrown. This exception will be thrown, for example, when an entity bean with the given primary key (in this case the ticker argument) already exists.

❏ The `findByPrimaryKey()` method locates and returns the entity bean with the specified primary key. In the case of the `Stock` entity bean, the primary key is the ticker symbol. One very nice feature of the `findByPrimaryKey()` method is that all you have to do is declare the method in the home interface. The deployment tool generates the code to implement it. Note that if the desired entity bean doesn't exist, a `FinderException` will be thrown.

Now let's look at the entity bean interface, `Stock.java`:

```
...
public interface Stock extends EJBObject {
  // The public business methods on the Stock bean
  // These include the accessor methods from the bean

  // Get the ticker. Do not allow ticker to be set through the
  // interface because it is the primary key.
  public String getTickerSymbol() throws RemoteException;

  // Get and set the name
  public String getName() throws RemoteException;
  public void setName(String name) throws RemoteException;
}
```

There are setter and getter methods for the name CMP field, but only a getter method for the tickerSymbol field. This is because we don't want the primary key to be altered after the entity bean instance has been created, so we make the setTickerSymbol() method unavailable in the bean interface. The methods of a remote interface must declare that they throw RemoteException, but the same methods in the bean class, as we see below, are not required to throw that exception.

Next we'll look at the entity bean class, StockBean.java:

```
...
public abstract class StockBean implements EntityBean {

    // Keeps the reference to the context
    private EntityContext _context;

    // The abstract access methods for persistent fields
    public abstract String getTickerSymbol();
    public abstract void setTickerSymbol(String ticker);

    public abstract String getName();
    public abstract void setName(String name);
```

Why are the two pairs of setter and getter methods for the CMP fields declared abstract? The answer is that the implementation code is created by the deployment tool, because that behavior is specific to the EJB server and database server implementation.

```
    // Standard entity bean methods
    public String ejbCreate(String ticker, String name)
      throws CreateException {

      setTickerSymbol(ticker);
      setName(name);
      return null;
    }
```

The constructor-like ejbCreate() method takes the arguments passed in and initializes the CMP fields with those values. There are a few things worth pointing out here:

❏ This is where tickerSymbol, the primary key field, gets initialized.

❏ The value of the tickerSymbol field is set via the setTickerSymbol() method of this bean class. This is the same method that we removed from the bean interface earlier to prevent clients from changing the primary key value.

❏ It is standard for the ejbCreate() method to return a null value.

```
    public void ejbPostCreate(String ticker, String name)
      throws CreateException { }
```

The ejbPostCreate() method gives you a chance to do extra initialization after the CMP fields are initialized, but before the entity bean is used by other beans. For example, manipulating container-managed relationship fields is not allowed in an ejbCreate() method, but is allowed in an ejbPostCreate() method. Container-managed relationships will be covered in the next chapter.

```java
public void setEntityContext(EntityContext ctx) {
  _context = ctx;
}

public void unsetEntityContext() {
  _context = null;
}

public void ejbRemove() { }
public void ejbLoad() { }
public void ejbStore() { }
public void ejbPassivate() { }
public void ejbActivate() { }
}
```

The rest of the methods are called by the EJB container during key points in the entity bean's lifecycle. For example:

❑   The setEntityContext() is called by the EJB container after the entity bean instance is created. The EntityContext passed is in the environment in which the entity bean is running. This is analogous to the relationship of an Applet and the AppletContext in which it is running, for example.

❑   The ejbRemove() method is called by the EJB container after the remove() method of the home interface or bean interface is called, and just before the entity bean is deleted. Implementing this method gives you the opportunity to do extra cleanup if desired.

The Session Bean

Let's turn our attention to the StockList session bean, which uses our entity bean. The session bean home interface, StockListHome.java, should be quite obvious with the single create() method.

Now the session bean interface, StockList.java:

```java
...
public interface StockList extends EJBObject {
  // The public business methods on the StockList bean
  public String getStock(String ticker)
    throws FinderException, RemoteException;
  public void addStock(String ticker, String name)
    throws CreateException, RemoteException;
  public void updateStock(String ticker, String name)
    throws FinderException, RemoteException;
  public void deleteStock(String ticker)
    throws FinderException, RemoteException;
}
```

The four methods in that interface will be used by the client to carry out the Get, Add, Update, and Delete stock operations shown in the GUI client. Notice that they throw either the FinderException or the CreateException located in the javax.ejb package. These exceptions are the mechanism in which we will tell the client that an EJB operation failed. For example, when calling the updateStock() method, if the supplied ticker didn't exist, it would throw the FinderException.

And now, on to the session bean class, StockListBean.java. To support the functionality we have built into the GUI client, the following methods of the session bean are employed, respectively:

- getStock()

- addStock()

- updateStock()

- deleteStock()

Each of these methods calls the getStockHome() method of the session bean to get a home interface reference to the Stock entity bean. The code in that method is the same as we've used in past examples to get a home interface reference to a session bean from our clients. Why do each of these methods call getStockHome(), as opposed to calling it once and putting it in an instance variable? The reason is that we specified when using the deployment tool that the session bean should be stateless. Therefore it cannot be trusted to retain the home interface reference.

```
public String getStock(String ticker) throws FinderException {
  try {
    StockHome stockHome = getStockHome();
    Stock stock = stockHome.findByPrimaryKey(ticker);
    return stock.getName();
  ...
  }
}
```

After the getStock() method gets a Stock entity bean home interface reference, it calls the findByPrimaryKey() method of the home interface, passing in the desired ticker symbol. If successfully found, it asks the Stock entity bean for the value held in its CMP name field, and returns the value:

- The addStock() method gets the Stock entity bean's home interface reference and calls its create() method.

- The updateStock() method uses the findByPrimaryKey() method to get the desired Stock entity bean reference, and uses a CMP method to update the name field.

- The deleteStock() method uses the findByPrimaryKey() method to get the desired Stock entity bean reference. It then calls the remove() method that the Stock interface inherited from the EJBObject interface. It is worth pointing out that the remove() method exists in both the home interface and bean interface. It is also worth noting that, as with some other methods noted previously, the code for the remove() method is generated for you.

The source code for StockClient.java, as well as the source code for all the examples in this book, may be downloaded from the Apress web site. The StockClient class gets a reference to a session bean as shown below:

```java
private StockList getStockList() {
   StockList stockList = null;
   try {
      // Get a naming context
      InitialContext jndiContext = new InitialContext();

      // Get a reference to the StockList JNDI entry
      Object ref  = jndiContext.lookup("ejb/beans.StockList");

      // Get a reference from this to the Bean's Home interface
      StockListHome home = (StockListHome)
         PortableRemoteObject.narrow(ref, StockListHome.class);

      // Create a StockList object from the Home interface
      stockList = home.create();
   } catch(Exception e) {
      e.printStackTrace();
   }

   return stockList;
}
```

It also calls the session bean's methods as needed by the user interface. The methods that call the session bean's methods catch either the FinderException or CreateException thrown from the enterprise beans in order to alert the user to these conditions. This is seen, for example, in the addStock() method below:

```java
private void addStock() {
   // Get the ticker
   String ticker = _ticker.getText();
   if (ticker == null || ticker.length() == 0) {
      JOptionPane.showMessageDialog(this, "Ticker is required");
      return;
   }

   // Get the name
   String name = _name.getText();
   if (name == null || name.length() == 0) {
      JOptionPane.showMessageDialog(this, "Name is required");
      return;
   }

   // Add the stock
   try {
      _stockList.addStock(ticker, name);
      JOptionPane.showMessageDialog(this, "Stock added!");
   } catch (CreateException fe) {
      JOptionPane.showMessageDialog(this, "Already found!");
   } catch (Exception e) {
      e.printStackTrace();
   }
}
```

The Deployment Descriptor

Here is an excerpt of the `ejb-jar.xml` file that holds the deployment descriptor for both the StockList and Stock beans. This excerpt reflects some choices that we made in the deployment tool:

```
...
<display-name>StockListJar</display-name>
<enterprise-beans>
  <session>
    <ejb-name>StockListEjb</ejb-name>
    <home>beans.StockListHome</home>
    <remote>beans.StockList</remote>
    <ejb-class>beans.StockListBean</ejb-class>
    <session-type>Stateless</session-type>
    <transaction-type>Bean</transaction-type>
    <security-identity>
      ...
    </security-identity>
  </session>
  <entity>
    <ejb-name>StockEjb</ejb-name>
    <home>beans.StockHome</home>
    <remote>beans.Stock</remote>
    <ejb-class>beans.StockBean</ejb-class>
    <persistence-type>Container</persistence-type>
    <prim-key-class>java.lang.String</prim-key-class>
    <reentrant>false</reentrant>
    <cmp-version>2.x</cmp-version>
    <abstract-schema-name>Stocks</abstract-schema-name>
    <cmp-field>
      <description>no description</description>
      <field-name>name</field-name>
    </cmp-field>
    <cmp-field>
      <description>no description</description>
      <field-name>tickerSymbol</field-name>
    </cmp-field>
    <primkey-field>tickerSymbol</primkey-field>
    <security-identity>
      ...
    </security-identity>
  </entity>
</enterprise-beans>
<assembly-descriptor>
  ...
  <container-transaction>
    <method>
      <ejb-name>StockEjb</ejb-name>
      <method-intf>Remote</method-intf>
      <method-name>getTickerSymbol</method-name>
    </method>
    <trans-attribute>Required</trans-attribute>
  </container-transaction>
  ...
</assembly-descriptor>
</ejb-jar>
```

You'll notice that both the session and entity beans are defined in the `<session>` and `<entity>` elements, respectively.

Also, the following snippet specifies that the `Stock` bean will use container-managed persistence:

```
<persistence-type>Container</persistence-type>
```

And this snippet specifies that one of the CMP fields will be `tickerSymbol`:

```
<cmp-field>
  <description>no description</description>
  <field-name>tickerSymbol</field-name>
</cmp-field>
```

The following snippet specifies that the primary key is a `String`, and that the `tickerSymbol` field is the primary key:

```
<prim-key-class>java.lang.String</prim-key-class>
...
<primkey-field>tickerSymbol</primkey-field>
```

In this section, we learned about, and walked through an example of, an entity bean that uses container-managed persistence. In the next section, we'll learn how to develop entity beans that don't rely on the EJB container to provide persistence.

Developing BMP Entity Beans

In the event that container-managed persistence is not an option, perhaps for one of the reasons mentioned previously, entity beans must supply their own persistence mechanism. Such entity beans use a technique that is appropriately named **bean-managed persistence** (**BMP**).

The following example demonstrates this technique by converting the `Stock` entity bean in the previous example from a CMP entity bean to a BMP entity bean. Let's see how this works.

Try It Out   Creating an Entity Bean That Uses BMP

This example application demonstrates how to develop an entity bean that uses bean-managed persistence. Everything, including the GUI client behavior, is the same as the previous example. In fact, only one Java source file changed: `StockBean.java`. This file contains the source for the bean implementation class, and may be downloaded from the Apress web site. We won't show it here due to its size.

Building and Deploying the BMP Example

The process to build and run this example is almost the same as the previous example, and all of the Java source filenames are the same. Follow the steps from the previously example for compiling, configuring, and deploying the application (with the suggested differences noted below).

1. Create a new application directory with beans and client subfolders. Copy the code files into their respective directories.

2. After compiling the files start the J2EE Server, Deployment Tool, and PointBase.

3. Create a new application EAR file, the application name we will use in this example is: StockListBmpApp.

4. Create and populate the bean JAR using StockListBmpJar as the JAR Display Name. The steps for the creation of the session bean will stay the same as in the previous example.

5. In the Entity Settings page of the wizard, shown below, select Bean-Managed Persistence. Change the Primary Key Class to String:

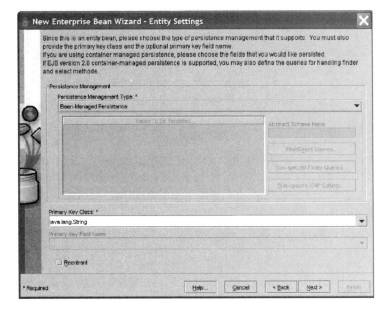

6. As in the previous example, after finishing the wizard, select StockEjb in the left-hand panel. In the Transactions tab on the right, select the Container-Managed option.

7. Select the application (StockListBmpApp) in the left-hand panel. Enter the same JNDI Names in the JNDI Name tab as you did in the previous example:

    ❑ Give the Stock entity bean the JNDI Name ejb/beans.Stock

    ❑ Give the StockList session bean the JNDI Name ejb/beans.StockList

8. Now select StockEjb in the left-hand panel, and the Resource Refs tab on the right. Click the Add button and enter a Coded Name of jdbc/StockDB as shown below. This allows the JNDI name, java:comp/env/jdbc/StockDB, to be used in the StockBean class to obtain a reference to the underlying data source. This occurs in the StockBean.java listing mentioned earlier, in the following statement:

```
DataSource ds = (DataSource) ctx.lookup("java:comp/env/jdbc/StockDB");
```

The concept of Coded Name *will be covered later in this chapter.*

9. Now enter the JNDI Name of the database by typing jdbc/PointBase in the Sun-specific settings for jdbc/StockDB panel as shown below. Be sure to press the *Enter* key after filling in this, or any other, text field in the reference implementation.

10. Remember to do a File | Save All now, and periodically.

11. Because the Stock bean uses bean-managed persistence, before we can actually deploy the application we have to create a table for use as its underlying data store. To do this, we'll use the PointBase Console by invoking the following command at the command line:

```
> %J2EE_HOME%\pointbase\tools\serveroption\startconsole.bat
```

12. The dialog shown below should appear, in which you should select the Open specified Database radio button, and enter the following into the labeled text boxes:

Driver: com.pointbase.jdbc.jdbcUniversalDriver

URL: jdbc:pointbase:server:///localhost:9092/sun-appserv-samples

User: PBPUBLIC

Password: PBPUBLIC

13. In the screen shown on the next page, enter the following SQL commands into the Enter SQL Commands panel, and click the Execute All icon. The results should be similar to what you see in the ExecuteAll tab of the screenshot on the following page.

```
drop table stock;

create table stock
(tickerSymbol varchar(10) constraint pk_stock primary key,
name varchar(50));
```

14. Exit the PointBase console by selecting File | Exit.

15. You may now deploy the application and create the client JAR file in the usual manner (by invoking the Tools | Deploy menu item).

16. To run the client, first set the classpath to use the client JAR. To do this, enter the following from the command prompt:

```
> set CLASSPATH=.;%J2EE_HOME%\lib\j2ee.jar;%J2EE_HOME%\lib\
➔ appserv-rt.jar;StockListBmpAppClient.jar
```

You can enter the following command to run the client that uses the beans we've built:

```
> java -Dorg.omg.CORBA.ORBInitialHost=localhost -
➔ Dorg.omg.CORBA.ORBInitialPort=3700 client.StockClient
```

The application will look the same as the CMP version.

How It Works

Looking at the code for this BMP entity bean we begin to appreciate what the EJB container does for us when using container-managed persistence. In this example, as with CMP, a table in the database is dedicated to our BMP entity bean. Each row represents a bean instance. Here's a list of things that the entity bean is responsible for when managing its own persistence:

❏ The BMP entity bean must supply implementations for the persisted field's getter and setter methods. In our example, this consists of using instance variables to hold these values as seen in the getTickerSymbol(), getName(), and setName() methods, shown below:

```java
public String getTickerSymbol() {
  return tickerSymbol;
}

public String getName() {
  return name;
}

public void setName(String name) {
  this.name = name;
}
```

❏ The implementation of the findByPrimaryKey() method declared in the home interface *must* be supplied. This is seen in the ejbFindByPrimaryKey() method below. Notice that JDBC is used to enable this find method:

```java
public String ejbFindByPrimaryKey(String primaryKey)
  throws FinderException {

  boolean result;

  try {
    String stmt =
      "select tickerSymbol " + "from stock where tickerSymbol = ? ";
    PreparedStatement pstmt = connection.prepareStatement(stmt);
    pstmt.setString(1, primaryKey);

    ResultSet rs = pstmt.executeQuery();
    result = rs.next();
    pstmt.close();
  }
  catch (SQLException ex) {
    throw new EJBException("ejbFindByPrimaryKey: " + ex.getMessage());
  }

  if (result) {
    return primaryKey;
  } else {
    throw new ObjectNotFoundException
      ("Ticker " + primaryKey + " not found.");
  }
}
```

❏ The `ejbCreate()` method, rather than simply tucking away arguments into instance variables, uses JDBC to insert the corresponding row into the table. This method is shown below:

```
public String ejbCreate(String tickerSymbol, String name)
  throws CreateException {

  try {
    String findstmt =
      "select tickerSymbol " +
      "from stock where tickerSymbol = ? ";
    PreparedStatement pfindstmt =
      connection.prepareStatement(findstmt);
    pfindstmt.setString(1, tickerSymbol);

    ResultSet rs = pfindstmt.executeQuery();
    boolean findresult = rs.next();
    if (findresult) {
      throw new CreateException("Ticker already exists!");
    }

    String stmt = "insert into stock values ( ? , ? )";
    PreparedStatement pstmt = connection.prepareStatement(stmt);

    pstmt.setString(1, tickerSymbol);
    pstmt.setString(2, name);

    pstmt.executeUpdate();
    pstmt.close();
  } catch (SQLException ex) {
    ex.printStackTrace();
    throw new EJBException("ejbCreate: " + ex.getMessage());
  }

  this.tickerSymbol = tickerSymbol;
  this.name = name;

  return tickerSymbol;
}
```

❏ The `ejbRemove()` method, shown below, is responsible for deleting the row that represents the entity bean's instance from the table:

```
public void ejbRemove() {
  try {
    String stmt = "delete from stock where tickerSymbol = ? ";
    PreparedStatement pstmt = connection.prepareStatement(stmt);

    pstmt.setString(1, tickerSymbol);
    pstmt.executeUpdate();
    pstmt.close();
  } catch (SQLException ex) {
    throw new EJBException("ejbRemove: " + ex.getMessage());
  }
}
```

❑ In a bean's lifecycle, the values of its fields are often changed by the application. As a result of this, the EJB container calls the `ejbLoad()` and `ejbStore()` methods, shown below, when it deems appropriate to keep the state of the entity bean in sync with the underlying data store. The BMP entity bean performs SQL SELECT and UPDATE statements via JDBC to implement these methods:

```java
public void ejbLoad() {
   try {
      String stmt = "select name from stock where tickerSymbol = ? ";
      PreparedStatement pstmt = connection.prepareStatement(stmt);

      pstmt.setString(1, tickerSymbol);
      ResultSet rs = pstmt.executeQuery();

      if (rs.next()) {
         this.name = rs.getString(1);
         pstmt.close();
      } else {
         pstmt.close();
         throw new NoSuchEntityException("Ticker: " +
            tickerSymbol + " not in database.");
      }
   } catch (SQLException ex) {
      throw new EJBException("ejbLoad: " + ex.getMessage());
   }
}

public void ejbStore() {
   try {
      String stmt =
              "update stock set name = ? " +
              "where tickerSymbol = ?";
      PreparedStatement pstmt = connection.prepareStatement(stmt);

      pstmt.setString(1, name);
      pstmt.setString(2, tickerSymbol);
      int rowCount = pstmt.executeUpdate();
      pstmt.close();

      if (rowCount == 0) {
         throw new EJBException("Store for " +
            tickerSymbol + " failed.");
      }
   } catch (SQLException ex) {
      throw new EJBException("ejbStore: " + ex.getMessage());
   }
}
```

❑ The `setEntityContext()` method is called by the EJB container after an entity bean is created. Since this entity bean uses JDBC to manage its persistence, we take this opportunity to get a JDBC connection. This connection is obtained within the private `getDatabaseConnection()` method in the listing above. We close the JDBC connection when the `unsetEntityContext()` method is called by the container. These methods are shown below:

```java
public void setEntityContext(EntityContext ctx) {
  context = ctx;

  try {
    getDatabaseConnection();
  } catch (Exception ex) {
    throw new EJBException("Unable to connect to database. " +
      ex.getMessage());
  }
}

public void unsetEntityContext() {
  context = null;
  try {
    connection.close();
  } catch (SQLException ex) {
    throw new EJBException("unsetEntityContext: " + ex.getMessage());
  }
}

private void getDatabaseConnection()
  throws NamingException, SQLException {

  InitialContext ctx = new InitialContext();
  DataSource ds =
    (DataSource) ctx.lookup("java:comp/env/jdbc/StockDB");
  connection =  ds.getConnection();
}
```

In this section we learned about, and walked through an example of, an entity bean that uses bean-managed persistence. In the next section, we'll learn about the concept of **local interfaces** and will retrofit the container-managed persistence example from earlier in this chapter.

EJB Local Interfaces

Local interfaces are a relatively new feature of EJBs, and were created primarily to increase performance among enterprise beans that exist in the same EJB container. Consider a case in which an application has several beans, where each bean instance holds references to several others. Calling each other's home and bean interface methods, since they utilize stubs and Java RMI, can be resource-intensive and have less than optimal speed. Local interfaces address these issues. For example, a session bean that calls the methods of an entity bean that has local interfaces exists within the same JVM as the session bean. Local interfaces, therefore, can be much faster and use fewer resources because they use Java memory references rather than Java RMI to pass data.

Remote interfaces must still be used when the caller of a bean is outside of the EJB server that the bean is running in. Because of this, we use the guidelines listed below to decide whether an enterprise bean should have local or remote interfaces:

❑ When a session bean's methods are invoked from a client that is external to the EJB server, that session bean should have remote interfaces.

❑ When a session bean's methods are only invoked from another bean from within the same EJB server, that bean should have local interfaces.

❑ Entity beans should have local interfaces.

Understanding EJB Local Interfaces

Up to now, the home interface of each of our enterprise beans has been a *remote* home interface. The bean interface of each of the enterprise beans has been a *remote* bean interface, more commonly known as a remote interface. There is a counterpart to each of these interfaces that is lighter weight, and potentially faster:

❑ The counterpart of the remote home interface is known as the **local home interface**. Instead of extending the EJBHome interface, a local home interface extends the EJBLocalHome interface.

❑ The counterpart of the remote interface is known as the **local interface**. Instead of extending the EJBObject interface, a **local interface** extends the EJBLocalObject interface.

The local home interface and the local interface are used in much the same way as their remote counterparts, and they are available to session beans as well as entity beans. The class diagram shown below depicts these interfaces in the context of the next example:

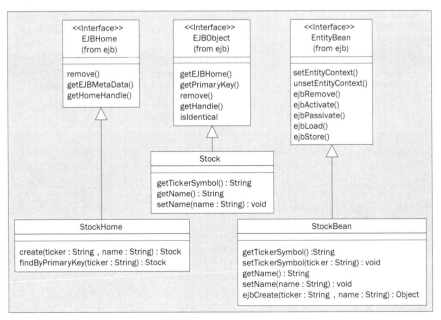

Try It Out   Create an Entity Bean That Has Local References

In this example, we're going to change the `Stock` entity bean into one that has a local home interface and a local interface. For brevity when speaking about this, we say that this bean has **local interfaces**.

We'll leave the `StockList` session bean alone, letting it continue to have remote references. This is because the `StockList` bean needs to be accessed from a client that is external to the EJB container in which the bean resides.

We'll also leave the `StockClient` unscathed so that the application will have the same behavior as the previous example.

Building and Running the Example

The only source files that changed from the previous example are `Stock.java`, `StockHome.java`, and `StockListBean.java`. The rest of the files have not been changed, and all are mentioned below.

The following source files define the `Stock` entity bean, and are contained in the `beans` package:

❑   `LocalStock.java` (was `Stock.java`, but now changed to being a local interface)

❑   `StockBean.java`

❑   `LocalStockHome.java` (was `StockHome.java`, but now changed to being a local home interface)

Note that we called the entity bean by the name `Stock`, even though the bean interface is now named `LocalStock`. This is because we're referring to the bean's abstract schema name, for which we'll continue to use the name `Stock`. Recall that we assign that name in the Deployment Tool.

These source files define the `StockList` session bean, also contained in the `beans` package:

❑   `StockList.java`

❑   `StockListBean.java` (changed to using the `Stock` bean's local home interface)

❑   `StockListHome.java`

The final source file defines the user interface client, and is contained in the `client` package:

❑   `StockClient.java`

1.   Create a new application directory with `beans` and `client` subfolders. Into these folders put the correct code files.

2.   Compile these source files, and start the J2EE server, the Deployment Tool, and PointBase.

3.   Create a new application EAR, calling it StockListLocalApp.

4.   Add the bean JAR, call it StockListJar.

5. Add the session bean class files as before. Only include the `StockList`, `StockListBean`, and `StockListHome` class files. Make it a stateless session bean.

6. When you run the wizard to create the JAR for the entity bean, ensure you choose only the class files of the `Stock` bean, as shown below:

7. Click OK and then Next. You then get to the General page in the New Enterprise Bean Wizard:

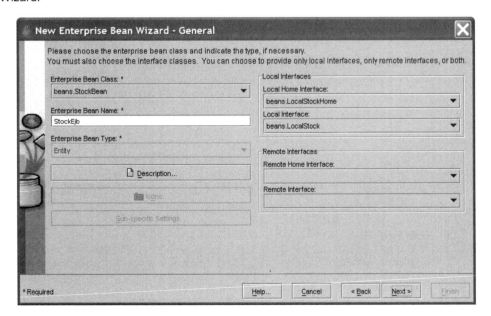

Make the same choices that you did in the previous example, but instead of using the Remote Interfaces drop-downs, choose the beans.LocalStockHome and beans.LocalStock interfaces from the Local Interfaces drop-downs.

8. On the Entity Settings page:

Our entity bean uses Container-Managed Persistence 2.0.

❏ In the Fields To Be Persisted window, choose both fields to be CMP fields.

❏ Use the tickerSymbol field as the primary key for the Stock.

❏ Select java.lang.String in the Primary Key Class drop-down.

❏ Set the Abstract Schema Name to Stock.

9. After finishing the wizard, select StockEjb in the left-hand panel, and the Transactions tab on the right. Make sure that the Container-Managed option is selected.

10. With StockListEjb selected in the left-hand panel, select the EJB Refs tab. Click the Add button on that page to produce the following dialog:

Fill in the dialog with the information about the Stock bean's local interfaces:

❏ Coded Name: ejb/beans.Stock

❏ EJB Type: Entity

❏ Interfaces: Local

❏ Home Interface: beans.LocalStockHome

❏ Local/Remote Interface: beans.LocalStock

The only information in this dialog that we haven't covered yet is the Coded Name: field, which will be explained when we walk through the code.

11. Clicking the OK button will fill in a row of the table on the underlying page with the values that you entered. Select the row in the EJB's Referenced in Code panel. Select the Enterprise Bean Name radio button at the bottom of this screen, and select ejb-jar-ic.jar#StockEjb from the drop-down list.

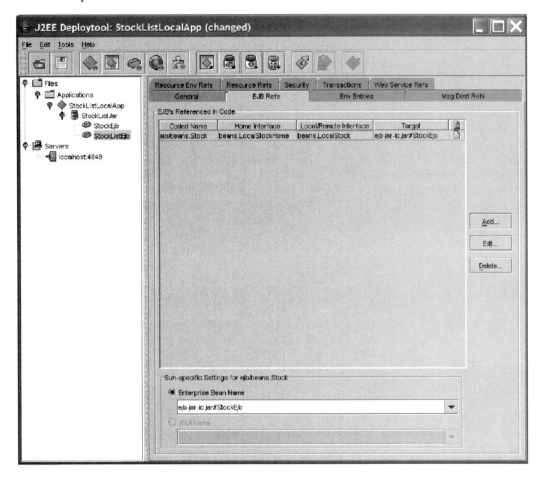

This information provides the linkage, internal to the EJB container, between the StockList session bean and the Stock entity bean that it accesses. This means that the StockList session bean doesn't have to use an external JNDI mechanism to get a reference to the home interface of the Stock entity bean, which means that performance is increased.

12. Select the StockListLocalApp node in the panel on the left, and then select the JNDI Names tab as shown below:

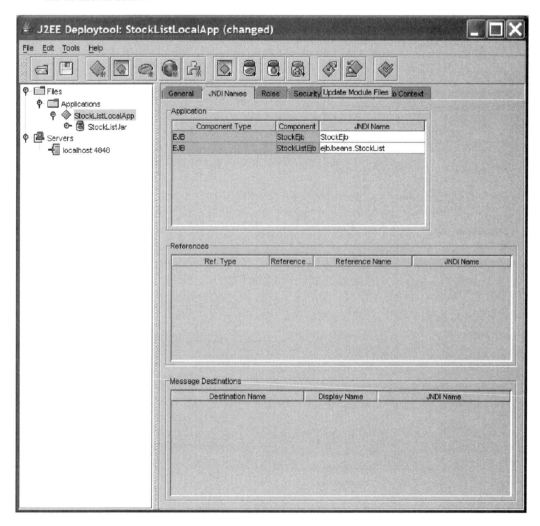

❏ Keep the default JNDI Name of StockEjb for the `Stock` bean. This bean will be accessed through a local reference.

❏ Enter ejb/beans.StockList as the JNDI Name for the `StockList` bean, as shown above.

13. Do a File | Save All. Select StockListJar in the left-hand panel, and click the Sun-specific Settings button at the bottom of the page. You'll enter the same values in the Sun-specific Settings and Create Field Mappings dialogs as you did previously:

❏ Specify jdbc/PointBase in the Database JNDI Name field.

❏ Select the Automatically Generate Necessary Tables option.

❏ Select PointBase in the Datasource Vendor drop-down list.

14. Deploy the application, making the client stubs JAR.

15. To run the client, set the classpath to use the client JAR: from the command prompt enter the following:

```
> set CLASSPATH=.;%J2EE_HOME%\lib\j2ee.jar;%J2EE_HOME%\lib\appserv-
� rt.jar;StockListLocalAppClient.jar
```

You can enter the following command to run the client that uses the beans we've built:

```
> java -Dorg.omg.CORBA.ORBInitialHost=localhost -
➫ Dorg.omg.CORBA.ORBInitialPort=3700 client.StockClient
```

For good housekeeping, make sure that you undeployed anything that was previously deployed.

How It Works

Only three source files and a deployment descriptor were altered in the making of this local interfaces example. Within those files, there were very few changes required to turn the previous example into a local interfaces example. We'll walk through them one at a time, beginning with LocalStockHome.java.

Making the Home Interface Local

Here are the modifications that we needed to make to the LocalStockHome file:

```java
package beans;

import javax.ejb.CreateException;
import javax.ejb.EJBLocalHome;
import javax.ejb.FinderException;

public interface LocalStockHome extends EJBLocalHome {
    // The create method for the Stock bean
    public LocalStock create(String ticker, String name)
        throws CreateException;

    // The find by primary key method for the Stock bean
    public LocalStock findByPrimaryKey(String ticker)
        throws FinderException;
}
```

There are a couple of things (other than the interface name) that changed in the home interface to make it local:

❑ The interface now extends EJBLocalHome instead of EJBHome.

❑ The methods of the interface don't declare that they throw RemoteException, because they are not accessed remotely.

Making the Bean Interface Local

Let's check out the changes to `LocalStock.java`:

```java
package beans;

import javax.ejb.EJBLocalObject;

public interface LocalStock extends EJBLocalObject {
    // The public business methods on the Stock bean
    // These include the accessor methods from the bean

    // Get the ticker. Do not allow ticker to be set through the
    // interface because it is the primary key.
    public String getTickerSymbol();

    // Get and set the name
    public String getName();
    public void setName(String name);
}
```

As with the home interface, there are a couple of things that changed in the remote interface to make it local:

❑   The interface now extends `EJBLocalObject` instead of `EJBObject`.

❑   The methods of the interface don't declare that they throw `RemoteException`, because they are not accessed remotely.

Using Local Home Interfaces vs. Remote Home Interfaces

To see how to access a local home interface, let's look at the new `StockListBean.java`:

```java
...
public class StockListBean implements SessionBean {

    // The public business methods, these must also be coded in the
    // remote interface.

    public String getStock(String ticker) throws FinderException {
        try {
            LocalStockHome stockHome = getStockHome();
            LocalStock stock = stockHome.findByPrimaryKey(ticker);
            return stock.getName();
        } catch (FinderException fe) {
            throw fe;
        } catch (Exception ex) {
            throw new RuntimeException(ex.getMessage());
        }
    }

    public void addStock(String ticker, String name) throws CreateException {
        try {
            LocalStockHome stockHome = getStockHome();
            stockHome.create(ticker, name);
```

```
      } catch (CreateException ce) {
        throw ce;
      } catch (Exception ex) {
        throw new RuntimeException(ex.getMessage());
      }
    }

    public void updateStock(String ticker, String name)
      throws FinderException {
      try {
        LocalStockHome stockHome = getStockHome();
        LocalStock stock = stockHome.findByPrimaryKey(ticker);
        stock.setName(name);
      } catch (FinderException fe) {
        throw fe;
      } catch (Exception ex) {
        throw new RuntimeException(ex.getMessage());
      }
    }

    public void deleteStock(String ticker) throws FinderException {
      try {
        LocalStockHome stockHome = getStockHome();
        LocalStock stock = stockHome.findByPrimaryKey(ticker);
        stock.remove();
      } catch (FinderException fe) {
        throw fe;
      } catch (Exception ex) {
        throw new RuntimeException(ex.getMessage());
      }
    }

    private LocalStockHome getStockHome() throws NamingException {
      // Get the initial context
      InitialContext initial = new InitialContext();

      // Get the object reference
      Object objref = initial.lookup("java:comp/env/ejb/beans.Stock");
      LocalStockHome home = (LocalStockHome) objref;
      return home;
    }

    // Standard ejb methods
    public void ejbActivate() {}
    public void ejbPassivate() {}
    public void ejbRemove() {}
    public void ejbCreate() {}
    public void setSessionContext(SessionContext context) { }
}
```

Recall that when using the Deployment Tool to configure the StockList session bean, we selected the **Enterprise Bean References** option that allowed you to enter information about the local interfaces of the Stock entity bean. One of the entry fields is called **Coded Name**, which holds a shorthand name for the name that the StockList session bean will use to lookup the local home interface. This **Coded Name**, when appended to java:comp/env/, produces a JNDI name that can reference another bean in the same EJB container. Here is the code that uses this JNDI name:

```
      Object objref = initial.lookup("java:comp/env/ejb/beans.Stock");
      LocalStockHome home = (LocalStockHome) objref;
```

Since the JNDI lookup is internal to the EJB container, it is very efficient for a bean to use. Also, notice that the cast is to a different class (LocalStockHome), and it is more straightforward than in the previous remote interface example where the complexities of Java RMI had to be dealt with, as shown below:

```
Object objref = initial.lookup("ejb/beans.Stock");
StockHome home = (StockHome)
    PortableRemoteObject.narrow(objref, StockHome.class);
```

Another thing worth noting in this class is that the methods of the local home interface return local bean references. This is demonstrated by the findByPrimaryKey() method invocation shown below. By the same token, the methods of a remote home interface return remote bean references.

```
LocalStockHome stockHome = getStockHome();
LocalStock stock = stockHome.findByPrimaryKey(ticker);
```

The Deployment Descriptor

Here is an excerpt from the deployment descriptor. The differences between this deployment descriptor and the one for the previous example are due to fact that the Stock entity bean now has local interfaces:

```
...
<display-name>StockListJar</display-name>
<enterprise-beans>
  <session>
    <ejb-name>StockListEjb</ejb-name>
    <home>beans.StockListHome</home>
    <remote>beans.StockList</remote>
    <ejb-class>beans.StockListBean</ejb-class>
    <session-type>Stateless</session-type>
    <transaction-type>Bean</transaction-type>
    <ejb-local-ref>
      <ejb-ref-name>ejb/beans.Stock</ejb-ref-name>
      <ejb-ref-type>Entity</ejb-ref-type>
      <local-home>beans.LocalStockHome</local-home>
      <local>beans.LocalStock</local>
      <ejb-link>StockEjb</ejb-link>
    </ejb-local-ref>
    ...
  </session>
  <entity>
    <ejb-name>StockEjb</ejb-name>
    <local-home>beans.LocalStockHome</local-home>
    <local>beans.LocalStock</local>
    <ejb-class>beans.StockBean</ejb-class>
    <persistence-type>Container</persistence-type>
    ...
  </entity>
</enterprise-beans>
<assembly-descriptor>
  ...
</assembly-descriptor>
</ejb-jar>
```

Notice the XML elements used to specify the local interfaces:

```
<local-home>beans.LocalStockHome</local-home>
<local>beans.LocalStock</local>
```

The remote interfaces version was:

```
<home>beans.StockHome</home>
<remote>beans.Stock</remote>
```

Also, the StockList session bean uses a different mechanism to get a reference to the Stock bean's home interface since it is now a local home interface. As noted previously, this mechanism is still JNDI, but it is *internal* to the EJB container, which, as we've said before, makes the whole process much more efficient. The following lines in the deployment descriptor make the local interfaces of the Stock entity bean available to the StockList session bean. It does this by linking the JNDI name java:comp/env/ejb/beans.Stock with the local interfaces of the Stock entity bean:

```
<ejb-local-ref>
  <ejb-ref-name>ejb/beans.Stock</ejb-ref-name>
  <ejb-ref-type>Entity</ejb-ref-type>
  <local-home>beans.LocalStockHome</local-home>
  <local>beans.LocalStock</local>
  <ejb-link>StockEjb</ejb-link>
</ejb-local-ref>
```

In this section, we discussed how to develop entity beans that have local interfaces, but the same concepts apply to session beans as well. We converted the previous container-managed persistence example that used remote interfaces into one that uses local interfaces.

In the next section, we'll explore a very powerful capability of Enterprise JavaBeans: the ability to use **SQL queries** on entity beans.

The EJB Query Language

Entity beans provide an object-oriented abstraction to an underlying database, complete with the ability to create business methods that operate on the data contained in the entity beans. One problem with this is that the abstract schema can become quite complex, making it very tedious and slow to do query-like operations that span multiple entity beans using Java code. EJB-QL lets you embed queries with SQL-like syntax into entity beans that can be accessed via methods of the entity beans. The results of EJB-QL queries are often entity bean references, which can be directly operated upon, so you get the combined advantages of object-orientation and SQL.

If you need a quick start guide to EJB-QL then please see Appendix B.

EJB-QL Find vs. Select Methods

There are two ways to implement EJB-QL in entity beans:

❑ **EJB-QL find methods** in the entity bean's home interface

❑ **EJB-QL select methods** in the entity bean class

Find methods are a natural extension of the concept of having the `findByPrimaryKey()` method in the home interface. As you recall, this method comes for free with entity beans—it's generated for you. You may want other methods in the home interface that find certain entity bean instances. Consider a fictional astronomy application that has an entity bean named `Planet`. A find method could be declared in the home interface and implemented via EJB-QL that returns only the planets with a given number of moons. This find method could have the following signature:

```
public Collection findByNumMoons(int moons) throws FinderException;
```

If that method were called with an argument having the value of 0, it would return a `Collection` containing two `Planet` entity bean references, representing Mercury and Venus, the two planets with no moons. The EJB-QL behind it could be something like this:

```
SELECT OBJECT(p)
   FROM Planet p
   WHERE p.numMoons = ?1
```

This query will:

❑ Take the argument passed into the method (in this case 0), which is represented by the `?1` portion of the query. This is just like the concept of SQL parameters.

❑ Find all of the entity bean instances with the abstract schema name of `Planet` whose `numMoons` field contains the value of 0. This is indicated by the `WHERE p.numMoons = ?1` portion of the code snippet.

❑ Return a collection of references to `Planet` entity bean interfaces.

The `SELECT OBJECT` portion of the above snippet indicates that the result will be an entity bean reference or collection of references. The `(p)` indicates that the type of entity bean reference returned will be one with an abstract schema name of `Planet`. That association was indicated by the `Planet p` portion.

The EJB-QL query is placed in the deployment descriptor, as the next example we see will demonstrate.

Find methods can also return a single entity bean reference, rather than a `Collection`. In this case, the entity bean's interface would be declared as the return type of the find method, and the EJB-QL query would be designed to return only one entity bean. For example, a find method in our fictional astronomy application that gets a planet by its diameter could have the following signature:

```
public Planet findByDiameter(int diameter) throws FinderException;
```

Select methods use EJB-QL as well, but are not declared in the home interface. Rather, they are declared in the entity bean class, and only available to other methods of the bean class. We'll discuss, and create, an example using select methods in the context of container-managed relationships in the next chapter.

Let's put these concepts into practice by working through an example of developing find methods.

Try It Out Create Entity Beans That Use EJB-QL Find

This example will highlight the development of EJB-QL find methods by adding two such methods to the `Stock` entity bean. To demonstrate the functionality supplied by the find methods, the `StockList` bean and `StockClient` application will be changed quite a bit. Here is a screenshot of the user interface that we will be using for this modified application:

When the client starts up, the scrolling panel is populated with radio buttons that represent all of the stock entity beans. If you select one of the stocks and click the Get button, a message dialog appears with the ticker symbol and name of the stock. When the 3 Letter Tickers Only checkbox is selected, only the stocks with three-letter ticker symbols appear in the scrolling panel.

Building and Running the Example

The names of the source files are the same as the previous example, and the process of building, configuring, deploying, and running the example is nearly the same as well.

1. Create a new application directory and create the `beans` and `client` subfolders within it.

2. Copy the code files from the download into their respective folders and then compile them.

3. Start the J2EE server, PointBase, and the Deployment tool.

4. Create a new application EAR calling it StockListApp and add an EJB jar, calling it StockListJar.

5. The creation of the session bean is the same as for the last example.

When creating the entity bean there are a couple of additional steps involved, as if there weren't enough already! They are as follows:

❑   Entering the EJB-QL queries for the find methods

❑   Loading the database with CMP field data for the Stock entity beans

Entering the EJB-QL Queries for the Find Methods

The first additional step will occur when you are configuring the Stock entity bean and get to the Entity Settings page of the Edit Enterprise Bean Wizard shown below:

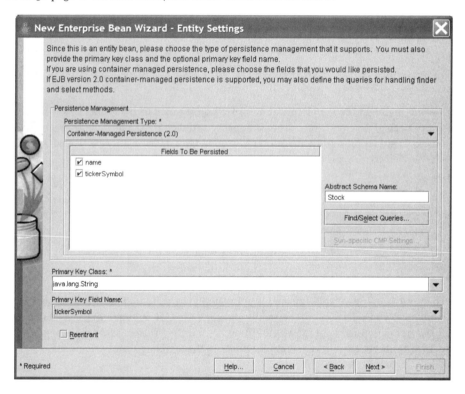

1. After filling in the information shown above, click the Find/Select Queries button to enter the queries for the two find methods. The dialog box shown below will appear, preloaded with the find methods that it found while reflecting upon the local home interface of the Stock bean:

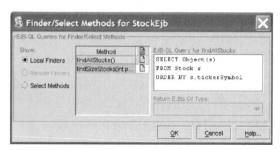

2. Select the findAllStocks entry in the Method panel, and enter the query shown below in the EJB-QL Query textbox:

```
SELECT Object(s)
FROM Stock s
ORDER BY s.tickerSymbol
```

This query will select all of the Stock entity beans, and return them in tickerSymbol order. Now select the findSizeStocks entry and enter the following query:

```
SELECT Object(s)
FROM Stock s
WHERE LENGTH(s.tickerSymbol) = ?1
ORDER BY s.tickerSymbol
```

This query will select and return only the Stock entity beans whose tickersSymbols are the same length as the argument passed to the findSizeStocks() method.

3. Once you have finished with the bean creation, populate the EJB Refs, JNDI Names, and Sun-specific Settings as described in the last example.

4. Go ahead and deploy the application.

Before you are ready to run the client we will load the database with some Stock entity bean data:

Loading the Database with CMP Field Data for the Stock Entity Beans

To load the database, use the PointBase Console tool as described earlier in this chapter to invoke the following SQL commands:

```
insert into STOCKEJB values ('ABC', 'ABC Company');
insert into STOCKEJB values ('ZZZ', 'Zigby Zebras');
insert into STOCKEJB values ('ICS', 'Internet Corp of Slobovia');
insert into STOCKEJB values ('DDC', 'Digby Door Company');
insert into STOCKEJB values ('ZAP', 'Zapalopalorinski Ltd.');
insert into STOCKEJB values ('JIM', 'Jimco');
insert into STOCKEJB values ('SRU', 'Stocks R Us');
insert into STOCKEJB values ('SRI', 'Shelves and Radios Inc');
insert into STOCKEJB values ('FBC', 'Foo Bar Company');
insert into STOCKEJB values ('DDBC', 'Ding Dong Bell Company');
insert into STOCKEJB values ('UDE', 'Upn Down Elevator Company');
```

When you start the PointBase Console tool, make sure that the Connect To Database dialog contains the values that are described earlier, including this URL:

```
%J2EE_HOME%\pointbase\tools\serveroption\startconsole.bat
```

5. To run the client, set the classpath to use the client JAR: from the command prompt enter the following:

```
> set CLASSPATH=.;%J2EE_HOME%\lib\j2ee.jar;%J2EE_HOME%\lib\appserv-
➔ rt.jar;StockListAppClient.jar
```

You can enter the following command to run the client that uses the beans we've built:

```
> java -Dorg.omg.CORBA.ORBInitialHost=localhost -
➔ Dorg.omg.CORBA.ORBInitialPort=3700 client.StockClient
```

Play with the client UI to see these EJB-QL find methods in action. When you've done that, let's walk through the code for this example.

How It Works

The following four Java source files changed from the last example:

❑   LocalStockHome.java

❑   StockList.java

❑   StockListBean.java

❑   StockClient.java

The Stock entity bean's local interface and bean class didn't change, and the StockList session bean's home interface didn't change.

First, here is the Stock entity bean local home interface, LocalStockHome.java:

```
...
// General imports
import java.util.*;

public interface LocalStockHome extends EJBLocalHome {
   // The create method for the Stock bean
   public LocalStock create(String ticker, String name)
     throws CreateException;

   // The find by primary key method for the Stock bean
   public LocalStock findByPrimaryKey(String ticker)
     throws FinderException;

   // The find all method for the Stock bean
   public Collection findAllStocks() throws FinderException;

   // The find by size method for the Stock bean
   public Collection findSizeStocks(int siz) throws FinderException;
}
```

You'll notice that all of our find methods are declared here. The findByPrimaryKey() method is required and the implementation is generated for you. The other two find methods have EJB-QL behind them, which as we'll soon see are located in the deployment descriptor. Both of them return a Collection of local interface references to Stock entity beans. The findAllStocks() method returns all of the Stock references.

The findSizeStocks() method returns only those Stock entity bean references in which the tickerSymbol length is the same as the value passed in to the method. As you can see, EJB-QL is a very powerful feature that provides a lot of functionality with very little code!

Here is the StockList session bean's remote interface, StockList.java:

```
...
// General imports
import java.util.*;

public interface StockList extends EJBObject {
  // The public business methods on the Stock List bean
  public String[] getSizeStocks(int siz)
    throws FinderException, RemoteException;
  public String[] getAllStocks()
    throws FinderException, RemoteException;
  public String getStock(String ticker)
    throws FinderException, RemoteException;
}
```

As expected, this interface declares the methods that will be called by the client application. Here is the bean class for the StockList session bean, StockListBean.java:

```
package beans;

import javax.ejb.FinderException;
import javax.ejb.SessionBean;
import javax.ejb.SessionContext;
import javax.naming.InitialContext;
import javax.naming.NamingException;

// General imports
import java.util.*;

public class StockListBean implements SessionBean {

  // The public business methods. These must also be coded in the
  // remote interface.
  public String getStock(String ticker) throws FinderException {
    try {
      LocalStockHome stockHome = getStockHome();
      LocalStock stock = stockHome.findByPrimaryKey(ticker);
      return stock.getName();
    } catch (FinderException fe) {

      throw fe;
    } catch (Exception ex) {
      throw new RuntimeException(ex.getMessage());
    }
  }

  public String[] getAllStocks() throws FinderException {
    try {
      LocalStockHome stockHome = getStockHome();
```

```
            Collection stockColl = stockHome.findAllStocks();
            String[] stocks = new String[stockColl.size()];
            int j = 0;
            Iterator i = stockColl.iterator();
            while (i.hasNext()) {
               LocalStock stock = (LocalStock) i.next();
               stocks[j++] = stock.getTickerSymbol();
            }
            return stocks;
         } catch (FinderException fe) {
            throw fe;
         } catch (Exception ex) {
            throw new RuntimeException(ex.getMessage());
         }
      }

      public String[] getSizeStocks(int siz) throws FinderException {
         try {
            LocalStockHome stockHome = getStockHome();
            Collection stockColl = stockHome.findSizeStocks(siz);
            String[] stocks = new String[stockColl.size()];
            int j = 0;
            Iterator i = stockColl.iterator();
            while (i.hasNext()) {
               LocalStock stock = (LocalStock) i.next();
               stocks[j++] = stock.getTickerSymbol();
            }
            return stocks;
         } catch (FinderException fe) {
            throw fe;
         } catch (Exception ex) {
            throw new RuntimeException(ex.getMessage());
         }
      }

      private LocalStockHome getStockHome() throws NamingException {
         // Get the initial context
         InitialContext initial = new InitialContext();

         // Get the object reference
         Object objref = initial.lookup("java:comp/env/ejb/beans.Stock");
         LocalStockHome home = (LocalStockHome) objref;
         return home;

      }

      // Standard EJB methods
      public void ejbActivate() { }
      public void ejbPassivate() { }
      public void ejbRemove() { }
      public void ejbCreate() { }
      public void setSessionContext(SessionContext context) { }
   }
```

The getStock() method is the same as in the previous example.

The getAllStocks() method calls the newly created findAllStocks() method of the Stock entity bean's local home interface. The findAllStocks() method, you'll recall, returns a collection of local interface references to Stock entity beans. The getAllStocks() method then iterates over these references and returns an array of Strings containing all of the ticker symbols.

The getSizeStocks() method calls the findSizeStocks() method of the Stock bean's local home interface, passing in the same value for desired tickerSymbol length that it received. The getSizeStocks() method then iterates over these references and returns an array of Strings containing only the ticker symbols with the desired length.

Notice that the getSizeStocks() and getAllStocks() methods return an array of Strings rather than a Collection of Stock entity bean references. There are a couple of reasons for this:

❑   Local interfaces can't be referenced from outside of the EJB container.

❑   Even if we were using remote interfaces, referencing entity beans from a user interface rather than through a session bean is usually not the best architecture. Recall that reasons for this were discussed earlier.

There are challenges to be overcome when not allowing entity bean references to be accessed from the client. These challenges will be dealt with in the next chapter when we discuss the "Value Object" architectural pattern.

Turning our attention to the client, the source code for StockClient.java may be downloaded from the Apress web site. In the StockClient class, when deselecting the checkbox, the getAllStocks() method of the StockList session bean is called to provide the ticker symbols of all the Stock entity beans. When selecting the checkbox, the getSizeStocks() of the session bean is called, passing in a value of 3, which returns a subset of the Stock entity beans' ticker symbols. This is shown in the stateChanged() method below:

```
public void stateChanged(ChangeEvent ce) {
  try {
    if (_threeOnly.isSelected()) {
      String[] stocks = _stockList.getSizeStocks(3);
      populateStockPanel(stocks);
    } else {
      String[] stocks = _stockList.getAllStocks();
      populateStockPanel(stocks);
    }
  } catch (Exception e) {
    e.printStackTrace();
  }
```

Here is an excerpt from the deployment descriptor that shows the EJB-QL queries that we entered:

```
      ...
      <display-name>StockListJar</display-name>
      <enterprise-beans>
        <entity>
          <ejb-name>StockEjb</ejb-name>
            ...
          <query>
            <query-method>
              <method-name>findAllStocks</method-name>
              <method-params>
              </method-params>
            </query-method>
            <result-type-mapping>Local</result-type-mapping>
            <ejb-ql>SELECT Object(s)<BR>
FROM Stock s <BR>
ORDER BY s.tickerSymbol</ejb-ql>
          </query>
          <query>
            <query-method>
              <method-name>findSizeStocks</method-name>
              <method-params>
                <method-param>int</method-param>
              </method-params>
            </query-method>
            <result-type-mapping>Local</result-type-mapping>
            <ejb-ql>SELECT Object(s) <BR>
FROM Stock s <BR>
WHERE LENGTH(s.tickerSymbol) = ?1<BR>
ORDER BY s.tickerSymbol</ejb-ql>
          </query>
        </entity>
        <session>
          ...
        </session>
      </enterprise-beans>
      <assembly-descriptor>
        ...
      </assembly-descriptor>
    </ejb-jar>
```

As shown above, there is a <query> element subordinate to the <entity> element that defines the find methods, their parameters, and the EJB-QL query that gets executed. By the way, if you are interested in the details of any element of the deployment descriptor, or have a bad case of insomnia, the element definitions are located at http://java.sun.com/xml/ns/j2ee/ejb-jar_2_1.xsd. This URL is also at the top of every ejb-jar.xml file that complies with the EJB 2.1 specification.

Summary

This chapter was completely devoted to entity beans, which are the persistent data objects in an EJB application. We found out that entity beans share a common anatomy with session beans, but that there are some basic differences between them. Entity beans also have several features that session beans don't have, such as:

- ❑ Container-managed persistence (CMP)
- ❑ Primary keys
- ❑ Their very own query language: EJB-QL
- ❑ Container-managed relationships (CMR)

We saw that by using CMP, an entity bean type is mapped to its own database table, and the data for each individual entity bean is stored in a row of that table. The EJB container handles all of the database persistence functionality for you. This saves a huge amount of time when developing applications, thereby increasing a developer's productivity.

We learned that each entity bean has a primary key that uniquely identifies it. Every entity bean's home interface has a method named findByPrimaryKey() that uses this primary key to return the corresponding entity bean. We touched on the fact that primary keys enable container-managed relationships; a concept that will be covered in the next chapter.

We also examined local interfaces and compared them with the remote interfaces that we'd been using up to that point. As a result of their speed and resource usage advantages, we switched to using local interfaces for entity beans. We continued using remote interfaces for the session beans, however, because they needed to be accessed from a client outside of the EJB container. In an application with more than one session bean, the ones that aren't called from the outside (presumably called by other session beans) can be local as well. Using local interfaces when applicable can boost the performance of an application.

We discussed the EJB query language, which provides the ability to create SQL-like queries that operate upon entity beans. These queries are encapsulated in entity bean methods so that their functionality is available via a method call. We demonstrated the use of one variety of EJB-QL: find methods. On this note, there is an EJB-QL chapter in the EJB Specification that provides a complete reference for the EJB Query Language. To view it, download the Enterprise JavaBeans Specification, version 2.1 from http://java.sun.com/products/ejb/docs.html#specs.

In the next chapter, we'll demonstrate how to create relationships among entity beans using container-managed relationships. In that context, we'll cover how to implement EJB-QL select methods. We'll also cover more EJB topics such as using JDBC with session beans, message-driven beans, EJB Timers, and implementing design patterns in EJB applications.

Exercises

1. Referring to the class diagram in the next chapter of the fictitious "Audio CD Collection" application, implement an entity bean with remote references for `CompactDiscTitle`. Attributes should be: `name` (String, and it will be the primary key) and `price` (double). Write a stateless session bean that allows you to get, add, update, and remove a CD title. Write a client application to test the beans.

2. Modify the previous exercise to use local references for the `CompactDiscTitle` entity bean.

3. Modify the previous exercise implementing a finder that returns all CD titles in ascending order by name, and a finder that returns all CD titles within a certain price range in ascending order by name. Write a simple client application to test the new methods.

4. Modify the stock list example in this chapter to return a list of stock tickers that start with a string entered by the user. Order the list ascending by ticker symbol.

10

More EJB Topics

The previous chapter explored EJB **entity beans**, which are the persistent data objects in an EJB application. In this chapter, we will continue to deal with entity beans, and cover some more EJB-related topics.

In this chapter you will learn how to develop:

- ❑ Entity beans that have **container-managed relationships**
- ❑ EJB-QL **select methods**
- ❑ Sessions beans that leverage JDBC to augment EJB-QL

We'll kick things off by demonstrating how to create relationships among entity beans. In that context, we'll cover how to implement EJB-QL **select methods**.

Container-Managed Relationships

As mentioned in the previous chapter, entity beans have an **abstract schema** that defines the **container-managed relationships** (**CMR**) between entity beans. For example, consider a fictitious application that manages a personal CD collection (audio compact discs, not certificates of deposit). We'll call it the "Audio CD Collection" application. In the music CD domain, a few candidates for entity beans jump to mind:

- ❑ `CompactDiscTitle`
- ❑ `SongTrack`
- ❑ `MusicalGenre`
- ❑ `Artist`
- ❑ `RecordLabel`

These entity beans have relationships with each other. For example, a `CompactDiscTitle` is published by one `RecordLabel`, and a `RecordLabel` has many `CompactDiscTitles`. Therefore, in our abstract schema there is a **one-to-many relationship** between `RecordLabel` and `CompactDiscTitle` entity bean instances. To be able to *navigate* these relationships from one entity bean to another, the following methods would be useful:

❑ A method of the `CompactDiscTitle` entity bean that would return the `RecordLabel` entity bean instance for a given `CompactDiscTitle`. A logical name for this would be `getRecordLabel()`.

❑ Conversely, a method of the `RecordLabel` entity bean would return all of the `CompactDiscTitle` entity bean instances published by a given `RecordLabel`. A good name for this would be `getCompactDiscTitles()`.

The term "navigate" is used to describe the process of obtaining, from a given entity bean, a reference to a related entity bean (or collection of entity beans).

The **primary key** of each entity bean helps establish these relationships with the other entity bean. The crude beginning of an "Audio CD Collection" class diagram illustrates the entity bean concepts presented so far:

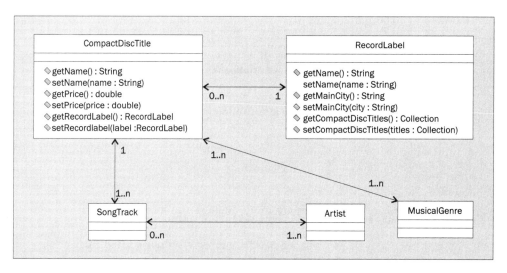

The CMP methods of the `RecordLabel` entity bean are `getName()`, `setName()`, `getMainCity()`, and `setMainCity()`. The `name` field is the name of the record company, and the `mainCity` field is where that record company is headquartered.

The CMR methods of the `RecordLabel` entity bean are `getCompactDiscTitles()` and `setCompactDiscTitles()`. CMR methods that interact with the "many" side of a relationship can use a `java.util.Collection` object to hold the bean interface references. For example, the `getCompactDiscTitles()` method returns a `Collection` of `CompactDiscTitle` bean interface references.

The primary key of the `RecordLabel` entity bean could be the `name` field, if that field was going to be unique among the `RecordLabel` entity bean instances.

Note the multiplicity notation on the relationships in the diagram, for example, a `RecordLabel` can have 0 or more (0...n in the diagram) `CompactDiscTitles`. A `CompactDiscTitle` can have only 1 `RecordLabel`.

The entity bean relationship multiplicity possibilities are:

- ❑ One-to-one

- ❑ One-to-many (which is also many to one depending on your perspective)

- ❑ Many-to-many

Each of these multiplicities can be **bi-directional** or **unidirectional**. The container-managed relationship between the `CompactDiscTitle` and `RecordLabel` entity beans in the diagram above is bi-directional. This is because there is a CMR getter method in both entity beans that accesses the entity bean(s) on the other side of the relationship. In a unidirectional relationship, only one of the entity beans would have a CMR getter method to access the other entity bean.

Also, with a many-to-many relationship, an additional database table exists behind the scenes that contains the primary keys from both of the entity beans in the relationship.

Now that we've discussed container-managed relationships, it's time to introduce a form of EJB-QL that can really exploit them: **EJB-QL select methods**.

Creating an EJB-QL Select Method

EJB-QL select methods are similar to finder methods in that they both are enabled by EJB-QL, but are different in a few ways, including:

- ❑ Finder methods are declared in an entity bean's home interface, but select methods are declared in its bean class.

- ❑ Finder methods are visible to other beans, but select methods are only accessible by methods of the same entity bean.

- ❑ Finder methods can return an entity bean reference or collection of references. In addition to these, select methods can return CMP field values and collections of these values.

- ❑ Finder methods have the form `findXxx()` but select methods use the naming convention `ejbSelectXxx()`.

For example, in the Audio CD Collection application above, let's say we want to know the names of the compact disc titles on record labels that have headquarters in a given city. To accomplish this we could declare the following select method in the `CompactDiscTitle` bean class:

```
public abstract Collection ejbSelectByRecordLabelCity(String city)
    throws FinderException;
```

If this method were called with an argument having the value of `Detroit`, a `Collection` of `Strings` would be returned that contains titles such as "Songs in the Key of Life" and "Cloud Nine," by Stevie Wonder, and The Temptations, respectively. The EJB-QL that provides the functionality for this method would be something on this order:

```
SELECT c.name
    FROM CompactDiscTitle c
  WHERE c.recordLabel.mainCity = ?1
```

This query will:

❑ Take the argument passed into the method (in this case `Detroit`), which is represented by the `?1` portion of the query.

❑ Find all of the entity bean instances of `RecordLabel` whose `mainCity` field contains the value of `Detroit`. This is indicated by the `WHERE c.recordLabel.mainCity = ?1` clause. The reason why `c.recordLabel.mainCity` represents the `mainCity` field of the `RecordLabel` entity bean is because:

    ❑ c represents the `CompactDiscTitle` entity bean, because of the `FROM` clause.

    ❑ `c.recordLabel` represents the `RecordLabel` entity bean instance that is related to the `CompactDiscTitle` entity bean. It is like calling the `getRecordLabel()` method on the `CompactDiscTitle` bean.

> *There is a caveat with using the dot operator to navigate between entity beans like we did just now; you can't navigate to the "many" side of a relationship using it. You can use operators like* IN *and* MEMBER OF *for that kind of functionality.* IN *is a standard SQL operator, and* MEMBER OF *is an EJB-QL operator. Notice that we used the dot notation to navigate through the "one" side of the relationship.*

❑ Return a collection of `Strings` containing the name field of the related `CompactDiscTitle` entity beans.

For more information on EJB-QL, take a look at Appendix B at the back of this book.

Now, let's work through an example that demonstrates both container-managed relationships and EJB-QL select methods.

Try It Out Create Entity Beans That Use CMR and EJB-QL Select

In this example, we're going to expand the `StockList` example from the previous chapter by adding an entity bean named `Analyst`. Each instance of the `Analyst` bean represents a stock analyst who assigns ratings to stocks. The `Analyst` entity bean and the `Stock` entity bean have a container-managed relationship that represents the stocks that a given analyst has rated.

Here is a screenshot of the Stock List application after Nancy the analyst rated the stock for Slobovia's largest Internet company:

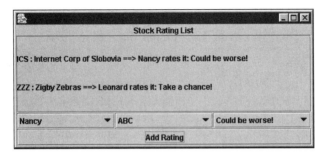

Shown below is a class diagram that depicts the enterprise beans involved in this application:

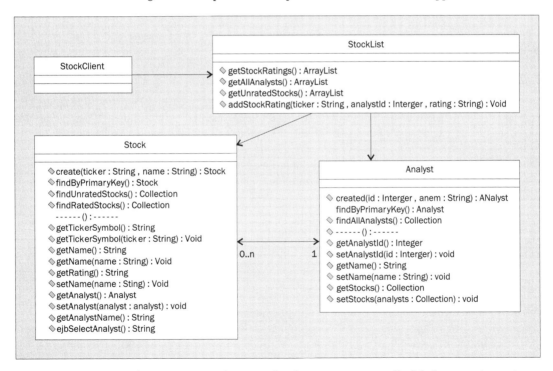

Note that the `Stock` and `Analyst` entity beans in the diagram represent all of their respective entity bean classes. To represent this, both of these classes have a dashed line that separates the home interface methods from the bean class methods.

Studying the diagram in a bit more detail, we see that the `StockClient` GUI uses methods of the `StockList` session bean to access and manipulate the `Stock` and `Analyst` entity beans. For example:

❑   To populate the drop-down listbox that contains the analyst's names, it calls the `getAllAnalysts()` method of the session bean.

❑   When the user clicks the Add Rating button, the `addStockRating()` method of the session bean will be called upon to create a relationship between the analyst and the stock being rated. That method will also set the value of the rating (for example, Could be worse! and Take a chance!) into the `rating` field of the `Stock` bean.

Turning our attention to the `Stock` bean, notice that in addition to the usual `create()` and `findByPrimaryKey()` methods, the `Stock` bean's home interface has a couple of EJB-QL finder methods.

As we'll examine shortly, the `Stock` bean also has an EJB-QL select method named `ejbSelectAnalyst()`. EJB-QL select methods can only be called from methods inside the same bean. We'll see, however, that the public `getAnalystName()` method offers the services of the `ejbSelectAnalyst()` method to other beans by calling it on their behalf. The `Stock` bean also has a couple of CMR methods, named `getAnalyst()` and `setAnalyst()`, that maintain its relationship to the `Analyst` bean. To round out the overview of the `Stock` bean, we'll also point out that it has three CMP fields (`tickerSymbol`, `name`, `rating`) represented by six CMP methods.

The `Analyst` bean has a similar set of methods, with the exception that it has no EJB-QL select method.

Building and Running the Example

Now we need to compile, configure, and deploy the application as we did in the previous chapter. The steps are basically the same but there will be some additional instructions intermingled, that pertain to container-managed relationships and EJB-QL select methods.

The names of the source files are the same as the last example of the previous chapter, with the addition of the three files that define the `Analyst` bean. These files are in the beans package, and are as follows:

❑   `LocalAnalyst.java`

❑   `AnalystBean.java`

❑   `LocalAnalystHome.java`

The Java source filenames carried over from the example in the previous chapter are:

❑   `LocalStock.java`

❑   `StockBean.java`

❑   `LocalStockHome.java`

- ❑ StockList.java

- ❑ StockListBean.java

- ❑ StockListHome.java

- ❑ StockClient.java (found in the client subdirectory)

Also, one Java program has been added to initially populate the entity beans. It is in the client package, and its name is: StockListAdder.java. All the code files for this example are available in the code download.

1. Open a command prompt in the application directory, (for example, StockListCmrApp), and set the classpath. As pointed out previously, on a default J2EE SDK 1.4 Windows installation the classpath would be set correctly by using the following command:

   ```
   > set classpath=.;%J2EE_HOME%\lib\j2ee.jar
   ```

2. Within the StockListCmrApp directory execute the following commands from the command prompt:

   ```
   > javac -d . client/*.java
   > javac -d . beans/*.java
   ```

3. Start the J2EE server, PointBase database server, and the Deployment Tool, as explained in Chapter 2.

4. Create the application EAR file by choosing New | Application from the File menu. Set the Application File Name to StockListCmrApp.ear and the Application display name to StockListCmrApp.

5. Start the Edit Enterprise Bean Wizard by choosing the File | New | Enterprise Bean menu item.

6. Follow the normal process for creating the bean JAR for the StockList session bean, setting the JAR Display Name to StockListCmrJar.

7. You'll also need to run through the **Edit Enterprise Bean Wizard** once for each entity bean. Shown below is the **Entity Settings** page of this wizard for the `Stock` bean:

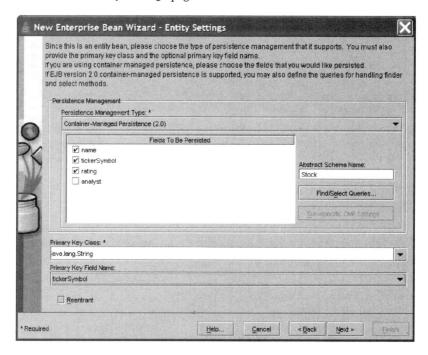

Notice that only the three CMP fields are checked. The `analyst` field is used for a container-managed relationship (CMR), so we'll leave it unchecked. As with the `Stock` bean in the previous example, the **Primary Key Field Name** is tickerSymbol, the **Primary Key Class** is `java.lang.String`, and we've chosen an **Abstract Schema Name** of Stock.

8. Click on the **Find/Select Queries** button, and we'll enter the queries for the finder methods, and select method mentioned previously:

In the dialog box shown, select the **findAllStocks** entry in the **Method** panel, and enter the query shown in the EJB-QL Query textbox:

```
SELECT DISTINCT OBJECT(s)
FROM Stock s
ORDER BY s.tickerSymbol
```

This query will select all of the Stock entity beans and return them in tickerSymbol order.

Now select the findRatedStocks entry and enter the following query for it:

```
SELECT DISTINCT OBJECT(s)
FROM Stock s
WHERE s.analyst IS NOT NULL
ORDER BY s.tickerSymbol
```

This query selects and returns only the Stock entity beans that have been rated. The ones that have been rated have a related Analyst. The DISTINCT keyword ensures that an entity bean isn't returned twice.

Now choose the Select Methods option, and choose the ejbSelectAnalyst entry. We'll enter the query for our EJB-QL select method, as shown below:

```
SELECT s.analyst.name
FROM Stock s
WHERE s.tickerSymbol = ?1
```

This query selects and returns the name of the Analyst that rated the Stock whose tickerSymbol was passed into the ejbSelectAnalyst() method.

Since this method doesn't return an EJB, choose None in the Return EJBs of Type drop-down list:

9. Shown below is the General page of the Edit Enterprise Bean Wizard when configuring the Analyst entity bean. Create the Analyst entity bean using these settings:

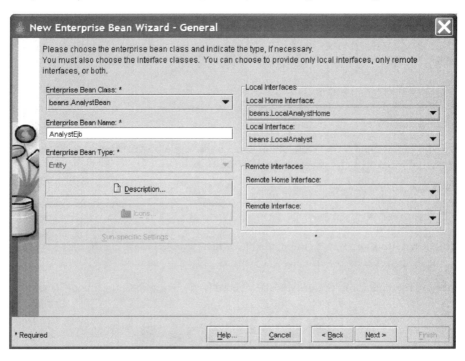

10. The Entity Settings page of this wizard when configuring the Analyst bean is shown below:

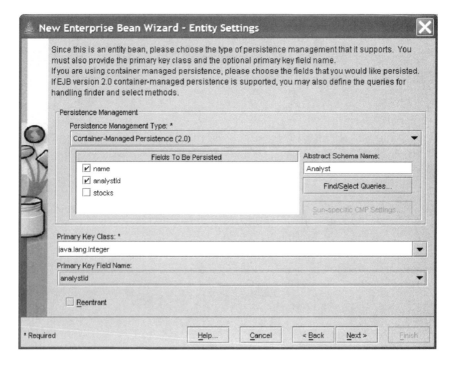

Only the two CMP fields are checked, name and analystId. The stocks field is used for a container-managed relationship (CMR), so we'll leave it unchecked. The Primary Key Field Name is analystId, the Primary Key Class is java.lang.Integer, and we've chosen an Abstract Schema Name of Analyst. Note that java.lang.Integer wasn't one of the choices in the Primary Key Class drop-down list, so you'll have to type it in.

11. Click on the Find/Select Queries button and we'll enter the query for the Analyst bean's EJB-QL finder method.

In the dialog box shown above, select the findAllAnalysts entry in the Method panel, and enter the query shown in the EJB-QL Query textbox, repeated below:

```
SELECT Object(a)
FROM Analyst a
ORDER BY a.name
```

This query will return all of the Analyst entity beans, and return them in name order.

12. After finishing the New Enterprise Bean Wizard for both entity beans, we need to define the container-managed relationship between them. To do this, select the EJB JAR (we used the name StockListCmrJar) from the tree in the left-hand panel, and click the Relationships tab as shown below:

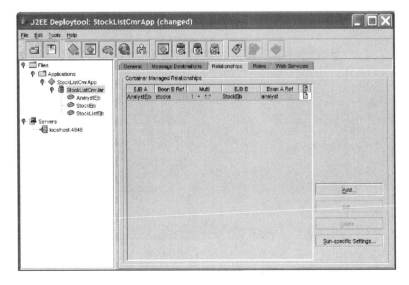

13. Click the Add button on the page shown above will enable you to define a relationship between the `Analyst` and the `Stock` entity beans in the dialog shown below. To do this, choose the options outlined here:

❑ As seen previously in the UML diagram for this example, there is a one-to-many relationship between these entity beans.

❑ On the "one" side (Enterprise Bean A) of the relationship is the `Analyst` bean, whose Enterprise Bean Name is AnalystEjb.

❑ To specify that `getStocks()` and `setStocks()` are to be the CMR methods that manage the relationship with the `Stock` bean, we'll choose stocks from the Field Referencing Bean B drop-down list.

❑ As we'll see from the `AnalystBean.java` source code in a moment, the `getStocks()` method returns a `java.util.Collection` (of `LocalStock` bean references). The `setStocks()` method takes a `java.util.Collection` (of `LocalStock` bean references) as its argument. Therefore, we'll choose a Field Type of `java.util.Collection`.

❑ On the "many" side (Enterprise Bean B) of the relationship is the `Stock` bean, whose Enterprise Bean Name is StockEjb.

❑ To specify that `getAnalyst()` and `setAnalyst()` are to be the CMR methods that manage the relationship with the `Analyst` bean, we'll choose analyst from the Field Referencing Bean A drop-down list.

❑ Since the other side of this relationship has a multiplicity of "one", the `getAnalyst()` and `setAnalyst()` methods return and take a `LocalAnalyst` bean reference, as opposed to a `Collection` of them. We'll see this in the `StockBean.java` source code. Therefore, we're not given a choice of Field Type.

❑ We can specify that whenever an `Analyst` bean is deleted, the `Stock` beans that are related to it should be automatically deleted. This is called a **cascading delete**, and can be specified by choosing the Delete When Bean X is Deleted option. We don't need that functionality in this example because we don't delete any `Analyst` beans. You'll want to think through the ramifications before choosing that option.

14. Now select AnalystEjb in the left-hand panel, and select the Transactions tab on the right. Make sure that the Container-Managed option is selected. Do the same for each of the other two beans (StockEjb and StockListEjb).

15. Select StockListEjb in the left-hand panel, and select the EJB Refs tab. You'll need to invoke the Add Enterprise Bean References dialog (by clicking the Add button) once for each entity bean. Shown below are the dialogs for both the Stock bean and the Analyst bean:

16. As shown below, select each row in the EJB's Referenced in Code panel and select the corresponding Enterprise Bean Name:

❑ ejb-jar-ic.jar#StockEjb for the Stock Bean.

❑ ejb-jar-ic.jar#AnalystEjb for the Analyst bean.

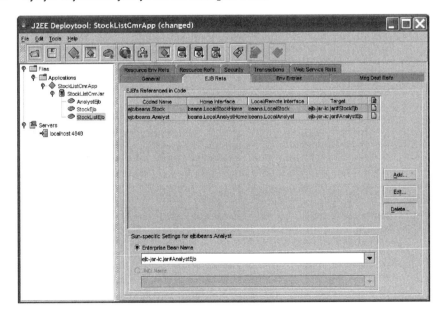

17. Do a File | Save All. Then select StockListCmrApp in the left panel, and select the JNDI Names tab. Give the StockListEjb component a JNDI Name of `ejb/beans.StockList`.

18. Select StockListJar in the left-hand panel, select the General tab, and then click the Sun-specific Settings button at the bottom of the page. You'll enter the same values in the Sun-specific Settings and Create Field Mappings dialogs as you've done previously, which are:

❑ jdbc/PointBase in the Database JNDI Name field of the CMP Resource panel. Remember to hit the *Enter* key.

❑ Select the Automatically Generate Necessary Tables option

❑ PointBase is selected in the Datasource Vendor drop-down list

19. Create the client JAR file and deploy the application by selecting the StockListCmrApp node in the tree in the left panel and selecting the Tools | Deploy menu item.

Before proceeding to the **Running the client application** step, we're going to populate the entity beans.

Loading the Database with CMP Field Data for Both Entity Beans

We're going to use a Java program this time to load the database, rather than using INSERT statements as in the last chapter. This program will use methods of the StockList session bean to create some Analyst and Stock entity beans. It will also use the StockList session bean to create a stock rating by associating a Stock entity bean with an Analyst entity bean and setting the rating field of the Stock entity bean. Here is the source code for this program that loads the database, StockListAdder.java:

```
package client;

import beans.StockList;
import beans.StockListHome;
import javax.naming.InitialContext;
import javax.rmi.PortableRemoteObject;

// General imports
import java.awt.*;
import java.awt.event.*;
import javax.swing.*;
import javax.swing.event.*;

public class StockListAdder {

    public static void main(String[] args) {
        try {
            InitialContext jndiContext = new InitialContext();

            // Get a reference to the StockList JNDI entry
            Object ref = jndiContext.lookup("ejb/beans.StockList");

            // Get a reference from this to the Bean's Home interface
            StockListHome home = (StockListHome)
                PortableRemoteObject.narrow(ref, StockListHome.class);
```

```
    // Create a StockList object from the Home interface
    StockList stockList = home.create();

    // Add analysts
    System.out.println("adding analysts");
    stockList.addAnalyst(new Integer(1),  "Fred");
    stockList.addAnalyst(new Integer(2),  "Leonard");
    stockList.addAnalyst(new Integer(3),  "Sarah");
    stockList.addAnalyst(new Integer(4),  "Nancy");
    System.out.println("analysts added");
} catch (Exception e) {
    System.out.println("exception adding analysts");
    e.printStackTrace();
}

try {
    InitialContext jndiContext = new InitialContext();

    // Get a reference to the StockList JNDI entry
    Object ref = jndiContext.lookup("ejb/beans.StockList");

    // Get a reference from this to the Bean's Home interface
    StockListHome home = (StockListHome)
      PortableRemoteObject.narrow(ref, StockListHome.class);

    // Create a StockList object from the Home interface
    StockList stockList = home.create();

    // Add stocks
    System.out.println("adding stocks");
    stockList.addStock("ABC",  "ABC Company");
    stockList.addStock("ZZZ",  "Zigby Zebras");
    stockList.addStock("ICS",  "Internet Corp of Slobovia");
    stockList.addStock("DDC",  "Digby Door Company");
    stockList.addStock("ZAP",  "Zapalopalorinski Ltd.");
    stockList.addStock("JIM",  "Jimco");
    stockList.addStock("SRU",  "Stocks R Us");
    stockList.addStock("SRI",  "Shelves and Radios Inc");
    stockList.addStock("FBC",  "Foo Bar Company");
    stockList.addStock("DDBC", "Ding Dong Bell Company");
    stockList.addStock("UDE",  "Upn Down Elevator Company");
    System.out.println("stocks added");
} catch (Exception e) {
    System.out.println("exception adding stocks");
    e.printStackTrace();
}

try {
    InitialContext jndiContext = new InitialContext();

    // Get a reference to the StockList JNDI entry
    Object ref  = jndiContext.lookup("ejb/beans.StockList");

    // Get a reference from this to the Bean's Home interface
    StockListHome home = (StockListHome)
      PortableRemoteObject.narrow(ref, StockListHome.class);
```

```
            // Create a StockList object from the Home interface
            StockList stockList = home.create();

            // Add ratings
            System.out.println("adding ratings");
            stockList.addStockRating("ZZZ", new Integer(2),
              "Take a chance!");
            System.out.println("ratings added");
        } catch (Exception e) {
            System.out.println("exception adding stocks");
            e.printStackTrace();
        }
    }
}
```

This class should already be compiled from when you compiled the client package.

1. To run `StockListAdder`, as well as `StockClient`, this would be the appropriate `classpath` for a default J2EE SDK 1.4 Windows installation:

    ```
    > set CLASSPATH=.;%J2EE_HOME%\lib\j2ee.jar;%J2EE_HOME%\lib\appserv-
    ➜ rt.jar;StockListCmrAppClient.jar
    ```

2. Run the application listed above to populate the beans by entering the following on the command line:

    ```
    > java -Dorg.omg.CORBA.ORBInitialHost=localhost -
    ➜ Dorg.omg.CORBA.ORBInitialPort=3700 client.StockListAdder
    ```

    When this command is run you will get the following output displayed in the command prompt:

    ```
    adding analysts
    analysts added
    adding stocks
    stocks added
    adding ratings
    ratings added
    ```

3. Now that the database is populated, let's run the client that uses the beans we've built, using the following command:

    ```
    > java -Dorg.omg.CORBA.ORBInitialHost=localhost -
    ➜ Dorg.omg.CORBA.ORBInitialPort=3700 client.StockClient
    ```

Congratulations! A screenshot of what the GUI client should look like is at the beginning of this example. Here it is again:

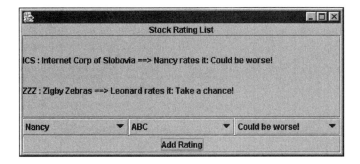

How It Works

In addition to the `StockListAdder.java` listing above, the source code for this example is listed below in ten Java source files:

For the `Analyst` entity bean:

❏ `LocalAnalyst.java`

❏ `AnalystBean.java`

❏ `LocalAnalystHome.java`

For the `Stock` entity bean:

❏ `LocalStock.java`

❏ `StockBean.java`

❏ `LocalStockHome.java`

For the `StockList` session bean:

❏ `StockList.java`

❏ `StockListBean.java`

❏ `StockListHome.java`

And for the `clients`:

❏ `StockClient.java`

Let's look at these and note some of the highlights after each listing, especially as they pertain to container-managed persistence and EJB-QL select methods.

Here is the Java source code for the implementation of the `Analyst` entity bean, `AnalystBean.java`:

```java
package beans;

import javax.ejb.CreateException;
import javax.ejb.EJBException;
import javax.ejb.EntityBean;
import javax.ejb.EntityContext;

import java.util.*;

public abstract class AnalystBean implements EntityBean {

    // Keeps the reference to the context
    private EntityContext _context;

    // The abstract access methods for persistent fields
    public abstract Integer getAnalystId();
    public abstract void setAnalystId(Integer id);

    public abstract String getName();
    public abstract void setName(String name);

    // The abstract access methods for CMR fields
    public abstract Collection getStocks();
    public abstract void setStocks(Collection stocks);

    // Business methods
    public void assignStock(LocalStock stock) {
      try {
        Collection stocks = getStocks();
        stocks.add(stock);
      } catch (EJBException ex) {
        ex.printStackTrace();
        throw ex;
      }
    }

    // Standard entity bean methods
    public Integer ejbCreate(Integer id, String name) throws CreateException {

        setAnalystId(id);
        setName(name);
        return null;
    }

    public void ejbPostCreate(Integer id, String name)
      throws CreateException { }

    public void setEntityContext(EntityContext ctx) {
      _context = ctx;
    }
```

```
      public void unsetEntityContext() {
        _context = null;
      }

      public void ejbRemove() { }
      public void ejbLoad() { }
      public void ejbStore() { }
      public void ejbPassivate() { }
      public void ejbActivate() { }
    }
```

The stocks CMR field is defined by the getStocks() and setStocks() methods listed above. As noted while building this example, these methods return and take a Collection of LocalStock bean references, respectively. They are declared abstract for the same reason that CMP methods are; the implementation code is created by the deployment tool because that behavior is specific to the EJB server and database server implementations. The java.util.* import is there because the Collection interface is in that package.

We've created a convenience method named assignStock() that adds a LocalStock reference to the "many" side of the relationship by performing the following steps:

❑   Use the getStocks() method to retrieve the Collection of related LocalStock references.

❑   Add the LocalStock reference argument to the Collection.

Since we've defined this relationship as bi-directional, the EJB container manages the other side of this relationship by using the setAnalyst() method of the Stock bean. Recall that we defined the relationship as bi-directional by declaring a CMR method in both entity beans that reference each other, and by specifying the relationship in the Add Relationship dialog of the Deployment Tool.

This assignStock() method is called by the StockList session bean when assigning a Stock entity bean to an Analyst entity bean.

Here is the Java source code for the local interface of the Analyst entity bean, LocalAnalyst.java:

```
    package beans;

    import javax.ejb.EJBLocalObject;
    import java.util.*;

    public interface LocalAnalyst extends EJBLocalObject {
        // The public business methods on the Analyst bean
        // These include the accessor methods from the bean

        // Add stock assignment
        public void assignStock(LocalStock stock);

        // Get the ID, no setter because primary key
        public Integer getAnalystId();
```

```
    // Get and set the name
    public String getName();
    public void setName(String name);

    // The public CMR methods on the Analyst bean
    // These include the CMR methods from the bean
    // No setters exposed to the local interface
    public abstract Collection getStocks();
}
```

In the local interface, listed above, we're exposing the getStocks() method to other classes, but notice that the setStocks() method is not declared. This protects the entity bean from having this relationship corrupted by other classes. This is a good time to point out that, although CMR methods are useful to the developer, they are mainly used by the EJB container to manage the entity bean relationships (hence the name).

Here is the Java source code for the local home interface of the Analyst entity bean, LocalAnalystHome.java:

```
package beans;

import javax.ejb.CreateException;
import javax.ejb.EJBLocalHome;
import javax.ejb.FinderException;

// General imports
import java.util.*;
public interface LocalAnalystHome extends EJBLocalHome {
    // The create method for the Analyst bean
    public LocalAnalyst create(Integer id, String name)
        throws CreateException;

    // The find by primary key method for the Analyst bean
    public LocalAnalyst findByPrimaryKey(Integer id)
        throws FinderException;

    // The find all method for the Analyst bean
    public Collection findAllAnalysts()
        throws FinderException;
}
```

There are no new concepts to discuss in the LocalAnalystHome interface listed above. Recall, however, that EJB-QL finder methods such as the findAllAnalysts() method are declared in the home interface, and that EJB-QL select methods are declared in the bean implementation class. We'll see one of these select methods in the next listing.

Here is the Java source code for the implementation of the Stock entity bean, StockBean.java:

```java
package beans;

import javax.ejb.CreateException;
import javax.ejb.EntityBean;
import javax.ejb.EntityContext;
import javax.ejb.FinderException;

public abstract class StockBean implements EntityBean {

  // Keeps the reference to the context
  private EntityContext _context;

  // The abstract access methods for persistent fields
  public abstract String getTickerSymbol();
  public abstract void setTickerSymbol(String ticker);

  public abstract String getName();
  public abstract void setName(String name);

  public abstract String getRating();
  public abstract void setRating(String rating);

  // The abstract access methods for CMR fields
  public abstract LocalAnalyst getAnalyst();
  public abstract void setAnalyst(LocalAnalyst analyst);

  // The abstract ejbSelect methods
  public abstract String ejbSelectAnalyst(String ticker)
    throws FinderException;
  // Business methods
  public String getAnalystName() throws FinderException {
    return ejbSelectAnalyst(getTickerSymbol());
  }

  // Standard entity bean methods
  public String ejbCreate(String ticker, String name)
    throws CreateException {

    setTickerSymbol(ticker);
    setName(name);
    return null;
  }

  public void ejbPostCreate(String ticker, String name)
    throws CreateException { }

  public void setEntityContext(EntityContext ctx) {
    _context = ctx;
  }

  public void unsetEntityContext() {
    _context = null;
  }
```

```
        public void ejbRemove() { }
        public void ejbLoad() { }
        public void ejbStore() { }
        public void ejbPassivate() { }
        public void ejbActivate() { }
}
```

The analyst CMR field is defined by the getAnalyst() and setAnalyst() methods listed above. As you might have noted while building this example, these methods return and take a LocalAnalyst bean reference, respectively. Recall that the relationship we defined in the Deployment Tool dictates that a stock can *only* be rated by *one* analyst, but an analyst can rate *many* stocks. Note that because their implementation code is generated by the deployment tool, the getAnalyst() and setAnalyst() methods are declared abstract.

We can also see the EJB-QL select method named ejbSelectAnalyst() in the listing above. It is declared as abstract because its implementation is generated for you. Note that, like EJB-QL finder methods, EJB-QL select methods throw a javax.ejb.FinderException.

EJB-QL select methods may not be directly called by methods outside of the bean in which they are located. To offer the services of the ejbSelectAnalyst() method to the StockList session bean, we created the getAnalystName() method. This method calls the EJB-QL select method, which returns the analyst's name.

Here is the Java source code for the local interface of the Stock entity bean, LocalStock.java:

```
package beans;

import javax.ejb.EJBLocalObject;
import javax.ejb.FinderException;

public interface LocalStock extends EJBLocalObject {
    // The public business methods on the Stock bean
    // These include the accessor methods from the bean

    // Find rated stock analyst name
    public String getAnalystName() throws FinderException;

    // Get the ticker, no setter because primary key
    public String getTickerSymbol();

    // Get and set the name
    public String getName();
    public void setName(String name);

    // Get and set the rating
    public String getRating();
    public void setRating(String rating);

    // The public cmr methods on the Stock bean
    // These include the cmr methods from the bean
    // No setters exposed to the local interface
    public LocalAnalyst getAnalyst();
}
```

In the local interface listed above, note that we're exposing the getAnalyst() CMR method to other classes, but that the setAnalyst() method is not declared.

Here is the Java source code for the local home interface of the Stock entity bean, LocalStockHome.java:

```java
package beans;

import javax.ejb.CreateException;
import javax.ejb.EJBLocalHome;
import javax.ejb.FinderException;

// General imports
import java.util.*;

public interface LocalStockHome extends EJBLocalHome {
    // The create method for the Stock bean
    public LocalStock create(String ticker, String name)
        throws CreateException;

    // The find by primary key method for the Stock bean

    public LocalStock findByPrimaryKey(String ticker)
        throws FinderException;

    // The find all stocks method for the Stock bean
    public Collection findAllStocks() throws FinderException;

    // Find rated stocks
    public Collection findRatedStocks() throws FinderException;
}
```

The EJB-QL finder methods are declared in the LocalStockHome interface listed above. Recall that EJB-QL select methods, however, are not declared in the home interface.

Here is the Java source code for the remote interface of the StockList session bean, StockList.java:

```java
package beans;

import java.rmi.RemoteException;
import javax.ejb.EJBObject;

// General imports
import java.util.*;

public interface StockList extends EJBObject {
    // The public business methods on the Stock List bean
    public ArrayList getStockRatings() throws RemoteException;
    public ArrayList getAllAnalysts() throws RemoteException;
    public ArrayList getUnratedStocks() throws RemoteException;
    public void addStockRating(String ticker,
                               Integer analystId,
```

```
                                    String rating) throws RemoteException;
     public void addAnalyst(Integer id, String name) throws RemoteException;
     public void addStock(String ticker, String name) throws RemoteException;
  }
```

The first four of these methods are used by the StockClient class, which provides the client UI. The last three methods are used by the StockListAdder class, which populates the entity beans initially. We'll discuss the implementation of these methods after the next code listing.

Let's examine some of the methods in the Java source code for the implementation of the StockList session bean, StockListBean.java:

```
package beans;

import javax.ejb.EJBException;
import javax.ejb.SessionBean;
import javax.ejb.SessionContext;
import javax.naming.InitialContext;

// General imports
import java.util.*;

public class StockListBean implements SessionBean {

  // The public business methods. These must also be coded in the
  // remote interface.

  public ArrayList getStockRatings() {
    try {
      // Get the initial context
      InitialContext initial = new InitialContext();
      // Get the object reference
      LocalStockHome home = (LocalStockHome)
        initial.lookup("java:comp/env/ejb/beans.Stock");

      // Get the stocks
      ArrayList stkList = new ArrayList();
      Collection stocks = home.findRatedStocks();
      Iterator i = stocks.iterator();
      while (i.hasNext()) {
        LocalStock stock = (LocalStock) i.next();
        String[] stockData = new String[4];
        stockData[0] = stock.getTickerSymbol();
        stockData[1] = stock.getName();
        stockData[2] = stock.getAnalystName();
        stockData[3] = stock.getRating();
        stkList.add(stockData);
      }
      return stkList;
    } catch (Exception e) {
      throw new EJBException(e.getMessage());
    }
  }
}
```

The getStockRatings() method, shown above, calls the findRatedStocks() method of the Stock entity bean's home interface to get references to the Stock beans that have been rated. This getStockRatings() method, then returns an ArrayList of String arrays. Each String array has four elements that contain the stock's ticker symbol, the stock's name, the name of the analyst that rated it, and the rating. The client UI uses this method each time it needs to display a current list of the stocks that have been rated. In the *Using Design Patterns in EJB Applications* section of the next chapter, we'll move away from using String arrays to pass data between clients and session beans in favor of using classes that are modeled after the Stock and Analyst entity beans. Note that in all of these methods, we're throwing an EJBException. This practice, and the topic of exception handling within EJBs in general, will be discussed in the context of the next example.

```
public ArrayList getAllAnalysts() {
   try {
     // Get the initial context
     InitialContext initial = new InitialContext();

     // Get the object reference
     LocalAnalystHome home = (LocalAnalystHome)
       initial.lookup("java:comp/env/ejb/beans.Analyst");

     // Get the analysts
     ArrayList analystList = new ArrayList();
     Collection analysts = home.findAllAnalysts();
     Iterator i = analysts.iterator();
     while (i.hasNext()) {
       LocalAnalyst analyst = (LocalAnalyst) i.next();
       Object[] analystData = new Object[2];
       analystData[0] = analyst.getAnalystId();
       analystData[1] = analyst.getName();
       analystList.add(analystData);
     }
     return analystList;
   } catch (Exception e) {
     throw new EJBException(e.getMessage());
   }
}
```

The getAllAnalysts() method, shown above, calls the findAllAnalysts() method of the Analyst entity bean's home interface to get references to all of the Analyst beans. It returns the data contained in the Analyst beans via an ArrayList of String arrays. The client UI uses this method when it needs to populate the drop-down list that contains the names of the analysts.

```
public ArrayList getUnratedStocks() {
   try {
      // Get the initial context
      InitialContext initial = new InitialContext();

      // Get the object reference
      LocalStockHome home = (LocalStockHome)
         initial.lookup("java:comp/env/ejb/beans.Stock");

      // Get the rated stocks
      Collection stocks = home.findRatedStocks();
      LocalStock[] ratedStocks = new LocalStock[stocks.size()];
      Iterator i = stocks.iterator();
      int ctr = 0;
      while (i.hasNext()) {
         LocalStock stock = (LocalStock) i.next();
         ratedStocks[ctr++] = stock;
      }
      // Get all stocks
      Collection allStocks = home.findAllStocks();
      ArrayList stkList = new ArrayList();

      // Eliminate the rated stocks
      Iterator j = allStocks.iterator();
      while (j.hasNext()) {
         LocalStock stock = (LocalStock) j.next();
         boolean rated = false;
         for (int k = 0; k < ratedStocks.length; k++) {
            String ratedTicker = ratedStocks[k].getTickerSymbol();
            if (stock.getTickerSymbol().equals(ratedTicker)) {
               rated = true;
               break;
            }
         }
         if (!rated) {
            stkList.add(stock.getTickerSymbol());
         }
      }
      return stkList;
   } catch (Exception e) {
      throw new EJBException(e.getMessage());
   }
}
```

The getUnratedStocks() method, shown above, calls the findRatedStocks() and findAllStocks() methods of the Stock entity bean's home interface. It uses the collections returned from these methods to identify the stocks that haven't been rated, and it returns an ArrayList of Strings containing ticker symbols. The client UI uses this method when it needs to populate the drop-down list that contains the ticker symbols for stocks that haven't been rated.

A good exercise for you at this point would be to create an EJB-QL finder method in the Stock bean named findUnratedStocks() that returns only the stocks that haven't been rated. Having this method available would simplify this getUnratedStocks() method considerably:

```
public void addStockRating(String ticker, Integer analystId,
    String rating) {
  try {
    // Get the initial context
    InitialContext initial = new InitialContext();
    // Get the home references
    LocalStockHome stockHome = (LocalStockHome)
      initial.lookup("java:comp/env/ejb/beans.Stock");
    LocalAnalystHome analystHome = (LocalAnalystHome)
      initial.lookup("java:comp/env/ejb/beans.Analyst");
    LocalStock stock = stockHome.findByPrimaryKey(ticker);

    // Get the local references
    LocalAnalyst analyst =
      analystHome.findByPrimaryKey(analystId);
    analyst.assignStock(stock);
    stock.setRating(rating);
  } catch (Exception e) {
    e.printStackTrace();
    throw new EJBException(e.getMessage());
  }
}
```

The addStockRating() method, shown above, takes two arguments; the ticker symbol of the stock being rated, and the ID number of the analyst rating the stock. These are the primary keys of the Stock and Analyst entity beans, respectively. This method uses these arguments to get references to a Stock bean and an Analyst bean. It then calls the assignStock() method of the Analyst bean that we examined earlier, passing in the reference of the Stock bean being rated. The client UI uses this method when the user clicks the Add Rating button. The StockListAdder class uses this addStockRating() method as well to set up an initial stock rating:

```
public void addAnalyst(Integer id, String name) {
  try {
    InitialContext initial = new InitialContext();

    // Get the object reference
    LocalAnalystHome analystHome = (LocalAnalystHome)
      initial.lookup("java:comp/env/ejb/beans.Analyst");
    analystHome.create(id, name);
  } catch (Exception e) {
    e.printStackTrace();
    throw new EJBException(e.getMessage());
  }
}

public void addStock(String ticker, String name) {
  try {
    InitialContext initial = new InitialContext();
```

```
            // Get the object reference
            LocalStockHome stockHome = (LocalStockHome)
              initial.lookup("java:comp/env/ejb/beans.Stock");
            stockHome.create(ticker, name);
        } catch (Exception e) {
            e.printStackTrace();
            throw new EJBException(e.getMessage());
        }
    }
```

The addAnalyst() and addStock() methods, shown above, take as arguments the values required for creating Analyst and Stock beans, respectively, after which they call the create() method of the proper home interface. The StockListAdder class uses these methods to create entity beans, and the client UI (the StockClient class) does not use them at all.

Shown below is the rest of the StockListBean.java listing; a standard refrain for our session bean implementation classes:

```
        // Standard ejb methods
        public void ejbActivate() { }
        public void ejbPassivate() { }
        public void ejbRemove() { }
        public void ejbCreate() { }
        public void setSessionContext(SessionContext context) { }
    }
```

Here is the Java source code for the home interface of the StockList session bean, StockListHome.java:

```
        package beans;

        import java.rmi.RemoteException;
        import javax.ejb.CreateException;
        import javax.ejb.EJBHome;

        public interface StockListHome extends EJBHome {
            // The create method for the StockList bean
            public StockList create() throws CreateException, RemoteException;
        }
```

As you can see the code is pretty simple.

Last but not least the Java source code for the GUI client, StockClient.java, may be downloaded from the Apress web site. It's not listed here because there isn't much code in there relevant to the EJB concepts we've been discussing. You might take a moment, however, to peruse that code, especially in areas where StockList session bean methods are being utilized. Doing so will help prepare you for the example in the *Using Design Patterns in EJB Applications* section of the next chapter, because it builds on this example.

Here is a relevant excerpt from the deployment descriptor:

```
...
<display-name>StockListCmrJar</display-name>
<enterprise-beans>
  ...
  <entity>
    <ejb-name>AnalystEjb</ejb-name>
    ...
  </entity>
  <entity>
    <ejb-name>StockEjb</ejb-name>
    ...
    <query>
      <query-method>
        <method-name>findAllStocks</method-name>
        ...
      </query-method>
      <result-type-mapping>Local</result-type-mapping>
      <ejb-ql>SELECT DISTINCT OBJECT(s)<BR>
              FROM Stock s<BR>
              ORDER BY s.tickerSymbol</ejb-ql>
    </query>
    <query>
      <query-method>
        <method-name>ejbSelectAnalyst</method-name>
        <method-params>
          <method-param>java.lang.String</method-param>
        </method-params>
      </query-method>
      <result-type-mapping>Local</result-type-mapping>
      <ejb-ql>SELECT s.analyst.name<BR>
              FROM Stock s<BR>
              WHERE s.tickerSymbol = ?1</ejb-ql>
    </query>
    <query>
      <query-method>
        <method-name>findRatedStocks</method-name>
        ...
      </query-method>
      <result-type-mapping>Local</result-type-mapping>
      <ejb-ql>SELECT DISTINCT OBJECT(s)
              FROM Stock s
              WHERE s.analyst IS NOT NULL
              ORDER BY s.tickerSymbol</ejb-ql>
    </query>
  </entity>
</enterprise-beans>
<relationships>
  <ejb-relation>
    <ejb-relationship-role>
      <ejb-relationship-role-name>AnalystEjb
      </ejb-relationship-role-name>
      <multiplicity>One</multiplicity>
      <relationship-role-source>
        <ejb-name>AnalystEjb</ejb-name>
```

```
        </relationship-role-source>
        <cmr-field>
          <cmr-field-name>stocks</cmr-field-name>
          <cmr-field-type>java.util.Collection</cmr-field-type>
        </cmr-field>
      </ejb-relationship-role>
      <ejb-relationship-role>
        <ejb-relationship-role-name>StockEjb</ejb-relationship-role-name>
        <multiplicity>Many</multiplicity>
        <relationship-role-source>
          <ejb-name>StockEjb</ejb-name>
        </relationship-role-source>
        <cmr-field>
          <cmr-field-name>analyst</cmr-field-name>
        </cmr-field>
      </ejb-relationship-role>
    </ejb-relation>
  </relationships>
  ...
</ejb-jar>
```

In the listing above, the <query> element in the <entity> element for StockEjb holds the EJB-QL
for the ejbSelectAnalyst() select method. Also shown are the descriptors for the container-
managed relationships that we defined earlier using the Add Relationship dialog of the Deployment
Tool.

In this section we've discussed, and walked through an example of, container-managed relationships
and EJB-QL select methods. In the next section, we'll use JDBC in the context of an EJB application.

Using JDBC with Enterprise JavaBeans

EJB-QL is an exciting technology that greatly enhances the functionality of Enterprise JavaBeans.
There are times, however, that you may want to use JDBC instead of EJB-QL:

❑   For example, EJB-QL is still a developing part of the specification. The EJB 2.1 specification
    added new keywords, which supports more complex queries. SQL is a much more developed
    specification, however, and functionality accompanies that maturity. In addition, SQL can be
    more straightforward than EJB-QL. When you need functionality not yet supported by the
    EJB-QL specification, or want a more understandable query, you might want to consider using
    JDBC.

❑   You may also want to use JDBC for performance reasons. Often, a JDBC query written
    especially for performance will execute faster than a similar EJB-QL query. When you
    encounter a poorly performing EJB-QL query, you might consider implementing the query in
    JDBC, along with the appropriate database tuning.

Let's look at an example of using JDBC within a session bean as an alternative to using EJB-QL.

Try It Out Using JDBC from Within a Session Bean

This example alters the previous example slightly to demonstrate the use of JDBC within the StockList session bean. To accomplish this, we're going to modify the getAllAnalysts() method of the StockListBean class that we walked through a bit ago. This modification will entail removing the call to the findAllAnalysts() method of the Analyst bean's home interface, and executing a JDBC query instead.

Building and Running the Example

The process to build and run this example is the same as the previous example, including all of the Java source filenames. The differences are:

1. When creating the application EAR file and the bean JAR use the names StockListJdbcApp.ear and StockListJdbcJar.

    When you Create Field Mappings, notice that the name field of the Analyst bean was mapped to the database field NAME9 (at least it was in the version of the J2EE Reference Implementation used as of this writing). As you'll see soon, we'll use this altered fieldname in a JDBC query.

    Before verifying and deploying, the next two steps use the same technique that we used in Chapter 9 to connect to the underlying database from an enterprise bean:

2. Select the StockListEjb node in the left-hand panel, and select the Resource Ref's tab as shown below. Add a Coded Name of jdbc/StockDB. This allows the JNDI name, java:comp/env/jdbc/StockDB, to be used in the StockListBean class to obtain a reference to the underlying data source. This occurs in the StockListBean.java listing below, in the following statement:

    ```
    DataSource ds = (DataSource) ic.lookup("java:comp/env/jdbc/StockDB");
    ```

    The concept of Coded Name *was covered in the previous chapter.*

3. Now enter the JNDI Name of the database by typing jdbc/PointBase in the Deployment setting for jdbc/StockDB panel as shown below:

4. Save, verify, and deploy the application, creating the client JAR file in the process.

5. To run StockListAdder, as well as StockClient, this would be the appropriate classpath for a default J2EE SDK 1.4 Windows installation:

```
> set CLASSPATH=.;%J2EE_HOME%\lib\j2ee.jar;%J2EE_HOME%\lib\appserv-
→ rt.jar;StockListJdbcAppClient.jar
```

6. Run the application to populate the beans by entering the following on the command line:

```
> java -Dorg.omg.CORBA.ORBInitialHost=localhost -
→ Dorg.omg.CORBA.ORBInitialPort=3700 client.StockListAdder
```

7. Run the application client using the following command:

```
> java -Dorg.omg.CORBA.ORBInitialHost=localhost -
→ Dorg.omg.CORBA.ORBInitialPort=3700 client.StockClient
```

Notice that it has the same GUI as the previous example, shown again below for your convenience:

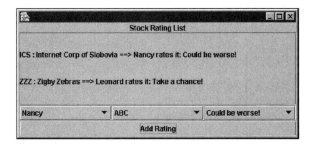

How It Works

Only one Java source file changed from the previous example. This file contains the implementation of the StockList session bean, StockListBean.java:

```
package beans;

import java.sql.Connection;
import java.sql.ResultSet;
import java.sql.SQLException;
import java.sql.Statement;
import javax.ejb.EJBException;
import javax.ejb.SessionBean;
import javax.ejb.SessionContext;
import javax.naming.InitialContext;
import javax.naming.NamingException;
import javax.sql.DataSource;

// General imports
import java.util.*;

public class StockListBean implements SessionBean {

  // The public business methods. These must be coded in the
  // remote interface also.

  public ArrayList getStockRatings() {
    try {
      // Get the initial context
      InitialContext initial = new InitialContext();

      // Get the object reference
      LocalStockHome home = (LocalStockHome)
        initial.lookup("java:comp/env/ejb/beans.Stock");

      // Get the stocks
      ArrayList stkList = new ArrayList();
      Collection stocks = home.findRatedStocks();
      Iterator i = stocks.iterator();
      while (i.hasNext()) {
```

```
          LocalStock stock = (LocalStock) i.next();
          String[] stockData = new String[4];
          stockData[0] = stock.getTickerSymbol();
          stockData[1] = stock.getName();
          stockData[2] = stock.getAnalystName();
          stockData[3] = stock.getRating();
          stkList.add(stockData);
       }

       return stkList;
    } catch (Exception e) {
       throw new EJBException(e.getMessage());
    }
  }

  public ArrayList getAllAnalysts() {
     try {
        // Make the SQL statements
        StringBuffer sql = new StringBuffer();
        sql.append("SELECT analystId, name9 ");
        sql.append("FROM AnalystEjb ");
        sql.append("ORDER BY name9");
        // Get the DB connection, statement, and resultset
        Connection conn = makeConnection();
        Statement stmt = conn.createStatement();
        ResultSet results = stmt.executeQuery(sql.toString());

        // Get the analysts
        ArrayList analystList = new ArrayList();
        while (results.next()) {
           Object[] analystData = new Object[2];
           analystData[0] = new Integer(results.getInt(1));
           analystData[1] = results.getString(2);
           analystList.add(analystData);
        }

        results.close();
        stmt.close();
        conn.close();

        return analystList;
     }
     catch (Exception e) {
        throw new EJBException(e.getMessage());
     }
  }

  public ArrayList getUnratedStocks() {
     try {
        // Get the initial context
        InitialContext initial = new InitialContext();

        // Get the object reference
        LocalStockHome home = (LocalStockHome)
           initial.lookup("java:comp/env/ejb/beans.Stock");
```

```java
      // Get the rated stocks
      Collection stocks = home.findRatedStocks();
      LocalStock[] ratedStocks = new LocalStock[stocks.size()];
      Iterator i = stocks.iterator();
      int ctr = 0;
      while (i.hasNext()) {
        LocalStock stock = (LocalStock) i.next();
        ratedStocks[ctr++] = stock;
      }

      // Get all stocks
      Collection allStocks = home.findAllStocks();
      ArrayList stkList = new ArrayList();

      // Eliminate the rated stocks
      Iterator j = allStocks.iterator();
      while (j.hasNext()) {
        LocalStock stock = (LocalStock) j.next();
        boolean rated = false;
        for (int k = 0; k < ratedStocks.length; k++) {
          String ratedTicker = ratedStocks[k].getTickerSymbol();
          if (stock.getTickerSymbol().equals(ratedTicker)) {
            rated = true;
            break;
          }
        }
        if (!rated) {
          stkList.add(stock.getTickerSymbol());
        }
      }
      return stkList;
    } catch (Exception e) {
      throw new EJBException(e.getMessage());
    }
  }

  public void addStockRating(String ticker,
                             Integer analystId,
                             String rating) {
    try {
      // Get the initial context
      InitialContext initial = new InitialContext();

      // Get the home references
      LocalStockHome stockHome = (LocalStockHome)
        initial.lookup("java:comp/env/ejb/beans.Stock");
      LocalAnalystHome analystHome = (LocalAnalystHome)
        initial.lookup("java:comp/env/ejb/beans.Analyst");
      LocalStock stock = stockHome.findByPrimaryKey(ticker);

      // Get the local references
      LocalAnalyst analyst = analystHome.findByPrimaryKey(analystId);
      analyst.assignStock(stock);
      stock.setRating(rating);
    } catch (Exception e) {
      e.printStackTrace();
```

433

```
            throw new EJBException(e.getMessage());
      }
   }

   public void addAnalyst(Integer id, String name) {
      try {
         InitialContext initial = new InitialContext();
         // Get the object reference
         LocalAnalystHome analystHome = (LocalAnalystHome)
            initial.lookup("java:comp/env/ejb/beans.Analyst");
         analystHome.create(id, name);
      } catch (Exception e) {
         e.printStackTrace();
         throw new EJBException(e.getMessage());
      }
   }

   public void addStock(String ticker, String name) {
      try {
         InitialContext initial = new InitialContext();

         // Get the object reference
         LocalStockHome stockHome = (LocalStockHome)
            initial.lookup("java:comp/env/ejb/beans.Stock");
         stockHome.create(ticker, name);
      } catch (Exception e) {
         e.printStackTrace();
         throw new EJBException(e.getMessage());
      }
   }

   private Connection makeConnection()
      throws NamingException, SQLException {

      InitialContext ic = new InitialContext();
      DataSource ds = (DataSource) ic.lookup("java:comp/env/jdbc/StockDB");
      return ds.getConnection();
   }

   // Standard ejb methods
   public void ejbActivate() { }
   public void ejbPassivate() { }
   public void ejbRemove() { }
   public void ejbCreate() { }
   public void setSessionContext(SessionContext context) { }
}
```

As shown in the listing above, the getAllAnalysts() method executes a JDBC query to get the data from the all of the Analyst beans. This is in contrast to invoking the findAllAnalysts() method of the home interface of the Analyst bean as the previous example did. Note that in the makeConnection() method we're using the resource reference (jdbc/StockDB) that we specified in the Deployment Tool to get a reference to the data source.

Notice that most of these methods catch an `Exception` and throw an `EJBException` (located in the `javax.ejb` package) with the message from the original exception being passed into its constructor. EJB methods of a production application should be more discriminating in their exception handling. There are three main exception-handling scenarios that should be dealt with:

❑   When a checked exception can occur that is defined by the application (as opposed to those defined in the standard Java libraries), a good approach is to declare that the EJB method throws that exception. This allows that exception to be thrown to the caller to communicate the exception condition.

❑   When a checked exception can occur that is defined by standard Java libraries, the preferred approach is to wrap that exception, or the message contained within it, in an `EJBException`. An example of a checked Java library exception is the `SQLException` that could occur as a result of the `executeQuery()` method in the `getAllAnalysts()` method shown above.

❑   Unchecked exceptions (`java.lang.RuntimeException` and its subclasses) should typically not be caught, but rather allowed to be handled by the EJB container.

Summary

In this chapter, we continued the discussion of entity beans from the previous chapter, covering concepts such as **container-managed relationships,** EJB-QL **select methods**, and using JDBC to augment EJB-QL.

❑   Container-managed relationships are a huge convenience to the developer, because the work in maintaining the relationships is performed by the EJB container. These relationships can be one to one, one to many, and many to many. In addition, each kind of relationship can be uni-directional or bi-directional.

❑   EJB-QL select methods are similar to EJB-QL finder methods in that they provide for using a SQL-like language to query entity beans. We pointed out some major differences, however, in the areas of: where they are declared, visibility, what they can return, and naming convention.

❑   EJB-QL is a very powerful feature of EJBs, but there are times when it is advantageous to use JDBC as well. The most compelling reason for using it is *performance*, especially when querying many rows across several entity beans.

In the next chapter we'll cover more EJB topics such as implementing design patterns in EJB applications, developing message-driven beans, and using the new EJB Timer Service. We're also going to modify a JSP example from Chapter 5 to use the EJBs that we've been developing for the `StockList` examples.

Exercises

1. Using the class diagram in this chapter of the fictitious "Audio CD Collection" application, implement the CompactDiscTitle and RecordLabel entity beans using local references, including the container-managed relationship. Implement a stateless session bean that allows you to add record labels and CD titles. Write a simple client application to test your beans.

2. Modify the previous exercise, adding a method to the session bean that uses JDBC to find all CD titles ordered by name. Change the client application to execute this method.

11

Design Patterns and Message-Driven Beans

The previous chapter introduced EJB container-managed relationships, and the use of JDBC in session beans. In this chapter, we will move on to some more advanced topics and another type of bean. You will learn about:

❑ What **design patterns** are, and how they can be applied in EJB applications.

❑ How to combine JSP and EJB technologies in one application. To demonstrate this, we'll fuse together the StockList example from the servlets chapter, Chapter 5, with an EJB-based version of the StockList application.

❑ Message-driven beans and the underlying Java Message Service (JMS) API.

❑ How to use the EJB Timer Service.

We'll start off by introducing the subject of design patterns, and how they can facilitate the development and maintenance of EJB applications.

Using Design Patterns in EJB Applications

When object-oriented software design is compared to designing a house, we know that software objects are analogous to some of the construction materials, or components, used to build the house. These materials or components range in size and complexity, some examples being a simple nail, a light switch, or a gas furnace.

Continuing this analogy, software **design patterns** are analogous to some of the concepts and styles used in house building. For example, when designing a house, an architect may specify that it have a gable roof, as opposed to, say, a hip roof or a gambrel (barn-style) roof. These well known roofing styles, or patterns, can be used to facilitate the task of designing and building a house–the architect doesn't have to invent a roofing style each time he or she designs a house, and the builder is familiar with implementing the design pattern of a gable roof. Not so coincidentally perhaps, roof trusses themselves are often built using a template, or pattern.

The concept of software design patterns became well known as a result of a book published in 1994 named *Design Patterns, Elements of Reusable Object-Oriented Software*. It was written by Erich Gamma, Richard Helm, Ralph Johnson, and John Vlissides (the "Gang of Four"), and it has a good starter set of software design patterns. Other works have been created since then that offer additional design patterns for the general object-oriented software domain, a well as for specific domains such as J2EE applications. One such work is Sun Microsystems' Java BluePrints Patterns Catalog, which can be viewed from the following link: http://java.sun.com/blueprints/patterns/catalog.html. Other resources are listed at the end of this chapter.

Software design patterns describe solutions to specific software design problems, such as:

❑   Designing an application in such a way that the client UI doesn't have to worry about the architecture or location of the application logic layer of an application. We'll demonstrate shortly how a couple of common patterns, specifically the **façade** and **value object** design patterns, can be employed to address this design problem. A given design pattern, by the way, can have several names. For example, the **value object** pattern is also known as the **transfer object** pattern and **data transfer object** pattern.

❑   Providing the ability to create an instance of a class that is vendor- or product-specific, in a generic way. We'll look at a very simple case of a pattern that enables this, known as the **factory pattern**.

❑   Designing a method in such a way that it will create and return the same instance of a class to any method that calls it. We'll see how the **singleton** design pattern can be used to enable this.

We'll build upon the now familiar `StockList` example to demonstrate the design patterns mentioned above.

Try It Out   Implementing Design Patterns

This example introduces the **façade**, **value object**, and **singleton** patterns to the previous `StockList` example. These design patterns will be explained in the context of this example.

Shown below is a class diagram for this example. The dashed lines indicate dependencies between classes in the direction of the arrow. For example, methods of the `StockClient` class hold references to `StockVo` instances. As the class name reveals, we'll implement the façade pattern with the help of the `StockListFacade` class. The singleton pattern will be employed in that class as well. The `StockVo` and `AnalystVo` classes will be used to implement the value object pattern:

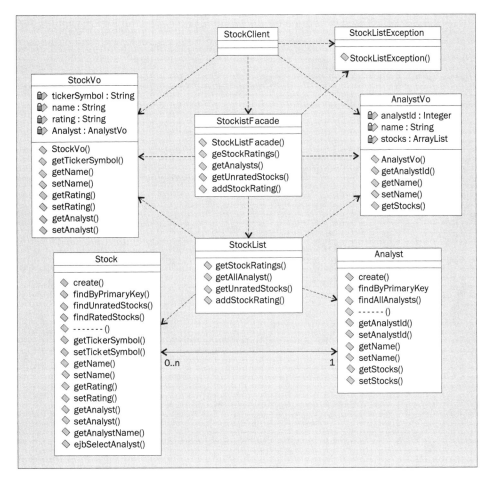

In this example, there are four new Java source files, as seen in the class diagram above. These are:

- ❑ StockListFacade.java

- ❑ StockListException.java

- ❑ AnalystVo.java

- ❑ StockVo.java

In addition, four Java source files from the CMR example were modified:

- ❑ StockList.java

- ❑ StockListBean.java

- ❑ StockClient.java

- ❑ StockListAdder.java

1. Firstly, you will need to type in the code (or download it from the Apress web site) for the
`StockListFacade.java` source file, in which you can see an implementation of the façade
pattern:

```
package facade;

import beans.StockList;
import beans.StockListHome;
import vo.AnalystVo;
import vo.StockVo;
import javax.naming.InitialContext;
import javax.rmi.PortableRemoteObject;

// General imports
import java.util.*;

public class StockListFacade {
  // Reference to singleton facade
  private static StockListFacade stockListFacade;

  // The reference to the stock list bean
  private StockList stockList;

  // private constructor - makes connection to session bean
  private StockListFacade() throws StockListException {
    try {
      // Get a naming context
      InitialContext jndiContext = new InitialContext();

      // Get a reference to the StockList JNDI entry
      Object ref  = jndiContext.lookup("ejb/beans.StockList");

      // Get a reference from this to the Bean's Home interface
      StockListHome home = (StockListHome)
        PortableRemoteObject.narrow(ref, StockListHome.class);

      // Create a StockList object from the Home interface
      stockList = home.create();
    } catch(Exception e) {
      throw new StockListException(e.getMessage());
    }
  }

  // The business methods. No exposure to actual implementation
  // on the server and the communication method between client and
  // server is hidden to the client.

  public ArrayList getStockRatings() throws StockListException {
    try {
      ArrayList ratings = stockList.getStockRatings();
      return ratings;
    }
    catch (Exception re) {
      throw new StockListException(re.getMessage());
    }
  }
```

```
public ArrayList getAllAnalysts() throws StockListException {
  try {
    ArrayList analysts = stockList.getAllAnalysts();
    return analysts;
  }
  catch (Exception re) {
    throw new StockListException(re.getMessage());
  }
}

public ArrayList getUnratedStocks() throws StockListException {
  try {
    ArrayList stocks = stockList.getUnratedStocks();
    return stocks;
  }
  catch (Exception re) {
    throw new StockListException(re.getMessage());
  }
}

public void addStockRating(StockVo stock)
  throws StockListException {
  try {
    stockList.addStockRating(stock);
  }
  catch (Exception re) {
    throw new StockListException(re.getMessage());
  }
}

public void addAnalyst(AnalystVo analyst)
  throws StockListException {
  try {
    stockList.addAnalyst(analyst);
  }
  catch (Exception re) {
    throw new StockListException(re.getMessage());
  }
}

public void addStock(StockVo stock) throws StockListException {
  try {
    stockList.addStock(stock);
  }
  catch (Exception re) {
    throw new StockListException(re.getMessage());
  }
}

public static StockListFacade getFacade()
  throws StockListException {
  if (stockListFacade == null) {
    stockListFacade = new StockListFacade();
  }

  return stockListFacade;
}
}
```

2. Next up, enter the code for `StockListException.java`:

```
package facade;

public class StockListException extends Exception {

  public StockListException(String msg) {
    super(msg);
  }
}
```

3. And now `AnalystVo.java`:

```
package vo;

import java.io.Serializable;
import java.util.*;

public class AnalystVo implements Serializable {

  // Holds references to the attribute data
  private Integer analystId;
  private String name;

  // Holds references to the relationships
  private ArrayList stocks;

  public AnalystVo(Integer analystId, String name) {
    this.analystId = analystId;
    this.name = name;
    stocks = new ArrayList();
  }

  // Get analyst ID. No setter because primary key
  public Integer getAnalystId() {
    return analystId;
  }
  // Get, set name
  public String getName() {
    return name;
  }

  public void setName(String name) {
    this.name = name;
  }

  // Get stocks
  public ArrayList getStocks() {
    return stocks;
  }
}
```

4. And finally, enter `StockVo.java`:

```java
package vo;

import java.io.Serializable;
import java.util.*;

public class StockVo implements Serializable {

    // Holds references to the attribute data
    private String tickerSymbol;
    private String name;
    private String rating;

    // Holds references to the relationships
    private AnalystVo analyst;

    public StockVo(String tickerSymbol, String name, String rating) {
        this.tickerSymbol = tickerSymbol;
        this.name = name;
        this.rating = rating;
        analyst = null;
    }

    // Get ticker symbol. No setter because primary key
    public String getTickerSymbol() {
        return tickerSymbol;
    }

    // Get, set name
    public String getName() {
        return name;
    }

    public void setName(String name) {
        this.name = name;
    }
    // Get, set rating
    public String getRating() {
        return rating;
    }

    public void setRating(String rating) {
        this.rating = rating;
    }

    // Get, set analyst
    public AnalystVo getAnalyst() {
        return analyst;
    }

    public void setAnalyst(AnalystVo analyst) {
        this.analyst = analyst;
    }
}
```

5. Next, we need to modify the source code for the `StockList` session bean to see how it uses value objects. Here is the `StockList` session bean's remote interface, `StockList.java`:

```
package beans;

import vo.AnalystVo;
import vo.StockVo;
import java.rmi.RemoteException;
import javax.ejb.EJBObject;

// General imports
import java.util.*;

public interface StockList extends EJBObject {
   // The public business methods on the Stock List bean
   public ArrayList getStockRatings() throws RemoteException;
   public ArrayList getAllAnalysts() throws RemoteException;
   public ArrayList getUnratedStocks() throws RemoteException;
   public void addStockRating(StockVo stockVo) throws RemoteException;
   public void addAnalyst(AnalystVo analystVo) throws RemoteException;
   public void addStock(StockVo stockVo) throws RemoteException;
}
```

6. Every method in the interface shown above either takes value objects as an argument, or returns value objects (actually in these cases, an `ArrayList` of them). So let's see how they are used by the new, value object-enabled version of the session bean's implementation class, `StockListBean.java`:

```
package beans;

import vo.AnalystVo;
import vo.StockVo;
import javax.ejb.EJBException;
import javax.ejb.SessionBean;
import javax.ejb.SessionContext;
import javax.naming.InitialContext;

// General imports
import java.util.*;

public class StockListBean implements SessionBean {

   // The public business methods. These must be coded in the
   // remote interface also.

   public ArrayList getStockRatings() {
      try {
         // Get the initial context
         InitialContext initial = new InitialContext();
         // Get the object reference
         LocalStockHome home = (LocalStockHome)
            initial.lookup("java:comp/env/ejb/beans.Stock");

         // Get the stocks
         ArrayList stkList = new ArrayList();
```

```
            Collection stocks = home.findRatedStocks();
            Iterator i = stocks.iterator();
            while (i.hasNext()) {
              LocalStock stock = (LocalStock) i.next();
              StockVo stockVo = new StockVo(stock.getTickerSymbol(),
                stock.getName(), stock.getRating());
              LocalAnalyst analyst = stock.getAnalyst();
              AnalystVo analystVo = new AnalystVo(analyst.getAnalystId(),
                analyst.getName());
              stockVo.setAnalyst(analystVo);
              stkList.add(stockVo);
            }
            return stkList;
          }
      catch (Exception e) {
        throw new EJBException(e.getMessage());
      }
    }
```

In the getStockRatings() method shown above:

❑   A call is made to the findRatedStocks() method of the Stock entity bean's home interface,
    which returns a Collection of Stock entity bean references.

❑   We iterate over that Collection and create a StockVo instance from the fields of each entity
    bean, populating an ArrayList with the StockVo references:

    ❑   Since the client UI is going to display information from the related Analyst entity bean,
        we use the getAnalyst() CMR method of each Stock bean to get a reference to the
        Analyst bean. An AnalystVo instance is then created from the fields of the Analyst
        bean, which is then associated with the StockVo instance via its setAnalyst() method.

❑   The ArrayList that contains StockVo references, each of which holds an AnalystVo
    reference, is serialized and streamed back to the caller. Recall that the caller in this case is the
    StockListFacade class.

If you decide to implement the idea of having methods in your value objects that mimic CMR
methods, care should be taken not to carry the idea too far. You probably don't want to stream a
graph of value objects back to the client in one method invocation that contains the data from all of
the entity beans in the application, for example.

445

7. The other methods that return an `ArrayList`, shown below, are similar in nature to the `getStockRatings()` method:

```
public ArrayList getAllAnalysts() {
   try {
     // Get the initial context
     InitialContext initial = new InitialContext();
     // Get the object reference
     LocalAnalystHome home = (LocalAnalystHome)
       initial.lookup("java:comp/env/ejb/beans.Analyst");

     // Get the analysts
     ArrayList analystList = new ArrayList();
     Collection analysts = home.findAllAnalysts();
     Iterator i = analysts.iterator();
     while (i.hasNext()) {
       LocalAnalyst analyst = (LocalAnalyst) i.next();
       AnalystVo analystVo = new AnalystVo(analyst.getAnalystId(),
          analyst.getName());
       analystList.add(analystVo);
     }
     return analystList;
   }
   catch (Exception e) {
     throw new EJBException(e.getMessage());
   }
}

public ArrayList getUnratedStocks() {
   try {
     // Get the initial context
     InitialContext initial = new InitialContext();
     // Get the object reference
     LocalStockHome home = (LocalStockHome)
       initial.lookup("java:comp/env/ejb/beans.Stock");

     // Get the rated stocks
     Collection stocks = home.findRatedStocks();
     LocalStock[] ratedStocks = new LocalStock[stocks.size()];
     Iterator i = stocks.iterator();
     int ctr = 0;
     while (i.hasNext()) {
       LocalStock stock = (LocalStock) i.next();
       ratedStocks[ctr++] = stock;
     }

     // Get all stocks
     Collection allStocks = home.findAllStocks();
     ArrayList stkList = new ArrayList();

     // Eliminate the rated stocks
     Iterator j = allStocks.iterator();
     while (j.hasNext()) {
       LocalStock stock = (LocalStock) j.next();
       boolean rated = false;
       for (int k = 0; k < ratedStocks.length; k++) {
```

```
                String ratedTicker = ratedStocks[k].getTickerSymbol();
                if (stock.getTickerSymbol().equals(ratedTicker)) {
                  rated = true;
                  break;
                }
              }
              if (!rated) {
                StockVo stockVo = new StockVo(stock.getTickerSymbol(),
                  stock.getName(), null);
                stkList.add(stockVo);
              }
            }
            return stkList;
          }
          catch (Exception e) {
            throw new EJBException(e.getMessage());
          }
        }
```

The addStockRating() method, shown below, passes the primary key fields contained in the AnalystVo and StockVo value objects to findByPrimaryKey() methods. This is for the purpose of obtaining references to the entity beans from which these value objects were originally created:

```
public void addStockRating(StockVo stockVo) {
    try {
      // Get the initial context
      InitialContext initial = new InitialContext();
      // Get the home references
      LocalStockHome stockHome = (LocalStockHome)
        initial.lookup("java:comp/env/ejb/beans.Stock");
      LocalAnalystHome analystHome = (LocalAnalystHome)
        initial.lookup("java:comp/env/ejb/beans.Analyst");
      LocalStock stock =
        stockHome.findByPrimaryKey(stockVo.getTickerSymbol());
      // Get the local refs
      LocalAnalyst analyst = analystHome.findByPrimaryKey(
        stockVo.getAnalyst().getAnalystId());
      analyst.assignStock(stock);
      stock.setRating(stockVo.getRating());
    }
    catch (Exception e) {
      e.printStackTrace();
      throw new EJBException(e.getMessage());
    }
}
```

8. Turning our attention to the `addAnalyst()` method, shown below, we see that it takes an `AnalystVo` instance as its argument, which it uses to create an `Analyst` entity bean. The `addStock()` method is very similar in nature to the `addAnalyst()` method:

```java
public void addAnalyst(AnalystVo analystVo) {
  try {
    InitialContext initial = new InitialContext();
    // Get the object reference
    LocalAnalystHome analystHome = (LocalAnalystHome)
      initial.lookup("java:comp/env/ejb/beans.Analyst");
    analystHome.create(analystVo.getAnalystId(),
      analystVo.getName());
  }
  catch (Exception e) {
    e.printStackTrace();
    throw new EJBException(e.getMessage());
  }
}

public void addStock(StockVo stockVo) {
  try {
    InitialContext initial = new InitialContext();
    // Get the object reference
    LocalStockHome stockHome = (LocalStockHome)
      initial.lookup("java:comp/env/ejb/beans.Stock");
    stockHome.create(stockVo.getTickerSymbol(),
      stockVo.getName());
  }
  catch (Exception e) {
    e.printStackTrace();
    throw new EJBException(e.getMessage());
  }
}

// Standard ejb methods
public void ejbActivate() { }
public void ejbPassivate() { }
public void ejbRemove() { }
public void ejbCreate() { }
public void setSessionContext(SessionContext context) { }
}
```

Notice that the logic that creates an entity bean from a value object, and vice-versa, is contained in these session bean methods. Another appropriate place to put this logic would be in helper methods, perhaps located in a parent class of the entity beans' implementation classes. In that scenario, the session bean could call a hypothetical `getValueObject()` method of the entity bean, which would return a value object populated with the data in that bean.

9. Next, we will take a brief look at the client classes, beginning with the `StockListAdder` class, which initially loads the data into the entity beans via these value objects. Here's the source code listing for `StockListAdder.java`:

```java
package client;

import facade.StockListFacade;
import vo.AnalystVo;
import vo.StockVo;

public class StockListAdder {

  public static void main(String[] args) {
    try {
      StockListFacade facade = StockListFacade.getFacade();

      // Add analysts
      System.out.println("adding analysts");

      facade.addAnalyst(new AnalystVo(new Integer(1), "Fred"));
      facade.addAnalyst(new AnalystVo(new Integer(2), "Leonard"));
      facade.addAnalyst(new AnalystVo(new Integer(3), "Sarah"));
      facade.addAnalyst(new AnalystVo(new Integer(4), "Nancy"));
      System.out.println("analysts added");
    }
    catch (Exception e) {
      System.out.println("exception adding analysts");
      e.printStackTrace();
    }

    try {
      StockListFacade facade = StockListFacade.getFacade();
      // Add stocks
      System.out.println("adding stocks");
      facade.addStock(new StockVo("ABC", "ABC Company", null));
      facade.addStock(new StockVo("ZZZ", "Zigby Zebras", null));
      facade.addStock(new StockVo("ICS",
                                  "Internet Corp of Slobovia", null));
      facade.addStock(new StockVo("DDC", "Digby Door Company", null));
      facade.addStock(new StockVo("ZAP", "Zapalopalorinski Ltd.", null));
      facade.addStock(new StockVo("JIM", "Jimco", null));
      facade.addStock(new StockVo("SRU", "Stocks R Us", null));
      facade.addStock(new StockVo("SRI",
                                  "Shelves and Radios Inc", null));
      facade.addStock(new StockVo("FBC", "Foo Bar Company", null));
      facade.addStock(new StockVo("DDBC",
                                  "Ding Dong Bell Company", null));
      facade.addStock(new StockVo("UDE",
                                  "Upn Down Elevator Company", null));
      System.out.println("stocks added");
    }
    catch (Exception e) {
      System.out.println("exception adding stocks");
      e.printStackTrace();
    }
```

```
    try {
        StockListFacade facade = StockListFacade.getFacade();

        // Add ratings
        System.out.println("adding ratings");
        StockVo stockVo = new StockVo("ZZZ", null, "Take a chance!");
        stockVo.setAnalyst(new AnalystVo(new Integer(2), null));
        facade.addStockRating(stockVo);
        System.out.println("ratings added");
    }
    catch (Exception e) {
        System.out.println("exception adding stocks");
        e.printStackTrace();
    }
  }
}
```

To create and populate an `Analyst` entity bean, for example, the desired data is passed into the constructor of the `AnalystVo` value object. The new `AnalystVo` object is then passed into the `addAnalyst()` method of the `StockListFacade` class that we walked through previously. This is all performed in one method, as seen below:

```
facade.addAnalyst(new AnalystVo(new Integer(1), "Fred"));
```

The way that this client method got a reference to the `StockListFacade` instance is in the statement shown here, which was previously shown after discussing the singleton and factory design patterns:

```
StockListFacade facade = StockListFacade.getFacade();
```

10. And finally, here is the Java source code for our new "value object-ized" version of the GUI client, `StockClient.java`:

```
package client;

import facade.StockListFacade;
import vo.AnalystVo;
import vo.StockVo;

import java.util.*;

// Other general imports
import java.awt.*;
import java.awt.event.*;
import javax.swing.*;

public class StockClient extends JFrame
    implements ActionListener {
    private Integer[] _analystIds;
    private JButton _get = new JButton("Add Rating");
    private JPanel _stockPanel = new JPanel();
    private JComboBox _analysts = new JComboBox();
    private JComboBox _tickers = new JComboBox();
    private JComboBox _ratings = new JComboBox();
```

```java
public StockClient() {
  // Add the title
  JLabel title = new JLabel("Stock Rating List");
  title.setHorizontalAlignment(JLabel.CENTER);
  getContentPane().add(title, BorderLayout.NORTH);

  JPanel activityPanel = new JPanel(new BorderLayout());
  try {
    // Add the stock list
    buildStockList();
    JScrollPane scroller = new JScrollPane(_stockPanel);
    activityPanel.add(scroller, BorderLayout.CENTER);

    // Add the rating panel
    JPanel ratingPanel = new JPanel(new GridLayout(1, 3));
    // Add the analysts
    populateAnalysts();
    ratingPanel.add(_analysts);
    // Add the unrated stocks
    populateTickers();
    ratingPanel.add(_tickers);
    // Add the ratings to pick from
    _ratings.addItem("Run away! Run away!");
    _ratings.addItem("Could be worse!");
    _ratings.addItem("A bit of OK!");
    _ratings.addItem("Take a chance!");
    _ratings.addItem("Smashing!");
    ratingPanel.add(_ratings);
    activityPanel.add(ratingPanel, BorderLayout.SOUTH);

    getContentPane().add(activityPanel, BorderLayout.CENTER);
  }
  catch (Exception e) {
    e.printStackTrace();
  }

  // Add the buttons panel
  JPanel buttons = new JPanel(new GridLayout(1, 1));
  _get.addActionListener(this);
  buttons.add(_get);
  getContentPane().add(buttons, BorderLayout.SOUTH);

  addWindowListener(new WindowAdapter() {
    public void windowClosing(WindowEvent e) {
      System.exit(0);
    }
  });

  setSize(480, 250);
  setVisible(true);
}

private void buildStockList() throws Exception {
  ArrayList stoks = StockListFacade.getFacade().getStockRatings();
  _stockPanel.removeAll();
```

451

```java
        _stockPanel.setLayout(new GridLayout(stoks.size(), 1));
        for (int i = 0; i < stoks.size(); i++) {
          StockVo stokInfo = (StockVo) stoks.get(i);
          Box stokLine = Box.createHorizontalBox();
          String stokDesc = stokInfo.getTickerSymbol() + " : " +
            stokInfo.getName() + " ==> " +
            stokInfo.getAnalyst().getName() + " rates it: " +
            stokInfo.getRating();
          stokLine.add(new JLabel(stokDesc));
          _stockPanel.add(stokLine);
        }
        _stockPanel.invalidate();
        _stockPanel.validate();
      }

      private void populateAnalysts() throws Exception {
        ArrayList anlysts = StockListFacade.getFacade().getAllAnalysts();
        _analystIds = new Integer[anlysts.size()];
        for (int i = 0; i < anlysts.size(); i++) {
          AnalystVo analystData = (AnalystVo) anlysts.get(i);
          _analystIds[i] = analystData.getAnalystId();
          _analysts.addItem(analystData.getName());
        }
      }

      private void populateTickers() throws Exception {
        _tickers.removeAllItems();
        ArrayList tkrs = StockListFacade.getFacade().getUnratedStocks();
        for (int i = 0; i < tkrs.size(); i++) {
          StockVo stockVo = (StockVo) tkrs.get(i);
          _tickers.addItem(stockVo.getTickerSymbol());
        }
        _tickers.invalidate();
        _tickers.validate();
      }

      public void actionPerformed(ActionEvent ae) {
        // Get was clicked
        if (ae.getSource() == _get) {
          try {
            int anlystNo = _analysts.getSelectedIndex();
            if (anlystNo < 0) {
              JOptionPane.showMessageDialog(this, "No analyst selected!");
              return;
            }
            Integer aId = _analystIds[anlystNo];
            if (_tickers.getSelectedIndex() < 0) {
              JOptionPane.showMessageDialog(this, "No ticker selected!");
              return;
            }
            String tkr = (String) _tickers.getSelectedItem();
            if (_ratings.getSelectedIndex() < 0) {
              JOptionPane.showMessageDialog(this, "No rating selected!");
              return;
            }
            String rtg = (String) _ratings.getSelectedItem();
```

```
            StockVo stockVo = new StockVo(tkr, null, rtg);
            stockVo.setAnalyst(new AnalystVo(aId, null));
            StockListFacade.getFacade().addStockRating(stockVo);
            buildStockList();
            populateTickers();
        }
        catch (Exception e) {
            e.printStackTrace();
        }
    }
}

    public static void main(String[] args) {
        StockClient stockClient = new StockClient();
    }
}
```

As you can see from the last two source code listings shown above, the clients in an application that use these design patterns can be well shielded from the realities of the application logic tier. The client's view of the rest of the application is the abstraction provided by the façades and value objects.

Now we can build, load the database, and run the example. We used StockListPatternsApp.ear for the EAR filename, and StockListPatternsJar for the EJB JAR name. If you use these names, the client stubs JAR file will be given the name StockListPatternsAppClient.jar. The build process is identical to the one that we used for the first example in the previous chapter (the CMR and EJB-QL example), with a couple of tweaks:

1. In addition to the usual packages, beans and client, you'll need to compile the classes in the vo and facade packages. These additional classes may be compiled by using the following commands:

   ```
   > javac -d . vo/*.java
   > javac -d . facade/*.java
   ```

   The classes in these packages pertain to the value object and façade pattern, respectively. As pointed out in the CMR and EJB-QL example, on a default J2EE SDK 1.4 Windows installation the classpath for this step would be set correctly by using the following command:

   ```
   > set classpath=.;%J2EE_HOME%\lib\j2ee.jar
   ```

2. The other tweak to the process is to put the classes located in the vo package into the EJB JAR, as shown below, when you are configuring the StockList session bean. We do this because the StockList bean is dependent upon those classes as illustrated in the class diagram above:

And those are the only differences in the build, database loading, and execution process. The appearance and behavior of the client UI is the same as in both of the examples in the previous chapter.

How It Works

Now that you've seen the design patterns in action, let's take a look at how they work. The first piece of code uses the façade pattern.

The **façade pattern** hides the server side of an application from the client with a thin veneer, or façade. As seen in the class diagram above, the StockClient class is no longer directly dependent upon the StockList session bean, but instead only "knows about" the StockListFacade class. The client calls methods of the façade class as if it were the application logic layer, and the façade class invokes methods of the application logic layer (the StockList session bean in this case) as needed. This approach has several advantages, including:

❑   The location of the application logic layer of the application is hidden behind the façade, so if its location changes, only the façade has to know about it.

❑   The client is insulated from changes to the application logic layer by the façade. This tends to reduce maintenance by localizing the necessary changes to façade classes, rather than scattered all over the UI.

❑   Data can be cached in the façade. This is especially helpful in terms of optimization when the client and application logic layers are separated by a network. In this way, the façade can maintain state for the UI.

❑   During development, the façade methods can first be developed as stubs, mimicking the eventual functionality of the application tier methods. This facilitates simultaneous development of these tiers.

A disadvantage of using facades is that by introducing a façade layer between the client and the application logic, data is passed from the client to the façade and then from the façade to the application logic. Therefore the data is passed one more time than necessary, but in our opinion, the advantages far outweigh this disadvantage.

When the constructor for the `StockListFacade` class is called, it does the same thing that our client UIs have done in the past: get a reference to a session bean. It stores that reference in an instance variable so that methods of the façade, when invoked by the client, can use the reference to call methods of the session bean. Of course, larger applications would typically contain multiple façades and session beans.

Notice that each of the methods of the `StockListFacade` class throws a `StockListException`. The methods that call methods of the `StockList` session bean catch an exception and throw the `StockListException`, with the message of the original exception passed into the constructor. Techniques such as this allow the façade to further insulate the client from the implementation details of the application logic tier, never having to know about a `RemoteException`, for example.

The `StockListFacade` class employs another design pattern as well–the **singleton pattern**. Take a look at the `getFacade()` method and you'll see that it is responsible for creating and returning and instance of a class. Notice, however, that if an instance already exists it returns that instance. This is called the *singleton* pattern because only a *single* instance of the returned class exists. This is useful in cases such as this façade example because multiple client UI classes may need a reference to a `StockClientFacade` instance, but there is no need for more than one to exist. In fact, we wouldn't want more than one because each one would have a remote reference to the session bean, which consumes resources.

Note that in the case where the client is a servlet or JSP, if we wanted the façade to hold some state without having it shared by all the clients, we would use a modified singleton pattern in conjunction with an `HttpSession` object. The `getFacade()` method would return the `StockClientFacade` instance for a *given session*, creating one if it doesn't exist.

In addition to implementing the singleton pattern, the `getFacade()` method implements a simple version of another design pattern known as the **factory pattern**. This pattern is characterized by a method, typically `static`, that creates and returns an instance of a class. The method that creates the instance is called a **factory method**, and it returns an object that is guaranteed to be of some type. This type is often either an interface that the object implements, or an abstract class that the object's class is a subclass of. This is preferable to directly using a constructor in some cases, because the returned class can be vendor-specific but created in a generic way.

As you have seen in the `StockClient.java` listing, the clients of this particular façade class call `StockListFacade.getFacade()` to obtain an instance of the `StockListFacade` class.

The Value Object Pattern

For reasons mentioned in Chapter 8, it is usually not good practice to allow clients to have remote references to entity beans. These reasons can be summarized as follows:

❑ Calling entity bean methods directly circumvents the business logic contained in session beans, and tends to push the business logic into the UI code.

❑ Session beans can protect the UI from changes to the entity beans.

❑ Restricting client access to session beans conserves server and network resources.

However, as we saw in the CMR example, awkward mechanisms were employed in their absence. For example, ArrayLists of arrays of Strings were used to pass entity bean data between the client and the application logic tier. The **value object pattern** addresses this problem by providing classes that are modeled after the entity beans. These classes are mainly used to carry entity bean data between tiers. There are two value object classes in this example: the AnalystVo class represents the Analyst entity bean, and the StockVo class represents the Stock entity bean. To keep them separate from other classes, we've put them in their own package, named vo.

The AnalystVo value object class contains an instance variable for each of the CMP fields of the Analyst entity bean. Its constructor takes all of these fields as arguments (although some value object implementations we've seen have only a no-argument constructor, and some have both forms of constructors). The AnalystVo value object also contains a getter and setter method for each of the non-primary key fields. It has only a getter for the primary key field because that field won't be changed.

Although not typical of value object pattern implementations, our value object also models container-managed relationships. To do this, it contains an instance variable that is capable of referencing an ArrayList of StockVo instances.

Since value objects are designed to carry data between tiers, they must implement the Serializable interface of the java.io package.

While we're looking at value objects, let's briefly describe the value object that represents the Stock entity bean, StockVo.java. All of the things that were said about the AnalystVo class apply to this StockVo class as well. Due to the nature of the CMR relationship in the Stock entity bean, the analogous methods in this value object return and take a single instance.

If you take another look at the StockListFacade class listing, you'll notice that these value object classes are passed into and returned by these methods, either as individual objects or inside of ArrayList objects. The classes in this example that manipulate them most, however, are the ones associated with the StockList session bean, and the client classes.

Using JSP and Servlets with EJBs

All of the EJB examples shown up until this point have had clients that were one of the following types:

❑   Simple command-line Java application

❑   Java Swing application

To tie things together a bit, now we're going to demonstrate an example EJB application whose client UI consists of JSPs and servlets. To facilitate this, we'll use the patterns discussed in the previous section. In fact, all the code in this example is exactly the same as in the previous example, with one exception: instead of using the StockClient class as the client UI, we'll use a modified version of the JSP and servlets-based StockList example from Chapter 5.

Try it Out   JSP/Servlets Client on the StockList EJBs

Since the EJB portion of the application is identical to the previous example, you can use the same process to build and configure it. You can use the same process to build the JSP and servlets portion of the application that you used in Chapter 5. There is one additional step, however, which is to add the façade and value object classes to the WAR file while in the Web Application Wizard. These files are:

❑   `StockListFacade.java`

❑   `StockListException.java`

❑   `AnalystVo.java`

❑   `StockVo.java`

None of the source code changed for the session and entity beans, façades, and value objects. The only source code that did change was JSP and servlet code. Those changes were for the purpose of adapting the UI portion of the previous JSP and servlets-based StockList application to using our façades and value objects. The modified source files are:

❑   `StockListServlet.java`

❑   `RatingsForm.jsp`

❑   `AddRating.java`

❑   `AnalystForm.jsp`

The StockList application was first presented in Chapter 5. It has been rewritten here to use the façade and value objects. The general flow will be reviewed here, however, for the purpose of pointing out the use of façades and value objects.

457

The entry point into the StockList web application was this HTML page, `index.html`:

```
<!DOCTYPE HTML PUBLIC "-//W3C//DTD HTML 4.01 Transitional//EN">
<html>
  <head>
    <title>Stocks and Analysts</title>
  </head>

  <body>
    <h1>Stocks and Analysts</h1>
    <p>
      <a href="/stock/StockList/AnalystForm">See all Analysts</a>
    <p>
      <a href="/stock/StockList/RatingsForm">See all Ratings</a>
    <hr>
  </body>
</html>
```

When one of the links is clicked, `index.html` submits a request to a servlet called `StockList`, which is in the following `StockListServlet.java` listing:

```
package web;

import javax.servlet.*;
import javax.servlet.http.*;
import java.io.*;
import java.util.*;
import facade.*;

public class StockListServlet extends HttpServlet {
    public void doPost(HttpServletRequest request,
                    HttpServletResponse response)
    {
      doGet(request, response);
    }

    public void doGet(HttpServletRequest request,
                    HttpServletResponse response)
    {
      try {
          ArrayList data = null;
          RequestDispatcher dispatcher;
          ServletContext context = getServletContext();
          StockListFacade facade = StockListFacade.getFacade();
          String name = request.getPathInfo();
          name = name.substring(1);
          System.out.println("name="+name);
          if ("AnalystForm".equals(name)) {
            data = facade.getAllAnalysts();
            request.setAttribute("data", data);
          } else if ("RatingsForm".equals(name)) {
            data = facade.getStockRatings();
            request.setAttribute("data", data);
            request.setAttribute("analysts", facade.getAllAnalysts());
            request.setAttribute("unrated", facade.getUnratedStocks());
```

```
          } else if ("AddRating".equals(name)) {
            //nothing to do here, just forward request
          } else {
            name = "Error";
          }

          dispatcher = context.getNamedDispatcher(name);
          if (dispatcher == null) {
            dispatcher = context.getNamedDispatcher("Error");
          }
          dispatcher.forward(request, response);
      } catch (Exception e) {
          e.printStackTrace();
      }
    }
  }
}
```

Here is the RatingsForm.jsp source code:

```
<!DOCTYPE HTML PUBLIC "-//W3C//DTD HTML 4.01 Transitional//EN">
<html>
  <head>
    <title>Stock Ratings</title>
  </head>

  <body>
    <h1>Stock Ratings</h1>
  <%@ page import="java.util.*, vo.*" %>
<%
    ArrayList stocks = (ArrayList) request.getAttribute("data");
    if (stocks != null && stocks.size() > 0) {
%>
    <form action="/stock/StockList/AddRating" method="post">
    <table border="1">
      <tr>
        <th>Ticker</th>
        <th>Analyst</th>
        <th>Rating</th>
      </tr>
<%
      for (int i = 0; i < stocks.size(); i++) {
        StockVo stockInfo = (StockVo) stocks.get(i);
        String ticker = stockInfo.getTickerSymbol();
        String analyst = stockInfo.getAnalyst().getName();
        String rating = stockInfo.getRating();
%>
    <tr>
      <td><%= ticker %></td>
      <td><%= analyst %></td>
      <td><%= rating %></td>
    </tr>
<%
      }
%>
    </table>
    <table>
```

```
            <tr>
            <td>
              <select name="analysts">
<%

              ArrayList analysts =
                      (ArrayList) request.getAttribute("analysts");
              for (int i = 0; i < analysts.size(); i++) {
                AnalystVo analyst = (AnalystVo) analysts.get(i);
%>

                <option value="<%= analyst.getAnalystId() %>">
                    <%= analyst.getName() %>
<%

              }
%>

              </select>
            </td>
            <td>
              <select name="stocks">
<%

              ArrayList unratedStocks =
                  (ArrayList) request.getAttribute("unrated");
              for (int i = 0; i < unratedStocks.size(); i++) {
                StockVo stock = (StockVo) unratedStocks.get(i);
%>

                <option value="<%= stock.getTickerSymbol() %>">
                    <%= stock.getTickerSymbol() %>
<%

              }
%>

              </select>
            </td>
            <td>
              <select name="ratings">
                <option value="Run away! Run away!">Run away! Run away!
                <option value="Could be worse!">Could be worse!
                <option value="A bit of OK!">A bit of OK!
                <option value="Take a chance!">Take a chance!
                <option value="Smashing!">Smashing!
              </select>
            </td>
            </tr>
            <tr>
            <td>
              <input type="submit" value="Submit Rating">
            </td>
            </tr>
        </table>
        </form>
<%
        } else {
%>
        No stock information found
<%
        }
%>
        <hr>
      </body>
</html>
```

Here is the `AddRating.java` source code:

```java
package web;

import javax.servlet.*;
import javax.servlet.http.*;
import facade.*;
import vo.*;

public class AddRating extends HttpServlet {
    public void doPost(HttpServletRequest request,
                        HttpServletResponse response)
    {
        try {
            String analyst = request.getParameter("analysts");
            Integer id = new Integer(analyst);
            String ticker = request.getParameter("stocks");
            String rating = request.getParameter("ratings");

            StockVo stockVo = new StockVo(ticker, null, rating);
            stockVo.setAnalyst(new AnalystVo(id, null));
            StockListFacade facade = StockListFacade.getFacade();
            facade.addStockRating(stockVo);

            request.setAttribute("data", facade.getStockRatings());
            request.setAttribute("analysts", facade.getAllAnalysts());
            request.setAttribute("unrated", facade.getUnratedStocks());

            ServletContext context = getServletContext();
            RequestDispatcher dispatcher =
                context.getNamedDispatcher("RatingsForm");
            dispatcher.forward(request, response);
        } catch (Exception e) {
        }
    }
}
```

Like the `StockList` servlet, the `AddRating` servlet shown above uses the methods of the `StockListFacade` class to access the services of the `StockList` session bean.

The other option available from the main page is the Analyst Management Form, whose UI logic is in the AnalystForm.jsp file, shown below:

```
<!DOCTYPE HTML PUBLIC "-//W3C//DTD HTML 4.01 Transitional//EN">
<html>
  <head>
    <title>Analyst Management</title>
  </head>

  <body>
    <%@ page import="java.util.*,vo.*" %>
    <h1>Analyst Management Form</h1>
    <form action="/stock/servlet/ProcessAnalyst" method="POST">
      <table>

<%
ArrayList anlysts = (ArrayList) request.getAttribute("data");
if (anlysts == null) {
%>
        <h2> Attribute is null </h2>
      <%
      } else {
        for (int i = 0; i < anlysts.size(); i++) {
        AnalystVo analystData = (AnalystVo) anlysts.get(i);
%>
      <tr>
        <td>
          <input type="checkbox" name="checkbox"
                    value="<%= analystData.getName() %>"
        </td>
        <td>
            <%= analystData.getName() %>
        </td>
      </tr>
    <%
        }
      }
      %>
      </table>
      <input type="submit" value="Delete Selected" name="delete">
      <p>
      <input type="text" size="40" name="addname">
      <input type="submit" value="Add New Analyst" name="add">
    </form>

    <hr>
  </body>
</html>
```

Again, note the use of the AnalystVo value object.

And that's all the code over and done with. After building and deploying the application, remember to populate the entity beans by running the StockListAdder application as before. You can run this application by pointing your browser to the following URL:

http://localhost:1024/stock/index.html

Here is a screenshot of this web application after Fred the Analyst rated the stock for the world's smallest tricycle infomercial company, Zapalopalorinski Ltd.:

How It Works

The StockList servlet uses the static StockListFacade.getFacade() method to get the singleton StockListFacade instance, as seen above. It uses that façade reference to get the data, and then forwards to a JSP for display. The request is forwarded based on the extra path information passed with the request. If getPathInfo() returns "/AnalystForm", the request is forwarded to AnalystForm.jsp. If getpathInfo() returns "/RatingsForm", the request is forwarded to RatingsForm.jsp. If getpathInfo() returns "/AddRating" the request is forwarded to the AddRating servlet.

The RatingsForm JSP creates a form that POSTs a request to the StockList servlet. This request is forwarded to the AddRating servlet. Take a moment to examine the use of value objects in the RatingsForm JSP shown above. After adding the rating, the AddRating servlet forwards to the RatingsForm JSP to display the new data.

This example again illustrates some of the advantages of using the façade and value object patterns in your web application. JSPs are primarily designed to provide a data visualization layer for a web application. Servlets are primarily designed to receive and respond to requests. By encapsulating the data access details in the façade and value objects, the JSPs and servlets don't need to worry about which EJB to access or how to access the EJBs. The JSPs and servlets don't even need to know that the data came from an EJB. The data could come directly from a database, or a flat file, or over the network.

Before we leave this chapter, let's take a look at two more EJB concepts: **message-driven beans** and **EJB timers**.

Developing Message-Driven Beans

As discussed in Chapter 8, in addition to session beans and entity beans, there is a type of EJB known as **message-driven beans**. Message-driven beans exist for the purpose of receiving and processing **asynchronous messages**. These messages could be from external systems, or from components of the same application. The reason that they are called *asynchronous* is that they can arrive at any time, as opposed to being a direct result of a remote method invocation for example. Similar to the way that UI event handling works, message-driven beans "listen" for asynchronous messages that have been sent to it. It is worth noting that, unlike calling a remote method, the sender of the asynchronous message doesn't block and wait for a response.

Message-driven beans are enabled not only by the EJB container, but by a facility in J2EE known as the **Java Message Service** API, or JMS for short. The diagram below shows the context in which the next example will operate, and will serve as a basis for our discussion of the JMS API:

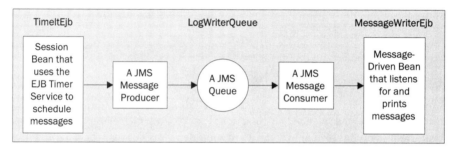

Introduction to the Java Message Service API

The JMS API is a Java API, located in the `javax.jms` package, which provides an interface for applications that require the services of a messaging system. A messaging system enables messages containing text, objects, and other message types to be sent and received *asynchronously*. This is in contrast with the remote procedure call (RPC) model that we've been using so far for EJBs, where interactions between components occur *synchronously*.

An implementation of a messaging system that complies with the JMS API is called a **JMS provider**. The J2EE SDK 1.4 has a JMS provider that we'll be using to enable the example in this section, and several vendors have commercial implementations available for use in enabling messaging in enterprise applications.

In the diagram above, the `TimeIt` session bean on the left sends asynchronous messages to the `MessageWriter` message-driven bean on the right. Both of these beans have been created for this example (they aren't Java library classes). These `TimeIt` and `MessageWriter` beans are known as **JMS clients** because they are *clients* of the underlying messaging system.

Messaging systems enable asynchronous communication by providing a **destination** for messages to be held until they can be delivered to the recipient. The circle in the middle, `LogWriterQueue`, is the destination that holds messages from the `TimeIt` session bean, which are bound for the `MessageWriter` message-driven bean. There are two types of destinations in JMS:

❏   A **queue** is used to hold messages that are sent from one JMS client to be delivered to another. This model of messaging is known as **point-to-point**.

❏   A **topic** is used to hold messages that are sent from potentially many JMS clients to be delivered to, potentially multiple, JMS clients. This model of messaging is known as **publish/subscribe**.

The example we will look at later in this section uses a queue type destination, which is reflected in the diagram. Also in the diagram above are boxes for a JMS **message producer** and a JMS **message consumer**. These represent classes in a JMS provider that work on behalf of the JMS clients to send and receive messages. As we'll see later, you don't have to create a JMS message consumer when working with message-driven beans, because the EJB container does that on the message-driven bean's behalf.

We'll have more to say about the JMS API when walking through the example code, so let's turn our attention to another technology that will be used in the example, the EJB Timer Service.

Introduction to the EJB Timer Service

There is a new capability in the EJB 2.1 specification known as the **EJB Timer Service**. Its purpose in life is to provide enterprise beans with a way to be notified of time-based events. This is useful, for example, if you want a session bean to initiate a process at 2:00 every morning to gather data from external system. These events can be triggered as follows:

❏   At a particular time. Perhaps you could have your EJB notified on July 28, 2061 at midnight that it should do something special (to celebrate the next date that Halley's Comet will be closest to the Sun).

❏   After a given elapsed time.

❏   On a recurring basis, after a given time interval.

These timer services are provided by the EJB container, and are defined by four interfaces located in the `javax.ejb` package:

❏   An EJB implements the `TimedObject` interface when it wishes to be notified of time-based events. The `TimedObject` interface contains one method, `ejbTimeout()`, which is called when a timer "expires".

❏   The `TimerService` interface provides access to the EJB Timer Service to an enterprise bean. It contains methods that create `Timer` objects, and that retrieve the `Timer` objects that have been created.

❏   Objects that implement the `Timer` interface implement the time-based logic described above (expiring at a specific time, elapsed time, or interval). Methods of the `Timer` interface allow you to get information about a `Timer` object, and to cancel the `Timer` as well.

❏   A `TimerHandle` can be used to retrieve a `Timer` object. Our example doesn't use that interface.

Let's go ahead and look at an example that demonstrates the technologies (message-driven beans, the JMS API, and the EJB Timer Service) mentioned above.

Try It Out Using an EJB Timer to Invoke a Message-Driven Bean

The diagram from earlier in this section depicts the behavior of this *Try It Out* example, which is as follows:

❑ The TimeIt session bean uses the EJB Timer Service to be notified every 10 seconds.

❑ Each time the TimeIt bean is notified, it uses the JMS API to create a JMS message producer.

❑ The TimeIt bean uses the JMS message producer to create and send a message that it wants delivered to the MessageWriter message-driven bean. In our example, this message is a text message that contains the date and time that the message was sent.

❑ The JMS message producer sends the message to the LogWriterQueue, which is an arbitrarily-named JMS queue created for this example.

❑ A JMS message consumer, which is created and managed by the EJB container, receives the text message.

❑ The EJB container calls the onMessage() method of the MessageWriter message-driven bean, passing the text message into the method.

The MessageWriter bean creates a String, concatenates the text message received, and sends it to System.out. Note the System.out is managed by the J2EE Server (j2ee), so we'll start it up in a special way to see the output.

To build the example, we have the following new .java files:

❑ TimeItHome.java in the timer package

❑ TimeIt.java in the timer package

❑ TimeItBean.java in the timer package

❑ TimeItTester.java in the timer package

❑ MessageWriterBean.java in the msg package

We'll implement the code involved in this example according to the flow of the message being sent.

Firstly, here is the home interface of the `TimeIt` session bean, `TimeItHome.java`:

```
package timer;

import java.rmi.RemoteException;
import javax.ejb.EJBHome;
import javax.ejb.CreateException;

public interface TimeItHome extends EJBHome {
  // The create method for the timer bean.
  public TimeIt create()
     throws CreateException, RemoteException;
}
```

And here is the remote interface of the `TimeIt` session bean, `TimeIt.java`:

```
package timer;

import java.rmi.RemoteException;
import javax.ejb.EJBObject;

public interface TimeIt extends EJBObject {
  // The public business method on the timer bean
  public void startTimer() throws RemoteException;
}
```

The remote interface only has one business method, named `startTimer()`. This method will be invoked by the `TimeItTester` client application, seen in the `TimeItTester.java` listing shown below, just to get things started up:

```
package timer;

import javax.naming.InitialContext;
import javax.rmi.PortableRemoteObject;

public class TimeItTester {
  public static void main(String[] args) {
    try {
      // Get a naming context
      InitialContext jndiContext = new InitialContext();

      // Get a reference to the SimpleSession JNDI entry
      Object ref  = jndiContext.lookup("ejb/timer.TimeIt");

      // Get a reference from this to the Bean's Home interface
      TimeItHome home = (TimeItHome)
       PortableRemoteObject.narrow(ref, TimeItHome.class);

      // Create a SimpleSession object from the Home interface
      TimeIt timeIt = home.create();

      timeIt.startTimer();

    } catch(Exception e) {
      e.printStackTrace();
    }
  }
}
```

Now we'll get to code that is the heart of the example–using the EJB Timer Service. Here is the implementation of the `TimeIt` session bean, contained in `TimeItBean.java`:

```java
package timer;

import javax.ejb.SessionBean;
import javax.ejb.SessionContext;
import javax.ejb.TimedObject;
import javax.ejb.Timer;
import javax.ejb.TimerService;
import javax.jms.Queue;
import javax.jms.QueueConnection;
import javax.jms.QueueConnectionFactory;
import javax.jms.QueueSender;
import javax.jms.QueueSession;
import javax.jms.Session;
import javax.jms.TextMessage;
import javax.naming.InitialContext;

// General imports
import java.text.*;
import java.util.*;

public class TimeItBean
    implements SessionBean, TimedObject {
    // Save a reference to the context
    private SessionContext ctx;

    // public business method to start the timer
    public void startTimer() {
        TimerService timerService = ctx.getTimerService();
        // After initial five seconds, then every ten seconds
        Timer timer = timerService.createTimer(5000, 10000, "timer");
    }

    // timer ejb method - timer expires - send message to queue
    public void ejbTimeout(Timer timer) {
        QueueConnection queueConnection = null;
        try {
            InitialContext jndiContext = new InitialContext();
            // Look up the connection factory
            QueueConnectionFactory queueConnectionFactory =
                (QueueConnectionFactory) jndiContext.lookup
                ("jms/QueueConnectionFactory");
            // Look up the queue (destination)
            Queue queue = (Queue) jndiContext.lookup("jms/LogWriterQueue");
            // Get a connection from the factory
            queueConnection = queueConnectionFactory.createQueueConnection();
            // Create a session
            QueueSession queueSession = queueConnection.createQueueSession(false,
                Session.AUTO_ACKNOWLEDGE);
            // create a sender for the session to the queue
            QueueSender queueSender = queueSession.createSender(queue);
            // Create a text message
            TextMessage message = queueSession.createTextMessage();
```

```
        // Create the message - a string to print on the other side
        SimpleDateFormat sdf =
          new SimpleDateFormat("yyyy.MM.dd 'at' HH:mm:ss.SSS");
        // Set the text of the message
        message.setText("log entry, the time is: " + sdf.format(new Date())));
        // Send the message
        queueSender.send(message);

    }
    catch (Exception e) {
      System.out.println("Exception in message: " + e.toString());
      e.printStackTrace();
    }
    finally {
      if (queueConnection != null) {
        try {
          queueConnection.close();
        }
        catch (Exception e) {}
      }
    }
  }

  // Standard ejb methods

  public void setSessionContext(SessionContext context) {
    ctx = context;
  }

  public void ejbCreate() {}
  public void ejbRemove() {}
  public void ejbActivate() {}
  public void ejbPassivate() {}
}
```

Here is the listing for our message-driven bean, `MessageWriterBean.java`. There aren't any home or bean interface listings to show because message-driven beans do not use them:

```
package msg;

import javax.ejb.MessageDrivenBean;
import javax.ejb.MessageDrivenContext;
import javax.jms.JMSException;
import javax.jms.Message;
import javax.jms.MessageListener;
import javax.jms.TextMessage;

public class MessageWriterBean
    implements MessageDrivenBean, MessageListener {

  // Abstract method from message listener. Here is where the
  // work is done.
  public void onMessage(Message message) {
    TextMessage msg = null;
    try {
```

```
        if (message instanceof TextMessage) {
          msg = (TextMessage) message;
          System.out.println("Got message: " + msg.getText());
        }
        else {
          System.out.println("Got message of type: "
              + message.getClass().getName() + " ==> ignored!");
        }
      }
      catch (Throwable te) {
        te.printStackTrace();
      }
    }

    // Standard ejb methods
    public void ejbCreate() { }
    public void ejbRemove() { }
    public void setMessageDrivenContext(MessageDrivenContext mdContext) { }
  }
```

Now let's build and run the example.

1. Set your classpath as follows:

   ```
   > set classpath=.;%J2EE_HOME%\lib\j2ee.jar
   ```

2. You can use the following commands to compile these files:

   ```
   > javac -d . timer/*.java
   ```

   ```
   > javac -d . msg/*.java
   ```

3. Internally, it seems that the J2EE application server utilizes PointBase in providing EJB timer services. For this example to execute properly, it is necessary to make sure that PointBase is started up before the J2EE server is. So if that's not the case, shut down the J2EE server, start up PointBase if it isn't running, and restart the J2EE server.

4. You'll use the Deployment Tool to configure and deploy the beans. We used TimerMessageApp.ear for the EAR filename, and TimerMessageJar for the EJB JAR name. The client stubs JAR file will be generated with the name TimerMessageAppClient.jar.

   You'll go through the New Enterprise Beans Wizard twice: once for the TimeIt stateless session bean, and once for the MessageWriter message-driven bean.

5. Using this wizard for the TimeIt session bean will be the same as usual for a session bean. Please note that even though we put the TimeItTester client code in the same package (named timer) as the beans, you shouldn't put the TimeItTester.class file in the bean JAR.

   When using the New Enterprise Beans Wizard for the MessageWriter message-driven bean, take note of the instructions that follow.

6. Since message-driven beans don't have home and bean interfaces, you'll only need to add the `MessageWriterBean.class` file (located in the `msg` package) to the bean JAR:

7. You'll choose `msg.MessageWriterBean` as the Enterprise Bean Class, and Message-Driven Bean as the Enterprise Bean Type. Again, there are no home or bean interfaces to choose, as shown below:

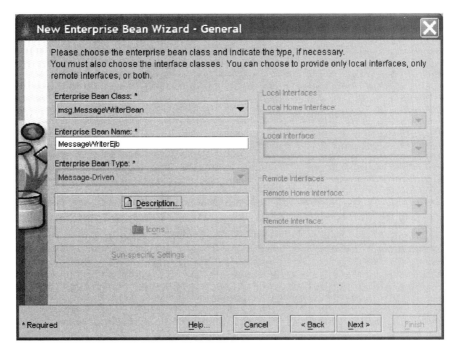

8. In the Message-Driven Bean Settings dialog, shown below, do the following:

❑ Select the JMS option from the Messaging Service drop-down list

❑ Select javax.jms.Queue from the Destination Type drop-down list.

❑ Type PhysicalQueue into the Target Destination Name field.

❑ Type jms/QueueConnectionFactory into the Connection Factory JNDI Name field.

❑ Don't click the Next button just yet.

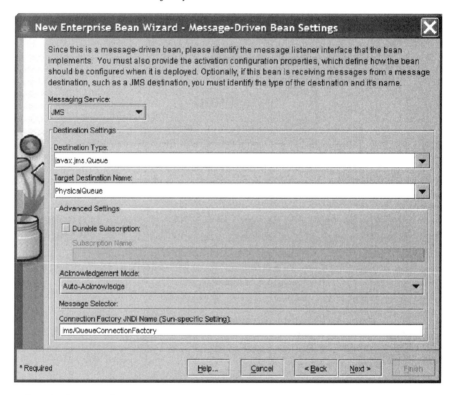

9. Now select the Non-JMS option from the Messaging Service drop-down list on that page. In the Message-Driven Bean Settings page below, javax.jms.MessageListener is chosen in the Message Listener Interface drop-down list. This is the interface that specifies the onMessage() method:

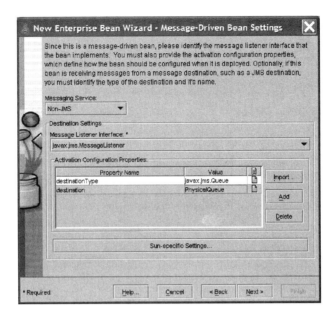

Use the Add button, shown above, to add each of two Activation Configuration Properties:

❏ The destinationType property, which as explained previously is `javax.jms.Queue`

❏ The destination property, which is PhysicalQueue

The message-driven bean will listen for messages arriving at the destination specified in these properties.

10. Now click the Sun-specific Settings button and enter jmsra into the Resource Adapter field as shown below, and click OK. A resource adapter is analogous to a JDBC driver, and in this case allows the JMS provider to interact with the J2EE server:

11. After finishing the wizard, select MessageWriterEjb in the left panel, and select the Transactions tab. Choose Container-Managed and let the Transaction Attribute default to Required.

12. Now select TimeItEjb in the left panel, and select the Transactions tab. Choose Container-Managed and select the Not Supported option in the Transaction Attribute column for both of the TimeItEjb methods. These methods can be accessed by clicking the Remote and Bean radio buttons on that page.

13. Do a File | Save All. Select TimerMessageApp on the left, and in the screen shown below, assign the following:

   ❏ JNDI name jms/LogWriterQueue to the MessageWriter bean.

   ❏ JNDI name ejb/timer.TimeIt to the TimeIt bean

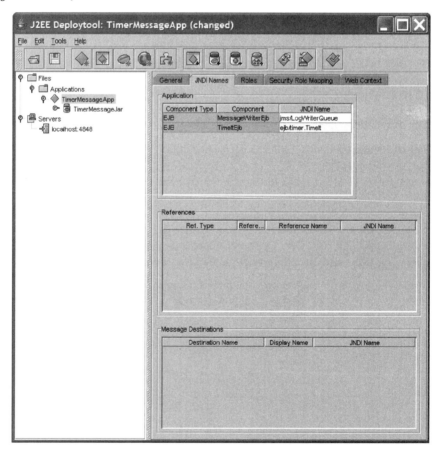

14. Before deploying the application, we need to create the LogWriterQueue. We're going to do this using one of the J2EE SDK 1.4 administration tools called asadmin. To create the LogWriterQueue, we'll execute the following commands from the operating system prompt. These are available in the Apress download for your convenience in files named CreateQ1.bat, CreateQ2.bat, etc. Each one will prompt you for your J2EE server password:

```
> asadmin create-jms-resource —user admin  ->
  —resourcetype javax.jms.QueueConnectionFactory  ->
  —property imqAddressList=localhost jms/QueueConnectionFactory

> asadmin create-jmsdest —user admin  ->
  —desttype queue PhysicalQueue

> asadmin create-jms-resource —user admin ->
  —resourcetype javax.jms.Queue  ->
  —property imqDestinationName=PhysicalQueue jms/LogWriterQueue

> asadmin reconfig —user admin
```

15. Now you can deploy the application, create the client stubs, and run the `timer.TimeItTester` client to test it out. These would be the appropriate commands for a J2EE SDK 1.4 Windows installation:

```
> set CLASSPATH=.;%J2EE_HOME%\lib\j2ee.jar;  ->
  %J2EE_HOME%\lib\appserv-rt.jar;TimerMessageAppClient.jar

> java -Dorg.omg.CORBA.ORBInitialHost=localhost  ->
  -Dorg.omg.CORBA.ORBInitialPort=3700 timer.TimeItTester
```

After five seconds, and every ten seconds thereafter, a message sent from the `TimeIt` session bean to the `MessageWriter` message-driven bean should appear in the J2EE server's log file. The log file is named `server.log` and is located in a subdirectory of J2EE_HOME. On our installation, the location of the server log file is:

```
%J2EE_HOME%\domains\domain1\logs\server.log
```

Here is some sample output:

```
Got message: log entry, the time is: 2004.11.14 at 18:29:30.124
Got message: log entry, the time is: 2004.11.14 at 18:29:40.144
Got message: log entry, the time is: 2004.11.14 at 18:29:50.057
Got message: log entry, the time is: 2004.11.14 at 18:30:00.000
Got message: log entry, the time is: 2004.11.14 at 18:30:10.177
```

16. To stop the messages, simply undeploy the application. To delete the queue, use the following commands from the operating system prompt. These are available in the Apress download for your convenience in files named `DeleteQ1.bat`, `DeleteQ2.bat`, etc.:

```
> asadmin delete-jms-resource —user admin jms/QueueConnectionFactory

> asadmin delete-jmsdest —user admin —desttype queue PhysicalQueue

> asadmin delete-jms-resource —user admin jms/LogWriterQueue
```

How It Works

Let's first look at how the EJB Timer Service is implemented in the `TimeItBean` class.

The `setSessionContext()` method of the session bean, shown below, is called by the EJB container after the session bean is created. The container passes in a `SessionContext` object, which represents the EJB container context in which the session bean is running. This is analogous to a servlet having access to its `ServletContext` object, which was discussed in Chapter 5.

```
public void setSessionContext(SessionContext context) {
    ctx = context;
}
```

The reason that we suddenly care about the `SessionContext` of session beans is that we'll use it, as seen in the `startTimer()` below, to get access to the EJB Timer Service. Recall that the `startTimer()` method is the one and only business method of this `TimeIt` session bean.

We'll use the `TimerService` object to create a `Timer` object that is supposed to expire, trigger, fire, go off, however you want to say it, in 5 seconds, and every 10 seconds thereafter:

```
public void startTimer() {
    TimerService timerService = ctx.getTimerService();
    // After initial five seconds, then every ten seconds
    Timer timer = timerService.createTimer(5000, 10000, "timer");
}
```

You might want to take a few moments at this point to examine the J2EE SDK 1.4 Java API documentation for the overloaded `createTimer()` method of the `TimerService` class. These will familiarize you with how to create `Timer` objects with the different types of time-based logic (expiring at a specific time, elapsed time, or interval) described above. By the way, one of the exercises at the end of this chapter specifies creating the different types of timers.

Whenever a timer fires, the `ejbTimeout()` method of the enterprise bean gets invoked. In our example, this method uses the JMS API to send an asynchronous message to a message-driven bean, so let's now turn our attention to that subject. Note that the `ejbTimeout()` method is part of the `javax.ejb.TimedObject` interface, which the `TimeItBean` class implements.

Next, we focus on how we use the Java Message Service API by reviewing the code we just saw in the `MessageWriterBean` class.

According to the diagram and description of this example's behavior given above, one thing that our `ejbTimeout()` method needs to do is to create a JMS message producer that can send messages to the `LogWriterQueue`. In order to do that, it will need a couple of **administered objects**, which are resources that are typically administered by JMS provider-specific administration tools. These administered objects are:

❑   A **connection factory**, which is used to create a connection to the JMS provider, discussed previously. As its name implies, a connection factory uses the factory design pattern that we covered earlier in this chapter.

❑   A **destination**, which in this case is a `javax.jms.Queue` that we're calling `LogWriterQueue`.

To begin the process of creating a JMS message producer, in the `ejbTimeout()` method we use JNDI to look up a connection factory as shown below. The connection factory that we're using here is a `QueueConnectionFactory`, because we'll be sending messages to a Queue:

```
InitialContext jndiContext = new InitialContext();
// Look up the connection factory
QueueConnectionFactory queueConnectionFactory =
   (QueueConnectionFactory) jndiContext.lookup
   ("jms/QueueConnectionFactory");
```

As seen below, we also use JNDI to look up the `LogWriterQueue` destination, which is an administered object. Recall that we used the `j2eeadmin` tool to create the `LogWriterQueue` destination:

```
// Look up the queue (destination)
Queue queue = (Queue) jndiContext.lookup("jms/LogWriterQueue");
```

Shown below, the `QueueConnectionFactory` is used to create a `QueueConnection` object, which is used to create a `QueueSession` object. For more information on these classes of the `javax.jms` package, consult the J2EE API documentation:

```
// Get a connection from the factory
queueConnection = queueConnectionFactory.createQueueConnection();
// Create a session
QueueSession queueSession = queueConnection.createQueueSession(false,
   Session.AUTO_ACKNOWLEDGE);
```

The `createSender()` method of the `QueueSession` object is passed a reference to our `LogWriterQueue`, and it creates a `QueueSender` object that can send messages to that destination, as shown below. The `QueueSender`, being a subinterface of `MessageProducer`, is represented by the JMS message producer in the example's diagram earlier:

```
// create a sender for the session to the queue
QueueSender queueSender = queueSession.createSender(queue);
```

As seen below, a `TextMessage` object is created by calling the `createTextMessage()` method of the `QueueSession` object. This particular message type is a `TextMessage`, but you can look at `javax.jms.Message` (its superinterface) in the J2EE API documentation to see a description of the other four message types available in JMS.

The String to be sent is built, placed into the TextMessage object, and sent to the destination (our LogWriterQueue), as shown below:

```
// Create the message - a string to print on the other side
SimpleDateFormat sdf =
  new SimpleDateFormat("yyyy.MM.dd 'at' HH:mm:ss.SSS");
// Set the text of the message
message.setText("log entry, the time is: " + sdf.format(new Date()));
// Send the message
queueSender.send(message);
```

We're not going to send any more messages until the next time the ejbTimeout() method is called, so we'll close the QueueConnection, which closes the QueueSession and QueueSender that were created earlier. This all happens in the code located in the finally block of the example:

```
finally {
  if (queueConnection != null) {
    try {
      queueConnection.close();
    }
    catch (Exception e) {}
  }
}
```

Now it's up to the JMS provider to deliver the message to the LogWriterQueue, and on to our MessageWriterBean, which is a message-driven bean.

Finally, we take a quick look at the code used for our message-driven bean, in MessageWriterBean.java. There aren't any home or bean interface listings to show because message-driven beans do not use them.

As seen in the listing for the MessageWriterBean class, message-driven beans must implement a couple of interfaces:

❑ MessageDrivenBean–Contains message-driven bean lifecycle methods.

❑ MessageListener–Contains the onMessage() method. This is the method that is called when a message arrives for a message-driven bean.

The onMessage() method of this example is expecting a TextMessage, and will use the getText() method to obtain the String that was sent. Then, regardless of the message type received, we print something to System.out.

Summary

In this chapter, we continued the discussion of EJBs from the previous chapter, covering the following concepts:

❏   Software design patterns

❏   Utilizing JSPs and servlets with EJBs in an application

❏   Message-driven beans

❏   The Java Message Service (JMS) API

❏   EJB Timer Service

Design patterns describe solutions to specific design problems, and improve developer productivity by leveraging these solutions. They are analogous to patterns such as roof styles when designing a house. There are many design patterns in use today, and new ones are continually being identified and documented by developers. The four that we discussed were façade, value object, factory, and singleton.

The design patterns example was fused with a JSP and servlets example from a previous chapter to show how JSPs, servlets, and EJBs could be used in the same application.

Message-driven beans are one of the three types of enterprise beans (session and entity are the other two). They are the mechanism to use when you want an EJB application to receive asynchronous messages via an underlying JMS provider (messaging system).

The new EJB Timer Service is useful when you have EJB application functionality that needs to be executed at defined times or time intervals.

Resources

More information about J2EE Patterns may be found in the following resources:

❏   *Core J2EE Patterns*, by Alur, Crupi and Malks

❏   *EJB Design Patterns*, by Floyd Marinescu

❏   http://java.sun.com/blueprints/patterns/catalog.html

More information on the Java Message Service API is at:

❏   http://java.sun.com/products/jms/

Exercises

1. Write a message-driven bean that takes a word and writes it to `System.out`. Write a simple application that writes to a message queue to test the message bean. Remember that `System.out` messages will go to the server log file.

2. Write a stateless session bean that implements the EJB Timer Service. Try using several of the different types of timers. Write an appropriate message to `System.out` to verify the timer is working.

12

Web Services and JAX-RPC

In the previous chapter we wrapped up the main part of our discussion about Enterprise JavaBeans. This chapter, and the chapter following, will cover another mechanism that is used to enable distributed applications–**web services**.

In this chapter you will learn:

❑ What web services are

❑ Fundamental concepts regarding web services, including the web services protocol stack

❑ Some guidelines for when to use web services

❑ How we can enable web services using SOAP and JAX-RPC

❑ How to use J2EE SDK 1.4 tools to configure and deploy an application that contains web services

❑ Describing web services using WSDL

❑ What SAAJ is

❑ The three ways that a client can invoke web service methods

Understanding Web Services

A web service consists of functionality that is available to applications via protocols associated with the Web. Example protocols that are commonly associated with the Web are HTTP (which, as we saw previously, is used for transmitting requests and responses between web clients, such as browsers, and web servers), XML, and SOAP (we'll be looking at XML and SOAP a little later on in this chapter.) Using these protocols, an application can make use of the functionality provided by a web service. For example, a bookseller named Apress might have a web service running on its web server that provides the ability to order books. We'll call this web service ApressBookService. An application could use this service when it needs to look up a price or order a book. This ApressBookService web service would have **operations**, each of which performs some functionality. For example:

❑ A getPrice operation could take the ISBN number of a book as input and would return the price of the book.

❑ An orderBook operation might take an ISBN and a credit card number, and process an order for a book, including having it shipped.

In the same way as the ApressBookService web service above, organizations and individuals can offer services to applications over standard, ubiquitous protocols such as XML, SOAP, and HTTP. The availability of web services over such protocols makes them an attractive choice for developing distributed applications, which can be composed of web services offered by other divisions in a company, or by other organizations.

For an example of some web services that are currently available, check out **www.xmethods.com**. This site is one of several that allow developers to post information about a web service that they have developed, including a description of the service and instructions on how to use it. To give you a flavor of the kinds of web services being developed, some interesting examples listed on this site at the time of writing include:

Web Service Name	Description
Air Fare Quote Search	Searches major airlines in real time to find the best available prices direct from their web sites.
BabelFish	Interface for AltaVista's Babelfish (language translator) service.
Bible Webservice	Retrieves Biblical text.
Delayed Stock Quote	20 minute delayed stock quote.
Domain Name Checker	Checks whether a domain name is available or not.
eBay Price Watcher	Checks current bid price of an eBay auction.
FedEx Tracker	Access to FedEx Tracking information.
Generate Bar Codes	This service generates (Interleaved 2 of 5) Bar Code images.
Get Currency Exchange	Returns the value of a given number of units changed from one currency to another.
Great Circle Distance	Great circle distance between 2 points of longitude, latitude.
Image Converter	Convert from one type of image to another.
Shakespeare	Takes a phrase from the plays of William Shakespeare and returns the associated speech, speaker, and play.
USA Zip Code Information	Gets USA State Code, City, Area Code, Time Zone, Zip Code by State Code, or City, or Area Code.
Weather–Temperature	Current temperature in a given U.S. zip code region.

The ability for parts of a distributed application to communicate with each other, and call each other's methods, like web services, should be familiar to you from the EJB chapters earlier in this book. In fact, many standards have evolved that enable clients on one machine to invoke the operations or methods of a server on another machine. Examples of this are:

❑ Remote Procedure Calls (RPC). There are a few flavors of RPCs, including:

   ❑ Distributed Computing Environment (DCE) RPCs

   ❑ Sun RPCs (interestingly enough, Sun was a pioneer of RPCs in the early 1980s)

❑ Common Object Request Broker Architecture (CORBA)

❑ Distributed Component Object Model (DCOM)

❑ Java Remote Method Invocation (RMI), which enables EJBs

Each of these standards are excellent, but each are, to some degree, platform or programming language dependent. To enable a future in which any application can invoke the methods of any other application (governed by security policies, of course), we need a standard that:

❑ Is available with most of the popular programming languages

❑ Can be used on almost any hardware/operating system platform

❑ Uses communication protocols that are ubiquitous

❑ Encourages communication over ports that are not likely to have firewall issues

Web services promise to help us realize that future, as they meet all of the criteria listed above: web services can be created in Java, C++, C#, Visual Basic, and many other programming languages. They can be used on most, if not all, major hardware operating system platforms. In addition, they typically run over TCP/IP and HTTP, both of which are ubiquitous. Because of this wide availability, we can all write applications that offer method-based services, and we can expect to be able to call the methods of applications that others have written. These applications can be deployed within the confines of a company's intranet, extranet, or on the Internet.

The RPC model is one way of implementing web services. In this model, a web service application makes an interface available to clients on the network, very similar to the EJB session bean model. Client programs can then find and invoke methods of this interface as if it were residing on the same machine. The data communicated between the client and the web service is expressed using Simple Object Access Protocol (SOAP) and XML.

The other way of implementing web services is using a messaging model. Each application can send SOAP messages to another, without expecting a return value as a caller of a method would. The applications communicate asynchronously, as did the components of the message-drive beans example in the previous chapter. We'll focus most of our attention on the RPC model of web services.

Why Use Web Services?

The cross-platform nature of Java facilitates distributed applications running on multiple hardware and operating system platforms. If all of the components of a distributed application are written in Java, then using EJBs with Java RMI is a good choice. However, web services are a great choice for integrating applications that are written in various languages, because most major platforms have support for SOAP, which is the protocol used in web services for passing object data from one application to another. This enables, for example, an application developed in Java to use the web service operations of an application developed in Perl.

A subtler advantage to web services is that they typically use HTTP as an underlying communication protocol. Because of this, they can easily and naturally be implemented over the TCP/IP ports most commonly open in firewalls, for example 80, 8080, and 443. Ports 80 and 8080 are used for standard browser-to-web server HTTP traffic, and port 443 is used for encrypted, secure HTTP traffic.

Because web services are so conducive to interoperability, legacy system vendors can expose functionality so that other systems can have access. For example, many banks have web access to accounts, including the ability to perform transactions such as transferring money between accounts. But wouldn't it be nice to be able to use your personal finance software to perform these transactions in real time, no matter what institutions those accounts are in? If every bank had a common set of secure web services that wraps their account management systems, then that could be a reality.

The use of web services in personal finance brings up the important issue of security. Applications that share sensitive information with each other need to do so securely. This is addressed in web services in a similar manner to other web-based applications: that is, through the use of network traffic encryption and user authentication.

Let's take a look at an architectural view of web services, in the form of a protocol stack.

The Web Services Protocol Stack

The diagram below shows the protocols used in web services, from highest to lowest level, reading downward. We've omitted layers lower than HTTP, most notably the ones that employ TCP/IP and Ethernet technologies.

Layer	Technology
Service Discovery	UDDI
Service Description	WSDL
Messaging	SOAP
Encoding	XML
Transport	HTTP

Let's cover these protocols from the bottom up.

Transport Layer

The typical transport layer is Hypertext Transfer Protocol (HTTP), the protocol over which most Web traffic travels. As you may recall, HTTP was discussed in the context of servlets and JSPs, in Chapter 5. Web services can also be carried over e-mail messages, using Simple Mail Transport Protocol (SMTP).

Encoding Layer

All web service traffic is expressed in Extensible Markup Language (XML). For information on XML, see the *Resources* section at the end of this chapter or the Apress book, titled *XML Programming: Web Applications and Web Services with JSP and ASP* (ISBN 1-59059-003-1).

Messaging Layer

All application data sent via web services is enclosed in Simple Object Access Protocol (SOAP) messages. SOAP is based entirely upon XML, and contains structures such as the SOAP envelope, and within that, the SOAP header and SOAP body. The SOAP body, for example, contains all of the instance data of the objects that are being transported. The following code is an example SOAP message for the getPrice operation of the fictional ApressBookService discussed previously.

```
<SOAP-ENV:Envelope
    xmlns:SOAP-ENV="http://schemas.xmlsoap.org/soap/envelope/"
    <SOAP-ENV:Body>
        <m:getPrice xmlns:m="http://ws.apress.com">
            <isbn>1590593413</isbn>
        </m:getPrice>
    </SOAP-ENV:Body>
</SOAP-ENV:Envelope>
```

A Java application can use the API defined in the SAAJ (SOAP with Attachments API for Java) to create, send, and receive SOAP messages. This API is contained in the javax.xml.soap package, which is included in the J2EE SDK 1.4. As you'll see a little later, we'll be using a facility known as JAX-RPC that lets us develop at a higher level of abstraction. JAX-RPC uses the SAAJ API under the covers to produce and consume the SOAP message. You can learn more about SAAJ from the SAAJ 1.1 specification, which is available for download at the URL provided in the *Resources* section of this chapter.

Service Description Layer

The functionality provided by a given web service is described by the Web Services Description Language (WSDL). When using JAX-RPC (which will be covered later in this chapter), web services are implemented in Java, with WSDL using XML to describe the interfaces, methods, arguments, return values, and the URL of a web service. To get a feel for WSDL parlance:

❑   A WSDL **port** element is analogous to a Java **interface**.

❑   A WSDL **operation** element is analogous to a Java **method**.

❑   WSDL **part** elements (contained inside of message elements) are analogous to Java **arguments** and **return values**.

We'll see an example of a WSDL file a little later in this chapter.

Service Discovery Layer

Web services can be registered for use, and then discovered at run-time. For example, a client application seeking a web service that offers the functionality of a thesaurus could check to see which applicable web services are registered. This is known as Universal Description, Discovery, and Integration (UDDI). UDDI registries hold information about businesses and the web services that they offer. These UDDI registries are hosted by various vendors and are available on the Internet, but could also be located within a corporate intranet. A list of UDDI registries available on the Internet, as well as more information on UDDI, is available at http://www.uddi.org. There is also an API known as JAXR (Java API for XML Registries) that provides a uniform interface to registries such as UDDI. To learn more about UDDI and the JAXR API, please see the appropriate URLs in the *Resources* section of this chapter.

Emerging Layers

Some emerging layers of the web services stack deal with issues such as security, client identity, transaction coordination, web service user interfaces, and business process workflow. These are very important issues with regard to the use of web services in mission-critical applications.

Developing Web Services in Java

There are a number of toolkits that may be used to develop web services in the Java programming language. One such toolkit is the very popular open-source implementation of SOAP called Apache AXIS. AXIS is from the Apache Software Foundation (http://www.apache.org/), an organization that provides support for open-source projects.

Another such toolkit is the Java API for XML-based RPC (JAX-RPC), which provides a Java API for developing and implementing web services. JAX-RPC handles all the details of the SOAP layer, via SAAJ, enabling development in terms of remote procedure calls. JAX-RPC is available in the J2EE SDK 1.4 that we've been using to build and run the examples throughout this book.

SAAJ and JAX-RPC are also contained in the Java Web Services Developer Pack. The Developer Pack is a toolset for developing web service-related applications, and is meant to be used in conjunction with the J2SE (version 1.3.1_04 or later). It is available from Sun's Java web site at the link provided in the *Resources* section of this chapter. You do not need to download this pack for the examples in this book, because all of the required technologies are available in the J2EE SDK 1.4.

Understanding JAX-RPC

JAX-RPC is a remote procedure call-based programming model introduced in the J2EE 1.4 platform. Its purpose in life is to provide an API for Java applications to communicate with each other using the SOAP protocol. As illustrated below, the programming model of JAX-RPC is very much like EJBs and Java RMI in that the details of the underlying over-the-wire protocols are hidden behind **web service stubs**. A stub implements the same interface as the web service that exists remotely, and it communicates with a **web service tie** on the server. The tie calls the methods of a web service, and communicates the return value and any exceptions encountered back to the client through the stub.

> **Ties are also referred to as skeletons, a familiar term in traditional RPC programming.**

This interface that both the stub and the web service implements is known as the Service Definition Interface. The communication between the stubs and the ties is SOAP, typically over HTTP.

Developing Web Services Using JAX-RPC

Let's begin developing web services. Our first web service is going to be a very simple one; on par with a "Hello World!" application, named SimpleService:

Try It Out   Create a Simple Web Service with JAX-RPC

Because this is the first web services example, and we haven't learned to build and deploy web services yet, we're going to create our code files now, and run them later. There are three Java source files and three XML files for this example.

These files should be organized in a subdirectory structure as shown below. Also shown in this structure are the three XML files that will be used in the build process. These three XML files are created by the application developer and will be used by the deployment and compile tools. We'll be creating these later in the chapter, or, along with the Java source code, they can be downloaded from the code download for this book.

1. The first Java source file that we need to create is the web service interface for this example. The file name is `SimpleServiceIF.java` and it is represented as the Service Definition Interface (in the figure shown opposite):

```
package webservices;

import java.rmi.Remote;
import java.rmi.RemoteException;

public interface SimpleServiceIF extends Remote {
   // the service methods
   public String getEchoString(String clientString)
      throws RemoteException;
}
```

2. The next file that we need to create is the class that implements the web service interface, `SimpleServiceImpl.java`:

```
package webservices;

public class SimpleServiceImpl implements SimpleServiceIF  {

   // the service method implementations

   public String getEchoString(String clientString) {
      return clientString + " back at you!";
   }
}
```

3. Now we need to create the file that will be the client we'll be using to test the web service, `SimpleServiceClient.java`:

```
package client;

import webservices.SimpleServiceIF;
import webservices.SimpleService_Impl;

import javax.xml.rpc.Stub;

public class SimpleServiceClient {
  public static void main(String[] args) {
    try {
      Stub stub = (Stub)
          (new SimpleService_Impl().getSimpleServiceIFPort());
      SimpleServiceIF myProxy = (SimpleServiceIF)stub;
      System.out.println("got service!");

      // loop through the words
      for (int i = 0; i < args.length; i++) {
        String returnedString =
          myProxy.getEchoString(args[i]);
        System.out.println("sent string: " + args[i]
          + ", received string: " + returnedString);
      }
    } catch(Exception e) {
      e.printStackTrace();
    }
  }
}
```

This web service has one method, which takes a `String` as input. It concatenates the `String`: " back at you!" to the input `String`, and returns the resultant `String`.

We'll build and run this example later in the chapter, but first we're going to examine how it all works.

How It Works

We have three Java source files to walk through here. We'll start with the Service Definition Interface, and then cover the web service implementation class, followed by the client. We'll examine the three XML files when we build the example.

The Service Definition Interface

The interface defined in `SimpleServiceIF.java` is the Service Definition Interface, which is used both at development-time and at run-time.

❑ At development time it will be used as input to generate the WSDL file. Recall that the WSDL file describes the interfaces, methods, arguments, return values, and the URL of a web service.

❏ At run-time it is the interface that is implemented by the stub and the web service implementation.

Our web service declares one method in its interface:

```
public String getEchoString(String clientString)
   throws RemoteException;
```

Since a web service is remote by definition, its interface must:

❏ Extend java.rmi.Remote and

❏ Declare that its methods throw java.rmi.RemoteException.

Supported Data Types

Notice that the getEchoString() method takes a String as input and returns a String. Because the arguments and return values of web services are described by WSDL, only Java types that can be represented by WSDL may be used in the method signatures of a JAX-RPC application. Fortunately, all of the Java primitive types and their associated wrapper classes are supported. As a refresher, these are:

Primitive Type	Wrapper Class (in java.lang)
Byte	Byte
short	Short
int	Integer
long	Long
float	Float
double	Double
boolean	Boolean

Additionally, the following Java classes are supported:

Package	Supported Class
java.lang	String
java.math	BigInteger BigDecimal
java.util	Date Calendar Many of the collection classes, such as ArrayList and HashMap

491

Arrays of primitive types and classes listed above are supported as well. Classes whose fields are composed exclusively of JAX-RPC supported data types can be supported as well. For more details on this you can consult the JAX-RPC Specification, which is listed in the *Resources* section of this chapter.

The Web Service Implementation Class

The implementation of our web service is contained in `SimpleServiceImpl.java`, which implements the `SimpleServiceIF` interface. As you can see from the listing above, other than this fact there is nothing special about this implementation class. The JAX-RPC tools and runtime classes do the heavy lifting!

A Web Service Client

The client for our web service is the `SimpleServiceClient.java` code. The `main()` method takes an array of `String` arguments and loops through these arguments, calling the `getEchoString()` web service method with each one.

As explained previously, a client communicates with a web service method via stub and tie classes. In our code example, we use the `getSimpleServiceIFPort()` of a class named `SimpleService_Impl` to obtain a reference to a stub that implements the Service Definition Interface. In this case, the stub implements the `SimpleServiceIF` interface, and the reference is held in the variable named `myProxy`.

```
Stub stub = (Stub)
    (new SimpleService_Impl().getSimpleServiceIFPort());
SimpleServiceIF myProxy = (SimpleServiceIF)stub;
```

By the way, the `SimpleService_Impl` class and the stub classes that it returns are generated in the build process that we'll walk through soon.

Continuing on, the `getEchoString()` method of the stub class is then called, which communicates the argument via SOAP to the tie. This calls the web service implementation, which returns the value via the tie to the stub, and back to the client:

```
String returnedString =
    myProxy.getEchoString(args[i]);
```

The returned value ends up in the `returnedString` variable, which we print out just to prove that the round trip to the web service was achieved:

```
System.out.println("sent string: " + args[i]
    + ", received string: " + returnedString);
```

The Three Ways to Invoke Web Service Methods

There are actually three ways for a client to invoke the methods of a web service:

Probably the most common way, which the example above employed, is known as static stubs. It is also referred to as generated stubs. Using this model, the stubs are created at development time, which we'll see when we build the example shortly.

There is another model, known as **dynamic proxy**, in which the stub classes are created at runtime instead of during development. The Service Definition Interface, however, is created at development time. We'll walk through an example of this in the next chapter.

There is also a Dynamic Invocation Interface (DII) call interface model in which the client can call a web service for which it has no Service Definition Interface or stubs. This is much like Java reflection, in that method signatures are dynamically created and subsequently invoked. The SimpleCalculatorApp example, from Chapter 8, will be transformed into a web service example that employs the DII in the chapter following this one.

Let's take a macro view of a build and deploy process for web services, and then we'll apply it to this example.

The Essential Steps for Building and Deploying Web Services

You'll be using two tools supplied with the J2EE SDK 1.4. One of these tools, the Deployment Tool, has been used throughout this book already. The other one, wscompile, will be used to create the WSDL file and the client stubs. All of the J2EE SDK tools, including the ones we have just mentioned, are located in the bin directory of the J2EE SDK installation.

To create a web service using JAX-RPC with the J2EE SDK 1.4, you can follow these steps:

1. Create the Service Definition Interface and the web service implementation class in the Java programming language, and compile the source files.

2. Create the WSDL file with the wscompile command line tool.

3. Start the J2EE Server and create the J2EE EAR file with the Deployment Tool.

4. Create the WAR file and configure the web service with the Deployment Tool.

5. Create the application server-specific deployment descriptor with the Deployment Tool.

6. Run the Verifier Tool.

7. Deploy the web service.

8. Build the web service stubs classes.

9. Create the client in the Java programming language and compile the source files.

10. Run the web service client.

Let's apply the steps listed above to build and deploy the example.

Try It Out   Compiling the Java Source Files for the Web Service

To build the following example, we'll first compile the two `.java` files that define and implement our web service:

❑   `SimpleServiceIF.java` (in the `webservices` package)

❑   `SimpleServiceImpl.java` (in the `webservices` package)

Later, we'll also compile the `.java` file that provides the client functionality:

❑   `SimpleServiceClient.java` (in the `client` package)

To compile these Java files, set the `classpath` to:

❑   The current directory, and

❑   The `j2ee.jar` file that is in the `lib` directory of the Java 2 SDK, Enterprise Edition 1.4 (J2EE SDK 1.4) installation.

❑   In addition, we'll put the `jaxrpc-impl.jar` file on the `classpath` that is in the `lib` directory of the J2EE SDK 1.4 installation. This will be needed for a compile that occurs later in this chapter.

For example, on a default J2EE SDK 1.4 Windows installation, the `classpath` would be set correctly by using the following command:

```
> set classpath=.;%J2EE_HOME%\lib\j2ee.jar;%J2EE_HOME%\lib\jaxrpc-impl.jar
```

With the directory that the `client` and `webservices` directories are rooted in (this example has used `SimpleServiceApp`) as the current directory, execute the following command from the command prompt:

```
> javac -d . webservices/*.java
```

The Java class files for the web service should end up in the same directory as the source files. We'll compile the client class in the *Compiling the Client* step.

At this point we need to create the WSDL file because it will, in turn, be used to create other files needed by this example.

Try It Out Create the WSDL File for the Simple Web Service

The drawing shown below illustrates this step:

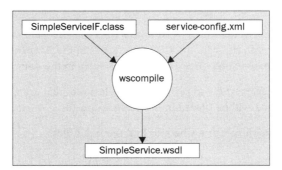

The inputs to this step are the `SimpleServiceIF.class` file that was created by the compile in the previous step, and the `service-config.xml` file shown below.

1. We need to create this XML file now and save it in the SimpleServiceApp root folder for our application, as shown in the diagram of the file layout, previously:

    ```xml
    <?xml version="1.0" encoding="UTF-8"?>
    <configuration
      xmlns="http://java.sun.com/xml/ns/jax-rpc/ri/config">
      <service
        name="SimpleService"
        targetNamespace="urn:simpleService"
        typeNamespace="urn:simpleService"
        packageName="webservices">
        <interface name="webservices.SimpleServiceIF"/>
      </service>
    </configuration>
    ```

    This `service-config.xml` file provides input to the `wscompile` tool, giving it some of the information that it needs to create the `SimpleService.wsdl` file. This information, as seen above, is the name of the web service, namespaces to be used in the WSDL file, the Java package name in which the web service classes reside, and the fully qualified name of the service definition interface.

2. To create the WSDL file, we'll use a command-line tool that comes with the J2EE SDK 1.4 named `wscompile`. This tool's purpose in life is to create WSDL, stub, and tie files. Here we'll just be using it to generate the WSDL file, which contains XML. To do this, with the current directory set as indicated above, type the following command:

    ```
    > wscompile -define -nd . -classpath . service-config.xml
    ```

So, let's take a look at what we've accomplished here.

How It Works

This command takes the `service-config.xml` file shown above, and the interface defined in the `SimpleServiceIF.class` file, and it generates the `SimpleService.wsdl` file.

❑ The –define option tells the tool to read a Java RMI interface and create a WSDL file that defines a web service. In this case the RMI interface is in the `SimpleServiceIF.class` file as indicated by the `webservices.SimpleServiceIF` entry in the `service-config.xml` file.

❑ The –nd option indicates where to place any non-class files that are generated. In this case, the `SimpleService.wsdl` will be placed in the current directory.

❑ The –classpath option specifies where to find the input files.

Documentation on the wscompile tool is included in the J2EE SDK 1.4 installation.

An excerpt shown below of the generated `SimpleService.wsdl` file has an XML representation of the interface, method, parameters, and return types defined by the `SimpleServiceIF` interface. As previously noted, the nomenclature used in the WSDL file includes ports, operations, messages, and parts. For example, the `<operation>` element defines the `getEchoString` operation and the `<message>` elements define the parameters and return type of that operation:

```
<?xml version="1.0" encoding="UTF-8"?>
<definitions name="SimpleService"
             targetNamespace="urn:simpleService"
             xmlns:tns="urn:simpleService"
             xmlns="http://schemas.xmlsoap.org/wsdl/"
             xmlns:soap="http://schemas.xmlsoap.org/wsdl/soap/"
             xmlns:xsd="http://www.w3.org/2001/XMLSchema">
    <types/>
    <message name="SimpleServiceIF_getEchoString">
      <part name="String_1" type="xsd:string"/>
    </message>
    <message name="SimpleServiceIF_getEchoStringResponse">
      <part name="result" type="xsd:string"/>
    </message>
    <portType name="SimpleServiceIF">
      <operation name="getEchoString" parameterOrder="String_1">
        <input message="tns:SimpleServiceIF_getEchoString"/>
        <output message="tns:SimpleServiceIF_getEchoStringResponse"/>
      </operation>
    </portType>
    <service name="SimpleService">
      <port name="SimpleServiceIFPort" binding="tns:SimpleServiceIFBinding">
        <soap:address location="REPLACE_WITH_ACTUAL_URL"/>
      </port>
    </service>
</definitions>
```

Note that when you are developing a new web service, you can modify the `service-config.xml` (shown at the beginning of this step) to reflect the name of the web service, and the package and name of the interface class. As an example, if you were developing a web service named WeatherService, and the package name was web_services, your service-config.xml file would look something like this:

```
<?xml version="1.0" encoding="UTF-8"?>
<configuration
    xmlns="http://java.sun.com/xml/ns/jax-rpc/ri/config">
    <service
        name="WeatherService"
        targetNamespace="urn:weatherService"
        typeNamespace="urn:weatherService"
        packageName="web_services">
        <interface name="web_services.SimpleServiceIF"/>
    </service>
</configuration>
```

Now that the WSDL file has been created, we'll use the Deployment Tool to configure and deploy the web service.

Try It Out   Creating the J2EE EAR File

Let's go ahead and start up the application server that comes with J2EE SDK 1.4 because we'll be deploying our web service soon. Instructions for starting it up are given in Chapter 2.

Now we'll use the Deployment Tool that comes with the J2EE SDK 1.4 to configure and deploy the web service. Instructions for starting it up are also given in Chapter 2.

After the Deployment Tool starts up, we'll create the J2EE Enterprise Application Resource (EAR) file in which the application will be packaged. When everything is completed, the web service will be packaged in a web application resource (WAR) file, which we'll stick in our EAR.

Try It Out   Creating the WAR File and Configuring the Web Service

1. Start by creating a new Application EAR file, and name it SimpleServiceApp.ear, placing it in your SimpleServiceApp directory, and setting the display name to be SimpleServiceApp.

2. One of the files we'll be putting in the WAR file is mapping.xml, which is another configuration file. The code for this file is as follows:

```
<?xml version="1.0" encoding="UTF-8"?>
<java-wsdl-mapping xmlns="http://java.sun.com/xml/ns/j2ee"
        xmlns:xsi="http://www.w3.org/2001/XMLSchema-instance"
        xsi:schemaLocation="http://java.sun.com/xml/ns/j2ee
http://www.ibm.com/webservices/xsd/j2ee_jaxrpc_mapping_1_1.xsd"
        version="1.1">
    <package-mapping>
        <package-type>webservices</package-type>
        <namespaceURI>urn:simpleService</namespaceURI>
    </package-mapping>
</java-wsdl-mapping>
```

Make sure you enter this code and save it in your `SimpleServiceApp` directory before continuing.

3. Now we'll create the WAR file in which the web service classes and resources will be packaged. To do this, make sure that SimpleServiceApp is selected in the tree on the left. From the File menu choose the New menu item, and then the Web Component menu item.

You will be asked by the wizard to choose where you want the WAR file to be placed. We're going to put it in our newly created SimpleServiceApp EAR file, so make the related choices that you see below. Also on this page is a place to enter the name for the WAR Display Name that you would like to appear in tools like this Deployment Tool. Let's call it SimpleServiceWar:

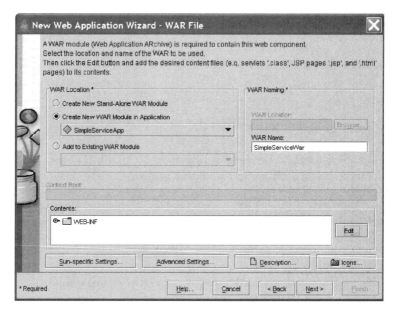

4. Next, click the Edit button on this page to pick the files that you want to put in the WAR file. In the Available Files panel of the dialog box shown below, navigate to the base directory of this SimpleServiceApp example. Choose the following files and click the Add button:

❑ The Service Definition Interface (`SimpleServiceIF.class`), located in the `webservices` directory.

❑ The Web Service Implementation class (`SimpleServiceImpl.class`), located in the `webservices` directory.

❑ The WSDL file (`SimpleService.wsdl`).

❑ The J2EE JAX-RPC mapping file (`mapping.xml`). The purpose of this file is to associate the Java package in which the web service class files are located with the namespace of the web service in the WSDL file. This is seen in the `<package-mapping>` element shown above.

Those four files should now appear in the Edit Contents of SimpleServiceWar panel as seen below.

5.   Closing the dialog box and clicking the Next button should make the page shown below appear. This page lets you choose the type of web component that you want. Here, because it is a web service, we'll indicate that we want it to be a Web Services Endpoint:

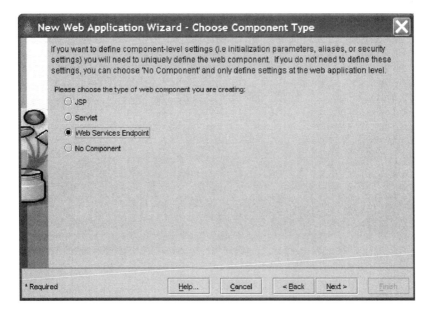

6. The next page of the wizard, shown below, lets you define the new web service. For this, we'll supply four pieces of information:

❑ Firstly, we'll indicate the name of the WSDL file (`SimpleService.wsdl`).

❑ Secondly, we'll indicate the name of the J2EE JAX-RPC mapping file (`mapping.xml`).

❑ The third piece of information that we'll supply to the page shown below is the name that we'll give the web service. SimpleService should be filled in for you already.

❑ Finally, we'll give it the name for the service that you would like to appear in tools like this Deployment Tool. SimpleService should be filled in for you already as well.

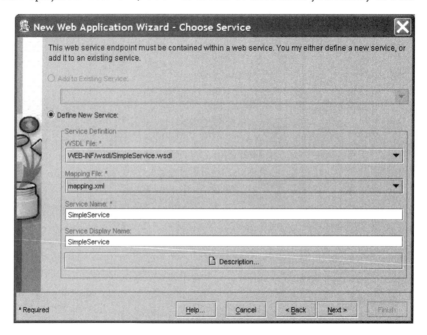

7. The next page of the wizard is shown below. In the Service Endpoint Implementation drop-down list, you'll choose the fully qualified name of the Java class that implements the web service, in this case webservices.SimpleServiceImpl. The other fields will be loaded with default values as seen below, and we'll keep the defaults:

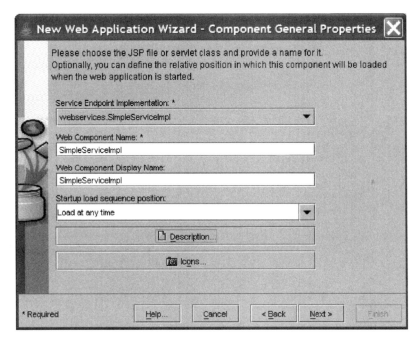

8. In the next page of the wizard, shown below, we'll enter information about the interface for the web service. There are five fields to fill out on this page:

❑ Service Endpoint Interface: An **endpoint** in web services parlance is the URL address of a web service. The Service Endpoint Interface that is implemented at the endpoint is what we've been referring to as the Service Definition Interface. The fully qualified name of this interface for our web service is webservices.simpleServiceIF, so choose that name from the drop-own list.

❑ WSDL Port Namespace and Local Part: These uniquely identify the web service port in the WSDL file, and associate it with the Service Endpoint Interface chosen above. Choose urn:simpleService and SimpleServiceIFPort, respectively.

❑ Port Component Name and Port Component Display Name: We'll use the class name of the Service Endpoint Interface for both of these fields, so enter SimpleServiceIF in each one.

❑ Let the Endpoint Address URI field remain the default. We'll change it later.

9. Click Next and Finish to leave the wizard, and the screen should look like the one shown below:

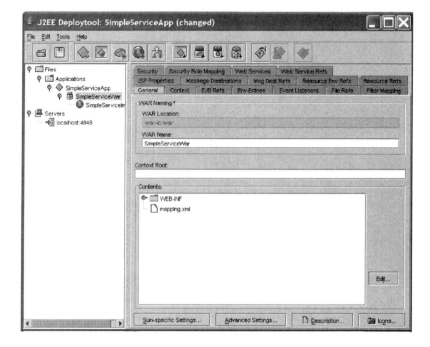

10. Now select SimpleServiceApp from the tree in the panel on the left, and select the Web Context tab in the panel on the right. In the Context Root column of the Web Context tab, enter simple-jaxrpc beside the SimpleServiceWar entry, as shown in the screenshot below. As you'll see when we examine the `client-config.xml` file, the URL for our web service will be http://localhost:8080/simple-jaxrpc/simple. The Context Root is the base directory for its WAR file, so simple-jaxrpc will become part of the URL.

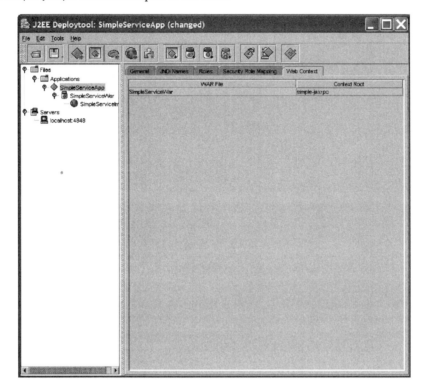

11. Now we're going to create an alias that will be part of our web service's URL. Select the SimpleServiceImpl node in the left panel, and select the Aliases tab. Click the Add button and assign an alias of /simple as shown below.

12. With the SimpleServiceImpl node in the left panel still selected, click the Endpoint tab. Select the endpoint named simple from the Endpoint Address drop-down as shown below.

13. Go ahead and save the application by selecting Save | All from the File menu. Run the Verifier Tool by selecting Verify J2EE Compliance from the Tools menu. Using the Verifier Tool is explained in the *Developing Session Beans* section of Chapter 8.

Try It Out Deploying the Web Service

Before we deploy, as a good housekeeping measure, we'll make sure that no other applications are deployed. There is no problem with having more than one application deployed at a time, but this will ensure that we don't have two of our example web services deployed with the same endpoint.

1. To verify that no other applications are deployed, select localhost:4848 in the tree in the left panel, and click the Undeploy button for any applications that are listed in the table.

2. To deploy the J2EE application that contains our web service, select SimpleServiceApp from the tree in the left-hand panel, and choose Deploy from the Tools menu. As a result, you should see the Deploy Module dialog, shown below. In this dialog, you are asked for your User Name and Password. Leave the Return Client Jar option unchecked.

505

3. After clicking the OK button, the following dialog will appear. Your SimpleServiceApp should successfully deploy, including the web service that we created. The web service is now ready for a client to invoke its one and only method. Click the Close button when it becomes enabled:

If you have any problems deploying, then follow the instructions in the *Troubleshooting the Deploy* section of Chapter 8.

After the web service is deployed, we'll turn our attention towards building and running the client.

Try It Out   Final Configuration and Test of the Web Service

Before we can compile the client application, we need to create the stub classes, because the client application is dependent upon them. Recall that the client calls methods of the stub, which communicates on its behalf via SOAP to the tie, which invokes methods of the web service. To create the stub classes:

1. Verify that your classpath is set as described in the *Compiling the Java Source Files for the Web Service* section earlier in this chapter.

2. We need to enter the code for the last of our XML configuration files, client-config.xml. Enter the following code and save the file:

```
<?xml version="1.0" encoding="UTF-8"?>
<configuration xmlns="http://java.sun.com/xml/ns/jax-rpc/ri/config">
  <wsdl location="http://localhost:8080/simple-jaxrpc/simple?WSDL"
        packageName="webservices"/>
</configuration>
```

3. With the base directory of the example (this explanation has used `SimpleServiceApp`) as the current directory, create a subdirectory named `stubs` (if it doesn't already exist). If it does exist, go ahead and delete everything within it for the sake of good housekeeping.

4. With the base directory of the example as the current directory, execute the following command from the command prompt. This is the same `wscompile` command-line tool that we previously used to create the WSDL file. This time, however, we're using the `–gen:client` option, which causes stub files to be generated.

```
> wscompile –gen:client -d stubs -classpath . client-config.xml
```

This form of the `wscompile` command takes as input the `client-config.xml` file shown above, and the WSDL of the web service. It gets the WSDL from the deployed web service by accessing its endpoint URL with the string "?WSDL" appended to the end. This URL is contained in the `<wsdl>` element of the `client-config.xml` file. The `packageName` attribute in the `client-config.xml` file indicates what package the generated stub files should be located in.

As a result of the `wscompile`, the Java class files for the stub should be generated and placed in a new `webservices` directory subordinate to the `stubs` directory.

5. Now we can compile the client class, being careful to add the `stubs` directory to the `classpath`. To do this on a Windows platform, for example, the command would look like this:

```
> javac –classpath %classpath%;stubs -d . client/*.java
```

The Java class files for the client should end up in the same directory as the source files.

6. To run the client, we'll need a few extra libraries on the `classpath`. By the way, this command file is in the Apress download for this chapter to save you the trouble of typing it in:

```
> java -classpath %classpath%;stubs; ->
%J2EE_HOME%\lib\jaxrpc-impl.jar;%J2EE_HOME%\lib\xsdlib.jar; ->
%J2EE_HOME%\lib\saaj-impl.jar; ->
%J2EE_HOME%\lib\commons-logging.jar; ->
%J2EE_HOME%\lib\endorsed\xercesImpl.jar; ->
%J2EE_HOME%\lib\endorsed\dom.jar client.SimpleServiceClient Hi Bye
```

The `SimpleService` web service will be invoked once for each of the command-line arguments. If you run the client with the command line arguments shown above (`Hi` and `Bye`), it should produce the following output:

507

How It Works

Congratulations! You've created and invoked a web service. The web service Java code and XML files are pretty straightforward, but building and deploying can seem like a chore the first couple of times that you do it (as you may have noticed).

By the way, because web services are invoked via HTTP, you can ping a web service via a web browser. For example, if you enter the endpoint of the web service followed by "?WSDL", the server will respond by sending you the WSDL for the web service. To try this, paste the following URL in your web browser with the web service deployed:

> http://localhost:8080/simple-jaxrpc/simple?WSDL

You may recall that this is the same URL that the wscompile tool used to get the WSDL for creating the client stubs.

Summary

In this chapter, we discovered that web services are a way to create distributed applications whose components communicate with each other over protocols associated with the Web. This application functionality can be offered via web services over the public Internet, or limited for use within a corporate intranet or extranet.

We saw that some of the advantages of web services are:

❑   They promote the development of distributed applications whose components are written in various languages, and deployed on various hardware and software platforms.

❑   They communicate over protocols and ports that are used by the Web, so they can be implemented relatively easily.

This chapter has also touched upon the fact that the availability of web services over the public Internet makes security, in the form of data encryption and user authentication, an important issue.

We then explored the web services protocol layers, which employ technologies such as HTTP, XML, SOAP, WSDL, and UDDI. An introduction to JAX-RPC was given, and web service concepts such as stubs and ties were explained in that context. Finally, we developed a simple web service and client, using the J2EE SDK 1.4 Deployment Tool and JAX-RPC implementation.

Now that we've explored web services and JAX-RPC, in the next chapter we'll cover some more topics germane to web services.

Resources

Here are some good resources for learning about XML:

- http://java.sun.com/xml/docs.html
- http://www.xml.org/
- http://www.xml.com/

You can learn more about JAX-RPC from the JAX-RPC Specification, which can be downloaded from the following page:

- http://java.sun.com/xml/downloads/jaxrpc.html

You can download the SAAJ specification from the following page:

- http://java.sun.com/xml/downloads/saaj.html

You can learn more about UDDI and the JAXR API from these web sites, respectively:

- http://www.uddi.org/
- http://java.sun.com/xml/jaxr/

The Java Web Services Developer Pack is available from Sun's Java web site on the following page:

- http://java.sun.com/webservices/webservicespack.html

Exercises

1. Write a JAX-RPC web service that takes a word and returns it spelled backwards.

2. Write a JAX-RPC web service that takes two numbers and a string operator value of "+" or "–". Apply this operator to the numbers.

13

More J2EE Web Services Topics

The previous chapter gave us an introduction to web services, including concepts such as the web services protocol stack and the layers contained within. We discussed JAX-RPC and developed a web service application using the J2EE SDK 1.4, including the JAX-RPC implementation.

In this chapter, we'll cover more topics germane to developing J2EE web services, including how web services and EJBs play well together, additional JAX-RPC concepts, and some dynamic aspects of web services.

In this chapter you will learn:

❑   How to implement a session bean as a web service

❑   How to develop **dynamic proxies** for web services

❑   How to create a stateful web service

❑   About the **JAX-RPC endpoint model**

❑   How to use the **DII** (**Dynamic Invocation Interface**) to call web services dynamically

We'll start by revisiting EJBs and take a look at how we can combine knowledge of EJBs with the deployment of web services.

Implementing a Session Bean as a Web Service

There is a relatively new capability in the EJB specification that provides for making the methods of a stateless session bean available via a **web service endpoint**. Note that the specification only requires that *stateless* session beans implement a **web service endpoint**, not *stateful* session beans. We do have a stateful web service example in this chapter, but it is implemented in a different way.

In the first example in this chapter, we'll be building on some of the techniques we've already learned. This example demonstrates how to take a stateless session bean and deploy it as a web service. In order to accomplish this we'll give the session bean a web service endpoint. Because we're dealing with an EJB that will become a web service, this example uses EJB concepts as well as web services concepts that we've learned in previous chapters:

❑ The EJB concepts, and some of the code for this example, come straight out of the *EJB Fundamentals* chapter. Specifically, we're going to use some of the session bean code and build process from the first *Try It Out* example, which was the *SimpleSessionApp* session bean example in Chapter 8.

❑ The web services concepts, and some of the code for this example, come from the previous chapter. We'll use some code and build process from the *SimpleServiceApp* example as well.

Recall that the *SimpleSessionApp* example referred to above is a stateless session bean that takes a String argument, concatenates the string: " back at you!", and returns the resultant string. The *SimpleServiceApp* does the same thing, except for the fact that it is a web service. Let's take a look the code that we'll borrow from each of these examples:

Try It Out   Creating a Web Service with a Session Bean

1. We'll start by using the session bean class code from the *SimpleSessionApp* example, which is in the Java source file, SimpleSessionBean.java:

```
package beans;

import javax.ejb.SessionBean;
import javax.ejb.SessionContext;

public class SimpleSessionBean implements SessionBean {
  // the public business method. this must be coded in the
  // remote interface also.
  public String getEchoString(String clientString) {
    return clientString + " back at you!";
  }

  // standard ejb methods
  public void ejbActivate() {}
  public void ejbPassivate() {}
  public void ejbRemove() {}
  public void ejbCreate() {}
  public void setSessionContext(SessionContext context) { }
}
```

Note that we're not going to use the session bean's **home interface** or **bean interface** classes. This is because the client in this example is a web service client. It will be invoking the methods of the **service definition interface** which is very similar to the **bean interface**, and it won't be using the **home interface** at all. Of course, you could leave those interfaces in, which would enable the deployed bean to be invoked via a web service client as well as via an EJB client. This is often a better approach, as it provides more flexibility as to how the session bean may be used.

2. The service definition interface is taken from the *SimpleServiceApp* example, `SimpleServiceIF.java`:

```
package webservices;

import java.rmi.Remote;
import java.rmi.RemoteException;

public interface SimpleServiceIF extends Remote {
  // the service methods
  public String getEchoString(String clientString)
    throws RemoteException;
}
```

3. The client for this example, `SimpleServiceClient.java`, is very similar to the client in the *SimpleServiceApp* example in the previous chapter: the basic difference is that we're going to take this opportunity to demonstrate how to use **dynamic proxies** mentioned in the previous chapter:

```
package client;

import webservices.SimpleServiceIF;

import java.net.URL;
import javax.xml.namespace.QName;
import javax.xml.rpc.Service;
import javax.xml.rpc.ServiceFactory;

public class SimpleServiceClient {
  public static void main(String[] args) {
    try {
      String serviceName = "SimpleBeanService";
      String urlString =
        "http://localhost:8080/simplebean?WSDL";
      String nameSpaceUri =
                "urn:simpleBeanService";
      String portName = "SimpleServiceIFPort";

      URL wsdlUrl = new URL(urlString);

      ServiceFactory serviceFactory = ServiceFactory.newInstance();

      Service jaxService =
        serviceFactory.createService(wsdlUrl,
                new QName(nameSpaceUri, serviceName));
```

```
            SimpleServiceIF myProxy = (SimpleServiceIF) jaxService.getPort(
                    new QName(nameSpaceUri, portName),
                    SimpleServiceIF.class);

            System.out.println("got service!");

            // loop through the words
            for (int i = 0; i < args.length; i++) {
              String returnedString =
                myProxy.getEchoString(args[i]);
              System.out.println("sent string: " + args[i]
                + ", received string: " + returnedString);
            }
        } catch(Exception e) {
          e.printStackTrace();
        }
      }
    }
```

We'll also be using slightly modified versions of the `service-config.xml` and `mapping.xml` files from the *SimpleServiceApp* example that we created in the previous chapter. These files will be listed in the place where we build and deploy the example.

Let's go ahead and build the example, using a fusion of the session bean and web service build processes described below.

To build this example, we'll begin by following the process defined in the *Essential Steps for Building and Deploying EJBs* section of the *EJB Fundamentals* chapter. You'll also notice that a lot of the steps in this example are the same as in the previous chapter. We'll coach you through this here, pointing out variations as they come up.

Here are the steps that will be followed for building and running this example:

❑ Compile the Java source code.

❑ Create the WSDL document.

❑ Start the J2EE Server and create the J2EE EAR file with the Deployment Tool.

❑ Create and populate the bean JAR.

❑ Configure the web service.

❑ Run the Verifier Tool.

❑ Deploy the web service.

❑ Run the web service client.

There are three Java source files in this example, and we'll compile all of them now, even the web service client. Do you remember why we didn't compile the client program in the previous web service example until later in process? It was because the static stubs first had to be generated due to the fact that the client depended upon them. In this example, we're going to demonstrate **dynamic proxies** which don't use static subs, so there are no dependency issues. Note that there is no relationship between this example being a session bean with a web service endpoint, and the client using a dynamic proxy. We could have just as easily used either of the other two client models (**static stubs** and **DII**) introduced in the previous chapter.

Here are the three .java files:

❑ SimpleSessionBean.java (in the beans package)

❑ SimpleServiceIF.java (in the webservices package)

❑ SimpleServiceClient.java (in the client package)

These files should be organized in the following subdirectory structure. Also shown in this structure are the two XML files that will be used in the build process:

4. To compile these Java files, set the classpath to:

❑ The current directory, and

❑ The j2ee.jar file that is in the lib directory of the Java 2 SDK, Enterprise Edition 1.4 (J2EE SDK 1.4) installation.

For example, on a default J2EE SDK 1.4 Windows installation, the classpath would be set correctly by using the following command:

```
> set classpath=.;%J2EE_HOME%\lib\j2ee.jar
```

5. With base directory of the example as the current directory, execute the following commands from the command prompt.

```
> javac -d . beans/*.java
> javac -d . webservices/*.java
> javac -d . client/*.java
```

At this point we'll borrow a step from the Web Services and JAX-RPC chapter. Because our session bean will be a web service, it will need a WSDL document, and to create that document, we need a `service-config.xml` file. Here is the `service-config.xml` file that we're using as input to the wscompile:

```
<?xml version="1.0" encoding="UTF-8"?>
<configuration xmlns="http://java.sun.com/xml/ns/jax-rpc/ri/config">
  <service
       name="SimpleBeanService"
       targetNamespace="urn:simpleBeanService"
       typeNamespace="urn:simpleBeanService"
       packageName="beans">
       <interface name="webservices.SimpleServiceIF"/>
  </service>
</configuration>
```

6. Now, to create the WSDL, with the current directory set as indicated above, type the following command:

```
> wscompile -define -nd . -classpath . service-config.xml
```

This will create a file named `SimpleBeanService.wsdl` that we'll put in the bean jar shortly. Now, back to the session bean build process:

7. After starting the J2EE server and Deployment Tool, create an Application EAR file and name it SimpleBeanServiceApp.ear.

8. Invoke the Add Enterprise Bean Wizard by selecting File | New | Enterprise Bean from the menu.

In the EJB JAR page of the New Enterprise Bean Wizard, use SimpleBeanServiceJar as the JAR Display Name. Click the Edit button on that page, and add the following files to the SimpleBeanServiceJar panel shown in the dialog below.

❑ The session bean implementation class (`SimpleSessionBean.class`). Recall that for this example, we don't need the two interface files that are normally included in session beans.

❑ The **service definition interface** (`SimpleServiceIF.class`) for the web service.

❑ The WSDL file (`SimpleBeanService.wsdl`) for the web service.

❑ The J2EE JAX-RPC mapping file (`mapping.xml`) for the web service. Here is the `mapping.xml` file that we're using for this example:

```
<?xml version="1.0" encoding="UTF-8"?>
<java-wsdl-mapping xmlns="http://java.sun.com/xml/ns/j2ee"
     xmlns:xsi="http://www.w3.org/2001/XMLSchema-instance"
     xsi:schemaLocation="http://java.sun.com/xml/ns/j2ee
         http://www.ibm.com/webservices/xsd/j2ee_jaxrpc_mapping_1_1.xsd"
     version="1.1">
    <package-mapping>
        <package-type>beans</package-type>
        <namespaceURI>urn:simpleBeanService</namespaceURI>
    </package-mapping>
</java-wsdl-mapping>
```

In the General page of the wizard, shown below, since the session bean interfaces aren't needed, we won't choose them from the General page shown below. Do, however, select beans.SimpleSessionBean from the Enterprise Bean Class drop-down, and specify that this is a Stateless Session bean. Also, enter SimpleSessionEjb as the Display Name:

The more inquisitive among us will have clicked the drop-downs in the Remote Interfaces panel to see if those interfaces were available to be chosen. They're not available in the drop-downs because we didn't add them in the previous dialog (I had to check).

9. The next page in the Wizard, shown below, is a pivotal one. From it, we'll indicate that our session bean should be a web service, and we'll be led into some pages that we saw in the Creating the WAR File and Configuring the Web Service section of the Web Services and JAX-RPC chapter. To do this, select Yes in the Expose Bean as a Web Service Endpoint panel:

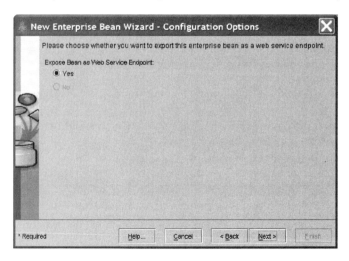

10. From the next page of in the New Enterprise Bean Wizard, shown below, select the `SimpleBeanService.wsdl` and `mapping.xml` files from the drop-down lists. Use SimpleBeanService for the Service Name and Service Display Name:

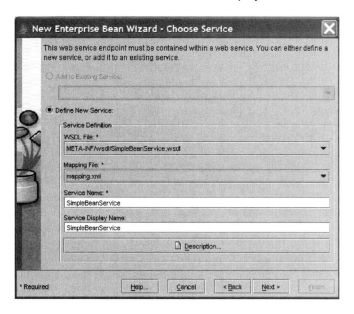

11. From the next page, select webservices.SimpleServiceIF from the Service Endpoint Interface drop-down list. Choose urn:simpleBeanService for the WSDL Port Namespace, and SimpleServiceIFPort for the WSDL Port Local Part. For a refresher on what these fields mean, refer to the *Creating the WAR File and Configuring the Web Service* section of the previous web services chapter. Enter SimpleServiceIF in the Port Component Name and Port Component Display Name fields. Enter simplebean in the Endpoint Address field as shown below. The complete URL for our web service will be:

```
http://localhost:8080/simplebean
```

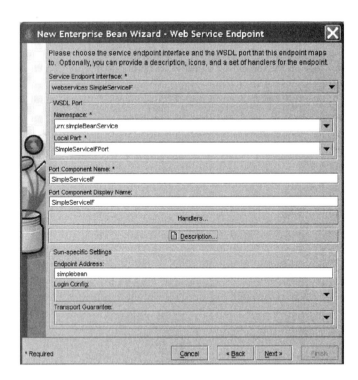

It is not necessary to visit the JNDI Names tab and give the session bean a JNDI name. The reason for this is that we'll be using the web service endpoint, shown above, to locate the session bean rather than using JNDI.

12. Save the application by selecting Save All from the File menu.

13. The last step before we deploy is to run the verifier tool (start by choosing the Tools | Verify J2EE Compliance menu item).

14. Deploy the application in the usual way (using the Tools | Deploy menu item). Do not select the Return Client Jar check box, because we'll be using web services stubs to communicate to the service. Deploying causes the web service to begin running, listening for requests from clients:

15. If you have any problems deploying, then follow the instructions in the *Troubleshooting the Deploy* section of Chapter 8.

16. We've already compiled our client class, and we don't need to build Stub classes here, because we're going to use **dynamic proxies**. We do, however, need several files on the classpath, so set the following classpath on the command line. By the way, this is in a command file in the Apress download for this chapter to save you the trouble of typing it in:

```
> set CLASSPATH=.;%J2EE_HOME%\lib\j2ee.jar; ->
%J2EE_HOME%\lib\jaxrpc-impl.jar; ->
%J2EE_HOME%\lib\xsdlib.jar; ->
%J2EE_HOME%\lib\saaj-impl.jar; ->
%J2EE_HOME%\lib\commons-logging.jar; ->
%J2EE_HOME%\lib\endorsed\xercesImpl.jar; ->
%J2EE_HOME%\lib\endorsed\dom.jar
```

17. To run the client, enter the following on the command line, including some arguments like the ones shown below:

```
> java client.SimpleServiceClient Faith Hope Love
```

You should see the following:

```
C:\3413\Ch13\SimpleBeanServiceApp>java client.SimpleServiceClient Faith Hope Lov
e
got service!
sent string: Faith, received string: Faith back at you!
sent string: Hope, received string: Hope back at you!
sent string: Love, received string: Love back at you!

C:\3413\Ch13\SimpleBeanServiceApp>
```

How It Works

The Deployment Tool took care of deploying the session bean in such a way that it may be accessed via a web service endpoint. Now we're going to examine the client code that dynamically accesses this web service without the benefit of a pre-existing client stub.

Let's revisit the Java source code for the web service client, `SimpleServiceClient.java`:

```java
package client;

import webservices.SimpleServiceIF;

import java.net.URL;
import javax.xml.namespace.QName;
import javax.xml.rpc.Service;
import javax.xml.rpc.ServiceFactory;

public class SimpleServiceClient {
  public static void main(String[] args) {
    try {
      String serviceName = "SimpleBeanService";
      String urlString =
        "http://localhost:8080/simplebean?WSDL";
      String nameSpaceUri =
                "urn:simpleBeanService";
      String portName = "SimpleServiceIFPort";

      URL wsdlUrl = new URL(urlString);

      ServiceFactory serviceFactory = ServiceFactory.newInstance();

      Service jaxService =
        serviceFactory.createService(wsdlUrl,
                new QName(nameSpaceUri, serviceName));

      SimpleServiceIF myProxy = (SimpleServiceIF) jaxService.getPort(
                new QName(nameSpaceUri, portName),
                SimpleServiceIF.class);

      System.out.println("got service!");

      // loop through the words
      for (int i = 0; i < args.length; i++) {
        String returnedString =
          myProxy.getEchoString(args[i]);
        System.out.println("sent string: " + args[i]
          + ", received string: " + returnedString);
      }
    } catch(Exception e) {
      e.printStackTrace();
    }
  }
}
```

Rather than generating a stub for our web service at build time, this client manufactures a stub at run-time. An advantage to this approach is that the location of the web service doesn't have to be known at build time (recall that in the *Building the Web Service Stubs* section of the previous chapter, the endpoint URL was specified in the `client-config.xml` file at build time). Rather, the endpoint URL of the web service can be supplied at run-time, perhaps passed in on a command-line or obtained from a database. A stub created dynamically at run-time is known as a **dynamic proxy**. Here is the statement that creates this dynamic proxy:

```
SimpleServiceIF myProxy = (SimpleServiceIF) jaxService.getPort(
            new QName(nameSpaceUri, portName),
            SimpleServiceIF.class);
```

The `jaxService` variable contains a reference to an instance of the `java.xml.rpc.Service` class, which represents a web service. Its purpose in life is to create proxies that may be used to call the methods of the web service that it represents. We'll back up in a moment and explain how the `Service` instance was created, but for now let's discuss the `getPort()` method of the `Service` class. The `getPort()` method takes two parameters:

❑   The **qualified name** of the web service **port**, which as discussed previously is analogous to a Java interface. The qualified name is represented by the `QName` class in the `javax.xml.namespace` package, and consists of the values that we gave it in the WSDL Port panel of the Web Service Endpoint page of the New Enterprise Bean Wizard. Those values are defined in the following statements of our client program:

```
String nameSpaceUri =
        "urn:simpleBeanService";
String portName = "SimpleServiceIFPort";
```

❑   The **service definition interface**, which in this case is defined in `SimpleServiceIF.class`.

If there are problems creating the proxy, the `getPort()` method will throw a `javax.xml.rpc.ServiceException`. As a result of the call to the `getPort()` method, the variable named myProxy contains a proxy whose methods will invoke the methods of our web service. As with the example in the previous chapter which used **static stubs**, the object that is referred to by myProxy implements the `SimpleServiceIF` interface. Therefore, the following code can be identical to the previous example even though the proxy was created in a different manner.

```
String returnedString =
    myProxy.getEchoString(args[i]);
```

As promised, backing up a bit, let's take a look at how the instance of the `Service` class was created. First off, there is a class in the `javax.xml.rpc` package named `ServiceFactory` whose job is to create instances of the `Service` class discussed previously. The following statements create a `Service` object for our web service:

```
ServiceFactory serviceFactory = ServiceFactory.newInstance();

Service jaxService =
    serviceFactory.createService(wsdlUrl,
            new QName(nameSpaceUri, serviceName));
```

523

The newInstance() method of the ServiceFactory class is a static method that returns an instance of the ServiceFactory class. The createService() method of the ServiceFactory object is then called, passing in a couple of arguments:

❑ An instance of the java.net.URL class that represents the URL of the WSDL document for our web service. This is how the resultant Service object knows the details of how to create the proxy, such as what web service **operations** (methods) are available. It is given this information dynamically from the WSDL document of the deployed web service. The WSDL URL is defined in the following statements of our client program:

```
String urlString =
    "http://localhost:8080/simplebean?WSDL";

URL wsdlUrl = new URL(urlString);
```

❑ The **qualified name** of the web service definition. This name consists of the values that we gave it in the Service Definition panel of the Choose Service page of the New Enterprise Bean Wizard. Those values are defined in the following statements of our client program:

```
String nameSpaceUri =
            "urn:simpleBeanService";
String serviceName = "SimpleBeanService";
```

If you want to display the WSDL of the deployed web service in your browser, you can do so by going to the following URL:

http://localhost:8080/simplebean?WSDL

By doing this you'll see the WSDL document, as shown below, that describes our web service so that the dynamic proxy can be created:

Notice that all of the **operations** are described, including parameters and return values. Notice also that three of the values from the WSDL document were passed into the `ServiceFactory.createService()` and `Service.getPort()` methods in order to identify the desired web service and port.

In this section we learned about, and walked through an example of, a stateless session bean that is exposed as a **web service endpoint**. We saw that the EJB specification enables us to use the now familiar EJB component model to create web services. This example also demonstrated how to use dynamic proxies to call a web service without having to generate stubs at build time.

In the next section, we'll learn how to create a web service that maintains state. In the process, we'll learn about the **JAX-RPC service endpoint model**, and how to use the **dynamic invocation interface** (DII) to call web services in an even more dynamic way.

Implementing a Stateful Web Service

In the *EJB Fundamentals* chapter, we demonstrated the concept of stateful session beans by creating a simple calculator whose session bean remembers a running total. In this section we're going to modify the calculator example by implementing it as a web service instead of a session bean.

Can Web Services Be Stateful?

Web service *can* be stateful, but some application developers would argue that web services should not be stateful. Often, the rationale for this argument is that state is stored for a given user's session, and that there is currently no standard, interoperable way of associating SOAP messages with a particular session.

With that caveat in mind, we're going to go ahead and demonstrate the ability to create a stateful web service using JAX-RPC. In the process, we're going to introduce the **JAX-RPC service endpoint model**, which enables that functionality.

The JAX-RPC Service Endpoint Model

As discussed previously in this book, Java servlets and EJBs have lifecycles. As you know, Java applets have lifecycles as well. Each of these Java components, for example, is notified by their respective containers when they are first created. Web services enabled by JAX-RPC also have a lifecycle, known as a **service lifecycle**. This **service lifecycle** is a feature of the **JAX-RPC service endpoint model**.

The current version of the JAX-RPC service endpoint model is underpinned by Java servlets. The underlying servlet layer provides facilities needed by the service endpoint model, for example, lifecycle method invocations and access to the HTTP session. The JAX-RPC service endpoint model has two major features:

❑   A **service lifecycle**, which consists of two methods: init() and destroy().

❑   A servlet **endpoint context**, which exposes to the web service the context in which it is operating.

Both of these features are defined by interfaces in the javax.xml.rpc.server package. Let's explore these a bit.

The Service Lifecycle

A JAX-RPC web service may implement the ServiceLifecycle interface, which defines two methods that are called by the JAX-RPC runtime system at different points in the web service's lifecycle:

❑   When the web service endpoint is instantiated, the init() method will be called. As with the Java servlet lifecycle, implementing the init() method gives the web service an opportunity to initialize itself and connect to resources. Passed into this method is an object that represents the **endpoint context**, which will be discussed shortly.

❑   When the JAX-RPC runtime system decides that the web service endpoint is no longer required, it calls the destroy() method of the web service. As with the Java servlet lifecycle, implementing the destroy() method gives the web service an opportunity to release resources.

The Endpoint Context

When the init() method of a web service endpoint is called, a java.lang.Object is passed in that exposes the context in which it is operating. In a JAX-RPC implementation that is enabled by Java servlets, this object implements the ServletEndpointContext interface. According to the API documentation for the ServletEndpointContext interface, the JAX-RPC runtime system is required to provide appropriate session, message context, servlet context, and user principal information per method invocation on the endpoint class. The web service can use this object to do things such as:

❑   Get a reference to the ServletContext object. This is accomplished by calling the getServletContext() method, which we have already discussed back in Chapter 5.

❑   Find out about the user that is calling the web service. This can be performed by calling the getUserPrincipal() method. This returns an object that implements the java.security.Prinicipal interface. Please consult the J2EE API documentation for information on this interface.

❑   Get a reference to the HttpSession object, which was discussed when we covered servlets in Chapter 5. This object can be accessed via the getHttpSession() method. We'll use the HttpSession object in the upcoming stateful calculator example to maintain the state of a web service session.

526

Try It Out Creating a Stateful Web Service

This example, similar to the calculator example in the Chapter 8, mimics some very simple operations on a calculator: adding, subtracting, and keeping a running total. To keep the running total we'll use features of the JAX-RPC service endpoint model that we just finished discussing. This example will also show how to use the third model that we discussed in the Web Services and JAX-RPC chapter of invoking a web service, known as **Dynamic Invocation Interface** (**DII**). Like dynamic proxy, this model does not use generated stubs. We'll also demonstrate the ability of JAX-RPC to carry exceptions thrown from the web service to the client. Let's build and run the calculator web service example, and then we'll walk through the code.

You can use a subset of the process defined in the previous chapter to build and run this example. The *Building the web service stubs classes* step is omitted because we're not generating stubs at build time. Also, the separate *Compiling the client* step will be combined with Step 1. This is due to the fact that there are no stub classes for the client class to be dependent upon. Here are the steps that we'll use to build this example:

❑   Compile the Java source files.

❑   Create the WSDL file with the `wscompile` command line tool.

❑   Start the J2EE Server and create the J2EE EAR file with the Deployment Tool.

❑   Create the WAR file and configure the web service with the Deployment Tool.

❑   Run the Verifier Tool.

❑   Deploy the web service.

❑   Run the web service client.

The Java source and XML files are organized in the following directory structure. Their listings appear in the text of this example. They also may be downloaded from the Apress web site for your convenience:

1. To compile these Java files, set the `classpath` to:

   ❏ The current directory, and

   ❏ The `j2ee.jar` file that is in the `lib` directory of the Java 2 SDK, Enterprise Edition 1.4 (J2EE SDK 1.4) installation.

   ❏ In addition, we'll put the `jaxrpc-impl.jar` file on the `classpath` that is in the `lib` directory of the J2EE SDK 1.4 installation.

   For example, on a default J2EE SDK 1.4 Windows installation, the `classpath` would be set correctly by using the following command:

   ```
   > set classpath=.;%J2EE_HOME%\lib\j2ee.jar;%J2EE_HOME%\lib\jaxrpc-impl.jar
   ```

2. With the directory that the client and webservices directories are rooted in (this explanation has used `CalculatorServiceApp`) as the current directory, execute the following commands from the command prompt:

   ```
   > javac -d . webservices/*.java
   > javac -d . client/*.java
   ```

   The Java class files should end up in the same directories as the source files.

3. Next we need to create the WSDL file. Here is the `service-config.xml` file that you'll use as input to the `wscompile`:

   ```
   <?xml version="1.0" encoding="UTF-8"?>
   <configuration
       xmlns="http://java.sun.com/xml/ns/jax-rpc/ri/config">
       <service
           name="CalculatorService"
           targetNamespace="urn:calculatorService"
           typeNamespace="urn:calculatorService"
           packageName="webservices">
           <interface name="webservices.CalculatorServiceIF"/>
       </service>
   </configuration>
   ```

   With the current directory set as indicated above, type the following command:

   ```
   > wscompile -define -nd . -classpath . service-config.xml
   ```

4. Time to create the application! Start the J2EE server and the Deployment Tool. When creating the application EAR file (from the File | New | Application menu item), name it CalculatorServiceApp.

5. So, the next step is to create the WAR file and configure the service. Here are the contents of the `mapping.xml` that you'll use in this step:

```
<?xml version="1.0" encoding="UTF-8"?>
<java-wsdl-mapping xmlns="http://java.sun.com/xml/ns/j2ee"
    xmlns:xsi="http://www.w3.org/2001/XMLSchema-instance"
    xsi:schemaLocation="http://java.sun.com/xml/ns/j2ee
        http://www.ibm.com/webservices/xsd/j2ee_jaxrpc_mapping_1_1.xsd"
    version="1.1">
    <package-mapping>
        <package-type>webservices</package-type>
        <namespaceURI>urn:calculatorService</namespaceURI>
    </package-mapping>
</java-wsdl-mapping>
```

6. Start the New Web Application Wizard by choosing the File | New | Web Component menu item. In the WAR File page of the New Web Application Wizard, enter CalculatorServiceWar as the WAR Name. Click the Edit button.

7. In the Available Files panel of the Edit Contents of CalculatorServiceWar dialog box, navigate to the base directory of this CalculatorServiceApp example. Choose the following files and click the Add button:

❑ The **service definition interface** (`CalculatorServiceIF.class`).

❑ The web service implementation class (`CalculatorServiceImpl.class`).

❑ The WSDL file (`CalculatorService.wsdl`).

❑ The J2EE JAX-RPC mapping file (`mapping.xml`).

8. In the Choose Component Type page of the New Web Application Wizard, indicate that we want it to be a Web Services Endpoint.

9. In the Choose Service page of the New Web Application Wizard you'll supply these four pieces of information:

❑ The name of the WSDL File: `CalculatorService.wsdl`

❑ The name of the Mapping File: `mapping.xml`

❑ The Service Name: CalculatorService

❑ The Service Display Name: CalculatorService

10. In the Component General Properties page of the New Web Application Wizard:

❑ Choose webservices.CalculatorServiceImpl from the Service Endpoint Implementation drop-down.

❑ Verify that CalculatorServiceImpl is entered in the Web Component Name and Web Component Display Name fields.

❑ Verify that Load at any time is selected in the Startup load sequence position drop-down list.

11. In the Web Service Endpoint page of the New Web Application Wizard, do the following:

❑ Choose webservices.CalculatorServiceIF from the Service Endpoint Interface drop-down list.

❑ In the WSDL Port Namespace and Local Part fields, enter urn:calculatorService and CalculatorServiceIFPort, respectively.

❑ Enter CalculatorServiceIF in the Port Component Name and Port Component Display Name fields.

❑ Let the Endpoint Address field default. We'll change it later.

12. After finishing the wizard, select CalculatorServiceApp from the tree in the panel on the left, and select the Web Context tab in the panel on the right. In the Context Root column of the Web Context tab, enter calc-jaxrpc beside the CalculatorServiceWar entry.

13. Now we're going to create an alias that will be part of our web service's URL. Select the CalculatorServiceImpl node in the left panel, and select the Aliases tab. Click the Add button and assign an alias of /calc.

14. With the CalculatorServiceImpl node in the left panel still selected, click the Endpoint tab. Select the endpoint named calc from the Endpoint Address drop-down.

15. Save, verify, and deploy the web service. Leave the Return Client Jar option unchecked.

16. We need several files on the classpath, so set the following classpath on the command line. By the way, this is in a command file in the Apress download for this chapter to save you the trouble of typing it in:

```
> set CLASSPATH=.;%J2EE_HOME%\lib\j2ee.jar; ->
%J2EE_HOME%\lib\jaxrpc-impl.jar; ->
%J2EE_HOME%\lib\xsdlib.jar; ->
%J2EE_HOME%\lib\saaj-impl.jar; ->
%J2EE_HOME%\lib\commons-logging.jar; ->
%J2EE_HOME%\lib\endorsed\xercesImpl.jar; ->
%J2EE_HOME%\lib\endorsed\dom.jar
```

17. Finally, we need to run the client. Use the following command to run the client:

```
> java client.CalculatorServiceClient
```

To operate the calculator GUI, shown here, type a number into the textbox, press the = button, then enter a second number, select an operation (+ or −) from the drop-down, and click the = button. The running total will be displayed beside the Calculator value label. This calculator is no "Deep Thought" computer, but it did give me the answer 42 as a result of subtracting 58 from 100.

To demonstrate the ability to throw exceptions from the web service back to the client, an exception will be thrown and displayed in a dialog if the answer is a negative value, as shown below.

Also, you might want to start up a second calculator client to show that the state of the running total is kept by the web service for each calculator.

How It Works

To see how this example works, we'll first look at the Java source code for the web service interface, `CalculatorServiceIF.java`:

```java
package webservices;

import java.rmi.Remote;
import java.rmi.RemoteException;

public interface CalculatorServiceIF extends Remote {
  // the service methods
  public void clearIt() throws RemoteException;
  public void calculate(String operation, int value)
    throws Exception, RemoteException;
  public int getValue() throws RemoteException;
}
```

The web service interface defines three methods that are implemented by the web service implementation, `CalculatorServiceImpl.java`:

```java
package webservices;

import javax.servlet.http.HttpSession;
import javax.xml.rpc.ServiceException;
import javax.xml.rpc.server.ServiceLifecycle;
import javax.xml.rpc.server.ServletEndpointContext;

public class CalculatorServiceImpl
  implements CalculatorServiceIF, ServiceLifecycle {

  private ServletEndpointContext _endpointContext = null;

  // service lifecycle methods
  public void init(Object context) throws ServiceException {
    _endpointContext = (ServletEndpointContext) context;
  }
```

```java
  public void destroy() { System.out.println("destroying"); }
  // the service business method implementations
  public void clearIt() {
    HttpSession session = _endpointContext.getHttpSession();
    session.setAttribute("balance", new Integer(0));
  }

  public void calculate(String operation, int value)
    throws Exception {
    // get the balance
    HttpSession session = _endpointContext.getHttpSession();
    Integer val = pluckValue();
    int bal = val.intValue();

    // if "+", add it
    if (operation.equals("+")) {
      bal = bal + value;
      session.setAttribute("balance", new Integer(bal));
      return;
    }

    // if "-", subtract it
    if (operation.equals("-")) {
      bal = bal - value;
      if (bal < 0) {
        throw new Exception("Balance less than 0");
      }
      session.setAttribute("balance", new Integer(bal));
      return;
    }

    // if not "+" or "-", it is not a valid operation
    throw new Exception("Invalid Operation");
  }

  public int getValue() {
    return pluckValue().intValue();
  }

  private Integer pluckValue() {
    HttpSession session = _endpointContext.getHttpSession();
    Integer val = (Integer) session.getAttribute("balance");
    if (val == null) {
      val = new Integer(0);
    }
    return val;
  }
}
```

Service Lifecycle and Endpoint Context

Before discussing the three methods that implement the `CalculatorServiceIF` interface, we're going to look at the code that pertains to the **JAX-RPC service endpoint model** discussed above. Recall that this model defines two methods in its **service lifecycle** that need to be implemented when the web service implements the `ServiceLifecycle` interface as this one does.

The first of these methods is the `init()` method. In this implementation we cast the **endpoint context** reference to a `ServletEndpointContext` and tuck it away into this web service's only instance variable:

```
public void init(Object context) throws ServiceException {
  _endpointContext = (ServletEndpointContext) context;
}
```

We'll use this **endpoint context** later to access the `HTTPSession` object in which we'll maintain the calculator's running total. Note that this method can throw a `ServiceException`, which is in the `javax.xml.rpc` package, if it has any problems initializing.

The other **service lifecycle** method is `destroy()`, in which we supply a nearly empty implementation. If we had, for example, connected to resources in the `init()` method that needed to be released, the `destroy()` method would have been an appropriate place to do that. An example resource would be a JDBC connection to a database.

The Implementation of the Calculator Web Service Interface Methods

The three methods of this web service that are defined in the `CalculatorServiceIF` interface, therefore having the ability to be called from the calculator client, are `clearIt()`, `calculate()` and `getValue()`.

The `clearIt()` method clears the running total by setting it to the value of 0, as seen in the code below. It does so by getting a reference to the `HttpSession` object from the `ServletEndpointContext` instance that was supplied to the `init()` method earlier. It then sets a session attribute, arbitrarily named `balance`, to the value of 0. Recall that session attributes must be objects, which is why we're using the `Integer` wrapper class.

```
HttpSession session = _endpointContext.getHttpSession();
session.setAttribute("balance", new Integer(0));
```

The `calculate()` method takes two arguments, performs a calculation, and stores the result in the session. The two arguments are:

❏ An operator (either "+" or "–")

❏ The value to be added or subtracted from the running total

This `calculate()` method uses the `private` method named `pluckValue()` to get the running total from the session, returning 0 if it didn't exist, as shown below:

```
private Integer pluckValue() {
   HttpSession session = _endpointContext.getHttpSession();
   Integer val = (Integer) session.getAttribute("balance");
   if (val == null) {
      val = new Integer(0);
   }
   return val;
}
```

If the result of a subtract operation causes the running total to be negative, an `Exception` is thrown, which is propagated to the client via the JAX-RPC runtime and SOAP:

```
if (operation.equals("-")) {
   bal = bal − value;
   if (bal < 0) {
      throw new Exception("Balance less than 0");
   }
   session.setAttribute("balance", new Integer(bal));
   return;
}
```

The `getValue()` method uses the `pluckValue()` method to supply the client with the current running total. For the client's convenience it converts the wrapped value stored in the session to a primitive type, as shown here:

```
public int getValue() {
   return pluckValue().intValue();
}
```

The Dynamic Invocation Interface (DII)

The client for this example calls the methods of the web service in a completely dynamic way. To demonstrate this, here is the Java source code for the client, `CalculatorServiceClient.java`:

```
package client;

import java.rmi.ServerException;
import javax.xml.namespace.QName;
import javax.xml.rpc.Call;
import javax.xml.rpc.ParameterMode;
import javax.xml.rpc.Service;
import javax.xml.rpc.ServiceFactory;

// general imports
import java.awt.*;
import java.awt.event.*;
import javax.swing.*;

public class CalculatorServiceClient extends JFrame
   implements ActionListener {
```

```
private JButton _clear = new JButton("Clear");
private JButton _equals = new JButton("=");
private JTextField _topNumber = new JTextField("0");
private JTextField _bottomNumber = new JTextField("0");
private JComboBox _operator = new JComboBox();
private Call _call;

public CalculatorServiceClient() {
  // get the Call
  try {
    _call = this.getCall();
  }
  catch (Exception e) {
    e.printStackTrace();
  }

  // add the title
  JLabel title = new JLabel("My Simple Calculator");
  title.setHorizontalAlignment(JLabel.CENTER);
  getContentPane().add(title, BorderLayout.NORTH);

  // add the calculation panel
  JPanel calcPanel = new JPanel(new GridLayout(2, 2));
  calcPanel.add(new JLabel("Calculator value"));
  _topNumber.setEditable(false);
  calcPanel.add(_topNumber);
  _operator.addItem("+");
  _operator.addItem("-");
  calcPanel.add(_operator);
  calcPanel.add(_bottomNumber);
  getContentPane().add(calcPanel, BorderLayout.CENTER);

  // add the buttons
  JPanel buttonPanel = new JPanel(new GridLayout(2, 1));
  _equals.addActionListener(this);
  buttonPanel.add(_equals);
  _clear.addActionListener(this);
  buttonPanel.add(_clear);
  getContentPane().add(buttonPanel, BorderLayout.SOUTH);
  addWindowListener(new WindowAdapter() {
    public void windowClosing(WindowEvent e) {
      System.exit(0);
    }
  });

  setSize(300, 150);
  setVisible(true);
}

public void actionPerformed(ActionEvent ae) {
  // if equals was clicked, run the calculation
  if (ae.getSource() == _equals) {
    runCalculator();
  }
```

```
      // if clear was clicked, clear the calculator
      if (ae.getSource() == _clear) {
        clearCalculator();
      }
   }

   private Call getCall() throws Exception {
      ServiceFactory factory = ServiceFactory.newInstance();
      Service service =
        factory.createService(new QName("CalculatorService"));
      Call call = service.createCall();
      call.setPortTypeName(new QName("CalculatorServiceIF"));
      call.setTargetEndpointAddress(
        "http://localhost:8080/calc-jaxrpc/calc");
      call.setProperty(Call.SOAPACTION_USE_PROPERTY,
        new Boolean(true));
      call.setProperty(Call.SOAPACTION_URI_PROPERTY, "");
      call.setProperty("javax.xml.rpc.encodingstyle.namespace.uri",
        "http://schemas.xmlsoap.org/soap/encoding/");
      call.setProperty(Call.SESSION_MAINTAIN_PROPERTY,
        new Boolean(true));
      return call;
   }

   private void runCalculator() {
      try {
        // get the bottom value to be added to the calculator
        int operVal = 0;
        String textVal = _bottomNumber.getText();
        if (textVal != null) {
          try {
            operVal = Integer.parseInt(textVal);
          }
          catch (NumberFormatException nfe) { }
        }

        // get the operator
        String oper = (String) _operator.getSelectedItem();

        // invoke the service to calculate the new value
        Object[] calcParms =
          new Object[] { oper, new Integer(operVal) };
        _call.removeAllParameters();
        _call.setReturnType(null);
        _call.setOperationName(new QName("urn:calculatorService",
                                         "calculate"));
        _call.addParameter("String_1",
          new QName("http://www.w3.org/2001/XMLSchema", "string"),
          ParameterMode.IN);
        _call.addParameter("int_2",
            new QName("http://www.w3.org/2001/XMLSchema", "int"),
                      ParameterMode.IN);
        Object ret = _call.invoke(calcParms);

        // invoke the service to display the new value
        Object[] getParms = new Object[0];
```

```
        _call.removeAllParameters();
        _call.setOperationName(new QName("urn:calculatorService",
                                        "getValue"));
        _call.setReturnType(
          new QName("http://www.w3.org/2001/XMLSchema", "int"));
        Integer getRet = (Integer) _call.invoke(getParms);
        _topNumber.setText(getRet.toString());
      }
      catch (ServerException se) {
        JOptionPane.showMessageDialog(this, se.getMessage());
      }
      catch (Exception e) {
        e.printStackTrace();
      }
    }

    private void clearCalculator() {
      try {
        // invoke the service to clear it out
        Object[] parms = new Object[0];
        _call.removeAllParameters();
        _call.setReturnType(null);
        _call.setOperationName(new QName("urn:calculatorService",
                                        "clearIt"));
        Object ret = _call.invoke(parms);
        _topNumber.setText("0");
        _bottomNumber.setText("0");
        _operator.setSelectedIndex(0);
      }
      catch (Exception e) {
        e.printStackTrace();
      }
    }

    public static void main(String[] args) {
      CalculatorServiceClient calcClient =
        new CalculatorServiceClient();
    }
}
```

Using the **dynamic invocation interface** (**DII**), the client doesn't need **static stubs**. You may recall that the **dynamic proxy** example didn't need **static stubs** either. Unlike **dynamic proxy** however, when using the **DII** the client doesn't even need a web service interface. In fact, it is possible to create a generic web service user interface that dynamically configures its functionality based upon the WSDL document of the web service with which it happens to be interacting.

As its predecessor in Chapter 8, this calculator client is a Java Swing application with GUI components and event handler methods. The client needs to call methods of the web service, so it creates an object that implements the `Call` interface of the `javax.xml.rpc` package. We'll dynamically configure this `Call` object to be able to use our calculator web service. The code that creates the `Call` object and performs this configuration is in our `getCall()` method which is called from the constructor, and progressively shown below.

As with the dynamic proxy example earlier in this chapter, a `ServiceFactory` is created. This `ServiceFactory` instance is then used to create an object that implements the `Service` interface that represents our `CalculatorService`:

```
ServiceFactory factory = ServiceFactory.newInstance();
Service service =
   factory.createService(new QName("CalculatorService"));
```

Now we'll create the `Call` object by calling the `createCall()` method of the Service interface:

```
Call call = service.createCall();
```

To configure the `Call` object for our calculator web service, we'll use methods of the `Call` object itself. First, as seen below, we'll tell it the name of the port type from the WSDL document:

```
call.setPortTypeName(new QName("CalculatorServiceIF"));
```

Next, we'll give the `Call` object the **web service endpoint** on which it will invoke methods.

```
call.setTargetEndpointAddress(
   "http://localhost:8080/calc-jaxrpc/calc");
```

The `Call` interface defines several constants, including the ones seen below, that can be used as properties. We'll set some properties of the `Call` object that specify that we'll be using SOAP and that provide some configuration. If you create a client that uses DII, you can use the following statements "as is":

```
call.setProperty(Call.SOAPACTION_USE_PROPERTY,
   new Boolean(true));
call.setProperty(Call.SOAPACTION_URI_PROPERTY, "");
call.setProperty("javax.xml.rpc.encodingstyle.namespace.uri",
    "http://schemas.xmlsoap.org/soap/encoding/");
```

Finally, as seen below, we'll tell the `Call` object that we want the client and the web service to maintain a session. This is very important in our case because as discussed previously, the calculator web service uses the `HttpSession` object associated with that session to store the running total on behalf of the client.

```
call.setProperty(Call.SESSION_MAINTAIN_PROPERTY,
   new Boolean(true));
return call;
```

Please note that the **static stubs** model provides for specifying that a session be maintained as well: you can call the _setProperty() method of the Stub interface to configure the Stub object, and one of the properties is Stub.SESSION_MAINTAIN_PROPERTY.

Using DII to Invoke Methods

Now that the Call object knows about the calculator web service, we'll begin invoking the web service's methods. When the "=" button is clicked on the calculator GUI client, two things are passed to the calculate() method of the calculator web service: The operator (either "+" or "–"), and the value to be added or subtracted from the running total. Because we don't have the benefit of a web service interface, we need to tell the Call object about the method that it is about to invoke. This is a very similar programming model to invoking methods using Java reflection. Let's progressively walk through some statements from the client's runCalculator() method that demonstrate this:

First, a java.lang.Object array is loaded with the arguments that will be passed into the calculate() method of the web service. Note that before the code snippet below is executed, the oper variable contains a String that represents the operation, and the operVal variable is an int that contains the value to be added or subtracted. The int must be wrapped in order to be able to live inside the Object array:

```
Object[] calcParms =
    new Object[] { oper, new Integer(operVal) };
```

Next, because we're going to reuse this Call object for invoking methods with different signatures, we'll do a little clean up: we'll remove the method parameters associated with the last method for which it was configured (if there was one).

```
_call.removeAllParameters();
```

Now we'll begin telling the Call object about the calculate() method of the calculator web service. The statement below says that it has no return type:

```
_call.setReturnType(null);
```

The following statement says that in the WSDL document, the namespace of the calculator web service is urn:calculatorService and the operation name is calculate:

```
_call.setOperationName(new QName("urn:calculatorService",
                                "calculate"));
```

539

Now we'll tell the Call object that the calculate() method has two parameters. The first one is a String, and the second one is an int. The parameter types are represented by the types in the XML Schema specification, whose namespace is the URI in the snippet below. Note: Although normal programming practices would dictate putting literals like some of the ones below into constants, we've not followed that practice here for the sake of clarity.

```
_call.addParameter("String_1",
    new QName("http://www.w3.org/2001/XMLSchema", "string"),
    ParameterMode.IN);
_call.addParameter("int_2",
        new QName("http://www.w3.org/2001/XMLSchema", "int"),
                    ParameterMode.IN);
```

To invoke the calculate() method, we'll pass the Object array that contains the arguments, which is referred to by the calcParms variable, into the invoke() method of the Call object:

```
Object ret = _call.invoke(calcParms);
```

Because our calculator web service maintains the running total, the client then calls the getValue() method of the web service to retrieve the running total and subsequently display it. The code below accomplishes this using the same techniques as we did to call the calculate() method.

```
Object[] getParms = new Object[0];
_call.removeAllParameters();
_call.setOperationName(new QName("urn:calculatorService",
                                    "getValue"));
_call.setReturnType(
    new QName("http://www.w3.org/2001/XMLSchema", "int"));
Integer getRet = (Integer) _call.invoke(getParms);
_topNumber.setText(getRet.toString());
```

When the user presses the Clear button, the clearIt() method of the calculator web service is called, which sets the running total to 0. Because the clearIt() method has no parameters and no return value, configuring the Call object is more concise than usual, as shown below:

```
Object[] parms = new Object[0];
_call.removeAllParameters();
_call.setReturnType(null);
_call.setOperationName(new QName("urn:calculatorService",
                                    "clearIt"));
Object ret = _call.invoke(parms);
```

As you can see, using the **dynamic invocation interface** is a little more work. It also can be harder to debug because the compiler can't help enforce that you're calling the web service interface methods correctly. DII can be invaluable, however, when coupled with Universal Description, Discovery, and Integration (UDDI) mentioned in the previous chapter. In that environment, web services are discovered dynamically, and often must be used without having a perfect understanding of their interfaces, therefore requiring dynamic invocation.

Summary

In this chapter, we continued covering some topics that are pertinent to web services in the context of J2EE:

- ❑ We demonstrated how to implement a session bean as a web service, giving it a **web service endpoint**. This provides the ability for a client written in virtually any language, running on most any platform, to be able to invoke the methods of EJBs.

- ❑ Two models that enable the client to dynamically deal with web services were explored: **dynamic proxies** and the **dynamic invocation interface** (**DII**). Both models allow flexibility by using a proxy created at run-time rather than a stub generated at build time. The DII model allows even more flexibility by not requiring a web service interface. Instead, it uses a model much like Java reflection to dynamically invoke web service methods at run-time.

- ❑ Covered also was the **JAX-RPC service endpoint model**, which defines a web service lifecycle and the ability for the web service to get in touch with its context. This enabled us to demonstrate a stateful web service, which was a modified version of the stateful session bean-based calculator from an earlier chapter.

Web services are a relatively new technology that has wide appeal in the Information Technology industry. It is far from being a mature technology, however, and we'll see much growth in the areas of development tools, deployment platforms, and web services-related standards. As this happens, developing mission-critical enterprise applications that utilize web services will become easier, to the point that the underlying web services infrastructure will become all but invisible to the developer. A great place to find out about developing standards surrounding web services is the World Wide Web Consortium (W3C) web site, which is http://www.w3.org. The W3C is the main policy-making body in the area of the Web, including web services.

Exercises

1. Write a stateless session bean that takes a word and returns it spelled backwards. Implement it as a web service, and use static stubs for the client.

2. Modify the previous exercise to use a dynamic proxy for the client.

3. Modify the previous exercise to use dynamic invocation interface (DII) for the client.

4. Write a stateful web service that takes one word at a time and appends it to the previous words received to make a sentence. Return the entire sentence each time a word is added.

Installing Tomcat

Although you can use the J2EE 1.4 server for all the examples in this book, there is another server you can use for the examples in the JSP and servlet chapters. To be correct, this other server is actually the same one used by the J2EE server for JSPs and servlets, but you can install it in a stand-alone mode so that you can run JSPs and servlets without a running a full J2EE server. This server is named Tomcat, and when running in this mode, it is referred to as **Tomcat stand-alone**.

Getting Tomcat

Tomcat is a part of the Apache Jakarta Project. Copies of Tomcat can be obtained from the Apache web site at http://jakarta.apache.org/tomcat/index.html.

For most of the JSP and servlet examples, you will be able to use either of two versions of Tomcat. At the time this was written, the stable version of Tomcat was version 4.1.29. The beta version was version 5.0.14. Which version of Tomcat you use depends on which features you need. Most of the JSP and servlet examples are based on the Servlet Specification 2.3 and JSP Specification 1.2; for these examples, you can use Tomcat 4.0 or any later version. However, a few of the JSP examples use features specified by the JSP Specification Version 2.0. For these examples, you must use Tomcat 5.0 or later. This is summarized below:

Servlet Version	JSP Version	Tomcat Version
2.3	1.2	4.0 or later
2.4	2.0	5.0 or later

After deciding which version you want to use, follow the links on the Tomcat web page to the directory that contains the Tomcat binaries. For Tomcat 4.1, this means clicking the Binaries link under Downloads on the left of the main Tomcat page, and then clicking the link for Tomcat 4.1.xx, where xx is the current stable version number. The download files for Tomcat 5 can be found in the same location.

It is, of course, possible that these locations might be changed by the time you read this. If so, you can still access the download directories using the links on the Apache Jakarta web site. Whenever possible, make sure to use a mirror site to download your files.

If you are installing to Windows, you should download either the .exe or .zip files for the version you want. If you are installing to Linux you can download a .tar.gz or a .zip file. Other Unix versions will use the .tar.gz file. Finally, for any platform, you can download the full source of Tomcat and compile it yourself.

Also, note that you will need a version of Java 2 for Tomcat. The Tomcat web page recommends using Java 2 version 1.4 JDK. Check the Tomcat web page for the requirements for using earlier versions of the JDK. Ensure you have an environment variable named JAVA_HOME that points to your JDK installation on your machine.

Binary Installation to Windows

The simplest installation for Windows is to download the .exe distribution. This is an installation program that handles all of the installation tasks for you. Simply double-click the .exe, and the installer will run. The installer runs as a wizard, and for the most part you can simply accept the default options at each step. The installer will extract and copy all the files to their correct locations, and configure the environment variables for you. It will also create Start menu shortcuts for starting and stopping the server.

If you downloaded the zipped distribution file, start by extracting the files in the .zip archive to a directory. One good choice would be to unzip the files using the default directory name, jakarta-tomcat-4.1.xx, into the same location as your Java Standard and Enterprise development kit directories. For example, you might have the following directory structure in the root of your C: drive:

After unzipping the files, you will need to set the environment variables yourself. You need to create an environment variable named CATALINA_HOME which will point to the location of Tomcat. For example, if you installed Tomcat to the default directory as suggested, you would set CATALINA_HOME to C:\jakarta-tomcat-4.1.29. In Win 9x and WinME, you will do this through the autoexec.bat file. For WinNT and Win2000 this is done on the System dialog, which you can access via Start | Settings | Control Panel and choosing the System option. Then, select the Advanced tab, and click the Environment Variables button. Installing Tomcat this way does not create Start menu shortcuts, but you can access the startup.bat and shutdown.bat files for starting and stopping the server in the Tomcat /bin directory.

One other thing you need to do for Win 9x and WinME is to ensure there is enough environment memory. Navigate to the Tomcat /bin directory and right-click the startup.bat and shutdown.bat files, select Properties, then select the Memory tab, and finally, set the Initial Environment to 4096.

Binary Installation to Linux/Unix

If you downloaded the .tar.gz or .zip distribution file, start by creating a directory for the installation and extracting the files to that directory.

If you are using an RPM for Linux, create an installation directory and copy the RPM to that directory. The RPM can be installed using the rpm program with the name of the .rpm file. For example, to install Tomcat 4.1.29, the command would be:

```
> rpm—iv tomcat4-4.1.29-full.1jpp.noarch.rpm
```

After installing the files, you will need to set an environment variable. The variable is named CATALINA_HOME and it will point to the location of Tomcat. For example, if you installed Tomcat to /usr/local/tomcat you would set the variable with this command in the bash shell:

```
> CATALINA_HOME=/usr/local/tomcat
> export CATALINA_HOME
```

If you are using a different shell, use the command that is appropriate for that shell. The scripts for starting and stopping the server are in the Tomcat /bin directory.

Source Installation

You can install and compile the source files of Tomcat if you are so inclined. However, this is not really necessary if all you want to do is use Tomcat as a server for JSPs and servlets. Since this book is about developing web applications, and not developing servers, we will not cover the steps in building a Tomcat server from sources. If you would like to explore this option, there are detailed instructions for Tomcat 4.1.x at http://jakarta.apache.org/tomcat/tomcat-4.1-doc/BUILDING.txt and for Tomcat 5.0.x at http://jakarta.apache.org/tomcat/tomcat-5.0-doc/building.html.

Running Tomcat

After installing Tomcat, start the server using the Start menu, batch file, or script file for your system. When the server is running, you can open a browser to the Tomcat web page at http://localhost:8080. If the Tomcat installation is successful, you should see a web page like this:

For the most part, if you follow these directions, you should have no problems installing Tomcat. If you do encounter any problems though, check your Java installation and ensure that the JAVA_HOME and CATALINA_HOME environment variables are set. If you are using Win 9x or WinME, ensure the environment memory space is set correctly as explained earlier. If that doesn't help, check the Tomcat web page at http://jakarta.apache.org/tomcat/index.html for documentation on installing and running Tomcat. This document contains additional troubleshooting steps that may help. You might also try one of the Tomcat mailing lists. At the time of publication, subscription information could be found here: http://jakarta.apache.org/site/mail2.html#Tomcat.

B

SQL and EJB-QL

The **Structured Query Language**, SQL, and the **Enterprise JavaBeans Query Language**, EJB-QL, are two techniques for accessing data that can be used in J2EE 1.4 programming. They are briefly introduced and summarized in this appendix.

SQL is relevant to data access techniques using JDBC, which was first introduced in Chapter 6, where we looked at several examples of how SQL code should be incorporated in your Java code. EJB-QL provides an alternative data access methodology specific to Enterprise JavaBeans, which were covered in Chapters 8 to 11, and more specifically entity EJBs, which were described in Chapter 9.

SQL

SQL, the Structured Query Language, is a standardized query language for retrieving or updating data held in a relational database management system. At the time of writing, the current version of SQL is SQL99, sometimes referred to as SQL3.

> *SQL is a topic that merits a book to itself. This appendix covers selected topics only. For a full introduction to SQL see* Instant SQL, *by Apress, ISBN: 1-86100-845-7.*

Many database management systems had proprietary methods of data retrieval and manipulation before SQL was disseminated, so database vendors provide somewhat variable support for SQL99. However, all the big name databases provide significant SQL99 support. It is important, nonetheless, that you check which aspects of SQL99 are supported by the database management system that you plan to use.

RDBMS products differ in how they handle *case*. Some products are case sensitive, for example in table names, whereas others are not. If there is any likelihood of you, or your client, wanting to transfer data to another product at a future date, it is a good idea to have a consistent naming scheme for tables, columns, and so on, in order that you don't end up with differing case in names in different parts of your code. That can cause problems, and much wasted time, when you switch products.

Similarly it is a good idea to adopt consistent use of case when writing SQL code. One convention, which you may recall from Chapter 6, is to use upper case for all SQL commands and lower case for table and column names. This style will be used in the code in this appendix. In addition, each clause of a SQL statement is expressed on a separate line, making the SQL code easier to read.

In practice, when working for a client, you will likely need to adopt the case convention in existing databases and code. When moving code from a non-case-sensitive RDBMS to a case-sensitive RDBMS be aware that code such as:

```
SELECT * FROM presidents
```

and:

```
SELECT * FROM Presidents
```

which will work identically in a non-case-sensitive RDBMS may cause difficult-to-diagnose problems in a case-sensitive RDBMS, depending on whether the table is named presidents or Presidents.

To understand the SQL approach to an RDBMS, we need to understand the objects and relationships that, conceptually, make up an RDBMS. A relational database provides a logical framework to allow the storage of pieces of data and the relational model includes a hierarchy of objects listed here:

- ❏ Clusters
- ❏ Catalogs
- ❏ Schemas
- ❏ Objects
- ❏ Columns
- ❏ Domain-defined data types and user-defined data types
- ❏ Rules and assertions

A **cluster**, as described in the SQL99 specification, broadly corresponds to an RDBMS product and is a named set of **catalogs** available in a SQL session. The SQL99 specification indicates that access permissions may be controlled at the cluster level, but some database vendors implement permissions only at the catalog level, which is described next, and at lower levels of the hierarchy.

A **catalog** is a uniquely named set of schemas. Some database products, for example Microsoft's SQL Server and Oracle, use the term **instance** to broadly correspond to a SQL99 catalog.

548

A **schema** is a uniquely named set of objects and data owned by an individual user.

Most usage of SQL takes place at the **object** level and below. Objects include tables, views, modules, and routines (such as stored procedures, which are used in Chapter 9).

SQL objects consist of one or, usually, more **columns**. A typical database table will consist of several columns, each of which contains, for each row, a piece of data of a particular **data type**. Data types may be domain-defined, which are standard SQL-recognized data types, or may be defined by a user, which are **user-defined data types**. Each piece of data in a column must comply with the constraints on its possible values imposed by the specified data type. Data types vary among vendors, but usually you will easily be able to identify a data type in any RDBMS, which corresponds to a SQL99 data type.

In the sections in this appendix, we will look primarily at how to use SQL to work with table objects, and to execute queries that select data from one or more columns in one or more tables. First, let's briefly look at the data types that are recognized in SQL99.

SQL Data Types

SQL data types are essentially **constraints** on the types of data that may be stored in a column and on *how* that data is actually stored in the RDBMS.

Careful consideration of what data types are appropriate is an important part of the analysis and design of a new database.

As with many aspects of RDBMS, the use of data types varies among RDBMS packages. Check the documentation to determine the precise rules.

String Data Types

String data is one of the most commonly used data types.

String data of fixed length is specified using the CHAR keyword. For example, to declare the last_name column as accepting text of exactly 20 characters in length we could write:

```
last_name CHAR(20)
```

Such declarations are used when creating columns for tables, as described in the next section. A CHAR declaration commonly is padded with spaces to the stated number of characters if the user-supplied string is shorter.

Commonly, a character string is declared to be of **variable length**. For example, to declare the last_name column as being a variable-length string up to 20 characters in length we could write:

```
last_name VARCHAR(20)
```

Some database packages use LONG, TEXT, or MEMO in place of VARCHAR. A VARCHAR is stored more efficiently than a CHAR in terms of disk space, but performance during sorts of VARCHAR data is likely to be slower. Some database systems don't allow indexes to be created on VARCHAR data types, which further impacts performance.

In addition, the NCHAR and NVARCHAR data types support multi-byte or Unicode characters.

All string data types, when referred to in SQL code, must be surrounded by paired apostrophes.

Numeric Data Types

At the risk of stating the obvious, numeric data types store numbers. Think carefully about the likely extreme values that may need to be stored when deciding among the list of data types listed here:

Data Type	Description
BIT	Single bit value, which can be 0 or 1
DECIMAL	Floating-point values with specified level of precision
FLOAT	Floating-point values
INT 4-	byte integer value
REAL	4-byte floating-point value
SMALLINT	2-byte integer value
TINYINT	1-byte integer value

Check your RDBMS documentation to confirm which data types it supports.

In addition, many RDBMS store a MONEY or CURRENCY data type.

Date and Time Data Types

Date and time data types vary between RDBMS. Likely types include DATE, DATETIME, and SMALLDATETIME.

Binary Data Types

Binary data types can be used to store data such as graphic images. Support may include BINARY, LONG RAW, RAW, and VARBINARY data types. Again, it's a good idea to check the documentation of your RDBMS to confirm allowable byte length.

Working with Tables

Creating and manipulating tables is a relatively infrequent but essential use of SQL, since typically a table will be created once and then used with unchanged structure over extended periods of time. Changes to table structure, assuming that the database design has been well thought out, will be rare.

Creating a Table

In SQL a table is created using the CREATE TABLE statement. The general format for a simple CREATE TABLE statement is:

```
CREATE TABLE tablename
(
 columnDefinitions
);
```

If we wanted to create a table called presidents with four columns, last_name, first_name, birth_date and gender, we would use code like this:

```
CREATE TABLE presidents
(
   last_name VARCHAR(20) NOT NULL,
   first_name VARCHAR(20) NOT NULL,
   birth_date DATETIME NOT NULL,
   gender VARCHAR(6)
);
```

The CREATE TABLE statement causes an RDBMS to create a new table. The code in parentheses defines the columns to be created in that table. For each column, we declare the column name (note the use of all lower case), its data type, and permitted number of characters, and then specify, for example, whether or not it is allowed to contain NULL values.

Specifying Default Values

In some circumstances, you may find it useful to specify a default value for a column. In our presidents table we might want to acknowledge the historical situation and allow for future possibilities by including a gender column in the presidents table, with a default value of Male. We could do that using code like the following:

```
CREATE TABLE presidents
(
   last_name VARCHAR(20) NOT NULL,
   first_name VARCHAR(20) NOT NULL,
   birth_date DATETIME NOT NULL,
   gender VARCHAR(6)DEFAULT 'Male'
);
```

A default value can also be specified for columns that are marked as not accepting NULL values:

```
gender VARCHAR(6) NOT NULL DEFAULT 'Male'
```

Updating the Structure of a Table

If we have designed our tables with enough careful thought, the need to alter the structure of a table should be an infrequent one. However, SQL provides an ALTER TABLE statement for such situations. If we wanted to add a death_date column to our presidents table, we could do so using the following code:

```
ALTER TABLE presidents
ADD death_date DATETIME
;
```

Be aware that RDBMS products differ significantly in what alterations in structure they will allow. To avoid difficulties at a later date, it is good practice to take more care when designing the table structure when the data store is created.

Similarly, if you had created a column for death_date, and later decided you wanted to delete it, then you could remove it using the following code:

```
ALTER TABLE presidents
DROP COLUMN death_date;
```

Deleting a column is not something you will do often, nor is it something to do lightly. If you don't have a backup then once you drop the column, it and all of its data is gone forever! So be careful...

If you feel that you really want to carry out substantial restructuring of a table, it may be more appropriate to create a new table and use the INSERT SELECT statement (not described in detail in this appendix) to copy data from the existing table, verify that the desired data has copied, rename the original table and then rename the new table to the name of the original table. You can expect to need to recreate any stored procedures, indexes, and so on.

Deleting Tables

Deleting or dropping a table is also not something to be done lightly. The SQL syntax to drop our presidents table would look like this:

```
DROP TABLE presidents;
```

When you execute this statement, you probably won't see any confirmation dialogs, nor is there any way to undo the statement. Executing this statement will permanently remove the table and all of its data.

Handling Null Values

In a relational database, a value in a particular field (the intersection of a row and column) may contain a NULL value. A NULL value signifies an absent or unknown value. A NULL is *not* the same as an empty string, a sequence of space characters, or a value containing numeric zero.

When a column is created it can be specified as allowing or disallowing NULL values. In a table called presidents, we might want to specify that the death_date column is allowed to contain a NULL value (the default situation), since not all US presidents will have died at any selected time. On the other hand, we would likely want to specify that a last_name column and a first_name column are not allowed to contain NULL values (they should always contain data for each row in the database). We could achieve both desired constraints using the following code:

```
CREATE TABLE presidents
(
    last_name VARCHAR(20) NOT NULL,
    first_name VARCHAR(20) NOT NULL,
    birth_date DATETIME NOT NULL,
    death_date DATETIME
);
```

Let's move on to examine how we can use SQL to query existing tables and, later, to update data contained in such tables.

Selecting Data from Tables

Querying data in an existing table is likely to be the most common SQL task that you will carry out. Such SQL queries are based on the SELECT statement.

The simplest form of the SELECT statement is shown here:

```
SELECT * FROM presidents;
```

This selects all columns from the presidents table, as indicated by the * wildcard. Since there is no WHERE clause, all rows contained in the presidents table are retrieved.

If, as is more usual, you wish to retrieve selected columns from the presidents table, you use what is known as a *projection*. You simply replace the * wildcard by a comma-separated list of the columns you want to retrieve. Specifying selected columns is also likely to be a more efficient query than using the * wildcard. If you wanted to retrieve the last_name and first_name columns of the presidents table, you could do so using the following code:

```
SELECT last_name, first_name FROM presidents;
```

Filtering Data in Queries

In practice, it is unlikely that you will want to retrieve all rows from a table. In SQL, you can filter out unwanted rows by specifying those rows you do want to see using a WHERE clause in conjunction with a SELECT statement. For example, if we wanted to retrieve the rows that contained data concerning presidents Theodore Roosevelt and Franklin Roosevelt, we could use the following SQL:

```
SELECT * FROM presidents
WHERE last_name='Roosevelt'
;
```

The * wildcard signifies that all columns are retrieved from each row of the presidents table. The WHERE clause filters the results so that only those rows containing the value Roosevelt in the last_name column are retrieved.

The WHERE clause can use a number of operators in filtering data in addition to the = operator used in the preceding example. The following table shows the operators which can be used in a WHERE clause:

Operator	Description
=	Exact equality
<>	Inequality
!=	Inequality
<	Less than
<=	Less than or equal to
!<	Not less than
>	Greater than
>=	Greater than or equal to
!>	Not greater than
BETWEEN	Between two stated values (inclusive)
IS NULL	A NULL value

You will most probably have noticed that there is some duplication in the available operators. For example, we can use the !> or <= operators to signify that values less than or equal to a specified value are to be included. As you may have guessed, this is another area where vendors may differ in which SQL syntax they support. Again, you will want to check the RDBMS documentation carefully.

If you wanted to select information about all US presidents except the two presidents Roosevelt you could use the following code:

```
SELECT last_name, first_name
FROM presidents
WHERE last_name <> 'Roosevelt'
;
```

Since the content of the `last_name` column is character data, we need to use paired apostrophes to delimit the value used in the `WHERE` clause. If the string value itself contains an apostrophe, then that will need to be escaped. The escape character varies between RDBMSs—in SQL Server the apostrophe is used while in Oracle the backslash is used.

Similarly, if you wanted to retrieve information about presidents whose birth year was between 1800 and 1900 inclusive, you could use code like the following:

```
SELECT last_name, first_name
FROM presidents
WHERE birth_year BETWEEN 1800 AND 1900
;
```

In this case, the value contained in the `birth_year` column is numeric so no delimiters are need for the values to which the `BETWEEN` operator is applied. Notice the `AND` keyword which is used in a `WHERE` clause of this type.

Sorting Data from Queries

Rows of data retrieved by an SQL query cannot be assumed to be in any particular order. If you want to sort the rows of data in a particular way you must specify the criteria for ordering the data by using an `ORDER BY` clause in conjunction with a `SELECT` statement.

If we wanted to select all columns of information about all US presidents from the `presidents` table and order them by last name we could do so using the following code:

```
SELECT * FROM presidents
ORDER BY last_name
```

The `ORDER BY` clause can be used together with the `WHERE` clause. For example, if the year of appointment was stored in an `appointment_year` column, we could display the surname and first name with the year of appointment of all US presidents whose surname begins with the letter R or later using the following:

```
SELECT last_name, first_name, appointment_year FROM presidents
WHERE last_name>'R'
ORDER BY appointment_year;
```

If we want to sort the rows returned by a query by more than one criterion, we can do so by combining the two columns in the order needed. In this example, the rows are ordered alphabetically by last_name and then by the first_name:

```
SELECT last_name, first_name
FROM presidents
ORDER BY last_name, first_name;
```

Where there is more than one US president with the same last name (Adams, Roosevelt, Bush) the ordering would be strictly alphabetical.

Wildcards and Regular Expressions

In addition to using the comparison operators described earlier, SQL provides facilities to allow you to retrieve data based on text *patterns*, similar to the pattern matching you can carry out using the regular expression support in Java.

The LIKE keyword allows text pattern searches. The % pattern matches zero or more text characters. So, to retrieve data from the presidents table about presidents whose last name begins with the letter B you could use the following code:

```
SELECT last_name, first_name
FROM presidents
WHERE last_name LIKE 'B%'
;
```

Notice that the text pattern is contained in paired apostrophes. The pattern B% matches any text string which begins with the upper case B, and that contains zero or more other characters. Therefore when that pattern is used to match the last_name column, which contains presidential surnames, data on all presidents whose surname begins with B is retrieved.

If we wished not to retrieve data on President Buchanan, but only on those whose surname begins with the characters "Bus", we could refine the search like this:

```
SELECT last_name, first_name
FROM presidents
WHERE last_name LIKE 'Bus%'
;
```

Data on both presidents Bush would be retrieved.

The underscore character, _, can also be used in text patterns and matches exactly one character. So, if we used a pattern like that in the following code:

```
SELECT last_name, first_name
FROM presidents
WHERE last_name LIKE 'Bu__'
;
```

We would retrieve the surname Bush. If the USA had had a president John Bull, then data on that fictional president would also be retrieved, since the pattern `Bu__` matches any string that is exactly four characters long and begins with the characters Bu.

If you plan to use the `LIKE` keyword, then be aware that support for this keyword depends on the RDBMS package you use.

Some database management systems also explore fuller regular expression syntax, sometimes associated with the `LIKE` keyword, and sometimes, for example MySQL, using the `REGEXP` keyword.

If we wanted to retrieve data from a MySQL database on presidents whose surname begins with the letters K or R we could use the following SQL code:

```
SELECT last_name, first_name
FROM presidents
WHERE last_name REGEXP "^[KR]."
;
```

Notice the `REGEXP` keyword, and that the text pattern is, in MySQL at least, contained in paired double quotes. The ^ character at the beginning of the pattern indicates that the text pattern matches the beginning of the data and the square brackets indicate a **character class**. Any character in the character class that occurs at the beginning of the data in the column will match. The . metacharacter serves a similar function to the % character with the `LIKE` keyword. Regular expression support in your favorite database management system may not have the functionality that MySQL supports, or may use different metacharacters inside text patterns.

Calculated Fields

Many pieces of data are reported exactly as they are held in the data store. However, sometimes you will want to retrieve data that combines data from more than one column. SQL provides **calculated fields** to achieve that functionality. Calculated fields can be created by combining string or numeric values.

A **field** often means the same as a column, and does so in this case. Occasionally, in discussions of databases, you may meet the term field used to refer to the intersection of a particular row and column. That is not the usage in the term "calculated field".

For example, you might hold address data in separate columns but want to display a city, regional code, and postal code together in an address. SQL code to achieve that might look like the following:

```
SELECT city+ ', ' + regional_code + ', ' + postal_code
FROM address
;
```

The + operator in the SELECT statement concatenates the string values contained in the city, regional_code, and postal_code columns. Depending on the data type used to create the city, regional_code, and postal_code columns you may have to trim out space characters contained as padding in the named columns, using the SQL RTRIM() function:

```
SELECT RTRIM(city)+ ', ' + RTRIM(regional_code) + ', ' + RTRIM(postal_code)
FROM address
;
```

If you declared the columns to be of type VARCHAR, then there will be no padding space characters and the RTRIM() function will be unnecessary.

Calculated fields also allow us to perform simple mathematical calculations to produce calculated fields.

For example, you may want to display a product catalog with item price, tax rate, and tax rate information. In that case, you would want to use an **alias** for the calculated field. So, to fill the tax rate field we could use code like this:

```
SELECT product_name, product_code,
item_price, tax_rate,
item_price * tax_rate AS taxed_price
FROM product_catalog
WHERE status = 'current'
;
```

Notice the AS keyword in the SELECT clause. In the third line of the SQL code, the value of the item_price and tax_rate columns are multiplied together to produce a calculated field with the **alias** of taxed_price.

Most database management systems will support standard mathematical operations of addition, subtraction, multiplication, and division using the standard mathematical operators, +, −, *, and /. Of course, Java provides the syntax to carry out these and more complex calculations. The choice of whether you use SQL or Java to achieve any desired calculations will depend on your level of comfort with the two languages, as well as other factors.

SQL Functions

A number of functions can be used in SQL to manipulate character, numeric, or date/time data. In an earlier example, you saw the RTRIM() function, which can be used to remove padding space characters from character data columns of fixed width.

SQL functions can be used to extract part of a string (that is, a substring), to convert data types, return a number's ceiling, retrieve the current date, and so on. Unfortunately, the implementation and syntax of SQL functions varies greatly among database packages. If you are familiar with the corresponding Java functions, as you are likely to be if you are reading this book, it may well be more convenient to ignore the SQL functions in many situations where you are using JDBC. If you do decide to use SQL functions then be sure to carefully consult the documentation for the database management system in order to determine the appropriate syntax.

In practice, if you want your JDBC code to be portable, it is highly advisable to use the Java functions rather than the SQL functions. One exception to that general advice is SQL's aggregate functions, which are pretty uniformly supported by popular database management systems:

❑ AVG( )–Returns the arithmetic mean value of a column

❑ COUNT( )–Returns the number of rows which contain a value in a named column

❑ MAX( )–Returns the largest value in a column

❑ MIN( )–Returns the smallest value in a column

❑ SUM( )–Returns the sum of the values in a named column

These SQL aggregate functions avoid the need to retrieve, perhaps across a slow network, all rows in a table and perform the corresponding calculations in Java. The retrieval and calculation of data is likely to be much more efficiently carried out by the database management system.

If you wanted to find the highest priced product in a product catalog you might use code like the following:

```
SELECT MAX(product_price)
FROM product_catalog
WHERE status = 'current'
;
```

Many other retrieval techniques are possible in SQL but those mentioned in the preceding sections will give you a start in how to use SQL syntax.

Inserting New Rows into a Table

As well as retrieving data, SQL can be used to insert new values in a database.

The most straightforward technique to insert data into a table is to insert a complete new row. This is done using the INSERT statement.

For example, in late 2000, we might have needed to add information about the election of the second president Bush. If the row contained data in `last_name`, `first_name`, and `election_year` columns, we add the information using code like the following:

```
INSERT INTO presidents
(last_name, first_name, election_year)
VALUES ('Bush', 'George', 2000)
;
```

If we also wanted to store a middle name but weren't (at the time) aware of the newly elected president's middle name we would need, to avoid ambiguity, to use an explicit NULL value, and we could do that using the following code:

```
INSERT INTO presidents
(last_name, first_name, middle_name, election_year)
VALUES ('Bush', 'George', NULL, 2000)
;
```

In the two preceding examples, each column was named. If you are totally confident of the ordering of column names, you can omit the column names, using code like the following:

```
INSERT INTO presidents
VALUES ('Bush', 'George', NULL, 2000)
;
```

Of course, if you make even a slight error in the ordering of column data then an error will be generated unless all columns happen to have compatible data types. Omitting column names increases the likelihood of data values being swapped around.

If we need to correct a mistake in an existing row we need to use a different technique using the UPDATE statement.

Updating Data in Tables

When you use UPDATE statements, be very careful to include a WHERE clause, and also make sure that the WHERE clause is appropriately tightly defined. If you omit the WHERE clause, then every row in the chosen table will be updated in the way defined. For example:

```
UPDATE presidents
SET middle_name = 'Walker'
;
```

This code would assign the middle name "Walker" to every US president in the table, which is not what we intended to do! The existing data for middle name for all presidents, whether NULL or an actual value, would be overwritten. You have been warned! Mistakes of this type make you very glad that you have a recent backup of your valuable data. You do have a recent, full backup, don't you?

The WHERE clause is used to ensure that the UPDATE statement is appropriately applied. Thus, we could change the middle name of the president elected in 2000 using the following code:

```
UPDATE presidents
SET middle_name = 'Walker'
WHERE election_year = 2000
;
```

The preceding code makes the reasonable assumption that only one president was elected in the year 2000.

Deleting Data from a Table

We are unlikely to want to permanently delete information from our presidents table, because it is of historical interest. However, in an e-commerce setting, we might choose to delete information about obsolete products. To achieve that you would use the DELETE statement.

Be very, very careful not to omit the WHERE clause in a DELETE statement. Look at this example:

```
DELETE
FROM product_catalog
;
```

This code has potentially just deleted all the data in every row in your product_catalog table. If you don't have a very recent, usable backup, you may want to start writing your resignation letter...

Suppose we wanted to delete a product with product ID of ABC123, we could use the following code:

```
DELETE
FROM product_catalog
WHERE product_ID = 'ABC123'
;
```

The WHERE clause confines the deletion to the specified row in the table.

Joins

A **join** is the combining of results from more than one table in a query. This is a crucial technique for RDBMS systems for all but simple queries. Let's consider how this works by reviewing the basics of relationships in an RDBMS.

Relational database tables each have a primary key, which uniquely identifies each row in the table. Suppose you had several orders from one customer over a period of time. It would be inefficient and error-prone to enter customer address data into each order individually. If order data was held in an orders table, then the corresponding customer data would be held in a customers table. A mechanism is needed to express the fact that a particular customer in the customers table is the customer for a particular order in the orders table. If the customers table contains a customer_id column that is the table's primary key, then we can create a customer_id column in the orders table as a foreign key. This expresses the fact that a particular order is linked to a particular customer.

Let's assume that we want to retrieve all orders for a particular customer. We will assume that an order can be made up of only a single type of product, and that the orders table contains the following columns: order_id, product_id, product_quantity, customer_id, and order_date. To simplify, we will assume that the customers table consists of customer_id, customer_name, and customer_address columns. We can use a SELECT statement similar to the following:

```
SELECT order_id, product_id, product_quantity, order_date, customer_name,
       customer_address
FROM orders, customers
WHERE orders.customer_id='ABC123'
AND orders.customer_id = customers.customer_id
;
```

This will retrieve all orders for the customer who has the ID of 'ABC123'.

The SELECT statement is similar to several you have seen earlier in this appendix, but notice that some of the columns are in the orders table, and some columns (customer_name and customer_address) are in the customers table. This is indicated by the FROM clause which specifies both the orders and customers tables. We need to filter the retrieved rows, so we do that using a two part WHERE clause. The first part of the WHERE clause specifies that we want data on the customer whose customer_id is 'ABC123'. The second part specifies that all retrieved rows from the customers table must have a customer_id column equal to the customer_id column in the orders table. This uses notation which will be familiar to you—a . separates the name of the table object from the name of the column object:

```
orders.customer_id = customers.customers_id
```

So far so good, but suppose we also want to retrieve price data, which is held in a separate `prices` table. We need a join that retrieves data from three tables. The following code will achieve that:

```
SELECT order_id, product_id, product_price, product_quantity, order_date,
       customer_name, customer_address
FROM orders, customers, prices
WHERE orders.customer_id='ABC123'
AND orders.customer_id = customers.customer_id
AND orders.product_id = prices.product_id
;
```

Notice the additional `AND` clause:

```
AND orders.product_id = prices.product_id
```

This clause expresses our desire to retrieve only products relevant to our query.

SQL allows us to construct joins from arbitrary numbers of tables.

EJB-QL

Enterprise JavaBean Query Language, EJB-QL, is a relatively new method of data access, having first been introduced in the EJB version 2.0 specification. In EJB version 1.1, vendors provided their own, non-standard query language for finder methods of entity EJBs, which meant that applications that used container-managed persistence had to be partly rewritten if they were moved from one vendor's EJB container to another.

The Enterprise JavaBeans query language, EJB-QL, is used to define data queries for entity EJBs in a portable way. EJB-QL is specified in the EJB specification (from EJB version 2.0 on), therefore all EJB 2.x implementations must conform to that specification. In that respect, EJB-QL offers better portability than SQL, which, as mentioned in the first part of this appendix, is implemented in significantly varying ways on different database management systems.

EJB-QL is a query specification language for the finder and setter methods of entity EJBs. EJB-QL is confined to queries against in-memory objects, and thus, differs from SQL in that EJB-QL cannot be used as a general purpose query against a database. Additionally, EJB-QL queries must be defined properly if container-managed persistence is to work correctly. Each EJB-QL query is specified in the `ejb-jar.xml` file, as will be described later in this section.

An EJB-QL query consists of the following:

❑ A `SELECT` clause which specifies the type or values of objects to be selected

❑ A `FROM` clause which specifies the domain (or table) from which objects are to be selected

❑ An optional `WHERE` clause which is used to filter the results returned by the query

❑ An optional `ORDER BY` clause which is used to sort the data returned by the query

If you have read through the section on SQL in this appendix, you will likely recognize the similarities of the syntax between some of the SQL you were introduced to and the syntax of EJB-QL.

A common form of an EJB-QL query is:

```
SELECT OBJECT(variable)
FROM abstractSchemaName [AS] variable
[WHERE value comparison value]
[ORDER BY ...]
```

To understand how EJB-QL works, let's think briefly about what an entity bean is.

An entity bean is a representation of data stored persistently in a database table. Data in an RDBMS is held in tables, and data in those tables can have relationships expressed using primary keys and foreign keys. Since entity beans represent data stored in database tables, it shouldn't be surprising that entity beans can similarly have corresponding relationships between them.

The relationships between entity EJBs are expressed in an XML deployment descriptor file. Typically, the EJB container will use the information in the deployment descriptor to create queries in a language such as SQL, which actually queries the data store.

The deployment descriptor file contains a `<relationships>` element for each entity enterprise bean which has relationships with other entity beans. Nested inside the tags of the `<relationships>` element are further elements which express where a particular piece of data is situated in the RDBMS (the `<cmp-field>` element is used for that when persistence is container-managed) and which express relationships among entity beans (the `<cmr-field>` element performs this function when persistence is container-managed).

An EJB-QL query references entity beans by their name in the appropriate abstract schema. The mapping of abstract schema names to an entity bean takes place in the `ejb-jar.xml` deployment descriptor file. Inside each `<entity>` element there will be an `<abstract-schema-name>` element that is used for that purpose:

```
<ejb-jar>
 <enterprise-beans>
  <entity>
   <ejb-name>MyPresidentsEntityBean</ejb-name>
   ...
    <abstract-schema-name>
     MyPresidentsSchema
    </abstract-schema-name>
     ....
    <query>
     <query-method>
      <method-name>findBySurname</method-name>
       <method-params>
        <method-param>java.lang.String</method-param>
       </method-params>
     </query-method>
     <ejb-ql>
```

```
                  <![CDATA[SELECT OBJECT(o) FROM MyPresidentsSchema AS o WHERE o=?1]]>
               </ejb-ql>
             </query>
            ...
       </entity>
      </enterprise-beans>
     ...
    </ejb-jar>
```

In addition, query methods for an EJB inside the same `<entity>` element are described using the `<query-method>`, `<method-name>`, `<method-params>`, and `<method-param>` elements. The preceding code corresponds to a finder method named `findBySurname`, which takes a single `java.lang.String` parameter.

As you have seen, the CDATA section in the `ejb-jar.xml` file contains the actual EJB-QL query:

```
<ejb-ql>
 <![CDATA[SELECT OBJECT(p) FROM MyPresidentsSchema AS p]]>
</ejb-ql>
```

The query is nested inside `<ejb-ql>` start and end tags. The CDATA section indicates to an XML processor that the content need not be well-formed XML, and is not to be processed as XML.

The EJB-QL query shown will return all rows from the database object that corresponds to the `MyPresidentsSchema` abstract schema.

The SELECT Clause

The SELECT clause may contain an **identification variable**, which requires an OBJECT operator. A SELECT clause must not use the OBJECT operator to qualify path expressions (discussed later).

The SELECT clause can be filtered using a WHERE clause. If we wished to retrieve data only for presidents whose surname is 'Bush' we could use the following EJB-QL query:

```
SELECT OBJECT(p)
FROM MyPresidentsSchema AS p
WHERE p.last_name = 'Bush'
```

Notice that the FROM clause associates the identifier variable p with the abstract schema name `MyPresidentsSchema`. The abstract schema name is specified in the deployment descriptor as you saw a little earlier.

The WHERE clause filters the query results so that only those results which match the supplied parameter are returned to the client.

Navigation Operator

In EJB-QL the **.** operator is termed the **navigation operator**, which is similar to how objects are navigated in Java itself. The **.** operator allows us to navigate paths which are expressed in **path expressions**.

Input Parameters

You may use input parameters in an EJB-QL query. The number of input parameters must not exceed the permitted number of parameters for the corresponding EJB finder method. An EJB-QL query need not make use of all the parameters permitted by a finder method.

Each input parameter is indicated by a preceding literal ?, followed by an integer value beginning at 1. In other words the first two input parameters are expressed as ?1 and ?2 respectively.

In an earlier EJB-QL example you just saw, a literal query could be constructed like this:

```
SELECT OBJECT(p)
FROM MyPresidentsSchema AS p
WHERE p.last_name = 'Bush'
```

Using an input parameter we can more flexibly construct the query as follows:

```
SELECT OBJECT(p)
FROM MyPresidentsSchema AS p
WHERE p.last_name = ?1
```

When an appropriate parameter is supplied, we can retrieve records for presidents with any specified surname.

Where there may be duplicate data, such as in the surnames of presidents we can use multiple parameters as appropriate. To retrieve data on the younger George Bush we could use the following query (assuming appropriate declaration of a second parameter in the deployment descriptor):

```
SELECT OBJECT(p)
FROM MyPresidentsSchema AS p
WHERE p.last_name = ?1 AND p.election_year=?2
```

Wildcards

You may use the LIKE keyword together with the % and _ characters as described under SQL earlier in this appendix. As a recap, the % character stands for zero or more characters and the _ character stands for any single character.

Functions

EJB-QL has string and numeric functions, which are listed below. All EJB 2.1-conformant EJB containers will support the following functions.

The string functions are:

❑ CONCAT(String, String)–Concatenates two strings and returns a String

❑ SUBSTRING(String, start, length)–Returns a String

❑ LOCATE(String, String [, start])–Returns an int

❑ LENGTH(String)–Returns an int

The numeric functions are:

❑ ABS(number)–Returns an int, float, or double of the same data type as the argument to the function

❑ SQRT(double)–Returns a double

❑ MOD(int, int)–Returns an int

Aggregate Functions

EJB-QL has the following aggregate functions: AVG(), SUM(), COUNT(), MAX(), and MIN(). The AVG() and SUM() functions must have a numeric argument. The other aggregate functions have an argument corresponding to the data type of the corresponding EJB field.

Values which contain NULL are eliminated before the aggregate functions are applied. The DISTINCT keyword can be used to eliminate duplicate values in conjunction with the EJB-QL aggregate functions.

Using Relationships

We can use EJB-QL to exploit relationships that are specified in the deployment descriptor.

Suppose we had an entity bean with abstract schema name ActsSchema, which contained information on all acts passed by the US Congress, and included information about which president was in office at the time. We could construct the following query:

```
SELECT OBJECT (p)
FROM MyPresidentsSchema AS p, IN (p.ActsSchema) AS a
WHERE a.president_surname = ?1
```

Notice the IN clause, which includes the syntax p.ActsSchema expressing that there is a relationship between the MyPresidentsSchema, identified by the identifier variable p and the abstract schema ActsSchema. Of course, if this is to work the necessary declarations for ActsSchema need to be present in the ejb-jar.xml deployment descriptor.

There is much more to EJB-QL than has been explained in this brief description. Further information on EJB-QL is contained in the EJB 2.1 specification, which can be downloaded from the Sun web site at http://java.sun.com/products/ejb/docs.html.

J2EE Glossary

Component

Definition: Essentially the building blocks of a J2EE application, components are specific software units, supported by a container, and configurable at deployment-time. The four types of components defined within J2EE are EJBs, web components, applets, and application clients.

Where used: In all J2EE applications.

Container

Definition: A software entity that provides services to components, including life cycle management, security, deployment, and runtime services. A container of a specific type of components, such as EJB, Web, JSP, servlet, applet, or application client, will provide the services its components need. For example, servlet containers will need to support HTTP as a protocol for requests and responses, while JSP containers need to provide the same services as servlet containers, plus an engine to interpret and process JSP pages into servlets.

Where used: In J2EE applications.

CORBA

Definition: Common Object Request Broker Architecture, CORBA, is a standard architecture for distributed object systems, a model specified by the Object Management Group. It allows a distributed, heterogeneous collection of objects to interoperate, regardless of platform or programming language.

Where used: In distributed object systems where language and platform-independence is critical.

Distributed Application

Definition: An application composed of a variety of components running in separate runtime environments, often on different platforms, and connected over a network. Distributed application types include two-tier (client-server), three-tier (client-middleware-server), and multi-tier or n-tier (client-multiple middleware-multiple servers).

Where used: Wherever different components of an application need to be connected to each other over a network.

Enterprise JavaBeans

Definition: A server-side component model for Java, a component architecture designed to enable developers to build and deploy scaleable, secure, multi-platform, business-critical applications that are object-oriented, reusable, and distributed. It allows the enterprise developer to focus on writing business logic without the need to write code that handles such tasks as transactional behavior, security, connection pooling, or threading, since the architecture delegates these tasks to the server vendor.

Where used: In distributed business applications that will operate on any server that provides the Enterprise JavaBeans APIs.

EJB Container

Definition: A container (see *Container*) for EJB components, providing a scaleable, secure, transactional environment in which enterprise beans can operate. It is the container that handles the object lifecycle, including creating and destroying an object as well as handling the state management of beans. When a bean is installed in a container, the container provides an implementation of the bean's EJBHome interface and the bean's remote interface. The container will also make the bean's EJBHome interface available in JNDI, the Java Naming and Directory Interface. An EJB container is provided by an EJB or J2EE server.

Where used: In any distributed application that uses EJBs.

EJB Server

Definition: A collection of services and resources needed to support an EJB installation. These services include management of distributed transactions, management of distributed objects and distributed invocations on these objects, as well as low-level system services. Since the J2EE architecture assumes that an EJB container is hosted by an EJB server from the same vendor, it does not specify the contract between these two entities. Each EJB server may host one or more EJB containers.

Where used: In distributed applications that employ one or more EJB containers.

Java 2 Enterprise Edition (J2EE)

Definition: A platform that creates an environment for developing and deploying multi-tiered web-based enterprise applications. It allows developers to create standardized, modular components, and provides those components with a complete set of services, application programming interfaces (APIs), and protocols that automatically handle many of the details of application behavior, without the need for complex programming. J2EE adds to the features of the Java 2 Platform, Standard Edition by including full support for EJB components, Java servlets API, JavaServer Pages, and XML.

Where used: In distributed transactional enterprise applications in which the developer needs to reduce the costs and time of development, and use the speed, security, and reliability of server-side technology.

Java IDL

Definition: The Java Interface Definition Language, IDL, is a technology for distributed objects, providing CORBA interoperability and connectivity capabilities for the J2EE platform. Similar to RMI (Remote Method Invocation), which supports distributed objects written entirely in the Java programming language, Java IDL enables objects to interact regardless of whether they're written in Java or another programming language. It uses CORBA's IDL to map Java to all other languages supported by CORBA.

Where used: In distributed applications in which objects written in Java will need to interact with objects that may be written in other programming languages.

JavaServer Pages (JSP)

Definition: A web technology that combines the tasks of page designing and programming. JSPs use template data, custom elements, scripting languages, and server-side Java objects to return dynamic content to a client. The developer writes the template data in HTML or XML, adding inline Java code, within special tags, to provide the dynamic content. These tags also allow JSPs to interact with Enterprise JavaBeans from a number of sources and display them. The beans can also be filled by using the input parameters of HTTP requests. Application servers compile JSPs into servlets.

Where used: To develop and maintain dynamic web pages that leverage existing business systems.

JDBC

Definition: An API that allows connectivity between J2EE applications and virtually any tabular data source. Typically, the data source is a SQL relational database (RDBMS), but the JDBC API also provides access to such data sources as flat files and spreadsheets.

Where used: Whenever a distributed application needs to access enterprise data.

Module

Definition: A software unit that is the smallest deployable and usable unit of J2EE components. It consists of one or more components of the same container type and one deployment descriptor that contains meta-information about the components. The three types of modules are EJB, web, and application client. Modules can be deployed as stand-alone units, assembled as packages of related components, or assembled into a single application module.

Where used: Throughout all J2EE applications.

Resource Manager

Definition: A J2EE component that manages the lifecycle of a resource type. This primarily involves providing access to a set of shared resources, including connection pooling, transaction support, and network communication. A resource manager provides and enforces the ACID transaction properties (atomicity, consistency, isolation, durability) for specific data and operations. An example of a resource manager is a relational database, which supports the persistent storage of relational data. The resource manager typically operates in a different address space or on a different machine from the clients that access it.

Where used: In enterprise applications where data and other operational resources require lifecycle management.

RMI

Definition: Remote Method Invocation. A strictly Java-to-Java technology that allows an object running in one Java virtual machine to invoke methods on an object running in a different Java virtual machine. The JVMs can be on the same or on different hosts. The object in the first program can make a call on a remote object in the second program once it has obtained a reference to the remote object.

Where used: Wherever distributed applications will involve only Java technology from end to end, or where provision is made, such as through RMI-IIOP, for Java technology to operate seamlessly with other languages.

Servlet

Definition: A component-based Java program that provides a simple, consistent mechanism for extending and enhancing the functionality of a web server and for accessing existing business systems. Servlets generate dynamic content and interact with web clients using a request-response paradigm. They have access to the entire family of Java APIs. Since servlets are server and platform-independent, they allow the developer to select servers, platform, and tools of choice. Think of a servlet as a GUI-less applet that runs on the server side.

Where used: To enhance the functionality of a web server in accessing distributed enterprise systems.

Servlet Container

Definition: A container (see *Container*) that provides network services for sending requests and responses, as well as decoding requests, and formatting responses. Servlet containers are required to support HTTP as a protocol for requests and responses, but may additionally support other request-response protocols such as HTTPS.

Where used: Wherever servlets are part of a distributed application.

Secure Sockets Layer

Definition: A security protocol designed to enable private communications over a non-private network such as the Internet. It uses public key encryption and digital certificates to establish a secure connection between a client (such as a web browser), and a web server, to prevent eavesdropping or tampering with communications within and between distributed applications. Servers are always authenticated and clients are optionally authenticated. Web pages that are secured with SSL will likely display a 'closed padlock' or other symbol to indicate that SSL has been enabled. By convention, such web site addresses will start with https:// rather than the usual http://.

Where used: In virtually all distributed enterprise applications, especially those in which communications include private or sensitive material.

Transaction

Definition: An indivisible unit of work that modifies data while ensuring its integrity. A transaction encloses one or more program statements, all of which must either complete (a commit) or be rolled back, ensuring that the data always remains in a consistent state. When a transaction commits, the data modifications made by its statements are saved. If any of the statements within a transaction fail, the transaction rolls back, undoing the effects of all statements in the transaction. Transactions control the concurrent access of data by multiple users.

Where used: In any application in which data is modified.

Web Application

Definition: An application written to be deployed over the Internet. This includes not only those built with Java technologies such as JavaServer Pages and servlets, but also those built with non-Java technologies such as CGI and Perl. Distributable web applications use J2EE technology, written to be deployed in web containers distributed across multiple Java virtual machines running on the same host or different hosts.

Where used: Whenever a distributed application will be deployed over the Internet.

Web Container

Definition: A container (see *Container*) that provides a runtime environment for web components, including security, concurrency, lifecycle management, transaction, deployment, and other services. A web container provides the same services as a JSP container plus a federated view of the J2EE platform APIs. A web container is provided by a web or J2EE server. A distributed web container is one that can run a web application that is tagged as distributable and that executes across multiple Java virtual machines running on the same host or on different hosts.

Where used: In any distributed application that includes web components.

Web Server

Definition: Software that provides a collection of services and resources for accessing the Internet, an intranet, or an extranet. A web server hosts web sites, provides support for HTTP and other protocols, and executes server-side programs. Within the J2EE architecture, a web server provides services, such as HTTP message handling, to a web container. Since the J2EE architecture assumes that a web container is hosted by a web server from the same vendor, it does not specify the contract between these two entities. Each web server may host one or more web containers.

Where used: Whenever web containers form part of an application, essentially whenever any part of the application involves a network.

XML

Definition: The eXtensible Markup Language (XML) is a universal syntax that allows developers to describe and structure data, independent of the application logic. Unlike HTML, which has fixed tags that deal mainly with style or presentation, XML tags are defined as needed. XML can be used to define unlimited languages for specific industries and applications. XML documents need to be transformed into a language with style tags under the control of a stylesheet before they can be presented by a browser or other presentation mechanism. Since XML and Java are both portable and extensible, they are an ideal combination for web applications.

Where used: In conjunction with J2EE technology, whenever an enterprise application needs to consume and generate information that is exchanged among different servers that run on varied system platforms.

Index

E

XYZ